# THE LOEB CLASSICAL LIBRARY

FOUNDED BY JAMES LOEB, LL.D.

EDITED BY

## E. H. WARMINGTON, M.A., F.R.HIST.SOC.

PREVIOUS EDITORS

# LIBANIUS

## I

# LIBANIUS
## SELECTED WORKS

WITH AN ENGLISH TRANSLATION,
INTRODUCTION AND NOTES BY

### A. F. NORMAN
THE UNIVERSITY OF HULL

IN THREE VOLUMES

I

## THE JULIANIC ORATIONS

CAMBRIDGE, MASSACHUSETTS
HARVARD UNIVERSITY PRESS
LONDON
WILLIAM HEINEMANN LTD
MCMLXIX

Printed in Great Britain

PA
4226
.A2
1969
v.1

# CONTENTS OF VOLUME I

# PREFACE

THE present volume contains all the orations of Libanius that bear directly on the career of Julian, with the exception of the fragmentary *Oration* 60 (*The Monody on the Temple at Daphne*). A volume of orations of the post-Julianic period and one of selected letters will complete the whole.

The reduction of the massive corpus of the works of Libanius into the confines of a three volume selection necessarily involves a choice that may appear invidious. It has, for instance, proved impossible to include any of those declamations for which Libanius was renowned in his lifetime and among the Byzantines generally, or of the *Hypotheses* of the orations of Demosthenes, upon which his fame rested until fairly recent years. Considerations of space also preclude the insertion of two highly individual compositions, *Orations* 11 and 1 (The *Antiochikos* and the *Autobiography*), but English translations of these are readily available (*cf.* Bibliography). The criterion of selection has been the relevance of these compositions to the understanding of the life and society of his age and of the development of his career and personality. On both counts the orations on Julian are of the highest importance.

The text is based on Foerster's magisterial work

# LIBANIUS

on the manuscripts described in his Teubner Edition, but since several of the standard works of reference, those of Sievers and Seeck, for instance, antedate Foerster's work, it has been necessary to supplement his paging and sections by reference, in the Orations, to the pagination of Reiske's edition and, for the Letters, to the enumeration of Wolf, to enable the reader to pick a way through the rather cumbersome combination of reference characteristic of more recent works on Libanius.

In the typing of this volume my thanks are due to Mrs. K. W. Peacock for her ready and invaluable assistance.

A. F. N.

# INTRODUCTION

On July 18th A.D. 362 Julian arrived in Antioch for his final preparations for the Persian campaign, to be greeted with a mixture of emotions by the inhabitants and an air of expectant unease.

Julian was born in A.D. 331, son of Constantine's half-brother ; his mother died at his birth and his father in the murders following Constantine's death in A.D. 337, which only he and his elder brother Gallus escaped. Responsibility for the massacre he always laid firmly at the door of his cousin Constantius II. As princes of the blood and therefore objects of suspicion, the two boys owed their preservation to the Christian church and, in particular, to the Arian bishop, Eusebius. After his death, in A.D. 341/2,[a] they were relegated to a quasi-exile on the imperial estate of Macellum in Cappadocia, and there Julian languished for six years. The early literary

---

[a] Seeck's dating of the Macellum period to A.D. 345/51 (*Untergang*, iv, pp. 205 ff.) accepted by Festugière (*Antioche*, p. 64) is disproved by Lib. *Or*. 18. 13 ff.—the account of Julian's relations with Libanius in Nicomedeia. Libanius was there in the period A.D. 344/9, and the only time, on Seeck's view, for this acquaintance to be made is therefore A.D. 344/5. But at the age of 13/14, Julian had not yet reached the age for rhetor training, and the term πρόσηβος is inapplicable. Bidez (*Vie*, pp. 38 f., 55) and Baynes (*J.H.S.* 45, 1925, pp. 251 ff.) adopt the dating 342/7 for Macellum, and this allows Julian to be in Nicomedeia at the end of Libanius' term, and at an age when attendance at a rhetor was normal.

education, begun in Constantinople under his pedagogue Mardonius, was here consolidated and amplified by due instruction in Christian practice and doctrine, so that Julian, enthusiastic and visionary, could at this time aspire to the priesthood. The Arian George of Cappadocia furthered his studies by the loan of items from his library, including works of pagan, and particularly of neo-Platonist, philosophy, so giving Julian his first insight into an entirely new world of experience and exciting his eager curiosity.

The sojourn at Macellum ended after Gallus was summoned to court in A.D. 347. Julian returned to Constantinople where he attended Nicocles' school, but for all his discreet deportment he could not fail to attract attention. He was once again packed off to Nicomedeia under his teacher and watch-dog, Hecebolius—contact with Libanius, the Sophist there, being forbidden him.

In A.D. 351 his position was suddenly changed, with the elevation of Gallus to the rank of Caesar, and for the first time he could pursue his interests without interference. The illicit readings of neo-Platonism now bore fruit, and he betook himself first to Pergamum, and thence to Maximus of Ephesus for instruction and conversion. His attachment to the doctrines and practice of the neo-Platonist thaumaturges was immediate and final.[a] Henceforth Maximus was his mentor, the forbidden rituals of initiation, purification and divination of a militant paganism were his inspiration. He succeeded in keeping his apostasy secret, but he was inevitably involved in the disgrace and fall of his brother

---

[a] Related by Eunapius, *V.S.* 473 ff., dated by his own reference to A.D. 351, *E.L.F.* No. 111.

# INTRODUCTION

Gallus (for which *cf.* Amm. Marc. Bk. 14). Some idea of the prolonged strain under which he laboured can be gathered from the bitter narrative of his *Letter to the Athenians*. In autumn A.D. 354, he was summoned to court at Milan, the target for the innuendo and malice of the ruling clique among the courtiers, and there he cooled his heels for some time, never entirely free from danger and denied access to his cousin until the Empress Eusebia unexpectedly took up his cause. In consequence Constantius' suspicions were allayed, and early in A.D. 355, to his great delight, Julian was sent to Athens to further his studies. Here his association with the neo-Platonist Priscus served to confirm the work begun by Maximus in Ephesus, and that with Basil and Gregory was to result in the uncharitable exaggeration of Gregory's *Invectives*,[a] which became the stock portrayal of the Apostate in the orthodox Church historians.

His period in Athens was short: by autumn he was recalled to court. The crisis in the West following usurpations and barbarian inroads had finally convinced Constantius that an imperial presence was required there. Despite his suspicions and hesitations, he elevated Julian to the rank of Caesar, as he had done Gallus before him, invested him before the army,[b] married him off to another of his sisters, Helena, and arranged for him to be the figurehead of the government of Gaul. In mid-winter A.D. 355 Julian entered his province at the head of a force of 360 troops, twenty-four years old, a tiro in arms, to show the imperial presence in Gaul or—as his friends suspected—to find his death.

[a] Greg. Naz. *Or.* 5. 23 : *cf.* Socr. *H.E.* 3. 23.
[b] *Cf.* Amm. Marc. 15. 8.

# LIBANIUS

The usual precautions were taken to keep Julian from displaying any initiative in his new office. Although he received the honour of the consulship, the control of affairs lay with the officials nominated by Constantius, and his every action was under the scrutiny of the ubiquitous agents of the secret service. He did, however, discover a loyal and capable subordinate in Salustius, and although in a subordinate capacity he took part in the campaign of A.D. 356.[a]

By the composition of the *Panegyrics* upon Constantius and upon the Empress (*Or.* 1 and 3), he made an open profession of his loyal acceptance of his position in winter A.D. 356–7, and the tactful replies of his friends acknowledging his presentation copies served to confirm this attitude under the scrutiny of the secret service (*e.g.*, Libanius to Paul "the Chain," *Ep.* 370). In the same winter, independent military action was forced upon him by the Germans, who kept him under siege in his own headquarters, ignored by his local commander, Marcellus. In consequence, Julian's prestige was enhanced by his successful resistance and the uncooperative Marcellus replaced. His independence in the direction of the affairs of Gaul became firmly established in A.D. 357 by reason of the incompetence of Constantius' generalissimo, Barbatio. Julian had been instructed to act in concert with him, but Barbatio, taking independent action in Upper Germany, was soundly thrashed and retired, leaving Julian isolated to bear the full brunt of the German invasion. At Strasburg Julian gained his first major success over the Germans, captured their leader whom he sent to Con-

[a] Amm. Marc. 16. 1-3 ; Lib. *Or.* 18. 43 ff.

stantius, invaded Germany proper and forced the minor chieftains to come to terms, before returning to Gaul.

This eager and successful assumption of the responsibilities of his position marks the point that sets him upon a collision course with the suspicious and vacillating Constantius. Although he continued to show due deference to his Augustus, Julian knew from recent history that to retreat from his new position of power would be fraught with danger to himself and disastrous to his provinces. In fact, for the consolidation and reconstruction of Gaul fresh campaigns in Germany were necessary, together with the resumption of the British corn trade with the Rhine. Thus in A.D. 358 a campaign in Lower Germany resulted in the submission of more German chieftains and the controlled return of their Gallic prisoners, a course of events to be repeated in A.D. 359.

The survival of Gaul was thus assured, but with it came the resurgence of Gallic nationalism that had been so potent in the preceding century. An absent Augustus afforded the provinces and armies little effective direction or protection. A Caesar in their midst had proved that they could withstand external pressures, and the successes of the last three years had concentrated upon him the enthusiasm and loyalties of both provincials and the army. Such unanimity could not fail to be reported by Constantius' agents, and provided the seeds of discord. This situation had, indeed, been foreseen by Julian: in the winter of A.D. 358/9, a second affirmation of loyalty came from his pen, the second *Panegyric* on Constantius (*Or.* 2), but its effect was almost immediately lost by the feud that broke out between Julian and his praetorian prefect Florentius over corruption in the civil administration. Florentius, piqued at Julian's refusal to support his oppressions, reported to court that the quaestor Salustius was exercising an improper influence over his Caesar, and so secured his recall. This was a slight from his superior that Julian could not fail to resent. His friend's departure was speeded with his *Or.* 8 (*Consolatory Address on Salust's Departure*).

The break came in A.D. 360. Constantius, after serious reverses in the Persian war, had to re-establish the Eastern armies, and after Julian's pacification of Gaul and elimination of the German problem, the only obvious reservoir of man-power was in the armies of Gaul. Reasonable though this assessment might be, the demands for reinforcement, both in their content and in the manner of their transmission, served to precipitate the final crisis. The pick of Julian's troops were to be withdrawn for Eastern service, regardless of the restrictions in the articles of service of many of them : the orders were handed direct to Julian's subordinates without reference to him. In addition, Constantius' agent was stupid enough to insist that the drafts should concentrate on Paris, the site of Julian's headquarters, despite his protests about the size of drafts and the unsuitability of rendezvous. The aggrieved soldiery were duly concentrated with orders to march, and the inevitable mutiny occurred. Once again a provincial army took matters into its own hands and proclaimed Julian Augustus willy-nilly. Even so, Julian was unready to take up arms yet to support his claim to his new position, and, in the

usual way of such usurpations, a protracted series
of negotiations took place throughout the whole of
A.D. 360 : caught between his angry troops and the
demands of Constantius, he could not give way, even
if he now wanted to do so.

In fact, he did not : recent history showed only too
clearly the fate reserved for unsuccessful usurpers,
and in the face of Constantius' demand for complete
submission, his only course was to go on. At this
time, the last tenuous tie with his cousin was broken
with the death of Helena. Whatever his feelings
towards her, it is a fact that after her death he never
touched another woman, and he increasingly com-
ported himself with an ascetic paganism, consulting
his gods for indications of their will. In his state of
nervous exaltation and his rigorously frugal regimen,
such indications were not slow in coming. Already
at Paris he had been visited by the Genius Populi
Romani : now at Vienne, on the occasion of his
quinquennalia, he was reassured by another vision
that announced the imminent death of Constantius.
With such, and other, tokens of divine support he at
last felt himself ready to move against Constantius—
but even so, the time for dissembling was not yet
done. He found it politic to attend church in this
very orthodox community.

The spring of A.D. 361 saw him in action at last, and
again Constantius made the move that gave him
the initiative by entering into communication with
Julian's old enemy, the German Vadomarius, and
engaging him to invade Rhaetia ; Julian's punitive
expedition against the Alemanni set him well on his
way to the East. Instead of delivering his main
thrust in the direction usually taken by usurpers from

Gaul and advancing into northern Italy, he was now half-way to the capital of the Danubian provinces, and this position was consolidated by his surprise advance and journey down-river. A sudden descent captured Sirmium, and Julian moved on to Naissus, the birthplace of his grandfather, there to guard the pass of Succi.

Here he had need to regroup, and since he had by-passed large concentrations of Constantius' supporters, to bring some form of decent administration into his newly acquired provinces. Most notable is the string of manifestos dispatched to the various communities, Greek and Roman, in justification of his rebellion. The surviving example is the *Letter to the Athenians*, but Corinth, Rome, Sparta and others received copies of this polemic also, and it forms the basic material for Libanius' account of Julian's career in *Or.* 18. As a further gesture to the intelligentsia and nobility of Rome proper, where his letter received an unfavourable reception, the rhetor Mamertinus was nominated consul for A.D. 362 (hence the *Gratiarum Actio*), the senator Maximus appointed prefect of Rome " to oblige Vulcatius Rufinus," and Symmachus treated with an uncommon deference. In the event, the campaign of propaganda proved unnecessary : Constantius died in Cilicia early in November while marching to engage him. This was the crowning mercy that confirmed him as sole Augustus without recourse to family feud or bloodshed, and after his earlier expressions of bitterness against Constantius, an emotional reaction set in with this revelation of divine protection. He proclaims to his friends his unwillingness to have resorted to force (*E.L.F.* No. 26 ; 28), and renders

# INTRODUCTION

thanks to the gods of his salvation without fear or
dissimulation (*E.L.F.* No. 29). The body and memory
of Constantius received full honour : abuse of the
dead emperor and his policies was no longer for him,
and even the more rancorous of his supporters found
it politic to preface any detraction of Constantius
with studied apology, as Libanius does. The whole
tenor of his first six months in Constantinople is that
of conciliation and reconstruction. The *Letter to
Themistius*, written before his imperial entry into the
capital, is an exposition of the monarch as subject to
law, directed by philosophy, and the proponent of
the rule of reason, and the rule of reason denied the
rightness or the efficacy of any kind of persecution.
The old religion was freed of the bans to which it had
been subjected, and its ritual and practices once
more became part of a *religio licita*, so that sacrifice
and divination once more became possible. The
Christians were treated with a tolerant and neutral
impartiality, into which it is unnecessary and un-
generous to read any deep Machiavellian designs.
The banished, whether Novatian, Donatist, Arian or
Orthodox, were allowed to return to their seats from
which sectarian bigotry had expelled them in large
numbers. In the event, the return of such exiles and
their claim for restitution of their rights was to create
widespread discord and opposition, but there is no
reason to believe that it was ordered with this
end in view. Simultaneously, every effort was made
to secure decent administration, not least in fiscal
matters—a foretaste of which had been given to the
Illyrian provinces during the days of waiting at
Naissus. The upper-class municipal society was to be
conciliated, no less than the senatorial class, by a

definition of rights and obligations. By mid-March, a full-scale piece of legislation had been framed dealing with curial recruitment, municipal properties, *munera extraordinaria* and other dues, reversing the trend towards a centralized officialdom of the previous generation. This same army of officials was drastically reduced (*cf.* Lib. *Or.* 2. 58) and the ubiquitous *agentes-in-rebus* and imperial notaries almost entirely disbanded. The purge of the palace took place without delay : all the paraphernalia of royalty was dispensed with—barbers, cooks, eunuchs and the rest, that had battened on the old régime. All was affability and efficiency, directed to the welfare of the Empire and its subjects. Men of education and good antecedents, Celsus in Cilicia, or the rhetor Belaeus in Arabia, for instance, were promoted to positions of office, and a less autocratic or bigoted monarch could hardly be imagined. No matter what their persuasion, the meritorious were offered a welcome with him : pagans like his old friends the doctor Oribasius or Salust, Christians of every breed —the orthodox Basil (Julian, *Ep.* 32), the heretic Aëtius (*Ep.* 46), the sophistic Prohaeresius (*Ep.* 31), Caesarius brother to the egregiously eloquent Gregory Nazianzen (*cf. R.E.* iii. 1299, *s.v.*)—and the principal devotees of neo-Platonist doctrine and practice like Priscus and Maximus—all received some conciliating, even affectionate, marks of attention. The one blot on his scutcheon was the series of courts-martial held at Chalcedon where not only the guilty agents of the previous reign like the eunuch Eusebius and the murderous Paulus, but the efficient and even innocent, like Ursulus, were condemned. Here Ammianus speaks with downright disapproval and even Libanius had much ado to make a decent justification.

Such universal tolerance and beneficence was all very well in theory, but in practice it soon fell foul of long-established vested interests. Recruitment to the *curiae* meant the abolition of immunities gained during the past generation, notably those of the Christian clerics : the restoration of municipal properties equally involved losses to important individuals and religious organizations ; so did the reopening of the pagan temples and the resumption of pagan sacrifices and rituals, for which financial provision had to be made. Opposition from the Christian communities grew apace. Nor did conciliation reach the local level : the return of the exiled heretics or orthodox produced a ferment in the various cities. Even by Christmas A.D. 361, the Alexandrians had lynched the Arian bishop, George, and members of the administration (*cf. E.L.F.* No. 60)— and this serious disturbance, though occurring in a city noted for its excessive violence, symbolizes the general unrest. Overriding all else was the need of a speedy solution to the political and religious problems of empire, for Julian as heir to Constantius had also inherited the war with Persia. Yet it was not religious conflict or self-interest that alone provoked criticism. Philosophy, in its popular manifestation of Cynicism, also took him to task upon his imperial conduct; in particular an impudent busy-body named Heracleios presented himself before him with a diatribe on the art of government, of which a highly irreverent use of myth formed a part. The myth for any professed follower of Plato was an integral part of the philosophic method, and Julian, outraged at the

tone and content, took himself off and composed in
haste his two discourses, *Against Heracleios* (*Or.* 7)
and *On the Mother of the Gods* (*Or.* 5), in which
the myth appears as an ethical allegory of autobio-
graphical content in the first and a complete meta-
physical explication in the second. The occasion of
these discourses is, significantly enough, about the
time of the feast of Attis and the Hilaria, at the
vernal equinox ; and equally significant is the ending
of *Or.* 5 where the " eradication of the stain of
atheism " and the recognition of the gods is the
necessary prerequisite for the welfare of the empire,
its survival and his own future. It is evident that the
pressures both from without and within were moving
him from his first professions of tolerance, and the
advent of Maximus at Constantinople was enough
to confirm this direction of his actions. A second
blast against these non-conformist philosophers
followed before mid-summer (*Or.* 6, *Against the Ignorant Cynics*). Here was a rallying of the ranks,
an attempt to synthesize the divergent pagan
philosophies into one acceptable faith in order to
place Roman society on a sound basis before his
departure from Constantinople for the Persian
campaign that he had already begun to devise. The
time for compulsion was fast approaching. This
growing ambitiousness in matters of faith was
indeed accompanied by measures for the public well-
being : the exactions of officials, great or small, on
the public post and the number of recipients of its
privileges were drastically reduced (*E.L.F.* No. 67) :
the financial exactions enforced in more equitable
manner, and methods of evasion curbed (*E.L.F.* Nos.
68, 71) : the presentation of *aurum coronarium* by the

# INTRODUCTION

provincial communities was made a voluntary
matter (*E.L.F.* No. 72), and the demands of the
military were repressed (*E.L.F.* No. 63). Finally,
on June 17th A.D. 362, a few days before his departure, Julian introduced a seemingly innocuous piece
of legislation upon the status of the teaching profession (*Cod. Th.* 13. 3. 5 : *E.L.F.* No. 61). Teachers
must have qualifications both moral and professional :
their appointment was to be subject to a unanimous
decree of the municipal councillors and then referred
to the emperor for ratification. Such centralizing
tendencies ran surprisingly counter to the whole tenor
of Julian's legislation up to date, for his programme
seemed to have as its objective the orderly return of
a defined system of duties and privileges. The reason
for them soon became apparent. Julian explained
his intention in a letter (*Ep.* 42: *E.L.F.* No. 61 c) that
defined the moral rôle of the teachers, explained how
the Galileans disdained the content of the literature
they professed to teach, and banned them from
practising the profession while ever they adhered to
their creed. The choice for such teachers was quite
clear—their religion or their profession. Prohaeresius
at Athens chose to give up his practice : not so
Hecebolius, whose record of conversions and re-
conversions in these years gained him the nickname
of " Euripus ". This innocent measure, one of the
first to be repealed after Julian's death (*Cod. Th.*
13. 3. 6 ; 11 January A.D. 364) was greeted with unqualified approval by the hard-core pagan teachers
like Libanius and a chorus of shocked outrage by the
Christians, and elicited even from Ammianus an
expression of protest, but in the context of his
theocratic aspirations and of the shortness of time

available to him, it was a logical step. He had tried
conciliation and the voluntary principle, so as to leave
a unified empire at his back, and this—as the
criticisms of the Cynics, the unrest among the
Christians and unease among certain communities
had shown—had failed. If these non-cooperative
elements would not be absorbed into his system, they
must be excluded from it, for the good of the body
politic. But in no sense did he wish to present this
alternative as a persecution : his object was to cure
a social ailment, not to punish it, and the cure could
come only with the offer of a reasonable alternative.
So, upon his departure from Constantinople, he
writes a series of letters to his chosen priests instructing them in the manner and content of the duties
demanded of them by their priesthood. The letters
to the priest (? Theodorus, *E.L.F.* No. 79 [*cf.* No
78]), to his uncle Julianus, now Comes Orientis
(*E.L.F.* No. 80), to Callixeina, priestess of the Mother
of the Gods whom he was to visit at Pessinus (*E.L.F.*
No. 81), give details of their duties : the rather later
fragments (also to Theodorus, *E.L.F.* No. 89 a, b)
present the principles of organization and ideology
of the new state religion as he conceived it—the
selection of priests, the austerity of their manner of
life, the manner of ritual and purification, and the
necessity for good works. This was the chief priest of
the Roman world issuing an encyclical to his subordinates, and adopting all the accoutrements and
the organization of the Galilean church to forward
his ideal. The priests of his state cult were appointed
without delay, Chrysanthius in Lydia (Eunap. *V.S.*
501), Arsacius of Galatia (*E.L.F.* No. 84 a), Bacchius,
Clematius, Seleucus (*cf.* Seeck, *B.L.Z.G. s.v.*), even

# INTRODUCTION

Theodora, widow of the Thalassius who had once had so much responsibility for the fall of Gallus (*E.L.F.* Nos. 85, 86). The whole of the East was in the throes of a rapid and drastic spiritual reorganization under the eyes of its demanding ruler, and even in the far West, it is tempting to see the restoration of the old " column cult " at Cirencester by the *rector* of Britannia Prima as a mark of this all-embracing redirection of militant paganism. Yet by the time he had reached Antioch in mid-July, it was borne in upon him that his programme was highly unpopular : Cappadocia he found hostile or ignorant (*E.L.F.* No. 78), and the shrine of Pessinus was ignored by the Galatians (*E.L.F.* No. 84 a).

Julian appeared in Antioch in the midst of the celebrations of the Adonia, and for the events thereafter, besides the fulminations of the Fathers of the Church, at least three eyewitnesses have left their accounts, Ammianus, Julian himself in the *Misopogon* and Libanius, both at the time in *Or.* 12-16, and in later accounts in the *Epitaphios* and the *Autobiography* (119-135). It is this last that best summarizes the relationships between the sophist and the emperor in the nine months' stay in Antioch, and gives the view of the educated pagan upon the programme.

In the period from A.D. 358 Libanius had suffered from a succession of private distresses and nagging ill-health. Julian's accession to the throne and the abolition of the restrictions on pagan worship evoked an enthusiastic welcome from him (*Or.* 1. 119) ; but the uncertainties of the situation with regard to Julian's attitude to certain members of his own family in consequence of the fall of Gallus made him advise caution. He refused to make the first move, preven-

ted by a stiff-necked pride and sense of honour that
needs to be assessed in the light of his regard for his
antecedents and his profession. Sixty years before,
the family property had been confiscated. Could he
decently be seen among the emperor's entourage
without the imputation of self-seeking? Two years
before, his professional standing had been grossly
impugned by the previous administration. Could he,
in decency, make any overture, or indeed welcome
any, until this slight had been removed? This was
a point of honour from which he could not budge.
So, despite overtures from members of Julian's court
(Maximus, Seleucus, *Epp.* 694, 697, 716), Libanius,
however great his approval for the emperor and his
policies might be, maintained a silence that piqued
Julian (*Or.* 1. 120) and puzzled later commentators.
The first meeting (described in *Or.* 1. 120 and *Ep.* 736)
occurred in consequence of Libanius' necessary
presence, as sophist of the city, among the deputation
of welcome upon Julian's arrival in Antioch. Here the
initiative clearly came from the side of the court, and
Julian's reaction, when the presence of Libanius was
pointed out to him, was significantly to compliment
him in the traditional sophistic style with a request
for an oration, a request to which the *Prosphone-
tikos* (*Or.* 13) is the answer. Even so, this does not
mark full association. Libanius speaks of Julian's
flatterers at court and at the performance of the daily
sacrifices in the Palace gardens, and asserts that
someone was opposing any resumption of their
intimacy (*Or.* 1. 120 ff.),[a] and even after an exchange

---

[a] Sievers (*Das Leben des Libanios*, p. 92) suggested that
this was Nicocles; Geffcken (*Kaiser Julianus*, p. 114)
Themistius (wrongly: he was not in Antioch). It remains

of letters with Julian, Libanius remained conspicu-
ously aloof. Only after the intervention of Priscus
was their association resumed ; and, significantly,
not until some time after Julian's arrival and the
delivery of *Or.* 13 does Libanius record the can-
cellation of the professional slight imposed upon him
by the previous administration (*Ep.* 740). The intercourse thereafter he represents as a disinterested
association concerned with literary and current
political topics, and he persistently disclaims any
motives of self-seeking (*Or.* 1. 125, *Ep.* 1154, *Or.* 51.
30) ; in fact, he gained some notoriety by his refusal
of the honorary title of quaestor with which Julian
invested him (*E.L.F.* No. 96, Lib. *Or.* 2. 8, Eunap.
*V.S.* 495 f.). Libanius, in fact, was enjoying the
opportunity of displaying the independence he always
associated with his professional position. His narrative of events before New Year A.D. 363 (*Or.* 1. 125-
130) gives two examples of this attitude. First occurred his suit on behalf of Aristophanes, the whole
tenor of which was an appeal for the unity of Hellenism directed to the propagator of that policy. The
plea (*Or.* 14) was sent to Julian, who read it with
admiration and consented to the rehabilitation of
Aristophanes (*E.L.F.* Nos. 96, 97), who, incidentally,
remained almost aggressively loyal to Julian's
memory in the days of persecution that followed his
death (*Ep.* 1264). The second case was Libanius'
defence of the city council at the time of the price
edict of November A.D. 362, where Libanius faced
the wrath of the emperor and the threats of his

most likely, despite Bidez (*Vie*, p. 400), that it was the arrogant and demanding Maximus. Libanius was not one of the
neo-Platonist coterie.

courtiers unabashed. What remains unmentioned in this narrative, not unexpectedly, since it was directed ostensibly to his fellow citizens, the majority of whom were Christian, is any mention of the religious quarrel between Julian and the *curia*.

In fact, if ever there was need of the unity of Hellenism, for which Julian was planning and to which Libanius appealed in *Or.* 14, it was precisely now, when relations were going from bad to worse between the emperor and the whole community of Antioch. Even before his arrival, it had been forecast that the harvest of A.D. 362 would be bad (*Epp.* 699, 713), but the situation was undoubtedly aggravated by the advent of the army. Almost on his arrival he was met by a popular clamour that there was famine in the midst of plenty (*Misopogon*, 368 c ff.), and he referred the matter to the attention of the councillors. After three months (*i.e.*, by October/November) they had done nothing, and he suspected that they were making the position worse by hoarding and profiteering. He therefore took emergency measures, importing large amounts of grain from neighbouring provinces, making allocations from his own commissariat, and simultaneously imposing by edict taxation and a fixed price that was two-thirds of that current earlier in the summer. What he failed to do was to institute any system of rationing. To his surprise, none of this corn appeared on the open market at this price : he asserted that these *principales* of Antioch had begun black market operations, bought up the corn cheap and were making a fortune from such operations. Hence his summary though short-lived arrest of the *curia* for attempting to thwart his will and the advent of Libanius as its spokesman. The philosophic

# INTRODUCTION

Julian, it appeared, was set on the same course that his brother had taken eight years before in the face of curial incapacity or antipathy.

In another field of municipal affairs also he found, upon his arrival in Antioch, that his policies of reconstruction had fallen foul of local intransigence and vested interest. Although he had remitted, on his accession, a large debt and arrears of tribute, the policy of recruiting new members conflicted with the " closed shop " interests of the local *principales*. Permitted to enrol two hundred members to supplement the numbers of the council, they had deliberately and for their own gain allowed evasion on the part of eligible nominees, or had connived at the enrolment of unsuitable candidates (367 d ff.). Strict enforcement of Julian's recruitment followed (*Cod. Th.* 12. 1. 51 of 28 August)—a measure of which Ammianus (25. 4. 21) strongly disapproved. Of three thousand allotments of waste land that he had allocated to the *curia* at their request, all had been monopolized by the ruling clique and none had found its way to the poorer members of the order, so that he had been compelled to cancel this grant (370 c ff.). It is this monopoly of the perquisites of municipal office (for they already had ten thousand allotments of land), unmentioned by Libanius in his *Autobiography*, but often criticized in his later orations (esp. *Or.* 48, 49) that arouses Julian's ire. In fact, his account of municipal mismanagement in the *Misopogon* reads very much like an incitement of the commons to act against the local potentates who misgoverned them.

It was in the field of religion, however, that these local potentates showed their apathy or ill-will most pointedly and in a manner that met with Julian's deepest displeasure. Before his arrival, his uncle Julianus had begun the religious programme (*E.L.F.* No. 80, Lib. *Ep.* 712) and upon his arrival Julian, in addition to Mithraic sacrifices in the palace, visited all the shrines of the city with due ritual (Lib. *Or.* 15. 79). The popular reaction to such acts of piety, however, soon became one of hostility, not merely because of Julian's energetic promotion of his paganism and his lack of interest in their amusements, but because in times of scarcity they saw the mass slaughter of sacrificial victims and had to encounter the tipsy soldiery, who got drunk in the celebrations (Amm. 22. 12. 6 f.). In August, however, the reactions of the local potentates became equally clear. The celebration of the feast of Apollo at Daphne that he then attended he found boycotted by the municipal councillors, and no public offerings forthcoming (*Misop.* 361 d ff.)—a most outrageous snub. In his effort to purify the precincts of the Daphnaean temple by the removal of the body of the martyr, Babylas, this antagonism was increased : and when on the following night, the temple, with its cult statue, was demolished by fire, he suspected arson, and finally attributed responsibility to the Christians. A commission of inquiry, of which Libanius was a member (*Ep.* 1376), could find no culprit, and Julian alleged against the council that they neglected or condoned the outrage. Libanius composed and delivered his *Monody on the Daphnaean Temple* (*Or.* 60, preserved in fragments by Chrysostom) but this could not save the community from punishment, for the Great Church of Antioch was closed and its sacred vessels confiscated

# INTRODUCTION

(*cf.* Chrysostom, *P.G.* 50. 530 ff. [*Hom. de S. Babyla*] ;
Theodoret, *H.E.* 12. 4 ; Sozom. *H.E.* 5. 8). The
persecution of the Christian community had indeed
begun. Nor was Antioch the only centre of opposition and unrest in these months. Bostra (*E.L.F.* No.
114) receives a letter of supercilious tone and content
that formally disclaims any intention of persecuting
the Christian clergy while yet imputing to them
responsibility for leading their communities into
violence and error. In October, Athanasius was again
banished from Alexandria (*E.L.F.* No. 110), a penalty
increased, upon appeal, to banishment from Egypt
altogether (*ibid.* Nos. 111/2). The property of the
Church in Edessa is confiscated : the Christians are
to learn poverty and decent behaviour, and so not to
lose their chance of the kingdom of heaven to which
they still aspire. Equally significantly, the Edessenes
are warned against creating any disorder (*E.L.F.* No.
115).

By December, Julian was only too well aware that
his programme of conciliation and reconstruction had
developed into one of all-out warfare to conquer this
religious opposition. His recognition of the fact
found expression in literary productions characteristic of himself that yet—despite the commendations
of Libanius—could only elicit the ridicule and dislike
of both the vulgar and the sophisticated. The
composition of the *Caesars* at the Saturnalia is
perhaps typical : in this work, Romulus, the personi-
fication of that Genius Populi Romani that had set
him on his course in Paris, sets the stage for the great
debate : Philosophy, in the person of Marcus
Aurelius, gains the verdict of the gods : the Christians, in the person of Constantine and his sons, in a

LIBANIUS

bitter parody of the Gospels, can sin, be purified by
baptism and return to sin once more (336 a, b): his
own guide is Mithras. This exposition of the ethical
and political creed of the ruler is closely followed
by the *Discourse on Helios the King*, in which the posi-
tive conception of his solar religion and metaphysic
finds clearest expression. The outraged tone of the
*Caesars* and the devout sincerity of *Helios the King* are
his personal reaction to the stubborn resistance he
encountered in his public programmes, and serve to
confirm him upon his predetermined course. And
such confirmation was indeed needed. The omens
were not always good, nor was success to be easy. On
January 1 the sacrificing priest collapsed and died
at the altar, and Libanius, called upon, despite his
hesitations (*Ep.* 785), to deliver his address to Julian
as consul (*Or.* 12), cannot disguise the fact, in his later
account, of the latent recriminations and dissatisfac-
tions that overshadowed the occasion (*Or.* 1. 127 ff.).
Moreover, despite the repeated assertions that the
orator makes concerning the success of Julian's
campaign of conversion in the army, often with the
help of donatives, evidences of disaffection were to be
observed in the first months of the year, with open
opposition to his religious ordinances among his
crack troops and conspiracies in his imperial guard
(Amm. 22. 11. 2 ; Theodoret, *H.E.* 3. 15. 4 ff.) ; and
after the deaths of his intimates Felix and Julianus,
the malicious populace saluted him with the pointed
*double entente*, Felix Julianus Augustus (Amm.
23. 1. 4 f.), and other lampoons against him (Lib. *Or.*
16. 30). Julian, in exasperation, began to take
measures for the discomfiture of the Christians in
general and the Antiochenes in particular, despite the

# INTRODUCTION

restraining efforts of Libanius (*Or*. 1. 131). He engaged upon the composition of his final discourse *Contra Galilaeos* (preserved in part in the refutation of Cyril of Alexandria, *P.G.* 76), and actively promoted the reconstruction of the Temple at Jerusalem (Amm. 23. 1 ; *E.L.F.* No. 134, *cf.* No. 89, p. 295 c), in order to secure the support of the Jews and at the same time irritate the bigoted Christians who opposed him. Finally, on the religious front, he published the ordinance banning funerals in day-time (*Cod. Th.* 9. 17. 5 of 12 February 363 ; *E.L.F.* No. 136 a, b). Despite the initial appeal to ancient tradition, the motivation is purely that of neo-Platonist religion and purification, requiring the prevention of any taint from the dead affecting the temples of the gods or the gaze of the Olympians. Against Antioch, both commons and council, Julian composed his bitter complaints in the self-satire the *Misopogon* late in February. Whatever the justice of his allegations of opposition from the volatile city—it may perhaps be best described as a case of mutual incompatibility —there were two features in this work that could not fail to inspire alarm in the councillors of Antioch. First, he proclaimed his intention of transferring his seat of government from Antioch to Tarsus, a bitter blow to Antiochene vanity (364 d) and to its future standing. Secondly, in announcing this transfer, he proclaimed that he left Antioch to experience divine justice, or, failing that, to indulge in an orgy of riot and self-destruction, as it had done under Gallus (370 b, c). And, as foretaste of what they could expect, he appointed Alexander as *consularis* of Syria, not because of any merits of character, but because he was the only sort of person fitted for a rebellious and greedy city. On March 5th he left on his campaign, still refusing to have anything to do with the councillors. They, in alarm at last, escorted him from the city with all ceremony, and received a rebuff for their pains (*Or.* 1. 132) ; on presenting themselves to him further along his route, their reception was little different (*E.L.F.* No. 98), and as Julian had predicted, they had recourse to Libanius to present their plea for reconciliation in due form. The result was *Oration* 16, addressed to the Antiochenes, upbraiding them for their misconduct, and urging them to earn the emperor's pardon by conforming to his policies, and a companion piece, *Oration* 15, addressed to the emperor, constituting a plea for forgiveness and an assurance to the emperor of the city's contrition. Neither oration was ever actually delivered. The composition of *Oration* 15 follows the receipt in Antioch of the news of Julian's first successes, and from *Or.* 17. 37 it is clear that this oration had not reached Julian at the time of his death and therefore remained undelivered. The companion oration (*Or.* 16), apparently composed immediately after this, also remained unpublished, according to the testimony of Socrates (*H.E.* 3. 17). The background of the composition of each is clearly that of the worried uncertainty in Antioch under the government of the heavy-handed Alexander.

After his penetration deep into the heart of Persia, however, Julian was mortally wounded on June 26th, deserted in a last vision by the Genius of the Roman People. The pietistic tradition of a conquering Christianity was to attribute to him a death-bed confession that the Galilean had conquered, a fiction that finds no place in the contemporary accounts.

# INTRODUCTION

The general psychological reaction to the news was immediate and explosive, and was to be followed by the violent political and religious repercussions of the reign of Valens. The first feeling of despair caused Libanius to contemplate suicide (*Or.* 1. 135), but this he put aside as unworthy of himself and of Julian. In any case, he had a duty to perform—the composition of funeral orations in his memory. Loyalty, affection and professional pride no doubt inspire him to this demonstration of piety, but there is no doubt of the sincerity and depth of his emotions. He was unable to resume his composition because of his grief (*Or.* 17. 38; *Ep.* 1430), and in fact he did not begin his declamations until after the New Year (*Ep.* 1128). He was offended by the indecent transports of joy with which the news had been received, not least in Antioch (*Epp.* 1119, 1187), and the epithet " Hellene " comes readily to his lips to rally the faithful (*e.g.*, *Epp.* 1120. 2; 1211. 2; 1431. 5). But as the persecution increases and he sees Julian's priests and officials brought to account, his expressions of outraged grief are tempered with resignation and despondency : " The gods were wiser than we " (*Ep.* 1210) ; the ἀλιτήριοι have it all plain sailing (*Ep.* 1157) ; he grounds arms, not from any change of heart but from the dictates of prudence (*Ep.* 1211. 4-5) ; and after his considerable risks and discomforts, he recommends a more passive attitude (*Ep.* 1533). Such passive resignation—and this is a characteristic feature of pagan attitude towards the excesses of the established order in the fourth century—does not, however, involve disloyalty to Julian or his memory. He provides support and commiseration for the victims of Christian oppression and deplores the ravages committed against the temples (*Epp.* 1307, 1518); years afterwards he is prepared formally to break off a friendship with Polycles because of his criticisms of Julian (*Or.* 37. 2 ff.), and even after a generation, Julian's memory is still green (*Ep.* 947. 5).

In such a frame of mind, he began the preliminaries for the work he had set himself to do. For the period up to November A.D. 361 he had no need for more than the *ipsissima verba* of the *Letter to the Athenians*. What he required was an account of the events of A.D. 363. Late in A.D. 363 he records (*Ep.* 1220. 7-9) that he had applied for information to his friends who had returned from the campaign but had received no support. Some of the soldiery hitherto unknown to him provided him with details of dates, distances and topography, but he had been unable to obtain a complete and coherent account. From Philagrius (*Ep.* 1434) he requests his diary of the campaign : " You will inform me of bare facts : I will clothe them in the garb of oratory." Seleucus is encouraged (*Ep.* 1508) to compose the history of the events of which he had been an eyewitness, a piece of advice that may actually have borne fruit (*cf.* Suidas, *s.v.* " Seleucus"), and despite the onset of gout and migraine Libanius had composed both orations by the autumn of A.D. 365.[a]

---

[a] The argument of Petit (*Vie municipale*, pp. 185 f.), whereby he dates *Or.* 18 to A.D. 368, is unconvincing. The alleged literary contretemps with Themistius (*Or.* 5. 66 a of 1 January 364, contradicted by Libanius, *Or.* 18. 279, which in turn is contradicted by Themistius, *Or.* 8. 114 c) would prove, if anything, that the *Epitaphius* is to be dated *before* 368. In the internal references (17. 30 ; 18. 287 [persecution of Maximus] ; *ib.* 290 [barbarian invasions] ; *ib.* 292 [earth-

# INTRODUCTION

The *Monody*, a form of rhetorical lamentation dear to Libanius and firmly embedded in the sophistic tradition, is a highly personal and deeply emotional tribute adorned with all the traditional devices of his art, and, with his *Monodies* on Nicomedeia (*Or.* 61) and on the Daphnaean Temple (*Or.* 60), is one of the three surviving examples from his pen. The tradition had been set by Aristeides with his *Monody on Smyrna*, and had been elaborated with Libanius' own *Monodies* on the deaths of Aristaenetus and his uncle Phasganius; and the method of publication that he describes for each of these works may indicate that followed in these orations. With the *Monodies* on Nicomedeia and Aristaenetus, the declamation took place before four friends who then distributed it among others (*Ep.* 33). A similar course was followed in the publication of his *Monody upon Phasganius*, though for a different reason (*Ep.* 283).[a] It may be assumed that this also applied in the present speeches, especially in view of the dangers with which he felt himself surrounded under Jovian's reign and which increased under that of Valens (*Or.* 1. 137 ff.).

If the *Monody* is an expression of personal loss, the *Epitaphios* is something more. Derived from the tradition of the classical funeral speeches, in its form it must adhere to the sophistic rules of panegyric and follow the pattern laid down in the text books of

quakes]), the events are those up to the end of July 365. The dangers of composition thereafter, because of the revolt of Procopius (*Or.* 1. 163) preclude the attribution of these speeches to any later date. Equally, the dating by Socrates (*H.E.* 3. 22) to the reign of Jovian is too early.

[a] On the methods of publication of Libanius' orations *cf.* Petit, " Recherches sur la publication et la diffusion des discours de Libanius," *Historia,* 5, 1956, pp. 479 ff.

# LIBANIUS

Hermogenes or Menander, so that it begins, as required, with family, and proceeds in strict order to deal with education, character and achievements. But the content of the achievements and assessment of the protagonist place it in the class of controversial didactic, along with the *Autobiography*. Such oratory, though restricted in its publication, had a practical end in view (*Or.* 2. 70 ff.). If the *Autobiography* reveals, in the career of Libanius, the unqualified merits of his system and an exposition of the cultural virtues of Hellenism, the *Epitaphios* represents, in the person of Julian, a paragon of such virtue, both moral and political, whereby the way to personal salvation is revealed and the state and society purged of grossness and error and brought to perfection. It is, in part, this ideally utilitarian intention that here affects Libanius' handling of the narrative of Julian's elevation in Paris (18. 97) as compared with those of *Or.* 13 and 12. 50 (described by Petit [*art. cit.*] as " laïcisation ") and of the famine in Antioch (18. 195), as compared with the accounts contemporary with the event (15. 29 ; 16. 21) or the more self-interested résumé of the *Autobiography* (1. 126). Not merely was the audience different but the intention with which each oration was composed also differed. Practical considerations of immediate importance to the Antiochenes have been replaced by a more academic exposition of the rule of right reason, and Libanius consciously aspires to demonstrate that practical philosophy upon which Julian had, at parting, complimented him (1. 131). The *Epitaphios* therefore ends with a bitterly critical account of the disasters suffered or expected by Roman society in consequence of its renunciation of

# INTRODUCTION

Julian's ideals. Pagans must no doubt continue to conform to the dictates of the law, just as Julian had done as emperor, but cannot be expected to agree that such dictates are now right or proper in direction or content. Such a protest, however, is not to be construed as an incitement to extra-legal action such as the Christians had habitually taken and which Libanius finally threatened would be taken in the *Pro Templis*. In such a context, the exclusion of any account of Julian's militant programme is hardly surprising.

The reign of Valens (A.D. 364–378), with its continued repression of the values of Hellenism and its disastrous conclusion at Adrianople, showed, if anything could, the rightness of Julian's course and the appalling consequences of its neglect. This submerged criticism came to the surface with the advent of Theodosius to the Eastern throne, and Libanius emerged from his obscurity once more to emphasize the necessity of a system of rights and obligations in which all Romans could share without fear of religious or social persecution. This is expressed in *Or.* 24 on the *Punishment of the Murder of Julian* in A.D. 379. Taking as his premise the circumstances of Julian's death—and a hardening of view can be seen on this topic, beginning with a confession of mystification in A.D. 364 (*Ep.* 1187. 2), proceeding to an imputation of Christian responsibility in the *Epitaphios* (18. 275), and culminating in certainty, in this oration (24. 6 ff.), despite the differences from other accounts then current, like that of Ammianus—he demands here that the moral law be enacted. Once the premise is granted, the oration no longer marks an " astounding deformation of his thinking " (Petit,

*Vie municipale*, p. 211), but is in the tradition of the views of crime and punishment that had informed Greek thought since the days of Homer, who is the foundation of his educational system, and had been confirmed by the ideas of purification based on Plato and now current among the neo-Platonists. There is the epic cycle of offence, divine anger and retribution, and the continuance of defilement in the world by reason of Julian's death and its subsequent neglect. Any relief can come only from a rigorous examination, though long delayed, and by the punishment of the guilty. Here once more are the arguments for which Arnobius had once criticized his pagan adversaries, but in addition there is an appeal to imperial *esprit de corps*. Any attack upon a lawful emperor that goes unpunished weakens the position of the lawful successors who fail to live up to their duty of punishment. The tradition of the Hellenic moral law is cleverly wedded to the conception of imperial self-preservation, calculated to influence the new emperor to reverse the disastrous tendencies of the previous reign.

# THE LIFE OF LIBANIUS

THE main events in the life of Libanius may be gathered from his Autobiography (*Or.* 1) and the additional information of letters and orations. Born in Antioch in A.D. 314 [a] of good municipal family and left fatherless by the age of ten, he had by the time he was fifteen planned for himself a career in rhetoric. In A.D. 336, with family permission finally granted, he went to complete his education at Athens, where he studied for the next four years. Impatient of professorial incompetence, resolutely pagan and innately priggish, he was rapidly marked out for promotion there because of his natural ability, but by A.D. 340/1 he had broken away to become a private teacher in the new society of Constantinople. Here his meteoric success inevitably aroused envy, and on the occasion of the riots of A.D. 342 sophistic rivals and disapproving officials combined to force his withdrawal under a cloud.[b] By A.D. 344 he was installed as professor in Nicomedeia, a post which he held with conspicuous success for the next five years, and there he made the acquaintance both of the future saint, Basil, and, at second-hand, as he narrates in *Or.* 18. 13 f., of the young Julian. In A.D. 349, after the delivery of the panegyric on the reigning emperors (*Or.* 59), he received an imperial summons to return

[a] *Cf.* Sievers, pp. 207 f.    [b] Eunapius, *V.S.*, p. 495.

as official sophist to Constantinople, and this he reluctantly obeyed. Despite more sophistic successes he became ever more ill at ease in the atmosphere of the Christian court until, after a short visit home in A.D. 353, he returned to Antioch to settle there permanently in the course of the next winter.

Very soon afterwards he was appointed official teacher there, a post for which he had evidently intrigued and which he had been half promised before his arrival, and with his ambition thus fulfilled, he never left the place thereafter. In Antioch his literary successes, upon which he continually plumes himself, once more continued, but again he had to contend with rivalries and intrigues, both professional and political. The last years of the reign of Constantius see him approaching the height of his rhetorical powers, the panegyric upon Antioch (*Or.* 11) being the most notable composition of the period, but, probably because of his known connections with Julian, rapidly losing official favour. At this time he was never able to " direct the city according to his nod," as his predecessor Zenobius had done, and his melancholia was increased by a succession of domestic troubles and bereavements.

From this slough of despond he was rescued by the advent of Julian to the throne. Without subscribing to the extremes of reactionary paganism, he welcomed the new régime with a fervent and undisguised enthusiasm. The social, religious and, above all, educational principles of the new emperor matched his own, and for the first time since Nicomedeia he could imagine himself undertaking his ideal rôle as the sophist of his city, and as the leader and publicist of its aspirations. This period of intimacy with

# THE LIFE OF LIBANIUS

Julian remains the high-water mark of his literary achievement and, indeed, of his whole career, representing as it does the true expression of his conception of the relationship between sophist and emperor. For all that, he remained non-conformist enough to refuse the honorary quaestorship then offered him,[a] and he employed his new-found opportunity for independence to temper the excesses of religious extremism with counsels of moderation and tolerance.[b] Even so, this harmony was soon marred. In the feud which arose between Julian and Antioch, he felt himself in duty bound to act as spokesman for his erring fellow countrymen before the emperor he so much admired, and the revulsion of popular feeling and the religious reaction which followed Julian's death left him bitterly disillusioned. He saw his rôle almost completely reversed, his task now being to justify his dead emperor to an ungrateful and hostile public.

In the years after A.D. 365 he was more than once accused of complicity in the conspiracies which were concocted against Valens, but, for all the gossip about him, nothing was proved. However, his avowed devotion to paganism and his intimacy with Julian made him an obvious target, and he lived dangerously and in growing disfavour and obscurity throughout the reign of Valens, the only certain composition of this period being the *apologia pro vita sua* embodied in the original Autobiography of A.D. 374. Not until after Valens' death in battle at Adrianople in A.D. 378 does he emerge once more to become the mouthpiece of a pagan revival, but, significantly enough, his first call for a restoration

[a] *Or.* 2. 8; Eunapius, *V.S.* 495 f.  [b] *Epp.* 757, 763, 819.

of Julian's memory (*Or.* 24) is followed closely by the confession of his own unpopularity, not least on this account (*Or.* 2). However, for the next dozen years he remains at his post, devoting his eloquence to forceful and, in the main, enlightened criticisms of various aspects of contemporary society. Although he was never entirely disinterested in his statements, his remarks upon the decline of the municipal administration, prison conditions, forced labour and religious bigotry, coupled with his own genuine humanity, provide a valuable and horrifying commentary upon the good intentions and grim performance of administrators, as they are revealed in the Codes. The excesses of cruelty and the reign of terror that he abhorred are never far from the scene, and could be applied equally by or against every section of the community. The councillors are, in turn, the petty oppressors of their fellows, as in *Or.* 48-49, and themselves the victims of outrage by the commons or the host of officials, as in *Or.* 19-23). The officials are lifted up and cast down in bewildering succession, and the commons alternately riots or is ground down under violent repression. Even education was under attack, and that for a man of his profession and ideals was the bitterest of pills, and, despite the receipt of an honorary prefecture in A.D. 383,[a] he shows in repeated complaints an increasing disappointment and frustration. Whether the reason lies in the personality of Libanius himself or in the deficiencies of the governors, every official in these years, with but one exception (*Or.* 41), is represented as finally falling short of the standard of conduct demanded by Libanius. His last known oration is

[a] *Cf.* Petit, *Byzantion*, 21. 293.

dated to A.D. 392, and his last letters to the following year, after which nothing more is known of him. The recent suggestion of Lacombrade,[a] identifying him with the unnamed nonagenarian mentioned by Synesius and so implying that he was still living in A.D. 404, is incapable of proof.

His personal life remained throughout subordinate to the demands of his profession. His deliberate adoption of a sophistic career set him apart from his fellows of curial standing, and his inheritance of curial land, together with his tenacious retention of his sophistic immunity from the obligations attached to it, emphasized this separation. He had expected to marry his cousin, but she died just before he returned home, and thereafter he held as concubine a woman of lower class, probably a slave, by whom he had his only son Arabius, later known as Cimon. From the time of Julian (*cf. Or.* 17. 37) a major preoccupation was with his son's succession to his estate, since the product of such a union was in law illegitimate. In A.D. 381/2 Cimon received the grant of testamentary succession, and this was increased in A.D. 388 by the right to receive the family property in his father's lifetime—a grant that immediately rendered him liable to curial service. To avoid such a dubious and expensive station Libanius had first hoped to establish Cimon in the immunity of a teacher, but the son opted for a career as a lawyer as a more favourable alternative, and was enrolled on the staff of the governor for a time. Finally under renewed threat of impressment by the council, he sought the sure refuge of imperial office and senatorial rank. He was initially successful in obtaining nomination to a post

[a] *Mél. Hen. Grégoire*, 2. 361 ff.

in Cyprus, which would have given him the immunity
he sought, but this appointment was not confirmed
and his application for enrolment into the senate was
rejected out of hand, because of his mother's low
status. Mortified, he made his way home from Constantinople, broke a leg in an accident on the journey
and, in A.D. 391, died. This was the major tragedy
of Libanius' latter years, for him comparable only
to the death of Julian. Coupled with his quarrel
with the town council in consequence of his inheritance under the will of his friend Olympius (*Or.* 63),
his support of his assistants Eusebius and Thalassius
in their attempts to avoid curial service, and the
council's decision to support the institution of a chair
of Latin in Antioch, it sours and embitters him, so
that his last writings convey a note of gloom and
disillusion.

He enjoyed ill-health. At the age of twenty he
suffered from shock as a result of a thunderbolt
(*Or.* 1. 9 ; *Ep.* 727), and this incident left him with
a migraine that affected him at intervals throughout his life, a tendency to hypochondria which he
modelled deliberately, in part at least, upon the behaviour of the second-century sophist, Aelius Aristeides, and the consciousness that by this accident
he had been placed on the same plane as others of
his heroes of the Second Sophistic who had been
similarly afflicted. The onset of gout in his early
forties combined with this, and though he used it as
an excuse to return home, it did in fact render him
increasingly liable to chronic depression and over-
strain. He suffered a nervous collapse after Julian's
death, and the combination of pressures under which
he worked in the 380's brought about a recurrence in

A.D. 386, which serves to explain the morbid touchiness that soured his relations with so many of his contemporaries (*e.g.*, *Or.* 36 ; 54). On the other hand, the biography by Eunapius emphasizes the force of personality and the charm that he exercised as a teacher. Vain, cantankerous and opinionated he may be, but he remained consistently and austerely devoted to the practice of his religion, and enthusiastically loyal to his profession, so that the memory of Julian, in whom he found the embodiment of his Hellenic ideal, remained for him an ever-present inspiration.

# THE WORKS OF LIBANIUS

THE writings of Libanius have commended themselves, in different aspects, to succeeding generations
of students. In his own day, he ruefully acknow-
ledges his unpopularity with an ever-growing section
of his society, but even so claims for himself pre-
eminence for his declamations (*Or.* 1. 155) and for the
artistry of his correspondence (*Or.* 13. 52). This
judgement Christian Byzantium was ready to confirm by its eagerness to imitate and to attribute its
imitations to him, as shown in the spurious correspondence between him and St. Basil (*Epp.* 1580 sqq.
of Wolf's Edition : Foerster, Vol. 11, pp. 572-597).
His standing among scholars of the 16th and early
17th centuries was no less high. Erasmus translated
the *Legatio Menelai* (*Decl.* 3) into Latin, Ben Jonson
used *Decl.* 26 (*The Misanthrope*) as material for the
*Epicene*, and the enthusiasm of Morell in his task of
editing and translating these declamations was such
that he could not be induced to leave it, even to visit
his wife on her death-bed. However, despite the
work of Gothofredus, where for the first time the
importance of Libanius as a commentator on problems of history and society was revealed, the reaction
had already set in. Bentley, in *Phalaris*, speaks of
the emptiness and deadness of the *Letters*, and
describes them as the works of " a dreaming pedant,

his elbow upon his desk." Gibbon goes further : for him the writings of Libanius are " the vain and idle compositions of an orator who cultivated the science of words, the productions of a recluse student, whose mind, regardless of his contemporaries, was incessantly fixed on the Trojan War and the Athenian commonwealth." This inaccurate and unfavourable judgement has prevailed until comparatively recent days. In the older British universities, for instance, any mention of Libanius was confined to a study of the *Hypotheses*, and even then with more regard to the oratory of Demosthenes than for the scholarship of Libanius. However, in Germany Sievers and Seeck both succeeded in demonstrating his value as a historical source, while his relevance for the history and practice of education attracted Walden and Schemmel and, more recently, P. Wolf and Festugière. The most striking recent development has been the belated rediscovery, as exemplified in the works of P. Petit and A. H. M. Jones, of his true value as a social commentator.

The *Declamations* attributed to him are found in Vols. 5-7 of Foerster's Teubner edition, and number 51, of which 44 are to be accepted as genuine.[a] These cover the whole field of sophistic invention, with the traditional treatment of topics philosophic, mythological, historical and social. The most outstanding is his *Apology of Socrates (Decl.* 1), and this alone may be regarded as having any relevance to contemporary matters, if the thesis of Markowski be accepted.[b] He argues, with great plausibility, that this is composed as a covert justification of the career of Julian. *Decl.*

[a] Spuria : Nos. 17, 34, 40, 43, 45, 49, 51.
[b] " De Libanio Socratis defensore " (repr. 1968).

27 also is of interest as being yet another exercise in the sophistic line of descent from Menander's *Dyscolus*, while *Decl.* 26, as already mentioned, plays its own small part in the history of English literature. Minor literary exercises illustrative of the sophist's art (*Progymnasmata*) appear in the Teubner Edition, Volume 8. Of the works there attributed to him the following are genuine :

Chriae 1-3 (of four).

Refutationes 1-2.

Confirmationes 1-2 (of three).

Loci Communes 1-5.

Laudationes 1-8 (of nine), No. 7 (*The praises of agriculture*) in theme and treatment akin to Themistius, *Or.* 30.

Vituperationes 1-8 ; for Nos. 5 and 6 *cf. Or.* 7 and 8.

Comparationes 1-5.

Ethopoeiae 20 (of 27, Nos. 13, 20, 22, 24-27 being spurious).

Descriptiones 1-7 (Nos. 8-30 being spurious). Nos. 2 and 4 are of interest as descriptions of murals in the Town Hall of Antioch, and No. 5 (*Description of the New Year*) is a companion piece to *Or.* 9.

Thesis No. 1 (of three ; εἰ γαμητέον—a problem he faced in real life).

The *Letters* of the Libanian corpus are contained in Volumes 10 and 11 of the Teubner Edition. Of over 1600 attributed to him, some 1540 or more are genuine, all of these save 20 covering the years A.D. 355–365 (*Epp.* 19-839, 1113-1542), and A.D. 388–393 (*Epp.* 840-1112). Despite Bentley's strictures, these letters, written to friends and acquaintances of both high and low degree, set the man firmly in his social context and are an invaluable commentary upon contemporary events.

The *Orations*, of which 64 survive, range in date from A.D. 349 to A.D. 392, and in style from purely sophistic exercises to the extremes of official panegyric and of personal abuse. His most individual composition is his own autobiography (*Or.* 1), but his oratorical powers revealed themselves at their peak in his orations on Antioch and on Julian. Thereafter a growing tone of social and personal criticism emerges, and the disappointed orator voices a sincere, if often self-interested, opposition to many of the municipal problems and administrative defects of his time.

The following is the list of the works of Libanius arranged in chronological order, as far as can be determined [a] :

A.D.

349 : *Or.* 59, Panegyric on Constantius and Constans (2. 201).

c. 352 : *Hypotheses* of the orations of Demosthenes (8. 575).

355–365 : Letters, Nos. 19-839, 1113-1542.

358 : *Or.* 61, Monody on Nicomedeia (4. 323).

360 : *Or.* 11, Antiochikos (1. 412).

361 : *Or.* 31, For the teachers (Wolf, *Schulwesen*, 94 f.).

361 : *Or.* 64, For the dancers (4. 406).

[a] References, unless otherwise stated, are to volumes and pages of Foerster's Teubner Edition.

# THE WORKS OF LIBANIUS

# LIBANIUS

A.D.

385 : *Or.* 50, About forced labour (3. 469).

386 : *Or.* 36, About the practice of magic (3. 225).

late 386 : *Or.* 33, Against Tisamenus (3. 163).

late 386 : *Or.* 45, About the prisoners (3. 357).

late 386 : *Or.* 30, For the temples (Petit, *Byzantion*, 21. 310).

spring 387 : *Or.* 19-23, On the riots in Antioch (2. 372).

spring ? 388 : *Or.* 51-52, On the governors' levées (Pack, *Studies*, 124).

388 : *Or.* 32, Against Thrasydaeus (3. 147).

summer 388 : *Or.* 56, Against Lucianus (Pack, *Studies*, 123).

autumn 388 : *Or.* 48-49, On the town councils (Pack, *Studies*, 123).

autumn 388 : *Or.* 35, To those who refuse to speak (3. 207).

after 387/8 : *Or.* 25, On slavery (2. 534).

after 387/8 : *Or.* 34, Against the criticisms of the pedagogue (3. 188).

after 387/8 : *Or.* 3, To his students, about his speech (1. 263).

after 387/8 : *Or.* 58, About the carpeting (4. 175).

after 387/8 : *Or.* 38, Against Silvanus (3. 250).

388–392 : Letters, Nos. 840-1112

389 : *Or.* 54, Against Eustathius, about his honours (4. 70).

389 : *Or.* 63, For Olympius (4. 384).

390 : *Or.* 4, On not talking nonsense (1. 279).

lii

# THE WORKS OF LIBANIUS

A.D.

390 : *Or.* 42, For Thalassius (Petit, *By-zantion*, 21. 297).

391 : *Or.* 47, On the protection rackets (3. 401).

392 : *Or.* 9, On the New Year (Schmid, *Philol.* 83. 447).

392 : *Or.* 46, Against Florentius (Seeck, *Rhein. Mus.* 73. 84 ff.).

*Orations of unknown date:*

A.D.

after 360 : *Or.* 55, To Anaxentius (*Or.* 55. 15).

after 366 : *Or.* 37, To Polycles (3. 236).

after 366 (? *c.* 374) : *Or.* 62 : Against those who deride his teaching system (4. 342).

? late 370's : *Or.* 40, To Eumolpius (3. 277).

? early 380's : *Or.* 39, Consolatory to Antiochus (3. 264).

between 380 and 392, an Olympic year (? 384) : *Or.* 53, On invitations to the festivals (4. 50).

before 389 : *Or.* 44, To Eustathius of Caria (antedates *Or.* 54).

? 392 : *Or.* 57, Against Severus (Norman, *B.Z.* 51. 76).

after 382 (? 392/3) : *Or.* 41, To Timocrates (Norman, *B.Z.* 51. 76).

? late : *Or.* 5, Artemis.

? late : *Or.* 6, On insatiability (1. 322).

? late : *Or.* 7, Ill-gotten gains more grievous than poverty (1. 322).

? late : *Or.* 8, On poverty (1. 322).

# BIBLIOGRAPHY

## Manuscripts

The results of Foerster's work upon the manuscripts of Libanius are embodied in his text and the
detailed introductions to the several orations in his
Teubner edition. This work is fundamental to all
later studies, replacing as it does the earlier work of
Reiske.

The Julianic orations of Libanius each survive with
varying manuscript density, indicative of the taste
for Libanian oratory among the later Byzantines.
Thus for *Or.* 12, 27 mss. survive; for 13, 48; for 14,
27; for 15, 32; for 16, 33; for 17, 59; for 18, 49; for
24, 26. Sixteen mss. are common to all these orations,
and of these Foerster used as the basis of his text:

C : Chisianus R VI. 43 of 11th/12th centuries.
A : Monacensis 483 (once Augustanus) : basically
    of the 10th century but for *Or.* 12. 1-63
    (ἐπειδὴ), 14. 16 (ἰδίων)—15. 42 (κεκρατηκὼς ἄσ),
    18. 38 (ἀλλὰ τότε)—50 (τὰς δ'), this has been
    replaced by a 13th-century hand. For 18. 50-
    298 (μέγιστον) the text is lacking.
P : Vaticanus Palatinus 282, of 14th century.
U : Urbinas 126; dated to 1316 A.D.
V : Vindobonensis XCIII, of 12th century (with
    scholia).
I : Marcianus Append. XCI. 2, of 14th century.

# LIBANIUS

M : Marcianus 437, of 15th century.
B : Barberinus II. 41, of 15th century.

The basic MSS. are grouped broadly into two families, with considerable variation in the different orations. Thus for 12-16, CAP consistently show the characteristics of one family, VIBM those of the other, and U, despite a connection with I, shows traces of a mixed tradition. For 24, however, the first family is represented by CAPBM, the second by VUI. Only CAV remain throughout free from any mixture of tradition, so that their importance is of the greatest.

## EDITIONS

The editio princeps, the Ferrara edition of Soterianus Capsalis (1517), contains 12, 14, 15 of these orations. Morel (*Libanii Orationum, Tomus II*, 1627), using the Ferrara edition, supplemented by P, Par. 3016, and Vat. 939, published 12-15, 17 and an incomplete version of 18. Olearius (Leipzig, 1702), using a transcript of Bodl. Barocc. 219, first published 24, and this, with *Or.* 2, an incomplete version of 16 (1-36) and 18 complete, appeared in Fabricius, *Bibl. Gr.* vii. 145-378 (Hamburg, 1715). The first consolidated edition of these orations was undertaken by J. J. Reiske and was produced after his death by his widow (*Libanii Sophistae Orationes et Declamationes* [4 vols.] : Altenburg, 1791). For this A and the Wolfenbüttel Codex were used in conjunction with the editions of Morel and Ferrara. However, the actual text is often that of Morel, with the many conjectures that Reiske had previously advanced in his *Animadversiones*, vol. V (Leipzig, 1766), mainly appearing in the notes ; but it remained the standard text until superseded by Foerster's Teubner text (Leipzig, 1903–1927; 12 vols.) These orations appear as part of vol. II of Foerster's edition. An unpublished edition of ten orations, by E. Monnier (*c.* 1860), in which 16 and 24 appear, exists in copies in the Sorbonne and Dumbarton Oaks (*cf.* Petit, *Libanius et la vie municipale à Antioche*, p. 8 ; Downey, *P.A.P.S.* ciii [1959], pp. 654-655). Cobet's textual work, which first appeared in *Mnemosyne,* is collected in *Miscellanea Critica* (Lugd. Bat., 1876) and *Collectanea Critica* (1878).

## TRANSLATIONS

The orations edited by Morel and Fabricius were accompanied by Latin translations, that of Morel being very indifferent. The translation offered by Fabricius was the competent work of Olearius. The sole English translation of any of these orations is that of 17 and 18 by C. W. King in the Bohn Library's *Julian the Emperor* (London, 1888).

## HISTORICAL SOURCES

Other than Libanius himself, the chief ancient sources for the career of Julian are :

Julian : ed. W. C. Wright, 3 vols. (Loeb), 1913.

Julian : *Epistulae, Leges, Fragmenta,* ed. Bidez and Cumont (Paris ; Les Belles Lettres and O.U.P.), 1922 = *E.L.F.*

Julian : *Œuvres complètes,* ed. Bidez, Rochefort, Lacombrade (Paris ; Les Belles Lettres), 2 vols. in 4, 1924–1964.

Ammianus Marcellinus : *Histories,* ed. Rolfe (Loeb), 3 vols. (especially Books 15-25).

# LIBANIUS

Chrysostom (John): *Oration on S. Babylas*, Migne, *P.G.* 50. 545 ff.

Codex Theodosianus : ed. Mommsen.

Eunapius : *Lives of the Sophists*, ed. Wright (Loeb).

Eunapius : *Histories*, ed. Müller (*F.H.G.*, vol. V), Didot.

Gregory Nazianzen : *Orations* 4-5 (Invectives against Julian), Migne, *P.G.* 35. 531 ff. Translated by King in *Julian the Emperor*.

Mamertinus : *Gratiarum Actio Juliano* (*Panegyrici Latini*, O.C.T.).

Socrates : *Historia Ecclesiastica*, Bk. 3, c. 1-23.

Sozomen : *Historia Ecclesiastica*, Bks. 5 and 6. 1-2.

Themistius : *Orationes*, ed. Dindorf, 1832 (repr. 1961).

Themistius : *Orationes*, ed. Downey, vol. 1 (Teubner), 1964.

Zosimus : *Histories*, ed. Mendelssohn, 1887 (repr 1963), Book 3.


## Modern Literature

An exhaustive bibliography dealing with Julian, Libanius and the history of Antioch is to be found in P. Petit, *Libanius et la vie municipale à Antioche*, Paris, 1955, and in G. Downey, *A History of Antioch in Syria*, Princeton, 1961.

Other literature particularly relevant to the present volume is :

P. Allard : *Julien l'Apostat*, Paris, 1906–1910.

J. Bidez : *La Vie de l'empereur Julien*, Paris, 1930.

P. de Jonge : " Scarcity of corn and corn prices in Ammianus Marcellinus," *Mnemosyne* (Ser. 4), i, pp 238-245 (1948).

# BIBLIOGRAPHY

G. Downey : " Julian the Apostate at Antioch," *Church History*, viii (1939), pp. 305 ff.

G. Downey : " Julian and Justinian and the unity of faith and culture," *ib.* xxviii (1959), pp. 7 ff.

G. Downey : *Economic Crisis at Antioch under Julian* (in *Studies in Social and Economic History in honour of A. C. Johnson*), Princeton, 1951.

W. Ensslin : " Kaiser Julians Gesetzgebungswerk und Reichsverwaltung," *Klio*, xviii (1923), pp. 104-199.

A. J. Festugière : *Antioche païenne et chrétienne*, Paris, 1959.

R. Foerster and K. Muenscher : " Libanius," *P.W* xii. 2. 2485-2551.

J. Geffcken : *Kaiser Julianus*, Leipzig, 1914.

A. H. M. Jones : *Social and Economic History of the Later Roman Empire*, Oxford, 1964.

J. Misson : *Recherches sur le paganisme de Libanius*, Louvain, 1914.

A. D. Nock : " Deification and Julian," *J.R.S.* xlvii (1957), pp. 114-123.

A. F. Norman : *Libanius' Autobiography*, ed. with translation and comment, Oxford, 1965.

L. Petit : *Essai sur la vie et la correspondance de Libanius*, Paris, 1866.

P. Petit : " Recherches sur la publication et la diffusion des discours de Libanius," *Historia*, v (1956), pp. 479-509.

A. Rostagni : *Giuliano l'Apostata*, Turin, 1920.

O. Seeck : *Die Briefe des Libanius zeitlich geordnet*, Leipzig, 1906 (repr. 1966).

O. Seeck : *Geschichte des Untergangs der antiken Welt*, Berlin, 1897–1921 (repr. 1967).

G. R. Sievers : *Das Leben des Libanius*, Berlin, 1868.

# LIBANIUS

E. A. Thompson : *The historical Work of Ammianus Marcellinus*, Cambridge, 1947.

Gore Vidal : *Julian* (a novel), 1964.

E. von Borries : "Julianos," *P.W.* x. 26 ff.

# ORATION 13

# ΠΡΟΣΦΩΝΗΤΙΚΟΣ ΙΟΥΛΙΑΝΩΙ

R 405　1. Ἐπανήκει μετὰ τῶν ἱερῶν, ὦ βασιλεῦ, καὶ τὸ F ii
τιμᾶσθαι τὴν τῶν λόγων τέχνην, οὐ μόνον ὅτι
μέρος τῶν ἱερῶν οὐκ ἐλάχιστον ἴσως οἱ λόγοι, ἀλλ᾽
ὅτι καὶ πρὸς τὴν τιμὴν τῶν θεῶν ὑπ᾽ αὐτῶν ἐκι-
νήθης τῶν λόγων. οὓς οὖν τῶν παρόντων ἀγαθῶν
αἰτίους εἶναι συμβέβηκε, τούτοις ἔδει δήπου καὶ
χώραν ἐν βασιλείοις εἶναι. 2. ἤκουσιν οὖν ὥσπερ
εἰς πομπήν τινα κεκοσμημένοι συγχαίροντες αὐτοῖς
τε καὶ πᾶσιν ἀνθρώποις, τὸ μὲν μῆκος εἰς αὖθις
ἀποθέμενοι, μεθ᾽ ὥρας δέ σοι | καὶ δρόμου φανῆναι F 6
βουλόμενοι, δοῦναι δὲ χάριν Ἑρμοῦ τε καὶ Μουσῶν
καὶ τῆς σῆς κεφαλῆς. εἰ γὰρ τὴν ἀπὸ τοῦ νεύματος
θεῖο ψῆφον, ἅπαντα ἕξει καλῶς. 3. ἐπέρχεται δέ
μοι μόνῳ θαρρεῖν ἐξ ἁπάντων ὁπόσοι τι τοιοῦτον
ἐτόλμησαν, οὔ τι κατὰ τὴν ῥώμην τῶν λόγων
R 406 οὐδ᾽ ὡς | μᾶλλον ἑτέρου λαβόντι τὴν τέχνην, ἀλλ᾽
ὅτι τὰ τῶν ἐρωμένων ὁποῖά ποτ᾽ ἂν ᾖ, καλὰ
φαίνεται τοῖς ἐρῶσι καὶ τὸ δοκιμάζειν ἀφέντες ὡς
ἐπὶ θαυμαστοῖς βοῶσι. 4. σὺ δ᾽ ἡμῖν πάλαι σαυτὸν
ἐνταῦθα κατέστησας, ᾧ γε καὶ σοφιστὴς ἅπας ἐπὶ
λόγοις εἰσιὼν παρέχει φόβον, μή τι βέλτιον ἐμοῦ

---

a Oration 13, requested by Julian at the first meeting with
Libanius upon his arrival in Antioch (July A.D. 362), and
referred to in Ep. 736: μικρὰ δὲ αὐτὸν ἀναπαύσας καὶ τὴν πόλιν
ἁμίλλαις ἵππων εὐφράνας, ἐκέλευέ με λέγειν καὶ εἶπον παρακληθείς,

2

# AN ADDRESS TO JULIAN [a]

1. In company with the worship of the gods, Sire, there has also returned the reverence for the practice of eloquence, not merely because eloquence is perhaps no small part of such worship, but also because you have been inspired towards reverence for the gods by eloquence itself. So there must surely have been room in your palace for it, since it has come to pass that it is responsible for our present blessings.[b] 2. Hence it comes, as though garbed for some triumphal procession, rejoicing in its own good fortune and in that of all mankind. Lengthy discourse it postpones for the future, in its desire to appear before you with speed and vigour and to grant us the grace of Hermes, the Muses and yourself, for if your verdict is one of approval, all will be well. 3. Of all who have essayed such a task as this, I, and I alone, have been induced to take courage, not through any special powers of eloquence on my part, nor through any surpassing skill, but because any object of affection is lovely to the lover's eye, so that, abjuring minute examination, he hails it as a nonpareil. 4. And you have long held a place here among us, and, in consequence, the arrival of each fresh sophist to display his eloquence inspires in me the dread that he may

οὐκ ἐνοχλήσας, ὁ δὲ ἐτέρπετο βεβαιῶν μοι τὸ προοίμιον· ἔφην γὰρ αὐτὸν ἐν προοιμίῳ πάντα τἀμὰ καλὰ νομιεῖν ὑπὸ τοῦ ἐρᾶν (cf. § 3). καὶ οὕτως ἐξέβη.

[b] Cf. Or. 18. 157 ff.

LIBANIUS

τύχῃ φθεγξάμενος καὶ τὴν δόξαν ἣν εἶχες μεταστήσας ἀπέλθῃ.

5. Ἆρ' οὖν μοι καιρὸν ἔχει κατὰ τὸν Λέσβιον
Ἀλκαῖον ποιήσασθαι τὴν ἀρχήν ; ἦλθες ἐκ περά-
των γᾶς, οὐκ ἐλεφαντίνῃ χρυσοδέτῳ καλ-
λωπιζόμενος λαβῇ, καθάπερ ἐκεῖνος ἐποίησεν, ἀλλ'
ἀτεχνῶς χρυσῇ ψυχῇ κατευθύνων τὴν οἰκουμένην,
μεγάλα μὲν ἐκ τοῦ γένους ἔχων τὰ παραδείγματα,
μικρὰ δὲ τοῖς σαυτοῦ | καὶ τὰ μέγιστα ἀποφήνας. F
6. οἷον γάρ τι τὸ τῶν Αἰακιδῶν γενέσθαι φασίν,
ἀγαθὸς μὲν αὐτὸς Αἰακός, οἱ δὲ ἐξ ἐκείνου γνωρι-
μώτεροι τοῖς ἔργοις, εἰς Ἀχιλλέα δὲ τὸ σπέρμα
προβὰν καθ' ὑπερβολὴν ἐξέλαμψε, τοιοῦτόν τι καὶ
τὸ νῦν· γενναῖοι γενναιότερον ἔτεκον καὶ τὴν ἡδί-
στην ἧτταν ἡττήθησαν καὶ κοινὴν ταύτην ἁπάντων
ἐποίησαν. ὅταν γὰρ οἱ τῶν ἄλλων ἀμείνους δεύ-
τεροί του γένωνται, μειζόνως τούτους ἀπέφηναν
ἐκείνου δευτέρους, ὧν ἦσαν αὐτοὶ καλλίους. 7.
πόρρωθεν δὲ ἄρα καὶ πρὸ τῆς βασιλείας ἦρξω
κρατεῖν. οὐ γὰρ ὅμοια τὰ ἐν παισὶ σοί τε καὶ τοῖς
ἄλλοις, οὐδὲ αἱ κρηπῖδες παραπλήσιαι. τῶν γε
R 407 μὴν εὐθὺς ἐν ἁλουργίσι τραφέντων | ὁ τὰ πρῶτα
μετασχὼν ἰδιώτου τάξεως ἐμπειρότερος εἰς ἀρχήν,
ἐξ ἀγορᾶς ἔχων τὴν μάθησιν ὧν διοικήσειν ἔμελλεν.
8. οὑτωσὶ μὲν τῶν πρὶν ἢ λυσιτελεῖν βασιλευσάντων

---

ᵃ Alc. *fr.* 33 (Bergk.).
ᵇ Notably Constantius Chlorus, his grandfather : *cf. Or.*
18. 8, 59. 14 ff.  Eutrop. 10. 1. 2.
ᶜ For Julian's schooldays in Constantinople *cf. Or.* 18.
11 ff.
ᵈ Per contra, the same argument is used to justify heredi-

4

prove a better orator than I, and may depart after upsetting the opinion you used to hold of me.

5. So may I fittingly begin with the words of Alcaeus of Lesbos ? [a] " Thou hast come from the ends of the earth," though not, as he put it, with parade of " swordhilt ivory with gold o'erlaid," but with heart of pure gold directing the world aright, and though you have great models in your own family, you prove even the greatest of them to be but petty in comparison with your own. 6. Legend has it, with regard to the descendants of Aeacus, that though Aeacus himself was a man of might, his offspring were more renowned for their deeds until, when the line of descent came to Achilles, it blazed forth with glory unsurpassed. Now we see just such another example : noble sires [b] begat a nobler son and themselves suffered this most happy reverse and extended it to all men alike, for when, excelling others, they are themselves inferior to someone else, they prove those whom they excel to be yet more inferior to him. 7. So you began your supremacy long ago, even before your reign began, for your childhood days were not like those of the others, nor was the basis of your career at all similar.[c] In fact, the holder of a private station originally is more experienced with regard to administration than those brought up from birth in the purple, since he has a practical knowledge of the problems with which he will have to deal.[d] 8. So you are superior to those who ascended the throne before it was proper for them to do so, for you came to it

tary monarchy, *Or.* 59. 12 f. Constantine and his sons are implicitly criticized here, for Constantine began his imperial career by usurpation and his sons were elevated to the throne in boyhood. Julian however, was now over 30, and of better education than any of his predecessors.

# LIBANIUS

κρατεῖς, ὅτ' ἄμεινον, ἐπὶ τοῦτο ἥκων· τοὺς δ' αὖ
μετὰ σοῦ[1] τοῦτο ἐσχηκότας νικᾷς ἑτέρωθεν, μᾶλλον
δὲ καὶ τούτους κἀκείνους ἀπὸ τῶν αὐτῶν νικᾷς,
παιδείας καὶ λόγων, οἷς εὐθὺς ἐκ νέου τὴν ψυχὴν
ἀρδόμενος ὑπὸ τῶν τὸ μέλλον ἐπισταμένων θεῶν
πόρρωθεν ἐδημιουργοῦ πρὸς τὴν παροῦσαν τύχην
δεινὸν ἡγουμένων, εἰ τὸν μὲν ἐφ' ἅρμα | ἀναβησό-  F 6
μενον σὺν τέχνῃ τοῦτο δέοι ποιεῖν ἢ βεβλάφθαι
μετὰ τῶν ἵππων, ὁ δὲ τῆς οἰκουμένης τὰς ἡνίας
ληψόμενος σὺν ἀμαθίᾳ τοσαύτης ἡνιοχήσεως ἅπτοι-
το καὶ τοῖς ἐσθήμασι τῶν ἀρχομένων κρείττων ὢν
ἐν τῷ καλλίονι λείποιτο.

9. Ἐγίγνοντο τοίνυν ἀρχαὶ τούτῳ τοῦ μανθάνειν,
ὅτε περ τοῦ παιδεύειν ἐμοί, καὶ πεφυκὼς ἐξ ὧν
ἴσμεν πάντα ἀφελὼν ὄγκον ἐβάδιζεν εἰς διδασκάλου
καταστήσας αὐτὸν ἐν τῷ τῶν ἄλλων μέτρῳ καὶ δι'
ὧν μὲν ἐτίμα τὸ περὶ ταῦτα ἴσον ἠγαπᾶτο, νίκην
δὲ κἀνταῦθα λαμπρὰν ἀνῃρεῖτο, σπορὰν μὲν τὴν
αὐτὴν τοῖς ἄλλοις δεχόμενος, ἐν δὲ τῷ τόκῳ τὴν
νεότητα παριών.   10. δοκῶν δὲ βασιλείᾳ πανταχόθεν πρέπειν καὶ κινῶν ἐπὶ τοῦτο τὰς τῶν ὁρώντων
γλώττας, ἵνα μὴ τοιοῦτος ῥέῃ λόγος ἐν ὁμίλῳ
R 408 πολλῷ καὶ | πόλει φρόνημα ἐχούσῃ, πέμπεται τῇ
Νικομήδους ἐνδιατρίψων, ὡς ἀσθενεστέρᾳ.   11. τὸ
δὲ ἦν ἀρχὴ τῶν μεγίστων ἀγαθῶν αὐτῷ τε καὶ τῇ
γῇ· ἦν γάρ τις σπινθὴρ μαντικῆς αὐτόθι κρυπτό-
μενος μόλις διαφυγὼν τὰς χεῖρας τῶν δυσσεβῶν.

---

[1] σοῦ MSS., Re. : νοῦ F.

[a] Libanius began his career as a private teacher in Constantinople in A.D. 340/1 (Or. 1. 31 ff.).   Here, as in Or. 18,
he omits any mention of Julian's relegation to Macellum,

6

when it was better so. It is for another reason that
you excel those who have obtained it as you have
done, or rather it is for the same reasons that you are
superior to both types, because of your education and
the eloquence with which the gods in their knowledge of the future nurtured your soul from your
youth up, long since fashioning you for your present
station. They felt it to be wrong that, while any
intending chariot driver must perform this function
skilfully or come to grief along with his team, the
aspirant to the reins of government over the whole
world should venture on such a great career in
ignorance of it and, though more impressive than his
subjects in his dress, he should be lacking in the
nobler attributes.

9. He began his learning at about the same time
as I began my teaching.[a] Though sprung of the stock
we know, he put aside all pride and made his way to
the schoolroom, placing himself on the same level as
others, and by his respect for the principle of equality
here he earned affection and yet gained a glorious
victory, for the seed sown in him was the same as in
others, but in its fruits he surpassed all young students. 10. On every count he was held to be fitted
for the throne and he inspired observers to make this
comment : so, to prevent the spread of such talk
among the mass of the people in a proud city, he was
sent to stay in Nicomedeia, as being a place of less
importance. 11. But this was the cause of untold
blessings both for himself and for the world, for there
was hidden there a spark of prophetic fire that had
barely escaped the hands of the disbelievers. Hence,

but resumes with his second departure from Constantinople
for Nicomedeia c. A.D. 348.

ὑφ' | ᾧ δὴ πρῶτον τἀφανὲς ἀνιχνεύων τὸ σφοδρὸν F 6
μῖσος κατὰ τῶν θεῶν ἐπέσχες ὑπὸ τῶν μαντευ-
μάτων ἡμερούμενος. 12. ὡς δὲ ἧκες εἰς Ἰωνίαν
καὶ εἶδες ἄνδρα καὶ δοκοῦντα καὶ ὄντα σοφὸν καὶ
περὶ τῶν τὸ πᾶν δὴ τοῦτο τεκτηναμένων τε καὶ
διατηρούντων ἤκουσας καὶ πρὸς τὸ κάλλος τῆς
φιλοσοφίας ἔβλεψας καὶ τοῦ ποτιμωτάτου τῶν
ναμάτων ἐγεύσω, ταχέως ἀποσεισάμενος τὴν
πλάνην καὶ διαρρήξας ὥσπερ λέων τὰ δεσμὰ καὶ
τῆς ἀχλύος ἀπαλλαγεὶς ἀλήθειαν μὲν ἀντέλαβες
ἀγνοίας, τὸ δὲ γνήσιον τοῦ νόθου, τοὺς δὲ παλαιοὺς
ἄρχοντας ἀντὶ τοῦ νεωστὶ κακῶς εἰσκωμάσαντος.
13. μιγνὺς δὴ τοῖς ῥήτορσι τὸν ἀμείνω χρόνον,[1] καὶ
R 409 γὰρ τοῦτο θεῶν ἔργον | εἰς μέγεθός σοι τὴν διά-
νοιαν διὰ τοῦ Πλάτωνος ἀγόντων, ὅπως ὑψηλῇ
γνώμῃ μέγεθος ὑποδέξαιο πραγμάτων, ἤδη τοίνυν
ἰσχύων ἑκάτερα, δρόμῳ τε γλώττης καὶ μαθήσει
τῶν ὄντων, πρὶν ἢ βοηθεῖν ἔχειν τοῖς ἱεροῖς ἐμήνυες |
ὅτι καιροῦ διδόντος οὐκ ἀμελήσεις, δακρύων μὲν ἐπὶ F 6
τοῖς κειμένοις, στένων δὲ ἐπὶ τοῖς σεσυλημένοις,
ἀλγῶν δὲ ἐπὶ τοῖς ὑβρισμένοις, διδοὺς τοῖς πλησίον
ὁρᾶν ἐν τῇ παρούσῃ λύπῃ τὴν ἐσομένην βοήθειαν.
14. τοιαύτης δὲ ἐλπίδος ἀναφυομένης ἅπαν ὅσον
ἔκκριτον καὶ νοῦν ἔχον ἐν ἠπείρῳ καὶ νήσοις μετὰ
σοῦ ταῖς εὐνοίαις ἐτάττετο συγκατασκευάζοντες
τὴν βασιλείαν οὐχ ὅπλοις οὐδὲ ξίφεσιν, ἀλλ' εὐχαῖς

---

[1] χρόνον mss. : χορόν F. (conj. Re.).

---

[a] Bidez (*Vie de l'empereur Julien*, p. 57), suggests that this
influence towards divination was associated with Libanius,
who was teaching there until A.D. 348/9.

[b] Julian obtained full freedom of movement only with

Sire, as you first began to seek out hidden lore, you were soothed by its utterances and checked the violence of your hatred for the gods.[a] 12. Upon your arrival in Ionia, you beheld a man wise both in repute and in reality,[b] heard of the gods who fashioned and maintain this whole universe, gazed upon the beauty of philosophy and tasted of its sweetest springs. Then you quickly cast off your error and, lionlike, burst your bonds, released yourself from darkness and grasped truth instead of ignorance, the real instead of the false, our old gods instead of this recent intruder and his baneful rites. 13. To this more auspicious season you linked oratory, and this too was the doing of the gods, who led your intellect to greatness through the study of Plato for you to undertake great issues with exalted spirit, and confirmed now both in fluent speech and in knowledge of truth, even before you could succour our religion, you began to indicate that if opportunity offered you would not neglect it. You wept at the ruin of our temples, lamented at their rape, grieved at their violation, and allowed those about you to observe in your present pain the aid to come.[c] 14. With the revival of such hopes, all the elite of intellect on continent and island aligned itself with you in good will, and united in preparing for you the throne, not by force of arms or point of sword, but by hidden

Gallus' appointment as Caesar in A.D. 351. He immediately went to Julianus, the neo-Platonist at Pergamum, and thence to Maximus of Ephesus, where his conversion was immediate and complete: cf. Eunap. V.S. 473 ff., Julian, E.L.F. No. 111. For Maximus see also Lib. Or. 18. 155, 12. 33 f.

[c] An indication of the strength of the pagan " underground " movement against Constantius' religious policies, and of Julian's readiness to support it.

9

# LIBANIUS

λανθανούσαις καὶ κρυπτομέναις θυσίαις, μάντις τε
ἅπας ἐνεργὸς ἦν ἐπιθυμῶν προμαθεῖν τὸ νῦν ὁρώ-
μενον. θεοὶ δὲ εὐμενεῖς ἐπένευον. 15. οὕτω πολὺ
πρὸ ταυτησὶ τῆς χλαμύδος ἐβασίλευες καὶ τὴν
ἀρχὴν εἶχες ἔργῳ καὶ πρὸ τοῦ σχήματος. ὅταν
γὰρ ᾖ τὸ¹ βουλόμενον ἄρχεσθαι, κἂν μήπω τὸ
ποθούμενον ἐφεστήκῃ, ταῖς τῶν ἐπιθυμούντων
γνώμαις ἐν τάξει τοῦ κρατοῦντός ἐστι. 16. θεοὶ
δέ σε τῆς μεταβολῆς ἀγασθέντες καὶ ὧν ὑπὲρ
αὐτῶν ἐγνώκεις τε ἤδη καὶ δράσειν ἔμελλες μι-
σθοὺς τοὺς μὲν ἐδίδοσαν, τοὺς δὲ ἡτοίμαζον.
ἡτοίμαζον μὲν τὸ σκῆπτρον, ἐδίδοσαν δὲ τὴν σωτηρίαν, ὅτε δὴ τῆς θαλάττης ἀναταραχθείσης ἐκ
πνευμάτων συκοφαντικῶν καὶ σκάφους τοῦ μὲν
καταδύντος, τοῦ δὲ περικλυζομένου καὶ τοῦ κύμα-
τος ὑπὲρ τῶν τοίχων αἰρομένου | Διοσκούρους ἄνω- F
θεν ἐκ κοινοῦ βουλευτηρίου πέμψαντες ἐξήρπασαν
τοῦ κλυδωνίου τὸ πλοῖον.

R410  17. | Καὶ ταυτὶ μέν, ὡς ἐνῆν, μάλιστα σκιάσας
διῆλθον ἐν ᾧ σοι τρόπῳ χαριούμενος ᾔδειν· μεγα-
λοψυχίας γὰρ δὴ περιουσίᾳ καὶ τοῖς ἠδικηκόσιν ὧν
πέπονθας ἠφίεις τὴν μνήμην. ὃ πειράσομαι μὲν
ἐν τῷ λόγῳ φυλάττειν, οὐκ ἐώντων δὲ παντελῶς
τῶν πραγμάτων ἔστω συγγνώμη.

18. Πάλιν τοίνυν ἐνεθυμήθην ὅτι καὶ ὅσα σοι τῆς
τιμῆς ἀφαιρεῖν ἐδόκει, καὶ ταῦτα τῆς καλλίονος
μοίρας ἦν γνώμη θεῶν. ὅτε γοῦν ἀφῃρέθης τὴν
τοῦ βαδίζειν ὅποι βουληθείης ἐξουσίαν, ἐν τοιούτῳ

¹ <τῳ> τὸ F.

---

ᵃ Cf. Julian, Or. 7. 231 d. For Christian suspicions (post
eventum) cf. Socr. H.E. 3. 1. 16 ff., Greg. Naz. Or. 4. 30 ff.

prayer and secret sacrifice, and every seer was engaged upon his task, desiring foreknowledge of what we now see; and the gods gave their gracious approval. 15. So you were emperor long before you donned this imperial robe, and you held sway in fact even before assuming this guise; for when there exists in any man the wish to be ruled, even if the object of his longing be not yet placed over him, it is yet enthroned in the hearts of its devotees. 16. And the gods rejoiced at your conversion and began to present to you and to prepare for you the rewards for the activities you had determined upon and were to fulfil on their behalf.[a] They prepared for you the throne and presented you with salvation: at a time when the sea surged under storms of slander, when ships that sailed thereon were submerged or on beam ends, and waves rose high over the gunwales, they sent the Dioscuri from the council chamber of the gods in heaven and snatched your bark from the midst of the breakers.[b]

17. The details of this I have refrained from developing, as far as possible, so casting my narrative as I knew would please you; for in your sublime generosity you granted pardon for the memory of injuries received even to those who had injured you. This attitude I shall try to maintain in my narrative, but if the facts utterly forbid it, Sire, pray forgive me.

18. Yet again it occurs to me that all that seemed to rob you of distinction has, by will of heaven, actually been part of your nobler destiny. At any rate, when deprived of the power of moving freely to

[b] Covert reference to Julian's dangerous position after the fall of Gallus in A.D. 354: cf. Or. 18. 24 ff., Amm. Marc. 14. 2. 7 ff., Julian, Ep. ad S.P.Q.Ath. 272 ff.

11

χωρίῳ κατεκλείσθης ἐφ᾽ ὃ πάντως ἂν ἔδραμες
ἐξουσίας ὑπαρχούσης. εἰς γὰρ τὴν ἀρχαιοτάτην
καὶ σοφωτάτην καὶ θεοφιλεστάτην καὶ κοινὴν ἐρωμένην ἀνθρώπων τε καὶ θεῶν, τὰς Ἀθήνας,
ἐπέμπου, καὶ παραπλήσιον ἦν ὥσπερ ἂν εἰ δίκην
ἀπαιτῶν ἕνα τῶν Φαιάκων Ἀλκίνους ἐν τῷ κήπῳ
καθείρξας εἶχεν. 19. ἐγίγνετο δὴ ταὐτὸ σόν τε
καὶ τῆς πόλεως κέρδος. σύ τε γὰρ ἑώρας τὴν
πόλιν ἥ τε πόλις ἐκτᾶτο σύμμαχον ἀνάγκαις
ἀγράφοις ταῖς ἀπ᾽ εὐνοίας κατειλημμένον εὖ ποιεῖν
διὰ πάντων | τὴν λῆξιν τῆς Ἀθηνᾶς. ὦφθαι δὲ F
ὑπὸ σοῦ τὴν πόλιν ἔφην, ὅτι δὴ γέμων ἐκ τῆς
Ἰωνίας λόγων οὐδὲν ἐδεήθης τῆς μητροπόλεως εἰς
R 411 σοφίαν, ἀλλ᾽ | οὗ μανθάνειν νόμος ἐνταῦθα δεικνύ-
ειν εἶχες ἃ κομίζων ἀφῖξο.

20. Τὰ δὲ ἐπὶ τούτοις ἔτι μείζω τὴν ἀπόδειξιν
ἔχει τοῦ βουλαῖς δαιμόνων διοικεῖσθαί σοι τὸν βίον,
καὶ ὡς περιστάντες ἐφρούρουν τε φιλοπόνως καὶ
φόβων ἔλυόν τε καὶ πρὸς δύναμιν ἦγον, οὐ κατὰ
μικρὸν ἐργαζόμενοι τὴν μετάστασιν ἐν μήκει
χρόνων, ἀλλ᾽ ἀγχιστρόφῳ μεταβολῇ τὴν βασιλείαν
δόντες, ὁποῖα τὰ τῶν θεῶν, οὐδὲν χρῄζοντα διατριβῆς, ἀλλὰ συνάπτοντα τοῖς ἐγνωσμένοις τὸ
πέρας. 21. οὕτω δὴ καὶ σὲ μετὰ μὲν τοῦ τρίβωνος
Ἀθήνηθεν ἀνέστησαν, ἐν δὲ τῇ κρατούσῃ κατὰ
νόμον ἐσθῆτι ταχέως ἔδειξαν ἀπιστεῖν τε τοῦ

---

[a] Cf. Or. 12. 36. For Julian at Athens cf. Or. 18. 27 ff.,
Julian, ibid. 273 c ff., Amm. Marc. 15. 2. 8. (A.D. 355).

[b] The gardens of Alcinoüs gave fruit throughout the year ;
Homer, Od. 7. 112 ff.

[c] Athens, the legendary metropolis of Ionia, had been
for centuries the foremost university centre of Greece, a

12

whatever place you wished, you were confined in the place to which you would quickly have made your way were the power yours.[a] You were sent to the most ancient, sapient and reverend of cities, the beloved of gods and men alike, to Athens, and it was just like Alcinoüs, seeking to punish one of the Phaeacians, keeping him confined in his garden.[b] 19. The same situation, then, was profit both to the city and yourself, for you viewed the city and the city gained an ally, bound by the unwritten ties of kindliness to bestow continual favour upon the inheritance of Athena. The city, I said, was viewed by you, for you were so filled with eloquence from Ionia that with regard to wisdom you had no need of its mother city, and you could display in what is normally the home of learning those gifts that you had brought with you at your coming.[c]

20. The events that followed show still more clearly that your life has been ordered by divine counsel, and that the gods have girt you about and watched over you with loving care, freeing you from fear and elevating you to power, not effecting it by gradual process of change over a long period of time, but granting you empire in a sudden upheaval[d]—the usual way of the gods, that brooks no delay but attaches immediate fulfilment to their decrees. 21. So they removed you from Athens in your student's gown and promptly revealed you in the dress usual to

place it still struggled to maintain. Its specialization, however, was in rhetoric, which was regarded as of less account than philosophy, and this for most pagans was represented by Neoplatonism.

[d] This expression of triumph is deliberately resumed in the pathos of the lament of *Or.* 18. 284 : a borrowing from Thuc. 2. 53.

# LIBANIUS

διδόντος ἀναγκαζομένου καὶ πειθομένου πιστεύειν
καὶ νῦν μὲν ἀνειργομένου, νῦν δὲ παρακαλουμένου,
τὸ μὲν ἐξ ὧν αὐτῷ συνῄδει πεπονθότος, τὸ δὲ ἐκ
τῆς σῆς φύσεως δεχομένου, πολλάκις ἐφ᾽ ἑκάτερον
μεταπίπτοντος, ἕως ὁ φόβος ὑπεχώρησε τῇ πίστει.
22. οὐ μὴν ἐκ τῶν λείων καὶ ἧττον ἐπιπόνων,
ὥσπερ εἰκὸς πῶλον τό γε πρῶτον ὑπαγόμενον
ζυγῷ, τῆς βασιλείας | ἥπτου ἀλλ᾽ ὥσπερ εἰ πρῶτον F 7
πλέων ἀπὸ τοῦ Σικελικοῦ πορθμοῦ τὴν πρώτην
ἀναγωγὴν ἐποιοῦ, χαλεπωτάτου γε πορθμοῦ, ὡς
Ὅμηρός τε δηλοῖ καὶ μαρτυρεῖ Θουκυδίδης, οὕτως
ἀπὸ τῆς ἑσπέρας, ᾗδ᾽ ἐστὶ πολέμου χωρίον, ἀρχὴν
ἐβάλου τῶν βασιλικῶν ἄθλων. 23. καὶ τὸ μὲν
σχῆμα ἦν δεχομένου μέρος τῶν ὄντων, τὸ δὲ ἔργον
R 412 τὰ μήπω | παρόντα κτωμένου. ἐπορεύου γὰρ ἐπ᾽
ὀνόματα πόλεων μᾶλλον ἢ πόλεις καὶ ποιήσων
πόλεις ἢ χρησόμενος οὔσαις· ὥστε ἐῴκεις οἰκιστῇ
γῆν ἔρημον οἰκίζοντι τῶν προσοικούντων οὐκ
ὄντων. 24. τοῦ γὰρ τῶν βαρβάρων ῥεύματος
ἐπικλύσαντος τὴν Γαλατῶν εὐδαιμονίαν, μᾶλλον
δὲ πεποιηκότος τῶν βαρβάρων τὰ τούτων, οὐ γὰρ
πάντα ἐφεξῆς ἔφθειραν ἀλλ᾽ εἶχον ὅσα ἐξῆν ἄγειν
καὶ ἦσαν ἰσχυρότεροι τοῖς ἔνθεν προσγενομένοις,
οὐκ ἠγάπησας εἰ στήσαις τὴν ὕβριν, οὐδὲ τὸ μή
τι παθεῖν ἀρκεῖν ἡγήσω, καίτοι καὶ τοῦτο ἦν

---

<sup>a</sup> For Julian's departure from Athens and elevation to
the rank of Caesar cf. Or. 18. 31, Julian, Ep. ad S.P.Q.Ath.
275 a b, Amm. Marc. 15. 8. 2 ff., Zos. 3. 1.
<sup>b</sup> As the murderer of Julian's kinsmen, a charge often
levelled by Julian and Libanius.
<sup>c</sup> For Constantius' suspicions cf. Julian, ibid. 277 d, 281 d,
Zos. loc. cit., Lib. Or. 12. 44, 18. 36 ff.

the emperor.[a] Constantius, who presented it, was inevitably distrustful and yet induced to trust you, now restrained by his own guilty conscience,[b] now encouraged by the loyalty of your nature, and his attitude often wavered until finally fear gave way to confidence.[c] 22. Yet it was on no smooth and easy course, such as you might expect a colt to be given when first put between the shafts, that you began your reign. Like a sailor starting on his maiden voyage from the Sicilian strait, that most hazardous of passages, as Homer proves and Thucydides confirms,[d] so from the west, the seat of war, you launched out upon the start of your imperial duties. 23. Your outward seeming was that of receiving part of what we then had : in reality, you were getting something that was not yet there. Your journey took you to cities that existed more in name than in fact, not to acquaint you with living communities but to create new ones. You were like some founding father, colonizing a region deserted and barren of neighbouring peoples. 24. For the barbarian flood had inundated the wealth of Gaul, or rather had rendered up to the barbarians all that Gaul possessed, for they blazed no trail of destruction but held possession of all that they could get and grew stronger on what they acquired from it.[e] You were not content merely to stay their outrages, nor did you consider it enough just to take no harm, though to be sure the

[a] Homer, *Od.* 12. 73 ff., 235 ff. Thuc. 4. 24. Julian was appointed Caesar in November and left for Gaul in midwinter, A.D. 355/6.

[e] For the overrunning of Gaul by the Alemanni since the revolt of Magnentius and his defeat at Mursa in A.D. 353 *cf.* Julian, *ibid.* 279 a ff., Zos. *loc. cit.*, Amm. Marc. 15. 8. 1 ff., 16. 2. 12, Lib. *Or.* 12. 44 ff., 18. 34 ff.

μέγιστον ἐν μέσῳ ληφθέντα τοῦ πυρὸς κρείττω γενέσθαι τῆς φλογός, ἀλλ' εἰ μὴ πικρὰν αὐτοῖς καταστήσαις τὴν ἡδονὴν ἣν ἥδοντο νικῶντες καὶ τὴν λείαν ἐπιζήμιον ἣν ἀπῆγον τρυφῶντες, οὐκ ἠξίους εἰς τὸν ἥλιον ἐλευθέρως βλέπειν, ἀντὶ τῶν ἐκδεδωκότων ὁ πειρώμενος ἀνασώζειν αἰσχυνόμενος.

25. Ἐνταῦθα δὴ τοῦ λόγου γενόμενος Ὅμηρος μὲν | ἂν εἶπεν· ἔσπετε νῦν μοι Μοῦσαι Ὀλύμ- F 7 πια δώματ' ἔχουσαι, ἐγὼ δὲ σοῦ δεηθείην ἂν εἰπεῖν ὅπως ἕκαστα πέπρακται. δεῖ δὲ οὐδέν σοι πρὸς ταῦτα στόματος, ἀλλ' ἀποχρήσει δοῦναι τὴν συγγραφὴν ἣν ὧν αὐτὸς ἔπραξας συνέθηκας ὁ R 413 αὐτὸς γενόμενος | καὶ στρατηγὸς καὶ συγγραφεύς. 26. ἀλλ' ἐκεῖνα μέν μοι χορηγήσει πρὸς μῆκος λόγου μικρὸν ὕστερον, ἐπειδὰν εἰς τὸ πᾶν ἀφεῖναι πέλαγος ὁ θεὸς ἐπιτρέπῃ, νῦν δὲ τὸ κεφάλαιον τῶν εἰργασμένων, καὶ γὰρ εἰς ἅπασαν ἐξέδραμε τὴν οἰκουμένην, εἰρήσεται.

27. Τοὺς μὲν διώκοντας φεύγοντας ἔδειξας, τοὺς ἐπηχότας δὲ ἐλαύνοντας, τοὺς μὲν ἁρπάζοντας ἀποδιδόντας, τοὺς δὲ ἀφαιρεθέντας κομιζομένους, καὶ μετήλλαξας φόβον καὶ θάρσος, ῥώμην καὶ ταπεινότητα, τὸ μὲν τρέμειν εἰς τοὺς ἐναντίους ἀπώσας, τὴν δὲ ἐκείνων ὑπεροχὴν εἰς τοὺς οἰκείους μεταστήσας. 28. οὐκ ἔστιν ὅπως ταῦτα σὺ χωρὶς τῆς Ἀθηνᾶς εἰργάσω, ἀλλ' ἔχων Ἀθήνηθεν τὴν θεὸν καὶ βουλῆς κοινωνὸν καὶ πράξεων συνεργόν, ὥσπερ Ἡρακλῆς ἐπὶ τὸν ἀλλόκοτον | κύνα, πάντα μὲν εἶδες τοῖς F 7

---

[a] Homer, *Iliad*, 2. 484.
[b] Julian wrote an account of the Battle of Strasburg

16

first preoccupation of anyone encircled by flames is not to get burned. But you could not endure to look upon the sun with level gaze if you did not make sour for them their joy in victory, and turn to their despite the loot with which they so exultantly made off. It was not those who had surrendered it, but you who attempted to retrieve it, that felt the disgrace.

25. At this point of the narrative, a Homer would have said, " Speak to me now, ye Muses, who live in Olympian dwellings." [a] I, however, would fain beg of you to tell how everything came to pass. Nor is there need for you to utter a word about it : it will suffice to provide the history that you composed about your own campaigns, a general turned historian.[b] 26. Yet such topics will serve as matter for full-scale oratory on some occasion hereafter, when heaven commands me to launch out upon the main.[c] For the moment I shall relate your achievements in summary, for their renown has traversed the world.

27. You revealed the hunters hunted and their cowering quarry in pursuit, ravagers restoring plunder and the ravaged recovering it : you have changed fear and courage, strength and weakness, about, so that you have thrust panic into your foes and transferred their ascendancy into your own subjects. 28. You could never have effected this without the help of Athena. You got her from Athens to be your comrade in counsel and partner in action, just as Heracles did when he went for the monster Cerberus [d] : in the light of reason you

(Argentoratum) in A.D. 357, cf. Julian, Epistulae, Leges, Fragmenta, ed. Bidez-Cumont ( =E.L.F.), pp. 212 f.
[c] A promise partly fulfilled in Or. 12 (To Julian as Consul) and completed with great pathos in Or. 18 (the Epitaphios).
[d] Cf. Homer, Iliad. 8, 366 ff., Od. 11. 623ff.

λογισμοῖς ὀρθῶς, πάντα δὲ τοῖς ὅπλοις ἐπετέλεσας
γενναίως, οὐ πέμπων στρατιώτας ἐκ χαρακώματος
οὐδ᾽ ἐν σκηνῇ καθήμενος περὶ τῶν ἐν τῇ μάχῃ
πυνθανόμενος, ἀλλὰ καὶ ποδὶ χρώμενος καὶ χεῖρα
κινῶν καὶ δόρυ σείων καὶ ξίφος ἕλκων, αἵματι τῶν
ἐναντίων παρακαλῶν τοὺς στρατιώτας, ἐν μὲν
ταῖς σκέψεσι βασιλεύων, ἐν δὲ τῷ τάττειν στρατηγῶν, ἐν δὲ ταῖς συμπλοκαῖς ἀριστεύων.   29.
τοιγαροῦν πολλάκις ἐπανῆλθες χρῄζων περιπλῦναι
414 τὰ ὅπλα | γέμοντα φόνου βαρβαρικοῦ, καί σε
διεδέξατο τράπεζα τῶν πολλῶν οὐ διαφέρουσα·
πλείω μὲν γὰρ πράττειν ἠξίους, μᾶλλον δὲ τρυφᾶν
οὐκ ἠνείχου.   30. τίνες οὖν οἱ τούτων καρποί ;
Γαλατῶν αἱ πόλεις ἀνίσταντο θεωρούντων μὲν
ἡμῶν, οἰκοδομούντων δὲ τῶν βαρβάρων.   ὥσπερ
γὰρ ἦν ἕτεμον Σπαρτιᾶται γῆν Τεγεατῶν, ταύτην
εἰργάζοντο τοῖς νενικηκόσι χοίνικας ἔχοντες, οὕτως
ἃς οἶδε κατήνεγκαν πόλεις αὐτοὶ ποιεῖν ἠναγκάζοντο, καὶ χεῖρες αἱ μαθοῦσαι κατασκάπτειν ἀνορ-
θοῦν ἐπαιδεύοντο.   31. λεὼς δὲ τοῖς ἄστεσιν οὐκ
ἐκ τῶν ἀγρῶν οὐδὲ σύμμικτος οὐδὲ τῶν ἐπιτυ-
χόντων, ὥστε τὰ μὲν ἄψυχα τοῖς πρὶν ἐοικέναι,
τὸ δὲ κυριώτερον χεῖρον εἶναι τοῦ πρόσθεν, ἀλλ᾽
ἀπέδωκας πάσῃ μηχανῇ τὰς μὲν οἰκίας τῷ τόπῳ,
ταῖς δὲ οἰκίαις τὰ σώματα.   καὶ κατῇσαν ἄνδρες
καὶ γυναῖκες καὶ παῖδες | ἐκ δουλείας ἀδίκου πρὸς F
εὐδαιμονίαν ἀρχαίαν, καὶ παρ᾽ οἷς ἐτράφησαν ἐν
οἰκετῶν τάξει, παρὰ τούτων ἐτρέφοντο πάλιν ἐν

---

ᵃ Cf. Herod. 1. 66.   For Julian's reconstruction of Gaul

saw all correctly, by force of arms you performed all nobly ; you sent no soldiers out from their lines to fight while you sat in your tent and heard of the fighting by hearsay, but by stamp of foot and move of hand, by poise of spear and grasp of sword, you encouraged your men with the blood of the foe, an emperor in strategy, a commander in tactics, a hero in combat. 29. In sober truth, you often returned requiring your gear to be cleaned, covered as it was with the blood of the barbarian, and a table, no different from that of the rank and file, then received you. While demanding of yourself the performance of greater deeds than theirs, greater luxury you refused. 30. So the fruits of all this are that the cities of Gaul have risen again, by the labours of the barbarian, as we look on. For, just as the shackled Spartans worked for their conquerors the land they had tried to wrest from Tegea,[a] so they too were compelled to rebuild the cities they had ruined, and their hands, schooled in devastation, were taught to engage in reconstruction. 31. The population for these towns was not drawn from the peasantry, nor yet was it a motley throng composed of any Tom, Dick or Harry. In consequence, the restoration of the inanimate features of the cities to their former state was not accompanied by a deterioration in their more vital element, but you used every endeavour to restore the homes to the locality and their inhabitants to their homes. Men, women and children began to return from base slavery to the prosperity of times past, and they were still maintained, but now as masters, by those same folk who had once main-

and the restoration of Gallic captives *cf.* Julian, *ibid.* 280 c, Lib. *Or.* 18. 75 ff., Amm. Marc. 17. 10 ff., 18. 1 ff.

# LIBANIUS

δεσποτῶν νόμῳ. ἡ δὲ τροφὴ σῖτος ἦν, μισθὸς
εἰρήνης. 32. πολλῶν δὲ ἀγγέλων ὡς τὸν πρεσβύτερον θεόντων ᾔτησε μὲν στρατιὰν οὐδείς, νίκην
δὲ πάντες ἐμήνυον. ὁ δὲ λόγος φερόμενος εἰς
Μήδους ἐνέπεσεν. εἶθ᾽ οἱ μὲν εὔχοντό σε περὶ τὸν
R 415 Ῥῆνον μένειν, οἱ δ᾽ αὖ περὶ Ῥῆνον διαβῆναί σε
τὸν Τίγρητα καὶ σφίσι μὲν ἕτερον ἀντιταχθῆναι,
σὲ δὲ καὶ Πέρσαις ἐπιδεῖξαι τὴν αἰχμήν.
33. Ἄγαμαι δὲ τῶν στρατιωτῶν ἐκείνων, οἳ
στεφανούμενόν σε τοῖς τροπαίοις ὁρῶντες οὐκ
ἤνεγκαν μὴ περιθεῖναι τὸν ἐκ λίθων στέφανον
δεινὸν νομίζοντες τὸ μὴ συμβαίνειν τοὔνομα τοῖς
ἔργοις μηδὲ συνᾴδειν τὴν τιμὴν ταῖς νίκαις.
καλούσης τοίνυν αὐτῆς τῆς ἀνδραγαθίας τὸ γέρας
εὖ ποιοῦντες ἠκολούθησαν, ὥσπερ ἀρίστῳ στρα-
τιώτῃ σκευὴν ἀμείνω διδόντες ἀντὶ τῆς χείρονος.
34. ταυτὶ δὲ ταῖς μὲν φαινομέναις ἀνάγκαις ὑπ᾽
ἐκείνων ἐδρᾶτο, ταῖς δὲ κρυπτομέναις ψήφοις ὑπὸ
τῶν θεῶν ἐκυροῦτο τῶν τε συμπαραταξαμένων
αὐτῷ τῶν τε ἄνωθεν τεθεαμένων τὰς μάχας. ὢ
νυκτὸς ἐκείνης ἱερᾶς, ὢ φιλονεικίας ὁπλιτῶν
ἐνθέου, ὢ θορύβου πομπῆς ἡδίονος, ὢ μακαρίας
ἀσπίδος ἣ | τὸν τῆς ἀναρρήσεως ἐδέξατο νόμον F 7
πρεπωδεστέρα σοι παντὸς εἰωθότος βήματος. ὡς
καλὸν μὲν σοῦ τὸ διωθεῖσθαι τὴν δόσιν, κάλλιον
δ᾽ ἐκείνων τὸ κατεπείγειν τὴν λῆψιν, ἐπιεικὲς δὲ
τὸ περὶ τοῦ πεπραγμένου τὸν θυμούμενον πραΰνειν,
R 416 ἀνδρεῖον δὲ | τὸ μὴ πρὸς βίαν τοῦ δοθέντος
ἐκπεσεῖν. 35. ὅτε δὴ πολλῶν ἐθνῶν μυρίοις

---

[a] Julian, *ibid.* 284 a ff., gives his own version of his
proclamation as Augustus in Paris in A.D. 360. Amm.
Marc. 20. 4 gives the most detailed and impartial account,

20

tained them as slaves. And their maintenance was
corn, a reward of peace. 32. Many messengers sped
to your senior colleague, but none requested an army
of reinforcement : all bore tidings of victory. The
news spread and burst upon the Persians, and then
they prayed for you to stay in the Rhineland, while
the Germans prayed for you to cross the Tigris and
for someone else to be pitted against them, while
you bared your blade against the Persians too.

33. Blessings upon those soldiers who saw you
crowned with victories and could not forebear to
place upon your head the jewelled crown ! They
thought it shameful for your title not to match your
deeds and for your station not to be attuned to your
victories. So your very valour invited its reward,
and they rightly followed its lead, as in the presentation to a fine soldier of finer gear instead of the second
rate. 34. This action, that they performed in consequence of what they regarded as necessity, was
ratified by the secret decisions of the gods, who
ranged themselves at his side and from heaven
gazed upon his battles. Ah, holy night, inspired
discontent of the soldiery and tumult more joyous
than any triumph ! Ah, blessed shield, that received
the ritual of proclamation more fittingly for you than
any usual dais ! How noble it was of you to reject
the offer ; how nobler of them to insist on its acceptance, how sensible to seek the abatement of your
anger at the deed, and how steadfast not to be
diverted from their offer into violence.[a] 35. And

from which it is clear that the situation was to some extent
manipulated by Julian. The three accounts given by
Libanius (*Or.* 12. 59 ff., 13. 33 f., 18. 95 ff.) are analysed by
Petit, " Recherches sur la publication et la diffusion des
discours de Libanius," *Historia*, 5 (1956), pp. 479 ff.

21

# LIBANIUS

ταλάντοις ἐπὶ σὲ παρακληθέντων τὸν ἡγούμενον
αὐτῶν ῥᾳδίως ἑλὼν τῇ τῶν κακούργων περιέβαλες
αἰκίᾳ διδάσκων ἐν ταῖς πλευραῖς μὴ τοιαῦτα
κερδαίνειν, σὺ μὲν ἴσως ἐγέλας ἐπιβουλευόμενος,
ἡμεῖς δὲ ἐφροντίζομεν εἰ καὶ θαρρεῖν ὑπῆρχεν. ὁ
δὲ πάντα ὁρῶν τε καὶ ἀκούων Ἥλιος οἶδεν ἃ τότε
ἐφρονοῦμεν καὶ τί τῷ πολέμῳ τὸ πέρας ᾐτοῦμεν.
οἷα δὲ φιλόδωρος θεὸς ἔδωκέ τε καὶ κάλλιον ἤ τις
ἂν ἤλπισεν. 36. οὐ γὰρ ἐπέτρεψε συμπεσεῖν
στρατῷ στρατὸν οὐδὲ γυμνῶσαι σίδηρον οὐδὲ ἐξ
ἀλλήλων οἰκείους ἀριστεῦσαι οὐδὲ φοινιχθῆναι γῆν
φόνῳ φιλτάτων οὐδὲ τελεσθῆναι νίκην τοῖς νικῶσι
λυπηρὰν οὐδὲ τοὺς αὐτοὺς καὶ κρατεῖν καὶ δακρύειν, ἀλλ᾽ ἀποστήσας τῶν πραγμάτων τὸν ἕτερον,
ᾧ καιρὸν εἶχεν ἀπελθεῖν, ὑπὸ τῷ τεχνίτῃ τοῦ
βασιλεύειν τὰ πάντα ἐποίησεν, ὥστε σοί τε καθαρὸν
αἵματος γενέσθαι τὸ κράτος ἐκείνῳ τε | τιμηθῆναι F 76
τὸν νεκρὸν ἐκ τοῦ τρόπου τῆς τελευτῆς. 37.
καίτοι κἂν εἰ σιδήρῳ κριθῆναι τὴν ἔριν ἐδέησεν,
οὐκ ἂν ἑτέρως τὸ πρᾶγμα ἔπεσεν, ἀλλ᾽ ἐρρύη μὲν
ἂν αἷμα, βραχὺ δὲ τοῦτο καὶ μικρόν. πλὴν γὰρ
ὀλίγων κομιδῇ λόχων οἵπερ ἦσαν κεκολακευμένοι,
R 417 ὁ στρατιώτης ἅπας συνέπνει | καὶ ἐδόκει μὲν ἐπὶ
σὲ τρέχειν, ὑπὸ δὲ σοὶ τεταξόμενος ἠπείγετο. 38.
τί οὖν ἄν τις τῶν πάντων μάλιστα θαυμάσειε;
πότερον τὴν τοῦ δικαίου φυλακὴν ἢ τὴν τῶν
ἑπομένων ἀρετὴν ἢ τὴν καινὴν ὁδὸν καὶ τὸ προσ-

---

[a] Vadomarius : Amm. Marc. 21. 3 ff., cf. Julian, ibid.
279 c ff., 286 a.

[b] Constantius died at Mopsucrene in Cilicia in November A.D. 361. To Julian (E.L.F. No. 28, 382 b c) and to
Libanius this was a divine dispensation, for Julian became
indisputably sole Augustus, and the empire was saved from

22

when many tribes had been summoned to oppose
you by enormous payments, you captured their
leader[a] without difficulty and inflicted upon him
the disgrace reserved for felons, teaching him, by the
lash upon his ribs, not to make money in this way.
Though you, Sire, perhaps laughed such plots to
scorn, we could not but wonder whether there was
room for confidence. The all-seeing all-hearing Sun
knows what our feelings then were, and what the end
of the war for which we prayed, and this the gracious
god granted, and more gloriously than any could have
hoped. 36. For he did not allow the clash of army with
army or the baring of the sword, nor did he let kinsmen win their spurs over kinsmen, the staining of
the earth with the blood of their dear ones, or the
fulfilment of a victory disastrous for the victors,
where success and lamentation became synonymous.
He removed from the scene that rival, whose destiny
it was to depart, and placed the whole world under a
specialist in empire. Thus your dominion was kept
free of bloodshed, and the dead man was honoured
in consequence of the manner of his dying.[b] 37. And
yet if the conflict had had to be resolved by the
sword, the result would have been no different. Blood
would have flowed, but not much, and not for long.
Except for very few regiments which had been mis-
led, the whole army was of one mind, resolved to take
your side and insisting on being under your command.
38. What then of all these occurrences would excite
most admiration—your maintenance of the right,
the valour of your followers, the novelty of your

yet another bout of civil war. Constantius was buried with
full imperial honours, Julian himself assisting at the ceremony : Amm. Marc. 21. 16. 20, Lib. *Or.* 18. 120.

δοκώμενον κατὰ γῆν ἐλθεῖν[1] περιπλεύσαντα τὸ
πλέον δοῦναι[2] τῆς κινήσεως αἴσθησιν μετὰ τὴν
κτῆσιν ἢ τὸν ἐκπλήξαντα γένη βαρβαρικὰ πλοῦν[3]
ἢ τὸ τῶν κομιζομένων δώρων ἐπὶ τὴν ὄχθην
κάλλος ὠνουμένων ἑκάστων παραμεῖψαι τὴν σφετέ-
R 418 ραν | τὸν στόλον ; 39. ἐγὼ μὲν ἐραστής εἰμι τοῦ
ποταμοῦ, καί μοι φαίνεται τοῦ καλοῦ μὲν καλλίων
Ἐνιπέως, τοῦ γεωργοῦ δὲ χρησιμώτερος Νείλου
δεξάμενος | εὐμενεῖ τῷ πόρῳ πλοῖα φέροντα πᾶσιν F 77
ἐλευθερίαν. 40. εἴπω τι τῶν εἰρημένων λαμπρότερον; Κιλίκων μὲν ἠγνόουν οὐκ ὀλίγοι τὸ παρὰ
σφίσι συμβάν, σὺ δ' ἐκ μέσων Ἰλλυριῶν ἑώρας
τὴν τύχην, μᾶλλον δὲ ἐκ μέσων Γαλατῶν ἐπὶ τὸν
κλῆρον ἔπλεις κληρονόμου γνώμῃ ναυπηγησάμενος
τὸ πρῶτον, οὐ πολεμίου μίσει, καὶ συνέβη δὴ
πάντων καινότατον, αὐτὸς ἐγίγνου τοῖς ἀγγέλοις
ἄγγελος. καὶ ἃ μηνύσοντες ἦλθον ἀκούσαντες
ἀπῆλθον. 41. καὶ οὐ τὰ μὲν τοῦ δαιμονίου τοιαῦτα,
αἱ δὲ πόλεις ἥττω τῆς προσηκούσης ἡδονῆς[4]
ἥσθησαν, ἀλλ' εἰ πάντες ἄνθρωποι νοσήματι κοινῷ
τῶν ὀφθαλμῶν ἐστερημένοι θεοῦ τινος ἐξαίφνης
εὐνοίᾳ τὰς ὄψεις ἀπέλαβον, οὐκ ἂν μειζόνως

[1] ἐλθεῖν F. : ἔχειν mss.
[2] δοῦναι F., Morel (Monacensis gr. 13 = Mo) : δόντα Re.
(other mss.).
[3] ἢ τὴν παρὰ τῶν Ἀντιοχέων σοι πρέπουσαν κωμῳδίαν : here
inserted by Morel from Mo. Re. rejected as gloss.
[4] ἡδονῆς mss. : ἡδονὴν F. (conj. Re.).

---

[a] For Julian's advance along the Danube in summer A.D.

progress whereby, though expected to take an over-
land route, you sailed along allowing observation of
your movements, for the most part, only after attaining your objective, or that voyage that inspired panic
among savage tribes, or the wondrous gifts they
brought to the river bank, each of them purchasing
the diversion of the armada from their lands ? [a]
39. That river I adore : to me it is more beautiful
than Enipeus in its beauty [b] and more kindly than
the fertilizing Nile, for it received on its propitious
stream the vessels that brought freedom to all men.
40. And, to mention something even more notable
than my story so far, though many among the
Cilicians were unaware of what had happened in their
midst, you observed the event from the depths of
Illyria, or rather, of Gaul,[c] whence you sailed to your
inheritance, for the building of your fleet was originally begun from your standpoint as the heir, not from
hatred of your enemy. Hence there resulted the
strangest paradox of all, that you yourself announced
the tidings to the bearers of it, and they departed
after hearing the news they had come to deliver.
41. Nor was it the case that this was the handiwork
of god while the cities had less joy in it than was
proper. Their celebrations could not have been
surpassed if all mankind had been afflicted with
blindness in a universal disease and then suddenly,
through the kindness of some divinity, had its sight

361 *cf. Or.* 18. 111, Amm. Marc. 21. 8 ff., Zos. 3. 10, Mamertinus, *Grat. Act.* 6 ff.
    [b] The vale of Tempe, in Thessaly.
    [c] While at Vienne Julian had obtained foreknowledge
by divination of Constantius' imminent death (Amm. Marc.
21. 1. 6). This was confirmed by an omen before he received
news of it at Naissus, *ibid.* 22. 1. 2.

ἐχόρευσαν[1]· οὐ γὰρ φόβος ἠνάγκαζε πλάττεσθαι
τὴν χαράν, ἀλλ' ἐπὶ τῆς ἑκάστου ψυχῆς ἡ πανήγυρις
ἤνθει, καὶ πᾶν ἰδίᾳ λυποῦν ἀσθενέστερον ἦν τοῦ
καιροῦ, βοὴ δὲ ἐκ παντὸς χωρίου πρὸς οὐρανὸν
γεγηθότων ἤρχετο τοῦτο μὲν ἐξ ἄστεων, τοῦτο δὲ
ἐξ ἀγρῶν, καὶ οἰκιῶν καὶ θεάτρων καὶ ὀρῶν καὶ
πεδίων, φαίην δ' ἂν ὅτι καὶ παρὰ τῶν πλεόντων ἐκ
ποταμῶν τε καὶ λιμνῶν καὶ θαλάττης μέσης. 42.
ὅπερ γὰρ Ἀσκληπιὸν φασιν Ἱππολύτῳ γενέσθαι,
τοῦτ' αὐτὸς ἐγένου τῷ τῆς οἰκουμένης σώματι. |
R 419 τεθνεῶτάς τε ἀνέστησας καὶ βασιλείας ὄνομα νῦν, F 7
εἴπερ ποτέ, προσέλαβεν ἔργον. δίκην μὲν ἐπράξω
παρ' ὧν μὴ λαβεῖν ἄδικον, αἰτίαν δὲ οὐκ ἐπήνεγκας
οἷς ὑπῆρχεν ἀναχώρησις. ἵππων δὲ καὶ ὀρέων
διαδοχὰς ὑπὲρ μεγίστων δὴ τὸ πρῶτον συστάσας
τριβομένας ἔπαυσας ὑπὸ τῶν ἐλαυνόντων. 43. οἱ
δὲ τῶν ἐθνῶν ἄρχοντες ὑπὸ λημμάτων οὐκ ἄρχον-
ται, φόβος δὲ καὶ τιμῆς ἐλπίς, ἡ μὲν ἐπεγείρει
πρὸς ἀρετήν, ὁ δὲ εἴργει πονηρευμάτων. πᾶν μὲν
ἀνάλωμα μάταιον ἐκβέβληται, πᾶς δὲ πόρος οὐκ
εὐπρεπὴς λέλυται, πᾶσα δὲ δόσις εὔλογος τετίμηται.
μόνος γὰρ οἶσθα καλῶς καὶ δοῦναι καὶ μὴ δοῦναι,
μτοῖς ἀχίμοις μὲν διὰ τῶν δωρεῶν παραμυθούμενος
τοὺς πόνους, θαυματοποιῶν δὲ τέχνας οὔτε καταλύσας οὔτε θαυμάσας,[2] τὸ μὲν οὐ σαυτοῦ νομίζων,

---

[1] ἐχόρευσαν mss., Re. : ἐχάρησαν F. (conj. Cobet).

[2] καταλύσας οὔτε θαυμάσας F. : κατέλυσας οὔτ' ἐθαύμασας
mss., Re.

---

[a] Cf. Or. 1. 119, Amm. Marc. 22. 2., Zos. 3. 11.

[b] Cf. Pausanias 2. 27. 4.   In later legend, Hippolytus, as a
chaste huntsman and a favourite of Artemis, was raised

26

restored. Fear did not compel them to simulate gladness, but joy blossomed forth in all men's hearts and every private grief paled into insignificance at the event. Glad cries rose to heaven the whole world over, as men began to rejoice in town and in country, in houses, theatres, hills and plains, and, I would declare, on rivers, lakes and the high seas, from those who sailed thereon.[a] 42. You were, for the body of our world, what in legend Asclepius was for Hippolytus.[b] You restored the dead to life, and now at last the title of emperor has gained fulfilment. You punished all whom it was wrong to let go scot-free, but levelled no charge against anyone who had any reason to escape.[c] You ended the ill treatment by the drivers of the relays of horses and mules originally organized for services of state.[d] 43. The governors of the provinces are governed by no thought of gain, but fear keeps them from wrong-doing and hope of distinction spurs them on to virtue.[e] Every vain expense has been rejected, every sordid source of income stopped, every justifiable grant honoured; for you, and you alone, have full knowledge of what and what not to give, as you console your soldiers for their labours by your gifts[f] and, with regard to the wonder-workers, you neither suppress their craft, since you consider it of benefit to the communities, nor wonder

from the dead by Asclepius. Italian legend then transferred him to the grove of Diana at Aricia.

[c] For the trials at Chalcedon cf. Or. 18. 152, Amm. Marc. 22. 3.

[d] The reform of the *cursus publicus*, Feb. A.D. 362 : *Cod. Th.* 8. 5. 12, 11. 16. 10 (*E.L.F.* No. 67).

[e] Cf. Or. 18. 194 : Julian, *E.L.F.* p. 86, ll. 15 ff.

[f] Cf Cod. Th. 7. 4. 7-8, 6. 24. 1 (Jan. and Aug. A.D. 362 = *E.L.F.* Nos. 63, 116-117). *Misop.* 370 b.

# LIBANIUS

τὸ δὲ δήμοις συμφέρειν. 44. τράπεζα δέ σοι
μετρία | καὶ σύσσιτοι Πλάτωνος ὁμιληταί, μεθ' ὧν F 7
ἐγρήγορας ὑπὲρ γῆς ἁπάσης καὶ θαλάττης, καὶ
παρεδρεύει Διὶ μὲν ἐν οὐρανῷ Δίκη, σοὶ δὲ τῶν
ἐπὶ γῆς οἱ σοφώτατοι χαίροντες τῇ φορᾷ τῆς
ψυχῆς ἣν παρ' ἡμέραν ἐκφέρεις. 45. ἡ δὲ φορὰ
ποικιλωτέρα παντός, οἶμαι, λειμῶνος. ἧς ἐστὶ
μὲν καὶ τὸ ταῖς πόλεσιν ἐπανορθῶσαι τὴν πενίαν |
R 420 ἐξεληλαμέναις ἀρχαίων τε καὶ δικαίων κτημάτων,
ὃ τοὺς μὲν ἰδίους οἴκους μεγάλους ἐποίησε, τοῖς
δὲ κοινοῖς περιέχεεν ἀμορφίαν, ἔτι δὲ τὸ τοῦδε
κάλλιόν τε καὶ μεῖζον, τὸ δοῦναι πάλιν θεοὺς
ἀνθρώποις ἐπιτρόπους πάλαι τοῦ γένους ἄνευ τῶν
μεγάλων κυβερνητῶν εἰκῆ φερομένου καὶ περιρ-
ρηγνυμένου ταῖς πέτραις. 46. καὶ γέγονεν, ὥσπερ
ἐν ἐκλείψεσιν ἡλίου, τοῦ μὲν ἐνοχλοῦντος ἀπαλλαγή, τῆς δὲ ἀκτῖνος ἐπάνοδος, τὸ δὲ αὐτὸ καὶ
κόσμος πόλεσιν, ὥσπερ οἱ στέφανοι, καὶ σωτήριον,
ὥσπερ τὰ φάρμακα. δι' ὧν γὰρ γίγνονται καλλίους,
διὰ τούτων ἐπ' ἀσφαλοῦς ὁρμοῦσι. καὶ σοὶ χάρις
ὀφείλοιτ' ἂν οὐχ ἥττων ἢ Πελασγῷ τῷ Ἀρκάδι.
R 421 τοῦ γὰρ τὴν ἐκ τῶν ναῶν | καταδεῖξαι τιμὴν | τὸ F 8
σβεσθεῖσαν ἐπαναγαγεῖν οὐκ ἔλαττον.

47. Νῦν καιρὸν ἂν ἔχοι τοῦ ζῆν ἐπιθυμεῖν καὶ
θύειν ὑπὲρ μακροτέρου βίου. νῦν γὰρ ὡς ἀληθῶς
ἔστι ζῆν, ὅτ' εὐδαιμονίας αὖραι τὴν γῆν ἐπι-

---

*a Or.* 18. 126. Julian himself was expert in divination :
*cf.* § 48.  *b Cf.* Amm. Marc. 25. 4. 1-15.
*c* Julian's edict of March A.D. 362 whereby civic property
28

at it, since you consider that beneath you.[a] 44. Your
table is a modest one, and your companions there
pupils of Plato : with them you have kept watch and
ward over land and sea alike, and, as Justice is
enthroned at the side of Zeus in heaven, so the wisest
men on earth are seated at your side, rejoicing in the
harvest of the spirit that you yield each day.[b] 45.
This harvest has, to be sure, more variety than any
meadow, for it amends the poverty of the cities
which have been driven from their old and lawful
possessions, whereby private houses have become
great and those of the community rendered ugly.[c]
Still more noble and more notable is the restoration
of the gods as the overseers of mankind, since the
human race, without its mighty helmsmen to guide
it, has long been carried aimlessly hither and thither
and broken on the rocks.[d] 46. There has occurred, as
in the sun's eclipse, the removal of impediment and
the return of light, and for the cities this same is
both the crown that adorns them and the salve that
cures them, for the same things that cause their
beauty to increase, cause them to ride safe at anchor.
And no less gratitude would be due to you than
Pelasgus the Arcadian [e] earned, since the restoration
of honours suppressed is of no less importance than
their revelation in the temples of the gods.

47. Now would be the time to desire life and to
offer sacrifice for a longer span, for now we can truly
live, when the breezes of happiness waft over the

was restored to the cities, *Cod. Th.* 10. 3. 1.  Lib. *Or.* 16. 19,
*Ep.* 828, Amm. Marc. 25. 4, Sozom. 5. 3 ( =*E.L.F.* No. 47).
    [d] His edict of toleration (Jan. A.D. 362), *cf. E.L.F.* No.
42.
    [e] The hero from whom the Arcadians claimed descent,
Paus. 8. 1. 4.

πνέουσιν, ὅτε σῶμα μὲν ἀνθρώπου, ψυχὴ δὲ θεοῦ
βασιλεύει, ὅτε πῦρ μὲν ἐπὶ βωμῶν αἴρεται, καπνῷ
δὲ ἀὴρ ἱερῷ καθαίρεται, ἑστιῶσι δὲ ἄνθρωποι
δαίμονας καὶ δαίμονες ἀνθρώποις ὁμιλοῦσι. καί
μοι δοκεῖ μηδὲν ἂν γενέσθαι ταῖς πόλεσι πλέον
αὐτοῦ τοῦ Διὸς ἑλομένου τὰ τῇδε διοικεῖν ὑποδύν-
τος ἀνθρώπου τύπου. οἷς γὰρ ἂν ἐχρῆτο τότε,
κατὰ ταὐτὰ νῦν ἀρχόμεθα. 48. βλέπει μὲν γὰρ
ὀξὺ καὶ τοῖς λογισμοῖς ἡμῖν ὁ βασιλεὺς παντὸς
Θεμιστοκλέους ὀξύτερον, εἶναι δέ τι πιστεύων ἐν
τοῖς κρείττοσι σοφώτερον ταῖς ἐκεῖθεν εἰσηγήσεσιν
ἄγει τὴν οἰκουμένην, οὐκ ἀναμένων χρησμοὺς
ἄνωθεν[1] οὐδὲ παραναλίσκων ἐν θεωρῶν ῥαθυμίᾳ
τοὺς χρόνους, ἀλλ᾽ ἀντὶ τῆς Πυθίας αὐτὸς αὑτῷ
καθιστάμενος, οὐκ ἀνασχόμενος βλέπειν εἰς ὀφρὺν
μάντεων οὐδὲ γνώμην ἑτέρων πρᾶγμα τοσοῦτον
ἐξάψαι, ἀλλ᾽ εἰδὼς ὅτι καὶ τοῦθ᾽ ἕν τι τῶν παρὰ
τῷ Χείρωνι μαθημάτων, καὶ | τὸν Ἡρακλέα F 8
μάντιν οὐχ ἧττον ἢ τοξότην ἐπιστάμενος παῖδα
R 422 τὸν Μελάμπουν ἀπέφηνας μετὰ[2] | τῶν θεῶν τὸ
μέλλον ὁρῶν. 49. ἐντεῦθεν καὶ μένεις καὶ βαδίζεις,
ὅτε βέλτιον, οὐχ ὑπὸ τῶν πεπραγμένων τὰς ἐκβά-
σεις μανθάνων, ἀλλ᾽ ἐπὶ προδήλῳ τῷ τέλει τοὺς
ἀγῶνας ἀναιρούμενος, στρατηγῶν μὲν τῶν τάξεων
αὐτός, στρατηγούμενος δὲ ὑπὸ τῶν κρειττόνων. 50.
ὁ μὲν οὖν Ἀγαμέμνων ἤκουσε παρά του τῶν

---

[1] ἄνωθεν mss., Re. : ἄλλοθεν F.
[2] διὰ τῶν θεῶν μετὰ τῶν θεῶν mss. μετὰ τῶν θεῶν om. Re.
διὰ τῶν θεῶν om. F.

---

[a] Thuc. 1. 138. The same point is made with pathos in
Or. 18. 281.
[b] For Julian's personal practice of divination cf. Amm.

earth, when there reigns one human of body and
divine in soul, when on the altars fire surges up and
the smoke of sacrifice purges the air, when men feast
gods and gods consort with men. The cities of the
world, I feel, would have nothing more to gain, even if
Zeus himself putting on human guise elected to direct
all things on earth, for our government now is according to the same principles as he would then employ.
48. Indeed our emperor is quick to observe, quicker
in appraisal than any Themistocles [a] : confident in the
reliance to be placed in the powers above, he leads
the world more wisely under their guidance. He does
not wait for the oracles from heaven nor does he waste
long periods as an idle spectator, but himself estab-
lishes himself in place of the Pythia and refuses to
gaze upon the lofty brow of seers [b] or to make so great
a duty dependent upon the will of others. In the
knowledge that this too was one of the articles of
Cheiron's teaching,[c] and in the awareness that
Heracles [d] was no less a prophet than an archer, you
proved Melampus a mere child and with god's help
you observed what was to be.[e] 49. Thus it happens
that you both wait and proceed when the time is ripe.
You do not learn of the future from the past, but you
undertake your hazards with the end already in full
view, yourself the leader of your regiments and led by
the command of heaven. 50. Agamemnon was told

Marc. 21. 1, 22. 12. The Pythia was the oracular mouthpiece of Apollo at Delphi, through whom the votaries
received their responses : *cf. Or.* 12. 60.

[c] Cheiron the Centaur, teacher of Jason and other heroes :
Pindar, *Pyth.* 4. 102 ff.

[d] Herod. 2. 83 tells of an Egyptian deity, identified with
Heracles, patron of divination.

[e] Melampus, nephew of Neleus, oldest of Greek seers and
ancestor of a family of seers, the Melampodidae.

ἡττόνων ὡς τύχης ῥοπῇ βελτιόνων ἄρχοι, μὴ
προσειληφέναι γὰρ τὴν ἀλκήν, νῦν δὲ ἐν τῇ τοῦ
κρατοῦντος ἀρετῇ καὶ τὸ τῆς ἐξουσίας ἐστί. καὶ
οὐδεὶς οὕτω δόξει γενναῖος, ὃς ἡγήσαιτ᾽ ἂν οὐ
δικαίως ἐν ἀρχομένοις εἶναι. 51. ὅ τι γὰρ παρ᾽
ἄλλῳ καλόν, τοῦτο παρὰ σοὶ μειζόνως. καὶ μόνος
συνείληφας ἃ τοὺς ἄλλους μεμερισμένα κοσμεῖ,
καὶ οὔτε ῥήτωρ οὔτε ὁπλίτης οὔτε δικαστὴς οὔτε
σοφιστής, οὐ τελεστικός, οὐ φιλόσοφος, οὐ μάντις
δύναιτ᾽ ἂν αὐτὸν πρὸ σοῦ θαυμάσαι. καὶ γὰρ πράττοντας οἷς πράττεις καὶ λέγοντας οἷς λέγεις ἐκά-
λυψας. 52. ὅς γε καὶ τὴν δοκοῦσαν ὥραν τῶν
R 423 ἐμῶν ἐπιστολῶν | παρελήλυθας. ἀλλ᾽ ἐνταῦθα μὲν
κοινὸν τὸ κέρδος, τουτὶ γὰρ | τὸ καλὸν ἐγὼ μὲν F 8
ἐφύτευσα, σὺ δὲ ἔθρεψας, αἱ δὲ πόλεις δρέπονται.

53. Δότε δή, θεοὶ σωτῆρες, τὸ γῆρας τοῦ Νέστο-
ρος τῷ βασιλεῖ, τὴν γὰρ δὴ γλῶτταν πάλαι
δεδώκατε, καὶ παῖδας, ὥσπερ ἐκείνῳ, καὶ τοσοῦτον
ἅπαντας τοὺς Ῥωμαίων ἡγησαμένους τῷ χρόνῳ
νικήσειεν ὅσονπερ ἤδη ταῖς ἀρεταῖς.

---

[a] By Diomede : Homer, *Iliad*, 9. 32 ff.
[b] Libanius claims, and Julian agrees, that he had influenced Julian's literary style, *cf. Or.* 15. 7, 18. 13 ff.
[c] Nestor outlived three generations of men : Homer,
*Iliad*, 1. 247 ff.
[d] In this, Libanius was to be disappointed : *Or.* 18. 294.

by one of his underlings that it was only by fortune's whim that he ruled over better men, for he had no more valour than they.[a] Now, however, our ruler's power is rooted in his valour, and none will seem so noble as to think himself undeservedly subject. 51. Whatever is noble in other men is present in you in greater measure. You alone have gathered to yourself all the several attributes that give renown to others. Neither orator, nor soldier, nor judge, nor teacher, nor initiate, nor philosopher, nor seer could have more admiration for himself than for you. Indeed their activities you have overshadowed by your actions, their oratory by your orations. 52. You have surpassed even the reputed merits of my own letters. But in this the gain belongs to all alike. I planted this glorious seed[b]; you nurtured it; the world plucks the fruit of it.

53. Grant then, gods of our salvation, that our emperor should enjoy an old age like that of Nestor[c] —for long ago you gave him eloquence such as his. Grant him children,[d] even as Nestor had, and may he so excel all the emperors of the Romans in length of life as he now does in virtue.

Julian never touched a woman after the death of his wife, Helena : Amm. Marc. 25. 4. 2. Nestor's descendants, the Neleidae, first found refuge in Athens and then led the colonization of Ionia.

# ORATION 12

## ΕΙΣ ΙΟΥΛΙΑΝΟΝ ΑΥΤΟΚΡΑΤΟΡΑ
## ΥΠΑΤΟΝ

R 366   1. Νῦν πρῶτον ὕπατον ἐν τῇ τοῦ πράγματος F
ὁρῶ στολῇ, καὶ καλῶς ὁ δαίμων ἀνεβάλετό μοι
τὴν θέαν, ὅπως τὸ τῶν σχημάτων σεμνότατον ἐν
τῷ κρατίστῳ τῶν βασιλέων πρῶτον ἴδω. καὶ γέγονε παραπλήσιον οἷον εἴ τῳ πρώτου μὲν Ὁμήρου ποιητῶν ὑπῆρξεν ἀκοῦσαι, πρῶτον δὲ ἅρμα
ἰδεῖν ὑπὸ Πέλοπος ἡνιοχούμενον. 2. ἔνι δέ τι καὶ
τούτων οὐ χεῖρον, τὸ τὴν πατρίδα μοι ταῦτα καὶ
δεδέχθαι καὶ δεῖξαι χωρίον | φίλτατον ποθεινο- F
τάτην ὄψιν. ἀλλ᾽ οὐδὲ ὃ τρίτον ἔχω προσθεῖναι
λείπεται τῶν εἰρημένων, ὅτι με μὴ τοῖς πολλοῖς ἐν
ἴσῳ θεωρὸν ἄφωνον ἔστησεν ἡ Τύχη τὴν μετὰ
R 367 σιγῆς ἡδονὴν | ἡδόμενον, ἀλλὰ καὶ λόγῳ μηνῦσαι
ταύτην ἔδωκε τοῖς τε παροῦσιν ὑμῖν τοῖς τε
ὕστερον ἐντευξομένοις. 3. ὑμεῖς δὲ ὅτι μὲν χαίρετε
τοῖς ὁρωμένοις, καὶ ταῖς εὐχαῖς δι᾽ ὧν αἰτεῖτε
ταῦτα πολλάκις ὀφθῆναι καὶ τοῖς προσώποις γέμου-

---

ᵃ *Oration* 12 : commissioned by Julian and delivered
before him in Antioch upon entering his fourth consulship,
1 Jan. A.D. 363. *Or.* 1. 127 ff. represents the occasion as a
rhetorical triumph for Libanius, but his account is obscured
by textual corruption and allusive conceits. Composition
of the speech, demanded by Julian despite a show of reluc-

36

# AN ADDRESS TO THE
# EMPEROR JULIAN AS CONSUL[a]

1. Now for the first time I see a consul in the dignity
of his station, and I am glad that Heaven has post-
poned my view of the spectacle, so that I may for
the first time see the most august office held by the
mightiest of emperors. It is almost as though one
could, of all poets, listen to Homer first, or behold
first a chariot driven by Pelops.[b] 2. No less important
is the fact that it is my own birth-place that has had
this privilege, and that so dear a spot has revealed a
sight so desirable. Yet a third consideration of equal
cogency is that Fortune has not set me here, like the
average person, a dumb spectator expressing myself
with silent feelings of pleasure, but that she has
granted me the ability to proclaim them both to you,
my present audience, and to future readers. 3. Your
pleasure at the sight is manifested by the prayers
which you offer for its frequent recurrence, and by

tance by Libanius, is mentioned in *Ep.* 785 : λόγος δὲ ὁ μὲν εἰς
τὴν πανήγυριν ἔτι μέλλει κρύπτεσθαι μὲν ἐθέλων, ἑλκόμενος δὲ εἰς
μέσον παρὰ τοῦ βασιλέως, καὶ ἴσως φανεῖται· δεῖ γὰρ ἐκεῖνον
κρατεῖν.

    [b] Legend ascribed to Pelops, among others, responsibility
for the foundation of the Olympic games : his chariot race
with Oenomaüs for the hand of Hippodameia was certainly
connected with the site, by tradition, and all three were
honoured there : *cf.* Pindar, *Ol.* 1. 75 ff.

σιν εὐθυμίας δηλοῦτε· πολὺ δ᾽ ἂν δείξαιτε κάλλιον,
εἰ συνεξορμήσαιτε[1] τοῖς λόγοις καὶ γένοιτο τῇ τοῦ
λέγοντος ἐφάμιλλος ἡ τῶν ἀκροωμένων βακχεία.

4. Πολλοὶ μὲν οὖν εἰσιν ἕτοιμοι τὴν πανήγυριν
ὑμνεῖν καὶ λόγους καθ᾽ ἡσυχίαν ἤκουσι συντε-
θεικότες, οἱ δὲ καὶ μένοντες οἴκοι τοὺς αὑτῶν
εὐφραίνουσιν ὁμοίως οἵ τε μᾶλλον οἵ τε ἧττον ἐν
δυνάμει τοῦ λέγειν. ὃ καὶ θαυμάσαι τις ἄν, ὅτι
μὴ τὸ μέγεθος τῶν πραγμάτων σιγᾶν ἠνάγκασε
τοὺς πολλούς, ἀλλὰ πᾶν μέτρον κινεῖται νῦν καὶ
τὴν ὑπόθεσιν οὐκ ὀκνεῖ. 5. ἔστι δ᾽ ὅ τις ἂν
ἠξίωσεν εἶναι τῆς σιωπῆς αἴτιον, τοῦτ᾽ αὐτὸ καὶ
τὸ πεῖθον τολμᾶν. εἰ μὲν γὰρ ἦσαν οἱ πρὸς ἀξίαν
ἐροῦντες, ὃ συμβαίνειν ἐπὶ τῶν μὴ λίαν ὑπερβαλλόν-
των πέφυκεν, οἱ συνειδότες αὑτοῖς ἀσθένειαν κέρδος
ἂν ἐποιοῦντο λαθεῖν. ἐπειδὴ δὲ οὐκ ἔστιν οὐδενὶ
τὴν ἧτταν διαφεύγειν, ἀλλὰ καὶ τὴν εὐδο|κιμοῦσαν  F
δύναμιν ἐλέγχει τῶν ἔργων ἡ φύσις, κοῦφον ἤδη
γίγνεται καὶ τῷ φαυλοτέρῳ μετὰ τοῦ βελτίονος
νενικῆσθαι καὶ τοῖς ἀμείνοσι μετ᾽ ἀλλήλων. 6. οὐ
γὰρ οὕτω τὸ τῶν πράξεων ἀπολειφθῆναι τοῖς
λέγουσι φαίνεται δεινόν, ὡς τὸ τοὺς μὲν ἰσχῦσαι,
τοὺς δὲ μὴ δυνηθῆναι. ὅπου δὲ τῶν ἐπαινούντων
τὰ τῶν ἐπαινουμένων καλὰ περιγίγνεται, δέξαιτ᾽
R 368 ἂν ἕκαστος εἰπὼν κοινωνῆσαι τῷ | κρείττονι τῆς
ἥττης ἢ τὴν ἡσυχίαν ἀγαγὼν μὴ μετὰ τῶν
εἰπόντων ἀριθμεῖσθαι.

7. Ἡ μὲν οὖν τοῦ βασιλέως ἀρετὴ καλεῖ πρὸς
ἑαυτὴν τὸν λόγον, ὁ δὲ τοῦ λόγου νόμος ἐπὶ τὸν

---

[1] συνεξορμήσαιτε F., Re. (V) : συνεξορμήσετε mss. except V.

the joy radiant upon your faces. A demonstration still more eloquent would be your active support of my speech, and for the enthusiasm of the audience to rival that of the speaker.

4. There are many persons prepared to celebrate the festival, who have come with speeches composed at leisure : there are others who, even though they stay at home, gladden the hearts of their own folk in like manner, no matter whether their qualifications in eloquence be great or small. Most noteworthy is the fact that the vastness of the subject has not reduced their numbers to silence, but that all means are now employed and there is no shrinking from the theme. 5. What might have been expected to induce silence is what actually inspires their venture. If there existed speakers to deal adequately with the subject, as is usual with matters of no outstanding merit, persons conscious of their own inability would have been only too glad not to attract attention. Here, however, none can avoid eclipse : the quality of the achievement is too much for eloquence even of the highest order, and so failure, in which his betters share, becomes for the less gifted a matter of little moment, as it does for better men, if they have each other for company. 6. A general inability to do justice to the subject is not so galling for orators as are occasions when some possess the gift while others do not. In laudatory addresses, whenever the virtues of the recipients prove too much for the speakers, everyone would prefer to speak out and reveal an incompetence in which his betters share, than to hold his peace and not be counted one of the speakers.

7. The genius of our emperor attracts my oration to itself, while the conventional form of the address

ὕπατον πρότερον ἄγει, πόθεν τε τὴν ἀρχὴν ἐνο-
μίσθη καὶ διὰ τί, καὶ ποῖ προῆλθε, καὶ τίς ὁ
καρπὸς τοῦ πράγματος. 8. τῶν γὰρ ἄνω βασιλέων
κατὰ μικρὸν τοὺς τῆς βασιλείας ἐκβαινόντων ὅρους
καὶ τὴν ἔννομον ἀρχὴν ἐξαγόντων εἰς τυραννίδος
ἐξουσίαν πόλις ἐλευθερίας ἐρῶσα καὶ πρόνοιαν μὲν
ἀρχόντων ἀγαπῶσα, δεσπότου δὲ ὕβριν οὐ δυνη-
θεῖσα φέρειν τὸν μὲν ὑπερόπτην ἐκεῖνον καὶ βαρὺν
καὶ ὄγκου γέμοντα καὶ ἀσελγείας ἐξέβαλε, φυλακὴν
δέ τινα τῆς ἐλευθερίας ἡ βουλὴ ζητοῦσα Λακωνι-
κόν τι μιμεῖται παράδειγμα καὶ παραδοῦσα τοὺς
μὲν μαχίμους ἐπετείοις στρατηγοῖς δυοῖν κοσμή-
σασα τῷ τῶν ὑπάτων ὀνόματι, τὸν δῆμον δ᾽
ἑτέροις ἄρχουσιν, ὅπως ἀλλήλους ἔχοιεν εἰς τὸ
σωφρονεῖν | ἀνάγκην, αὑτὴν ἐν μέσῳ κατέστησεν F
ἐφορῶσά τε τὰς ἑκατέρων γνώμας καὶ παρε-
σκευασμένη τοῖς ἀδικουμένοις ἐν ταῖς ταραχαῖς
ἀμύνειν. 9. εὗρε δὴ τοὺς ἐξιόντας φιλοπόνους καὶ
δικαίους καὶ φιλοκινδύνους, ταῦτα δὴ τὰ σά, τὰ
μὲν φύσεως δεξιότητι, τὰ δὲ εὐθυνῶν φόβῳ. ὧν
ὃν ἔφην προϊόντων τρόπον γίνεται βασιλεία πάλιν
καὶ τὰ αὑτῆς ἀπολαμβάνει, τὸ δὲ ὅπως, οὐ τοῦ
παρόντος καιροῦ λέγειν. ἢ τοὺς ὑπάτους παρα-

---

[a] Cf. Dion. Hal. 4. 73, who is probably Libanius' ultimate
source of information. Libanius knew no Latin and readily
ignored all things Roman in his devotion to Hellenism, in
this differing from Julian. Thus he passes over the period
from the kings until his own day at one bound.

[b] This garbled account of the origin of the tribunate and
the function of the senate shows the rationalizing influence

would have me deal first with the institution of the
consulship, its origins, its cause, its progress and its
results. 8. Now the early kings gradually overstepped
the bounds of their royal power and diverted their
constitutional monarchy into a tyrannical oppression.
Then the city, in her love of liberty, though readily
accepting the direction of a legitimate ruler, refused
to endure the caprice of a master, and so she expelled
that harsh, arrogant, brutal Superbus. In quest of
some protection for her independence, the Senate followed a precedent set forth by Sparta [a] and entrusted
to two annually elected generals the command of the
troops, giving them the honorific title of " consuls,"
and put the commons under other officials, so that
they should have one another as a restraining influence. It took up its position between them, super-
vising the attitude of each side and prepared to defend persons who suffered in political disturbances.[b]
9. It found the magistrates vacating office to be
industrious, ambitious, just and adventurous—your
own qualities, Sire—either from their own natural
characteristics, or from fear of being called to account.[c] Events proceeded in the manner I have
described until monarchy was re-established and
resumed its rightful place. As to the way in which
this occurred, it is no part of the present occasion to
relate. But the monarchy divested the consuls of

of the classical Greek theory of the " mixed constitution "
as applied to Rome.

[c] Further rationalization on the Greek model : *provocatio*
is here equated with the function of εὔθυνα as exercised by
the *boule* of democratic Athens. Libanius interprets the
*populus Romanus* in the light of municipal Antioch of his
own day, when the πόλις is to all intents and purposes
represented by the *boule* and the πολιτευόμενοι are the
βουλευταί : cf. Petit, *Vie municipale*, pp. 30 ff.

λύσασα τοῦ στρατηγεῖν ἐπὶ τῶν λοιπῶν ἐτήρησε
ποιήσασα τὸ γέρας ἄοπλον.

R 369   10. Εἶθ' ὁπότε μὲν βουληθεῖεν τῶν | σπουδαίων
λαμπρῦναί τινας, ἐδίδοσαν τὴν τιμήν, ὁπότε δὲ
αὐτῇ χαρίσασθαι τῇ τιμῇ, σφίσιν αὐτοῖς περιετί-
θεσαν αὐτὴν τῷ βασιλεῖ τὸν ὕπατον παραζεύξαντες,
ὅπως ἅμα μὲν ἡ τὸ σχῆμα εὑροῦσα τιμῷτο πόλις
οὔτ' ἀνηρημένου παντάπασι τοῦ νόμου τοῦ τε
πάντων κρατοῦντος μεταλαμβάνοντος ὡς καλοῦ,
ἅμα δὲ αὐτοῖς ἀθάνατος ἡ προσηγορία μένοι καὶ
τῶν ἀεὶ γινομενων ἀπιόντων ἑστήκοι παγίως κατὰ
παντὸς τοῦ χρόνου. ὥστ'[1] οὔτε λιθίνην οὔτε
χαλκῆν οὔτε ὀρειχαλκίνην, ἀλλ' οὐδὲ ἐξ ἀδάμαντος
στήλην εὑρήσεις μονιμωτέραν τῆς μνήμης ἣν τουτὶ
τὸ καλὸν | τῷ τυχόντι βεβαιοῖ. 11. κεῖται γὰρ F
οὐκ ἐν μιᾷ τινι πόλει, καθάπερ Ἀθήνησιν Ἁρμο-
δίῳ καὶ Ἀριστογείτονι, τῇ τῆς πόλεως ὑποκει-
μενον τύχῃ καὶ μετὰ ταύτης σωζόμενόν τε καὶ
διαφθειρόμενον, καίτοι καὶ πόλεως ἑστώσης πολλάκις αἱ ἐπιγραφαὶ[2] τῶν στηλῶν προαπεῖπον, ἀλλ'
αὕτη γε καὶ κατακλυσμὸν καὶ τὴν ἐκ πυρὸς ἂν
διαφύγοι διαφθορὰν μετὰ τῶν ἐκεῖνα διαφευγόντων
ἀνθρώπων, οὓς αἱ τῶν τόπων ῥύονται φύσεις, κἂν
R 370  τὰ πεδία γένηται πέλαγος, | οἵ γε ἐν σκοπέλοις
οἰκοῦντες ἢ πόλεις ἢ κώμας ἔχουσιν, ἐν οἷς μάλιστα
φυλάττουσι τοὔνομα καὶ διδάσκειν τοὺς ἔπειτα
δύνανται. 12. πολλὴν δὴ συγγνώμην ἔχω τοῖς
ἐρῶσι τοῦ πράγματος καὶ παρὰ τῶν θεῶν αἰτοῦσι
πρὸ τῶν ἄλλων ἀγαθῶν ἐπὶ τοῦδε κομισθῆναι τοῦ
δίφρου. ἐπεὶ καὶ οἷς ὑπῆρξεν εἰς ὑπάρχους τελέσαι

---

[1] ὥστ' Re. (mss. except VB) : ὡς F. (VB).
[2] ἐπιγραφαὶ F. (conj. Re.) : γραφαὶ mss.

42

their military command, reserving it for itself for the future and making the office a civilian one.

10. Thereafter, whenever the emperors wished to honour any deserving person, they would grant him this honour, and whenever they wished to raise the prestige of the office itself, they would assume it in person, linking the consulship with their imperial position. In this way the state which had first devised this rank would be honoured, since the tradition was not entirely discarded and the supreme ruler participated in it as a mark of esteem, and also their title would remain undying, firmly fixed for all time, though consuls come and go. So you will find no pillar of stone, bronze or orichalc, nor even of adamant, to be more enduring than the fame that this noble institution confirms for its recipient. 11. For it is confined to no single state, as the names of Harmodius and Aristogeiton[a] are confined to Athens, nor is it involved in the destiny of that city, living and dying with it. It must be admitted that, even in the lifetime of cities, inscriptions on pillars have often disappeared and vanished. This title, however, would survive deluge and destruction by fire in the company of those human beings who, saved by the accidents of geography, survive them. Even if the plains become open sea, at least the dwellers on the heights possess cities or villages, and on them they best preserve the name, and can pass it on to their descendants. 12. I can readily forgive admirers of the institution who pray Heaven that, rather than any other blessing, they may be carried upon this chair. Even those to whom it has fallen to be

---

[a] The Athenian tyrannicides adopted by democratic Athens as its heroes : cf. Thuc. 6. 54 ff., Herod. 5. 55.

πρὸς τοῦτο βλέπουσιν, ὡς τοῦτο ὂν ἆθλον ἐκείνου,
οἷς τε συνέβη τοῦδε πρὶν ἐκείνου τυχεῖν ἥκιστα
προσέχουσιν ἐκείνῳ νομίζοντες, ὅ τι ἂν ἐπὶ τῷδε
λάβωσιν, ἔλαττον εἰληφότες ἔσεσθαι. 13. τί γὰρ
ἂν γένοιτο σεμνότερον ἢ τὴν οἰκουμένην ἅπασαν
ἡλίου δίκην ἐπέχειν τῇ προσηγορίᾳ, καὶ πάντων
ἀνθρώπων ἐν στόμασιν εἶναι τοὔνομα | [ἢ¹] τὸ παρὰ F
τῶν γονέων τεθὲν πολλὰς ἀνάγκας τῆς μνήμης
ἐχούσης, δικαστήρια, γάμους, ἀγοράν, λιμένας,
χρέα, πράσεις, τοὺς συμβάλλοντας καὶ γραφο-
μένους συνθήκας, τοὺς διαφερομένους καὶ τὴν
πίστιν ἀπὸ τῶν γραμμάτων φέροντας, τοὺς κοινω-
νοῦντας, τοὺς διισταμένους, παίδων γενέσεις εὐδαιμόνων, παίδων ἐν διδασκαλείοις μαθήσεις ; ὧν
μία σπουδὴ βοῆσαι τοὺς ὑπάτους, ἐφ᾽ ᾧ δὴ καὶ
διαλύονται. 14. ὅπερ οὖν ἤδη τις ἔφη περὶ τοῦ
R 371 τῶν θεῶν ὑπάτου, | Διός, τὸ μεστὰς εἶναι πάσας
μὲν ἀγυιάς, πάσας δὲ ἀγορὰς καὶ λιμένας καὶ
θάλατταν, τοῦτ᾽ ἄν τις εἴποι καὶ περὶ τῶν ὁμωνύ-
μων τῷ θεῷ. καὶ γὰρ τὰ τούτων ὀνόματα
πᾶσαν μὲν ἤπειρον, πάντας δὲ μυχοὺς θαλάττης ἐπέρχεται καὶ ἀγροὺς καὶ καλύβας, καὶ ὅλως οὗ
γένος ἀνθρώπων ἥμερον, καλῶ δὲ ἥμερον τοὺς ἐν
τοῖς ἡμετέροις ζῶντας νόμοις, ἐνταῦθα ταῦτα καὶ
γνωρίζεται καὶ λέγεται καὶ τὸ κῦρος τοῖς με-
γίστοις παρέχει, καὶ βασιλεὺς ἀπὸ τῆς ἐκεῖθεν
προσθήκης οὐχ ἧττον ἀπανταχοῦ καθ᾽ ἑκάστην

---

¹ ἢ MSS., F. Re. would either omit ἢ (so *Animad-*

44

appointed prefects[a] look to the consulship as the reward for their efforts there, while those who hold the consulship before a prefecture pay little attention to this last, since they feel that whatever position they reach after holding the consulship will be the acceptance of a lesser station. 13. For what could confer greater dignity than that the whole world should revolve around this title like the sun, and that the name bestowed by our ancestors should be on the lips of all men, since reference to it must be involved in so many matters, court actions, weddings, the operations of markets and harbours, debts and sales, agreements and the signature of deeds, disputes and the production of depositions in writing, partnerships and dissolutions, the birth of happy children, and the education of children in school ? And these have but one thought—to cheer the consuls, which is of course the reason why they go on holiday.[b] 14. So, as was long ago said about Zeus, the consul of the gods [c]—that every street, every market square, every harbour and sea is filled with his presence —the same may be said of the namesakes of the gods. For indeed their title reaches every continent and every inlet of the sea, every farm and cottage, the whole civilized world, in fact—that is, all who live under our code of laws—and there it is an object of note and remark, endowing the greatest with its authority. Even an emperor's praises resound the more loudly everywhere every day because of the

---

[a] As Sallustius, Julian's colleague in the consulship.
[b] Cf. Or. 9 : Εἰς τὰς Καλάνδας.
[c] Cf. Aratus, Phaenom. 2 ff.

---

versiones) or insert μᾶλλον before it (so Edition). His first suggestion seems preferable.

ᾄδεται τὴν ἡμέραν. 15. τοσοῦτον δέ ἐστι τὸ τῆς
τιμῆς ὑπερβάλλον, ὥσθ' αἱ μὲν τῶν θεῶν ἑορταὶ
διῄρηνται τοῖς τόποις, καὶ τῶν ὁμόρων τοὺς μὲν
τούτῳ, τοὺς δὲ ἑτέρῳ πομπὴν πέμποντας ἴδοι τις
ἄν, καὶ τοὔνομα τοῦ τὴν θυσίαν δεχομένου πολὺ |
μὲν παρὰ τούτοις, πολὺ δὲ παρ' ἐκείνοις, οὐ ταὐτὸν F
ἑκάτερον, ὁ δὲ ὕπατος ἐν πανταχοῦ καὶ πολύ,
χρόνον ἐλάττω καὶ πλείω διορίζων, οὐκ ἐῶν τοὺς
νεωτέρους τὰ τῶν πρεσβυτέρων ἔχειν, ὁ δὲ πάλαι
κείμενος ἐν ταῖς δίκαις ὥσπερ ἀνίσταται, καὶ
συνδικάζει τοῖς ζῶσιν ὁ τεθνεώς. 16. εἰκότως ἄρα
παῖδες Ῥωμαίων καὶ πρὸ γήρως λιπαροῦ τίθενται
τὴν τιμὴν καὶ δοθείσης αἱρέσεως παρά του τῶν
κρειττόνων βίου τε μακροῦ καὶ ταύτης ἐπὶ ταύτην
ἂν ἐνεχθεῖεν. ὃ γὰρ τοὺς ἥρωας ἐπίστανται τῶν
ψυχῶν πριαμένους, τὸ μηδαμοῦ στῆναι τὴν |
R 372 μνήμην αὐτοῖς, τοῦτ' ἴσασιν ὑπάρξον σφίσιν ἀπὸ
μόνου τοῦ γέρως. 17. οὐδὲν τοσοῦτον ὁ Πυθόδω-
ρος, φαῦλον ἡ Χρυσίς, μικρὸν ὁ Αἰνησίας· Ἄργος
ἐκείνης, Ἀθῆναι τούτου, Λακεδαίμων ἐκείνου, καὶ
οὔτ' ἂν ὁ Λάκων ἐπεγράψατο τῷ ψηφίσματι τὸν
Ἀθηναῖον οὔτ' ἂν οὗτος τὸν Λακεδαιμόνιον, ἀλλ'
εἴσω τῶν ὅρων ἑκατέροις ἡ τῶν ὀνομάτων ἰσχύς.
ἔνι δέ τις καὶ τοῖς Ὀλυμπίοις μοῖρα περὶ βραχύ τι
καὶ αὐτὴ μένουσα. τούτῳ δὲ πᾶσαν μὲν τὴν
R 373 οἰκουμένην ὁ νόμος | ἀνέῳξε, πανταχοῦ δὲ τὴν
αὐτὴν ἐγκατέστησε δύναμιν. 18. καὶ τὸ τῆς
σελήνης πρὸς τοὺς ἀστέρας εἴποι τις ἂν ἐν καιρῷ,

---

ᵃ Homeric tags (*Od.* 19. 368, 23. 283) and situations
(*Iliad*, 9. 410 ff.).

46

prestige derived from it. 15. Festivals of the gods
are marked off by their geographical location :
neighbouring peoples can be seen in procession, one
to this god, one to that : the name of the deity to
whom sacrifice is offered is mighty in the eyes of the
one or the other, but it is never the same name for
both. But with the consulship, so exalted is the
renown of the position that it is universally one and
mighty. It defines periods of time great and small,
it forbids the young to usurp the prerogatives of the
old, and a consul long since passed away is, as it
were, resurrected in court, and the dead joins the
living in the formulation of the verdict. 16. Thus it
is with good reason that the descendants of the Romans prefer this honour to ripe old age[a] and, if given
a choice by any of the higher powers between it and
a long span of life, they would opt for this. They
know full well that what the heroes purchased with
their lives,[a] a fame immortal, will be theirs simply
from holding this position. 17. Pythodorus of Athens
does not count for very much : as for Chrysis of
Argos, she is a nonentity : Aenesias of Sparta is a
mere name.[b] Yet the Spartan would not have
entered the Athenian's name on any decree of his,
nor the Athenian that of the Spartan, but the importance of their names remained confined each to
its own state. The Olympic festival also has its own
certain share of fame, but even this is of short duration. Yet the law has opened wide the whole world to
the consulship and everywhere has endowed it with
the same authority. 18. The analogy of the moon and
the stars[c] could properly be applied, that, of all the

---

[b] Thucydides' (2. 2) emphatic dating of the start of the
Peloponnesian War.     [c] Cf. Sappho, fr. 3 (Bergk.).

ὅτι πολλοῖς εἴδεσι τῶν ἀγαθῶν | κοσμουμένων οὐκ F 1
ἔστιν ὅ τι μὴ κρύπτεται τῷ παρὰ τοῦδε φωτί.
μόνη γὰρ ἥδε τιμῶν καὶ βασιλέως ἥρμοσε τύχῃ.

19. Καὶ περὶ μὲν τοῦ πράγματος αὐτοῦ καὶ τῶν
ἀπ' αὐτοῦ τοῖς μετασχοῦσι γιγνομένων ἀπόχρη τὰ
εἰρημένα· πλείω μὲν γὰρ ἕτερος ἴσως γ' ἂν εἴποι,
μέμψιν δ' οὐκ ἂν ἀπειροκαλίας ἐκφύγοι. οἷς δὲ
ἡγοῦμαι τῶν βασιλέων αὐτὸ πρέπειν καὶ προσέτι
γε λυσιτελεῖν, ἐνταῦθα ὑπειπὼν ἐπὶ τὰ λοιπὰ
βαδιοῦμαι. 20. ἐγὼ νομίζω τὸν μὲν σὺν τέχνῃ
βασιλικῇ τὴν γῆν κατευθύνοντα καὶ τὰ μὲν Ῥωμαίων κρείττω ποιοῦντα, τὰ δὲ τῶν ἀντιπάλων
ἀσθενῆ, καὶ τοῖς μὲν εὐφροσύνας πορίζοντα, τοῖς
δὲ θρήνων ἀφορμὰς περιιστάντα, καὶ τὰ μὲν εὖ
διακείμενα φυλάττοντα, τὰ δὲ ὡς ἑτέρως ἐπανορ-
θοῦντα, τούτῳ μὲν καὶ προσήκειν ἐν τούτῳ γενέσθαι καὶ κέρδος εἶναι τὴν ἀίδιον μνήμην, ὥσπερ
Θησεῖ καὶ Πηλεῖ καὶ Παλαμήδει καὶ οἷς ἐμέλησεν
ἀρετῆς. 21. ὅσοι δὲ τὰ μὲν τῶν οἰκείων εἰς φαῦλον
κατάγουσι, τὰ δὲ τῶν ἐναντίων αἴρουσι καὶ συνεθί-
ζουσι νικᾶν μὲν ἐκείνους, αὐτοὺς δὲ φεύγειν, τοὺς
δὴ τοιούτους οὐχ ὅπως οἶμαι δεῖν τὴν ἐξ ὑπάτου
μνήμην διώκειν, ἀλλὰ καὶ τοῖς τὸ πρῶτον εὑροῦσι
γράμματα καταρᾶσθαι καὶ μισεῖν, ὅτι κακῶν
R 374 ἀπιόντων ἐπελάβοντο καὶ κατέσχον | καὶ τὴν ἀπὸ
τοῦ χρόνου λήθην | ἐκώλυσαν. 22. ὅσων γοῦν F
μαλακῶν ἐν ἀρχαῖς γενομένων αἱ τῶν συνθηκῶν
ἀναγνώσεις ἐπεισάγουσι τοὔνομα, συνεισέρχεται
καὶ ὁ τῶν κακῶν ὄχλος, καὶ τὸ τέλος αὐτοῖς

---

ᵃ Libanius naturally has recourse to Greek heroes as
the prototypes of his ideal Roman emperor : Theseus, the
legendary founder of Athens, Peleus, at whose wedding the

48

blessings arrayed in many forms, there is not one that is not hidden by the radiance of the consulship. For this is the only honour that befits the imperial station.

19. These remarks suffice for my narrative of the actual office and of the rewards which it bestows upon its holders, for another speaker might possibly deal with it at greater length, but without avoiding the reproach of vulgarity. I will now indicate briefly the type of monarch for whom I think it to be an honour, and an advantage moreover, and proceed to the remainder of my subject. 20. I believe that the man who governs the world with the skill of an emperor and strengthens the fortunes of Rome while crushing her enemies, who makes Romans to rejoice and gives their foes cause to mourn, who preserves good institutions and mends the bad, such a man deserves to hold this office and gains the reward of immortal fame, as did Theseus, Peleus, Palamedes[a] and all who were exponents of virtue. 21. But whoever[b] brings his people's fortunes low, while swelling the success of his foes, who has trained them to victory and himself to defeat, such as he should, in my opinion, not just refrain from aspiring to the fame that the consulship gives, but should damn with hatred the inventors of writing, for they pick upon troubles past, retain them and deny them the oblivion of time. 22. At any rate, the perusal of their treatises recalls the name of any who has been incompetent in office, and with it comes the recollection of a sea of troubles, so that the result is the loss

gods appeared as guests, and Palamedes, the wisest of the Greeks before Troy and the legendary inventor of the alphabet. Politics, religion and education are here interconnected. [b] Like Constantius.

γίγνεται τῆς λαμπρότητος ζημία. 23. τίσιν οὖν
οὕτω συμφέρει καὶ τὴν ἐσθῆτα ταύτην ἐνδῦναι
καὶ τὸ σκῆπτρον ἐνεγκεῖν καὶ τὸ φάρμακον μνήμης
ἀπαύστου πρὸς τὸ μέλλον ἀφεῖναι ; σοὶ καὶ ὅστις
σοὶ προσόμοιος ἢ γέγονεν ἢ γενήσεται. παῖδες δέ
σοι καὶ παίδων παῖδες καὶ οἱ ἀπ' ἐκείνων τῶν σῶν
γένοιντο καὶ ζηλωταὶ καὶ κληρονόμοι. 24. μὴ
γάρ μοι πᾶς ὕπατος γενέσθω βασιλεύς, ἐπειδήπερ
ἔξεστι καὶ ἔστιν αὐτὸς μὲν ὁ διδούς, αὐτὸς δὲ ὁ
λαμβάνων, ἀλλ' ὃς κατὰ τὸν πάλαι τῶν ὑπάτων
νόμον οὕτω προὔστη τῆς βασιλείας, ὡς εἰς εὐθύνας
καταστησόμενος τῆς ἀρχῆς, οἷος ἡμῖν αὐτὸς δέδει-
ξαι. 25. καὶ γὰρ εἰ μείζων λογιστῶν καὶ τοῦ
διδόναι λόγον ἀνθρώπων τισὶν ἡ Τύχη, θεούς γέ
σοι καθῆσθαι νομίζων δοκιμαστὰς ἀξίως τῶν ἐκείνων ὀφθαλμῶν ἅπαντα καὶ πράττεις καὶ λέγεις,
ὡς οὔτε τὸν ἥλιον οὔτε τὴν νύκτα λήσων. λαμ-
βανέτω δὲ καὶ πᾶς ὁ βουλόμενος ἐξέτασιν ὁμοίως
καὶ νέος καὶ γέρων.

26. Ἐρῶ δὲ ἐγὼ φαυλότερος ὑπὲρ ὀξυτέρου
ῥήτορος οὐκ ἀπ' αὐτῆς τῆς βασιλείας ἀρξάμενος,
ἀλλ' ἐπὶ | τὴν πρώτην ἡλικίαν ἀνενεγκὼν τὴν κρί- F
σιν, ὅπως ταύτην φαίνηται προσηκόντως λαβὼν καὶ
δείξας ἀρετὴν ἐπὶ τῆς ἐξουσίας. |

R 375　27. Ὅσα μὲν οὖν παιδαγωγῶν τε ἐγκειμένων
καὶ διδασκάλων φοβούντων ἐδέξατο τῇ ψυχῇ τὰ
πρῶτα τῶν ἱερῶν καὶ τὴν ῥίζαν ἔχοντα, ἔχων
50

of his fair fame. 23. For whom then is it such an advantage to don these robes, to grasp this sceptre, and to transmit to the future this elixir of immortal renown?[a] For you, Sire, and all who have been or shall be like you. And may your children, your children's children and all their seed for ever[b] be your rivals and your heirs. 24. And pray, let not every emperor become consul, for it is permitted and possible for him personally to be both giver and taker of it, but only him who, according to the old tradition of the consulship, has so far advanced in majesty as to brook a scrutiny of the office, such as you have revealed yourself to us to be. 25. Indeed if Fortune is above scrutiny and beyond the rendering of account to any human auditors, yet you think the gods are set as your examiners, and all your acts and words are done in a manner worthy of their gaze, since you will not be unobserved either by the sun or by the night. Then let any who will, young and old alike, undertake an assessment of yourself.

26. When I speak of him, it will be a case of a poorer speaker dealing with a better. I shall not begin my account merely with the commencement of his reign, but shall refer the investigation back to his earliest youth, so that he may be revealed as a deserving occupant of the throne and of proven ability in his position of authority.

27. Though I could discourse upon the learning he absorbed under pressure from his attendants and menaces from his teachers—a learning in which is contained the first essential and the foundation of

---

[a] Plato, *Phaedr.* 275 A.
[b] *Cf.* Homer, *Iliad,* 20. 308. In this prayer, Libanius was destined to be disappointed : *cf. Or.* 18. 179 ff.

εἰπεῖν[1] παραλείψω. καὶ γὰρ εἰ μηδὲ τότε τὸ τῆς
προθυμίας ἀπῆν, εἴς γε τὴν τῶν ἐφεστηκότων
ὀφρὺν ἡ δόξα τῶν πόνων ἔρχεται. 28. ἀλλ' ἐπειδὴ
προϊὼν ὁ χρόνος τὰς μὲν τοιαύτας ἀνάγκας ἔπαυσε,
βουλῆς δὲ κύριον ἐποίησεν, ὥσπερ τὸν Ἡρακλέα,
ὑπῆρχε δὲ καὶ διὰ τῆς λείας ἔρχεσθαι καὶ οὐκ ἦν
ὁ κωλύσων εἰς οἶνον ἐκφερόμενον καὶ κύβους καὶ
σωμάτων ἔρωτας, ἐπὶ τὸν ὄρθιον καὶ τραχὺν οἶμον
ὁρμᾷ, ποῖ φέρει μᾶλλον σκοπήσας ἢ δι' ὅσων
χαλεπῶν. 29. καὶ μέσος δυοῖν βασιλέοιν ἰδιώτης
ἐν Ἀστακίᾳ καθήμενος, ἔνθεν μὲν ἀνεψιοῦ τοῦ τὸ
πᾶν κράτος ἔχοντος, ἑτέρωθεν δὲ ἀδελφοῦ δευτέραν τάξιν εἰληφότος, ἐπέθετο κτήμασι βασιλείας
καλλίοσι, | φιλοσοφίᾳ καὶ λόγοις, οὕτω δὲ ψηφί- F
ζομαι παρὰ σοῦ μαθών, ὦ βασιλεῦ, τοῦ προτιθέν-
τος ἃ μαθὼν ἔχεις ὧν ἄρχεις ἐθνῶν. 30. ὁρῶν
δ' ὅτι ῥητορικὴ μὲν τὴν πρὸς τὰ πλήθη πειθὼ
δημιουργεῖ, φιλοσοφία δὲ περὶ τῶν σεμνοτέρων
εἰδέναι ποιεῖ, καὶ νομίσας δεινόν, εἰ περὶ μὲν τῶν
ἱκανῶς διαλέξεται, τὰ μείζω δὲ οὐκ εἴσεται,
R 376 συνῆγεν ἀμφοτέρας καὶ συνεκέραννε, | τὴν μὲν
διάνοιαν ὑψηλοτέραν ποιῶν τῇ τῶν οὐρανίων μαθήσει, τὴν δὲ γλῶτταν εἰς δρόμον ἀσκῶν τῇ τῶν
ῥητόρων ὁμιλίᾳ. 31. καίτοι τίς οὐκ ἂν ἀρκούσας
ὑπολαβὼν εἰς εὐδαιμονίαν ἀφορμὰς τὸν πατέρα,

---

[1] ἔχων inserted Norman. ἔχοντα, εἰπεῖν mss., F. ἔχων εἰπεῖν conj. Re.

---

[a] Study of the poets in primary education, Homer and
Hesiod especially, laid the foundation both for the study
of rhetoric and for the religious teaching of the Hellenic
παιδεία : cf. Festugière, Antioche, pp. 91 ff., 211 ff.

[b] Cf. Xen. Mem. 2. 1. 21, Cic. De Off. 1. 32, for Prodicus'

religion—I will refrain.[a] For even if he showed no lack of enthusiasm at that time, the report of his labours redounds to the credit of his supervisors. 28. But as the progress of time removed such constraints and made him independent of judgment, as in the case of Heracles,[b] it was open to him to tread the primrose path, and there was none to stop him diverging towards drinking, gambling and sex. Yet he set his feet upon the steep and rugged path, with his gaze fixed not on the intervening obstacles but upon his goal. 29. And there he settled in Astacia, a private citizen in between two emperors, here his cousin, the possessor of supreme power, there his brother, his immediate subordinate[c]: but he set himself to acquire something more noble than empire—philosophy and eloquence. Such, Sire, is my verdict, and I have learnt it from you who prefer the possessions of learning to the provinces you govern. 30. Observing rhetoric to be a means of persuading the masses whereas philosophy induces knowledge of matters more exalted, he thought it improper to discourse adequately on the one subject and yet show an ignorance of higher things. So he combined both studies and made an amalgam of them, elevating his intellect by a study of heavenly lore and at the same time, by his association with rhetoric, training his tongue to run trippingly. 31. Any ordinary person might have regarded himself as having opportunity enough for a successful career

allegory of the choice of Heracles between Pleasure and Virtue.

  [c] In A.D. 351, while Julian was still residing in Asia Minor, Constantius as Augustus held court in Constantinople and Gallus as Caesar in Antioch. Only then was he allowed full freedom of movement.

τὸν πάππον, τὸν θεῖον, τὸν ἀνεψιόν, τὸν ἀδελφόν,
τὰς διὰ τὸ γένος τιμὰς καὶ θεραπείας καὶ κολακείας, ἐσθίων καὶ πίνων καὶ καθεύδων διετέλεσεν
ἐπὶ μισθῷ τοῖς δεομένοις συμμαχῶν καὶ προστιθεὶς
ἀγροῖς ἀγρούς, χρυσῷ χρυσόν, σκεύη σκεύεσι,
τἆλλα τοῖς ἄλλοις ; ἀλλ' οὐχ οὗτος. 32. ἀλλ' ἐπαινῶν 'Αναξαγόρου τὸ τὴν μὲν πατρῴαν γῆν
ἄσπορον ἀφεῖναι, τὴν ψυχὴν δὲ εἰς καρποὺς παρα-
σκευάσαι τῶν μὲν ἠμέλει, τὴν δὲ ἐθεράπευε καὶ
κτήματος ἑνὸς ἀμετρίαν θαυμάσας, οὐ γὰρ ἀπο-
κρύψομαι, βιβλία πάντα πανταχόθεν ἐξείλκυσε καὶ
τὰ ταμιεῖα διηρευνήσατο ταῦτα[1] μᾶλλον ἢ τὰ τῶν
χρημάτων ἕτεροι. 33. φιλοσοφίας δὲ ἡμμένον καὶ
ἐπὶ τὸν ἐκείνης | παρακύψαντα λειμῶνα δόξαν περὶ F 2
τοῦ θείου παράσημον οὐκ ἐνῆν περιφέρειν, ἀλλ'
εὐθὺς τὴν κηλῖδα διέρρυψε[2] καὶ τοὺς ὄντας ἀντὶ
τοῦ δοκοῦντος ἐπέγνω πρὸς τὴν ἀλήθειαν ἡγεμόνι
φιλοσοφίᾳ χρησάμενος. 34. ἐκείνην ἐγὼ τὴν
ἡμέραν ἀρχὴν ἐλευθερίας τῇ γῇ καλῶ καὶ μακαρίζω
τόπον τε ὃς τὴν μεταβολὴν ἐδέξατο, καὶ τὸν τῆς
γνώμης ἰατρόν, ὃς κινδύνων τὸν κάλλιστον αὐτός
τε κινδυνεύσας καὶ τόνδε πείσας μετὰ τοῦ μαθητοῦ
τὰς Κυανέας διέπλευσεν. 35. εἰ μὲν οὖν προσεῖχε
τὸν νοῦν τοῖς τοῦδε γράμμασιν ὁ ἀδελφός, ἦν ἂν
νῦν συζυγία προστατῶν, καὶ γὰρ ἦν οἷος οὐ
R 377 βασιλεύων | βασιλεύοντα νουθετεῖν. ὡς δὲ ὁ μὲν

---

[1] ταῦτα Re. (mss. except V) : τούτων F. (V).
[2] διέρρυψε F. (corrections in IM) : διέρρυψε Re. (other
mss.).

---

[a] Julius Constantius, Constantius Chlorus, Constantine.
Constantius II and Gallus.
[b] Cf. Diog. Laert. 3. 2.

in his father, his grandfather, his uncle, cousin, and brother,[a] and in the honours, attentions and deference resulting from his family connections, and might have passed his time in eating, drinking, sleeping, in granting assistance, at a price, for those in need, and in accumulating lands, money, movables, and the like. Not he, though. 32. No! he supported Anaxagoras' maxim, to let the family estates lie fallow and prepare one's soul for fruition,[b] and so he eschewed all this and cultivated his intellect. In his regard—not to mince matters, in his inordinate regard for one type of acquisition only, he collected books of all kinds and ransacked their store with more zest than other men ransack stores of treasure. 33. Devoting himself to philosophy, after one glimpse of her fair meadow, he found it impossible to maintain false ideas about the divine. Straightaway he cleansed the smirch and, with philosophy as his guide to truth, he recognized the real gods instead of the false one. 34. That day I call the start of freedom for the world, and I bless the spot where this conversion took place and the healer of his mind, who personally undertook this noble hazard,[c] carried conviction with him and, in company with his disciple, passed through the Cyanean rocks.[d] 35. Thus, if his brother had paid attention to the letters he sent him, there would now be a pair of rulers,[e] for he, though no emperor himself, was fit adviser for an emperor. His brother was got rid of

[c] Maximus of Ephesus : cf. Or. 13. 12.
[d] The Cyanean rocks, the Symplegades of the Argo legend, were traditionally placed at the Bosporus.
[e] Gallus' deposition and execution took place in A.D. 354. In Or. 18. 25 Libanius denies the existence of any such compromising letters.

ἄκριτος ἀπεληλύθει λέγειν ἔχων τι περὶ τῶν πεπραγμένων, ἐπὶ δὲ τοῦτον ἐκτεῖναι τὰς μέμψεις ὁ
ἐκεῖνον ἀπεκτονὼς ἐβούλετο μέν, ἠπόρει δέ, φόνου
μὲν ἔσχεν,[1] πλάναις δὲ ἐκάκου δίκας λαμβάνων
ὧν ἐγκαλεῖν οὐκ εἶχεν. 36. οὕτω δὲ ἄρα τῆς ὑφ᾿
ἑαυτῷ γῆς | ἠπίστατο τὴν φύσιν ὥστε τὴν λῆξιν F 2
τῆς Ἀθηνᾶς τὰς τῶν Συρρακουσίων ἡγεῖτο λιθο-
τομίας καὶ λόγων ἐραστῇ τὸ χωρίον δεσμωτήριον,
ὥσπερ ἂν εἴ τις εἰς Θάσον τῶν φιλοίνων τινὰ
κομίσας καὶ κελεύσας μένειν τήκειν αὐτὸν ἡγοῖτο
τῷ τόπῳ, τὰ πάντων ἥδιστα χαριζόμενος ἐν τῇ
κολάσει. 37. μᾶλλον δὲ θεῶν τοῦτο δῶρον ἦν
βουλομένων φίλην τε πρὸ τῆς βασιλείας αὐτῷ
γενέσθαι τὴν πόλιν καὶ προεισενεγκεῖν χάριτας,
ὅπως ἂν ἐν τῷ βασιλεύειν ὀφειλέτης εἴη τῇ πόλει,
καὶ τὸ μέγιστον, ἵν᾿ Ἀθήνηθεν ἐπὶ τὸ σκῆπτρον
ἰὼν φέρηται παρὰ τῆς Ἀττικῆς, ὥσπερ ἄλλο τι
τῶν ἐκεῖ φυομένων, τὸ κρατεῖν βαρβάρων. 38. ὁ
μὲν οὖν δαίμων καλῶς ταῦτα διῴκει τῆς οἰκουμένης προμηθούμενος, ὁ δ᾿ ἡσυχίας ἐπιθυμίᾳ βασιλείαν ἔφευγε, μόνος ἀποδιδράσκων τὸ παρὰ τῶν
ἄλλων θηρευθέν, καὶ φόνον[2] καὶ βασιλείαν τὴν
τότε. τεκμήριον δέ, πλείω μὲν ἀφῆκε δάκρυα
καλούμενος ἐπ᾿ αὐτὴν ἐχόμενος τῆς ἐν ἀκροπόλει

[1] ἔσχεν αὐτόν F. (V).
[2] καὶ φόνον Re. (mss.) : στέφανον conj. F.

---

[a] Cf. Or. 13. 18. The Athenian captives were imprisoned in the Syracusan quarries : Thuc. 7. 86.

[b] The vintage wine of the Greeks came from Thasos.

[c] The date of Julian's departure from Athens for the court at Milan and elevation to the position of Caesar is A.D.

without trial for all that he could have given some account of his actions, and his murderer wanted to extend his accusations against our emperor here, but was at loss for the means. So he stayed his hand from murder, but vented his spleen by exiling him, punishing him for an offence he could not define. 36. Yet so little was his knowledge of the world he ruled that he mistook the inheritance of Athena for the quarries of Syracuse[a] and regarded the place as a prison for a lover of eloquence. It was just like taking a drunkard to Thasos[b] and telling him to stay there, under the impression that he would pine to death in the place, yet in the punishment granting him his heart's desire. 37. Or it should be regarded rather as a gift of the gods, who willed that the city should be his friend before ever he ascended the throne and that it should confer an advance of favour upon him so that, once on the throne, he should be in the city's debt and, most of all, that, on leaving Athens to grasp the sceptre, he should convey with him from Attica as a normal product of the place, the conquest of barbarians.[c] 38. So god, in his forethought for the world, arranged all this to perfection. He, however, in his desire for anonymity, sought to avoid elevation to the throne : he alone tried to escape what all but he pursued, the blood-shed[d] and the imperial station of those days. The evidence for this is that, on receipt of the summons, he shed more tears as he grasped the latticed gates

355. The classical allusion is to Athenian successes in the Persian Wars.
[d] A grim—and true—summary of the history of the house of Constantine. Besides the murders of Julian's kinsfolk in A.D. 337, execution or assassination had removed Priscus, Constantine II, Constans and Gallus.

κιγκλίδος ἤ τις ἂν ἐπὶ κώνειον ἀγόμενος, ἥδιστα
R 378 δ᾽ ἂν | πτερωθεὶς ἐξαίφνης εἰς Ὑπερβορέους ἀπ-
έδρα. στρέφων δὲ παρ᾽ ὅλην τὴν πορείαν λογι-
σμούς, εἴ πως ἀποκρούσαιτο τὴν πολύευκτον ἀρχήν,
| οὐ πρότερον ἐξέληξε πρὶν θεῶν τις ἐπελθὼν F 2
μετέστησε τὴν βουλὴν καὶ τὸν ὄκνον ἀφεῖλε διαρ-
ρήδην ἐπιτάξας ὑπομεῖναι τὴν λειτουργίαν. 39.
μάρτυρα δὲ τῆς ὁσιότητος αὐτὸν εἶχε τὸν ἐχθρόν.
ἵνα δὲ μὴ θαυμάσῃ τις ἐχθρὸν ἀκούων τὸν κοινού-
μενον τῆς ἀρχῆς, ἐρῶ τίς ἦν ὁ τῆς κοινωνίας νοῦς.
ἐκεῖνος γὰρ οὐχ ὅπως τινὰς ἀνθρώπων ἡδέως ἂν
εἶδεν ἐν θρόνοις βασιλικοῖς ἢ τοῖς ἁλουργοῖς ἐσθή-
μασιν, ἀλλ᾽ οὐδ᾽ ἂν ὀνείρατα ταύτην ἔχοντα τὴν
θέαν μετρίως ἤνεγκεν ἄν. πόθεν οὖν μετέδωκεν
ὧν περιείχετο; 40. κακῶς ἔπασχεν ὑπὸ τῶν
βαρβάρων πανταχοῦ, καὶ τὸ περικείμενον τοῖς
Ῥωμαίων ὅροις Μυσῶν λείαν ἐπεποίητο τὰ τῇδε,
μάλιστα δὲ τὸ περὶ τὴν ἑσπέραν ἐπόνει, καὶ
μικρὸν ἦν στρατηγὸς εἰς ἐπανόρθωσιν, ἀλλ᾽ ἔδει
βασιλέως ἐπισχήσοντος τὸ ῥεῦμα. 41. δραμεῖν
μὲν οὖν αὐτὸς οὐκ ἠπίστατο, κοινωνὸν δὲ τῆς
ἀνάγκης καλούσης τοὺς ἄλλους ὑπερπηδήσας τὸν
ἠδικημένον αἱρεῖται, τοῦ μὲν αἵματος ὁπόσον

---

[a] Cf. Or. 18. 21. The conceit is borrowed from Julian,
Ep. ad S.P.Q.Ath. 275 a. The mention of Athens leads
Libanius, ever the purist, to substitute the method of execution in classical Athens, the drinking of hemlock, for the
bloodier methods of his own day.

[b] A legendary people living in perfect happiness in the
extreme north. For their religious connections with Delos
cf. Herod. 4. 32 ff. Cf. also Strabo, Bk. 11, p. 711.

[c] The theme of this oration, specially composed for Julian,
was that of divine guidance and purpose: the theme of

of the Acropolis than any condemned man led to execution.[a] Had he but wings, he would gladly have made sudden flight to the Hyperboreans.[b] All the length of his journey, he pondered whether he could somehow rid himself of this much-prized position, nor did he cease until a visitation from heaven changed his mind and removed his reluctance by explicit injunctions that he should undertake the duty.[c] 39. As testimony to his sense of duty he had even his foe. And in case you are surprised at hearing his partner in empire called his foe, I will explain the reason for the partnership. It was not simply that Constantius found no joy in seeing anyone on the imperial throne, clad in regal purple : even to dream about it would have upset him dreadfully. So why did he give away any part of what he grasped so tightly? 40. On every side he was harassed by the barbarians. The peoples bordering on the Roman frontiers had created havoc in the East here, and the situation in the West was very desperate.[d] A general to restore order was useless: an emperor's presence was needed to stem the flood. 41. He personally was incapable of going to their aid. The crisis demanded a colleague on the throne. So he disregarded the rest and chose the one he had wronged, not unmindful of the blood

the parallel narrative in *Oration* 18 is one of praise and justification of Julian. Hence the differences of emphasis. *Cf.* Petit, *Historia*, 5, pp. 479 ff.

[d] Constantius had inherited the Persian War from his father, and it continued intermittently throughout his reign. The situation in the west became disastrous in consequence of the revolts of Magnentius and Vetranio (A.D. 350/3) and Silvanus (A.D. 354). The proverb Μυσῶν λεία—a prey for all and sundry—originated from the Greeks' conception of the Mysians as weak and effeminate. *Cf.* also ὁ Μυσῶν ἔσχατος, *Or.* 14. 26 ; Plat. *Theaet.* 209 B.

ἐξέχεεν οὐκ ἐπιλελησμένος, πιστεύων δὲ τῷ κατηγορεῖν ἔχοντι μᾶλλον ἢ τοῖς ὀφείλουσι χάριτας.
καὶ οὐκ ἐψεύσθη. λαβὼν γὰρ | Ἀθηναίων λογι- F 2:
σμὸν καὶ τὸ στῆθος πλήξας καὶ κελεύσας μὴ
R 379 μνησικακεῖν οἷος ἦν | ἀδόλως συμπονεῖν.

42. Αἱ μὲν πρὸ τῆς βασιλείας εὔθυναι τοιαῦται,
πάντα ἂν λογιστὴν ἐπαινέτην λαβοῦσαι. δοκιμά-
ζωμεν δὲ καὶ τὸν κυβερνήτην τὸν ἤδη κινοῦντα
τοὺς οἴακας. ὁ μὲν οὖν ἐκπέμπων ἐπὶ πολεμίους
εὖ πράττοντας οὐ νίκην αἰτῶν οὐδὲ κράτος οὐδὲ
ἀριστεύειν ἐξέπεμπεν. 43. εὐθὺς γὰρ αὐτῷ μετά-
μελος εἰσῄει λογισμὸν οὐκ ἔχων, ἐπεὶ καὶ οὓς
συναπέστειλεν ἐν τάξει συμβούλων κωλυτὰς ἔργων
γενναίων οὐ παραινέτας ἐξέπεμπε, Φοίνικα δὲ
ἐξαιρῶ[1] τοῦ λόγου, τοιγαροῦν εὐθὺς ἀφείλκετο,
μᾶλλον δὲ ἐφοβεῖτο τὴν τοῦ συνάρχοντος εὔκλειαν
ἢ τὴν τῶν ἐναντίων ὕβριν, καὶ τὸ μὴ τοῦτον
ἐπαινεθῆναι τοῦ πληγῆναι τοὺς πολεμίους ἥδιον ἦν.
44. ἀλλ' ἐκείνου κατηγορεῖν ἐμοὶ μὲν οὐχ ἡδύ, τῷ
λόγῳ δὲ ἀνάγκη. διαστῆσαι γὰρ τὴν εὐφημίαν
ἀπὸ τῶν μέμψεων οὐκ ἔστιν. ὁρμηθεὶς τοίνυν ἐξ
Ἰταλίας σὺν ὁπλίταις ἐλάττοσιν ἢ τετρακοσίοις
ἐν ἀκμῇ τοῦ χειμῶνος, τὴν δὲ τῆς ὥρας ὑπερβολήν,
ἣν ἐνιαυτοῦ κύκλος ἐφίστησι τοῖς τόποις, οἱ μὲν
ὑμῶν ἤνεγκαν, οἱ δὲ ἀκηκόασι, | σὺν εὐχαῖς μὲν F 24

---

[1] ἐξαιρῶ F. (conj. Gasda) : ἐξαίρω Re. (mss.).

---

[a] Cf. Or. 15. 37 ff. Libanius' models, the orators of the
fourth century b.c., made much of Athens' generosity towards erstwhile aggressors. Libanius adds an Homeric touch
(Od. 20. 17).

[b] Salustius, his quaestor (cf. Julian, loc. cit. 281 d, Or. 8.
240 ff.), introduced by a Platonic tag (Phaedr. 242 b).

that he had spilled but placing more reliance on his potential accuser than on those under obligation to him. Nor was he deceived. Taking a leaf out of the Athenians' book,[a] Julian smote his breast, bade himself bear no malice and prepared loyally to play his part in the task.

42. Such then is the examination of his career before he ascended the throne, and it would win the commendation of all who assess it. Now let us scrutinize him as the pilot at the helm. Well, Constantius, in sending him out to face the victorious foe, did so with no wish that he should win a battle, a campaign or a triumph. 43. For immediately an irrational change of mind affected him: those whom he sent with him ostensibly as counsellors were to act not as advisers, but to prevent any notable action, though I expunge from this account the Phoenician,[b] for he was immediately withdrawn. He was more alarmed at his partner's fame than at the insolence of the foe, and more pleased that Julian should fail to gain renown than that the enemy should escape defeat.[c] 44. I take no pleasure in accusing Constantius, but my narrative demands that I do so, for it is impossible to separate the praise from the blame. Well, setting out from Italy in the depths of winter with fewer than four hundred infantry [d]—and you have, some of you, either experienced the extremes of climate that the circling year brings in those regions [e] or have heard tell of them—Julian offered up prayers as he set foot

---

[c] Cf. Or. 18. 36, Socr. H.E. 3. 1, Zos. 3. 3.

[d] Cf. Or. 18. 37, Zos. loc. cit., Julian, Ep. ad S.P.Q.Ath. 277 d, 281 d.

[e] A comment specially designed to interest some of Julian's closest intimates, e.g. Priscus, Alypius (for whom cf. Amm. Marc. 23. 1. 2).

61

ἐπέβη τῆς ὁμόρου, γῆν δὲ ὁρῶν Γαλατῶν μὲν
καλουμένην, ἐσπαρμένην δὲ ὑπὸ βαρβάρων οἳ μετὰ
τῆς πρότερον ἀρουμένης καὶ τὰς πόλεις αὐτὰς
κατενεγκόντες ἐγεώργουν, τὸν χειμῶνα μὲν ἀνή-
λισκεν εἰς βουλήν, ὡς δὲ τῆς ὡραίας ἐπὶ τὰ ἔργα
καλούσης ἐβόα μὲν αὐτὸς καὶ συνῆγε καὶ συνεκρότει
καὶ παρεθάρρυνε τοὺς ἐπτηχότας, ὑπεσκέλιζον δὲ
τὴν ὁρμὴν οἱ ἵππαρχοι καὶ λοχαγοὶ καὶ ταξίαρχοι
πληροῦντες ἐντολὰς δεσπότου, νικᾷ νίκην ἡμῖν ὁ
R 380 βασιλεὺς πρὸ | τῆς ἐν τοῖς ὅπλοις τὴν ἀπὸ τῆς
καρτερίας καὶ τοῦ ταῦτα πράως ἐνεγκεῖν, κἀνταῦθα
τὸ τῆς παιδείας ἀπήντα κέρδος, Ἡρακλῆς τε
χείρονος ἀνδρὸς ὑπακούων Ἄρης τε ἐνιαυτοῦ πλέον
ὑπ' ἀνθρώπων ἐμπλήκτων δεθείς. 45. ἀλλὰ γὰρ
ἔδει καὶ τὸν Ἄρη λυθῆναί ποτε καὶ τοῦτον. ὡς
γὰρ ὁ μὲν ἐν τοῖς κωλύμασιν ἔστενε μέν, οὐκ
ἠρεθίζετο δέ, τὰ δὲ πράγματα ἀπωλώλει, τοῖς δὲ
βαρβάροις ηὐξάνετο τὸ φρόνημα, τῶν δ' ἐπηρεα-
ζόντων ὁ κίνδυνος οὐκ ἠνείχετο, λαβὼν ὁρμᾷ[1] |
δύναμιν μικράν τε καὶ πολιορκεῖσθαι μαθοῦσαν. F
46. ὑμεῖς μὲν ἴσως ἐπιθυμεῖτε καὶ παράταξιν
ἀκοῦσαι καὶ στρατοπέδου φύσιν καὶ κέρας ἑκάτερον
καὶ φάλαγγα καὶ παράκλησιν καὶ τῶν ἐναντίων
τέχνας καὶ στρατὸν φανερὸν καὶ κρυπτομένους
λόχους καὶ προοίμιον συμβολῆς καὶ ζέουσαν μάχην
καὶ τραυμάτων εἴδη καὶ φυγὴν καὶ δίωξιν καὶ γῆν
ἀφανῆ νεκροῖς, ἐγὼ δὲ τὴν μὲν τῆς διηγήσεως

---

[1] ὁρμᾷ conj. Herwerden, approved F. (vol. III, p. xxxxii):
οἶμαι Re., F. (Text.), mss.

---

[a] Heracles and Eurystheus : cf. Homer, *Iliad*, 19. 133,
*Od.* 11. 621 f.

on the soil of the neighbouring province. There he saw a land called Gaul, but where the barbarians sowed their seed, for after overwhelming the cities they were tilling their land also, besides that which they farmed before. He spent the winter in council, but when the opening of the campaign season invited action, he himself raised the battle cry, collected his forces and drilled them, encouraging the faint-hearted. Then the squadron leaders, the brigadiers and the colonels sought to hamper his effort in fulfilment of their master's commands, but our emperor, before ever he triumphed in battle, triumphed here as a result of his constancy and patience in the face of such treatment, in this reaping the reward of his schooling, a Heracles serving a lesser man[a] and an Ares held in chains for more than a year by men infatuate.[b] 45. Yes, but this Ares too had to be set free some time. For though grieving at this constraint, he was not provoked, but, with our fortunes ruined and the barbarians' arrogance increasing, the danger from their insolence became unendurable and he advanced with a force small in number and well used to standing siege. 46. You perhaps are eager to hear of the character and deployment of the army, of the formation on flank and centre, the address to the troops and the stratagems of the foe, of regiments exposed to view and hidden ambuscades, of the start of the fighting and the heat of battle, of casualties, flight and pursuit, and of the earth hidden by the bodies of the slain.[c] Such detailed narrative

[b] Otus and Ephialtes kept Ares imprisoned for 13 months: cf. *Iliad*, 5. 385 ff.

[c] For the battle of Strasburg (A.D. 357) cf. *Or*. 18. 53 ff., Amm. Marc. 16. 12.

R 381 ἀκρίβειαν, ὅταν καὶ περὶ τῶν ἄλλων | ἱκανῶς
διεξίω, κομιῶ· νῦν γὰρ δὴ πάντα συντέτμηται, καὶ
ὁ λόγος ἔοικε σκιρτήμασι τῇ πανηγύρει πρέπουσιν.
47. ὥσπερ οὖν Ὀλυμπιονίκης οἴκαδε σπεύδων ἀπὸ
τῆς Πίσης ἐρωτώμενος ὑπὸ τῶν ἐντυγχανόντων
τῆς νίκης τὸν τρόπον τοῦτο μὲν ἀποδώσειν ὑπ-
ισχνεῖται, συγχαίρειν δὲ αὐτῷ πρὸς τὸ παρὸν ἀξιοῖ
δεικνὺς ἅμα τὸν στέφανον, οὕτω καὶ νῦν τὰ ἀπὸ
τοῦ πολέμου λέγομεν ὑπερβάντες τὰς μάχας. 48.
καρπουμένων γὰρ τὴν ἡμετέραν τῶν βαρβάρων καὶ
πόλεις μὲν πέντε δεούσας πεντήκοντα καθῃρη-
κότων, | ἀποτετμημένων δὲ τῆς γῆς τὸ πλέον καὶ F 2
κεκτημένων, τῶν δὲ φανερωτάτων ἐν Γαλάταις
γενῶν οἰκτρῶς ἐκεῖ δουλευόντων, ἤδη δὲ μείζω
περίνοιαν τῶν πολεμίων εἰληφότων ὁ στρατηγι-
κώτατος οὗτος καὶ τῶν ἀφ' οὗ γεγόνασιν ἄνθρωποι
πολέμων γέμων οὐ φορητὸν ἡγησάμενος εἰ πλείους
μὲν χιλίων[1] τριήρεις ἐνίκων περὶ Σαλαμῖνα τρια-
κόσιαι, τὸ δὲ τῶν βαρβάρων νέφος αὐτὸς σὺν ὀλίγοις μὴ τρέψαιτο, προσπίπτει μὲν ὡς ἀγαπήσων
εἰ τῆς χώρας ἐξελάσειεν, ἡ νίκη δὲ αὐτὸν ἐπὶ τὴν
ἐκείνων προήγαγε καὶ διαβὰς Ῥῆνον ποταμόν,
R 382 ὕδωρ ἐλέγχον ἐκ τῶν γεννωμένων ἀδικίαν | μητέ-
ρων, φιλονεικήσας ζῶντας λαβεῖν εἰδὼς ἀγαλλο-
μένους θανάτῳ τοσούτους σαγηνεύσας ἤγαγεν ὥσθ'
ἡμῖν μὲν ἐπίπονον τὴν ἐκείνων γενέσθαι τροφήν,
τοῖς δὲ ὑπολειφθεῖσιν ἄφθονον τὴν οἴκοι προκεῖ-
σθαι. 49. δείσας δὲ τὸ τῆς νίκης μέγεθος καὶ τὴν

---

[1] χιλίων inserted F. (conj. Re.).

[a] This account is derived from Julian himself (loc. cit.
279 a). Zosimus (3. 1, 3. 5. 1) gives the number in round
figures as 50 and 40.

I will present when I deal in full with all his other
achievements. Now, in fact, all has been compressed
and my oration frolics, as it were, in a manner suited
to the holiday. 47. Just as an Olympic victor hurries
home from Pisa and, if asked by any who meet him
about the manner of his winning, promises them a
full account but, for the present, merely requests
their congratulations as he displays the crown, so I
pass over the fighting and narrate the aftermath of
the war. 48. The barbarian was tilling Roman soil :
he had sacked forty-five of our cities,[a] had appropri-
ated the greater part of the land and was in occupation of it: the most famous states of Gaul lay there
in abject slavery, and our enemies had begun to
entertain more insolent designs. Then did our great
commander here, with full knowledge of all the wars
that have taken place since the human race began,
find it intolerable if, when three hundred ships at
Salamis could beat over a thousand, he and his
handful of men could not rout the clouds of barbarians. So he fell upon them, content if he should expel
the foe from our domains, but his victory advanced
him against theirs. He crossed the Rhine, the river
whose water proves, in the persons of their children,
the misconduct of the mothers,[b] and in his eagerness
to take captives, since he knew that they gloried in
death, so many did he catch and bring back prisoner
that we had difficulty in providing for their maintenance. For the remnants that he left behind there
was ample store at home. 49. He was more afraid of

---

[b] According to legend, the Rhine provided a test of marital
loyalty of the local women by drowning their illegitimate
children and allowing the legitimate to float to safety : cf.
[Julian], E.L.F. No. 191 (383 d), Or. 2. 81 d, Greg. Naz.
P.G. 37. 1516, Anth. Pal. 9. 125.

τοῦ ἔργου λαμπρότητα μᾶλλον ἢ τοὺς ἐν τῇ μάχῃ
κινδύνους οὐ προσέθηκε τῷ τροπαίῳ πομπὴν καὶ
ταῦτα ἐν δεσμοῖς ἔχων τὸν ἄρχοντα τῶν πολεμίων,
οὕτως ἐπεξῆλθε κρατῶν, | οὐδὲ κύπτοντα τοῖς F
πεπορθημένοις ἔδειξεν οὐδ' ἐπικατέσφαξε ταῖς
κειμέναις τῶν πόλεων τὸν κατενεγκόντα καλλωπι-
ζόμενος τῷ φόνῳ ἀλλ' ἀναμνησθεὶς Ἀχιλλέως, ᾧ
τὸ νικᾶν ἤρκει, παρεχώρει τῶν λοιπῶν τῷ πρεσβυτέρῳ πανταχοῦ τὰς ἀφορμὰς παραιρούμενος τῶν
φθόνων. 50. οἰηθεὶς δὲ ὅτι τὸ χρῆμα τῶν πόλεων
οὐ ταὐτὸν ἀνθρώπῳ πάσχει, τοῖς μὲν γὰρ ἄλυτος ἡ
τελευτή, τὰς δὲ ἔστιν ἀναβιώσασθαι, χεῖρα ὀρέγει
ταῖς κειμέναις. αἱ δὲ ἀνίσταντο καὶ αὐτίκα κῆρυξ
διέπλει τὸν ποταμὸν κελεύων ἐπὶ τὰ σφέτερα
αὐτῶν κατιέναι τοὺς ἑαλωκότας, οἱ δὲ ἔθεον, οὐκ
ἀνὴρ ἀντ' ἀνδρὸς λυθείς, ἀλλ' οἱ μὲν ἔμενον οἱ[1]
ἐκείνων, οἱ δὲ ἐπανῆεσαν ὑπὸ τῶν ἑλόντων προπεμ-
R 383 πόμενοι. | οὕτως αὐτοὺς ἐπαίδευσε πάντα ὑπα-
κούειν ἡ μάχη. 51. εἰ δὲ τὸ προσθεῖναι πόλιν ταῖς
ἀρχαίαις εὐεργεσία κοινὴ τοῦ τῆς οἰκουμένης
αὐξανομένου σώματος, τό γε τὰς ἀνῃρημένας
ἀποδοῦναι πόσῳ λαμπρότερον; ἐν ᾧ καὶ τὴν γῆν
ἔστιν οἰκίζειν καὶ τὴν αἰσχύνην λύειν. οὐ γὰρ τὸ
μὴ ποιῆσαι τὴν οὐκ οὖσαν δεινόν, τὸ δὲ τὴν πρὶν |
οὖσαν περιιδεῖν ἐρριμμένην διπλῆς ἐντεῦθεν περι- F
ισταμένης ζημίας, ὀνειδῶν τε καὶ βλάβης. ὡς
ἐκεῖνό γε τὸ πτῶμα φαινόμενον τοῖς τε βαρβάροις
ἂν ἦν εἰς τόλμαν παράκλησις τοῖς θ' ἡμετέροις εἰς

---

[1] [οἱ] F.

[a] Chnodomarius: Julian, *Ep. ad S.P.Q.Ath.* 279 d, Amm.

the completeness of his victory and the fame of his
achievement than of the perils of battle, and so he
did not celebrate a triumph after his success, even
though he held the enemy chieftain in chains. He
thus continued on his conquering way; he did not
parade his captive with downcast head before the
victims of his ravages, nor did he revel in bloodshed
and slaughter over those fallen cities their destroyer,
but he followed the example of Achilles, for whom
victory was enough, and handed him over to his senior
colleague, so removing all grounds for enmity.[a]
50. Considering also that the destinies of cities are
not identical with those of men, for man's end is
irrevocable while they can be revived, he stretched a
protecting hand over the wasted towns. They began
to rise again, and a herald crossed the Rhine forthwith,
bidding the captives return to their own homes, and
they came hastening back. Nor were they released
on an exchange of man for man ; they, the enemy
prisoners, that is, stayed with us while ours were set
upon their homeward way by their captors, who were
so schooled by battle as to obey in all things. 51. If
the addition of a city to the existing number is a
blessing to mankind, since the fabric of the world is
thereby increased, then far more glorious is the
restoration of cities laid in ruins, for thus the land can
be peopled and the shame removed. Failure to found
a non-existent city is no shame, but to ignore the
destruction of a previously existing town involves the
double penalty of disgrace and damage. The occurrence of such a disaster would have been an invitation
to the barbarians for further attempts, and to our own

Marc. 16. 12. 66.   He was imprisoned in Rome, where he
soon died.   The Homeric reference is to *Iliad*, 9. 330 ff.

ἀτολμίαν ἀνάγκη, κἂν εἰ μὴ νῦν, ἀλλ᾽ ὕστερόν γε
τοὺς μὲν ἂν ἔθελξε, τοὺς δὲ παρώξυνε. σὺ δ᾽ ὅπως
οἱ μὲν ἀεὶ τρέμοιεν, οἱ δ᾽ ἀεὶ θαρροῖεν, τρόπαιον
ἀκίνητον τὰς πόλεις ὤρθωσας. 52. καὶ διὰ τὴν
σὴν καὶ γνώμην καὶ τύχην καὶ μόχθους καὶ τέχνας
R 384 οὐ καθ᾽ ἑκάτερον τοῦ πολέμου | τὸ στόμα τοῖς
βαρβάροις ὑπῆρχε κρατεῖν, ἀλλ᾽ οἱ μὲν ἔδρων, οἱ
δὲ ἔπασχον, ἔπασχον μὲν οἱ περὶ Ῥῆνον, ἔδρων δὲ
οἱ περὶ Τίγρητα, καὶ τῇ μὲν εἰσέρρεον,[1] τῇ δὲ
ἔπιπτον· οἷόν τι περὶ Ποτίδαιαν γενέσθαι φασὶν
Ἀριστέως μὲν τοῦ Κορινθίου τρεψαμένου τὸ καθ᾽
ἑαυτὸν καὶ ἐλαύνοντος, θατέρου δὲ κέρως, ἕως εἰς
τὸ τεῖχος κατεκλείσθη, φεύγοντος. 53. εἰ δὲ μὴ
σὺ τότε ἀντέκρουσας, οὐδὲν ἂν ἐκώλυσε τοὺς
βαρβάρους ἑκατέρους τὴν ἐν ποσὶν ἀεὶ κτωμένους
περὶ τὸν Βόσπορον ἀλλήλοις τελευτῶντας συμ-
μῖξαι. νῦν δ᾽ ἡ τῶν ἑτέρων ἧττα τοὺς μὲν ἀπ-
ώλεσε, τοὺς δὲ φροντίζειν ἐποίησε καὶ συνεσκίασε
τὴν ἀπὸ τοῦ νικᾶσθαι Ῥωμαίους αἰσχύνην φήμης
φήμην παραμυθουμένης καὶ λόγου λόγον καταλαμ-
βάνοντος. |

54. Σὺ μὲν οὖν ἀπὸ τοῦ τροπαίου πάλιν ἐπὶ τὰς F
Μούσας ἐτρέπου, καθάπερ ἀθλητὴς ἐπὶ παλαίστραν
ἀπὸ στεφάνου, καὶ τὰ ὅπλα καταθέμενος ἀνελάμ-
βανες τὰ βιβλία, παρ᾽ ὧν ὁρμηθεὶς καὶ τὴν νίκην
ἀνείλου· πλήθει γὰρ ἀντιταττομένη σοφία κρείττω

---

[1] εἰσέρρεον F. (conj. Re., correction in Pl): εἰσέρρει other
MSS.

[a] Cf. Homer, Iliad, 10. 8.
[b] From A.D. 357, while Julian was recovering the west,
Constantius suffered serious reverses against the Persians,

people an inevitable cause for despondency, to them a spur to greater efforts, to us a paralysing agent, if not now, yet at some future time. You, Sire, have raised up the cities, a trophy immovable, that the foe should ever feel fear and we confidence. 52. Through your resolution and fortune, your toil and skill, it has been ensured that the barbarians should not be victorious in both the jaws of war simultaneously,[a] but that they should experience both success and failure, failure on the Rhine and success on the Tigris, with casualties here and advances there— a situation like that reported at Potidaea, when Aristeas of Corinth drove all before him in rout while the other wing fled in disorder for the protection of the city wall.[b] 53. If you had not offered such spirited resistance at that time, there would have been nothing to prevent both barbarian peoples from extending their occupation over the lands that lay successively in their path and ending by meeting each other at the Bosporus.[c] As it is, the defeat of the one has destroyed them, and given the other food for thought too. It has helped overshadow the disgrace of defeats sustained by the Romans, and the report of the one consoles us for the other ; the tale of it cuts short the tale of defeat.

54. As an athlete after winning the crown returns to the wrestling school, you returned from your triumph and devoted yourself once more to the Muses. You put aside your weapons and took up the books under whose inspiration you had gained your victory, for wisdom, when opposed to mere numbers,

with the loss of such strongpoints as Amida and Bezabde. The classical allusion is to Thuc. 1. 62.

[c] The bitter comments upon Jovian's treaty of A.D. 363 (*Or.* 18. 279 f.) deliberately recall this passage.

ποιεῖ τὸν συνετώτερον. 55. ἀφικνοῦνται δέ σοι
τῆς δόξης αἰρομένης οὐκ ὀρχησταὶ καὶ μῖμοι
γέλωτος ἀφορμὰς κομίζοντες οὐδ' αὐληταὶ καὶ
R 385 κιθαρῳδοὶ δείπνων χρησίμους ἐξελαύνοντες | λό-
γους, ἀλλὰ σμήνη τε ῥητόρων καὶ φιλόσοφος
Ἀθήνηθεν, καλὸς μὲν ἰδεῖν, καλλίων δὲ χρήσασθαι,
πλεῖστον μὲν ἀνθρώπων ἔχων νοῦν, ἐν δὲ λόγοις
ἄριστος εἶναι μᾶλλον ἢ δόξαι βουληθείς. 56. ὃς τὰ
μὲν ἐπαινέσας, περὶ δὲ τῶν συμβουλευσάμενος
ἀπηλλάττετο δῶρον λαβών, ὃ μόνος βασιλέων δέ-
δωκας, ἔπη τὸν ἄνδρα μηνύοντα. εἰ δὲ Πεισίστρα-
τον ἐπαινοῦμεν ὑπὲρ τῆς τῶν ἑτέρῳ πεποιημένων
συλλογῆς, ποῦ θήσομεν τὸν Ὁμήρου μιμητήν;

57. Ἀλλὰ γὰρ οἷς τοὺς πολεμίους ἐξέκοπτες,
μετὰ | τῶν κρατουμένων τὸν διὰ σοῦ νικῶντα
ἡνίας. οὕτω δύσμαχόν ἐστι νόσημα φθόνος καὶ
τὴν τῶν ὠφελούντων δύναμιν ὁ κερδαίνων μισεῖ.
ὃς δὴ καὶ τότε ἐπὶ τόνδε πάλαι πεφυτευμένος
ἀνέδραμε καὶ τὸν σπινθῆρα προήγαγεν εἰς φλόγα.
58. τὸ πρῶτον ἐψίλωσε φίλων, ὡς βλάψων ἐν ταῖς
βουλαῖς, ὁ δὲ ἦν ὁμοίως εὔβουλος, μετὰ ταῦτα
χειρὸς συχνῆς, ὡς ἀσθενῆ ποιήσων, ὁ δὲ ἦν οὐδὲν
ἧττον ἰσχυρός. πάντας ἐκάλει τὰ Περσικὰ προ-
ϊστάμενος, εὐφημότατα ἀνθρώπων ἐκδιδοὺς μετὰ
τοῦ βασιλέως τὰς πόλεις. ὁ δ' ἦν μὲν πέρα τοῦ
μετρίου πρᾷος, ἐρῶ γάρ, καὶ βαδίζειν ἐκέλευεν,
R 386 οἰμωγαὶ δὲ γυναικῶν | ἀντελαμβάνοντο τῶν σωμά-

---

[a] Priscus, the Neo-Platonist, visited Julian at Paris : cf.
Julian, E.L.F. No. 13.
[b] The first redaction of the Homeric poems was undertaken upon the orders of Peisistratus (c. 535 B.C.) : cf. Paus.
7. 26. 13.

gives power to the man of understanding. 55. As your fame grew, there arrived not dancers and actors with the material for ribald laughter, not pipers and harpists who expel elevating conversation from the dining table, but swarms of orators and a philosopher from Athens, fine as a person, finer as an acquaintance, intellectually without equal, and in eloquence intent upon the reality rather than the appearance of excellence.[a] 56. He bestowed praise here and counsel there, and then departed with a gift which you alone of all emperors have granted, a poem in his honour. If we praise Peisistratus for his collation of another man's compositions, in what category shall we place the disciple of Homer?[b]

57. Yet, by your overwhelming victory over the enemy, you caused distress not merely to the vanquished but to him who conquered by your agency. Such an intractable disease is envy, where the person helped hates the helper's power. At that very time, long nurtured against our emperor here, it sprang up and fanned the spark into flame. 58. First of all, he stripped him of his friends, to harm him in his counsels; but he remained as full of good counsel as before.[c] Then he stripped him of a large part of his forces, to weaken him; but he remained no less strong. Then he called for his whole force, putting forward the pretext of operations against Persia and under these most specious terms betraying both the emperor and the cities. His reaction was one of what I can only call unreasonable restraint; he bade his troops march, but the laments of their womenfolk affected them. These, who had but now

[c] Cf. Julian, Ep. ad S.P.Q.Ath. 282 c ff. For a fuller account cf. Or. 18. 90 ff., Amm. Marc. 20. 4, Zos. 3. 8.

τῶν. αἷς ἀναπεπνευκυίαις ἄρτι κῦμα δεύτερον
συνίστατο, τὸν δὲ οὐδὲ ταῦτα ἀντιτείνειν ἔπειθε.
59. πῶς δὲ μέγας γίγνεται βασιλεύς; ἐνταῦθα γάρ
μοι δοκοῦσιν ὀξύτερον βλέψειν οἱ κριταί· οὔτ᾽
ἐβιάζετο στρατιώτης οὔθ᾽ ἡττᾶτο στρατιωτῶν
βασιλεὺς οὐδ᾽ οὕτως ἐπεπαίδευτο τὸ ἀρχόμενον
κακῶς ὥστε τὸν ἄρχοντα γνώμῃ προσπεσὸν ἄγειν.
ἀλλὰ τίς δὴ λόγος ἀληθέστερος ;[1] θεὸς[2] | μὲν F
ἐξώρμησεν ἐκείνους οὐδὲν προεσκεμμένους, ἀλλ᾽
ἔφθασε τὸν λογισμὸν ἡ φωνή. θεοῦ δὲ τοῦτο.
πρόσταξις ἧκεν ἀδελφὴ τῆς προτέρας προστιθεῖσα
θαλαττίῳ χλαμύδος βαφῇ λιθοκόλλητον ταινίαν |
R 387 φέρουσάν τι καὶ αὐτὴν καρποῦ θαλαττίου. ὁ δὲ
ἔβλεπε πρὸς οὐρανόν, καὶ ἦν ὁμοίως ἥ τε δόσις ἥ
τε λῆψις ἄμφω βουλὴ δαιμόνων. 60. ὥσπερ οὖν
οὐ τῆς Πυθίας ἡγούμεθα τοὺς χρησμούς, ἀλλὰ τοῦ
πέμποντος ἐπὶ τὸ στόμα τὰ λόγια, οὕτω νῦν τῶν
ἐκείνους τε κεκινηκότων τοῦτόν τε πεπεικότων
κοσμῆσαι τὴν κεφαλὴν κεκρίσθω μᾶλλον τὸ ἔργον
ἢ ὧν τὰς γνώμας ὡς ἐβούλοντο διέθηκαν. εἰκός
γέ τοι τοὺς ἐπινεύσαντας ἐρωτωμένους καὶ τὴν
γένεσιν ὡς καλῷ τῷ πράγματι παρασχεῖν. ἄδικον
μὲν γὰρ τιμὴν οὐκ ἂν ἐπήνουν, δικαίαν δ᾽ ἂν
εἰσῆγον. 61. οὐ μὴν τό γε νεῦμα τῶν θεῶν
ἕρμαιον ἐγένετο τῷ τετιμημένῳ, καθάπερ πάλαι
ταύτην ἐν αὑτῷ τὴν ἐπιθυμίαν τρέφοντι, ἀλλ᾽ ὡς
ἄν τις τῷ βραχυτέρῳ χαίρων, ἔμελλεν, ὤκνει, περὶ
τὸ πρόσθεν μέτρον διέτριβε, τὴν ἐνθένδε ψῆφον

---

[1] ἀλλὰ τίς . . . ἀληθέστερος ; F. (conj. Re.): ἀλλά τις
. . . ἀληθέστερος. mss.
[2] θεὸς F.: οἷος mss.: οἰωνὸς conj. Re.

recovered from one ordeal, were now faced with a second blow, but not even so was he induced to resist. 59. What then is it that makes an emperor great? Here I believe observers will bestow more searching scrutiny. Coercion was not applied to the troops, nor was the emperor coerced by them; his subjects were not so ill disciplined that they would attack their leader's decision and seek to direct him. What then was the true story? A god inspired them: they had no preconceived plan: their words were uttered before the thought was formulated—and that was god's work. Then came an injunction akin to the first, and this gave him, besides his cloak of sea purple, a diadem jewel-studded and itself adorned with sea pearls. He cast his gaze up to heaven, and both the gift and its receipt were heaven's will.[a] 60. It is not the Pythian priestess, but the god who puts the words into her mouth, whom we believe responsible for the oracles[b]: so now let our judgement be that this was the doing of the powers that inspired them and induced him to put the crown on his head rather than of men reaching their decision of their own free will. Indeed the likelihood is that inquiry was made of the gods, they gave their assent, and they set in motion an action of which they approved. For though disapproving of an honour undeserved, they would sponsor one well merited. 61. This is not to say that this divine assent came as a godsend to the object of their care, as if he had long nurtured such desires in his heart. He accepted it as a lesser evil, with reluctance and hesitation, adhering to his earlier course and awaiting the verdict of men after

[a] Cf. Or. 13. 33 ff. and note.
[b] Cf. Or. 13. 48 and note.

μετὰ τὴν ἄνωθεν ἔμενε. τὸν δὲ ἔκαμπτεν οὐδέν.
62. ἕως μὲν οὖν ὑπῆσαν ἐλπίδες καταλλαγῶν
ἀνεῖχεν. ἐπεὶ δὲ πόλεμος μὲν ἐκεκήρυκτο σαφής,
R 388 ἐπετειχίζετο | δ᾽ | Ἰταλία, παρεκαλεῖτο δὲ τὸ F
Κελτικόν, ἐκινεῖτο δὲ τὸ Σκυθικόν, ἐχώρει δὲ ὁ
πεζός, ἐπορεύετο δὲ ὁ τοξότης, κατεῖχε δὲ οὐδὲν
οὐδὲ ἐπέστρεφεν, οὐ Περσῶν ἵππος χρεμετίζων
περὶ τὸν Εὐφράτην, οὐ μηχαναὶ προσαγόμεναι
τείχεσιν, οὐ θρηνοῦσαι πόλεις, οὐκ ἐλπιζόμενον
πῦρ, ἀλλ᾽ ἐωνεῖτο τῇ Ῥωμαίων γῇ τὸν φόνον[1] τῶν
μεγίστων ἀφιστάμενος βαρβάροις, ἵνα μὴ μικρῶν
τῷ γένει, τότε δὴ τότε τοὺς ἀντικαθισταμένους
ἀφεὶς τὴν λεωφόρον σκοπεῖν αὐτὸς ἑτέραν ὁδὸν
ἀτριβῆ καὶ τραχεῖαν καὶ κρημνοῖς ἄπορον, ὥσπερ
τινὰ τῶν ἐν ἄστει χειροποιήτων δρόμων, ἤνυσεν
ἴσως Ἀπόλλωνος ἡγουμένου καὶ τὸ δύσβατον
λεαίνοντος κατὰ τὴν τάφρον τῶν Ἀχαιῶν. 63.
οὕτω δὴ τῶν ἁλισκομένων οὐκ αἰσθανομένων,
R 389 ὥσπερ τινῶν ἰχθύων | οὔπω τοῦ δικτύου συναχ-
θέντος, ἐπειδὴ καιρὸς ἦν, ἀνεφάνη πρῶτον ἐπιβὰς
τῶν ἐσχάτων καὶ διήνεγκεν οὐδὲν ὑφύδρου κολυμ-
βητοῦ κρυπτομένου μὲν ὑπὸ τοῖς νώτοις τῆς
θαλάσσης, λανθάνοντος δὲ | τοὺς ἐπὶ τῆς ἠιόνος F
ἕως ἂν βούληται. 64. οὕτω δὲ πλείω λόγον τοῦ
μὴ δοκεῖν ἀδικεῖν ἢ τῆς νίκης αὐτῆς ἐπεποίητο,

---

[1] φόνον mss. : φόβον F. (conj. Re.).

---

[a] For Constantius' preparations against Julian in A.D.
360/1 cf. Julian 286 a ff.

[b] The Gothic embassy of § 78 is apparently a consequence
of this manœuvre of Constantius.

that of heaven. However, Constantius remained inflexible. 62. So while ever a prospect of reconciliation existed, Julian stayed his hand. But once open war had been proclaimed, Italy put on a war footing, approaches made to the Celtic peoples[a] and the Goths roused to action against him,[b] when forces of infantry and archers advanced undeterred, and with no backward glance either for the Persian cavalry that neighed on the banks of the Euphrates, or for the siege engines that were brought against our fortresses, or for the laments of the cities and the expected holocaust, and when, at the cost of massacre for the Roman world, they surrendered our most important persons to barbarians, not to mention those of low degree,[c] then, and then only, did he leave his adversaries to watch the highroad while he set his feet upon another way,[d] pathless, steep and as precipitous as a man-made flight of stairs in a city.[e] Perhaps Apollo was his guide, smoothing the impassable ways, as he did around the ditch of the Achaeans.[f] 63. So they never noticed that they were caught like fish before the net is drawn tight. When the time came, he suddenly made his appearance on the frontier,[g] just like an underwater diver who is hidden under the surface of the sea and unobserved by watchers on shore for as long as he likes. 64. He had been far less interested in actual victory than in

[c] As at Amida (Amm. Marc. 19. 2-9), Singara and Bezabde (*ibid.* 20. 6-7).

[d] Refers to Julian's advance along the Danube in A.D. 361.

[e] τῶν . . . δρόμων, from its iambic rhythm, may embody a quotation from drama.

[f] *Cf.* Homer, *Iliad*, 15. 353 ff.

[g] For the surprise of Sirmium *cf.* Amm. Marc. 21. 9. 5 ff.

# LIBANIUS

ὥστ' ἐν μέσοις τοῖς δεινοῖς ἐμβεβηκὼς δι' Ἑλλήνων ἅπασιν ἀνθρώποις ἀπελογεῖτο πέμπων ἐπιστολὰς ἐκεῖσε κατὰ τοὺς ἑκάστων τρόπους μείζους,
ἐλάττους, τὸ μέσον ἐχούσας, ὡς ἔμελλον τοῖς
δεξομένοις ἁρμόσειν. 65. βουλευομένου τοίνυν ἐν
Παιονίᾳ περὶ τῆς Θρᾴκης, εἴτ' ἐμβολῆς εἴτε καθέδρας ὁ καιρός, καὶ τῷ πλήθει τῶν πολεμίων
ἀντιτάττοντος ἀρετὴν τύχη τις κρίνει τὸ ἔργον
ἡσυχαζόντων τῶν ὅπλων πρέπον ἐξευροῦσα τῇ
συγγενείᾳ πέρας. ἐπειδὴ γὰρ ἔδει κρατῆσαι τὸν
ἀμυνόμενον, ἐξήρπασε τὸν ἐπιόντα νόσῳ· καὶ τὸ
μὲν τρόπαιον οὕτω μέγα, στρατιωτῶν δὲ οὐδαμοῦ
τάφος. 66. ὑποχωρείτω τοίνυν τῷ βασιλεῖ καὶ |
R 390 Κῦρος ὁ μέγας ἐν θεοφιλῶν κρίσει. καὶ γὰρ εἰ τοῦ
ποιμένος ἔτυχεν εἰς σωτηρίαν, ἀλλὰ μεμάχηταί γε
τῷ πάππῳ καί τι καὶ πλέον, ὡς Ἰσοκράτης φησίν,
ὥσθ' ὁμοῦ Μήδους τε εἶχε καὶ συνεκαλύπτετο·
σοὶ δὲ καλλίων τοῦ κτηθέντος ὁ τῆς κτήσεως
τρόπος καθαρᾷ τῇ χειρὶ παρελθόντι πρὸς τὸ πᾶν.
67. τὸ δὲ ἔτι κάλλιον, τὴν γὰρ αὐτὴν ᾔσθησαν ἐπὶ
τούτοις ἡδονὴν οὕς τε ἦγες καὶ οἷς ἀπήντας· νόμῳ
μὲν γὰρ μεθ' ἑτέρων ἦσαν, φίλτρῳ δὲ μετὰ σοῦ
πυνθανόμενοι γνώμῃ μὲν εἶναι βασιλέα, πόνοις
δὲ συστρατιώτην. 68. καὶ τοῦτ' ἄρ' ἦν τὸ τὴν
κεφαλήν σου παρὰ τῶν κρειττόνων | ἄγεσθαι πρὸς F
ἀνάδημα, ὅπως ἀκολουθήσῃ τῷ στεφάνῳ μὲν ὀργή,
R 391 τῇ δὲ ὀργῇ κίνησις, τῇ κινήσει δὲ | ὁ σὸς δρόμος

---

[a] Julian, *E.L.F.* Nos. 20-22 : cf. *Ep. ad S.P.Q.Ath.* 268 ff.,
*ad Corinthios*, Lib. *Or.* 14. 29 f., *ad senatum Romanum*,
Amm. Marc. 21. 10. 7.

[b] Constantius died in Nov. A.D. 361 in Cilicia while on
his way to encounter Julian, who was consolidating his

76

avoiding the appearance of aggression, and in consequence in the midst of peril he sent messages of explanation to all men throughout Greece, of long, short or moderate length, as was likely to suit the character of the recipients.[a] 65. Then, in Pannonia, as he was taking counsel with regard to Thrace, as to whether it was the moment to deliver or await an attack, and as he deployed his valour in opposition to the masses of the foe, a stroke of fortune decided the issue without recourse to arms and devised an end that befitted the ties of kinship. He was on the defensive and would surely have gained the day, when fortune took off the attacker by illness, and so the triumph was complete at the cost of no soldier's life.[b] 66. Then let even Cyrus the Great give way to our emperor if it comes to any comparison of divine favour. He had a shepherd to save him, but he still fought his grandfather[c]; and worse still, as Isocrates says, he won Media and at the same time hid his face for shame.[d] For you, Sire, as you proceeded to supreme power with hands clean, the method of acquiring it was more glorious than its acquisition. 67. More glorious still is the fact that both your followers and your opponents rejoiced with the same joy at this event. Officially, they were on the other side, but their hearts were with you as they learned that you showed the spirit of an emperor and yet comradeship in their wars. 68. This then was why the powers above encircled your head with the diadem, that anger should follow upon your coronation, mobilization upon anger, your advance upon mobilization, and

position at Naissus before a move on Thrace: *cf.* Amm. Marc. 21. 15.

[c] *Cf.* Herod. 1. 110 ff.
[d] *Cf.* Isocr. *Or.* 9. 38.

# LIBANIUS

καὶ γένοιο δὴ τοῖς πράγμασι πλησίον. Εἰ δὲ
ὀκνεῖς, φησί, τὸν φόνον, θάρρει. καὶ τοῦτο ἡμῖν
μελήσει.

69. Οὕτω τοίνυν ὁσιώτατα ὢν ἴσμεν τῆς τε Εὐρώπης τὸ πλέον καὶ τὴν Ἀσίαν προσλαβὼν οὐδὲν
πρὸ τῶν ἱερῶν ἐσπούδασεν, ὥσπερ τις ἀγαθὸς
ναυπηγὸς τὴν τρόπιν πρὸ τῶν ἄλλων σκεπτόμενος.
ὥσπερ γὰρ ἐν τῷ ταύτης ἰσχυρῷ σῴζεται τὸ πλοῖον, οὕτως ἐν τῇ θεραπείᾳ τῶν κρειττόνων αἱ πόλεις.
διὰ τοῦτο νεὼς ἀνίστη καὶ βωμοὺς ἐποίει καὶ τὴν
αὑτοῦ πατρίδα συνείθιζε μὴ πολεμεῖν τοῖς καλοῖς
ἥκιστα ἀνεχομένην καπνοῦ λυσιτελοῦντος, ὥσπερ
τινὰ μητέρα νουθετῶν υἱός, ὃς αὐτῇ τὰ πρῶτα συν-
εξηπατημένος αὑτόν τε κἀκείνην ὕστερον ἀπήλλαξε
τῆς πλάνης.

70. Θαυμάζω τοίνυν ἔγωγε τῶν ἐν μνήμῃ
Περσῶν, ὅτι μὲν αὐτῶν κρατήσεις λεγόντων, ὅτι
δὲ κεκράτηκας οὐκ ἐνθυμουμένων, καὶ ταῦτα ἐπὶ
τῷ στόματι τοῦ Πόντου πρὸς τῷ Βοσπόρῳ καθήμενος καὶ ποιῶν ὃ νῦν ἐγώ, βιβλίον αὐτοῦ τῇ
μεγάλῃ βουλῇ δεικνύων. τίς οὖν ἡ νίκη ; 71.
R 392 γυμνώσας | μὲν ἐκεῖνος τῆς τῶν | ὁπλίτων ἀκμῆς F
τὴν ἑῴαν γῆν ἐπορεύετο τῷ φαυλοτάτῳ τῆς στρατιᾶς παραδοὺς τὰς πόλεις, οἳ φυλάκων ἔχοντες
σχῆμα τῶν φυλαξόντων ἐδέοντο, καὶ μετὰ τῶν
φρουρουμένων οἱ φρουροῦντες ἔτρεμον. τὴν μὲν
οὖν τῶν πόλεων ἁρπαγὴν οὔπω παροῦσαν ἐδοκοῦ-

---

[a] For Julian's divination before leaving Gaul of the imminence of the death of Constantius cf. Amm. Marc. 21. 2. 2, Lib. Or. 18. 118, Zos. 3. 9, Zonaras 13. 11.
[b] For the edict of toleration cf. E.L.F. No. 42.
[c] The senate at Constantinople, enrolled by Themistius

78

so you should be brought close to power. " If you shrink from killing," was their message, " take heart. This will be our concern."[a]

69. Having thus gained most of Europe and Asia besides more honestly than anyone we can recall, his first care was for religion.[b] In this he was like a skilled shipwright who before all else looks to the keel. In its strength lies the safety of the boat, and in the same way the safety of our cities lies in the worship of the gods. Thus he raised temples and built altars, and schooled his country not to fight against the good, when she was least patient of the smoke of sacrifice which was so beneficial for her. He was like a son reproving his mother, and removing both her and himself from error after originally being her companion in infatuation.

70. I am surprised at people who, when discussing the Persians, predict that you will beat them, without realizing that you have beaten them already, at that very time when you settled by the Bosporus at the mouth of the Pontus and did just what I am now doing—presented a composition of your own to the supreme senate.[c] The manner of the victory is as follows. 71. Constantius had stripped the eastern empire of its picked troops when he began his march. He entrusted the cities to the weakest of his forces who, protectors to all appearances, themselves needed protection. Thus both flock and watch-dog alike were in fear and trembling. We thus felt that we had before our eyes the sack of our cities, though it had not yet occurred, and that our

in A.D. 358/9, brought the new Rome into line with the old. μεγάλη differentiates the senate from the local *boulae* (*curiae*) of the municipalities.

# LIBANIUS

μεν ὁρᾶν, ἡ φυγὴ δὲ εἶχε τὴν σωτηρίαν. 72. καὶ
ἐμακάριζον οἱ μὲν ἐν μεσογείᾳ τοὺς ἐπὶ θαλάττῃ,
οἱ δὲ οἰκοῦντες κάτω τοὺς ναυκλήρους αὐτῶν καὶ
οὐδὲν ἦν εὐδαιμονέστερον τότε τοῦ κεκτῆσθαι
πλοῖον. Κυπρίων δὲ οἱ παρόντες ἐθεραπεύοντό τε
καὶ καταγωγὰς ὑπισχνοῦντο. ἦν δὲ ἀδεὲς οὐδὲ ἡ
θάλαττα ὡς ἔν τε τοῖς λιμέσιν ἐσομένων ὑπὲρ τῶν
νεῶν τραυμάτων ἔν τε τῷ πελάγει νεκρῶν τοῦ
καιροῦ τοὺς κακούργους ἀθροίζοντος. 73. ταύτας
δὴ τὰς μεταναστάσεις ἔσχεν ἡμέρα μία. ἡ γὰρ
αὐτὴ σοὶ μὲν ταῦτα ἔδωκεν, ἡμῖν δὲ θαρρῆσαι τὴν
μονὴν οὐ δυνάμεώς ποθεν ἐπελθούσης οὐδὲ τειχῶν
τοῖς μὲν γενομένων, τοῖς δὲ ἐπισκευασθέντων οὐδὲ
τῶν ἀντιπάλων λοιμῷ βεβλημένων, ἀλλὰ ψιλῆς
τῆς προσηγορίας ἐκβαλούσης τὸν φόβον, καὶ Τίγρητος ἀπέχων ἑβδομήκοντα σταθμούς, ὥσπερ ἄρας
R 393 εἰς μάχην σημεῖα, | τοὺς Πέρσας ἐτάραττες. 74.
ὁ δὲ κακῶς ἀπολούμενος Δημάρατος ὁ τὰ παρ'
ἡμῖν ἐπαινῶν πρὸς | ἐκεῖνον[1] ἀγαθὰ καὶ τοῦ F
χειμῶνος φάσκων αὐτῷ[1] παραδώσειν ὥσπερ ἐν
κύρτῳ τὴν πόλιν μεταβαλὼν τοὺς Πολυδάμαντος
ἠφίει λόγους οἷς ἐκεῖνος ἐχρῆτο φανέντος Ἀχιλλέως. ταύτην ὅστις εὖ φρονεῖ μεγάλην νίκην
προσερεῖ τῆς μελλούσης οὐ φαυλοτέραν. ἡ μὲν
γὰρ ἐκείνους θεῶν διδόντων δοριαλώτους ἄξει, ἡ
δ' ἡμᾶς ἐκώλυσε γενέσθαι, καὶ δι' ἐκείνης μὲν ὧν
πεπόνθαμεν ληψόμεθα δίκην, διὰ δὲ ταύτης οὐ
προσπεπόνθαμεν. 75. ἡττᾶται δέ, οἶμαι, πολέμιος

---

[1] ἐκεῖνον . . . αὐτῷ mss. (except for corrections in P and
Vat. 84) : ἐκείνους . . . αὐτοῖς F. (corrections as above).

---

[a] Demaratus, deposed king of Sparta, sought refuge with

80

safety lay in flight. 72. The inhabitants of the inland
area envied the luck of those by the sea ; and those
by the coast in turn envied those of their number who
owned a ship ; to possess a boat was at that time the
height of good fortune. Visitors from Cyprus were
overwhelmed with attentions and promised hospi-
tality, but even the sea was not without its perils ; in
the harbours people were sure to be wounded in the
struggle to get aboard, and on the high seas corpses
would float as pirate bands collected in this hour of
crisis. 73. Yet a single day was enough to put a stop
to this panic, for the same day that gave you your
present state gave us the courage to remain. Though
no reinforcements reached us at all, nor had we walls
built or building, though the enemy was not visited
by plague, your mere name cast out fear from us and,
though seventy day's march from the Tigris, you
caused panic among the Persians just as though you
had raised your battle standard. 74. That doubly
damned rogue, that second Demaratus who filled the
ears of the Persian king with the tale of our wealth
and who promised to betray to him during the winter
our city in thrall,[a] changed his tune, and his words
were those of Polydamas at the appearance of
Achilles.[b] Any sensible man will describe this as a
great victory, in no way less than the one to come. It
has kept us from captivity and ensured no more sufferings for us : your future triumph will, with heaven's
grace, lead our enemy captive and ensure for us vengeance for wrongs suffered. 75. An enemy, in fact,

Xerxes and acted as his adviser in the invasion of 480 B.C.
Similarly, the *protector* Antoninus deserted to the Persians
and acted as Sapor's adviser in the recent campaigns : *cf.*
Amm. Marc. 18. 5.

    [b] Homer, *Iliad*, 18. 247 ff.

οὐχ ἁλισκόμενος μόνον, ἀλλὰ καὶ ὅταν λήψεσθαι
μὲν ἐλπίσῃ, σωθεὶς δὲ ἀγαπήσῃ· τὸ γὰρ προσδοκη-
θὲν ἐν τοῖς εἰλημμένοις ἀριθμῶν ἀπεστερῆσθαι
νομίζει. 76. μία μὲν οὖν αὕτη τοῦ νενικῆσθαι τὸν
Μῆδον ἀπόδειξις, ἑτέρα δέ, καί μοι σύγγνωθι πρὸς
Διὸς εἴ τι τῶν ἀπορρήτων ἐκφέροιμι, βιάζεται γάρ
μοι τὸ στόμα καὶ γίγνεται τοῦ τείχους τῶν ὀδόντων
δυνατώτερον, γράμματα πρῴην ἧκεν Ἀσύρια δεόμενα κήρυκι καὶ πρεσβείᾳ ἀνοῖξαι τὴν ὁδὸν καὶ
τὰ διάφορα λόγῳ τεμεῖν. 77. ἐγὼ μὲν οὖν ᾤμην
αὐτὸν κροτήσειν καὶ ἑορτάσειν καὶ τάχους ἐπιμελεῖσθαι[1] καὶ συνέχαιρον δὴ πρᾶγμα ποιῶν πολ-
λάκις | ἡττημένου, ὁ δ' ἀπέρριψε τὴν ἐπιστολὴν F
ἀνδρειότερον Διομήδους δεινὸν νομίζων εἴ τις
ὀφείλων δίκας περὶ σπονδῶν διαλέξεται. 78.
τούτων δὲ οὐκ ἐλάττω τὰ πρὸς τοὺς ἥκοντας παρὰ
τῶν Σκυθῶν, οὓς ἐν τοῖς ὅρκοις ἀκριβολογου-
μένους λαβὼν ἐκέλευσεν ἀπελθόντας περὶ πολέμου
σκοπεῖν, καὶ διὰ μακροῦ δὴ χρόνου Ῥωμαῖος ἀνὴρ
ἠπείλησε βαρβάρῳ. 79. πόθεν δὴ τὸ τοῦ πολέμου |
R 394 μεταπέπτωκε πνεῦμα ; καὶ τί τὴν Ῥωμαίων
τύχην ἐπανήγαγεν εἰς τὸ Πέρσας φοβεῖν ; οὐ
πεζομαχία τις οὐδ' ἱππομαχίας πόνος οὐδ' ὅπλων
καινότης οὐδ' ἐπιτεχνήσεων εὕρεσις, ἀλλ' αἱ πυκναὶ
θυσίαι καὶ τὸ αἷμα τὸ πολὺ καὶ οἱ τῶν ἀρωμάτων
ἀτμοὶ καὶ θεῶν ἑστιάσεις καὶ δαιμόνων τοὺς πολεμίους συνέστειλαν. 80. διὰ τοῦτο χαίρει καλού-

---

[1] ἐπιμελεῖσθαι mss. : ἐπιμελήσεσθαι F. (conj. Gasda).

---

[a] Cf. Or. 18. 164 f. Here Assyria is used as an allusive
synonym for Persia. Other fourth-century writers continue
to use the term " Parthian " in the same way.

[b] Homer, Iliad, 9. 31 ff.

is worsted not just when he is caught, but whenever he hopes to succeed and then is thankful to come off with a whole skin. By counting chickens before they are hatched he feels that he has sustained loss. 76. This then is one proof that the Persians are defeated, but there is yet another. Pray, pardon me, Sire, if I broadcast news of any secret, but this forces me to speak and leaves me unable to keep my mouth shut. The other day a message from Assyria came requesting free entry for a herald and embassy and suggesting that differences be settled by nego-tiation.[a] 77. At this I thought that he would applaud and dance for joy and be all eagerness, and I began to offer congratulations, in this behav-ing like one who has suffered many a set-back, but he cast aside the message with more courage than Diomede,[b] for he thought it a disgrace that any-one who deserved to be punished should dare to talk of peace. 78. No less forthright was his reply to envoys from the Goths.[c] When he found them quibbling about the terms of their treaty, he told them to be off and look to their arms. For the first time for years a Roman has bearded a barbarian. 79. What then has caused this change in martial spirit? And what has caused the Romans to inspire fear among the Persians? No infantry battle, no cavalry activity, no innovation in armament or inven-tion of engines of war, but it is the many sacrifices, the frequent blood-offerings, the clouds of incense, the feasting of gods and spirits that has brought our enemies low. 80. Thus he rejoices in the title of priest

---

[c] Cf. § 62. It is uncertain whether there is any connection between this incident and the anecdote preserved by Eunapius (F.H.G. v, fr. 22. 1) = E.L.F. No. 94.

μενος ἱερεὺς οὐχ ἧττον ἢ βασιλεύς, καὶ τοὔνομα
τοῖς ἔργοις συμβαίνει· ὡς οὐ μᾶλλόν γε βασιλέας
τοῖς περὶ τὴν ἀρχὴν ἢ τοὺς ἱερεῖς ἁγιστείαις παρῆλθεν. οὐ λέγω τοὺς νῦν τοὺς ἀμβλυτέρους, ἀλλὰ
τοὺς πάλαι τοὺς ἐν Αἰγύπτῳ τοὺς ἀπηκριβωμένους.
οὐ γὰρ νόμων ἀνάγκαις ὑπηρετῶν νῦν μὲν ἔθυσε,
νῦν δὲ ἔληξεν, ἀλλ' ὀρθῶς εἰρῆσθαι νομίζων τὸ
δεῖν ἀπὸ θεῶν ἄρχεσθαι καὶ ἔργων καὶ λόγων, ἃ
τοὺς ἄλλους οἶδε ταῖς νουμηνίαις ἀναθέντας, ταῦθ'
ἑκάστης ἡμέρας εἶναι πεποίηκεν, αἵματι μὲν |
δεχόμενος ἀνίσχοντα τὸν θεόν, αἵματι δὲ παρα- F 3
πέμπων εἰς δύσιν καὶ ταὐτὰ[1] πάλιν νυκτερινοῖς
ἑτοιμάζων δαίμοσιν. 81. εἴσω δὲ τὰ πολλὰ κατ-
εχόμενος ὑπὸ τῆς τύχης, ἐπεὶ μὴ τρέχειν εἰς ἱερὸν
παρ' ἡμέραν ἔνεστιν, ἱερὸν ποιεῖται τὰ βασίλεια
καὶ τὸν κῆπον καθαρώτερον τῶν παρ' ἐνίοις
ἀδύτων, καὶ γίγνονται τοῖς μὲν δένδρεσιν ἡδίους
οἱ βωμοί, τοῖς βωμοῖς δὲ τὰ δένδρα. 82. τὸ δὲ
κάλλιστον, οὐ γὰρ ἐφ' ὑψηλοῦ καθήμενος ἢ χρυσαῖς
ἀσπίσι περικλειόμενος ἑτέρων χερσὶ θεραπεύει τοὺς
θεούς, ἀλλ' αὐτουργεῖ καὶ περιτρέχει καὶ σχίζης
R 395 ἅπτεται | καὶ μάχαιραν δέχεται καὶ ὄρνις ἀνέρρηξε
καὶ τὰ ἔνδον οὐκ ἠγνόησε, καὶ τούτων πίστις οἱ
δάκτυλοι τῶν ἐκεῖθεν τεκμηρίων γέμοντες. ἡγεῖται
γὰρ ἄτοπον, εἰ τὰ μὲν γραμματεῖα τοῖς ἄρξουσιν

---

[1] ταὐτὰ F. (conj. Re.) : ταῦτα MSS.

---

[a] For the moral requirements Julian expected of his
priests cf. E.L.F. No. 89 a and b (pp. 452 ff. and 288 ff.).

[b] Because of his excesses of sacrifice in time of famine,
Julian's unpopularity had increased during his stay in
Antioch, and his displays of religious activity and practice
of divination in a largely Christianized community had made
him an object of lampoons (Amm. Marc. 22. 12. 4 ff.), the

no less than in that of emperor, and the title is matched by his actions, for he has excelled priests in his performance of services to the gods as he has done emperors in government. Nor do I mean these spiritless priests of the present day but those in Egypt who have long been specialists in their art.[a] He did not comply with the dictates of convention and offer sacrifices on some occasions and refrain on others. He believed in the rightness of the statement that deeds and words must both begin with the gods; all the sacrifices that he knows other people make at the month's beginning he has ensured shall take place every day; he greets the rising of the sun and sees it to its rest with offerings of blood, and also prepares the same for the spirits of the night.[b] 81. Since, as a consequence of his station, he is mostly kept indoors and cannot hurry to the temple every day, he makes a temple of his palace, and his gardens are more holy than the actual temples are among some people.[c] The altars become the more pleasant because of the trees, and the trees because of the altars. 82. And, best of all, he is not enthroned on high or fenced around with golden shields, worshipping the gods by means of another's hands. He performs the sacrifice in person; he busies himself on the preparations, gets the wood, wields the knife, opens the birds and inspects their entrails. The proof of this is in his fingers which bear the evidence therefrom. It is absurd, he thinks, that he should handle personally messages to his future governors

mob dubbing him *victimarius* (*ibid.* 22. 14. 3). The insistence of the pagan Libanius upon the virtues of Julian's conduct in religion must be considered in the light of such opposition.

  [c] *Cf. Or.* 1. 121, 15. 71, 18. 177.

αὐτὸς ἐγχειριεῖ, ταῖς δ' αὐταῖς χερσὶν οὐ πληρώσει τὰ πρὸς τοὺς θεούς. 83. ἐντεῦθεν οὐ καθίζει βουλὰς στρατηγῶν καὶ λοχαγῶν καὶ ταξιαρχῶν ἐν τοῖς ἐπείγουσιν οὐδὲ τρίβει χρόνους ἐν σκέψεσιν, ἀλλ' ἐπὶ τοὺς διδασκάλους τῶν ἐν ἀδήλῳ καταφυγῶν ἀπήλλακται, ἐντεῦθεν γράμμα μὲν οὐδὲν ἀπὸ τῶν περάτων τῆς ἀρχῆς ἢ κομιδῇ σπάνια, πάντα δὲ ἔγνωσται, καὶ καθάπερ τὸν Ἥλιον λέληθεν οὐδὲν τῶν ἐπὶ γῆς, οὕτως οὐδὲ σὲ τῶν δρωμένων οὐδὲν αὐτοῦ διδόντος Ἡλίου. 84. ἔτι δὲ κἂν τοῖς ἐσχάτοις ὅσοι βάρβαροι τὴν ἡμετέραν ἀπὸ | τῆς F 3 ἔξω θαλάττης μέχρι τῆς τοῦ Πόντου παροικοῦσι ῥαχίας, τὰ ὅπλα κρεμάσαντες ἀλοκίζουσι τὴν γῆν |

R 396 τὰς μὲν ἐντεῦθεν καὶ παρ' ἡμῶν εὐπορίας ἀπεγνωκότες, εὐχόμενοι δὲ τῇ Δήμητρι. τῶν δ' ὑπηκόων ὅσοις ἔδει γενέσθαι κακῶς, τυραννίδος ἔρωτι σφᾶς αὐτοὺς ἀπώλεσαν, ἃ μὲν ἤλπισαν οὐ δυνηθέντες, ἃ δ' ἐφοβήθησαν ἁλόντες οὐ παθόντες, μόνοι ζῶντες ἐπὶ τοιούτοις βουλεύμασιν. 85. ἐγὼ δὲ Ξέρξην ἐθαύμαζον οὐκ ἀποκτείναντα τοὺς ἀντὶ τῶν ἀγγέλων ἐπὶ τὸν θάνατον ἥκοντας. κήρυκες |

R 397 ἠδίκηντο παρ' ὅλης πόλεως, εὐκαταφρόνητον τῷ Μήδῳ, καὶ ἅμα τὴν ἀνδρίαν τῶν αὐτοὺς διδόντων ᾐσχύνθη. ὁ δὲ τοὺς ἐπ' αὐτὸν ἃ μηδὲ εἰπεῖν θέμις συντεθεικότας μέχρι τῶν ἐλέγχων ἐκόλασε.

86. Καὶ ταῦτα, ὦ ἄνδρες, τῶν αὐτῶν ἐπικούρων ἡγώμεθα τῶν βελτιόνων εἰς φυλακὴν Ἄργου τοῦ

---

[a] This authoritarian attitude also emerges very clearly from Ammianus' account of his conduct of the Persian campaign.

[b] *i.e.*, the barbarians must reconcile themselves to agriculture: vocabulary hints at Aristoph. *Wasps*, 850.

[c] *Cf. Or.* 16. 19.

and yet not fulfil his duties towards the gods with the same hands. 83. As a result, he does not institute committees of generals, brigadiers and colonels to deal with matters of urgency, nor does he waste time in discussion, but he has recourse to his instructors [a] in secret lore, and so has done with problems. Hence it happens that, though no or very few dispatches arrive from the frontiers of the empire, yet he is aware of everything. Just as nothing on this earth, Sire, remains unnoticed by the sun, so by the gift of this very sun nothing happens of which you too remain unaware. 84. Moreover, all the barbarians bordering on our frontiers from the western ocean to the Pontic shores have put up their weapons and plough their fields and, despairing of battening upon those of our provinces too, they offer up their prayers to Demeter.[b] Those of your subjects who were destined to go wrong have brought their own ruin in their devotion to tyranny, but though unable to achieve their objective, when caught they failed to suffer the punishment they dreaded : they, and they alone, live to tell the tale after engaging in such conspiracies.[c] 85. I used to admire Xerxes for not executing those men who presented themselves to die as scapegoats for the death of his envoys.[d] His heralds had suffered at the hands of the state as a whole, a fact the Persian could easily have ignored, and he respected the courage shown by such self-sacrifice. Here our emperor, in dealing with the members of unspeakable plots against his person, exacted no punishment beyond proving their guilt.

86. This event, gentlemen, let us attribute to those same helpers whose protection is more effective than

[d] *Cf. Or.* 15. 40 : Herod. 7. 136.

# LIBANIUS

γηγενοῦς, οἳ φρουροῦσι μὲν αὐτὸν μετὰ δορυφόρων,
φυλάττουσι δὲ τοὺς δορυφόρους αὐτούς, κἂν εὕρω-
σιν ἀντὶ κυνῶν λύκους, ἐμήνυσαν, οὐκ ἀσθένεσι
καὶ | σκολιαῖς ἐνυπνίων ὄψεσιν, ἀλλ᾽ ὥσπερ νῦν F 4
ἡμεῖς ἀλλήλους ὁρῶμεν καὶ φράσειεν ἂν ἄλλος
ἄλλῳ περὶ τοῦ λέγοντος, ὡς εὖ λέγοντος ἢ τοὐναντίον, οὕτως ἐκεῖνοι τούτῳ περὶ τῶν πρασσόντων
R 398 νεώτερα, τιμῶντες αὐτῷ τοὺς ὀφθαλμοὺς | τῇ
σφετέρᾳ θέᾳ καὶ οὐκ ἐῶντες ἀπιστεῖν Ὁμήρῳ
θεοὺς ἀνθρώποις ἀναμίξαντι καθάπερ ἑταίρους καὶ
φίλους. 87. πῶς δὲ οὐκ ἔμελλον ἔσεσθαί σοι φίλοι
μηδενὸς αὐτοῖς ἀμεληθέντος ἐν τῇ δεῦρο πορείᾳ
βωμοῦ; ὅς γε καὶ τῆς εὐθείας ὁδοῦ τοσοῦτον
ἐκδραμὼν εἰς Φρυγίαν ἐλθὼν τὴν τεκοῦσαν ἡμῖν
τοὺς θεοὺς πολλοῖς καὶ μεγάλοις τιμήσας ἐπανῆλθες. ἥκων τοίνυν παρ᾽ ἡμᾶς, ὡς μὲν ἄν τις φαίη
τῶν οὐδὲν εἰδότων, ἡσύχασας, ὡς δ᾽ ἂν ἐγώ, πεπο-
λέμηκας, καὶ τῶν εἰς τὴν νίκην φερόντων εὕρηταί τι
μεῖζον αὐτῆς τῆς μάχης. καὶ γὰρ οὕτως ἔχει. 88.
οὐκ ἦν ἡμῶν τὸν ἔμπροσθεν χρόνον ἡ Περσῶν
δύναμις οὔτε πλήθει μείζων οὔτε ἀλκῇ βελτίων
οὔτε τέχνῃ καλλίων οὔτε ὅπλοις ἰσχυροτέρα, ἀλλ᾽ ὃ
πάντα ταῦτα καὶ συνέχει καὶ διαφθείρει νῦν μὲν
παρόν, νῦν δὲ ἀπόν, ἐκεῖσε μεθειστήκει καὶ μετ᾽
R 399 ἐκείνων ἐπῄει, δαίμονες | πολέμου καὶ μάχης καὶ
τροπῆς κύριοι, καταπολεμοῦντες μὲν τοὺς ἀτιμά-
ζοντας, ἐπιρρωννύντες δὲ τοὺς αἰδουμένους. 89.
συνιόντων τοίνυν ἔτι τῶν στρατοπέδων ἀφανῆ παρ᾽

88

that of Argus the earth-born.[a] They join his guards in protecting him, and they guard against the guards also, and if they find any acting not as watch-dogs but as wolves, they signify the fact, not by any vague or oblique vision of dreams, but by actually telling him of any treachery. We now look at each other face to face; we could inform one another about the virtues or defects of the speaker; in exactly the same way they communicate with him, and honour his eyes with the sight of themselves, and they refuse to let us disbelieve Homer when he associates gods with humans as comrades and friends. 87. The gods were bound to be your friends, Sire, for you have ignored none of their altars in your journey here. For instance, you diverged from your direct route, visited Phrygia and bestowed upon our Mother of the Gods much signal honour before resuming your march.[b] And, upon your arrival here, though an ignoramus might describe your conduct as inactivity, in my opinion you have fought the good fight and devised a means of victory more decisive than actual fighting. The circumstances are as follows. 88. In days gone by, the might of Persia did not surpass our own in numbers; it was no more valiant, or proficient or strongly armed. The one factor whose presence unites all these qualities and whose absence ruins them, had deserted us and ranged itself on their side—those deities who control war, battle and rout, who crush those that spurn and strengthen those that revere them. 89. So, upon the meeting of the armies, their invisible weapons,

---

[a] Argus, the hundred-eyed, was set by Hera to guard Io : cf. Aesch. P. V. 568.

[b] Cf. Or. 18. 161 f., Amm. Marc. 22. 9. 5.

ἐκείνων ἐπὶ τοὺς ἡμετέρους ὁπλίτας ἐχώρει βέλη
τῶν ψυχῶν ἁπτόμενα, | τὰ μὲν Ἄρεος ἀφιέντος, τὰ F 4
δὲ τῶν Ἄρεος λοχιτῶν, τοῦ Δείμου, τοῦ Φόβου.
τούτοις δὴ τάς τε καρδίας ἐπλήττοντο τά τε ξίφη
τῶν χειρῶν μεθίεσαν, ἔπασχόν τε ὅπερ εἰκὸς
ἀνθρώπους, ἡττῶντο δαιμόνων. 90. εἰδὼς οὖν
ὀρθῶς ὅτι δεῖ στρατιώτην ἕκαστον προσκυνῆσαι
τούτους ὧν δεῖται μαχόμενος, ὡς τοῦτ' ὂν τῆς
παρασκευῆς κεφάλαιον, οὐκ ἀσπίδος οὐδὲ θώρακος
οὐδὲ ἀκοντίου, καὶ διαλεχθεὶς τοῖς θεοῖς ἄττα δὴ
καὶ διείλεξαι, συνέσει τῶν κρειττόνων τὴν δύναμιν
ὥπλισας, ἑκόντας ἐπὶ τοὺς βωμοὺς θέοντας καὶ
διαμαχομένους ὑπὲρ τοῦ λιβανωτοῦ.

91. Τῇ μὲν οὖν Ῥωμαίων ἀρχῇ τοιοῦτον τεῖχος
περιήλασας. εὖ δὲ ποιῶν καὶ τὸν ἄλλον μεταρρυθ-
μίζεις ὄχλον, τὸ τοῦ Πρωτέως εἰς ἑτέρους ἐργαζόμενος. νῦν γὰρ δὴ τὸ τὴν γῆν οἰκοῦν ἀπὸ συῶν
ἀτεχνῶς εἰς ἀνθρώπους μεταπλάττεται. 92. τούτων
R 400 δὲ | ἁπάντων αἴτιον οἱ λόγοι. ταυτὶ μὲν γὰρ ἔργα
φρονήσεως, φρόνησις δὲ λόγων, οὓς ἐδέξω τῇ
ψυχῇ πᾶσαν ἰδέαν, τοὺς μὲν δρόμῳ χωροῦντας,
τοὺς δὲ σχολῇ βαίνοντας, ἐπιστολάς, διαλεκτικούς,
κάλλος ἐπῶν· ὧν τοῖς μὲν ἐγκωμιάζεις, τοῖς δὲ
πείθεις, τοῖς δὲ ἀναγκάζεις, τοῖς δὲ θέλγεις, καὶ
νικᾷς τοὺς μὲν ῥήτορας τῇ φιλοσοφίᾳ, | τοὺς δ' αὖ F 4
φιλοσόφους τῇ ῥητορείᾳ, τῇ ποιήσει δὲ ἀμφοτέρους,
ὥσπερ αὖ τοὺς ποιητὰς ἀμφοτέροις ἐκείνοις καὶ
νὴ Δία γε πάντας οὓς ἔφην, θατέρᾳ φωνῇ τελεώτατα
ἐχούσῃ, λέγω δὲ οὐκ αὐτὸς ἐπαΐων, ἀλλά με

---

ᵃ Cf. Or. 18. 166 ff.   Homer, Iliad, 4. 440, 11. 37.

aimed by Ares and his henchmen, Panic and Fear,[a] were hurled against our troops and gripped their spirits. At this they were shaken at heart and let their swords fall from their grasp, and, as men are bound to be, they were worsted by gods. 90. Thus in the sure knowledge that every soldier must adore the gods he needs to help him in the fight, for this, not shield, breastplate or spear, is the ideal armament, and in communion with the gods, as you are, you armed your forces with understanding of these greater powers, and every man hastens of his own free will to their altars competing with his fellows with offerings of incense.[b]

91. This then is the bulwark you have made for the Roman empire. With saving grace you seek to correct the remainder of its population, inducing others to suffer a sea-change, for now the inhabitants of the world are being transformed from mere swine into human beings.[c] 92. The cause of all this is eloquence. It results from understanding, and understanding from eloquence, and with eloquence of every type you have furnished your intellect, with compositions rapid or leisurely, letters, dialogues and the beauties of verse. In these you produce works of panegyric, persuasion, injunction and charm. You excel the orators in philosophy, philosophers in oratory, and both alike in poetry. Similarly you excel poets in both these accomplishments and indeed all those just mentioned by your perfect Latinity, of which I cannot speak from my own knowledge, but from the conviction that our Carthaginian friend has

[b] For Julian's exclusion of Christians from the civil and military services cf. E.L.F. No. 50.

[c] Homer, Od. 4. 455 ff.

91

πέπεικεν ὁ Καρχηδόνιος ἐκεῖνος. 93. ὥστ᾽ εἴ σοι
συμβεβήκει ταῦτα κεκτῆσθαι βασιλείας ἄνευ, πολλοῖς ἂν βασιλέων ἐπιθυμίαν παρέσχες τὰ μὲν
αὐτῶν δοῦναι, τὰ δὲ σὰ λαβεῖν, καὶ εἴ γέ πως
ἐνῆν σοι δέκα γλώσσαις ἐκπέμπειν φωνήν, οὐδὲν
ἂν ἐδέου τῶν περὶ τὰς ἐπιστολὰς συμμάχων. 94.
τούτους δὴ τοὺς πολλοὺς καὶ καλοὺς καὶ ποικίλους
λόγους οὐ πρεσβυτέροις τῆς ἀρχῆς μόνοις ἐκτήσω
πόνοις, ἀλλ᾽ ἐτήρησας ἔτι καὶ νῦν τὴν ὑπὲρ αὐτῶν
ἀγρυπνίαν. καὶ οὐκ ἠνάγκασεν ἡ βασιλεία κεῖσθαι
μάταια τὰ βιβλία, ἀλλ᾽ ἡ μὲν νὺξ ἐπὶ τῆς πρώτης
ἔτι μοίρας, σὺ δὲ ᾄδεις πολὺ πρότερος τῶν ὀρνίθων
R 401 ἢ τίκτων λόγους | ἢ τὸν ἑτέρων τόκον λαμβάνων.
ὕπνου δὲ ἰσχὺς κεκράτηται κεκολασμένης γαστρός·
μετὰ μὲν γὰρ οἴνου καὶ πλησμονῆς ἄρχει βλεφάρων
ἐκεῖνος, ἄνευ δὲ τούτων οὐ μέγα δύναται. 95. τί
δὴ θαυμαστόν, εἰ σωμάτων ὠλιγώρηται κάλλος ἐν
τεττίγων μὲν τροφῇ, λόγων δὲ ἀπεργασίᾳ, θεῶν δὲ
συνουσίᾳ, πόνῳ δὲ συνεχεῖ; τὸ γὰρ ἐπὶ ταῦτα |
ἐρρυηκὸς ἀπήρτηται τῶν ἐκεῖθεν ἡδονῶν. καὶ F
κινδυνεύει τῇ πρὸς τὸ σωφρονεῖν παρασκευῇ τῶν
περὶ τῆς σωφροσύνης ἐπαίνων ἀπεστερῆσθαι· τὸ
γὰρ μηδ᾽ ἐγχωρεῖν ἐνταῦθα διαίτης τεταγμένον
δουλεύειν ἔρωτι πονηρῷ τὸ θαῦμα περιήρηκε. 96.
τοιοῦτος ἡμῖν ὁ βασιλεύς τε καὶ ὕπατος, νικῶν

---

[a] For Julian's various literary activities cf. Or. 17. 27, 18.
302, 24. 37 : also Amm. Marc. 16. 5. 7, where his facility in
Latin is noted. The identity of the Carthaginian is uncertain : he may be the Latin orator whose composition
preceded that of Libanius on this occasion (cf. Or. 1. 127 ff.).

[b] Homer, Iliad, 2. 489.

[c] " Grasshopper's food " was proverbially microscopic.

inspired in me.[a] 93. Thus, if you had possessed all
these attributes without coming to the throne, you
would have made many an emperor wish himself to
be in your shoes and you in his; and, had you ten
tongues to speak with,[b] you would need no one
to assist you in your correspondence. 94. This splen-
did variety of glorious eloquence you have acquired
not simply by your efforts before ascending the
throne: even now you continue to spend sleepless
nights upon it. Your imperial majesty has not compelled your books to lie idle, but while the night is yet
young you give utterance much earlier than do the
birds, either begetting works of your own or taking
up those begotten by others. Your appetites are
controlled and the power of sleep has been overcome,
for sleep holds sway over the eyes in conjunction
with wine and a full belly. Without these its power
is small. 95. What cause for surprise, then, that he
disregards physical attractions, when he lives on next
to nothing,[c] engages in literary composition, associates
with gods and performs unremitting toil ?[d] A dedi-
cation to these pursuits is far removed from physical
pleasure. In fact, because of this armour of self-
control, he may perhaps even lose the praise it
deserves, since the very impossibility of a life ordered
on these lines falling under the spell of ignoble passion detracts from the feeling of admiration. 96.
Such then is our emperor and consul, supreme by the

---

Cf. Plut. *Symp.* 4. 1. 1 ἐν ἀέρι καὶ δρόσῳ καθάπερ οἱ τέττιγες
σιτούμενον; Theocr. *Id.* 4. 16; Aristoph. *Nub.* 1360. The
proverb is personified in the legend of Tithonus.

[d] Cf. *Or.* 18. 170 ff., where this topic is elaborated. The
pathos of the *Epitaphios* is heightened by its deliberate
reminiscences of this panegyric, both in arrangement of
material and in use of vocabulary.

ἁπάσαις οὐ μόνον ἡμῶν ψηφιζομένων ἀλλὰ καὶ
θεῶν δικαζόντων, ἐμφράττων καὶ τὸ τοῦ Μώμου
στόμα τῇ τῆς ἀρετῆς ἀκριβείᾳ· ἐπεὶ καὶ τοῦτο
γενναῖον καὶ μεγαλόψυχον τὸ πολὺ τῇ τύχῃ λειπόμενον προελέσθαι[1] τὸν ὁμόζυγα καὶ μήτε τὸ σχῆμα
διαφυγεῖν οὐκ ὄντος ὁμοτίμου μήτ᾽ ἐπιθυμίᾳ τοῦ
R 402 σχήματος πρὶν | ἢ κάλλιον ἀποδεῖξαι τὸν ὁμότιμον.
97. πάντως δὲ καὶ Ξάνθος, ἀθάνατος ἵππος, οὐκ
ἠτίμαζε τὸν Πήδασον παραθέοντα. καὶ πρὸς
τούτῳ γε τῷ παραδείγματι τὴν Ἀθηνᾶν καὶ τὸν
Διομήδην ἐφ᾽ ἑνὸς ἴσμεν ἀγομένους ἅρματος,
δεινὴν θεὸν ἄνδρα τ᾽ ἄριστον.

98. Νῦν μοι δοκοῦσι καὶ γάμοι σωφροσύνῃ
συνέσεσθαι | καὶ πάντα συμβόλαια δικαιοσύνης F
μεθέξειν καὶ παῖδες ἐπ᾽ ἀμείνοσι τεχθήσεσθαι
χρηστοῦ τινος οἰωνοῦ τῆς σῆς προσηγορίας ἡγου-
μένης.

99. Τοῦτον ἐγὼ τὸν ἐνιαυτόν, εἴ τις ἦν ἀγὼν
ἐνιαυτοῖς, ὥσπερ ἀθληταῖς, καὶ κρίσις, δοκῶ μοι
πᾶσιν ἂν νικῆσαι τοῖς κριταῖς. ὕπατον μὲν γὰρ
ἐδέξαντο πολλοὶ καὶ δέξαιντό γε, πρῶτος δὲ οὗτος
ἐν μοναρχίᾳ. εἰ οὖν Σαπφὼ τὴν Λεσβίαν οὐδὲν
ἐκώλυσεν εὔξασθαι νύκτα αὐτῇ γενέσθαι διπλασίαν,
ἐξέστω κἀμοί τι παραπλήσιον αἰτῆσαι· Χρόνε,
R 403 πάτερ | ἐνιαυτοῦ καὶ μηνῶν, ἔκτεινον ἡμῖν
τουτὶ τὸ ἔτος οἷόν τε πλεῖστον, ὥσπερ ὅτε
Ἡρακλῆς ἐσπείρετο τὴν νύκτα ἐξέτεινας,

---

[1] προελέσθαι mss. : προσελέσθαι F. (conj. Cobet).

[a] Son of Night (Hesiod, *Theog.* 214), and spirit of ridicule
and blame : *cf.* Lucian, *Hermot.* 20.
[b] Sallustius ; p. p. Galliarum. Ammianus notes the novelty of this nomination ; *cf.* 23. 1. 1.

unanimous verdict not merely of our finding but of gods in judgement, who stops even the mouth of Momus [a] by his consummate virtue. For his generous and noble character is further demonstrated by his choice as colleague of a man of far lower station,[b] and by his refusal either to avoid the office because he has no peer, or, out of desire for it, to nominate a peer to himself before it was right and proper to do so. 97. In any case, Xanthus, that immortal steed, did not disdain his team-mate Pedasus [c]: and besides this example, we know that Athena and Diomede rode in the same chariot, " a dread goddess and a goodly man."[d]

98. Now, so it seems to me, marriage and decency will unite and all contracts will partake of justice, and children will be born to a better future, for your title ushers in some good portent.[e]

99. Were there competition between the years, as there is between athletes,[f] and decision upon the winner, this year would have been declared the winner by unanimous verdict. Many of them have welcomed a consul—and may they continue so to do —but this one leads the field in the monarchy. So, if nothing stopped Sappho of Lesbos from praying for her night to be made twice as long,[g] let me too make a similar prayer : "Chronos, father of the year and the months, extend this year for us as far as you can, as once you extended the night when Heracles

---

[a] Of the horses of Achilles, Xanthus and Balius were immortal, while Pedasus was mortal: Homer, *Iliad*, 16. 148 ff.

[d] *Ibid.* 5. 839.

[e] A theme resumed in the lament of *Or.* 17. 13.

[f] *Or.* 18. 283 develops this idea.

[g] Sappho, *fr.* 130 (Bergk).

καὶ δὴ καὶ ὅλως τῷ βασιλεῖ τὴν ζωὴν ὑπὲρ
τὸν ὅρον τοῦ Σόλωνος ἕλκε σαυτοῦ νομίζων
κόσμον ἀγαθοῦ βασιλέως γῆρας.  100. ταῦτα
αἰτῶ καὶ προσέτι τὴν ἡμετέραν στρατίαν ἐν Σούσοις δειπνῆσαι Περσῶν οἰνοχοούντων.  ταῦτα εὔ-
χεσθαι καλόν, ταῦτα εὔλογον προσδοκᾶν.  σὺν γὰρ
θεῷ καὶ αὐτοὶ κινησόμεθα.

101. Ἴθι δὴ νέμε τὴν ἐλευθερίαν πᾶσί γε χρηστοῖς
καὶ βελτίστοις οἰκέταις, οὓς τοσοῦτον τῶν ἐπ᾽
ἐλευθερίᾳ πώποτε ῥαπισθέντων εὐδαιμονεστέρους
θετέον ὅσον ἐκείνους τῶν ἐντελευτησάντων τῇ
δουλείᾳ. | μεταβάλλει γέ τοι τὴν τύχην αὐτοῖς F
ἀνὴρ ἀφ᾽ αὑτοῦ τῆς ἐλευθερίας ἀρξόμενος καὶ οὐκ
ἐάσας ἐνδυναστεῦσαι τῇ ψυχῇ τὴν δεσποτείαν τῶν
ἡδονῶν.  102. καὶ πλεονεκτοῦσι τῶν μὲν ἑτέρωθι |
R 404 λυθέντων ἐκ δουλείας τῇ τοῦ ὑπάτου σεμνότητι,
τῶν δ᾽ αὖ παρ᾽ ὑπάτοις τῇ τοῦ βασιλέως προσθήκῃ,
τῶν δ᾽ αὖ παρὰ τοῖς βασιλεῦσι τῇ τοῦ νῦν ὑπεροχῇ.

Οὕτω παραπλησίαν τῇδε πανήγυριν οὔπω πρότερον ἑωράκασιν οὔτ᾽ ἀνθρώπων οὔτε θεῶν ὀφ-
θαλμοί.

---

[a] The night was lengthened to enable Zeus to succeed in
his *affaire* with Alcmene : *cf.* Plautus, *Amph.*
[b] Herod. 1. 32.

was begotten.[a] And moreover, take our emperor's life beyond the limits Solon set,[b] and think the old age of a good emperor to be a credit to yourself." 100. This is my prayer, and that our army may feast in Susa with Persians waiting upon them.[c] It is right for this to be our prayer and reasonable for it to be our expectation. We too will march with god on our side.

101. Come, then! Grant freedom to all your good and trusty servants. They must be regarded as happier than all who ever suffered for freedom's sake, just as these are happier than those who end their days in slavery. Their destiny is changed by a man who has of himself laid the foundations of freedom and who has forbidden the tyranny of pleasure to dominate his soul. 102. Because of the consul's prestige they have the advantage over slaves released from bondage elsewhere; over those released under consuls, their advantage lies in the addition of the emperor's title, over those under the emperors, in the surpassing merits of the present ruler.

Thus a festival to compare with this has never before been looked upon by the eyes of either men or gods.

[c] Deliberately echoed in *Or.* 18. 282. Susa, the capital of Persia in classical times, is used instead of the contemporary, Ctesiphon.

# ORATION 14

# ΠΡΟΣ ΙΟΥΛΙΑΝΟΝ ΥΠΕΡ
## ΑΡΙΣΤΟΦΑΝΟΥΣ

R 424    1. Εἰδώς σε πολλήν, ὦ βασιλεῦ, τῶν τοῖς φίλοις F i
οὐ συναγωνιζομένων κατεγνωκότα κακίαν φίλος
ὢν αὐτὸς Ἀριστοφάνει τῷ Κορινθίῳ καὶ τὸν
ἄνθρωπον ὁρῶν ἐν τῇ παρὰ σοῦ προνοίᾳ τὰς
ὑπολοίπους κεκτημένον ἐλπίδας λέγειν δεῖν ᾠήθην
περὶ αὐτοῦ καὶ βοηθεῖν ὃν δύναμαι τρόπον. 2.
ἴσως μὲν γάρ τις καὶ γενήσεται πρᾶξις ἀπὸ τῶν
λόγων συμφέρουσα, καὶ | τυχών τινος ἀγαθοῦ τὴν F
αὑτοῦ κομιεῖται· εἰ δ᾽ ἄρα τοῦ δαίμονος ἡ δυσ-
μένεια δι᾽ ἣν ἐν πολλοῖς τεταλαιπώρηται κακοῖς
ἔτι καὶ νῦν ἐπηρεάζοι, τὸ γοῦν ἐμέ τε παρὰ σοὶ
διὰ τὴν σπουδὴν εὐδοκιμεῖν κἀκείνῳ τινὰ παραμυθίαν εἶναι τὸ μὴ περιῶφθαι δυστυχοῦντα παρὰ
R 425 τῶν | γνωρίμων ὑπάρξει. 3. εἰ μὲν οὖν μὴ καλῶς
ποιῶν ὁ δυσχερὴς ἐκεῖνος παρεληλύθει χρόνος,
λέγειν μὲν ἂν οὐδὲν ἐχρῆν, οὐ γὰρ ἦν ὁ καιρὸς
λόγων, ζητεῖν δὲ τῶν εὐνούχων τοὺς ὅ τι δόξειε

---

ᵃ Oration 14 : for the circumstances cf. Seeck, B.L.Z.G.
88 ff., Bidez-Cumont, Recherches sur la tradition manuscrite
des lettres de l'empereur Julien.    After Julian's arrival in
Antioch and probably before 22nd October, since no mention
is made of the burning of the temple at Daphne, Libanius
composed this apology for his disgraced friend Aristophanes,
who was then in Antioch.    He informed Julian that Priscus
would undertake delivery to him but, owing to delay on

# TO JULIAN ON BEHALF OF
# ARISTOPHANES

1. I KNOW, Sire, that you have often condemned for their cowardice people who fail to support their friends, and so, as a personal friend of Aristophanes of Corinth and seeing that he has his hopes for the future in some provision from yourself, I feel that I must speak on his behalf and assist him as best I can. 2. Perhaps there will result from my speech some satisfactory conclusion, and he will gain some advantage and come into his own again: but if, after all, the evil destiny that has caused him so much trouble in the past still uses him amiss, at least my stock will be higher with you because of my efforts, and he too may console himself somewhat with the thought that in his misfortunes he has not been entirely neglected by his friends. 3. Had not those evil days gone for good—and good riddance to them ! —there would be no necessity for making a speech now. It would be no time for speeches : he would have to seek out the all-powerful among the eunuchs,

Priscus' part, received a letter (*E.L.F.* No. 96. 374 b ff.) asking for it. He sent the speech, with *Ep.* 760 as covering note : Julian read it and replied immediately (*E.L.F.* No. 97), granting the plea. In return Libanius sends a letter of thanks (*Ep.* 758). Compare also *Or.* 1. 125 : τὸ τοῦ Ἀριστοφάνους λόγος ἦν οὐκ ἐῶν κακὸν τὸν οὐ τοιοῦτον δοκεῖν. *Ep.* 1154. 3 : Ἀριστοφάνει τὸ δοθὲν ἐκεῖνο τὸ μικρὸν ἔργον ἦν λόγου τινός, οὐκ ἐμὴ δέησις.

πράττοντας καὶ δανεισάμενον[1] ὡς πλεῖστον χρυσίον
ὠνεῖσθαι παρ' αὐτῶν τὰ μέγιστα· ἐπεὶ δὲ τοῖς
γιγνομένοις ὁ Ζεὺς αἰσχυνόμενος νοσοῦσαν μὲν
τὴν βασιλείαν ἔπαυσεν, εἰς δὲ τὴν ἀπὸ τῶν λογισμῶν διοίκησιν τὸ πρᾶγμα μετέστησε καὶ λέγειν
ἔξεστιν ὑπὲρ ὧν ἀγορὰ προὔκειτο, πολλῆς ἡγησά-
μην ἀργίας εἶναι μὴ χρῆσθαι τῇ φωνῇ τοῦ καιροῦ
ταύτην ἀπαιτοῦντος, ἄλλως τε καὶ σοῦ τῷ ῥήτορι
χαίροντος καὶ τῆς γνώμης οὐ μᾶλλον ὅπως
Ἀριστοφάνει τι τῶν κατὰ νοῦν ἔσται ζητούσης ἢ
ὅπως τῆς ὑπαρχούσης δόξης ἄξιόν τι ποιήσας
ὀφθήσῃ.

4. Γεγενῆσθαι μὲν οὖν ἐν χείρονι λόγῳ καὶ φήμῃ
τὸν ἄνθρωπον οὐκ ἀντιλέγω, καὶ γὰρ τοῦτο τῆς
δυστυχίας ἣ τά τε ἄλλα τοῦτον κατέβλαψε καὶ
δόξῃ | φαυλοτέρα τῶν ἔργων. ἀλλ' εἰ μὲν Ἀριστο- F
φάνης πρῶτος καὶ μόνος τοῦτο ἐπεπόνθει, σφόδρα
ἂν ᾐσχυνόμην· ἐπεὶ δὲ μετὰ τῆς τῶν ἀνθρώπων
φύσεως ἐξ ἀρχῆς εἰσῆλθε τὸ πολλοὺς μὲν πονηροὺς
R 426 ἐπιεικεῖς, πολλοὺς | δὲ τῶν μετρίων ὑπειλῆφθαι
μοχθηροτέρους, δέομαί σου, βασιλεῦ, τὸν τοῦ λόγου
μικρὸν χρόνον μεταστησάμενον ἀπὸ τῆς ψυχῆς
ἣν ἔχων δόξαν περὶ τούτου τυγχάνεις ἀκολουθῆσαι
τοῖς πράγμασι, κἂν μὲν ἐκεῖνα δεικνύῃ βέλτιστον,
οὕτω φρονεῖν, εἰ δὲ μή, μὴ μόνον ἀμελείας ἄξιον
ἀλλὰ καὶ δίκης ὑπολαμβάνειν. ἀνάσχου δὲ μικρὸν
ἄνωθεν ἀκούων, μῆκός τε γὰρ ἀφαιρήσω τῆς
διηγήσεως, καὶ σὺ μᾶλλον εὑρήσεις ἃ γνῶναι
δίκαιον.

---

[1] δανεισάμενον F. : δανεισαμένους Re. (mss.).

borrow all the money he could, and purchase from them everything that mattered. However, Zeus in disgust at such goings-on has put an end to that ailing regime [a] and he transformed public life to an administration based on reasoning and we can speak on matters relevant to an assembly. So I consider it sheer idleness not to employ my voice when the occasion demands it, especially since you are pleased with my oratory and are bent upon ensuring not so much that Aristophanes should obtain something to his liking as that you should be seen to act in a manner worthy of your present fame.

4. I do not deny that he has been held of less account and in low repute. Indeed, that is part of the misfortunes that have dogged him and, in particular, have given him a bad name that his conduct belies. If Aristophanes had been the first or the only man to be so affected, I would have very great qualms : but since it has been something inseparable from human nature right from the beginning for many a rascal to have a name for respectability and many a decent man to be thought a rogue, I pray you, Sire, that for the short duration of my speech you will rid yourself of any prejudice you may have against him, and concentrate upon the facts. Then if they prove him to be a good fellow, make your decision accordingly ; if they do not, then regard him as deserving not merely indifference but punishment. Bear with me while I give a brief recapitulation. My story will not be a long one, and you will the more easily discover all that you ought to know.

[a] Of Constantius, whom Libanius prudently refrains from mentioning by name.

5. Τούτῳ Μένανδρος μὲν ἦν πατήρ, τὰ πρῶτα
Κορινθίων, φίλος Ἑκάτῃ καὶ Ποσειδῶνι, πλέων
μὲν εἰς Αἴγιναν ὑπὲρ τῶν ἐκείνης ὀργίων, ἐλαύνων
δὲ εἰς Ἰσθμὸν ὑπὲρ τῶν τοῦδε μυστηρίων, ἐν μὲν
τῇ νήσῳ κορυφαῖος ὢν τοῦ θιάσου, ἐν δὲ τῇ
χερρονήσῳ συντελῶν ἀπὸ τῶν μικροτέρων, τελῶν
δὲ εἰς τὸ μέγα συνέδριον. 6. ὅτε δὴ καὶ πατὴρ
ἐγένετο τοῦτον γεννήσας, οὕτως ἦν φιλόπολις
R 427 ὥστε διαπράττεται τῆς οἴκοι βουλῆς εἶναι | μᾶλλον
ἢ τῆς Ῥωμαίων. ἀλλ᾿ Ἀριστοφάνης ὑπὸ τῆς
τύχης κεκώλυται τὸν πατέρα ζηλοῦν, | ὡς εἴσῃ F
προϊόντος τοῦ λόγου. 7. γενόμενος τοίνυν ἐξ
ἐκείνου τε καὶ τῆς τῶν φιλοσόφων ἀδελφῆς, Ἱερίου
λέγω καὶ Διογένους, τρέφεται μὲν ἐν ταῖς τούτων
χερσί, παιδεύεται δὲ ὑπὸ τοῦ πατρὸς λόγους τε καὶ
τὸ καλῶς ἀναλίσκειν διὰ παντὸς εἴδους δαπάνης
ἐρχόμενος ᾗ τὸ πρὸς τοὺς θεοὺς εὐσεβὲς ἀναμέ-
μικται. οἶδε ταῦτα Δημήτηρ καὶ Κόρη καὶ
Σάραπις καὶ Ποσειδῶν καὶ ὁ τὴν Λέρνην κατέχων

---

[a] He was a *principalis*, a member of the leading curial
class : cp. Sievers, *Das Leben des Libanios*, pp. 94, 130.

[b] Of Hecate Enodia : *cf.* Lucian, *Navigium*, 15, Paus.
2. 30. 2. He does not appear to have attained the *strategia*
at Corinth, a position equivalent to that of Syriarch in
Antioch, where the holder was president of the Isthmian
festival—or its 4th-century descendant here described by
Libanius, with pietistic intent, as " mysteries."

[c] μέγα distinguishes the senate from the local *curiae*.
At the time (*c.* A.D. 320–330) this could only be the senate
at Rome, that of Constantinople not being enrolled until
A.D. 358/9 by Themistius. The expenditure of presiding over
the old civic festivals had now become a *munus* undertaken
by the leading *principales*. Thereby this ruling class in the
cities enhanced their great importance. Other *munera* (*e.g.*,
choregiae and liturgies) of varying impact had to be under-

5. His father was Menander, a leading citizen of Corinth,[a] and a friend of Hecate and Poseidon, who sailed to Aegina to take part in her ritual and rode to the Isthmus to participate in his mysteries. In the island, he was the leader of the band of initiates,[b] but on the mainland he was a lesser contributor, being enrolled as a member of the supreme senate.[c] 6. Upon becoming the father of Aristophanes here, his patriotism was such that he succeeded in retaining membership of his own city council in preference to enrolment in that of the Roman Senate. Aristophanes, however, was not destined to follow in his father's footsteps, as you will hear, Sire, as my tale proceeds. 7. He was, then, the son of Menander by the sister of the philosophers Hierius[d] and Diogenes.[e] He was brought up by them and trained by his father in oratory and in noble extravagance, since he performed every kind of expenditure associated with piety towards the gods. Demeter and her daughter, Sarapis and Poseidon and Iacchus of Lerna all know

---

taken regularly by all members of the local *curiae*, but both the expenditure and the resultant prestige fell below those of such presidents (hence συντελῶν ἀπὸ τῶν μικροτέρων). The most common method of escape for decurions with the necessary income was nomination to the senate (τελῶν εἰς τὸ συνέδριον) where the entrant could normally expect to pay, in the form of the praetorship, a heavy entrance fee. In compensation, he could normally expect immunity from the regular round of personal and financial obligations to his own city, and could hope to profit by entering on an administrative career in the imperial service. *Cf.* Petit, *Vie municipale*, pp. 45 ff., 321 ff.

Menander is an example, like Libanius' uncle Phasganius, of that type of decurion who preferred to retain his municipal status rather than to embark upon a career of office, a course sincerely approved by Libanius.

[a] Seeck, *op. cit.* 175 ii.  [e] Sievers, *op. cit.* 94.

Ἴακχος καὶ πολλοὶ πρὸς τούτοις ἕτεροι δαίμονες
περὶ οὓς ἅπαντα φιλοτίμως ἐξεπλήρωσε. 8. καὶ
προῆλθεν, ὦ βασιλεῦ, δαπανῶν εἰς τὴν τοῦ καλου-
μένου στρατηγοῦ λειτουργίαν, καὶ τοῦτον αὐτὸς
εἶδον ἐν ἐκείνῃ τῇ στολῇ παραπεμπόμενον ὑπ'
εὐφημιῶν ἐκ Λακεδαίμονος ἀναστρέφων, οὔπω
μὲν ὢν τῷ νέῳ συνήθης οὐδὲ εἰδὼς εἴ ποτε ἔσομαι,
μακαρίζων δὲ τῷ τηλικοῦτον ὄντα κτᾶσθαι τὴν
παρὰ τῆς πόλεως τιμὴν ἐν ταῖς τοῦ πατρὸς φρον-
τίσιν. 9. ἔτι γὰρ ἔζη Μένανδρος. ὡς ἔδει γε καὶ
μέχρι γήρως ἐσχάτου. ἦ γὰρ ἂν Ἀριστοφάνης
πολλῶν μὲν ἀπήλλακτο πλανῶν, πολλῶν δ' ἂν
κινδύνων τῶν μὲν ἐν ταῖς ὁδοῖς συμβάντων τῶν δὲ
ἐν δικαστηρίοις οὐχὶ δικαίως, ἦν δ' ἂν τῶν
δυναμένων ἐν Κορίνθῳ μᾶλλον ἢ τῶν τὴν ἑτέρων
θαυμαζόντων δύναμιν.

10. Πόθεν οὖν ἐξέπεσε τῆς αὐτῷ προσηκούσης
τάξεως καὶ τὸν τοῦ πολιτευομένου βίον φυγὼν
ἧκεν εἰς τὸν τοῦ στρατιώτου; Εὐγένιος ὁ μικρὸς
γίνεται | παρὰ Κώνσταντι μέγας. λαβὼν δὲ ἐκ F
γάμου τινὸς ἀφορμὰς ἀναισχύντους εἰς τὸ τῶν
Ἀριστοφάνους ἀμφισβητεῖν χωρίων, οἶσθα δὲ ὡς |
R 428 πάντων μὲν ἐπεθύμουν οἱ τοιοῦτοι, πάντα δὲ
ἥρπαζον ἀναγκάζοντες ἢ τῶν ὄντων ἀφίστασθαι
τῷ βουλομένῳ λαβεῖν ἢ πολεμεῖσθαι, ὅδ' οὔτ'
ἐκεῖνο πειθόμενος, οὐ γὰρ ἦν ἐν μικροῖς ἡ ζημία,

---

<sup>a</sup> A good example of the pagan tendency towards syn-
cretism : cf. Nilsson, *Gesch. d. Gr. Rel.* ii, pp. 555 ff.

<sup>b</sup> The highest curial office at Corinth and, in keeping with
the traditional rate of magisterial benefaction, the most expensive of the local liturgies.

this well, as do many other deities besides, towards whom he zealously fulfilled all his obligations.[a] 8. He continued this career of expenditure and undertook the duties connected with the office of "Strategos."[b] I myself, on my return from Sparta, saw him escorted in such state with acclamation and applause, and though then unacquainted with the young fellow and unaware that I ever would be, I held him happy in obtaining from his city that honour, for the performance of which his father took the responsibility.[c] 9. Menander, you see, was then still alive, and it would have been better if he had lived on to a ripe old age, for then Aristophanes would have been spared many wanderings and the many dangers that beset him on the highroads and, unjustly, in the courts : he would still be one of the worthies of Corinth rather than an admirer of the worth of others.

10. How then was he expelled from his proper station, and how is it that he fled the life of a city councillor and took up a military career? That puny Eugenius rose to greatness under Constans.[d] As a result of some marriage, he impudently seized the opportunity of calling into question the ownership of Aristophanes' property. You know how greedy for everything such fellows were and how they tried to lay their hands on everything, forcing people either to relinquish their property to some would-be possessor or else to fight for it. Aristophanes refused to take the first course, for his loss would be a severe

---

[c] Cf. Or. 1. 23 : as a student in Athens between A.D. 336 and 340, Libanius visited Corinth, once while en route to the διαμαστίγωσις at the festival of Artemis Orthia in Sparta, and again when visiting the mysteries at Argos (cf. Iacchus of Lerna, above).

[d] Flavius Eugenius : Seeck, op. cit. 134 ii.

LIBANIUS

τοῦτό τε δεδοικὼς φυγὰς γίγνεται τῆς αὐτοῦ
νομίζων οὕτως ἂν τήν τε γῆν καὶ τὸ σῶμα δια-
σῶσαι. 11. τὰς μὲν οὖν ἐπιβουλὰς ὅσας ἐπ᾽
αὐτὸν ἐκίνησε καὶ ὡς οὐδενὸς ἀπέσχετο πειρώμενος αὐτὸν ὑπὸ χεῖρα λαβεῖν, καὶ βίαν καὶ
ταραχὴν ὧν ἐνέπλησεν αὐτῷ καὶ ἀγροὺς καὶ
οἰκίαν, ἐῶ. καὶ γὰρ σιωπῶντος οὐδὲν ἧττον
ἔγνωκας εἰδὼς ἐν οἷς ἔζων οἱ δυναστεύοντες τότε.
12. γενόμενος δὲ ἐν Συρίᾳ καὶ στὰς καὶ | ἀνα- F 9
πνεύσας οὐκ ἐπὶ τοὺς πλέον ἰσχύοντας ἢ τὸν ἐν
βιβλίοις βιοῦντα Φουρτουνατιανὸν καταφεύγει νομίζων παρ᾽ Ἕλληνος, οὕτω γὰρ ἐκεῖνον καλεῖν
ἄξιον, τεύξεσθαί τινος αἰδοῦς. ὃ καὶ γέγονεν.
ἀκούσας γὰρ ὅθεν τε ἥκοι καὶ ὅπως καὶ τί παθὼν
καὶ τί φοβούμενος, δέχεται τὸν ἄνθρωπον ἡμέρως
καὶ κατέστησεν εἰς ἄδειαν διὰ τοῦ σχήματος. 13.
ὁ δὲ ὢν ἤδη στρατιώτης σώματι μὲν ἀπείρῳ
τοιούτων πόνων διῆλθεν ἐφ᾽ ἵππων πολλάκις τὴν
οἰκουμένην ἐν τοῖς ἐπείγουσι τῶν καιρῶν εἰσφερό-
μενος τάχος, καὶ οὐδὲν ὧν ἦν ἀνάγκη θᾶττον
μαθεῖν βραδύτερον παρὰ τὴν τοῦδε μέλλησιν Κωνστάντιος ἤκουσε, πλὴν εἴ που συνετρίβη καταπεσών,
ὃ καὶ αὐτὸ τοῦ σπεύδειν σημεῖον. 14. ἐπαινού-
μενος δὲ τῶν πόνων τὰ προτεινόμενα κέρδη
διεωθεῖτο, καὶ οὐκ ἔστιν ὅστις ἐπιδείξει τοῦτον

ᵃ An example, despite these excuses, of a decurion resorting to flight.
ᵇ Seeck, *op. cit.* 159 : an influential pagan philosopher
and courtier, active under every emperor until A.D. 371 at
least, when he had attained the rank of *comes*. As with
Aristophanes and his kin, Libanius stresses the Hellenism
and intellectual gifts of Fortunatianus to win Julian's sympathy.

one, and he was afraid of the second, and so he exiled
himself from his own country, thinking that by so
doing he could preserve his estates and his person.[a]
11. All the plots that Eugenius contrived against him,
the utter unscrupulousness of his attempts to get
him in his clutches, the violence and turmoil with
which he filled his lands and home, all this I leave
on one side. Even if I leave it unsaid, you are none
the less aware of it, for you know the manner of life
of the persons who ruled the roost at that time. 12.
Aristophanes came and settled in Syria and breathed
again, for he sought refuge not with men of wider influence, but with Fortunatianus [b] who spent his life
among his books, for he thought that he would meet
with some respect from a Greek—for so it is proper
to call him. Nor was he disappointed, for upon hearing
whence he came and the circumstances of his coming,
all his misfortunes and all his fears, Fortunatianus
gave him a kindly reception and established him in
the immunity of an official post.[c] 13. And upon becoming a member of the services, though physically
untrained for such tasks, he often traversed the world
on horseback, and his contribution at times of urgent
crisis was speed. No information that required prompt
delivery ever came slowly to Constantius' ears by
reason of delay on his part, unless he happened to be
thrown and injured, which in itself was a sign of his
devotion to duty. 14. Though commended for his
efforts, he always refused the opportunities for gain
that were put in his way. Everywhere he will be seen

[c] He was enrolled as *agens-in-rebus*. In the normal
course of events, the precarious immunity from curial
obligations gained by his flight would thus receive official
sanction.

R 429 οὐκ ἐπιμελητὴν ὀρέων,[1] οὐκ ἄγγελον | ὑπάρχων,[2]
οὐ νίκης μηνυτήν, οὐκ ἄλλο τῶν τοιούτων ὑπηρετη-
κότα οὐδὲν ὃ τὰς μὲν πόλεις ἀπώλλυε, τοὺς δὲ
δοκοῦντας | διακονεῖν μετ' ἀμαξῶν χρυσὸν ἀγουσῶν F
ἀπέπεμπεν. οὐ μὴν Ἀριστοφάνης ἠξίωσε τοῖς
πατρῴοις τοιαῦτα προσθεῖναι χρήματα, ἀλλ' ἐτρέ-
φετο μὲν τοῖς οἴκοθεν ἐν ξένῃ, τὸ δὲ διαπεφευγέναι
τὸν κίνδυνον ἀρκοῦν ἡγεῖτο κέρδος ἐλευθέρῳ καὶ
πρέπον.

15. Ἐν τοιαύτῃ δὲ προαιρέσει ζῶντος ἐπεθύ-
μησε δυστυχῶς τῆς Αἰγυπτίων ἀρχῆς Παρνάσιος
καὶ μετέσχεν Ἀριστοφάνης τῆς τύχης, εἵπετο γὰρ
Μουσωνίου πέμποντος, διότι μέν, οὐκ οἶδα, τοσοῦτον δὲ ἐπίσταμαι ὅτι πέπονθε μὲν ἃ μέχρι νῦν, ὦ
βασιλεῦ, δακρύει, λαβεῖν δὲ μικρὸν μὲν ᾐτιάθη
χρυσίον, ἔλαβε δὲ οὐδὲ τόδε, πληγὰς μέντοι
πολλὰς καὶ χαλεπὰς καὶ πολλαχοῦ τῆς γῆς ταῖς
ἐκ μολύβδου σφαίραις ἃς ἡγήσατο Παῦλος εἰς
θάνατον ἀρκέσειν. καὶ ἅμα ταῦτά τε ἔπασχε καὶ
παρὰ Κορινθίοις ἐλειτούργει τὰ τῶν καλουμένων
R 430 στρατηγῶν· οὕτω | γὰρ Ἀνατόλιος ἔγνω. 16. τὸ
μὲν οὖν ἔγκλημα ἦν ὅτι μάντιν εἰσαγάγοι Παρνασίῳ
τῶν περὶ τοὺς ἀστέρας ἐχόντων τὴν τέχνην ἐροῦντά

---

[1] ὀρέων F. : ὁρίων mss. : ὁρίων ( = horreorum) Re.
[2] ὑπάρχων F., Sievers : ὑπάτων Re., mss.

---

[a] As agent in the *cursus publicus*. Contrast the complaints made against them, *Or.* 18. 135 ff.
[b] Prefect of Egypt, A.D. 358, fellow countryman of
Aristophanes, accused of treason before Modestus at Scythopolis on this charge; *cf.* Amm. Marc. 19. 12. Seeck, *op.
cit.* 231 i. [c] Seeck, *op. cit.* 218 i.

to have acted as remount officer,[a] bearer of dispatches from the prefects, bringer of the tidings of victory, without performing any of the other services that brought the provinces to ruin and sent home those so-called administrators with waggon loads of gold! No! Aristophanes could not bring himself to add money of this kind to his family fortune, but in a foreign land he maintained himself on the income sent from home, and he thought that ridding himself of danger was sufficient and fitting reward for a gentleman.

15. While he was living in this fashion, Parnasius [b] conceived his ill-starred desire for the governorship of Egypt, and Aristophanes was involved in his fall, since he accompanied him as a member of staff, seconded by Musonius,[c] for what reason I cannot say. Of this much, however, I am well aware, that his sufferings then are what he still bewails, Sire. He was charged with having taken a few paltry pieces of gold, though that he never did. What he did take was many a severe flogging with the leaden cat-o'-nine-tails in many parts of the province, and that, Paulus thought, would suffice to be the death of him.[d] So he suffered this, and simultaneously in Corinth he had to fulfil the obligations of the titular strategos, according to a decision reached by Anatolius.[e] 16. Now the charge was that he had introduced to Parnasius a soothsayer, one of those skilled in astrology, to inquire about one of those matters

[d] Paul " the Chain " (*ibid.* 233 ii), principal " hatchet-man " of Constantius, deeply involved in Gallus' execution. This fact predisposed Julian in favour of Aristophanes (*E.L.F.* No. 97).

[e] An example of curial duties being imposed as punishment. Anatolius (Seeck, *op. cit.* 59 i), pr. pr. (Illyricum) A.D. 357–360, had jurisdiction over such matters in Corinth.

τι τούτων ὑπὲρ ὧν οὐ νόμος μανθάνειν. ὁ δὲ τὸ
μὲν εἰσαγαγεῖν ὁμολογῶν, φάσκων δὲ τὴν μαν-
τείαν ἐπὶ τῶν ἰδίων τοῦ Παρνασίου | στῆναι πρὸς F
πάσας ἀνάγκας ἤγετο προσπαροξύνας τι καθ᾽
ἑαυτοῦ τὸν Παῦλον ῥήμασιν ἐκείνῳ μὲν προσή-
κουσιν ἀμείνοσι δὲ τότε σιγᾶσθαι.   17. τῆς τρα-
γῳδίας δὲ ἐκείνης εἰς ἔτος προβεβηκυίας τρίτον
καὶ μόλις λαβούσης τελευτὴν τοῖς μὲν ἄλλοις ὑπῆρξεν ἀπαλλαγή, μόνος δὲ οὗτος ἐκολάζετο περι-
γραπτοῖς ὅροις ὧν ἐκτὸς οὐκ ἦν κινεῖσθαι. καὶ
ἐπέμπετ᾽ ἂν δεδεμένος, εἰ μὴ θεῶν τις τὴν ταῦτα
παρανομοῦσαν (ἀρά μοι δώσεις τυραννίδα πρὸς σὲ
εἰπεῖν;) ἔστησε.

18. Τοιούτοις, ὦ βασιλεῦ, προσπαλαίσας Ἀριστοφάνης Κύκλωψι δεῖται σοῦ, καὶ ἡμεῖς δὲ συν-
δεόμεθα, πέμψαι παρὰ τοὺς οἰκείους χαίροντα καί
γε δυνάμενον διάγειν τῶν προγόνων ἀξίως.   19.
καὶ τίς, φήσεις, αὐτὸν κωλύει βαδίζειν;
πολλὰ καὶ μεγάλα· τὸ δεσμωτήριον, αἱ πληγαί,
ἡ ἀτιμία, τὸ γυμνωθῆναι πρὸς βάσανον, τὸ μικροῦ
R 431 πλησιάσαι τὸν | κοντὸν τοῖς νώτοις εἰ μὴ Μόδεστος
οἷς ἐβόησεν οὗτος ἐπὶ διακρούσει τῆς βασάνου
συνεχώρησε. ταῦτα αὐτὸν ἐμποδίζει, ταῦτα δε-
σμεύει, ταῦτα τῶν οἰκείων διείργει, ταῦτα ἂν μή
τις ἀνέλῃ, πᾶσαν οὗτος ὄψεται πόλιν πλὴν τῆς
οἰκείας.   20. οὐ γὰρ τὸ βασανισθῆναι μόνον, ὦ

---

[a] Aristophanes' frankness seems to have been disconcert-
ing : cf. Ep. 1264.
[b] From the Scythopolis trials until Constantius' death
late in A.D. 361. His punishment was relegatio. Libanius
is very daring in using the term τυραννίς about a legitimate
emperor before his successor. It was usually reserved for
usurpers : hence the apology.

where information is forbidden. While admitting that he had introduced the soothsayer, he maintained that the matter had to do only with Parnasius' private affairs, but he was compelled to undergo every kind of torture, since he had also incurred Paulus' anger by passing remarks applicable to him but, at the time, better left unsaid.[a] 17. That tragedy lasted three years until it finally drew to a close. All the rest were released, but he alone was punished by confinement to a definite locality and forbidden to leave it. And he would have been sent in chains had not one of the gods put a stop to such flagrant tyranny, if you will pardon the expression, Sire.[b]

18. Such were the monsters with whom Aristophanes had to contend. Now, Sire, he prays of you, and I join in his prayer, that you send him home rejoicing to his family, able to live in a manner worthy of his ancestry. 19. " Well," you will say, " who is stopping him from going ? " There are many serious considerations, Sire: imprisonment, flogging, dishonour, his stripping for the torture, the rod almost descending on his back, had not Modestus, influenced by his protests, agreed to defer the examination.[c] That is what is stopping him: that is what keeps him confined and separates him from his own kith and kin : and if this is not removed, he will see any country but his own. 20. It is not the actual

---

[c] Seeck, *op. cit.* 213 ff. Domitius Modestus, *Comes Orientis* and president of the court, a frequent correspondent with Libanius and an almost professional turn-coat.

The flogging of accused officials in examination by their superiors was common : that of decurions was at this time banned. Aristophanes must have protested his curial origins and so, though escaping the lash reserved for officials, he laid himself open to a forced performance of curial obligations.

βασιλεῦ, καταχεῖ τῶν πεπονθότων | ἀτιμίαν, ἀλλὰ F 9
καὶ ὅστις ἐγγὺς ἦλθε τοῦ παθεῖν τὸ τῆς ἐπιτιμίας
ἀκέραιον ἀπολώλεκε. κἂν εἰς ἔριν καταστῇ πρός
τινα καὶ φιλονεικίαν, ἀκούει τὰ τῶν πεπονθότων·
τὸν δὲ ἐκ τοῦ δεσμωτηρίου; τὸν δὲ ἐκ τῆς
βασάνου; τὸν τῷ μεταφρένῳ νενικηκότα
τοὺς ἄκμονας; τοῦτον δὲ ἐν τῷ βουλευ-
τηρίῳ περὶ κοινῶν φθέγγεσθαι πραγμάτων
δέον ἐν τῷ οἰκήματι πρὸς τοὺς δεσμώτας
περὶ τοῦ ξύλου; ταῦτα ἴσως ἐρεῖ τις τῶν νῦν
μὲν λαμπρῶν, πάλαι δὲ τοὺς Μενάνδρου θεραπευ-
όντων οἰκέτας. οὗτος δὲ ἄρα καταράσεται Μοδέ-
στῳ μὴ τεμόντι τὸν τράχηλον.

21. Τίς οὖν τούτων ἐπανόρθωσις; καὶ πῶς ἂν
ἄπρακτα τὰ πεπραγμένα γένοιτο; λυθῆναι μέν,
ὦ βασιλεῦ, καὶ μὴ γενέσθαι τὰ γεγενημένα τῶν
ἀμηχάνων, ἐξαλεῖψαι δὲ τὴν ἀπ᾽ αὐτῶν ἀτιμίαν
ἔστι. τούτου δ᾽ ἰατρὸς ἄλλος μὲν οὐδείς, μόνος
R 432 δὲ σύ· ὡς ἂν παραστῇ σοι | τὸν ἄνθρωπον ἀπο-
λαμπρῦναι τιμῇ τινι, κέκρυπται τὰ ὀνείδη, συν-
εσκίασται τὰ χείρω, γέγονεν ἔνδοξος, ἔχει τὴν
παρρησίαν, ἀπέθετο τὴν αἰσχύνην. 22. πρὸς γὰρ
τῷ τὰ δεύτερα τῶν προτέρων πεφυκέναι κρατεῖν,
ὡς ἔφη Πίνδαρος, τὸ τὸν τετιμηκότα τοῦ | περι- F 9
υβρικότος εἶναι βελτίω μεγάλην ἰσχὺν εἰς τὸ λή-
θην ἐπιθεῖναι τοῖς φαυλοτέροις ἔχει. καὶ δόξει
τὸ μὲν ὀρθῇ κρίσει δεδόσθαι, τὸ δὲ ἀνοήτῳ πικρίᾳ
πεπλημμελῆσθαι. ὅταν δὲ ὡς ἠδικεῖτο δι᾽ ὧν
ἔπασχε πεισθῶσιν ἅπαντες, οὐκέτ᾽ ὀνειδιοῦσιν ἃ πέ-

---

ᵃ A prolonged adaptation of Pindar, *Ol.* 2. 15 ff.

examination, Sire, that brings disgrace upon any who have undergone it: whoever has come anywhere near such an experience has thereby lost the fine flower of honour. If he gets into a quarrel or an argument with somebody, he will hear the comments reserved for those who have experienced it. " What ! This jailbird, this gallow's meat, whose back has had more of a hammering than any anvil, is he going to speak in the city hall on matters of public policy? He ought to be in jail, talking about the stocks with the rest of the old lags." That is what some of those who once curried favour with Menander's slaves and now have made themselves men of mark, may perhaps have to say of him, and he will curse Modestus for not cutting his throat for him.

21. What is the remedy for this, then? How can what is done be undone? It is impossible for a thing to be undone, Sire, and once it has happened it cannot be prevented, but it is possible for the disgrace resulting from it to be erased. For this, however, there is no other physician than yourself. If you decide to accord him some mark of honour, all the reproaches will be hidden, a veil drawn over all his misery, and he will be a man of reputation and independence, with his shame removed. 22. For besides the fact that it is natural, to adapt Pindar's words,[a] for the second stage to be better than the first, for a person to be honoured by someone better than those who have insulted him is an effective means of consigning unpleasantness to oblivion, for it will be thought that the grant of honour comes from reasoned judgement, whereas the insult was the error of irrational spite. As soon as all are convinced that his sufferings were unjustified, he will no longer be

πονθεν. οὐ γὰρ ἦν ἀδικοῦντος. 23. οὕτως ἔξεστί
σοι τῆς οἰκίας ἀφανίσαι τὴν ἀδοξίαν ποιήσαντι
τὰ τρίτα τοῖς πρώτοις παραπλήσια. τούτων γὰρ
ἐκείνοις ὁμοιωθέντων ὑποχωρήσει τὸ μέσον καὶ
δυσχερές, καὶ οὐδεὶς Κωνστάντιον καὶ δεσμὰ ἀλλὰ
σὲ περιάσει καὶ τὴν τιμήν. 24. τίς οὖν αὕτη
γένοιτ᾿ ἂν αὐτὸς κρινεῖς, ἡμεῖς δὲ εἰσόμεθα χάριν.
ὥσπερ γὰρ δοῦναι ῥάδιον ἦν ἂν δόξῃ παρασχεῖν,
οὕτω σοι τὸ τὴν δοθῆναι προσήκουσαν εὐχερὲς
εὑρεῖν. πολλοὶ δέ, ὦ βασιλεῦ, τιμῶν τρόποι καθ᾿ οὓς
καὶ μείζονος καὶ ἐλάττονος ἔστι τυχεῖν. ἡμεῖς
δὲ οὐ διοισόμεθα περὶ τοῦ μέτρου. πάντως ὅ τι
ἂν δῷς κοσμήσει τὸν εἰληφότα, καὶ μικρὸν οὐδὲν
R 433 οὐδὲ ταπεινὸν τῶν ἐκ | γενναίας καὶ θείας διδομέ-
νων ψυχῆς.

25. Εἰ δέ τις ἡμᾶς ὀχληροὺς εἶναι φήσει καὶ
πλείω σοι τῶν ἀναγκαίων ἀνατιθέναι βοηθεῖν
ἀξιοῦντας ταῖς τῶν καθ᾿ ἕκαστον τύχαις, ὥσπερ
οὐκ ὂν ἱκανὸν φορτίον τὰς ὑπὲρ τῶν πόλεων
φροντίδας, ἴστω τὸ μέγιστον | τῶν σῶν ἀγνοῶν. F
τοῦτο δ᾿ ἐστὶ τὸ καὶ μέχρι γένους ἑκάστου καὶ
ἀνδρὸς τὴν σὴν τετάσθαι διάνοιαν. τοῖς μὲν γὰρ
βραχυτέροις τὰς γνώμας καὶ τὸ περὶ τῶν ὅλων
ἀκοῦσαί του λέγοντος ἢ διαλεχθῆναι βαρύ, τὸν
μεγαλόψυχον δὲ χαίροντα τῷ πλήθει τῶν ὑπ᾿
αὐτοῦ πραττομένων ὁρῶμεν. 26. **καθεδεῖτ᾿ οὖν
ὁ βασιλεὺς ἡμῖν σκοπῶν πῶς ὁ δεῖνα καὶ
πῶς ὁ δεῖνα πράττει, καὶ φιλονεικήσει
μεθιστάναι τὰ λυπηρά; καὶ πῶς ἐξαρ-
κέσει; μάλιστα μὲν ὤφειλεν οἷόν τε εἶναι περὶ
πάντων αὐτὸν καὶ πυνθάνεσθαι καὶ βουλεύεσθαι**
116

reproached with them, for they did not arise from wrong-doing. 23. So, if you make his third state like his first, you can wipe out the disgrace that has come upon his house. When the first and the last are equal, the troubles in between will vanish, and no one will breathe a word about his imprisonment under Constantius. The talk will all be of the honour he enjoys from you. 24. Decide for yourself what this honour may be, and we will be grateful for it. It is easy for you to grant whatever you decide to give, and no less easy to discover the honour that may fittingly be granted. There are many kinds of honour, Sire, and one may obtain it in greater or lesser degree accordingly. We, however, will not quibble about the degree. Absolutely anything you care to grant will redound to the credit of the recipient, and nothing offered by a noble and divine soul can be petty or mean.

25. If any man asserts that we are tiresome and impose upon you more than we should in requesting you to assist individuals in distress, as though it were not burden enough already for you to look after the welfare of the empire, he should realize that he is ignorant of the most important element in your character, your interest in every family and individual. The insensitive find hearing or speaking of matters of universal import to be a bore, but we see the magnanimous taking pleasure in the number of his activities. 26. " Is our emperor, then, going to sit down and see how so-and-so is getting on? Will it be his intention to get rid of all their troubles? How on earth is he going to be able to do all that? " Ideally, by his ability to obtain first-hand information and to form his own opinion on every subject, and

καὶ κινεῖν τὰ μὴ καλῶς ἔχοντα. ἐπεὶ δὲ τοῦθ᾽
ἧττον δυνατὸν ἢ τὴν ἄμμον ἀριθμεῖν, τούς γε
δεξιωτέρους καὶ παρὰ τὴν ἀξίαν ἀτυχοῦντας οὐ
περιοπτέον. ὧν εἷς ᾿Αριστοφάνης. πολλὰ γὰρ
αὐτῷ τὰ βοηθοῦντα, καὶ οὐ Μυσῶν ἀνὴρ ἔσχατος
ἀλλ᾽ οἷος φέρειν φιλοτιμίαν τοῖς εὖ ποιεῖν αὐτὸν
προαιρουμένοις. ὡς δὲ οὐκ ἔστι σοι παρὰ φαῦλον
τὰ τοῦδε ποιήσασθαι γνῶναι ῥάδιον.

27. Πρῶτον μὲν Ἕλλην ἐστίν, ὦ βασιλεῦ· τοῦτο
δ᾽ ἐστὶν ἕνα τῶν σῶν εἶναι παιδικῶν. οὐδεὶς γὰρ
οὕτω τῆς αὑτοῦ πατρίδος ἐραστὴς ὡς σὺ τοῦ τῆς
Ἑλλάδος ἐδάφους ἐνθυμούμενος ἱερὰ καὶ νόμους
καὶ λόγους καὶ σοφίαν καὶ τελετὰς καὶ τρόπαια
ἀπὸ βαρβάρων. 28. ὄντος | δὲ ᾿Αριστοφάνει τού- F
R 434 του πλεονεκτήματος οὐ μικροῦ, κἂν εἰ | Μεγα-
ρεὺς ἐτύγχανεν ὢν ἢ Μήλιος ἢ Λήμνιος, μεῖζόν
ἐστι τὸ τῆς πόλεως εἰς αἰδῶ. Κορίνθιος γὰρ
οὑτοσί. καὶ οὐκ εἰς μύθους ἀποίσω τὸν λόγον
οὐδ᾽ Ἡλίου καὶ Ποσειδῶνος ἔριν οὐδ᾽ ἐπιγράμ-
ματά σοι δίειμι κοσμοῦντα νεκροὺς ἐκ ναυμαχιῶν
τεθαμμένους οὐδὲ δικαιοσύνην τῆς πόλεως καὶ τὸ
μετὰ τῶν ἠδικημένων ἀεὶ γίγνεσθαι, οὐχ ὡς μικρὰ
πρὸς δόξαν ὄντα τοῖς ἔχουσιν ἀλλ᾽ ὅτι καὶ τῶνδε
κάλλιον ἔχω λέγειν. 29. ἀνάμνησον γὰρ σαυτόν,
ὦ βασιλεῦ, τῆς ἐπιστολῆς ἣν Κορινθίοις ἔπεμψας,
ἄκων μὲν εἰς τὸν πόλεμον ἐμβάς, ἤδη δὲ τὸ πλέον

---

[a] Cf. Or. 12. 40 and note ; Plato, Theaetetus, 209 B.

[b] His loyalty to Julian's memory certainly justifies this
commendation : cf. Ep. 1264.

[c] All proverbially ill-fated : cf. Theocr. 14. 49, Suidas,
s.v. ὑμεῖς, ὦ Μεγαρεῖς ; Aristoph. Birds, 186 ; Ep. 1175.

[d] Cf. Favorinus ? [Dio], Or. 37. 106 R. A neat piece of
aposiopesis, having regard to Julian's expressed interest in

to remedy anything that is at fault. But since this
is as impossible as counting the grains of sand, at least
men of good character who are unluckier than they
deserve must not be neglected: and Aristophanes is
one of these. There are many considerations that
weigh in his favour, and he is no nincompoop,[a] but
the sort of man to stand up for anyone who chooses
to be his benefactor. It is easy to see that you
cannot underestimate him.[b]

27. First of all, Sire, he is a Greek—that is, one of
your chosen people. There has never been a man such
a lover of his country as you are of the soil of
Greece, as you reflect upon its religion, its laws, its
eloquence, its philosophy, ritual of initiation, and
trophies won from the barbarians. 28. Even if
Aristophanes had been a Megarian, Melian or
Lemnian,[c] he would have had this considerable
advantage: in fact, however, his city's name inspires
even more respect, for he is from Corinth. In my
argument I shall make no appeal to legend, nor dilate
upon the contest between Helios and Poseidon,[d] nor
upon the epitaphs of the dead buried there after
naval battles,[e] nor upon the city's fair dealing and
consistent support of the victims of aggression.[f] This
is not to imply that this has little bearing on the
renown of its possessors, but that there is a more
notable claim that can be adduced. 29. Just remind
yourself, Sire, of the letter you sent to the Corinthians
after embarking upon hostilities against your will, and

myth (*Or.* 7. 204 ff.) and, with the subsequent references to
Dio, marking Libanius' special appeal to Julian's appreciation of his work.

[e] On the fallen at Salamis: Simonides, *fr.* 96 ff. [Dio]
37. 109 R.

[f] *Ibid.* 108 R.

119

λαβών, οὔπω δὲ εἰς τέλος ἥκων· ἐν ᾗ σαφῶς
εὐεργέτας σαυτοῦ τοὺς Κορινθίους καλεῖς. ἀλλὰ
γὰρ αὐτοῦ μοι δεῖ τοῦ μέρους τῆς ἐπιστολῆς, καὶ
γὰρ ἂν ἡδίους τοὺς ἀκούοντας ποιήσαιμεν.   30.
πατρῴα μοι πρὸς ὑμᾶς ὑπάρχει φιλία. καὶ
γὰρ ᾤκησε παρ᾽ ὑμῖν ὁ ἐμὸς πατὴρ καὶ
ἀναχθεὶς ἔνθεν, ὥσπερ ἐκ Φαιάκων Ὀδυσ-
σεύς, τῆς πολυχρονίου πλάνης ἀπηλλάγη.
εἶτα μικρὰ διελθὼν περὶ πανούργου μητρυιᾶς,
ἐνταῦθα, φής, ὁ πατὴρ ἀνεπαύσατο. σεμνόν
γε τοῦτο Κορινθίοις, | ὥσπερ Ἀθηναίοις τὰ περὶ F 9
τὴν Δήμητρος πλάνην.   31. οἴου τοίνυν ἕνα τῶν
R 435 δεξαμένων | τὸν σὸν πατέρα τὸν Ἀριστοφάνους
πατέρα. τῶν γάρ, οἶμαι, πρώτων ἦν καὶ τῶν
ἀγόντων τὴν πόλιν ὥστε τῶν δημοσίᾳ πραττομένων
οὐκ ὀλίγον εἰς ἐκεῖνον ἤρχετο. πάντων δὲ ἀτοπώτατον εἰ πόλει μὲν ὅλῃ βλάβος ἀνδρὸς ἑνὸς γίγνεται
κατὰ τὸν Ἡσίοδον κακία, πόλεως δὲ ὅλης ἀρετὴ
μὴ δύναιτο ἄνδρα ἕνα ὠφελεῖν.   32. εἶεν. Ἱέριον
δὲ καὶ τὸν ἀδελφὸν ἆρ᾽ εἰ ζῶντες ἐτύγχανον, οὐκ
ἂν εἶχες περὶ σεαυτόν, ὥσπερ τὼ δαιμονίω τώδε,
τόν τε ἀπὸ τῆς Ἠπείρου καὶ τὸν ἐκ τῆς Ἰωνίας;
τί δ᾽; ἐκείνους οὐκ ἂν οἴει πάνθ᾽ ὑπὲρ Ἀριστοφάνους εἰπεῖν τε καὶ πρᾶξαι; πάνυ γε. καὶ γὰρ
ἤχθοντο βεβιασμένου στρατιώτου στολὴν ὑποδῦναι,
καὶ καιροῦ τυχόντες, ὅπως ἔσται τι βέλτιον αὐτῷ

---

[a] A manifesto, issued from Naissus simultaneously with
his *Letter to the Athenians* : *cf. Or.* 12. 64, 18. 113.   Zos. 3.
10.   Amm. Marc. 21. 10. 7.   These are the only surviving
fragments.

[b] Helena, concubine of Constantius Chlorus, mother of
Constantine, step-mother of Julius Constantius.

when you had already gained your objective for the most part but without attaining it completely. There you explicitly name the Corinthians as your benefactors. I must here cite the exact words of part of your letter, since that is how we may better please our audience.[a] 30. " I have an hereditary friendship with you," you wrote, " for my father lived among you and departed from among you, like Odysseus from the Phaeacians, after resting from his long wanderings." Then, after a few words about his wicked stepmother,[b] you went on, " Here my father found repose." This is indeed a source of pride for the Corinthians, as is for the Athenians the ending of Demeter's wanderings. 31. Consider, then, that Aristophanes' father was one of those who extended a welcome to your own father. He was certainly one of the magnates who directed the city, and much of the public business came his way.[c] It is quite absurd for us to agree with Hesiod that the wickedness of a single individual can harm the whole state,[d] and yet deny that the merits of the whole state can help an individual. 32. Very well ! But if Hierius and his brother were still alive, would you not have them among your entourage, as you have this gifted pair from Epirus and Ionia?[e] Do you not think that they would have left no word unsaid, nothing undone, to help Aristophanes? Obviously not ! They were sorely grieved when he was forced to don a soldier's dress, and if they had the chance, they would concern themselves for the

[c] Julius Constantius' retirement to Corinth occurred during the period A.D. 325–330.

[d] *Works and Days*, 240.

[e] Priscus of Epirus and Maximus of Ephesus—a neatly philosophic parallel.

προϋνοοῦντ᾽ ἄν. 33. μὴ τοίνυν, εἰ μὴ φωνῆς
ἀκούεις Ἀριστοφάνους τῶν θείων, ἧττον νόμιζε
χαριεῖσθαι τοῖν ἀνδροῖν εἰ δώσεις ἃ βουλομένοις
ἐστί. τοῦ μὲν γὰρ ἡμῖν διαλέγεσθαι γεγόνασιν
ἔξω, πρὸς δὲ τοὺς τῶν ἀνθρώπων κρείττους οἷς νῦν
ὁμιλοῦσι, μεμνήσονταί που¹ τῆς χάριτος. 34. πῶς
οὖν οὐ δεινόν, εἰ Ἀλέξανδρος, καὶ ταῦτα Θηβαίοις
ὀργιζόμενος, ὡς οἶσθα, τοὺς Πινδάρῳ κατὰ γένος
προσήκοντας ᾐδέσθη διὰ τὴν Πινδάρου μουσικήν, |
Ἀριστοφάνην δὲ μηδὲν ὀνήσει μήτε τῶν θείων ἡ    F ¹
φιλοσοφία μήτε τῶν σοὶ συνόντων οἷς ἴσα καὶ
γονεῦσι προσφέρῃ; ταυτὶ γὰρ ἃ νῦν λέγω Μάξιμον
νόμιζε λέγειν, Πρίσκον παραινεῖν. εἰ δὲ ἀπιστεῖς,
ἐρώτησον αὐτούς. ὁρᾷς ὡς ἐπιθυμοῦσι τυχεῖν
τινος ἀγαθοῦ τὸν ἄνθρωπον; 35. ἀλλ᾽ οὐδ᾽
R 436 Ἐλπίδιος, ὃν κατὰ σοφίαν | μὲν λείπεσθαι συμ-
βαίνει τοῖν ἀνδροῖν, τῇ δὲ περὶ τὸ θεῖον σπουδῇ
καὶ τῷ περὶ σὲ φίλτρῳ μάλιστα αὐτοῖν ἐοικέναι,
οὐδ᾽ οὗτος ὡς ὑπὲρ ἀλλοτρίων τῶν Ἀριστοφάνους
βουλεύεται ἀλλὰ καὶ τοῦθ᾽ ἕν ἐστι τῶν ἀγρυπνίαν
αὐτῷ φερόντων καὶ ποιησόντων γε ἡδονὴν εἰ
γένοιτο. 36. μετὰ τούτων ἐστὶ Φηλιξ ὁ καλὸς καὶ
γενναῖος, τούτῳ μὲν ἀρχαῖος ἑταῖρος, θεοῖς δὲ
νεωστὶ φίλος ἡγεμόνι σοὶ χρησάμενος ἐπὶ τὴν
γνῶσιν τῶν κρειττόνων· ὃς ἐπειδὰν ἤδη τὸν γνώ-
ριμον, ἐγκαλύπτεται τῶν δεινῶν οὔπω λελυκὼς
οὐδέν. 37. πρόσθες ἐκείνῳ τὸν χρηστὸν καὶ πάν-

¹ που MSS. : σου F.

---

ᵃ Seeck, op. cit. 170 ii.  His activity in the cause of
Aristophanes is mentioned, Ep. 758.
ᵇ Seeck, op. cit. 155 ii.  He died suddenly at the end of

improvement of his lot. 33. So, if you do not hear the actual voices of Aristophanes' uncles, do not think that you will be conferring any less favour upon them in granting them their wish. Though they have passed beyond the reach of human intercourse, they will surely remind the super-human beings with whom they now consort, of your kindness. 34. It would be a shame for Alexander, despite his anger against the Thebans, as you know, to show respect to Pindar's relatives because of Pindar's poems, and yet for the philosophy of Aristophanes' uncles and that of your own companions, whom you regard as though they were your parents, to avail him nothing, for you must imagine that my words now are the words of Maximus, my advice that of Priscus. If you disbelieve me, ask them. Don't you see how eager they are for him to obtain some benefit? 35. Elpidius also,[a] though less gifted in philosophy than either of them, is their equal in his zeal for religion and affection for yourself : he follows the fortunes of Aristophanes with an interest as keen as if they were his own, and this is the one matter that now causes him sleepless nights and will give him pleasure, if it should come about. 36. Our good and noble friend Felix is at one with them in this.[b] He is an old companion of Aristophanes and a recent convert to our gods, with you as his guide to the knowledge of things divine. Whenever he sees his friend he hides his head because he has not yet relieved him of any of his troubles. 37. Besides him there is Dorion, that fine

the year, closely followed by Julian's uncle, Julianus. Thereafter the Antiochenes saluted Julian with the malicious *double entente*, " Felix Julianus Augustus " (Amm. Marc. 23. 1. 5).

123

τας ἀνθρώπους ἀνηρτημένον τῇ καλοκἀγαθίᾳ Δω-
ρίωνα ᾧ τὴν ἀπὸ τῶν ἄλλων εὐφροσύνην ἀμ-
βλύνει τὰ περὶ τοῦτον οὐ μεταβεβλημένα. 38. καὶ
μὴν αὐτὸς ὁ λέγων παρὰ σοὶ μὲν οὐκ ἄτιμος,
τούτῳ δὲ ἐπιτήδειος ἀπ᾽ ἐκείνων τῶν χρόνων | ἐν F 16
οἷς τῶν τι¹ ἐμῶν συγγραμμάτων ἀναγινώσκων
ἐν Λυκείῳ λίθοις ἐβάλλετο παρὰ τῶν οὐκ οἰομέ-
νων αὐτοῖς τὴν ἀνάγνωσιν λυσιτελεῖν καὶ τοιαῦτα
ποιῶν οὐκ ἐμοὶ μᾶλλον ἢ τῷ χαίροντι τοῖς λόγοις |
R 437 ἐχαρίζετο. σὺ δ᾽ ἂν αὐτὸς εἴης ὁ χαίρων. οὐκοῦν
καὶ αὐτὸς ἂν μετ᾽ ἐμοῦ χάριν ὀφείλοις. ἐμοῦ
τοίνυν ἀποδιδόντος τῷ λέγειν ἀπόδος καὶ σὺ τοῖς
ἔργοις.

39. Οἱ μὲν οὖν ἀξιοῦντες τοσοῦτοι καὶ πάντες
φίλοι, οἶμαι δ᾽ εἰ τοῖς μὲν ἄλλοις ἔμελεν ἥκιστα
τοῦ πράγματος, εἷς δέ τις ἐκ τῶν ἠριθμημένων ἦν
ὃν οὗτος ἐλύπει δυστυχῶν, κἂν τοῦτον ἂν ἠδέσθης
τὸν ἕνα. δοὺς τοίνυν ἂν ἑνὶ τὴν χάριν, ὦ βασιλεῦ,
τοσούτοις οὐ δώσεις οὐδ᾽ ἡγήσῃ δεῖγμα τῆς
Ἀριστοφάνους ἐπιεικείας εἶναι τοιούτων μαρτύρων
χορόν; οἳ οὔτ᾽ ἂν ἠγνόησαν εἴπερ ἦν πονηρός,
οὔτ᾽ ἂν ἐπήνεσαν πρὸς δὲ τὸν πεπονηρευμένον.
40. εἰ γὰρ καὶ φίλος, ἀλλ᾽ οὐ σοῦ γε φίλτερος οὐδ᾽
αὖ τἀκείνου τῶν σῶν, ἀλλ᾽ οὐδὲ πάντες οὐδὲ τὰ
πάντων οὔτ᾽ ἔστιν οὔτε μὴ γένηται. μὴ τοίνυν
οἷς μὲν μοχθηροὶ βοηθοῦσι, τούτους ἡγοῦ τοῖς

¹ τι om. F. (CAPV).

---

ᵃ Mentioned, *Ep.* 823 : *cf.* Sievers, *op. cit.* 96.
ᵇ Feuding between factions supporting the various rhetors
at Athens was notoriously violent : *cf. Or.* 1. 19 ff., Eunap.
*V.S.* 483 ff., Himerius, *Or.* 69 (ed. Colonna). Libanius in

fellow who has attached everyone to himself by his nobility of character.[a] If there is no altering Aristophanes' plight, his happiness from other sources will be soured. 38. Moreover I, his advocate, am not without honour for you, and I have been his friend since the day when he gave a reading from my compositions in the Lyceum and was pelted with stones by the gentry who thought the reading to be against their own interests, and in acting so he obliged not so much myself as any devotee of learning.[b] You, Sire, might yourself be that man, and so you would be in his debt as much as I. If then I repay my debt by my words, repay yours by your actions.

39. So many, then, are they who put forward this plea, all of them your friends. In my opinion, if all the others did not care twopence about the business and yet there was just one of these afore-mentioned who was grieved at Aristophanes' troubles, you would defer to this one man. Thus, Sire, if you would grant this favour to any one of them, will you not grant it to them all? Will you not regard such a body of witnesses as proof of Aristophanes' good character? If he were a rogue, they would not have been unaware of it, and they would never have recommended him to your notice if he had been a rogue. 40. However much their friend he may be, he is not so much so as you are : his well-being is not so dear to them as yours, and not all of them taken together, nor the well-being of them all, are or ever can be. Well now, don't suppose that people whom rascals help really resemble their helpers, and then suppose that, when

later years laments the absence of such support from his own pupils (*Or.* 3. 22 f.). Julian (*E.L.F.* No. 97) approves Libanius' commendation of Aristophanes for such services.

βοηθοῦσιν ἐοικέναι, πάλιν δὲ ἡγοῦ μοχθηρὸν ὑπὲρ
οὗ ποιοῦνται τοὺς λόγους οἷς τὰ βελτίω σύνοισθα. |

41. Εἰ μὲν οὖν ἓν τοῦτο μόνον ὑπῆρχεν Ἀριστο- **F**
φάνει τὸ συνηγόρων τῶν ὑπὸ σοῦ πιστευομένων |
R 438 εὐπορεῖν, ἴσως ἂν ὀκνηρότερον διεκείμην. νῦν δ᾽,
ὦ βασιλεῦ, ταὐτὰ μὲν ἡμῖν ηὔξατο, ταὐτὰ δὲ
ἐμίσησε, τῶν αὐτῶν δὲ ἐπεθύμησεν. ἧκεν εἰς τὰ
λείψανα τῶν ἱερῶν κομίζων οὐ λιβανωτόν, οὐχ
ἱερεῖον, οὐ πῦρ, οὐ σπονδήν, οὐ γὰρ ἐξῆν, ἀλλὰ
ψυχὴν ἀλγοῦσαν καὶ φωνὴν ὀδυρομένην καὶ δεδα-
κρυμένην καὶ δακρύων ἀφορμὰς καὶ βλέπων εἰς
γῆν, τὸ γὰρ εἰς οὐρανὸν σφαλερόν, ἤτει παρὰ τῶν
θεῶν παῦσαι μὲν τὸ φθεῖρον τὴν οἰκουμένην, τὰ δὲ
Γαλατῶν ἀγαθὰ κοινὰ ποιῆσαι τῆς γῆς. 42. καὶ
ταύτης τῆς εὐχῆς οὐκ ὀλίγους αὐτῷ κοινωνοὺς
εἰργάσατο, πρὸς μὲν ἐκεῖνον ἐκπολεμῶν, εἰς δὲ τὴν
μερίδα τὴν ἡμετέραν εἰσάγων, κἂν τοῖς συλλόγοις
οὐκ ἀκινδύνους μὲν ἡδίστους δὲ αὐτῷ λόγους
ἀπέτεινεν οὔπω παρούσης ἑορτῆς ἑορτάζων οἷα
μὲν ἔσται τὰ τῶν στρατιωτῶν, οἷα δὲ τὰ τῶν
πόλεων, οἷα δὲ τὰ βασίλεια, τὰ δὲ τῶν ἀρχόντων,
τὰ δὲ τῶν λόγων, τὰ τῆς Ἀσίας, τὰ τῆς Εὐρώπης,
R 439 τὸ μέγιστον ἁπάντων, τὰ περὶ | τοὺς θεούς. 43.
εἰπέ που λέγων ὡς πρῶτος ἐνευδαιμονήσει | τῷ **F**
καιρῷ. βεβαίωσον τοίνυν αὐτῷ καὶ τὴν ἐλπίδα
καὶ τὴν μαντείαν καὶ μὴ περιίδῃς καταγελώμενον
ὑπ᾽ ἐκείνων οἷς ἦγε[1] τὰς προσδοκίας. δεῖ γὰρ

---

[1] ἦγε mss. : ἧδε F. : ἤλεγχε conj. Re.

---

ᵃ From A.D. 341 at least (*Cod. Th.* 16. 10. 3).

a man has as his advocates persons whom you know
to be of sterling worth, he is a rascal too.

41. Now, if it were the sole claim of Aristophanes,
that he has plenty of advocates who enjoy your
confidence, I might perhaps be rather half-hearted
in his defence. However, Sire, his prayers, his hates,
his desires are the same as my own. He came to what
was left of our temples with no incense or victim, no
burnt-offering or drink-offering—for that was not
allowed.[a] What he brought was a sorrowing heart,
and a voice of grief, anguish and tears. He gazed on
the ground, for it was a dangerous business to gaze
up to heaven, and he used to pray the gods to call a
halt to the ruination of the world [b] and to distribute
the blessings enjoyed by Gaul over the whole earth.
42. He ensured that many became his partners in
this prayer, by opposing that regime and leading
them over to our side.[c] In the literary clubs he would
utter words which, though dangerous, were a real
pleasure to him, as he enjoyed the delights of anticipation with joyful narration of the blessings to be
shared by the army, by the cities, the court, the
governors, rhetoric, by Asia and by Europe, and, last
but not least, by the religion of the gods. 43. He said
somewhere that he would be the first to share the
blessings of that event. Then confirm for him both
his hope and his prediction, and do not let him become
a laughing stock for those to whom he confided his

[b] Imperial *esprit de corps* again prevents Libanius from
naming Constantius outright.

[c] For the existence of this pagan " underground " movement in the period after Julian's elevation to the rank of
Caesar *cf.* Petit, *Libanius et la vie municipale*, pp. 203 ff.
Julian (*E.L.F.* No. 97) shows appreciation of the stress laid
on Aristophanes' piety here.

LIBANIUS

εἶναί τι πλέον τοῖς ἐπιθυμήσασι σὰ γενέσθαι τὰ
πάντα.

44.. Καὶ ὡς μὲν τοῖς πᾶσιν εὐθενεῖ τὰ τῶν
βουλευόντων πράγματα καὶ τῷ πλήθει τῶν προσ-
γεγενημένων καὶ τῷ μέτρῳ τῶν ἀναλωμάτων καὶ
τῷ πάλιν ἐπὶ τοῦ παλαιοῦ τετάχθαι σχήματος
ἀνωμολόγηται· Ἀριστοφάνης δὲ οὔτε ταῦτ' ἀγνοῶν
οὔτε φαῦλον ἡγούμενος τῆς αὑτοῦ προβεβλῆσθαι
καὶ σώζειν τε τὴν πατρίδα καὶ τὸν οἶκον τὸν
αὑτοῦ μείζω ποιεῖν φεύγει τὴν προστασίαν καὶ τὸ
R 440 πολιτεύεσθαι. | ἀλλ' ὅθεν ὁ καλὸν ἡγεῖται πράττειν
οὐ δύναται φράσω, κἄν με λάβῃς ψευσάμενον, μή
μοι δῷς ἕτερον παρρησίας λόγον.

45. Ἐκάκωσεν, ὦ βασιλεῦ, τὰ πράγματα τούτῳ
πρῶτον μὲν Εὐγένιος φόβον ἐμβαλὼν τοῖς διοικοῦσι
καὶ προδείξας ὡς ὁ μὴ φεύγων ἀπολεῖται παιόμενος
καὶ ἀγχόμενος, ἔπειθ' οὗτος μακραῖς καὶ χρονίοις
ἀπουσίαις δι' ἃς δένδρα τε ἐκκέκοπται καὶ γῆ
γεωργίας ἐστέρηται, τῶν δὲ ἀνδραπόδων τὰ μὲν
ἀπέδρα, τὰ δὲ ἀργεῖν ἔμαθε, τὰ δὲ κακουργεῖν,
γυνὴ δὲ τὰ τοιαῦτα θρηνεῖν μὲν δύναιτ' ἄν, διορ-
θοῦσθαι δὲ οὐ | πάνυ. ὁ δὲ δὴ τελευταῖος σκηπτὸς F
ὅσα ἦν ἐπίπλων ἐχόμενα πάντα ἐξανήλωκε μετα-
πεμπομένου τοῦδε χρυσία καὶ σκεύη κατακόπτον-
τος καὶ¹ θεραπεύοντος ἀπὸ τούτων πολλοὺς |
R 441 πανταχόθεν λύκους ἐπικειμένους. 46. οὐ δεῖ δὴ
θαυμάζειν εἰ τηλικοῦτον μῆκος οὕτω δεινῆς συμ-
φορᾶς ἠλλοίωσέ τι τῆς πατρικῆς εὐδαιμονίας ἀλλ'

---

¹ κατακόπτοντος καὶ mss. : καὶ κατακόπτοντος F.

ᵃ Following the edict of 13 March A.D. 362 (E.L.F. No.
47), by which abuse of the *cursus publicus* was removed
(*Cod. Th.* 11. 16. 10), civic lands restored (*ibid.* 10. 3. 1),
128

expectations, for the people who wanted you to become supreme should get some benefit.

44. It is now agreed that the situation of the councils is in every respect satisfactory, in the number of new members, in the amount of their contributions, and in their return to their previous status.[a] Aristophanes is not unaware of this, nor does he seek to avoid a position of responsibility in civic life because he thinks it of little account to be a leader of his community, the preserver of his city, and the sponsor of greater renown for his family. I will tell you the reason why he cannot fulfil his noble ambition, and if you find my story false, never grant me another free hearing.

45. The ruin of his fortune, Sire, was first Eugenius who inspired fear in his bailiffs, threatening that any who did not decamp would be put to death by the lash or the rope,[b] and secondly himself, by reason of his lengthy and prolonged absences, whereby his plantations have been felled, his lands have fallen out of cultivation, and of his slaves some have fled, others have learned to be idlers or rascals, and while his wife might deplore all this, there was nothing at all that she could do about it. The final blow is that everything that he could realize upon has gone, for he kept sending for money, turning his property into cash and fattening upon it the packs of wolves that beset him on every side. 46. No wonder, then, that the long period of such a disastrous plight has impaired his family fortunes. The real wonder is that

immunity from *collatio lustralis* and recruitment of new members allowed to the *curiae* (*ibid.* 12. 1. 50): *cf. Or.* 18. 146 ff. Ammianus (25. 4. 21) disapproved of this recruiting campaign, as did the Church historians, and for the same reason—self-interest.      [b] *Cf.* §§ 10 f. above.

ὅπως οὐ καὶ τοὺς ἀγροὺς καὶ τὴν οἰκίαν ἀπέδοτο μετὰ
τῶν ἄλλων ὑπὸ τοσούτων ἐσθιόμενος θηρίων. τίνα
δὴ βούλει τὸν ἄνθρωπον ἐπανελθόντα γενέσθαι καὶ
τί ποιεῖν; ἅψασθαι προστασίας μετὰ πενίας, ὦ
βασιλεῦ; μέγα μέντ' ἂν στενάξαι Μένανδρος ὑπὸ
γῆς, εἰ αἴσθοιτο τὸν υἱὸν αὐτῷ χρημάτων ἐνδείᾳ
πολλοῖς τῶν αὑτοῦ χειρόνων ἐξιστάμενον τῶν
πρωτείων. ἀλλὰ δι' ἐπιμελείας μὲν ἰάσασθαι τὰ
τραύματα, χρημάτων δὲ ἤδη συνειλεγμένων οὕτως
ἐκεῖσε παριέναι; καὶ τίς ἀνέξεται τῶν αὐτὸ τοῦτο
δεδοικότων μὴ σχολῇ θεραπεύσῃ τὸν οἶκον; 47.
R 442 δεῖ | δή τινος τιμῆς ἐξ ἧς ἀτέλειαν χρόνον τινὰ
καρπωσάμενος ἤδη μετὰ ῥώμης | εἰς τὸ λειτουρ- F
γεῖν ἀφίξεται. καὶ γὰρ εἰ τοῦτο φαίης ὡς δώσεις
ψιλὴν ἀτέλειαν ἐτῶν δή τινων καὶ τοῦτο προσήκει
στέργειν, ὅτι μὲν ταπεινότερον τοῦτο ἐκείνου καὶ
οὐκ ἀρκοῦσαν ἔχον τῷ τοσαῦτα πεπονθότι τὴν
παραμυθίαν ἐάσω, ἀλλὰ σοί γε οὐκ ἂν εἴη τοῦ
βελτίονος λόγου. 48. δῆλον γὰρ ὡς ἂν ἀτελὴς
περινοστῇ μηδ' ἐν ἄλλῳ τῳ τὴν ἀφ' ἑαυτοῦ παρεχό-
μενος χρείαν, ἄνισον δόξει τὸ πρᾶγμα, καὶ λυπήσει
τοὺς λειτουργοῦντας εἴ τις τῶν ἐκείνων ἀναλωμάτων θεωρὸς περίεισιν ὁμοίως τοῦ τε λειτουργεῖν
καὶ πάσης ἀφειμένος διακονίας. 49. καὶ πολλοὺς
γε τοὺς τῶν αὐτῶν ἀξιώσοντας τυχεῖν εὑρήσεις·
οὐ γὰρ ἀπορήσουσιν ὅθεν ἐνοχλήσουσιν. οἷς εἰ
μὲν ἅπασι τὴν ἀτέλειαν δώσεις, βλάψεις τὰς πόλεις,
εἰ δὲ οὐδενὶ πλὴν τοῦδε, πολλοὺς ἀνιάσεις. πάντα

130

he has not sold up lands and house along with the rest, since he has so many ravening beasts battening upon him. What do you want to become of the man on his return, and what do you want him to do? Aspire to the leadership of the city—and him in penury, Sire? Menander in the world below would be sore grieved to know that his son because of his financial straits had given up his position of primacy to many who are his inferiors. Would you suggest healing his smarts by means of some public duty and letting him resume his position when he has got enough money together? If people are afraid simply that he may have time to recover the fortunes of his house, will they ever put up with that? 47. He must have some form of honour whereby he may enjoy immunity for a time and then, when he has recovered his strength, may approach his civic obligations. If you say that you will grant him bare immunity for so many years and that he must be satisfied with that, leaving aside the fact that such a course is less generous than my alternative and is hardly consolation enough for such sufferings, I insist that you would not be well advised in so doing. 48. For obviously, if he roves around with a grant of immunity and provides no service of any other kind, the business will seem unfair, and it will rankle with those who undertake the duties towards the community, that anyone should remain a mere spectator of their own expenditure, released both from such burdens and from any part of the civic administration. 49. You will find many claimants for the same privilege, and they will have plenty of opportunity to make nuisances of themselves. If you grant immunity to them all, you will do harm to their cities : if you grant it to none save him, you will

δὲ ἄμεμπτα βουλοίμην ἂν εἶναι τὰ σά, καθάπερ τὰ
τῶν θεῶν. 50. ἵν᾿ οὖν μὴ Κορινθίων μὲν οἱ πολλοὶ
διὰ τὴν Ἀριστοφάνει δοθεῖσαν ἀτέλειαν διαφύγωσι
τὸ λειτουργεῖν, Ἀργεῖοι δὲ διὰ Κορινθίους, Σπαρτιᾶται δὲ διὰ τοὺς Ἀργείων ἀτελεῖς, τῶν δὲ ἄλλων
ἕκαστοι διὰ τοὺς πλησίον, γενέσθω τι τοιοῦτον
Ἀριστοφάνει παρὰ τῆς σῆς διανοίας ὃ τούτῳ μὲν
R 443 εὐσχήμονα | τὴν ἀνάπαυσιν οἴσει, τοὺς δὲ ἄλλους
οὐκ ἐάσει δαπανωμένους ἀγανακτεῖν ὡς ἂν ἐλατ-
τουμένους. 51. οὐ γὰρ ἑτέρως γε εἰ τιμηθείη τις,
τὸ μὴ πᾶσι γενέσθαι τὴν αὐτὴν τιμὴν ἐν ἐγκλήμασι
θήσονται, ἀλλ᾿ ἐκεῖνο μὲν λογιοῦνται τῇ τοῦ
λαβόντος πρὸς | τὸ ἔργον ὃ δεήσει πράττειν F
ἐπιτηδειότητι, μετουσίαν δὲ τῆς ἀτελείας οἱ
ζητοῦντες ἔσονται καὶ οὐ δόξουσιν ἀναισχυντεῖν.
ἵν᾿ οὖν μηδὲν ἕπηται τῇ δόσει δυσχερές, ἄλλῳ τῳ
τὸν ἄνθρωπον εὖ ποίει.

52. Τῶν δὲ ἐξ Αἰγύπτου χρημάτων ὅταν μνημο-
νεύσῃς καὶ τῶν κεκλοφότων ἕνα νομίζῃς Ἀριστοφάνην, ἐπαινῶ μέν σε τοῦ μίσους ὅτι μισεῖς τοὺς
ὅθεν οὐ δίκαιον λαμβάνοντας, ὅταν γὰρ τοῖς πάλαι
τὰ τοιαῦτα κεκερδακόσιν ὀργίλως ἔχῃς, οὐδ᾿
ἐνθυμηθῆναι περὶ τῶν πονηρῶν λημμάτων τὸ νῦν
ἐᾷς, πρόσαγε μέντοι ταῖς διαβολαῖς, ὦ βασιλεῦ,
τὴν ἀκριβεστάτην βάσανον. 53. ταῦτα γὰρ οἱ
νόμοι λέγουσι. δεῖ δὲ οὐδὲν οὔτ᾿ Αἰγυπτίους
δεῦρο καλεῖν οὔτε τοῦτον ἐκεῖσε πέμπειν ὑποσχή-
σοντα λόγον· πάλαι γὰρ ταῦτα κέκριται καὶ
βεβασάνισται, καὶ βουλόμενον εἰδέναι τὰ δημόσια
διδάξει γράμματα. ἐν τούτοις τοίνυν ἕνδεκα μὲν
καὶ διακοσίους στατῆρας ἐγκέκληται λαβεῖν, οὐχ

132

annoy a large number; and all your actions I would wish to be as blameless as those of the gods. 50. So then, that the majority of the Corinthians may not seek to avoid civic service because of the immunity granted to Aristophanes, and the Argives because of the immunity of the Corinthians, and the Spartans because of that of the Argives, in short, anyone at all because of that of his neighbours, let Aristophanes of your good will be granted something that will bring him an honourable respite and will not allow the others who have to meet financial obligations to be annoyed at coming off second best. 51. For if an honour of a different kind be granted, they will not resent the fact that the same honour is not enjoyed by all, but they will regard it from the point of view of the fitness of the recipient for the duty he has to perform : but there will be claimants for a share in this immunity, and they will not be regarded as impudent for so doing. Therefore, so that there may be no untoward consequences to your grant, favour him in some other way.

52. When you make mention of the money stolen in Egypt and regard Aristophanes as one of the thieves, I commend you for your loathing of illicit gain, for your anger towards old hands at this game now forbids the very idea of criminal embezzlement. But, Sire, bring the most searching examination to bear upon such charges. 53. That is what the laws bid us do. There is no need either to summon Egyptians here or to send him to Egypt to render an account. Examination was conducted and judgement passed long ago, and the public records will give information enough to any who wants to know. In them he stands accused of obtaining 211 staters,

ἁρπάσας οὐδὲ βιασάμενος ἀλλά τινος μισθὸν
ὠφελείας, ὡς ὁ συκοφάντης ἔφησεν, ἦν γὰρ δὴ
R 444 συκοφάντης, | λαβεῖν, ἀλλ' οὐκ ἀπολαβεῖν ἐθέλων.
54. ὡς δ' ὁ μὲν οὐκ ἐξήλεγχεν, ὁ δ' οὐδὲ τὴν
αἰτίαν ἔφερεν, ὑπῆρχε δὲ τῷ κατηγόρῳ Παῦλος
εἰς πλεονεξίαν, παρῄνουν δὲ | καὶ τῶν φίλων οἱ F
παρόντες ὑπομεῖναι μᾶλλον τὴν ἄδικον ζημίαν ἢ
τὴν ἐπὶ πλέον κρίσιν, οὕτως ἐποίησε. καὶ δανεισά-
μενος τῷ ψευσαμένῳ μὲν τὴν ἀναίδειαν ἔγκαρπον
κατέστησεν, ἔδωκε γὰρ τὸ χρυσίον, αὐτίκα δὲ ἐν
πολλῶν ἐδόκει χερσὶν ἔσεσθαι τοῦ παραδείγματος
μυρίους ἐγείροντος. 55. ὡς δὲ οὐδεὶς ἐφαίνετο
μέμψιν ἐπάγων, παραδόντες αὐτὸν στρατιώταις καὶ
κήρυκι κελεύσαντες δι' Αἰγύπτου πάσης τὸν μὲν
ἄγεσθαι, τὸν δὲ κηρύττειν εἴ τις Ἀριστοφάνει
προεῖτο μισθὸν ἥκειν ἀποληψόμενον, ἔπεμψαν. ὁ
δὲ τῇ περιουσίᾳ τῆς ἀληθείας κρείττων ἐγένετο
τῆς Αἰγυπτίων φύσεως· πάντες μὲν γὰρ εἶδον
ἀγόμενον, πάντες δὲ τοῦ κήρυκος ἤκουσαν, παρῄει
δὲ οὐδείς. 56. καίτοι τίς οὐκ ἂν τῶν ἡνίκα
ἠναγκάζοντο[1] δοῦναι λελυπημένων ἡδέως ἂν πάλιν
R 445 ἤνεγκε | τὸ χρυσίον οἴκαδε, καὶ ταῦτα Αἰγύπτιος ;
οὓς οὐκ ὀκνοῦντας ὁρῶμεν ὧν ἔδοσαν μνησθῆ-
ναι, ἀλλὰ μάλ' εὐχερῶς εἰσπράττοντας ἃ μὴ δέδοται.
ἀλλ', οἶμαι, τὸ μηδὲ σκιὰν ὑπεῖναι δωροδοκίας μηδ'
ὅθεν ἂν αἰτία γένοιτο πιθανὴ σιγᾶν ἠνάγκασε καὶ
συκοφάντου τόλμαν. 57. πότερ' οὖν τἀμφίβολον
ἐκεῖνο λῆμμα τὸ μικρὸν σημεῖον δεῖ ποιεῖσθαι μειζό-

―――――
[1] ἠναγκάζοντο Re., F. : ἠναγκάζετο mss.

[a] In company with most other ancient writers, Libanius
has little good to say of Egyptians : cf. the proverbial
Αἰγυπτιάζειν (Suidas).

134

not by violence or extortion, but obtaining them, according to the informer's story,—for there was an informer, of course—as reward for some assistance, though without claiming them as his due. 54. The action was failing and Aristophanes was quite cleared of guilt when the support of Paulus induced the plaintiff to press further claims. Even his friends there present counselled him to submit to an unjust punishment rather than a protracted law-suit, and he followed their advice. He raised a loan and turned this liar's impudence into a source of profit for him, for the money was handed over, but it seemed that he would soon be in the clutches of many more, since hordes of others would be stirred up by the example. 55. When no one turned up with any complaint, they handed him over to some officers and a herald with orders for him to be paraded through the length and breadth of Egypt, and for the herald to proclaim that any man who had handed any money over to Aristophanes should come and reclaim it. But by the power of truth he prevailed over the inborn character of Egyptians, for though they all saw him paraded before them and all heard the herald's announcement, not one of them put in an appearance. 56. Yet of all the people who resented being compelled to pay, everyone would have been glad to get his money back home, especially an Egyptian,[a] for we see them nothing loth to refer to any payments of money they have made and, in fact, only too prone to reclaim payments not made at all. Obviously, the absence of any suspicion of bribery and any justification of the charge caused even the hardiest of informers to hold his tongue. 57. So are we to assume this petty piece of peculation, itself not proven, to be an

135

νων ἃ μηδεὶς ἐγκέκληκεν, ἢ τὴν ἐν τοῖς κηρύγμασι
τῶν εἰωθότων συκοφαντεῖν σιωπὴν τοῦ μὴ δικαίως |
ἐγκεκλῆσθαι τὰ μικρὰ τεκμήριον; μᾶλλον γὰρ F
εἰκὸς τὸν οὐ παρ' ἄλλων εἰληφότα μηδὲ τοῦτο λαβεῖν ἢ τὸν τοῦτο θαυμάσαντα τῶν μειζόνων ἀποσχέ-
σθαι. 58. πᾶς γάρ, ὦ βασιλεῦ, φιλοχρήματος
μικρὸν οὐδὲν ἐξ Αἰγύπτου φέρεται. ῥεῖ γὰρ αὐτόθι
μετὰ τοῦ Νείλου καὶ τὰ κέρδη, καὶ τούτων οὐκ
ἀφανεῖς αἱ πηγαί. ὁ δὲ οὕτως ἦν ἄθλιος καὶ χρημάτων τε ἥττων καὶ τοῦ κερδαίνειν ἄπειρος ὥσθ'
ἕνεκα διακοσίων στατήρων αἰσχύνην κινδύνους ἔ-
χουσαν ὑπομένειν ᾑρεῖτο. 59. καὶ μὴν εἰ μὲν ἐπιθυμῶν λαβεῖν εἶτ' οὐκ ἔχων εἰς τοῦτο[1] συμπράττειν
δύναμιν οὐδὲ τὸν δώσοντα εἶχεν, ἀπολογίαν ἔχει
τὴν ἀσθένειαν αὐτήν· εἰ δ' ὢν κύριος πολλαχόθεν |
R 446 μισθαρνεῖν οὐκ ἐχρῆτο τῇ δυνάμει πρὸς πόρον,
πῶς ἂν μᾶλλον φανείη κρείττων χρημάτων; ἢ
τίς ἂν βασιλεὺς τούτῳ πράγματα ἐγχειρίσας αὐτὸν
αἰτιάσαιτο;

60. Ἥσθην δέ τινος εἰπόντος ἐν μέρει κατηγορίας
ὡς οὗτός ἐστι διειλεγμένος ἑταίρᾳ τινὶ τῶν ἐπὶ
σκηνῆς γυναικῶν. οὐ γὰρ οἶδα τίνας ἂν πρὸ
τούτων ἐζήτησε λόγους, εἰ συνήγορος ἦν. 61.
φέρε γάρ· εἰ ἐγὼ ποιῶν Ἀριστοφάνει τούτῳ νῦν
ἐγκώμιον μετὰ τὸν ἀπὸ τῶν ἄλλων ἔπαινον ἐπὶ τὸν
τῆς ἐγκρατείας προελθὼν | τόπον οὕτω πως F
διῆλθον, ὅτι οὗτος μέντοι πλείστην γῆν ἐπελ-

---

[1] τοῦτο mss. (τὸ τοῦτο I, corrected): τό τῳ F.

---

[a] Unlike those of the river itself : Herod. 2. 28.
[b] Pleas singled out by Julian in his reply : the second
is a neat man-of-the-world deviation from the conventional

indication of worse misdeeds of which no one has accused him, or is the silence of such habitual liars when these announcements were made not evidence for the fact that the accusation on the minor issue was itself baseless? It is much more probable that a man who extorted nothing from others should not have taken this either, than that he should have hankered after it and yet held aloof from more serious offences. 58. Any man who sets his mind on money, Sire, gets a vast amount of it from Egypt. The profits flow in there along with the Nile flood, and their sources are plain to see.[a] Then Aristophanes was so miserably venal and clumsy in his money grubbing[b] that he chose to endure the shame and its attendant dangers, all for 200 staters! 59. If he was desirous of taking bribes and then was incapable of managing it, and had no one ready even to offer him any, he has his very impotence as an excuse. But if he had the power to amass a fortune from many sources and did not use his influence for personal gain, how could he more clearly prove himself superior to the influence of money? What emperor would reproach himself for entrusting the management of his affairs to him?

60. I was pleased to find it said as part of the accusation against him that the mistress with whom he was intimate was a stage actress.[b] I don't know what arguments would have been sought in place of this by a counsel for the defence. 61. Just consider! If I delivered a panegyric on Aristophanes here and, after praising him on other counts, proceeded to the subject of his continence, and continued in some such vein as this, "He has travelled all over the world

κρείττων ἡδονῶν, which tactfully confesses the superiority of that philosophic ideal.

# LIBANIUS

θῶν καὶ πολλοῖς ὡμιληκὼς ἔθνεσι νέος ὤν,
ὅτε μάλιστα ψυχῆς τυραννοῦσιν ἔρωτες,
ὑπερόπται νόμων, οὐκ ἐπεβούλευσε γάμοις
οὐδὲ διέστησε τοὺς ὑπὸ τῆς Ἥρας ἐζευγ-
μένους οὐδὲ συνετάραξε Διὸς γαμηλίου
θεσμὸν οὐδ' ἐξ ὧν ἄλλους ἠδίκει τὰς ἡδονὰς
ἐπλήρωσεν, ἀλλ' ἐν ταῖς ἀφειμέναις εἰς
Ἀφροδίτης ἐξουσίαν τὰς τῆς φύσεως ἐκού-
φιζεν ἀνάγκας, εἰπέ μοι, τούτοις εἰ τὸν ἄνθρωπον
ἐσέμνυνον, ἆρ' ἂν ἐδόκουν ἀγνοεῖν ἐγκωμίων
ὁδοὺς ἢ ψυχῆς ἀρετὴν ἱκανῶς δεικνύειν; 62. καὶ
γὰρ εἰ μὲν φιλοσοφεῖν ἔφασκεν Ἀριστοφάνης καὶ
περὶ τῶν ἐν οὐρανῷ σκοπεῖν καὶ τὰ θεῖα ταῦτα δὴ
μετεχειρίζετο, γεωμετρίαν, ἀστρονομίαν, μουσικήν,
ἀριθμούς, τὸν Πλάτωνα, τὸν Πυθαγόραν, καὶ
καταδεδουλῶσθαι τὰς ἡδονὰς ἔλεγε καὶ πολὺ τῶν
ἄλλων ἡγεῖτο διαφέρειν, εἰκότως ἂν ἐπετιμᾶτο
χείρων τοῦ προσήκοντος δεικνύμενος· εἰ δὲ εἷς ἐστι
τῶν ῥητορικῶν ἤ, εἰ βούλει γε, στρατιωτῶν, τί ἄν
τις παρ' αὐτῷ ζητοίη τὰ τοῦ ἱεροφάντου, δέον
ἐπαινεῖν εἰ ταῖς ἐννόμοις ἠρκέσθη μίξεσιν; 63.
ἐγὼ μὲν γὰρ οὐδ' ἱερὰ τῶν κειμένων ἀνοικοδομεῖν
R 447 ὑπὸ ταῖς τοῦδε | φροντίσι φαίην ἂν πλημμελές.
ὁρῶ γὰρ οὐκ ὀλίγων τῶν νῦν ἐπ' ἐκείνων τεταγ-
μένων τόνδε σωφρονέστερον καὶ | οὐδένα τῶν F
θεῶν ὑβρισμένον ἀπεληλακότα τῆς ἐπιμελείας
οὐδένα. 64. ἀλλ' ἐφ' ἃ μὲν Ἀριστοφάνει χρῆσθαι

---

[a] Libanius recognizes the higher prestige accorded to
philosophy as the most exclusive vocation of later paganism.
This is appropriately tactful when presented to such a
fervent admirer of philosophy as Julian, whose final compli-

138

and is acquainted with many provinces. He is a young man, at an age when the sexual desires that ride rough-shod over convention hold sway in the soul, yet he has not intrigued against the married state, nor separated any whom Hera has united; nor has he disturbed the ordinance of Zeus, lord of wedlock, nor satisfied his pleasures by doing wrong to others, but he has relieved the demands of nature with women dedicated to the governance of Aphrodite,"—if I had made such claims for him, tell me, would I seem to be ignorant of the paths of panegyric or to be giving ample demonstration of his moral fibre? 62. If Aristophanes had claimed to be a philosopher, investigating the heavens and treating of such divine subjects as geometry, astronomy, music, number, Plato and Pythagoras, if he asserted that he had his desires under complete control and regarded himself as far superior to any one else, such a charge would be justified, for he would be proved below the required standard.[a] If, however, his sphere is rhetoric or, if you like, officialdom, why should conduct befitting a high priest be expected of him? He deserves commendation for contenting himself with such intercourse as is lawful. 63. I would venture to assert, indeed, that it would be not improper for our ruined temples to be restored by his contriving. I see his conduct to be more decorous than that of many who are now in charge of them,[b] and he has not dismissed from his consideration a single one of our violated gods. 64. As I have said, Sire, consider

ment to Libanius (*Or* 1. 131) emphasizes the general rule of the duality between these professions.

[b] As also did Julian : *cf.* the qualifications required of his priests (*E.L.F.* No. 89 b, pp. 288 c ff.).

LIBANIUS

βέλτιον, αὐτός, ὅπερ ἔφην, ἤδη βουλεύσῃ, σκληρὰν
δὲ αὐτῷ τὴν τύχην ἐπικειμένην καὶ κατενεγκοῦσαν
εἰς πᾶν ταπεινότητος διάλλαξον, πρὸς Διός, ὦ
βασιλεῦ, καὶ ποίησον ἡμερωτέραν, χεῖρα ὄρεξον
ἀνδρὶ πεπονηκότι, λόγων ἡμμένῳ, μεμνημένῳ,
Πειρήνης τροφίμῳ Δωριεῖ, Κορινθίῳ, Χαρίτων
μνήμονι, φίλων ἐπιμελεῖ, τὴν ἐκ τοῦ τοὺς θεοὺς
ἀτιμάζειν οὐ δεξαμένῳ τιμήν. 65. πόσου ποτ᾽
ἂν ἐπρίατο Γεώργιος ἐκεῖνος αὐτομολοῦντα τοῦτον
ἰδεῖν καὶ στάντα ἐπὶ τοῦ βήματος ὅθεν ἐκεῖνοι τὰς
R 448 γραῦς δημαγωγοῦσιν, ἐξειπεῖν | καὶ διασῦραι τὰ
ἀπόρρητα τῶν δαιμόνων, τὰ τῆς Ἰνοῦς, τὰ τοῦ
παιδός, τὰ Καβείρων, τὰ Δήμητρος; ποίαν οὐκ
ἂν προῦπιεν Αἴγυπτον ἀντὶ ταύτης τῆς κωμῳδίας;
παρὰ τίσιν οὐκ ἂν εὐνούχοις τὸν ἄνθρωπον ἀπέφηνεν ἰσχυρόν; ἧπτετ᾽ ἄν, εὖ ἴσθι, καὶ τῆς Κωνσταντίου κεφαλῆς, εἰ τὴν ἑαυτοῦ κεφαλὴν πρὸς
Γεώργιον ἤρειδεν. | 66. ἀλλ᾽ οὔτ᾽ ἀρχῆς οὔτε F
χρημάτων οὔτ᾽ ἀσφαλείας οὔτ᾽ ἐλπίδων ἀπέδοτο τὰ
κάλλιστα τῶν Ἑλληνικῶν, ἀλλὰ κἂν ταῖς κρίσεσιν
αὐταῖς ὁπότε δεήσειεν ὅρκου τοὺς θεοὺς ὤμνυ
φυλάττων ἀκριβέστερον ἀνδρὸς Σπαρτιάτου τάξιν,
οὐ πεπεισμένος μὲν ὡς σωθήσεται, νομίζων δὲ
καλὸν τὴν εὐσέβειαν ἐντάφιον. 67. εἶθ᾽ ᾧ τὸ
κινδυνεύειν κουφότερον τῆς μεταβολῆς, οὐδὲν ἐκ
τῶν νῦν καιρῶν ἔσται τὸ ἆθλον, ἀλλὰ περιόψει
ποιοῦντα τοῦθ᾽ ὃ ποιεῖν ἔγνωκεν, εἰ μὴ βοηθήσεις;
τί δὲ τοῦτο ἔστιν; εἰς πλοῖον ἐμβὰς πλανᾶσθαι

---

ᵃ George of Cappadocia, Arian bishop of Alexandria
usurping the seat of the exiled Athanasius and enjoying
140

for yourself how best to treat Aristophanes: remove the harsh fate that has befallen him and brought him to the depths of misery, and, in heaven's name, make it more bearable. Stretch out your protecting hand to a man who is in sore straits, a man wedded to learning, an initiate, a nurseling of Peirene, a Dorian, a Corinthian, mindful of the Graces, who has regard for his friends and has never won honour by dishonouring the gods. 65. How much do you think that fellow Georgius [a] would have given to see him desert his post and stand at the platform where such as they harangue the old crones, traducing the secrets of the gods, of Ino and her son, of the Cabeiri, or Demeter? Would he not have pledged him the whole of Egypt in return for such an entertainment? Would he not have made him a man of might among all those eunuchs? Rest assured that, if he had inclined himself towards Georgius, he would have embraced the cause of Constantius too. 66. Yet not for office or wealth or security or ambition did he barter all that is best of the heritage of Greece. Even in the actual trials, whenever he had to take the oath, he swore by our gods and stayed at his post more steadfastly than any Spartan, not won over by hopes of safety but regarding his piety as a noble memorial. 67. To him danger was less of an evil than a change of front. Is he then to have no reward from the present state of things? Will you ignore him as he embarks upon the course he has determined for himself if you refuse to assist him? That is, to board ship and sail

high favour under Constantius, was lynched at the first news of the emperor's death by the Alexandrian mob (24th Dec. A.D. 361). His conduct towards both orthodox and pagans had been highly provocative: Amm. Marc. 22. 11. 5 ff., Socr. *H.E.* 3. 2, Sozom. *H.E.* 5. 7, Julian, *E.L.F.* No. 141.

R 449 διανοεῖται | περὶ τὴν Ἰταλίαν, περὶ τὴν Λιβύην περὶ τὴν ἔξω θάλατταν. ἐπιστρέφει[1] δὲ αὐτὸν οὐδέν, οὐ παιδίον αἰσθανόμενον ἐπῶν, οὐ γυνὴ σώφρων, οὐ σήματα[2] προγόνων, οὐ θανάτου φόβος, οὐκ εἰ τὴν ψυχὴν ἐν ξένων ἀφήσει χερσίν, οὐκ εἰ τεθνεὼς ἄταφος κείσεται. τούτων γὰρ ἁπάντων ἡγεῖται πικρότερον εἶναι τὸ στένειν οἴκοι.

68. Σὸν τοίνυν, ὦ βασιλεῦ, μεταστῆσαι τὴν ψῆφον καὶ ποιῆσαι γλυκίω μὲν αὐτῷ τὴν πατρίδα, ποθεινὴν δὲ τὴν γυναῖκα, πλείστου δὲ ἀξίαν τὴν τοῦ παιδὸς θέαν, ὃς ζῶντος ἔτι τοῦ πατρὸς πέπονθε τὰ τῶν ὀρφανῶν | καὶ τὰ μέλλοντα φοβερώτερα. F προέεισι μὲν εἰς ἡλικίαν, δέος δὲ μὴ προσαγάγῃ τις μηχανήν, μήτηρ δὲ οἰκουροῦσα πρὸς τὰς ἔξω πάγας οὐκ ἂν ἀμύνοι, γνῶμαι δὲ παίδων εὐπαράγωγοι, δεῖ δὲ πατρός. 69. ἀπόδος τοίνυν, ὦ βασιλεῦ, τῷ νέῳ τὸν ὀφθαλμὸν τοῦ γεννήτορος καὶ γενοῦ σωφροσύνης αἴτιος. μὴ πλείτω πρὸς τὰ πέρατα τῆς γῆς Ἀριστοφάνης μετὰ δακρύων ἀλλὰ βαδιζέτω μετ᾽ εὐφροσύνης πρὸς τὸ τοῦ Πέλοπος χωρίον. ἐν μέσῃ Πελοποννήσῳ διηγείσθω τὰς σὰς ἀρετάς, ἔχει γλῶτταν ἀρκοῦσαν τοῖς ἔργοις, λεγέτω πρὸς τοὺς Ἕλληνας ἐν οἷς ζῆς καθ᾽ ἡμέραν ἃ τεθέαται. πορευέσθω μηνυτὴς τῶν πολλῶν καὶ μεγαλοπρεπῶν θυσιῶν ὧν τὰς μὲν R 450 ἡ πόλις | ἐδέξατο, τὰς δὲ ἡ Δάφνη, τὰς δὲ τὸ ὄρος, ἀγέλας ἐσφαγμένας, αἵματος ῥύακας, εὐωδίαν εἰς αὐτὸν ἀνατρέχουσαν αἰθέρα. εὐξάσθων ὅμοια καὶ

---

[1] ἐπιστρέφει Re. (mss.) : ἐπιστρέψει F.
[2] σήματα F. (PIV) : σχήματα Re. (other mss.).

round Italy, Libya and the outer ocean. Nothing deters him—not his son, now gaining his first acquaintance with the poets, not his faithful wife, nor the tombs of his ancestors, nor the fear of death, not the loss of his life at the hands of strangers nor the exposure of his unburied corpse. All this he thinks a fate less bitter than grieving at home.

68. So, Sire, it is for you to alter his decision, to make his country more pleasing to him, his wife more desirable, and the sight of his son all-important—his son, who has suffered an orphan's lot in his father's lifetime, and whose future is more forbidding still. He will advance to manhood, but it is to be feared that some trickery will be brought against him, and his mother, though managing at home, will not be able to protect him from snares outside. The minds of children are easily swayed, and he needs a father's care.[a] 69. Then, Sire, give back to the lad a father's eye and be responsible for his good behaviour. Do not let Aristophanes sail tearfully to the ends of the earth, but let him go on his way rejoicing to the land of Pelops. In the heart of the Peloponnese let him glorify your virtues,—he has eloquence enough for the task—and let him tell the Greeks, among whom you spend your daily life, of all that he has seen. Let him go to inform them of the many glorious sacrifices performed here in the city, in Daphne, and on the mountain.[b] Let him tell of the herds of victims slain, of the streams of blood that flow, and of the sweet savour that rises aloft to the very heavens. Let them

[a] Libanius here addresses Julian in the light of the personal experience of them both.

[b] From this passage it does not appear that the temple of Apollo had yet been burned down (22 October A.D. 362): for Zeus Cassius cf. Or. 18. 172 f.

# LIBANIUS

παρὰ σφίσιν ἰδεῖν ἐν Δελφοῖς, ἐν Πίσῃ, παρ'
Ἀθηναίοις, παρὰ τοῖς τοῦδε πολίταις, πανταχοῦ
τῆς Ἑλλάδος, κατ' ἤπειρον, ἐν νήσοις. 70. ταῦτα
μὲν καὶ αὐτὸς εὔχομαι καὶ μετασχεῖν γε τῆς
πορείας ἐκείνης. ὡς καλὸν ἐπ' Ἐλευσῖνος ἰδεῖν
μύστην Ἡρακλεῖ παρισούμενον καὶ τοῦτον αὐτὸν
Ἀριστοφάνην ὑπὲρ τοὺς ἄλλους πηδῶντα.

71. Τί φής, ὦ βασιλεῦ; πείθομεν ἢ ληροῦμεν;
ἤδη ψηφίζου τοσοῦτον προενθυμηθεὶς ὡς οὐ λήσει
τοὺς | ὄντας ἀνθρώπους οὔθ' ὁ λόγος οὔθ' ἡ ψῆφος. F
ἦν οὖν ἐρραψῳδηκέναι δόξω, τὸ μὲν ἐμὸν οὐ
πολλῆς φροντίδος, σκόπει δὲ αὐτὸς εἰ μηδὲν σοὶ
βλάβος τὸ δοκεῖν οὐκ εὖ φρονεῖν, ὃν περὶ πολλοῦ
ποιῇ.

---

[a] As a result of this oration, Aristophanes obtained an
office which Seeck identified as that of proconsul of Achaïa.
However, it is known that Praetextatus was appointed to
that position by Julian, and the suggestion is unlikely.

pray to see the like there also, in Delphi, Pisa, Athens, Corinth, and everywhere in Greece, both on continent and island. 70. This is also my own prayer, and I pray to take part in that journey. How fine a sight it would be to see at Eleusis an initiate who is the peer of Heracles, and Aristophanes excelling all the rest in his transports of delight.

71. Well, Sire? Do I win my point or am I talking nonsense? Make your decision now, in the foreknowledge that neither the plea nor the verdict will go unnoticed by men of real worth. If I be held to have composed a tissue of lies, my reputation is not of much consequence: but consider for yourself, whether anyone whom you value can, without harm to yourself, be thought to be in the wrong.[a]

Aristophanes showed a commendable loyalty to Julian's memory, and in A.D. 364 was already engaged in compiling a collection of his works (*Ep.* 1264). Bidez-Cumont suggest that the mss. tradition may ultimately be derived from this work of piety.

# ORATION 15

R 451    1. Ἦλθες,[1] Τηλέμαχε, γλυκερὸν φάος.
μέχρι τούτου μοι τῷ ἔπει χρηστέον, τὰ δὲ ἐφεξῆς
Εὐμαίῳ μὲν ἥρμοττεν εἰπεῖν, ἐμοὶ δὲ οὐκέτι, ἐπεὶ
καὶ ὄψεσθαί σε ἐφάμην καὶ νενικηκότα καὶ
ταῦτα ἃ πάντες ᾄδουσι δεδυνημένον.    2. εὖ γὰρ
ἴσθι πᾶσαν μὲν γνώμην, πᾶσαν δὲ γλῶτταν ἐπὶ
σαυτὸν ἀπὸ τῶν πρὶν ὑμνουμένων μεταστήσας,
καὶ οὔτε τὰ πρὸ τῶν Τρωικῶν | οὔτ' αὐτὸς οὗτος F 1
ὁ δεκέτης πόλεμος οὔτε τὸ γενόμενον ἐν τῇ
θαλάττῃ πρὸς τὸν τοῦ νῦν Πέρσου πρόγονον τοῖς
R 452 Ἕλλησιν | ἔργον οὔτε ἃ Ἀλέξανδρος ἐκλελυμένοις
προσπεσὼν ἔπραξε, τούτων οὐδὲν οὐδενὸς ἀνθρώπων κατέχει τὴν ψυχὴν οὐδὲ τὴν φωνήν, ἀλλὰ
πάντες πάντων ὡς μικρῶν ἀφέμενοι τῶν παρόντων
ἔχονται καὶ χαίρουσιν ἀκούοντές τε καὶ λέγοντες
ὁ μὲν τόλμαν, ὁ δὲ εἰσβολήν, ὁ δὲ διάπλουν, ὁ δὲ
τοὺς ἐν χερσὶ πεσόντας, ὁ δὲ καθέδρας, σοφίσματα,
ἀγῶνας.

    3. Ὑπὲρ μὲν οὖν τούτων μεγάλη τοῖς θεοῖς ἡ
χάρις, οἵ σε ἐπόρευσάν τε πρὸς τὸν βάρβαρον καὶ

---

[1] ἦλθες C, corrected from ἤλυθες PI : ἤλυθες AUVBM.
Thomas Magister (s.v. μεταξύ, p. 239. 13 R) quoted Ἦλθες
Τηλέμαχε as the beginning of the speech.

# THE EMBASSY TO JULIAN[a]

1. "You have come, Telemachus, sweet light of my eyes."[b] So far I may quote the verse. In what follows, the words would be appropriate to Eumaeus but not to me, for " I did think to see you again," victorious and endowed with this majesty that all men acclaim. 2. For rest assured that you have concentrated upon yourself from previous objects of renown the attention and the eloquence of everyone : events before the Trojan War, that ten-year struggle itself, the naval achievements of the Greeks against the ancestor of the present king of Persia, the deeds of Alexander in his attack upon them after their liberation—nothing of these exercises the imagination or the voice of any man.[c] Everyone rejects all this as so much triviality, clings to the present, and delights to hear or tell of your daring, your invasion, your crossing, of battle casualties, of ambush, stratagem and affray.[d]

3. For all this, then, we offer our hearty thanks to the gods who dispatched you against the barbarian,

[a] *Oration* 15.
[b] Homer, *Od.* 16. 23 ; 17. 41. *Cf.* Julian, *E.L.F.* No. 188 (376 d).
[c] Stock subjects of declamation in the Second Sophistic.
[d] This oration was composed after Julian's departure for the Persian campaign and upon receipt of news of his initial success in Mesopotamia.

κρείττω τῶν ἐναντίων ἔδειξαν καὶ πάλιν ἀπέσωσαν,
εὔχομαι δὲ τοῖς αὐτοῖς θεοῖς καὶ ἐμοὶ δοῦναι
κρατῆσαι τήμερον καὶ μὴ καταγέλαστον ἐνθένδε
ἀπελθεῖν. κρατήσαιμι δ' ἄν, εἰ πείσαιμί σε, μᾶλλον δέ, εἰ πείσαιμι, σὸν ἔσται τὸ κράτος τοῦ
παύσαντος τὸν θυμόν. 4. καὶ οὕτω δὴ νίκην νίκῃ
συνάψεις τῇ διὰ τῶν ὅπλων τὴν ἀπὸ τῆς | ἡμερότη-  **F 1**
τος, ἣν ἔπεμψέ με νῦν αἰτήσοντα πόλις ἀτυχής, εἰ
δὲ βούλει, προπετής, πόλις ἐπὶ μὲν τοῖς σοῖς
τροπαίοις ἡδομένη, ταῖς δ' αὑτῆς αἰτίαις αἰσχυνο-
μένη. 5. πεποίηκε δέ μοι τὴν χειροτονίαν οὔτε τὸ
γένει τῶν ἄλλων διαφέρειν οὔτε τὸ χρόνῳ προήκειν
οὐδὲ πλῆθος λειτουργιῶν οὐδὲ τὸ μὴ δύνασθαι τοὺς
ἄλλους λέγειν· εἰσὶ γάρ, εἰσὶν ἡμῖν ἄνδρες ἐν
παιδεύσει καὶ λόγοις τεθραμμένοι καὶ περὶ πραγμάτων ἱκανοὶ διαλεχθῆναι. 6. ἀλλ' ἐπὶ ταύτην με
τὴν πρεσβείαν κατέστησε πρῶτον μὲν τὰ τοῖς
διδασκάλοις ὑπὸ τῶν ὡμιληκότων ὀφειλόμενα χρέα·
πεπείκασι γὰρ αὐτοὺς ὡς ἐμὸς σὺ μαθητής, οὐκ
ἐμοῦ ταῦτα ἀλαζονευσαμένου πρὸς τὴν πόλιν, ἀλλ'
ἡ τῶν λόγων ὁμοιότης τὴν δόξαν ταύτην εἰσήγαγε
R 453 καὶ | οὐδ' ἂν οἱ χρησμοὶ μεταβάλοιεν, ὡς οὐ πρὸς
ἐμὲ σὺ βλέπων τοιαῦτα δημιουργεῖς. 7. ἐν μὲν
τοῦτο τοὺς ἀνθρώπους περιέστησέ μοι καὶ παρέ-
στησεν ἐλπίδας, ὡς αἰδεσθήσῃ τὴν συγγένειαν τῶν
λόγων, ἕτερον δὲ ἃ τιμῶν διατετέλεκας θέρος ὅλον

---

[a] Embassies were normally undertaken as a civic duty
by members of the highest curial class (*principales*). Their
rhetorical prowess was indication of the high standard of
education in Antioch, upon which Libanius naturally dilates :
cf. *Or*. 11. 133 ff.

[b] Cf. *Or*. 18. 14 ff., where he claims to have been πατὴρ

revealed you supreme over your foes and brought
you home again safe. To the same gods I offer my
prayer to grant me victory today and not to let me
depart a laughing stock. And victory would be mine
if I were to convince you ; or rather, if I were to
convince you, yours will be the victory for abating
your anger. 4. In fact, in this way you will link to a
victory gained by force of arms one won by clemency,
and for this I have been sent now to plead by a city
which is unfortunate or, if you would have it so,
precipitate, a city which rejoices in your triumphs
and is ashamed of the charges made against her. 5.
My selection for this office has been caused not by
any superiority of birth or seniority in age, nor yet
by the number of my public duties or the inability of
the rest to present a case. We have, we have indeed,
men reared in culture and eloquence and capable of
discoursing on matters of state.[a] 6. The prime reason
for my appointment to this embassy is the indebted-
ness of pupils towards their teachers. My fellow
citizens have persuaded themselves that you are my
pupil. Not that I have made any such boast to them :
the resemblances in our literary styles have caused
this idea, and not even oracular responses would
alter their opinion that your literary compositions
are performed with an eye upon my own. 7. Such is
the first consideration that induced them to come to
me and caused them to hope that you would respect
our kinship in oratory.[b] Another is the honour you
have continued to bestow upon me throughout a
whole summer and winter by invitation, summons

τῶν λόγων to Julian in Nicomedeia, even though Julian was
barred from attending his lectures and obtained notes at
second-hand.

καὶ χειμῶνα καλῶν, μεταπεμπόμενος, ἐπιστέλλων,
λέγοντος ἡδόμενος, ἀχθόμενος σιγῶντος. οὐδὲ τὴν
ἀγρυπνίαν ἠγνόησαν ἣν ἐρεῖν ποτέ μου μέλλοντος
ἠγρύπνεις διὰ τὰς ἐν ταῖς τοιαύταις ἐπιδείξεσι
τύχας. 8. τά γε μὴν περὶ τοῦ σίτου, δι' ὃν ἔστιν[1]
ἡμῖν ἡ πόλις, εἰ γὰρ μὴ τότε ἐκεῖνον ἔδωκας
ἐγκαλῶν ὁμοῦ καὶ | σῴζων, νῦν ἂν κενὴ σωμάτων  F
ἡ πόλις εἰστήκει, ταύτης τοίνυν τηλικαύτης εὐεργεσίας ἐμοὶ τὴν χάριν ἐκέλευες ἀπελθόντας ἔχειν,
ὃ καὶ ἐποίουν ἥκοντες μακαρίζοντες ἐμὲ καὶ σφᾶς
αὐτούς, τῶν μὲν τιμῶν ἐμέ, τῆς δὲ βοηθείας
αὐτούς. οὐ τοίνυν ἔμελλον ταῦτα εἰδότες ἑτέρωθεν
μεταπέμψεσθαι τὸν πρεσβευτὴν οὐδ' ἀμνημονήσειν
τοῦ δακρύσαντος παρ' Ἀχιλλεῖ γέροντος, ὃν πρὸ
τῶν ἄλλων ἐπιτήδειον ἡγεῖτο διαλλάττειν ἕτερος
γέρων. 9. οἱ μὲν οὖν[2] εἰκότως ᾑροῦντο ἐμὲ νομίζοντες οὕτως ἢ τεύξεσθαι τούτων ἐφ' ἃ πέμπουσιν
R 454 ἤ, τό γε | δεύτερον, οὐ δώσειν αἰτίᾳ χώραν, ὡς
οὐ καλῶς εἶδον ὃν ἑλέσθαι χρῆν. ἐγὼ δὲ εὐθὺς
μὲν ἐξωμοσάμην, ὦ βασιλεῦ, καὶ πᾶν ποιήσειν
πρότερον ἔφην ἢ τοῦτο, μεμνημένος ὅτι μ' ἐκέλευες φεύγειν τὸν ὑπὲρ τῆς πόλεως λόγον ὡς οὔτ'
αὐτὸς ἐνδώσων οὔτ' ἐμοὶ καλῶς ἔχον ἄπρακτον
ἀπελθεῖν. 10. προσκαθημένων δὲ ἀνθρώπων πολιτῶν καὶ συμφοιτητῶν καὶ συγγενῶν καὶ στενόντων
καὶ θρηνούντων καὶ διεξιόντων ἄθλους τῶν ἐμῶν
ὑπὲρ τῆς πόλεως προγόνων καὶ δεικνύντων |

---

[1] ὃν ἔστιν F.: ὃν ἔστιν Re. (mss.).
[2] οὖν F. (V): om. Re. (other mss.).

---

[a] For a similar emphasis on literary interests as the basis
of his relations with Julian in Antioch cf. Or. 1. 121 ff.

and correspondence, by your pleasure when I spoke and disappointment when I did not.[a] Nor are they unaware of the sleepless nights you spent, previous to the delivery of my orations, because of the vicissitudes that attend such declamations. 8. Moreover, with regard to the allocation of corn, the means by which our city still exists,[b]—for had you not made your grant then and saved us, despite your disapproval, it would now stand emptied of its inhabitants—you bade them go and show thanks to me for such consideration. And so they did, for they came and congratulated me upon the honour done me and themselves upon the assistance they received. Aware of all this, they were not likely to summon an envoy from elsewhere, nor to forget the old man weeping by Achilles' side whom another old man considered the most suitable person of all to effect a reconciliation.[c] 9. Their choice of me was natural. They thought that they would in this way succeed in their mission or, failing that, at least leave no room for accusations of ignorance as to where their choice should have lain. My first reaction, Sire, was to refuse: I would do anything rather than this, I said, for I remembered your injunction to me to refrain from pleading the city's cause, since you would not relent and I did not deserve to emerge unsuccessful.[d] 10. But I was besieged by my fellow citizens, my old schoolfellows and kinsmen. They, with tears and lamentation, recounted the labours of my forebears on the city's behalf: they pointed to the tombs of

[b] *Cf.* Julian, *Misop.* 369 a ff., Amm. Marc. 22. 13. 4.

[c] Homer, *Iliad*, 9. 162 ff. (Phoenix and Nestor).

[d] *Cf.* Julian's final words to the Antiochene embassy after his departure on campaign : *Or.* 1. 132 ; Jul. *E.L.F.* No. 98 (399 c).

LIBANIUS

τάφους μητρός, πατρὸς καὶ ἔτι τῶν ἀνωτέρω καὶ F
τῶν πάλαι καὶ τῶν πρῴην οἰχομένων νομίσας, ὦ
βασιλεῦ, μετὰ τούτων ἐκείνους παρεστάναι καὶ τὰ
μὲν ἱκετεύειν, τὰ δὲ τῇ μελλήσει μέμφεσθαι, τὰ
μὲν αἰσχυνθείς, τὰ δὲ δείσας Ἐρινῦς, ἃς ἀγανακτεῖν δεῖ νομίζειν πατρίδος ἀμελουμένης, ὥσπερ
ἀμέλει τοκέων, καὶ πρὸ τούτων τὴν σὴν γνώμην
φοβηθείς, μή με ἡγήσῃ θηριώδη καὶ δυσσεβῆ καὶ
τῶν τιμιωτάτων προδότην, ὑπὲρ[1] τούτων ἁπάντων
ἐπείσθην ἤ, τό γε ἀληθέστερον, ἠναγκάσθην ὑπα-
κοῦσαι κλάουσιν. 11. ἀλλὰ τί με ποιεῖν ἐχρῆν;
ἀπελαύνειν δεομένους; μὴ δοκεῖν ἀκούειν λεγόντων; μὴ δοκεῖν ὁρᾶν παρόντας; περιχυθέντων
ἀποπηδᾶν; εἰς ἀγρὸν ἐλαύνειν; ἐρήμους ἐᾶν
ἄνωθέν τε ταῦτα ἐφορῶντος ἡλίου καὶ γῆς δια-
στῆναι δυναμένης; 12. καὶ τίς ἂν ἦν εὐπρόσωπος
λόγος τοσαύτῃ κακίᾳ; ὅτι τραχὺς ὁ βασιλεὺς καὶ
δυσχερὴς τὸν τρόπον καὶ δίκας εἰδὼς λαμβάνειν
παρρησίας; ἀλλ' ᾔδεσάν μου τὴν ὑπὲρ αὐτῶν
R 455 τούτων πρὸς σὲ παρρησίαν ἀπὸ | δείλης πρωίας
μέχρι μέσων πολλάκις προελθοῦσαν νυκτῶν, ἐφ'
ᾗ τῶν μὲν φίλων τινὲς δείσαντες ὡς ἂν ἐκβαινούσῃ
τὸ μέτρον ἐπεῖχον, σὺ δὲ ἐκείνους ἐπεῖχες μὴ
ταῦτα ποιεῖν νομίζων εἶναι βασιλικὸν καὶ τῆς σῆς
αὐλῆς ἄξιον οὐ τὸ σιγώντων κρατεῖν, ἀλλὰ τὸ φερόντων εἰς μέσον ἃ φρονοῦσι περιεῖναι. 13. τοσ-

[1] ὑπὲρ Re. (CAPU ; corrected from ὑπὸ M, into ὑπὸ B) :
ὑπὸ F. (VI).

[a] Libanius' uncle, Phasganius, and his mother had both
died in autumn A.D. 359 : *Ep.* 96, *Or.* 1. 117. For his
parentage, *Or.* 1. 3 ff.

154

my mother, my father and their ancestors before them, of the long dead and the recently departed,[a] and I felt, Sire, that these too were present in their company, united with them in their pleas and reproaching me for my hesitation. So partly in shame, partly in fear of the avenging Furies, whose anger I must think is roused at any lack of patriotism, let alone of filial piety, and fearing, even more than them, the opinion you might hold of me, that you might think me brutal, impious and traitor to all that I hold dear,[b]—in view of all this, I was induced or, more correctly, was compelled to lend an ear to their complaints. 11. What else should I have done? Drive them away as they presented their pleas? Pretend not to hear what they said, not to see them before me? Start away from them as they came crowding round me and drive off to my estate? Leave them in the lurch, while ever the sun above observed it and earth could yawn? 12. What specious excuse could there be for baseness so great? The emperor's harshness and sour temper? His habit of punishing independence of speech? Yet they knew that I had employed such independence before you, often from early afternoon until midnight on their very own behalf, though some of your friends feared that I was going beyond all reason and tried to stop me, while you stopped them from doing so.[c] You regard it a sign of majesty and a credit to your court not to rule over men who refuse to speak their minds but to excel those who openly voice their opinions.[c] 13. So, with

[b] By choice of vocabulary here Libanius implies the existence of strong Christian opposition to Julian's policies among the *curiales* of Antioch.

[c] *Cf. Or.* 1. 126.

# LIBANIUS

αὐτῆς | τοίνυν ἀδείας ἀνεῳγμένης τῇ παρρησίᾳ τῷ F
σιγᾶν οὐδαμόθεν ἀπολογία. ἄνδρα δὲ ᾧ χαίρεις
καὶ ὃν ἐν τοῖς ἑταίροις ἠρίθμηκας, ἐξελεγχθῆναι
πονηρὸν καὶ μιαρὸν καὶ ὠμὸν καὶ βάρβαρον οὐδ᾽
ἂν σοὶ καλῶς εἶχεν, ὦ βασιλεῦ.

14. Διὰ ταῦτα ἥκω πρεσβεύων καί σου δέομαι
μὴ μεταξὺ λέγοντος ἀπαντᾶν μηδὲ τὴν ἄμαχον
ἐκείνην τῶν λόγων ῥώμην ἀντεξάγειν τοῖς ἐμοῖς.
δεῖ γάρ σε τήμερον χρηστὸν φανῆναι μᾶλλον ἢ
ῥητορικόν· ἃ δὲ δέομαί τε καὶ ὧν ἀξιοῦμεν τυχεῖν,
μίμησαι σαυτόν, ὦ βασιλεῦ, καὶ ποίησον τῇ
προτέρᾳ καθέδρᾳ τὴν δευτέραν παραπλησίαν. 15.
ἔστης παρ᾽ ἡμῖν ἀπὸ τῆς ἑσπέρας ἐλαύνων·
στῆθι καὶ νῦν ἀπὸ τῶν νενικημένων ἀναστρέφων.
παλαιὸν βασιλέων χειμάδιον ἡ πόλις. μεινάτω
τοίνυν ὁ περὶ τὸν χειμῶνα νόμος. 16. κάλλη μὲν
ἡμῖν οὐκ ἔστιν οἰκοδομημάτων, οὐ γὰρ εἴασεν ἡ
R 456 πάλαι Περσῶν ὕβρις πῦρ ἐπιφέρουσα | τοῖς
ἀνθισταμένοις, ἔστι[1] δὲ πολὺ τὸ οἰκούμενον ἀπο-
χρῶν καὶ πολίταις καὶ μετοίκοις καὶ ξένοις καὶ
βασιλεῖ καὶ | στρατοπέδῳ, τέχναι δὲ παντοῖαι καὶ F
πλῆθος ἐμπόρων καὶ πηγαὶ καὶ ποταμὸς καὶ
χειμὼν πρᾷος καὶ θέρος ἄλυπον καὶ γῆ πάντα
πολλὰ φέρουσα τῶν παρὰ τοῦ Διός, εἰ τύχοι. 17.
εἰς ἃ μοι δοκεῖτε βλέψαντες ὑμεῖς οἱ βασιλεῖς ἐν
τοῖς πρὸς τοὺς βαρβάρους πολέμοις τῇδε χειμά-

---

[1] ἔστι F. : ἔτι Re. (mss.).

[a] Cf. Aristoph. Ach. 440.
[b] Julian had threatened to use Tarsus as his winter quarters upon his return from the Persian campaign, so showing his disapproval of Antioch : cf. Or. 1. 132, 16. 53, Amm. Marc. 23. 2. 5.

156

such freedom open to frankness, there is no possible
excuse for silence. For a man whose company you
enjoy, whom you count as one of your friends, to be
proved base, despicable, brutal and uncivilized, would
be no credit to you either, Sire.

14. Hence I have come as their envoy, and I beg
of you not to engage me in debate while I am still
delivering my address: do not array the relentless
force of your eloquence against what I have to say,
for "today you must show yourself a man of merit"
rather than of eloquence.[a] The request I make, and
which I hope to obtain, is that you follow your own
lead, Sire, and make your residence here a second
time, as you did your first.[b] 15. On your march from
the west, you stayed with us. Stay with us now also
on your return from your triumphs. Our city has of
old been the winter quarters of our emperors. Then
let the custom of wintering here remain unimpaired.
16. We may have no noble buildings—the age-old
insolence of the Persians that fired all that stood
in its path has seen to that [c]—but we have a large
domain sufficient to maintain our citizens, permanent
residents and visitors from abroad, an emperor and
his army: we have industry of every kind and large
numbers of tradespeople, springs of water, a river,
a climate mild in winter and temperate in summer,
and a soil that gives rich yield of all that Zeus may
grant if he so pleases.[d] 17. You emperors, I feel, have
borne this in mind when you spend your winters here
during your campaigns against the barbarian, for our

---

[c] *Cf. Or.* 24. 38 and note.

[d] A résumé of the praises of Antioch as expressed in *Or.*
11. These same arguments are adduced in a similar situation in A.D. 387, when Antioch once again had disgraced
herself: *cf. Or.* 19. 51 ff.

ζειν, ὡς ἀρκούσης τῆς πόλεως ἀνασχέσθαι τὸν
ὄγκον τοῦ πράγματος, τὰς δ᾽ ἄλλας καὶ διατρέ-
χοντες θορυβεῖτε μὴ δυναμένας ἐνεγκεῖν τὸ φορτίον. ἡ μὲν γὰρ ἔοικεν ὁλκάδι μυριοφόρῳ μεγάλῃ
καὶ ἰσχυρᾷ, τὰς δ᾽ εἰκάσαις ἂν ἀκατίοις, οἷς πλέον
ἄχθος εἰ φιλονεικήσαις ἐνθεῖναι, κατέδυσας. 18.
νῦν οὖν ἥκομεν ὡς χάριν αἰτοῦντες τὴν λειτουργίαν
ζημίαν ἡγούμενοι τὴν περὶ ταῦτα ἀνάπαυσιν. ἐν
γὰρ τῷ¹ πάλαι μελέτην εἰληφέναι τοῦ πράγματος
ποθοῦμεν βασιλέως καθέδραν, ὥσπερ αἱ τίτθαι τὸν
περὶ τὰ παιδία πόνον τοῦ χρόνου προϊόντος ἐν
ἡδονῇ τίθενται κἂν ἡ τιτθεία λάβῃ τέλος δακρύουσιν. 19. εἰ μὲν οὖν ἐξ οὐρίων ἡμῖν τὸ κλέος
ἔτρεχεν, οὔτ᾽ ἂν ἕτερον εὐτρέπιστό σοι χωρίον
R 457 οὔτ᾽ ἂν λόγων ἔδει τοῖς ἀφιγμένοις, ἀλλ᾽ | ἃ τῶν
συνηδομένων ἐστὶ φθεγξάμενοι καὶ τῇ τοῦ δήμου
φωνῇ τὰ εἰωθότα χρησάμενοι σὺν χορείᾳ καὶ
κρότῳ καὶ σκιρτήμασιν ἤγομεν ἄν σε πρὸς τὸ
ἄστυ· | ἐπειδὴ δὲ πέπτωκεν εἰς χείρω δόξαν τὰ F
ἡμέτερα καὶ δοκοῦμεν οὐ προθύμως ὑπουργηκέναι
καὶ τὰ μὲν ἐρρᾳθυμηκέναι, τὰ δ᾽ ἐξεπίτηδες
ἠναντιῶσθαι καί, τὸ πάντων δεινότατον, ὠρχῆσθαι
κακῶς καὶ πανήγυρίν τινα πεποιῆσθαι πρόφασιν
πονηροῦ δρόμου, λείπεται λόγῳ βοηθεῖν τοῖς εἰς
τοιαύτας αἰτίας ἥκουσιν.

20. Ἐρῶ δ᾽ οὐχ ἃ λεγόντων ἀκήκοα προστιθέν-
των ὀδυρμοὺς τοῖς λόγοις. τίνα δὴ ταῦτα ἃ παρα-
λείπω; τίς ἡμῖν ἀδίκημά τι σύνοιδε; παριὼν² δει-
κνύτω καὶ τὸ διαβάλλειν ἀφεὶς ἐξελεγχέτω. τί

¹ ἐν γὰρ τῷ Re. (mss.) : ἐκ γὰρ τοῦ F.

158

city is capable of bearing the burden this imposes.
Even when you pass through other towns, you set
them at sixes and sevens, for they cannot take such a
strain. Our city is like a huge merchantman, sturdy
and strong ; them you may liken to so many rowing
boats, and you sink them if you insist on overloading
them. 18. So now we come to request that we be
favoured with this duty, for we feel that its cessation
is our loss. Long experienced in the job, we desire
our emperor's residence among us : we are like
nurses who, as time goes on, regard their duties towards their charges as a pleasure and burst into tears
if ever their nursing comes to an end. 19. If our
fame had been sped by favourable winds,[a] there
would have been no other place made ready to welcome you and no need for us to come and plead.
With cries of gladness and the usual acclamation from
the common folk, dancing, applauding, high stepping,
we would escort you into the town. However, we
have fallen into disrepute : we are held to have shown
no zeal in your service and to have been either careless or deliberately opposed to you, and, worst of all,
to have put on a shocking dance and turned a religious
holiday into an excuse for a disreputable racing
entertainment,[b] and in consequence I must plead for
a people involved in such accusations.

20. I will leave unsaid the remarks I have heard
them make with their voices choked with tears. I
leave aside statements such as these : " Who knows
of any wrong that we have done? Come out and show
it. Put aside slander and prove it. Of what neglect,

[a] Cf. Soph. Aj. 1083.
[b] Cf. Julian's complaints against Antioch, Misop. 346 b ff.

---

² παριὼν Re., F. : παρὼν mss.

μὲν ὠλιγωρήθη; τί δὲ ἐπεβουλεύθη; τί μὲν
μαλακίᾳ προείθη; τί δὲ πονηρίᾳ διεφθάρη; 21.
βασιλεὺς μὲν εὖ ποιῶν ἐκόλασε τῶν ὠνίων τὰς τι-
μάς, ἡ γῆ δὲ περὶ τὰς γονὰς ὑπὸ τῶν αὐχμῶν
ἠδικημένη μετὰ ἀφθονίας οὐκ ἔσχε βεβαιῶσαι τὸν
νόμον, αἱ δὲ τῶν κερδῶν ὑπερβολαὶ κεκωλυμέναι τὰς
ἐμπορίας κατέλυσαν. ἡμεῖς δὲ τῶν λειτουργούν-
των ἐσμέν, οὐχὶ τῶν καπηλευόντων. οὐ ταύτην
ἐγὼ κομίζω τὴν ἀπολογίαν. ὅτου γὰρ ἂν καταγνῷς,
ὦ βασιλεῦ, καὶ παρ' ἐμοὶ τοῦτον ἡλωκέναι δεῖ, κἂν
εἴπῃς· Ὁ δεῖνα ἠδίκηκε, ταῦτα καὶ αὐτὸς ψηφίζο-
μαι. |

22. Πόθεν οὖν ἐξαιροῦμαι τῆς ὀργῆς καὶ τοῦ | F
R 458 κινδύνου τὴν πόλιν, ἣν οὐκ ἂν καλέσαιμι δικαίαν;
ἔστι τι παλαιὸν νόμιμον ὑπὸ θεῶν μὲν κατα-
πεμφθέν, ὑφ' Ἑλλήνων δὲ τιμηθέν, πολλοὺς δ'
ἐν δικαστηρίοις σεσωκός, ὃ μυριάκις αὐτὸς πεποίη-
κας κύριον. ἔφθης εἰπὼν τὴν συγγνώμην καὶ
ῥῆμα μέλλον ἐγνώρισας, οὗ τὸ ἔργον οὐκ ὀλιγάκις
ἔπραξας. 23. ἡμάρτομεν, ὁμολογοῦμεν, καὶ γεγό-
ναμεν τῆς σῆς βουλήσεως βραδύτεροι. οἱ μὲν
ἡμῶν ἀμβλύτερον τοὺς σιτοποιοὺς ἐφύλαξαν, οἱ δὲ
ὅλως ἐκαθεύδησαν, οἱ δὲ ἐπεθύμησαν ἀργυρίου
πλείονος. ἔστω γάρ· τί οὖν; αἴτιον[1] δεῖ διὰ
τοῦτο γενέσθαι τὴν πόλιν; καὶ τὸ τῆς συγγνώμης
μέρος οὐδὲν ὀνήσει τοὺς ὃ τῆς ἀνθρωπείας ἐστὶ
φύσεως πεπονθότας, ἐξενεχθέντας τοῦ δέοντος;

---

[1] αἴτιον MSS. F. (crit. note) suggested ἄτιμον.

what intrigue are we guilty ? What have we disregarded in our slackness ? What ruin have we
caused by misbehaviour ? 21. The emperor kindly
cut the price of foodstuffs, but the soil experienced a
crop shortage as a result of drought and failed to support his edict with a good yield, and the ban on high
profits caused the bottom to drop out of the market.[a]
But we are town councillors, not market vendors."
This is not the excuse I present, for if you condemn
anyone, Sire, I must find him guilty too. If you state
that a person has committed an offence, that is my
verdict also.

22. How then do I remove from the danger of your
wrath the city that I could not describe as innocent?
There is an old principle that descends from the gods
above and is respected by Greeks, that has been the
salvation of many a man in courts of law and put into
operation by yourself time and again. When you
have spoken of forgiveness, you have taken the words
out of my mouth; you have discovered the term I
intend to employ, for you have so often put it into
practice.[b] 23. We did wrong, we confess. We have
been too slow in obeying your will. In supervis-
ing the bakers we were, some of us, too careless, or
fast asleep, or eager for more cash.[c] Admitted—but
what then? Must the city be held responsible on
this account? Will there be no scrap of forgiveness
to help people whose natural human frailty has been

[a] Cf. Or. 1. 126 : Jul. Misop. 368 d ff. : Amm. Marc.
22. 14. 1.
[b] For Julian's administration of justice cf. Amm. Marc.
22. 10.
[c] For the organization of the city's food supply in periods
of famine, and the part played by the curiales, cf. P. Petit,
Libanius et la vie municipale à Antioche, pp. 105-122.

καὶ ποῦ τὸ θεοὺς ἀνθρώπων εἶναι κρείττονας, εἰ
τὸ μηδὲν ἁμαρτάνειν καὶ παρὰ τούτοις ἀξιώσομεν
εἶναι; τίς δὲ πόλις ἢ ποῖον ἔθνος ἢ τίς ἀνὴρ ἕξει
σωθῆναι διὰ πάντων τοιαύτης ἀκριβείας τεταμένης;[1] 24. εἰ μὲν ἐξηρῆσθαι δεῖ τοῦ βίου τὴν
συγγνώμην καὶ πάντα ἐξετάζεσθαι πικρῶς καὶ τὸν
ἐφ᾽ ὁτῳοῦν ἁλόντα κολάζεσθαι, μενέτω τὸ μῖσος,
καὶ κάλει τὴν πόλιν ἐχθράν· εἰ δὲ νῦν, εἴπερ ποτέ,
προσήκει ταύτην ἀνθεῖν τὴν καταφυγήν, διὰ τί
μόνοι τῶν τοῦ καιροῦ καλῶν ἐξειργόμεθα;

25. Ἐνθυμοῦμαι δέ, ὅσα σε ποιεῖ φιλάνθρωπον·
πρῶτον μὲν Ἕλλην τις εἶ καὶ κρατεῖς Ἑλλήνων·
οὕτω | γὰρ ἥδιόν μοι καλεῖν τὸ τοῖς βαρβάροις F
R 459 ἀντίπαλον, | καὶ οὐδέν μοι μέμψεται τὸ γένος
Αἰνείου. 26. φρονεῖ δ᾽ ὁ μὲν βάρβαρος μέγα
λυττῶν καὶ ἀγριαίνων καὶ τὰ τῶν θηρίων μιμούμενος καὶ σφάττων ἐν δείπνῳ τὸν ὁμόφυλον καὶ
πίνων ἐπὶ τοῦ νεκροῦ, κἂν ἱκετεύῃ τις, ὁ μέν τις[2]
οὐδὲν ἤνυσεν, ὁ δὲ καὶ προσπαρώξυνεν. ἀλλ᾽
ἡμῖν ἡ μεγίστη σπουδὴ τῶν θηρίων ὅτι πλεῖστον
διεστάναι καὶ θυμὸς ἐξελύθη δάκρυσι καὶ τὸ τῆς
ὀργῆς ζέον ἐσβέσθη κλαυθμῷ καὶ τὴν ὧν ἔπαθε
μνήμην ἐξέβαλέ τις ἰδὼν αἰσχυνόμενον τὸν ἠδικηκότα. 27. οὕτω δὲ ἡμῖν ἡρμοσμένου τοῦ γένους
ἴσῳ μέτρῳ δεῖ τῶν μὲν βαρβάρων ἡμᾶς ἡμερωτέ-
ρους εἶναι, τῶν δ᾽ ἄλλων ἡμῶν τὴν σὴν ψυχήν.

---

[1] τεταμένης Re., F. (V and correction in I): τεταγμένης
other mss.

[2] [τις] F. (om. P, erased U).

---

[a] Libanius takes up, on behalf of Antioch, the argument
of Julian, *Misop.* 367 c. Both under and after Julian,
Libanius employs the term " Hellene " to denote his traditional culture, and in this pity and clemency both figure

162

carried to excess? What is the point of gods being superior to humans, if we expect mankind never to fall into error either? What city, what profession, what individual can hope for protection if such scrupulous exactitude be universally applied? 24. If forgiveness must be removed from the life of man, if everything must be rigorously examined and if anyone caught in default must suffer punishment, then let your ill-will remain and call our city your foe. But if, at this of all times, this type of protection ought to be effective, why are we alone barred from enjoying the glories of the age?

25. If I consider all the qualities which make up your humanity, first you are a Greek and rule over Greeks [a]—for so I prefer to describe the opponents of barbarism, and the descendants of Aeneas will not reprove me for it.[b] 26. The barbarian, in his pride, rages and ravens like a wild beast; he slays his kinsman at his table and drinks a toast over his dead body; supplication is either fruitless or spurs him on to worse frenzy still. But with us, our chief aim is to separate ourselves as far from brute beasts as we can; our temper is wrought upon by tears and our seething rage is quenched by lamentation, and we forget our injuries when we see the sinner shamed. 27. Such being our social order, we must be more humane than the barbarian, and in like measure you more than

largely, both when, as now, he puts forward a plea for Christians, and when, in later times, his arguments are for persecuted pagans: cf. *Epp.* 819, 1120, 1211, 1351, 1414, 1431. *Or.* 19. 13.
[b] He here tones down a normally strong prejudice against Rome and Romans: *e.g.*, *Or.* 1. 179 f., 11. 151, 174. This passage draws some of its inspiration from Julian, *Or.* 4 (*To Helios the King*) 153 a ff.

# LIBANIUS

διὰ τί ; ὅτι σε οὐ κυνηγέται πρόσηβον ὄντα
παραλαβόντες θηρία βάλλειν ἐδίδαξαν τὸ πολὺ τοῦ
χρόνου περὶ νάπας καὶ ὄρη καὶ κρημνοὺς ἐν
λεόντων καὶ κάπρων διατρίβοντα μάχαις, ἀλλ᾽
ἀνὴρ Λακεδαιμόνιος, ἱερεὺς δικαιοσύνης, ἡγεμὼν
παιδείας, εἰδώς, εἴπερ τις, τῆς Ὁμήρου γνώμης τὰ
ἀπόρρητα καὶ σύμπαντός γε τοῦ περὶ τὸν Ὅμηρον
χοροῦ, ὃν ἐδέξω μὲν νέος ὤν, ὡς εἰκὸς τὸν τηλικοῦτον, ἐπίστασαι δὲ νῦν, ὡς εἰκὸς τὸν φιλοσο-
φοῦντα. 28. καὶ μὴν καὶ ῥήτορας ἅπαντας καὶ
συγγραφέας, πολλῶν πραγμάτων διδασκάλους, ὧν
ὁ πόνος οὐδὲν τῶν ἀρχαίων ἀφῆκεν | ἀγνοηθῆναι F
προσπεριείληφας τοῖς ἀπὸ τῶν μέτρων χρησίμοις.
ὅ γε μὴν κολοφών, τὰ θεῶν θρέμματα, Σωκράτης,
Πυθαγόρας, Πλάτων καὶ ὅσοι ῥύακες ἀπ᾽ ἐκείνων
ἐρρύησαν, τούτων οὐδεὶς ἔξω τῆς σῆς διανοίας, ἣν
R 460 εἰσελθόντες ἐξειργάσαντο καλὴν καὶ | γενναίαν,
ὥσπερ οἱ παιδοτρίβαι τὰ σώματα. παρὰ τούτων
ἀπαιτῇ τήμερον τὴν πρὸς ἡμᾶς ἡμερότητα, καθάπερ
γῆ παρὰ τῶν γεωργῶν τοὺς καρπούς.

29. Εἰσὶ δὲ καὶ τούτων τινὲς αἰδεσιμώτεροι
πράκτορες. τίνες οὗτοι ; οἱ τὸν Ὄλυμπον οἰκοῦντες, μᾶλλον δὲ σοὶ συνοικοῦντες θεοὶ καὶ
δαίμονες, ὧν τὸν φίλον εἰς φιλανθρωπίαν ἀνάγκη
καθέλκεσθαι. καὶ γὰρ οὐχ ὅσον δέξασθαι θυσίαν
καὶ δι᾽ ὀρνίθων πετομένων ἢ ἀρνῶν σφαττομένων
μηνῦσαί τι τῶν κρυπτομένων οὐδὲ μέχρι μαντικῆς
ἡ μετ᾽ ἐκείνων σοι συνήθεια, καίτοι καὶ τοῦτο

---

ᵃ The contrast with the huntsman is with Constantius.
The Spartan is Nicocles : cf. Jul. Misop. 353 b ; Socr.
H.E. 3. 1. 10 ; Lib. Or. 1. 31 ff.
164

we common folk. The reason is that, when you were a lad, you had no huntsmen to take you in hand and teach you to strike down beasts, nor did you spend the greater part of your time in hills and glades and rocks fighting lions or wild boars. Your instructor was a Spartan [a] who initiated you in justice and led you in learning, who knew, if ever a man did, the mysteries of the genius of Homer and all of Homer's school. As a boy you took in Homer, as is natural for one of that age ; now you understand him, as is natural for a philosopher. 28. Moreover, besides the benefits of poetry, you have taken to yourself all the orators and historians, authorities upon so many subjects, whose work has left us in ignorance of nothing of classical times.[b] Above and beyond all else, those divine spirits Socrates, Pythagoras and Plato [c] and all the effluents from them, hold a place in your understanding. They have entered into it and have rendered it fine and beautiful, as physical instructors do with the bodies they train. As farmers demand crops of the soil, so do these demand of you today clemency towards us.

29. We have supporters even more revered than these—the gods who dwell in Olympus, or rather, the gods and spirits who dwell with you. Their friend must needs be drawn to friendship with humanity. Your association with them is not confined merely to their acceptance of sacrifice or the revelation of their secrets through the flight of birds or the slaughter of lambs, nor yet to mere divination, great though

[b] Cf. Socr. loc. cit. Liban. Or. 18. 21. A tactful confession of the superiority of philosophy over rhetoric.

[c] An adaptation of [Dio Chrys.] Or. 37. 32, one of Julian's favourite authors, and so most appropriate in an oration such as this.

# LIBANIUS

λαμπρόν, ἀλλ᾽ ὅσαπερ ἡμῖν παρ᾽ ἀλλήλων, τοσαῦτα
σοὶ πρὸς ἐκείνους. 30. οἳ καὶ καθεύδοντά σε ἀνή-
γειραν χειρὶ κινήσαντες καὶ λόχους ἔφρασαν καὶ
στρατείας καιρὸν καὶ παρατάξεως τόπον καὶ ποῖ
δεῖ προελθεῖν καὶ πόθεν ἀπελθεῖν. καὶ μόνος σὺ
τὰς ἐκείνων ἑώρακας μορφὰς εὐδαίμων εὐδαι-
μόνων | θεωρός, καὶ μόνῳ σοὶ φωνῆς θεῶν ὑπῆρξεν F
ἀκοῦσαι καὶ διανισταμένῳ πρὸς ἕκαστον τὸ
Σοφοκλέους λέγειν, νῦν μέν, Ὦ φθέγμ᾽ Ἀθάνας,
νῦν δέ, Ὦ φθέγμα Διός, νῦν δὲ Ἀπόλλωνος,
Ἡρακλέους, Πανός, πάντων θεῶν καὶ πασῶν. 31.
τοιαύτης οὖν ἑταιρίας καὶ συνουσίας ἠξιωμένος καὶ
τοιούτους ἔνδον ἔχων, οἷς συμβουλεύῃ περὶ τῶν
πραγμάτων, οὐκ ἄδηλον ὡς ὁμοιότητι τρόπων
ἐπεσπάσω τοὺς αὐτοὺς καὶ προστάτας καὶ φίλους.
ἀπὸ τοίνυν τούτων ἦν ἡ κατέχουσα τὸν Ἀχιλλέα
θυμούμενον, ὅτε λανθάνουσα τοὺς ἄλλους ἑωρᾶτο
μόνῳ δι᾽ ὃν ἀφῖκτο. 32. καὶ μὴν ὁ Ζεὺς οὐ
καταιβάτης μόνον, ἀλλὰ καὶ ἱκέσιος καὶ μειλίχιος.
ποιήσας τοίνυν τὸ τοῦ καταιβάτου πρὸς τοὺς
R 461 βαρβάρους, ὅπερ ἦν δίκαιον, μειλίχιος | ἡμῖν γε-
νοῦ, καὶ δέξαι τὰς ἱκετείας, ἐπεὶ καὶ παρὰ τοῖς
βαρβάροις ἑκατέραν ἐμιμήσω τοῦ θεοῦ τὴν δύναμιν
ἐμπίπτων μὲν ὥσπερ τις κεραυνὸς τοῖς ἀντι-
βλέπουσιν, οὐκ ἐπάγων δὲ τὸν σίδηρον τοῖς ἱκε-
τεύουσιν· οἳ τοσοῦτον ἑτέρως τὰ νῦν πράττουσιν,
ὅσον γῆν ἀντὶ γῆς μετειλήφασιν. ὧν[1] τἆλλα τε

---

[1] ὧν Re. (mss. except VI): ὡς F. (VI).

[a] Soph. *Ai.* 14. For Julian's vision of the *Genius Populi Romani cf.* Amm. Marc. 21. 2.
[b] Homer, *Iliad*, 1. 198 ff. (Athena).

the virtue of this may be. Your intercourse with them is as close as ours with each other. 30. They have shaken you with their hand and roused you from your sleep, have told you of ambushes, the time to march, the place of battle, the points of advance and of departure. You alone have seen them in physical manifestation, a blessed observer of the blessed. You alone have been privileged to listen to the voice of the gods and to rise and address each one with that greeting of Sophocles, " Voice of Athena "[a] or " Voice of Zeus," or of Apollo, Heracles, Pan and all gods and goddesses. 31. So when you are honoured with such company and society and have such as them close by you as counsellors on matters of state, it is obvious that you have, by likeness of character, embraced them as both protectors and friends. One of this company was she who restrained Achilles in his wrath when, unseen by the rest, she was observed only by him on whose account she had come.[b] 32. Zeus also is not merely the thunderer, but also the protector of suppliants and the gracious.[c] You have loosed your thunders against the barbarian, as he deserved : now be gracious to us and receive our supplications. Even with the barbarians you have imitated the god in both his aspects, for you fell like a thunderbolt on them when they opposed you and did not resort to the sword when they made supplication to you, and so different is their present state that they have gained other lands in exchange for those they held. They create no fear or injury, but

[c] The manifestations of Zeus are deliberately drawn from classical literature, such allusions enabling the flattery to appeal more directly to Julian's taste : Zeus Meilichios Thuc. 1. 126 ; Z. Kataibates, Aesch. *P.V.* 359, Aristoph. *Pax*, 42 ; Z. Hikesios, Soph. *Phil.* 484, Aesch. *Supp.* 616.

καὶ φόβος καὶ ὕβρις ἄπεστι καὶ τρέφονται καὶ θε-
ραπεύονται τῶν φρουρίων ἐγγύς, ἃ κατεσκάφασι.
| 33. πρὸς θεῶν, ὅταν Ἀχιλλεὺς ἀκούων περὶ τῆς F
φύσεως τῶν Λιτῶν καὶ ὡς στρεπτοὶ δέ τε καὶ
θεοὶ αὐτοί, μένῃ φυλάττων τὴν ὀργήν, οὐκ ἀγα-
νακτεῖς πρὸς αὐτόν, καὶ ταῦτα ἐρῶν τοῦ στρατιώτου, εἰ τοῖς θεοῖς κατὰ γένος προσήκων οὐ
μιμεῖται τούτους ἐξ ὧν ἐγένετο, ἀλλ᾽ αὐτὸς μὲν
ἔργον Ἀπόλλωνος τὸν λοιμὸν εἰδὼς ἐπὶ θυσίας
προτρέπει τὸν Ἀγαμέμνονα πιστεύων ἀρκέσειν τὰ
τοιαῦτα πρὸς μεταβολήν, αὐτὸν δ᾽ οὐκ ἀξιοῖ τοσούτοις καὶ τηλικούτοις δώροις ἀφεῖναι τὴν ὀργήν,
καὶ ταῦτα ἐγγύθεν ἔχων τὸ παράδειγμα τοῦτον τὸν
ἄρτι μὲν ἀναλίσκοντα τῇ νόσῳ τὸν στρατόν, μικρὸν δ᾽ ὕστερον διηλλαγμένον τῶν θεωρῶν ἡκόντων καὶ τεθυκότων; 34. ὃ δ᾽ αὖ τότε ἐποίησεν
ὁ θεὸς περὶ Ἴλιον, αὐτός τε καὶ οἱ λοιποὶ καθ᾽
R 462 ἡμέραν | ἔτι καὶ νῦν πράττουσι τῶν ἁμαρτανόν-
των μέν, εἰς εὐχὰς δὲ καταφευγόντων φειδόμενοι.
εἰ δὲ ἐφ᾽ ἑκάστῳ τῶν εὐήθως ὑπὸ τῶν ἀνθρώπων πραττομένων βέβαιον εἶχον τὴν ὀργὴν
καὶ μηδὲν ἦν ἱκανὸν πρὸς διαλλαγήν, ἠρήμωντ᾽
ἂν αἱ πόλεις ὀλίγων κομιδῇ διαφευγόντων τὰ παρ᾽ |
ἐκείνων βέλη. ἀλλ᾽ οἶμαι καὶ πλημμελοῦμεν καὶ F
ἱκετεύομεν καὶ σωζόμεθα. καὶ ὁ θεοείκελος
ἀκριβῶς τοῦτο ἔστιν οὐχ ὁ τοῖς θεοῖς τὴν μορφὴν
ἐοικώς, οὐ γὰρ οἷόν τε, ἀλλ᾽ ὅστις ἑτοίμως ἔχων
εὖ ποιεῖν οὐκ ἐπιθυμεῖ πανταχοῦ τιμωριῶν. 35.
διὰ τοῦτο τηροῦντος μὲν τὴν μῆνιν Ἀχιλλέως
ἀχθόμεθα καὶ μετὰ τῶν πρέσβεων τῶν οὐχὶ

---

*a* A summary of Julian's achievements in Gaul and

168

are maintained and protected near the garrisons they once destroyed.[a] 33. Good heavens! When Achilles hears of the nature of prayer, that " even the very gods are moved by it,"[b] and still remains obdurate in wrath, are you not out of patience with him, despite your admiration for him as a warrior? Though related to the gods by birth he does not follow the lead given by his forebears; he knows well enough that the plague is Apollo's work and he urges Agamemnon to sacrifice,[c] since he is sure that this will produce a change in the situation, and yet he does not deign to relax his anger for so many precious gifts,[d] even though he has to hand the example of the god who recently wasted the army by the plague and was a little later reconciled when its envoys came and offered sacrifice.[e] 34. Even now the behaviour of Apollo and the rest every day is exactly the same as it was on that occasion at Troy. Sinners who have recourse to prayer they spare. If they maintained their rancour unshakeable at every mistake of man's stupidity and if nothing sufficed to reconcile them, the cities would be deserted, for precious few would escape their bolts. But surely, we make mistakes, we make our supplication and we are saved. And any man who really approximates to the divine, does so not by any physical likeness, for that is impossible, but by his readiness to do good and his dislike of the indiscriminate use of punishment. 35. Thus, if Achilles maintains his anger, we feel aggrieved: we think, as the envoys did when they failed to

Germany (A.D. 356–360). *Cf.* Jul. 280 b ff.; Zos. 3. 3-8; Amm. Marc. 17. 8-10; 18. 2.
   [b] Homer, *Iliad*, 9. 497 ff.
   [c] *Ibid.* 1. 59 ff.    [d] *Ibid.* 9. 377 ff.    [e] *Ibid.* 1. 457 ff.

πεπεικότων ἀδικεῖσθαι νομίζομεν, χαίρομεν δὲ
τὸν Πρίαμον ὁρῶντες ἔνδον ὄντα παρ' αὐτῷ καὶ
συνδειπνοῦντα καὶ οὐδενὸς ὧν ἐσπούδαζεν ἀτυ-
χοῦντα. καὶ τοῦτον νομίζομεν ὡς ἀληθῶς ἐκ
Θέτιδος καὶ τῆς οἰκίας Αἰακοῦ, τὸν δὲ ἡδέως
ἐκεῖνον χαλεπαίνοντα καὶ ὁ σφόδρα αὐτὸν ἀγαπῶν
Πάτροκλος οἶσθα ὧν ἔφησεν εἶναι παῖδα. 36. καὶ
μὲν τοὺς θυέεσσι καὶ εὐχωλῇς ἀγανῇσι
φησὶν Ὅμηρος, σοὶ δ' ἔσται μὲν ὅτε θύσουσιν
ἄνθρωποι καὶ βωμοὺς ἱδρύσονται καὶ προσεύξονται
καθάπερ Ἡρακλεῖ, τὸν γὰρ ἔργων τῶν ἐκείνου
ζηλωτὴν εἰκός τοι καὶ τιμῶν τῶν ἐκείνου τεύξεσθαι,
νῦν δέ σοι παρ' ἡμῶν ἀνθ' ἱερείων καὶ καπνοῦ καὶ
κνίσσης σχῆμα ταπεινὸν καὶ ἀντιβόλησις καὶ δάκρυα.
R 463 νεῦσον δή, | πρὸς τῆς Ἀθηνᾶς, ἧς τὴν πόλιν F
ὥσπερ Ῥώμην ἑκατέραν ἐπιθυμεῖς ἰδεῖν, μετὰ τῆς
σαυτοῦ πατρίδος καὶ τῆς τὰ πολλὰ ταῦτα κτησα-
μένης πόλεως τὰς Ἀθήνας θαυμάζων. 37. ἐνθυμοῦ
τοίνυν, ὅτι τούτων τῶν Ἀθηναίων καλὰ μὲν
κἀκεῖνα, ναυμαχίαι μετὰ χρησμῶν κατορθούμεναι
καὶ πείθουσαι τοὺς βαρβάρους ἀγαπᾶν τοὺς
ἀρχαίους ὅρους, μᾶλλον δὲ συστέλλειν εἰς ἔλαττον
ἀναγκάζουσαι τοὺς ὅρους, κάλλιστον δὲ ἁπάντων
ἡ πρὸς τοὺς ἀτυχοῦντας φιλανθρωπία, δι' ἣν πρὸς
οὓς ἄρτι παρετάττοντο, ὑπὲρ τούτων πρὸς ἑτέρους
ἠγωνίζοντο. 38. ἔπασχον ὑπὸ Θηβαίων κακῶς·
εἶτ' ἔτρεχον εἰς Ἁλίαρτον ἐλευθερώσοντες Θη-

    <sup>a</sup> Homer, *Il.* 9. 624 ff.
    <sup>b</sup> *Ibid.* 24. 599 ff.
    <sup>c</sup> *Ibid.* 16. 34 f.        <sup>d</sup> *Ibid.* 9. 499.
    <sup>e</sup> On this passage *cf.* A. D. Nock, *J.R.S.*, 157, p. 122 :
*Deification and Julian.*
    <sup>f</sup> Rome : and Constantinople, Julian's birthplace, *cf.*

convince him, that he is not treating us properly,[a]
but we are pleased when we see Priam in his tent,
dining with him and successful in obtaining all his
requests.[b] Then we feel that he really is a son of
Thetis and of the house of Aeacus; but when he is
so ready to lose his temper—well, you know the
parentage Patroclus ascribes to him, much though
he loves him.[c] 36. Homer speaks of the gods as
being influenced " by incense and reverent vows."[d]
At some time or other men will offer sacrifice and
prayer to you, and set up altars as they do to Heracles,
for obviously his rival in action will obtain the same
honours as he.[e] At present, though, instead of sacrificial offerings, smoke and the scent of fat, we present
our dejection, pleas and tears. Grant us this favour,
Sire, in the name of Athena, whose city you long to
see as if it were one of the two capitals, for you
reverence Athens no less than your own birthplace
and that city which possesses this vast empire.[f]
37. Consider then: in the case of these Athenians,
though their renown is based upon their great feats
of arms—naval victories won under oracular guidance,[g] that induced the invader to remain content
with his former boundaries, or rather, forced him to
reduce them—yet their crowning glory lies in their
generosity towards the unfortunate. Because of this
they espoused the cause of their late opponents and
entered the fray against yet other foes. 38. They
suffered harsh treatment from the Thebans, but then
they marched out to Haliartus to liberate Thebans.[h]

Jul. *E.L.F.* No. 59 (443 bc), Lib. *Or.* 18. 11. For Julian's
regard for Athens *cf.* Jul. 275 ab, Lib. *Or.* 13. 18 ff.

  [g] Salamis, *cf.* Herod. 7. 141 f., 8. 96.
  [h] In the " Corinthian War," 395 B.C. *Cf.* Xen. *Hell.* 3.
5. 7 ff.

βαίους. οὐδὲν μετριωτέρων ἐπειρῶντο Κορινθίων
καὶ Κορινθίοις ἠδικημένοις ἐβοήθουν. ἔσωζον καὶ
τὴν Σπάρτην μετὰ Κριτίαν καὶ Δρακοντίδην καὶ
τὸ καθῃρημένον τεῖχος καὶ τὰς ἀφειλκυσμένας
τριήρεις καὶ τὸ πολὺ κώνειον καὶ τὰς φυγὰς καὶ
τὸν λιμὸν ἐκεῖνον καὶ τὸν φόνον. δι᾽ Ἐλευσῖνος
τῆς τετμημένης ἦλθον εἰς Πελοπόννησον οὐκ ἐπι-
τρέψοντες ἀπολέσθαι τὴν Λακεδαίμονα. 39. τῶν
γὰρ οἴκοι τὸν ἔλεον ἡγουμένων θεόν, οὗ τὸν
βωμὸν ἑώρακας Ἀθήνησιν, ὦ βασιλεῦ, μεμνῆσθαι
τῶν τοῖς καλοῦσι καὶ δεομένοις ἡμαρτημένων οὐκ
ἦν, ἀλλ᾽ ἢ | τὸν βωμὸν ἀνατρέπειν ἐχρῆν ἢ διηλ- F
λάχθαι. μίμησαι δὴ πόλιν, ἢν τὸ οἰκτείρειν τοὺς
εἰς αὐτὴν ἀδικήσαντας ἐποίησεν ἔνδοξον· μᾶλλον
δὲ ἀκολούθησον σαυτοῦ φιλανθρωπίαις, τούτου γὰρ
R 464 οὐδὲν εἶχον[1] μεῖζον εἰπεῖν. 40. εἰ | μὲν γὰρ μήπω
μανίαν ὑπηκόων πράως ἐτύγχανες ἐνεγκών, εἶπον
ἄν σοι Ξέρξην ἀφέντα μὲν τοὺς κατασκόπους,
ἀφέντα δὲ[2] τοὺς ἀντὶ τῶν κηρύκων, ἰδόντα δὲ
Θεμιστοκλέα τὸν ἔχθιστον ὡς φίλον καὶ τῷ μὴ
λαβεῖν δίκην προσθέντα τὸ καὶ δοῦναι δωρεάς,
Λάμψακον, Μυοῦντα, Μαγνησίαν, μετὰ[3] τὰς περιβοήτους[4] ἐκείνας[5] ναυμαχίας τὰς μὲν ἥττους, τὴν
δὲ ᾗ προσόμοιον οὐδέν, δι᾽ ἣν ἡ Σαλαμὶς ὑπὸ τοῦ

---

[1] ⟨ἄν⟩ εἶχον F. (text). F. withdraws the conjecture, vol.
iii, p. xxxxv.

[2] ἀφέντα δὲ F. (VBMI). Om. Re. (other mss.). Gasda
deletes ἀφέντα δὲ . . . κηρύκων.

[3] μετὰ F., Re. (*Animadv.*). Cobet: Μέγαρα μετὰ V, correction in I. μετὰ om. other mss.

[4] περιβοήτους F., Cobet: πρέσβεις PM ; followed by la-
cuna CA : π with erasure U : πολλὰς VI.

[5] ἐκείνας οὐ λογισάμενον P.

Their experience at the hands of Corinth was no better, but when Corinth was the victim of aggression they went to her help.[a] They tried to save even Sparta, after the destruction of their walls, the loss of their navy, the reign of terror under Critias and Dracontides with its many executions, exiles, starvation and murder.[b] Through a ravaged Eleusis they marched to the Peloponnese to prevent the destruction of Lacedaemon.[c] 39. In Athens they regarded Pity as a god[d]—and, Sire, you have seen its altar there—and so they could not reflect upon the wrongs committed by those who sent and implored their aid. Either they had to overthrow the altar or else be reconciled to them. Then imitate a city that has won such fame by pitying those who wronged her : or rather, follow your own humane inclinations, for I can present no more potent plea than that. 40. If you had never yet shown clemency towards your misguided subjects, I would have cited the example of Xerxes. He released the spies and also those who offered themselves in lieu of his heralds,[e] and he made a friend of Themistocles, his greatest enemy. So far from revenging himself upon him, he even bestowed gifts upon him, Lampsacus, Myus and Magnesia,[f] after all those famous battles, both the minor ones and that incomparable victory which

---

[a] In 394 B.C. ; Xen. *Hell.* 4. 2. 16 ff. Tod, *G.H.I.* vol. ii, No. 105.

[b] The rule of the Thirty at Athens, 404 B.C.: *cf.* Xen. *Hell.* Book 2. On hemlock as the method of execution *cf.* Xen. *Hell.* 2. 3. 56 ; Plato, *Phaedo,* 116 c ff.

[c] The Theban invasion of 370/69 B.C. : Xen. *Hell.* 6. 5. 33 ff.

[d] *Cf.* Paus. 1. 17. 1.

[e] Herod. 7. 146 : *ibid.* 134, *cf.* Lib. *Or.* 12. 85.

[f] Thuc. 1. 138.

# LIBANIUS

Πυθίου θεία προσείρητο. καὶ ταῦτα ἦν μεγαλοψυχίας, ἐμοὶ δοκεῖν, οὐκ ἐλπίδων μισθός, ἃς ὑπετίθετο δουλώσειν αὐτῷ τοὺς Ἕλληνας. τὸν γὰρ τῆς οἰκείας προδότην οὐκ ἂν | ἡγεῖτο περὶ τὸν F 1 βάρβαρον ἔσεσθαι χρηστόν. 41. εἶπον ἄν σοι μετὰ Ξέρξου καὶ τὸν Μολοττὸν Ἄδμητον, ὃς ἥδιστ᾿ ἂν¹ τὸν αὐτὸν τοῦτον ἄνθρωπον λαβὼν ὥστε ἀποκτεῖναι, λαβὼν καὶ ἔχων οὔτε τοῖς ἐξαιτοῦσιν ἔδωκε καὶ ὅπως ἔλθοι² παρ᾿ οὓς ἐβούλετο, ἔπραξε. 42. διεξῆλθον ἂν καὶ περὶ Φιλίππου τοῦ Ἀμύντου καὶ περὶ Ἀλεξάνδρου τοῦ Φιλίππου, ὧν ὁ μὲν Ἀθηναίων τοὺς Ἀργαῖον κατάγοντας κεκρατηκὼς ὥσπερ εὐεργέτας ἀπέπεμψεν οὐδὲν ἀξιώσας κατασχεῖν λάφυρον τῶν ἐκ τῆς νίκης αὐτῷ γεγενημένων, Ἀλέξανδρος δὲ πολλὰ παρὰ τῶν Ἀθήνησι ῥητόρων ἠδικημένος τά τε πράγματα ταραττόντων καὶ τοὺς δήμους κινούντων καὶ μαργίτην αὐτὸν ἀποκαλούντων καὶ ὑβριζόντων καὶ καταφρονούντων τῷ μὲν εἶναι πάντων κύριος ἀπέσφαξεν ἄν, εἴπερ ἤθελε, δεξάμενος δὲ πρεσβείαν εἴασε καὶ τηλικαύτην χάριν R 465 | ἔδωκε Δημάδῃ τῷ Δημέου.

43. Τούτων ἂν καὶ πολλῶν ἑτέρων ἐμνήσθην, εἰ μὴ τούτων ἐπεποιήκεις λαμπρότερα. νῦν δέ με τοῦ τὰ παλαιὰ παραδείγματα συλλέγειν ἀπήλλαξας ἤδη τούτων ὑπαρξάμενος, ἐφ᾿ ἃ νῦν ἥκομεν. ἢ γὰρ οὐχ οὗτος ἐκεῖνος ὁ τοὺς θήξαντας ἐπ᾿ αὐτὸν

¹ ἥδιστ᾿ ἂν F., Gasda : ἥδιστα Re. (mss.).
² ἔλθοι F. (correction in B) : ἔλθῃ Re. (other mss.).

---

[a] Herod. 7. 141 ff.
[b] Thuc. 1. 136 f.
[c] One of the first successes of Philip's reign, 359 B.C. : cf. Diod. Sic. 16. 3. Demosth. c. Aristocr. 30.

174

caused the Pythian god to call Salamis " divine."[a] This, I feel, he gave as the reward for his nobility of spirit, not for his hopeful promise to subject Greece to him, for he would never expect a traitor to his country to be loyal to the barbarian cause. 41. Along with Xerxes I would have mentioned Admetus the Molossian too. He would have been very glad to get hold of this same Themistocles and put him to death, but when he did get hold of him and had him in his power, he refused to hand him over to the Athenians as they requested and he ensured that he reached his desired destination.[b] 42. I would have narrated to you the story of Philip son of Amyntas also, and of his son Alexander. Philip defeated the Athenians when they tried to put Argaeus on the throne, and then he treated them as though they were benefactors, sent them away and did not deign to retain any of the booty that he had won as a result of his victory.[c] Alexander suffered much at the hands of the orators in Athens. They created trouble for him, they organized the democracies against him, they dubbed him " Don Quixote " and covered him with insult and obloquy. When absolutely supreme, he could have massacred them, had he wished, but instead he welcomed their embassy and let them be, granting this great favour to Demades son of Demeas.[d]

43. These examples and many more I would have cited, were it not that you had performed deeds even more famous. As it is, you have provided an example of the treatment that we now come to obtain, and so you have prevented me from collecting instances from past history. Was it not our emperor here who,

[d] After the destruction of Thebes, 335 B.C. : cf. Plut. Demosth. 23, Diod. Sic. 17. 15.

τὰ ξίφη καὶ | βεβουλευμένους ποῦ καὶ πότε δεῖ F 13
τὴν κοινὴν εὐτυχίαν ἐκτεμεῖν, ἐλέγξας μὲν καὶ
μεμψάμενος, τῶν ψυχῶν δὲ οὐκ ἀποστερήσας, ἐφ'
ᾧ καὶ μᾶλλον τὴν οἰκουμένην ἢ τοῖς τροπαίοις
ἐξέπληξε; νόμος ἦν τῇ τότε φιλανθρωπίᾳ¹ φέρειν
τῶν ἀρχομένων τὰς πλημμελείας. τήρει δή μοι
τὸν νόμον ἀκίνητον καὶ τοῖς ἐνεγκοῦσιν ἔπαινον
ἕτερα προστίθει. 44. καὶ γὰρ οὐδὲ τὰ πάντα
πονηρᾷ σπείσῃ πόλει οὐδὲ ἐξ ἀπονοίας καὶ
θρασύτητος καὶ ὕβρεως καὶ τῶν χειρίστων γιγνω-
σκομένη ἀλλ' εἰ δίδως εἰπεῖν, τοῦτο πρῶτον
ἐγκεκλημένη. διὸ καὶ συνειπεῖν ἐπείσθην νομίζων
ἔσεσθαι τὰ πρόσθεν τῶν τελευταίων παραίτησιν,
ἐπεὶ καὶ τῶν ἀνθρώπων τὸν μὲν παμπόνηρον καὶ
λυσιτελεστέραν ἡγούμενον τῆς ἐπιεικείας τὴν
κακίαν μισεῖν δεῖ καὶ ἀπολλύναι παντὸς εἵνεκα
βίου, τῷ δὲ ὅλως μὲν μετρίῳ, δεξαμένῳ δὲ αἰτίαν
πᾶς ἂν εἰκότως καὶ συνάχθοιτο καὶ βοηθοίη.

45. Ἡ πόλις αὕτη, ἵνα τὰ παλαιότερα παρῶ,
πυνθανομένη σου τὰς περὶ Ῥῆνον μάχας καὶ νίκας
καὶ λόγων ἀπεργασίας καὶ τὴν ἄλλην ἀρετὴν
δημοσίᾳ μὲν οὐκ ηὔξατο τοῖς θεοῖς σὴν γενέσθαι
R 466 τὴν γῆν, οὐ γὰρ | ἐξῆν, καθ' αὑτὸν δὲ ἕκαστος ἢ
κατὰ συμμορίας | τῶν ταῦτα βουλομένων αἰτοῦν- F 1
τες οὐ διέλιπον τὸν Δία τὰ μὲν φθείροντα τὴν

even after he had proved them guilty and had no
good word for them, refrained from executing those
who sharpened their swords against him and conspired as to how and when they might best cut short
the happiness of the whole world ? [a] Did he not
astonish the world more by this than by his triumphs ?
Characteristic of your clemency then was your patient
endurance of the errors of your subjects. Now maintain it unimpaired, and add fresh praise to that
already won. 44. Moreover, you will make your
peace with a city that is not wholly bad nor yet a by-
word for stupid, reckless insolence and misconduct
of the worst kind, but is here a first offender, if you
allow the term. For this reason I was induced to be
her advocate, since I thought our former services
would be some palliation for our late misconduct.
Even with individuals, where a man is an utter rogue
and decides that vice is more to his advantage than
virtue, he deserves to be hated and exterminated
because of his whole way of life ; but when a man is,
in general, decent, and yet has laid himself open to
blame, it would be natural for everyone to offer him
compassion and help.

45. This city,—leaving ancient history aside—on
hearing of your battles on the Rhine and of your
victories, of your literary compositions and all your
other high qualities, did not as a community offer
prayers to the gods for the world to become your
own, for indeed it could not. Yet all here, either
singly or in groups with this desire, ceaselessly prayed
Zeus to put an end to all that was ruining the empire

[a] Lib. *Or.* 18. 199.

---

[1] τῇ τότε φιλανθρωπίᾳ F., Re. : ἡ τότε φιλανθρωπία MSS.

ἀρχὴν παῦσαι, δοῦναι δὲ τῷ σώσοντι τὸ κράτος.
46. φοιτῶντος δὲ ἐκ Κιλικίας νῦν μὲν τούτου, νῦν
δὲ ἐκείνου τοῦ λόγου πρὸς μὲν τὸν μεμνημένον
ὑγείας ὠχρίων, ὁ δ᾽ ἕτερος ἦν ἑορτὴ νευόντων
ἀλλήλοις ἀφανῶς τὰ τῆς ἡδονῆς νεύματα. 47. οὐχ
οὕτω πλέοντες ἄνθρωποι κακῶς ἐπεθύμησαν ἅψασθαι γῆς ὡς οἶδε τῶν σῶν ἀπολαῦσαι φαρμάκων,
οὐχ οὕτω γέρων πατὴρ υἱῶν ἰδεῖν γενεὰν ὅλην
ἔκδημον γεγενημένην ὡς ἡ δύστροπος αὕτη πόλις
τὴν σὴν ἰδεῖν κεφαλήν, οὐχ οὕτως οἱ δουλεύοντες
καὶ παρὰ σφᾶς ἐλθεῖν τὴν Ἡρακλέους συμμαχίαν
ὡς ἡμεῖς ἐπὶ πᾶν ἐκταθῆναι τὴν πρὶν ἐν μικρῷ
βασιλείαν. 48. ὡς δὲ τὰ μὲν εἶχε τελευτήν, τὰ σὰ
δὲ ηὔξητο καὶ ὁ καιρὸς ἐδίδου δεῖξαι τὴν γνώμην,
ἤκουσαν οἱ θεοὶ βοῆς ἡλίκης οὐ πρόσθεν, τῶν μὲν
R 467 ἀνδρῶν ἐμπεπληκότων οὐ μόνον τὸ | θέατρον ἀλλὰ
καὶ τὰς τοῦ ὄρους λαγόνας, τῶν¹ γυναικῶν δὲ κατὰ
τὸν αὐτῶν νόμον οἴκοθεν ἑκάστης συνεκπεμπούσης
εὐφημίαν. 49. ἀπὸ τῶν ἐνταῦθα πεπραγμένων,
καὶ εἴ τις ἦν ὀνειροπολῶν τι νεώτερον, τῆς ἐλπίδος
ἀπέστη καὶ παρὰ τὴν ὄχθην Ὀρόντου τὰ σὰ
τιμήσειν ὀμώμοκεν, ὅ τε δὴ στρατὸς καὶ τὸ ῥεῦμα
τοῦ ποταμοῦ, ποιητὴς ἂν ἔφησε, γαννύμενον
ἐχώρει. 50. τούτων τὰ μὲν ὡμολόγηται, περὶ δὲ
τῶν ἐμοὶ πίστευσον. ἔμελλέ τις ἐν Ἐφέσῳ τοῦ |
περὶ σὲ φίλτρου δώσειν δίκην κἀνταῦθά τις F 1
ὑπωπτεύετο καὶ ἡ σύλληψις ἠλπίζετο. ἦσαν

---

¹ τῶν inserted Herwerden.

ᵃ Constantius, en route from the Eastern frontier to
oppose Julian in Thrace, first fell ill at Tarsus : ignoring
this illness, he went on to Mopsucrene, where he died, 3
Nov. A.D. 361 : cf. Amm. Marc. 21. 15.

and to grant dominion to its future saviour. 46. First one story, then another, came from Cilicia.[a] At the rumour of his recovery they grew pale: the receipt of news to the contrary caused rejoicing, and their nods and smiles revealed to one another the pleasure they felt. 47. Mariners in mid-ocean are not so dreadfully anxious to reach land as our people were to profit by the medicine you would give. No aged father was ever so eager to see all his far travelled family as this perverse city of ours was to see yourself. None in the bonds of slavery ever prayed Heracles to come to their rescue so much as we prayed for your empire, lately so small, to be extended over the whole world. 48. When that reign was ended and yours had been increased and when the times allowed us to demonstrate our feelings, the gods heards such a cry of jubilation as never before.[b] The men filled not just the theatre but the hill side above it, and the women at home each offered up a prayer of thanksgiving in their own fashion. 49. As a result of what happened here, even if anyone dreamed of being disloyal, he gave up this hope and by the side of the Orontes swore fealty to you, while the army and the river's flood, to use a figure of poetry, passed merrily by. 50. Part of this is no secret, but you must take my word for the rest. In Ephesus people were going to be punished because of their affection for you[c]: here too people were suspect and arrests were expected.

[b] Cf. Or. 1. 118 ff. Undertones of dissatisfaction in Antioch at the turn of events may, however, be discerned in the careful advice of Ep. 679.

[c] A covert allusion to Maximus of Ephesus, neo-Platonist philosopher and thaumaturge, Julian's teacher (cf. Eunap. V.S. 474 ff.), for whose safety Julian had expressed anxiety in A.D. 361. Cf. Julian. E.L.F. No. 26 (p. 415 a).

# LIBANIUS

κἀνταῦθα τῆς σῆς φύσεως μηνυταὶ διδάσκοντες ἃ
συνῄδεσαν, καὶ πολὺ τὸ πειθόμενον κηλούμενον
ἔρωτι. 51. βούλει με καλέσαι τούτου μάρτυρα τὸν
ὑπὸ σοῦ πάλαι μὲν στέγῃ, μετὰ ταῦτα δὲ γράμμασι,
τὰ τελευταῖα δὲ νῦν ἀρχῇ[1] τετιμημένον; ἢ βλάπτει
καὶ ἐμὲ καὶ τὸν μάρτυρα τὸ εἶναι πολίτας ἄμφω;
R 468 τῶν γε πλειόνων | ἡμεῖς, ὦ βασιλεῦ, καὶ συγ-
γενεῖς, ἀλλ' ὅμως μήποτε οὕτω θαυμάσαιμεν μὴ
πατρίδα, μὴ γένος, ὥστ' ἀληθείας τε καὶ σοῦ
ποιήσασθαι πρότερα. 52. καὶ τί δεῖ περὶ ταῦτα
διατρίβειν, ᾧ μάρτυς ὑπάρχει πιστότατος, ὃν μόνον
τῶν πάντων οὐκ ἂν ἐκβάλοις; τίνα δὴ λέγω
τοῦτον; αὐτὸν σέ. σὺ γάρ τι τῇ πόλει πρῴην
πρὸς ἐμὲ μεμφόμενος, Ἐγὼ δέ, ἔφης, αὐτὴν διε-
νοούμην ποιῆσαι μαρμαρίνην. οὕτω γὰρ εἶπες
τῷ ῥήματι. οὐκοῦν ἀφίκου φιλῶν. εἰ δὲ ἐφίλεις,
ἐπῄνεις. ἐπῄνεις δὲ οὐκ ἐχθράν, ἀλλ' ἀμειβόμενος[2]
φίλτρον· οὐ γάρ σε ἐλάνθανε τὰ τῆς ἑῴας ἐπὶ τῆς
ἑσπέρας καθήμενον οὐδὲ τίς μὲν ἠγάπα τὰ χείρω,
τίς δὲ ἐποίει[3] τὰ βελτίω. ὃ τοίνυν τῇ πόλει παρ-
εσκεύαζες κάλλος, τεκμήριον ἦν | τοῦ τὰ σὰ τὴν F 14
πόλιν ᾑρῆσθαι. 53. ἴσως τις ἀπήγγειλέ σοι μετὰ
τῶν ἄλλων νεὼς ἔτι πολλούς τε καὶ μεγάλους

---

[1] ἀρχῇ F. Conj. Re. ἄρει MSS.
[2] ἀμειβόμενος F. (VB, correction in I) : ἀμυνόμενος Re.
(other MSS.).
[3] ἐποίει MSS. ἐπόθει F., conj. Re.

---

[a] Libanius himself : cf. Julian's comment reported in Or.
1. 120 : ὁ τοὺς ἐκ τοῦ γράφειν ὑπομείνας κινδύνους ἐν ἀσφαλείᾳ
σιγᾷ.
[b] Celsus of Antioch, praeses Ciliciae in A.D. 362 : cf.
Seeck, BLZG, p. 105.
[c] Cf. Sueton. Aug. 28. Julian's acquaintance with Sue-

Here too there were some to tell all they knew and
to reveal your high qualities, and there were many
who were charmed by affection and believed them.[a]
51. Do you wish me to call as witness of this Celsus
who long ago had the honour of residing with you,
thereafter of corresponding with you, and finally
now of holding office under you?[b] Or is it to the detriment of both my witness and myself that we are
both native here? Admittedly, Sire, we are part of
the larger community and related to them, yet I trust
that we never be so devoted to family and country
as to prefer them to truth and our duty to you.
52. Yet why should I dwell on all this? I can adduce
the most cogent of all witnesses, the only one you
could not possibly reject. Whom, think you, do I
refer to? Your own self. Recently, in the complaints you addressed to me about the city, you told
me, " I intended to make it a city of marble." [c]
That is the very expression you used. In that case
you came with love in your heart. If you loved us,
you approved of us,[d] and your approval was not for
a town that was your foe : you were returning the
affection it felt, for while resident in the west you
were not unaware of the state of the east. You knew
who supported the cause of evil and who promoted
that of the good. So then, the glory you planned for
the city was evidence that she had taken your part.
53. Perhaps you received this news among others,
that we had many great temples still standing here,[e]

tonius is confirmed by his reference to another incident
(*Aug.* 16) in *Caesars* 325 cd.

[d] Julian's approval of Antioch was, however, limited : *cf.*
*Misop.* 366 d.

[e] *Cf.* § 79. Libanius, by implication, contests Julian's
arguments in *Misop.* 361 a.

παρ' ἡμῖν ἑστηκότας, ὃ τῆς τῶν ἐνοικούντων εὐσεβείας ἐποιοῦ σημεῖον, ὡς τῶν μὲν βουλομένων
R 469 καθαιρεῖν ὄντων, σεσωσμένων | δὲ τῶν οὐ κειμέ-
νων ταῖς τῶν ἀχθομένων τῇ καθαιρέσει μάχαις.[1]

54. Τί οὖν; πάντα ἐκεῖνα ἐξαλείψομεν εἰς ἓν
τοῦτο βλέποντες, καὶ περιέσται τῶν δεικνύντων
ἀρετὴν τὸ πραχθὲν ἐκ ῥᾳθυμίας; δίκασον ἡμῖν,
ὡς Λακεδαιμόνιοι,[2] ἐφ' ἑκάτερα τὴν ἐξέτασιν ἄγων
δὸς τῷ πλείονι τὴν ῥοπήν. ἀναμνήσθητι τοῦ σαυτοῦ νόμου τοῦ περὶ τῶν ψευδομένων· "Αν ψεύση-
ται, φησίν, ἅπαξ τῶν ἐμοί τις ὁμιλούντων, οἴσω·
κἂν δεύτερον ἴσα τολμήσῃ, καὶ τοῦτο ἀνέξομαι·
κἂν ἁλῷ τρίτον οὐ τἀληθῆ λέγων, οὔπω μεμίση-
ται· προστιθεὶς δὲ τέταρτον ἐξελήλαται. ἀλλ' ἡμῖν
γε μὴ τρὶς νέμε συγγνώμην, ἀλλὰ νῦν μόνον. ἔπ-
ειτά σοι παρέξομεν ἡμᾶς αὐτοὺς ἀμέμπτους. ἡ
γὰρ παροῦσα λύπη νήφειν παρακελεύσεται. 55. εἶτα
ἐρήσῃ· Τί γὰρ δέδιτε; ποίαν δήμευσιν οὐσίας;
ποίαν φυγήν; τίνας | σφαγάς; παίζεις, ὦ βα- F
σιλεῦ, πρὸς ἄνδρας ἀτυχοῦντας. τί φῄς; οὐ δημεύ-
εις οὐδὲ σφάττεις οὐδὲ φυγαδεύεις, ἀλλὰ μισεῖς
καὶ δυσμενεῖς νομίζεις καὶ καταλείπεις. τοῦτο
δέ ἐστιν ἡ μεγίστη δίκη· πολλὰ γὰρ ἐν ταὐτῷ
κατὰ τῆς πόλεως βοᾷς, ὅτι Φεύγω πόλιν μεστὴν ἁπάντων κακῶν, ὕβρεως, μέθης, ἀκρασίας,

---

[1] Punctuation F. (correction in M). ὄντων σεσωσμένων,
τῶν δὲ οὐ mss. ὡς τῶν μέν, τῶν βουλομένων καθαιρεῖν ἀπιόντων,
σεσωσμένων conj. Re.

[2] Λακεδαιμόνιοι F., conj. Re. Λακεδαιμονίοις mss.

[a] An obscure allusion, most probably referring to the

and you took that as a sign of the piety of the inhabitants, since, despite the existence of those who would demolish them, those that were not lying in ruin had been saved by the active opposition of people who disapproved of their demolition.

54. Well, then. Shall we concentrate upon this one incident and wipe out the memory of all our past credit? Shall one act of remissness prevail over everything that shows our virtue? Pass verdict upon us as the Spartans would.[a] Subject both good and bad to the test, and let the scale descend on the side that holds the more. Remember your own habit with regard to falsehood. It is this: "If any of my friends tells a lie once, I will put up with it. If he dares do the same again, even then I will endure it. Even if he be caught lying a third time, he has not yet incurred my hatred. But let him add a fourth time, I banish him." But do not grant us pardon three times—only just this once. Thereafter our behaviour towards you will be free from reproach, for our present distress will be a warning to us to be careful. 55. Then you will ask, "Why, what are you afraid of? Confiscations? Exile? Executions?"[b] You are making fun of men in their misfortune, Sire. You say you have no recourse to confiscation, execution or banishment, but all the time you hate us, think of us as your foes and forsake us. That is the worst punishment of all, for in one and the same breath you heap criticisms on the city. You declare that you are taking leave of a city that is crammed full of every kind of wickedness,—inso-

incident in Thuc. 5. 63, where Agis has his sentence remitted after failing to take Argos, 418 B.C. He begged to be given the chance of performing some service to the state that would wipe out his disgrace.

[b] Libanius adapts Julian, *Misop.* 364 c ff.

R 470 ἀσεβείας, φιλοχρηματίας, | θράσους καὶ μεθίσταμαι
πρὸς ἐλάττω πόλιν τοῦ τῆς δυνατωτέρας τρόπου
κατεγνωκώς. 56. οὕτως οὖν λαμπρῶς ἔτι ζῶντας
ἡμᾶς καὶ στηλίτας ποιῶν, ἃ παραλείπεις λέγων,
οἴει κρύψειν δι᾽ ὧν κολάζεις, ὥσπερ ἂν εἰ τήμερον
ἐκθεὶς κατ᾽ ἐμοῦ λόγον, ὡς εἴην ἀνοσιώτατος καὶ
σὸς ἐχθρός, ἔπειτα ἠξίους με εἰδέναι χάριν, ὅτι μὴ
τέθνηκα· ἐγὼ δὲ εἶπον ἄν σοι· Εἰρωνεύῃ, βασιλεῦ,
καὶ μείζω θανάτου τιμωρίαν εὑρὼν ὑποκορίζῃ τὸ
πρᾶγμα. μή μοι χαρίζου τὰ τοιαῦτα μηδ᾽ ἐπονεί-
διστόν μοι ποιῶν τὸν βίον ἐπίτρεπε ζῆν, ἀλλ᾽
ἀνασταύρωσον, καταπόντισον. λεγέτω μέ τις
κακῶς οὐκ αἰσθανόμενον, νῦν δὲ οὐκ ἀποκτενεῖς,
ὅπως μειζόνως ἀνιάσῃς ; ἔστιν, ὦ | βασιλεῦ, καὶ F 1
ζωὴ πολλάκις πικροτέρα τελευτῆς. 57. τάχα σοι
καὶ ἡ πόλις λέγει· Δήμευσον, ἀπόκτεινον· εἰ
βούλει, κατάσκαψον. μιᾶς ἡμέρας ἡ λύπη, τὸ δὲ
νῦν κακὸν πῶς οἴσω μακρὸν γιγνόμενον ; ἐξ-
άγιστος ἡ πόλις, ὡς ὁ Κιρραίων λιμήν, ἐπάρατος,
ὡς τὸ Πελασγικὸν ἐκεῖνο, καὶ κινδυνεύομεν τήμερον περὶ τῆς παρρησίας. ὡς γὰρ εἷς ἀνὴρ
R 471 ἁλοὺς ἑταιρήσεως ἄτιμος, οὕτως ἡ πόλις | ἡμῖν, εἰ
μείναις ὀργιζόμενος, ἄφωνος. ποῦ γὰρ ἔτι καὶ
πρὸς τίνας σεμνυνούμεθα ἢ παρ᾽ ἡμᾶς ἰόντας ἢ
παρ᾽ ἑτέρους ἰόντες ; κεκλείσεται πᾶς μὲν ἡμῖν
λιμήν, πᾶσα δὲ ἤπειρος, πᾶν δὲ γένος, καὶ δεήσει

---

a Cf. Demosth. Phil. 3. 45.
b As a result of the First Sacred War, 595 B.C.  Cf.
Aeschin. c. Ctes. 36. 107.
c The " Pelasgic Wall " was on the western side of the
Athenian acropolis.  The area around it was cursed—an
184

lence, drunkenness, intemperance, impiety, greed
and stubbornness,—and are shifting to a lesser town
in condemnation of the behaviour of the greater.
56. So by leaving us still alive [a] for all to see and
pillorying us and telling us of what you have left
undone, do you think to hide the manner of the
punishment you inflict? It is like spreading abroad
the tale against me today that I am an utter blackguard and your foe, and yet expecting me to be
thankful that you have not put me to death. I would
have told you, "Sire, you are not being fair. You
have devised a punishment worse than death and
then gloss over the matter. Do not give me any
favours like this. Do not make my life a thing of
shame and then let me live, but crucify me first, or
drown me. I may be abused for my stupidity, but
is not the object of your refusal to execute me simply
the infliction of a harsher penalty? Life itself, Sire,
can often be a harder thing to bear than death." 57.
Our city too perhaps may reply, "Employ your confiscations and executions. Raze us to the ground, if
you like. Our grief then is a matter of but a single
day. But how shall I endure my present long drawn
tale of woe?" Our city is an abomination like the
harbour of Cirrha,[b] accursed like the Pelasgicon of
old,[c] and today our very freedom of intercourse is at
stake. As any single individual, upon conviction for
prostitution, is disfranchised, so, if you remain angry
with us, our city is reduced to silence. Where and
with whom shall we have any credit, either with visitors
to us or as visitors to others? Every harbour will be
closed to us, every continent, every province, and

inheritance from primitive taboo: *cf.* Thuc. 2. 17, Herod.
6. 137.

τοὺς ἀποδημοῦντας κρύπτειν ὅθεν εἰσί, καὶ πλάττειν ἑαυτοῖς πατρίδας. 58. τοῖς μὲν ἀνδροφόνοις
εὕρηται καθάρσια τὸ μῦσος λύοντα, κἂν ἀφείς τις
τὴν τοῦ παθόντος χώραν ἑτέρωσε δράμῃ, τὸν
βοηθήσοντα καὶ παραμυθησόμενον εὗρε, τὸ δὲ
ἡμέτερον κακὸν πανταχοῦ πολεμίους εὑρήσει, καὶ
τὴν σὴν ἔχθραν ἡ οἰκουμένη μιμήσεται, κἂν ἔλθῃ
τις ὡς ἡμᾶς ξένος, διαδραμεῖται τὸ ἄστυ, καθάπερ
οἱ τὰς νοσούσας. 59. λήσει δὲ τοῦτο οὐκ Αἰθίοπας
ἀμφοτέρους, οὐ Κελτούς, οὐ Σκύθας, οὐ Περσῶν
τοὺς λειπομένους. ἡ γὰρ τοῦ θυμουμένου λαμ-
πρότης οὐκ | ἐᾷ λαθεῖν τοὺς μισουμένους, πρὸς δὲ F
καὶ τὸ μέγεθος τῆς μισουμένης πολὺν ποιεῖ τὸν
λόγον. καὶ γὰρ εἰ προσεπταίκαμεν, καὶ κατεγνώ-
σμεθα. ἀλλ' ἐν ταῖς μετὰ δύο τὰς πρώτας τετάγ-
μεθα, καὶ γίνεται τῇ πόλει ζημία τὸ βεβοῆσθαι,
ὥσθ' ὃ τὸν Καλλίξενον περιστῆναί φασιν, ἀποθανεῖν λιμῷ μισούμενον, τοῦθ' ἡμῶν τοῖς ἄλλοθι
φανεῖσι συμβήσεται παντὸς ὠθοῦντος, ἐκβάλλοντος,
ἐξελαύνοντος. 60. καὶ οὔπω τοσοῦτον τὸ κατ'
ὀλίγων[1] τῶν ἑτέρωσε ἐόντων γενησόμενον, ἀλλ'
ὅλῃ γε ἀνάγκη τῇ πόλει τὴν ἀσφάλειαν ἀπολωλέναι.
εὐτυχεῖν μὲν γὰρ διηνεκῶς ὄντας ἀνθρώπους
ἀμήχανον, ἀλλὰ καὶ λιμὸς καὶ λοιμὸς καὶ τὰ ἔτι
R 472 δεινότερα, τὰ | ἀπὸ τῶν σεισμῶν λυμαίνεται τὰς
πόλεις. ἐν δὲ τοῖς τοιούτοις καιροῖς ἓν φάρμακον

---

[1] τὸ inserted F. Conj. Re. (correction in M). ὀλίγων F.
(UV : correction in PBM) : ὀλίγον Re. (other mss.).

---

[a] Cf. Herod. 7. 70.

if we go abroad, we shall have to conceal our place of
origin and invent new birthplaces for ourselves. 58.
For the murderer a ritual of purification has been
evolved that purges the stain of guilt, and if he leaves
his victim's country and goes elsewhere, he finds
help and comfort. We, in our disastrous plight, will
find enemies everywhere, and the whole world will
follow your example and be our foe, and if any visitor
comes to us, he will go straight on, shunning the city
as though it were plague-stricken. 59. Neither tribe
of the Ethiopians,[a] nor the Celts, nor the Scyths nor
the Persians that survive[b] will be unaware of this.
The renown of the aggrieved party prevents the
object of such hatred from finding concealment, and
the tale is exaggerated to suit the greatness of the
hated city. Indeed, if we have offended, we have
already been condemned. We are one of those cities
next in line to the two capitals, and our renown is our
undoing.[c] The fate of Callixenus was, we are told,
to die by starvation loathed by all.[d] The same will
befall any of us who shows his face anywhere else,
for everyone will rebuff us, eject us, expel us. 60. And
it is not the consequences for the few who venture
abroad that matter so much now : the whole city,
in fact, must lose its security. For us humans unbroken happiness is beyond our reach : famine,
plague and, worse still, earthquakes ravage our
cities. Yet in such disasters there is one cure for the

[b] Further indication that Julian is already engaged on the
Persian campaign at the time of composition.
[c] Antioch is a *metropolis*, and inferior only to Rome and
Constantinople : *cf.* Auson. *Ord. Urb. Nob.* 4-5.
[d] The demagogue who demanded the trial of the generals
after Arginusae. Exiled thereafter, he returned after the fall
of the Thirty to suffer this fate : *cf.* Xen. *Hell.* 1. 7. 35.

LIBANIUS

τοῖς πληγεῖσιν, ἡ παρὰ τῶν προσχώρων προθυμία.
ἣν ἐὰν ἀφέλῃς, τὴν μόνην ἐλπίδα ἀνῄρηκας.
ἀναιρεῖται δὲ πῶς; ἐὰν οἱ παθόντες | πονηροὶ δο- F
κῶσι. τοῖς γὰρ τοιούτοις ἐπιχαίρειν, οὐκ ἐπαμύ-
νειν εἰώθασιν ἅπαντες. 61. μικράς γε ἡμᾶς καὶ
οἵας ἐνέγκαι ῥάδιον εἰσπράξῃ δίκας κοινὸν ἡμῖν
ἁπάντων ἀνθρώπων ἐπάγων πόλεμον, δι' ὃν ὀρθῆς
μὲν μενούσης τῆς πόλεως τεταπεινῶσθαι συμβήσεται, συμφορᾷ δὲ χρησαμένης τῶν βοηθησόντων
ἀπορεῖν. 62. εἶεν· τὰ μὲν παρὰ τῶν ἀστυγειτόνων
καὶ τῶν ἄλλων ἀνθρώπων πρὸς ἡμᾶς τοιαῦτα·
παῖδες δὲ σοὶ καὶ παίδων παῖδες οὐ δοκοῦσί σοι
τὸ μῖσος μετὰ τῆς ἀρχῆς ἐκδέξεσθαι¹ περὶ τὴν
ἡμετέραν καὶ τιμήσειν ἑτέρας καὶ ταύτην ἀτι-
μάσειν καὶ πάντα τρόπον κακώσειν; 63. ἐγὼ
μὲν γὰρ ἕως ὁ παρὼν τῶν πραγμάτων ἑστήξει²
κόσμος, καὶ τὴν τῶν ἀεὶ κρατούντων ἔχθραν
ἀθάνατον ἑστήξειν ἡγοῦμαι τῇ πόλει, κἂν ταλαι-
πωρούμενοι φθεγγώμεθα τὰ τῶν ἀλγούντων, εὐθὺς
ἥξειν ἡμῖν τὰ νῦν· Οὐ γὰρ οἶδε εἰσὶν οἱ τὸν
πρᾳότατον ἐξοργίσαντες καὶ πικρὰν αὐτῷ κατα-
R 473 στήσαντες τὴν ἑαυτῶν καὶ | ποιήσαντες ζητεῖν
τόπους ἑτέρους εἰς χειμερινὴν καθέδραν; εἶθ'
οὓς ἀπολωλέναι πάλαι προσῆκεν, εἰ μὴ τρυφᾶν
ἐξέσται, δεινὰ πεπόνθασιν; οὐ ποιήσει τις μικρὰν
ἐκ μεγάλης τὴν τύραννον, οὐ πένητας ἐξ εὐπόρων;
64. | δυσμένειαν οὖν, ὦ βασιλεῦ, φυτεύων ἡμῖν F
ἄπαυστον, δι' ἣν πάντας μὲν ὑπάρχους, πάντας δὲ
ἡγεμόνας πολεμίους ἕξομεν, ὡς ἐκ τῶν ἡμετέρων
188

victims in the eagerness of their neighbours to assist
them. Remove this, and you remove their only hope.
And removed it is, if the victims are of ill repute,
for everyone is in the habit of being pleased at their
misfortunes, not of assisting them. 61. Yes, the
punishment you will inflict upon us is certainly light
and easy to bear, when you rouse the hostility of all
mankind against us. Thus even if our city remains
still standing, it is bound to decline, and if it meets
with disaster, it will find none to aid it. 62. Well,
such will be our treatment at the hands of our
neighbours and the rest of the world. But do you
not think that your children and your children's
children will, upon inheriting the throne, inherit your
hatred for our city ? Will they not honour other towns,
and hold us in dishonour and do us all kind of injury ?
63. Yes, I think the hatred of successive rulers for
our city will remain unceasing as long as the present order of the world shall remain, and if, in our
misery, we give expression to our grief, this episode
will immediately be cited against us. " Why, aren't
these the people who roused the anger of the mildest
of emperors ? Didn't they make their own city re-
pulsive to him and cause him to seek another place
for his winter residence? They ought to have been
exterminated long ago : yet their cup of woe is full
if they cannot live on the fat of the land. Won't
someone reduce this tyrant city from her former
greatness, and make them poor instead of rich ? "
64. Though you sow the seeds of perpetual hatred
against us, Sire, and thereby we shall have every
prefect and governor as our foe since they think they

---

¹ ἐκδέξεσθαι F. (VU : corrections in PIM) : ἐκδέξασθαι Re.
(other MSS.). ² ἐστήξει F. Conj. Re. : ἑστήκει MSS.

κακῶν τοῖς βασιλεῦσι χαριουμένους, πείθειν ἐπι-
χειρεῖς ὅτι οὐ ταῦτα τιμωρία; τί γὰρ φήσομεν
ἐρωτώμενοι· Πόθεν μεμίσησθε;[1] μεταστήσομεν
ἐπὶ σὲ τὴν αἰτίαν; ἀλλ' οὐ δέχεται μέμψιν ἡ σὴ
φύσις, καὶ γίγνεται κατὰ τῶν ἐγκαλουμένων ἡ
τοῦ κατεγνωκότος ἀρετή. 65. ὥσπερ γὰρ οἱ τῶν
ἱερῶν ὑπὸ τῶν θεῶν διὰ τῶν χρησμῶν ἐκβαλλό-
μενοι σιγῶσιν, ὡς ἂν ὑπὸ τῶν ἅπαντα εἰδότων
ἐξεληλεγμένοι, οὕτως ὢν ἂν ὡς κακῶν μνησθῇς,
οὐκ ἔχουσιν ὡς συκοφαντοῦνται λέγειν. τοῖς σοῖς
οὖν, ὦ βασιλεῦ, καλοῖς ἑαλώκαμεν. σὺ δ' ἀπο-
κτείναις μὲν ἡμῶν μηδένα μηδέ γε στερήσαις μήτε
οὐσίας μήτε πατρίδος μηδέ γ' ἕτερος ἀνθ' ἑτέρου
γένοιο. 66. ὁρῶ δέ, ὡς ἐν μὲν τοῖς τοιούτοις
πάθεσι τὸ κοινὸν ἐκφεύγει τὰς αἰτίας τῶν ἐγκλημάτων ἐν τοῖς παθοῦσιν ἱσταμένων, ἃ δὲ σὺ[2]
βούλει ποιεῖν, ὅλην τὴν πόλιν περιβάλλει τῇ δίκῃ.
R 474 τὸ μὲν γάρ ἐστιν ἐν χρηστῇ πονηρούς | τινας F 1
πεφηνέναι, τὸ δὲ διὰ πάσης ἥκειν τὴν μοχθηρίαν.

67. Θαυμάζω δέ, εἰ θαυμαστόν σοι δοκεῖ τὸ μὴ
καλῶς ἡρμόσθαι τὰς πόλεις τοιούτου διδασκάλου
πολὺν δὴ χρόνον τυχούσας. οὐ πάντα ἦν ταραχῆς
καὶ ῥαθυμίας καὶ ἀμελείας μεστά; οὐχ οἱ μὲν
νόμοι γράμματα ἄλλως, ἀρχαὶ δ' ἐπωλοῦντο, τοῖς
δὲ ἀρχομένοις κρείττοσιν εἶναι τῶν ἀρχόντων

[1] μεμίσησθε F. (correction in B), Morel: μεμισῆσθαι Re.
(other mss.).
[2] ⟨σὺ⟩ F., conj. Re.

[a] Proverbial reference to the ban proclaimed by Apollo
against the killer of Archilochus, cf. Suidas, s.v., Lib. Or.
1. 74, Decl. 1. 180.
190

will be doing the emperors a favour by our misfortunes, yet do you try to make us believe that this is no punishment ? What reply shall we make if we are asked, " Why have you incurred this hatred ? " Shall we shift the blame onto you ? Yet you are beyond reproach, and the excellence of the judge discredits any whom he condemns. 65. Men whom the gods have expelled from their temples by means of their oracles are reduced to silence, as being convicted by the omniscient deity [a] : in the same way, any whom you describe as evil cannot assert that they are falsely accused. We thus stand condemned by your virtue, Sire. But I trust that you never proceed to execute any of us, nor yet deprive him of house and home, nor change your present mode of conduct. 66. In such tribulations, I observe, the community escapes blame, since the charges are concentrated upon the individual sufferers. Your intended procedure, however, embraces the whole body politic in the punishment. The normal implication is that some rogues have turned up in a city that is sound at heart ; your view is that corruption has permeated the whole.

67. What surprises me is that you are surprised at any disorderliness in the cities after their long experience under such a teacher.[b] Was not everything full of confusion, incompetence and neglect ? Was not law a dead letter and office bought and sold ? Was it not possible for the governed to ride roughshod over their governors, sending them bribes one

[b] Constantius (ὁ πάντα φθείρων, Ep. 697 : ὁ ὕπτιος, Or. 16. 37) reigned as Augustus from A.D. 337 to 361. According to Libanius, he possessed the τύχη but lacked the γνώμη of an emperor (ibid.), so that his reign became a νοσοῦσα βασιλεία or—more daringly—a παρανομοῦσα τυραννίς (Or. 14. 3, 17).

# LIBANIUS

ὑπῆρχε δείλης μὲν δῶρα πέμπουσιν, ἔωθεν δὲ
μονονοὺ ῥαπίζουσιν; οὐ τὸ μὲν δικαίως ἄρχειν
κατεγελᾶτο, τὸ δὲ μισθοφορεῖν ἐπῃνεῖτο; οὐ τὸ
μὲν καλὸν ἀσθενὲς ἐγεγόνει, τὸ δὲ ἡδὺ τὴν ἰσχὺν
εἶχεν; οὐχ ὁ πονηρευόμενος κύριος ἦν τοῦ μὴ
δοῦναι δίκην; 68. τί οὖν θαυμαστόν, εἰ τοσαύτης
ἐξουσίας εἰς κακίαν δεδομένης ἐγένετό τις τοῖς
τῶν πόλεων τρόποις ὑπὸ τοῦ καιροῦ λύμη; ἢ
τοὺς μὲν τῶν φαύλων μαθητὰς σοφιστῶν οὐκ ἔνι
γενέσθαι τεχνίτας ἀγαθοὺς λόγων, ὑπηλοῦ δὲ
ἀνδρὸς βασιλεύοντος σωφρονεῖν τὴν οἰκουμένην
ἔστι; καὶ τῇ μὲν τῶν ποιμένων ἀμαθίᾳ τὰ ποίμνια διαφθείρεται, ταῖς δὲ τῶν βασιλέων ῥᾳθυμί-
αις αἱ πόλεις παιδεύονται; | ὁποῖον ἂν ἐπιστήσῃς F
R 475 τοῖς ἵπποις ἡνίοχον, τοιοῦτον ἔλπιζέ | σοι τὸ ἅρμα
γενέσθαι. 69. διὰ τί νῦν μακαρίζομεν τὴν γῆν;
ὅτι παρῆλθεν ἐπὶ τὴν θεραπείαν αὐτῆς ἰατρὸς
ἄκρος. οὐκοῦν ὡς μεταθήσοντος τῶν πόλεων
τοὺς τρόπους καὶ δείξοντος ἀμείνους χαίρομεν. τί
οὖν δεῖ θαυμάζειν, εἰ πλημμελείας εὗρες, ἃς ἐκ
τοῦ παύειν εὐδοκιμεῖς; ἤδη τις ἵππον φαύλως
ἠγμένον ἐπρίατο πιστεύων αὐτὸν ἐπανορθώσειν τῇ
παρ' ἑαυτοῦ τέχνῃ. οὗτος οὖν εἰ τὴν πρώτην ἐπ'
αὐτὸν ἀναβὰς εὐθὺς ἠγανάκτει μὴ πάντα ἄριστον
ὁρῶν, οὔ σοι δοκεῖ δικαίως ἂν ἀκοῦσαι παρ'
αὐτοῦ λαβόντος φωνὴν ἐξ Ἥρας ὡς, Εἰδὼς μέντοι
ταῦτα ἐπρίω καὶ ὡς ἀπαλλάξων τῆς ἀταξίας διὰ

---

ᵃ Julian's criticisms of Antioch (*Misop.* 354 b ff.) and of
Constantius (Jul. *Or.* 7. 232 b ff.) are here combined by
Libanius to explain his countrymen's misconduct. Avarice
and reckless pursuit of pleasure are repeatedly imputed by

192

afternoon and next morning practically wiping the floor with them? Was not just administration laughed at and corruption commended? Virtue was out of fashion and it was a reign of pleasure, and rascals were able to get away scot-free.[a] 68. So what surprise is it that, with such free rein for wickedness, the conduct of the cities be somewhat tainted by the times? If pupils of bad teachers have no hope of becoming expert practitioners of eloquence, can the world retain any decency when a sluggard is on the throne? If flocks are ruined by the stupidity of their shepherds, are cities well schooled by the incompetence of the emperors? You can expect your chariot to be exactly as good as the driver you put in charge of it. 69. Why now do we call the world happy? Simply because an expert physician has come to tend it. We are glad, for he will alter the behaviour of the cities and improve it. What need for wonder, then, if you have found some shortcomings, for you have gained a name for repressing them?[b] People have before now bought a horse that has been considered no good, confident of being able to correct it by their own skill. If, the first time they mount, they are annoyed because they do not find it in tip-top condition, don't you think they deserve the horse to tell them, if it got the gift of speech from Hera,[c] " You knew all this when you bought me. You were going to get rid of my faults by employing the know-

Julian to Constantine and his sons (*e.g.*, *loc. cit.*, *Caesars*, 329 a, 335 b ff., *Misop.* 357 a ff.), although Ammianus remarks more impartially on the sobriety of Constantius' life.

[b] Refers not to Julian's curial legislation but to his religious policies. *cf. Or.* 18. 124 ff. (the cure of souls).

[c] Homer, *Iliad*, 19. 407.

τῆς ἐπιστήμης ἣν ἔχεις; δεῖ δὴ τῇ παιδείᾳ
χρόνου καὶ μελέτης, ὧν προϊόντων ἴσως φανοῦμαι
βελτίων. 70. βεβιώκαμεν ἀνειμένως, ὦ βασιλεῦ,
πάντες ἐπὶ τῆς ἔμπροσθεν ἐξουσίας. ἥκομεν ὑπὸ
ζυγὸν ἀκριβέστερον. πειρασόμεθα φέρειν. σύγγνωθι μικρὰ καὶ ποιήσεις ἀμείνους ἢ δεῖσθαι
συγγνώμης. καὶ ὅτι γε καινὸν οὐδὲν αἰτοῦμεν,
ἀλλ' ἤδη τοῦ συγγινώσκειν ὑπῆρξω, τῆς ἡμέρας
ἐκείνης ἀναμνήσθητι, ἐν ᾗ πονηρούς τε ἐκάλεις καὶ
σῴζειν ἠξίους. Ἥμαρτον μέν, ἀλλὰ | τρεφέσθων· F
ἐλύπησαν μέν, ἀλλὰ μὴ λιμωττόντων. δίδου
μέτρα μύρια καὶ προστίθει τρισχίλια. 71. ταῦτα
χαλάσαντος ἦν, ταῦτα οὐ τελέως μισοῦντος, ταῦτα
προσδοκῶντος μεταβολήν· οὐ γὰρ δὴ πόλιν ἀνιάτως
ἔχουσαν ἔμελλες φιλοπόνως φρουρήσειν, εἰ μὴ
κἀκεῖνα μισοῦντος ἦν ὄμβρων ἀμετρίαν ἐπιχειρεῖν
ἀνείργειν καὶ ῥύεσθαι τὴν γῆν τῶν ἐκεῖθεν κιν-
R 476 δύνων, | ὅτε τὸν πολὺν ἐκεῖνον ὑετὸν ὑπαίθριος τῷ
βωμῷ προσεστὼς ἐδέξω τῷ σώματι τῶν ἄλλων
ὑπὸ τῷ νεουργῷ συνειλεγμένων ὀρόφῳ δεδιότων
μὴ τοῖς καρποῖς βοηθῶν αὐτὸς ἰατροῦ δεηθῇς, ἀλλ'
οὐδὲν ἀπέστησέ σε[1] τῆς βοηθείας. 72. οὕτως
ὠλιγώρεις τῆς πόλεως· ὑπὲρ ἧς κἀκεῖνο προσέ-
θηκας, ᾐσθόμην γάρ· ἤρου τοὺς θεούς, εἰ πρὸς τὸ
θέρος ἥξομεν ἀστασίαστοι, γνώμην ἔχων εἰ προαί-

---

[1] ⟨σε⟩ inserted F. Conj. Re. (Animadv.): correction in I.

[a] For the famine of A.D. 362/3 cf. Petit, op. cit. pp.
109 ff. Libanius here adapts Misop. 368 c ff. for his own
argument.

ledge you have. Training needs time and practice.
Give me more of this and you will probably see some
improvement " ? 70. In the easy-going days of the
past, Sire, we all of us lived a life of indiscipline. Now
we have come under a firmer yoke, and we shall try
to bear it. Pardon our petty faults and improve us so
as to have no need of pardon. We ask for nothing
fresh, for already you have made a beginning of par-
doning us. Just recollect that day when you called us
rascals and yet saw fit to save us. " Their conduct has
been criminal, but let them be fed," you declared.
" They have angered me, but don't let them starve to
death. Give them 10,000 bushels, and another 3,000
for good measure." [a] 71. Those words were spoken in
an anger that was waning, not in utter hatred ; they
came from your anticipation of a change in us. You
would not have gone to such lengths to protect a
city that was beyond redemption, unless of course
that also was a sign of your hatred, when you tried
to ward off violent rainstorms and to protect the land
from damage resulting from them, when you stood
at the altar in the open air and yourself faced that
pouring rain. The others collected under the cover
of a freshly-made shelter and were afraid that, in
your concern for the crops, you would need a doctor
yourself, but nothing made you desist from rendering
such aid.[b] 72. Such was your contempt for our city !
On her behalf—as I saw for myself—you undertook
this further task too. You inquired of the gods
whether we would last until summer without disturbance, for you intended, in case of any indication of

[b] *Cf. Or.* 18. 177, where this incident appears as Julian's
intercession to Poseidon on behalf of Constantinople, lately
visited by earthquake.

σθοιτο¹ τις δεινόν, ἀπώσασθαι δι᾽ ὧν εἴωθας. εἶθ᾽
ὑπὲρ ὧν ὅπως μὴ ἀπολοῦνται πονεῖς, τούτους
ὅπως ἀθυμοῦντας ἀπολεῖς σκοπεῖς καὶ λιμοῦ μὲν
ἐξαιρεῖς,² λύπαις δὲ ἐκδίδως ; καὶ μένειν | μὲν βού- F 1
λει τὴν πόλιν ὡς οὐκ ἄχρηστον, αἰσχύνῃ δὲ περιβάλλει ὡς οὐδενὸς ἀξίαν ;

73. Ἀλλὰ πάντως ἡμᾶς δεῖ δοῦναι δίκην ;³
δεδώκαμεν, ὦ βασιλεῦ, καὶ ταύτην μεγάλην καὶ
μακράν, καὶ μὴν οὑτοσὶ πέμπτος τῇ τιμωρίᾳ.
στένοντες καὶ σκυθρωποὶ καὶ κατηφεῖς διηγάγομεν
οὐδὲν τῶν δεδεμένων ἄμεινον, πεπληγμένοι τὰς
ψυχάς, νέφους τὰ πρόσωπα γέμοντες, ὅμοιοι τοῖς
πενθοῦσι παίδων ἄωρον τελευτήν, δακρύοντες,
ὀδυρόμενοι, μισοῦντες ἡμᾶς αὐτούς, τοὔδαφος, τὸν
ἀέρα, τὸ ὕδωρ, τὰς οἰκίας, τοὺς ἐντυγχάνοντας,
ἀλλήλους ἐκτρεπόμενοι, κεντούμενοι τῆς νυκτός,
ὀδυνώμενοι μεθ᾽ ἡμέραν. 74. ἔσωσε μὲν Ἀλέξ-
R 477 ανδρος τὴν | πόλιν, ἔσωσεν, οὐκ ἂν ἄλλως φαίην,
ἀλλὰ μετὰ πικρῶν ῥημάτων τῶν μὲν τὴν βουλὴν
βαλλόντων, τῶν δὲ τὸν δῆμον τιτρωσκόντων οὐ
διὰ τὸ καθ᾽ ἡμέραν ἐξαμαρτάνειν, πᾶς γὰρ αὐτῷ
τὰ δίκαια παρῄνει φυλάττειν, ἀλλὰ δι᾽ ἓν ἐκεῖνο τὸ
σὲ παροξῦναι, καὶ ἀνθρώπων πάντων ἠθροισμένων
τοῖς μὲν ἄλλοις ἦν πρᾷος, ἐφ᾽ ἡμᾶς δὲ χειμάρρου
σφοδρότερος, ὥσθ᾽ ἡμῖν τὸν Κιμμερίων ἐκείνου
τοῦ χρόνου γεγονέναι βίον ἐν σκότῳ καὶ νυκτὶ

---

¹ προαίσθοιτό F. Conj. Re. (*Animadv.*) : πρόσθοιτό mss.
(except V, correction in P : πρόσθειτό).
² ἐξαιρεῖς F., Cobet : ἐξαίρεις Re. (mss.).
³ Punctuation : question Re. (mss.) : period F.

---

ᵃ The breach between Julian and Antioch began with the
burning of the temple of Apollo, 22 Oct. A.D. 362. The

196

trouble, to avert it by your usual means. So, when you exert yourself for us so that we may not die, will you seek to make us die of despair? Will you rescue us from starvation and consign us to misery? Do you want the city to remain in existence because it has its uses, and cover it with shame as being worthless?

73. Must we by all means be punished, then? Sire, we have been punished already, and a heavy, long drawn out punishment it is. It has been going on for five months now,[a] and we have spent our time in grief, misery and dejection, little better than prisoners, smitten to the heart, with gloom on our faces, like men who mourn for their children untimely dead, in tears and lamentation; we hate ourselves, our soil, our climate, our waters, our homes and all who meet us. We avoid each other's company; we feel the sting all night long, and each day we know the pain. 74. Alexander[b] saved the city, saved it, yes—but with harsh words aimed at the town council and wounding to the common folk. And it was not because of our daily misdeeds, for everyone took good care to behave himself, but simply because of what had provoked your anger. At the provincial assembly, his attitude to the rest was mild, but towards us he was as violent as a river in spate, and all that time we felt that we lived like Cimmerians, dwelling in the darkness of perpetual night, and that the sun would

date of composition is thus about mid-March, when Julian was now a fortnight away (having left Antioch on the Nones of March, A.D. 363). The language deliberately echoes *Misop.* 344 a (βαρύτητος, ἧς ἀνεχόμενοι μῆνα ἕβδομον τουτονί).

[b] The bigoted and violently pagan governor of Syria, appointed by Julian upon leaving Antioch. *Cf.* Seeck, *B.L.Z.G.* 53 iii. Petit, *op. cit.* pp. 276 f.

συνεχεῖ, τὸν δ' ἥλιον ἡμῖν ἐνομίζομεν οὐκ ἀνίσχειν.
75. τίνας ἔτι ζητεῖς | δίκας παρ' ἀνθρώπων F
ἀναλωμένων λύπῃ ; δὸς δὴ συγγνώμην, δός,
ὦ βασιλεῦ, μὴ πάντων ἐφεξῆς, ἀλλ' ὅσα ἐκ τῶν
ὠνίων ἔφυ. τῶν δὲ ἐν τῷ δρόμῳ τετολμημένων
σὺ μὲν πάλαι κατεγέλασας, ἡμεῖς δὲ ἀπαιτήσομεν
δίκας, ὡς ἀνιχνεύοντές γε τοὺς καταράτους οὐ
πεπαύμεθα. καὶ τοῦ λαβεῖν ἐσμὲν οὐ πόρρω.
σύγγνωθι δὴ πρὸς θεῶν, πρὸς δαιμόνων, πρὸς τῶν
τροπαίων, πρὸς αὐτῆς φιλοσοφίας. ἀπὸ μεγάλων
ἔργων ἥκεις. ἔστω σου καὶ τοῦτο μέγα. στεφάνω-
R 478 σον τὰς | νίκας τῇ φιλανθρωπίᾳ καὶ μὴ μόνους
ἡμᾶς[1] ἐν κοινῇ πάντων ἀνθρώπων πομπῇ καθίσῃς
κλάοντας.

76. Ἡμεῖς οἱ μισοῦντες σὲ καὶ σὴν βασιλείαν.
καὶ γὰρ ταῦτα ἀκηκόαμεν, Ἥλιε. τῶν μὲν ἔργων
σοι χωρούντων κατὰ νοῦν, τοῦ δὲ τῶν ἔργων οὔπω
φαινομένου λόγου πάντα ἀφέντες ἐν ἱκετείαις ἦμεν,
παῖδες, γέροντες, γυναῖκες, εὐθὺς μὲν καθ' ἑκάστην
ἀγειρόμενοι φυλήν, ἔπειτα εἰς ὅμιλος τὰ μέρη
γιγνόμενοι, πορευόμενοι μὲν δι' ἀγορᾶς μετὰ
λαμπρῶν τῶν εὐχῶν, ὑπερβαίνοντες δὲ τὰς πύλας
μετὰ μειζόνων, κυλινδούμενοι δὲ ἐν τῷ πεδίῳ τῷ

---

[1] ⟨ἡμᾶς⟩ inserted F., conj. Re.

[a] Cf. Homer, Od. 11. 14 ff.
[b] Cf. Or. 18. 195. Despite encroachment by imperial officials, the *curia* still possessed vestiges of disciplinary powers. Julian's criticism was that it was unwilling to use them.

198

never shine on us again.[a] 75. What punishment more
do you require of men consumed with grief? Grant us
pardon then, Sire, not for absolutely everything, but
for our short-comings with regard to our market.
As for the misconduct in the hippodrome, you
have long scorned that [b]; but we shall exact punishment for it, for we have spared no effort in tracking
the scoundrels down, and we are very near to arrest-
ing them. Then in the name of the gods and spirits,
of your victories, and of philosophy herself, pardon
us. You have come to us from mighty deeds. Let
this deed of yours be mighty too. Crown your victories with mercy, and do not reduce us alone to
tears in this triumph in which all the world shares.

76. We are the ones who hate you and your
majesty! Yes, by Helios, we have even heard that
remark passed. But as you proceeded successfully
upon your career, before the outcome was yet plain,[c]
we put all else aside, and joined in supplication, boys,
old men and women alike. First crowds gathered in
every ward of the city,[d] and then these sections
merged into one mass which passed through the city
square with a loud chorus of prayer. It went on
through the city gates and its prayers became louder
still until, as it moved up and down on the military

[c] A demonstration of loyalty held in Julian's absence on
the Persian campaign : cf. Or. 1. 133 : καὶ τούτων ἕκαστον
ἤγγελλε μὲν οὐδείς, τὴν δὲ τῶν ὁρώντων ἡδονὴν ἡδόμεθα πιστεύοντες, ἃ δὴ καὶ ἐγίγνετο, γενήσεσθαι.

[d] Antioch was, for local administration, organized into 18
φυλαί. These had corporate existence, with baths of their
own, and participated in the boxing competitions in honour
of Artemis (cf. Or. 11. 231, 11. 245, 19. 62, 5. 43 f.). They
were controlled by epimeletae, responsible for discipline,
police and services (e.g., lighting) : cf. Or 23. 11, 24. 26, 33.
35 f.

τὰς τοῦ πολέμου δεχομένῳ μελέτας μετὰ μεγίστων.[1]
ὅσοι δὲ ἡμῶν ἐν ἐπιστήμῃ | τοῦ θείου, καὶ τούτων F 1
ἐκοινώνουν καὶ πρὸς βωμοὺς ᾖσαν καὶ πάντα
R 479 τρόπον | θεραπεύοντες τοὺς δοῦναι νίκην κυρίους.
εἰ οὖν ταῦτα τῶν μισούντων, τίς ἡ τοῦ φιλεῖν
ἀπόδειξις; 77. ἀλλ' εἰσὶν οἳ δυσχεραίνουσί τι τῶν
σῶν. καὶ γὰρ πατέρας τινές. γένοιτ' ἂν οὖν τι
πατέρων γλυκύτερον; περὶ δὲ Ταρσέων, ὦ βασιλεῦ, πῶς ἔχεις; οὐδεὶς ἐκείνων ἀγροικότερόν τι
φθέγξεται· καὶ τίς ἐγγυᾶται χρησμός; τί οὖν,
ἂν ἐκδράμῃ τι ῥῆμα χαλκοτύπον ἢ σκυτοτόμον,
ἢ[2] ὃ τοὺς τοιούτους εἰκός; ζητήσεις πόλιν ἑτέραν
καὶ πάλιν ἄλλην; καὶ τὸ ποῦ δεῖ σε χειμάζειν ἐν
τοῖς ὑπηκόοις κείσεται; μήποτε τοσοῦτον ἰσχύσαιμεν.[3] ἀλλ' ἐγκάθιζε τοῖς μὲν βουλομένοις ὡς
εὐφραίνων, τοῖς δὲ οὐκ ἐθέλουσιν, ὅπως μάθωσιν
ἐθέλειν. δεῖ γὰρ τοὺς μὲν ἑκόντας γνώμῃ, τοὺς δὲ
ἄκοντας ἀνάγκῃ τὰ δέοντα ποιεῖν. 78. εἰ δὲ
σοφιστὴς ἡμῖν ἐτύγχανες ὤν, πάντως δ' ἄν, εἰ μὴ
τοῦτο ἦσθα τὸ μέγιστον καὶ θειότατον, ἀντηγωνί-
ζου μοι νῦν, ἔπειτα τῶν σῶν τις ὁμιλητῶν ἐβλά-
κευεν, ἆρ' ἂν ἐπέτρεπες; οὐκ ἔστιν· ἀλλ' εἰσήγετ'
ἂν τὸ σκῦτος. οὕτω δὴ καὶ νῦν ἅπασα πόλις μα-
θέτω βασιλέως ἐπιδημίαν φέρειν. 79. ἀλλὰ ταῦτα
μὲν περὶ τῶν τοῖς τοιούτοις βαρυνομένων, ἡμεῖς
| δὲ πάλαι τε ἐθάδες τῆς σὺν βασιλεῖ διαίτης καὶ F 1

---

[1] ⟨μετὰ μεγίστων⟩ inserted F.
[2] ἢ cancelled F., Re. (*Animadv.*).
[3] ἰσχύσαιμεν Re. (mss.) : ἰσχύσαιεν F.

---

[a] The military parade ground (τὸ πολεμικὸν γυμνάσιον :
Theodoret, *H.E.* 4. 26. 1) lay across the river and north of
the island palace. It was a favourite spot for Christian

parade ground, they reached a climax.[a] Those of us who were acquainted with religious procedure took part in them also, and approached the altars with all manner of offerings for the gods by whom victory is granted. Now, if this is the behaviour of men who hate you, how can they show their love? 77. Some people do resent some of your actions, I admit. In fact, some people resent their fathers, yet what could be dearer than one's father? But what do you think about Tarsus, Sire? Will there be no rude remarks from them? But how can you foretell that for certain? If some remark slips out, redolent of forge or tannery, or such as you can expect people of that sort to make, what then? Will you seek another city, and then another? Will it be left to your subjects to decide where you should have your winter quarters? Never let us take so much upon ourselves! Take up your residence among willing hosts to oblige them, among the unwilling, to teach them willingness, for duty must be done, by the willing voluntarily, by the reluctant under duress. 78. Were you one of the professors here,—and but for the supreme and revered position you hold, you would be my rival now—would you let it pass if one of your pupils grew lazy? Of course not. Out would come the whip. In the same way let every city now learn how to support an emperor's residence in it. 79. That is the line to take with people who resent such a thing: we however have long been used to associating with the emperor, and now our plea is not

prayer meetings conducted by the local saints (*cf.* Theodoret, *loc. cit.*, *H.R.* 1320 A, 1372 A)—as is here implied by Libanius with his distinction between the mass rally and the select religious procedure of his pagan worthies.

νῦν δεόμεθα μὴ στερηθῆναι τοῦ γέρως. ἱκετεύει
σε πόλις Ἰνάχου γένος ἔχουσα κατὰ ζήτησιν τῆς
R 480 Ἰοῦς | πλανηθέν, ἱκετεύει σε πόλις μέρος Ἀθηναίων
ἔχουσα, πόλις Μακεδόνων, πόλις Ἀλεξάνδρου τοῦ
τὰ αὐτά σοι δραμόντος, ἧς τὴν πηγὴν ἐθαύμασεν,
ἐξ ἧς ἡδέως ἔπιεν, ἱκετεύει σε πόλις πολλούς σοι
θεοὺς παρασχομένη συμμάχους, οἷς ἔθυσας, οὓς
ἐκάλεσας, μεθ' ὧν ἐστρατεύου, τὸν Ἑρμῆν, τὸν
Πᾶνα,[1] τὴν Δήμητρα, τὸν Ἄρη, τὴν Καλλιόπην,
τὸν Ἀπόλλω, τὸν Δία τόν τε ἐπὶ τῆς κορυφῆς καὶ
τὸν ἐν ἄστει, παρ' ὃν εἰσῆλθες ὕπατος, ὅθεν ἐξῆλθες
θαρρῶν, ᾧ γέγονας ὀφειλέτης. ἔχω σου γράμματα
παρὰ τῷ θεῷ κείμενα. ἧκε θύσων, ἀπόδος τὸ
χρέος καὶ θύσας μένε[2] τὸ τεταγμένον. 80. αὐτῶν
ἐκείνων νόμιζε ταῦτα ἀκούειν, αὐτοὺς ὁρᾶν οἵου
νῦν. ἴσως δὲ καὶ βλέπεις περιεστῶτας ἡγουμένου
τοῦ Διός, ὃς λαβὼν ἡμᾶς ἤδη σου μαχομένου
R 481 τρέμοντας ἐπέρρωσέ τε καὶ παρεθάρρυνεν | ἐναργεῖ
τεκμηρίῳ. τοῦτο δὲ ἦν, κύκνον τις ἑλὼν ἐν ταῖς
ὄχθαις τῆς λίμνης φέρων ἀνέθηκε τῷ θεῷ. ὁ δὲ
τῶν μὲν πτερῶν οὐ παρῄρητο, τὴν δὲ ἰσχὺν
ἀποβεβλήκει τῶν πτερύγων, οἷόν τι συμβαίνει
περὶ τοὺς κύκνους, ὅταν ἐκπεσόντες | τῆς ἐν τοῖς F
ἔλεσιν ἐλευθερίας ἀνθρώποις ὑποχείριοι γένωνται.

---

[1] τὸν Πᾶνα inserted F. (V) : om. Re. (other mss.).
[2] ⟨κατὰ⟩ inserted F. before τὸ.

---

[a] For the foundation legends of Antioch : Io, cf. Or. 11.
44 ff. (Cook, Zeus, 1, pp. 236 f.) : Athenians, cf. Or. 11. 58,
92 : Alexander, ibid. 72 ff., 88. Malalas, p. 234.

[b] For Julian's sacrifices at Antioch cf. Misop. 346 b f.,
Lib. Or. 18. 171 f. The Antiochenes dubbed him victimarius
for his pains : Amm. Marc. 22. 14.

[c] The patroness of Antioch : cf. Or. 1. 102.

to lose the privilege. Our city claims descent from the race of Inachus that wandered far in search of Io ; she has an Athenian element ; she is a city of Macedonians, of Alexander who trod the same path as yourself; he admired its spring and gladly drank of its water[a]; this city makes its supplication to you. She has given many gods to be your allies. You have sacrificed and made invocation to them,[b] and you have soldiered with them, Hermes, Pan, Demeter, Ares, Calliope,[c] Apollo, the Zeus of the mountain[d] and the Zeus in the city,[e] whose presence you entered as consul and left in confidence, and in whose debt you are. I have writings of yours that were deposited with the god. Then come and sacrifice ; repay your debt, and, after the sacrifice ordained, stay with us. 80. Think that you are listening to this from their very lips; think that you behold them now. Perhaps you even see them grouped around you with Zeus at their head. He recently found us fearful while you were in the thick of the fray,[f] and he gave us strength and confidence by a visible sign. A swan was caught on the banks of the lake and brought as offering to the god. Though its pinions had not been clipped, it had lost the power of its wings, as happens with swans when they leave the freedom of their marshes and fall into the hands of men. 81. For most

[d] Zeus Cassius : cf. Or. 18. 172. Amm. Marc. 22. 14. 4. The shrine was on the summit of Mt. Cassius, south of the city.

[e] Zeus Philius : cf. Or. 1. 122. In Or. 18. 172 Libanius attributes to Zeus Cassius the support here received of Zeus Philius. Julian evidently composed a thanksgiving oration to Zeus.

[f] i.e., during Julian's advance along the Euphrates in March.

LIBANIUS

81. τὸν μὲν δὴ ἄλλον χρόνον ἐπὶ γῆς ἦν οὐκ
ἐπιχειρῶν αἴρεσθαι. θυσίαν δέ τινα ποιουμένων
ἑβδόμῃ ἱσταμένου ὡς προσῆλθε τῷ ἱερῷ τὸ πῦρ,
ὁρμήσας ὁ κύκνος πρὸς τὸν ἀέρα τρὶς τὸν νεὼν
ὑπ' αὐτὰ τὰ γεῖσα τῷ πτερῷ περιδραμών, ἔπειτα
μετεωριζόμενος ἀναβὰς ἀφῆκεν αὐτὸν πρὸς τὴν ἕω.
καὶ αὐτίκα βοή τε¹ ἦν χαιρόντων, ἐξαλλομένων,
κυβιστώντων μνήμῃ τῆς τοῦ Διὸς μεταβολῆς, ἣν
εἰς τοῦτον τὸν ὄρνιν μεταστήσας ἑαυτὸν τὴν
Ἑλένην ἔσπειρεν, ἐδόκει τε πᾶσιν ἐπείγεσθαι
συνεξαιρήσων τὸ Περσικόν. 82. οὗτος μετ' ἐμοῦ
νῦν ἀγορεύει βουλόμενος τῇ μὲν πόλει γενέσθαι
διαλλαγάς, ἐμοὶ δὲ τὴν ἐκ τοῦ δοκεῖν πεπεικέναι
δόξαν. μὴ τοίνυν ἀτιμάσῃς μηδὲ ἐλέγξῃς ῥήτορα
ψήφῳ σῇ κεκοσμημένον. ἔδωκας τοὺς πυροὺς
ἐμοῦ δεηθέντος, λῦσον τὴν ὀργὴν ἐμοῦ δεομένου.
μὴ κάμῃς σεμνύνων ἄνθρωπον ἐκκρουσθέντα πολλάκις ὕπνου ταῖς περὶ σοῦ φροντίσι μηδ' ἀποπέμ-
R 482 ψῃς ἄπρακτον εἰς τὴν | πατρίδα κύπτοντα, ἐρυθρι-
ῶντα, ἐγκεκαλυμμένον, αἰσχυνόμενον μὲν τῶν
πολιτῶν τοὺς παρόντας, αἰσχυνόμενον δὲ τοὺς
ἀπόντας. 83. οἷς | ἐπειδὰν προαπαντῶντες ἐρω- F 15
τῶσι· Πεπείκαμεν, ὦ πρεσβευτά; τί ἀποκρί-
νωμαι; προσωπείου μοι δεήσει τότε ἢ νὴ Δία γε,
νυκτὸς εἰς τὴν εἴσοδον καιροῦ κρύπτοντος φοινισ-
σομένην παρειάν. οἴκοι δὲ γενόμενον ἀνάγκη
καθειργμένον μένειν, ὡς οὐκ οἴσω τοὺς εἰς ἐμὲ

¹ ⟨τε⟩ inserted F.

ᵃ Cf. Ep. 824 : ἐγὼ δὲ λιμοῦ μὲν τὴν πόλιν ἱκετεύων ἐξειλόμην,
. . . πεῖσαι δὲ ὡς οὐκ ἠδίκηται παρ' ἡμῶν ἐπεχείρησα μέν, ἀπ-
204

of the time it stayed on the ground without attempting to fly, but at the end of the first week of the month people were making a sacrifice. As the flame approached the offering, the swan rose up into the air and three times circled round the temple at cornice level, and then soaring aloft it flew away towards the east. And there arose a cry, as the spectators danced up and down for joy, remembering Zeus' transformation into such a bird on the occasion that he sired Helen. Everyone was agreed that he was hastening to assist in the destruction of Persia. 82. He is now my advocate, desiring reconciliation for the city, and for myself the credit of seeming to convince you. Do not then dishonour and disgrace an orator who has been honoured by your approval. At my request, you granted them grain[a]; at my request, abate your wrath. Do not be stiff-necked and weary out one who has often been robbed of sleep through concern for you, nor send me away to my homeland empty-handed and skulking, with blushing face and covered head, ashamed before my fellow citizens, whether present or absent. 83. When they come to meet me inquiring, " Have we won our case, ambassador ? ", what answer can I give them ? I will need a mask then, or else, by heaven, the cover of night, for my entrance into the city, to allow me to hide my burning cheeks.[b] When I reach home, I must stay confined there, for I shall be unable to bear their gaze as they point out to their neighbours

ἦλθον δὲ οὐ δυνηθείς. . . . λείπεται δὴ πρὸς διαλλαγάς, ἐφ' ὃ ἡμεῖς τετράμμεθα.

[b] The representation of this oration as a personal embassy to the absent emperor was recognized as an artistic fiction by Socrates, H.E. 3. 17 : τούτους μὲν τοὺς λόγους φασὶ γράψαντα τὸν σοφιστὴν μηκέτι εἰς πολλοὺς εἰρηκέναι.

# LIBANIUS

βλέποντας δεικνύντας τοῖς πέλας τὸν ἡττημένον.
84. ἀλλὰ γὰρ ἔστιν ἡμῖν ὄρη μεγάλα καὶ ὑψηλὰ
καὶ λάσια, ἀνθρακέων τινῶν δῆμοι καὶ ἄντρα καὶ
καλύβαι. παρὰ τούτους ἥξω μεταθέμενος τοὔνομα
καὶ στολὴν μεταλλάξας καὶ ὅσα ἂν ἐξῇ τῶν περὶ
τὸ πρόσωπον. ἐνταῦθα ἐπ' ἐρημίας κείσομαι
πόρρω τῆς πόλεως ἣν οὐκ ἔσχον ὀνῆσαι.

85. Χορηγῶν μὲν ἐγενόμην ἔκγονος, ὦ βασιλεῦ,
χορηγεῖν δὲ αὐτὸς ὑπὸ τῆς Τύχης ἐκωλύθην.
αἰσχρὸν δὲ ζῆν μηδὲν εὖ ποιεῖν τὴν αὐτοῦ δυνάμενον. ἐπειδὴ τοίνυν τῶν τερπουσῶν λειτουργιῶν
ἀπολέλειμμαι, δεῖξόν με τῇ σῳζούσῃ φιλοτιμού-
μενον. 86. καὶ μή μοι λεγέτω τις τὴν ἐν Κιλικίᾳ
παρασκευήν. βουλήθητι μόνον, καὶ πάντα ἕψεται. |
R 483 πέντε ἡμερῶν τὸ ἔργον καὶ καμήλων οὐ πολλῶν.
εἶδες ἡμᾶς ἠσθενηκότας, ὅρα καὶ δύναμιν ἔχοντας.
λάβε πεῖραν τοῦ τόκου τῆς γῆς, ἐπειδὴ καὶ τῶν
ἐναντίων. νῦν εἴσῃ σαφῶς εἴτε κακίας ἦν εἴτε
δυστυχίας ἐκεῖνα.

---

[a] Mt. Silpius provided refuge for oppressed members of
the commons (e.g., Or. 1. 226 f.) and Christian hermits
(Theodoret, H.E. 4. 28).

[b] Libanius was descended from one of the principal
families of Antioch, and might have been expected to become
a city councillor like the rest of his family (Or. 1. 3 ff.). He
would then have been liable to the performance of the
liturgies—services rendered by the *curiales* to the city—of

the man who lost their case for them. 84. However, we have great, high, forest-clad mountains, settlements of charcoal-burners, caves and cottages. There shall I retire under an assumed name, changing my dress and facial appearance as best I may, and there shall I dwell in the wilderness, far from the city that I could not aid.[a]

85. Though I am descended of men who held the post of choregos, Sire, Fortune has prevented me from undertaking such a duty myself. It is a wretched business to live and be unable to be of service to one's own community. Since, then, I am deprived of the services that delight them, show that I am honoured with a service that protects them.[b] 86. And let there be no talk of preparing your residence in Cilicia. Only wish it, and everything will follow. It needs five days and a few camels. You have seen us in our weakness : now see us in our strength. See for yourself what our land can produce, since you have seen what it could not. Now you will know for certain whether that was due to our fault or our misfortune.

which the most important and expensive was the *choregia* (the provision of public entertainment). Libanius normally speaks of this deprivation in pathetic tones (*e.g.*, *Or.* 1. 58, 11. 9, 55. 15), but he was in fact deliberate in his choice of a sophistic career (*cf. Or.* 1. 11 ff.) and tenacious of the immunity from such curial services that he obtained thereby.

# ORATION 16

# ΠΡΟΣ ΑΝΤΙΟΧΕΑΣ ΠΕΡΙ ΤΗΣ ΤΟΥ ΒΑΣΙΛΕΩΣ ΟΡΓΗΣ

R 484   1. Ἃ μὲν ὑπὲρ τῆς πόλεως, ὦ ἄνδρες Ἀντιοχεῖς, F ι
πρὸς τὸν αὐτοκράτορα διείλεγμαι καὶ ὡς οὔτ᾽
ἀγῶνος οὔθ᾽ ἱκετειῶν οὐδοτιοῦν παραλέλοιπα,
μεμαθήκατε τὰ μὲν αὐτοῦ μου διηγουμένου πρὸς
ὑμᾶς οὐχ ὡς ἄν τινος σεμνυνομένου μᾶλλον ἢ
παραμυθουμένου, τὰ πλείω δὲ τοῦ βασιλέως μεμη-
νυκότος ἐνταῦθά τε πρὸς τὸν ἱερέα λέγοντος
ἠνωχλῆσθαι παρ᾽ ἐμοῦ καὶ πάλιν ἐν τῷ σταθμῷ
πρὸς τὸ κοινὸν τὸ ὑμέτερον· | ἃ δὲ καὶ ὑμᾶς F ᴵ
ἀκοῦσαι δεῖ περί τε τῶν κατεχόντων δυσχερῶν καὶ
περὶ[1] τῆς τοῦ βασιλέως ὀργῆς καὶ πῶς ἂν ἐκείνην
τε παύσαιμεν καὶ δόξαιμεν γεγονέναι βελτίους,
ταῦτα πειράσομαι διελθεῖν. 2. ἔδει γὰρ ἐκεῖ μὲν
ὑμᾶς ἐξαιρεῖσθαι αἰτίας ἐπιχειρεῖν, ἐνταῦθα δὲ
R 485 μὴ | κρύπτειν ἅ τις ἂν ἡμᾶς αἰτιάσαιτο δικαίως.
τὸ μὲν γὰρ εἶχε συγγνώμην καὶ τετύχηκε καλῶς

---

[1] καὶ περὶ τῆς Re. (UBM) : περὶ om. F. (other mss.).

---

[a] *Oration* 16 : a companion piece to the preceding,
written at the same time. Socr. *H.E.* 3. 17, confirming *Or.*
17. 37, notes that neither was actually delivered. On these
orations *cf.* Petit, " Recherches sur la publication et la

# TO THE ANTIOCHENES: ON THE EMPEROR'S ANGER[a]

1. MEN of Antioch, you know of my speech before the emperor on our city's behalf, and how I left no form of ordeal or supplication untried.[b] Some of this you have learned from my own account to you, though my intention was not so much to preen myself upon it as to offer words of advice, but for the most part the information came from the emperor. Here in Antioch he told the priest that he had been pestered by my attentions, and again, at the post station, he told your council the same.[c] Now I shall try to give some account of what you should be told about the evils that beset us, the emperor's wrath against us, and the manner in which we can bring that to an end and be seen to have mended our ways. 2. There I had to try to free you from complaints made against you. Here I must not seek to conceal any accusation which may be justly levelled against you. Then my concern was with pardon for you, and fortunately it

diffusion des discours de Libanius," *Historia*, 5 (1956), pp. 479 ff.

[b] Not *Oration* 15, but personal intercessions made before Julian's departure, *cf. Epp.* 802, 815, 824.

[c] For Julian's final interview with the Antiochene *curia* at Litarba, the post-station, *cf.* Julian, *E.L.F.* No. 98 (399 bc), Amm. Marc. 23. 2. 4, Lib. *Or.* 1. 132. These speeches were composed in consequence of the rebuff administered there.

ποιοῦν, τῷ δ᾽ ἂν τὰ μέγιστα βλαβείημεν, εἰ
μείναιμεν ἐπὶ τῶν αὐτῶν ὡς οὐδὲν ἡμαρτηκότες.
3. καὶ ὅτι μὲν ἢ πάντας ἢ τοὺς πλείους ἀνιάσω διὰ
τῆς παρρησίας οὐκ ἀγνοῶ, πολὺ δέ γε βέλτιον
λυπηθέντας τοῖς λόγοις ἡσθῆναι τοῖς ἀπ᾽ αὐτῶν
ἔργοις ἢ νῦν τὰ τέρποντα ἀκούσαντας ἀντὶ μικρᾶς
ἡδονῆς πολλὴν καὶ μεγάλην ὑπομεῖναι ζημίαν. εἰ
μὲν γὰρ ἦν ἐπαινεῖν τε ὑμᾶς ὁμοῦ καὶ δι᾽ ὧν ἂν
τὸν κίνδυνον ἐκφύγοιμεν δεικνύειν, μανίας ἂν ἦν
δήπου μὴ τοῦτον αἱρεῖσθαι τῶν λόγων τὸν τρόπον·
ἐπειδὴ δὲ διὰ τῆς ἐν τῷ λέγειν χάριτος ἀνάγκη τὸ
συμφέρον ἀπολωλέναι, σωφρονούντων ἂν εἴη τὰ φέροντα τὴν σωτηρίαν πρὸ τῶν κολακευόντων ποιήσασθαι.

4. Δημοσθένης μὲν οὖν τοῖς αὑτοῦ πολίταις
παραινῶν ἀθυμοῦσι μὴ οὕτως ἔχειν ἠξίου μηδ᾽
ὡς οὐκ οὔσης χρηστῆς ἐλπίδος διακεῖσθαι τὰς
γνώμας· ἐγὼ | δὲ τοσοῦτον ἀπέχω τοῦ συμβου-  F 16
λεύειν ὑμῖν ἀποθέσθαι τὴν ἀθυμίαν, ὥστ᾽ οὐδ᾽
ἂν ἄλλως ἡγοῦμαι σωθῆναι τὴν πόλιν εἰ μὴ
προσθεῖμεν τῇ παρούσῃ καὶ τοὺς πώποτε δόξαντας
μεθ᾽ ὑπερβολῆς πεπενθηκέναι παρέλθοιμεν τῇ λύπῃ.
5. ὡς οὕτως ἔχει· εἰ μὲν ὡς περὶ κούφου τοῦ
παρόντος καιροῦ διανοηθείημεν, μεῖζον ποιήσομεν
τὸ κακόν, ἐνδειξάμενοι πᾶσιν ὡς οὐδὲν ἔσται
R 486 τοσοῦτον ἀπ᾽ οὐδενὸς | ὃ ταράξει τὴν πόλιν· ἂν δ᾽
ἀπογνῶμεν τὰ βελτίω καὶ λάβωμεν φόβον ὃν
εἰκὸς τοὺς ὑπὲρ αὐτῶν τῶν ἐδαφῶν εἰς κίνδυνον
ἥκοντας, πρῶτον μὲν ἄμεινον περὶ τῶν λοιπῶν
μετὰ τούτου βουλευσόμεθα τοῦ δέους. ἔπειτα καὶ
τοῦτ᾽ ἂν ἴσως ἀρκέσαι τῷ βασιλεῖ πόλιν δοκοῦσαν

succeeded. Now it would be disastrous for us if we maintain the same attitude and regard ourselves as innocent. 3. I am perfectly well aware that I shall displease all or most of you by my frankness, but it is far better for you to find my remarks disagreeable and yet be pleased with their consequences, than for you to listen to something you like and, for the sake of some paltry pleasure, suffer much severe punishment. If it were possible to speak favourably of you and at the same time to show how we could escape our danger, it would surely be madness not to choose this manner of address. However, since a comfortable discourse is bound to be to your detriment, it would be mere common sense to speak in terms conducive to your welfare rather than in tones of flattery.

4. When Demosthenes encouraged his fellow citizens in their despondency, he begged them not to behave so nor to adopt an attitude of hopelessness.[a] I, however, have no intention of advising you to lay aside your despondency. In fact I think our city cannot be saved in any other way than by our adding to it and outdoing in grief any who have ever been thought to have plumbed the depths of despair. 5. This is our situation. If we are disposed to regard our present crisis as a trifling matter, we shall make our troubles all the worse, for we prove to everyone that no one can do anything that holds terrors for the city. If, however, we give up any hope of better things and experience that fear natural to those who have embarked on a course hazardous for its very foundations, first, our future policies will be improved, with this fear to guide us, and secondly, the very fact that a city that has a name for great

---

[a] Demosth. *Phil.* 1. 2.

ἐπὶ μεγάλου φρονήματος εἶναι παρὰ πάντα τὸν
χρόνον ἐκπεπλῆχθαι καὶ ταπεινὴν γεγονέναι καὶ
πιστεύειν ὡς ἀπολεῖται.

6. Πολλαὶ μὲν οὖν ἀεὶ καὶ μεγάλαι συμφοραὶ τὴν
ταλαίπωρον ταυτηνὶ περιέσχον, καὶ ἴσως οὐ μετὰ
δεξιῶν συμβόλων ὁ Σέλευκος αὐτὴν ἐποίει. τῇ
γοῦν δυνάμει τῶν Περσῶν ἀπὸ τῶν ἡμετέρων
κακῶν εὐδοκιμεῖν ὑπῆρξεν, ὥσπερ παλαιστῇ τὸν
αὐτὸν ἀντίπαλον πολλάκις καταβαλόντι. πότε
γὰρ οὐκ ἐστράτευσαν ἐπὶ | τήνδε τὴν γῆν ; ἢ F 1
πότε ἐπελθόντες οὐκ ἀνῃρήκασιν, ἃ μὲν ἐδύναντο
κατασκάπτοντες, κατὰ δὲ τῶν λοιπῶν τῷ πυρὶ
χρώμενοι ; 7. φιλόνεικοι δὲ ἄρα ἦσαν οἱ ἡμέτεροι
πρόγονοι καὶ οὐκ εἰδότες δαίμοσιν ἐξίστασθαι
τόπων. οὓς ἐχρῆν ἐνθυμηθέντας ὅτι τις ἄρα
φθόνος πολεμεῖ τῷ χωρίῳ, μετὰ τὸ πρῶτον εὐθύς,
εἰ δὲ μή, τό γε δεύτερον πτῶμα ζητῆσαι γῆν
ἑτέραν, ὥσπερ οἱ Φωκαεῖς ἐκεῖνοι. νῦν δὲ ἀνίστα-
σαν καὶ πάλιν ἐδείκνυσαν πόλιν, οὐκ εἰδότες ὅτι
κακοῖς ἑτέροις ἑτοιμάζουσι τὸ ἄστυ.

8. Πολλῶν δὲ δὴ καὶ δεινῶν κατασεισάντων, ὦ
ἄνδρες πολῖται, πρότερον τὴν ἡμετέραν οὐδὲ μίαν
ἔγωγ᾽ ἂν τῇ παρούσῃ συμφορᾷ ἐξισοῦσθαι φαίην
ἄν. πρῶτον μὲν γὰρ οὐχ ὅμοιον ὑπὸ τῶν φύσει
πολεμίων πάσχειν κακῶς ἢ παρὰ τῶν οἰκείων

---

[a] Julian, at his departure, had appointed as governor of
Syria Alexander of Heliopolis, a heavy-handed martinet,
" not because he deserved the post, but because a governor
of his kidney was best suited to the greedy and insubordinate
Antiochenes." The end of the *Misopogon* contains a barely-
concealed threat to let the *curia* stew in its own juice (370 bc).

214

arrogance has for all time been humbled and panic stricken and is convinced of its imminent doom, may perhaps satisfy the emperor.[a]

6. Many great misfortunes have ever afflicted this poor city. Perhaps the omens were unpropitious when Seleucus founded it.[b] At any rate, the Persian empire has succeeded in winning prestige from our misfortunes, like a wrestler flooring the same opponent time and again. Always this land of ours has been the target for their attacks. Always in their invasions they have ravaged it, demolishing all they could and firing the rest.[c] 7. Our ancestors were obstinate indeed in their refusal to abandon the site to the gods. They should have recognized that there was some opposing influence hostile to the place, and, if not after the first disaster, at any rate after the second, they should have done as the Phocaeans of old did, and sought another land.[d] As it is, they rebuilt her, and once again revealed her as a city, heedless of the fact that they were merely making the town ready for further troubles.

8. Many and terrible indeed, my fellow countrymen, have been the disasters that in the past have shaken her to her foundations. Yet not one of them could I at any rate compare with the disaster that afflicts us now. In the first place, there is no comparison between disasters suffered at the hands of our natural foes and the hatred for us evinced by our

Moreover, besides the loss of prestige entailed by the proposed transfer of the imperial residence to Tarsus, Antioch was in some danger of losing her metropolitan status altogether.

[b] For the foundation by Seleucus I Nicator cf. Or. 11. 84 ff.
[c] Cf. Or. 15. 16, 24. 38 (and note).
[d] Herod. 1. 164.

215

καὶ ὧν εἰκὸς ἦν ἀπολαύειν τῆς προνοίας[1] μισεῖσθαι.
9. ἀλλ᾽ ὥσπερ πολλῷ δεινότερον ὑπὸ τοῦ πατρὸς
ἐλαύνεσθαι καὶ κατήγορον ἔχειν αὐτὸν τὸν γεγεν-
R 487 νηκότα τοῦ παρὰ | τῶν ἔξω τοῦ γένους ἐπιβουλεύ-
εσθαι, οὕτω μεῖζον κακὸν τῷ Ῥωμαίων βασιλεῖ
δοκεῖν ἀξίαν ἀναστάσεως εἶναι τὴν πόλιν ἢ παρὰ
τῶν βαρβάρων ἔργῳ τοῦτο παθεῖν. 10. τὸ μὲν γὰρ
ὁ τοῦ πολέμου νόμος οἶδε, | καὶ τῶν εἰωθότων τὸ F
πλῆθος,[2] τοῦ δὲ οὐ πολλὰ τὰ παραδείγματα. καὶ
τοῦ μὲν ἄν τις αἰτιάσαιτο τὴν τύχην, τὸ δὲ τῆς
γνώμης ἔλεγχον ἔχειν δοκεῖ. καὶ τὸ μὲν ἐλεεῖται
παρὰ τῶν ὁμοφύλων, καὶ βοηθεῖν εἰσιν ἕτοιμοι
τοῖς πεπληγμένοις, τῶν δ᾽ ἅπας τις ἂν τὴν φιλίαν
φύγοι τοῦ πολὺ τῇ γνώμῃ διεστάναι σημεῖον
ἐκφέρων τὸ μισεῖν. 11. οὔκουν εἰ μὴ πέπτωκεν
ἡμῖν ἡ πόλις προσήκει χαίρειν ἢ μετρίως τὴν
δυσκολίαν φέρειν, ἀλλ᾽ εἰ τὴν πρὶν ἀποβαλοῦσα
δόξαν ἐν ταῖς μοχθηροτάταις τέτακται μᾶλλον ἀλγεῖν ἢ εἰ τοὺς πολεμίους ἀπὸ τῶν τειχῶν ἑωρῶμεν.
ἐμοὶ γὰρ εἴη μάλιστα μὲν καὶ σώζεσθαι καὶ
σπουδαίῳ δοκεῖν, εἰ δ᾽ ἕλκοι πρὸς αὑτὴν ἡ κακία,
μετριώτερον, ὦ ἄνδρες πολῖται, τελευτὴ πονηρίας.
12. οὑτωσὶ μὲν οὖν εἰ καὶ θαρρεῖν ὑπῆρχε περὶ τοῦ
μέλλοντος, διά γε τὴν παροῦσαν αἰσχύνην ἔδει
καταδύεσθαι καὶ στένειν καὶ νομίζειν τῇ πόλει
σχῆμα προσήκειν οἷον ἐν τοῖς κήδεσιν οἶκον
R 488 ἕκαστον καταλαμβάνει, νῦν δ᾽ οὔσης | τῆς ἀδοξίας

---

[1] ἀπολαύειν τῆς προνοίας F. (CAPU) : τῆς προνοίας ἀπολαύειν
Re. (other mss.).
[2] πλῆθος Re. (mss. except Mo) : πάθος F., Cobet (Mo).

216

own kith and kin and people whose good will we would normally expect to enjoy. 9. It is a far more shocking thing to be persecuted by one's own father and to have one's parent as an accuser than to be assailed by those not of one's own kin. Similarly, it is a far worse thing for the Roman emperor to consider that our city is deserving of ruin than for us actually to experience it at the hands of the barbarian.[a] 10. That is one of the practices not unknown to war and an incident of not uncommon frequency : examples of this are few. There fortune could be blamed : here there is implied a disapproval of one's attitude. There the reaction of kinsfolk is one of pity and there is a readiness to help the afflicted : here everyone would avoid friendship with us, and publish his hatred as indication of his very different attitude. 11. Hence it is no matter for rejoicing or for making light of this ill-feeling if our city still stands. Rather should we be more grieved at the loss of our previous good fame and our relegation to the company of the most disaffected states than at the sight of the enemy from our battlements. My chief desire is for my preservation and the retention of my name for integrity, and, if the attractions of treason prevail, then, men of Antioch, death would be preferable to dishonour. 12. Thus, even if we have grounds for confidence for the future, we ought to be overwhelmed at our present disgrace : we ought to be in mourning and think that the city should assume the appearance that every household assumes in times of bereavement. Now our disgrace is so great that there is none to

---

[a] The emperor still holds the title of *pater patriae*, first bestowed on Augustus.

τοσαύτης οὐδ' ὁ μηδὲν πείσεσθαι τῶν ἀνηκέστων
ἐγγυώμενός ἐστιν, εἰ μή με λελήθατε χρησμοὺς
ἐκ Δελφῶν δεξάμενοι. 13. ἕως οὖν ἀκμάζει τῆς
ὀργῆς ταύτης ἡ φλόξ, τίς οὕτως ἀνδρεῖος ὅστις |
οὐκ ἀξιώσει τρέμειν; οὐκ ἴστε, ὡς ὅσα οἱ σει- F
σμοὶ δύνανται καὶ οἱ σκηπτοὶ καὶ αἱ τῆς θαλάττης
ἐκδρομαί, τοσαῦτα καὶ οὐδὲν ἐλάττω βασιλέως
θυμός; ἰσχύει γέ τοι τοῖς στρατεύμασι κατὰ τῶν
ὅπλα οὐκ ἐχόντων, κἂν ἀναρπάσαι[1] νεύσῃ πόλιν,
οἴχεται ἡ μεγίστη τῶν ἁπασῶν ἐν ἡμέρας σμικρῷ
μέρει χειρί, σιδήρῳ, πυρί, τοῖς ἄλλοις. 14. ὁ δὲ
ταύτην ὀκνῶν τὴν ὑπερβολὴν ἀφελὼν ἃ πόλεώς
ἐστι γνωρίσματα, κώμης σχῆμα περιέθηκε. βλέ-
ψατε δὴ εἰς Καππαδοκίαν ἐκείνην. ἐκεῖ πόλις
εὐδαίμων καὶ λαμπρὰ καὶ τοῦ δύνασθαι λέγειν
ἐπιμελουμένη καὶ χειμάδιον βασιλεῖ γεγενημένη
πολλάκις ἐξώσθη τοῦ τῶν πόλεων καταλόγου
δόξασά τι θρασύτερον ποιεῖν τῆς ἐξουσίας. τί
οὖν; οὐκ εὖ[2] φρονούντων ἀνθρώπων ἐστὶ πεφρι-
κέναι, δακρύειν, σκοπεῖν ὅπως τι τῶν ἡμαρτη-
R 489 μένων ἀναλύσομεν; | 15. εἶτ' ἀναστάς τις ἐν-
ταῦθα ἐρήσεται· Καὶ ποῦ τοῦτο | ἀδίκημα ἡμέ- F
τερον, εἰ μήτε ἔδωκεν ὅσα προσῆκεν ἡ γῆ τάς τε
ἐμπορίας ἔπαυσε τὰ περὶ τὰς τιμὰς τῶν ὠνίων
νεωτερισθέντα; ὁ δὲ τοσοῦτος[3] λόγος ἀτυχοῦντας
δείκνυσιν, εἰ μηδὲν ἀδικοῦντες μεμισήμεθα. ὥστ'

---

[1] ἀναρπάσαι Re., F. : ἁρπάσαι mss.
[2] τί οὖν; οὐκ εὖ F. (U unpunctuated) : τί οὖν εὖ Re. (mss.).
[3] τοσοῦτος Re. (mss. except V, P corrected) : τοιοῦτος F.
(other mss.).

---

[a] A warning appropriate and topical in A.D. 363, when

guarantee that we shall not suffer the most extreme penalty unless, unawares to me, you have had some oracle from Delphi. 13. So while this blazing wrath increases, who is so brave as to feel no tremor? Don't you know that the emperor's wrath is no less potent than earthquake,[a] thunderbolt and tidal wave? By his armies he prevails over the unarmed, and if he decides upon the destruction of a city, then the greatest of them is gone in less than half an hour by might and main and fire and sword and the rest. 14. And if he refuses to go to such extremes, he takes away all the paraphernalia of a city and gives it the status of a village. Just look at what happened there in Cappadocia. There a prosperous and famous city, that practised eloquence and had often been the imperial winter residence, was erased from the number of cities, since its conduct was held to be too undisciplined for its position.[b] So should not we, as loyal subjects, tremble and weep and consider some method of purging our error? 15. Then will any man rise to his feet and ask us here, " Well, how are we at fault, if the land has not produced the amount it should and if the innovations dealing with the prices of goods have paralysed business?"[c] Such a bold argument proves us unfortunate, in having incurred dislike without having done any wrong. So in either

earthquakes of uncommon severity occurred : *cf. Or.* 1. 134, Amm. Marc. 23. 1.

[b] Caesarea (*E.L.F.* No. 125 = Sozom. *H.E.* 5. 4. 1 ff., 5. 11. 8). The strong Christian element there had recently converted the Temple of Fortune to its own uses, and so roused Julian's anger against the city.

[c] Julian's price edict of October A.D. 362 : *cf.* Jul. *Misop.* 350 a ff., 368 c, Lib. *Or.* 18. 195.

ἐξ ἀμφοτέρων συνεστάλθαι καὶ θρηνεῖν νοῦν ἐχόν
των ἐστίν, εἴτ' ἐξεπίτηδες ἄρχοντα χρηστὸν ἠδική
καμεν εἴτ' οὐδὲν ἡμαρτηκότας δαίμων τις ἐχθρὸς
ταύτῃ περιβέβληκε τῇ δόξῃ. 16. ἀλλ' ἐπειδὴ παρ'
ὑμῶν μὲν τὸ μηδὲν ἠδικηκέναι πολύ, παρ' ἐκείνου
δὲ τὸ τὰ μέγιστα ἠδικῆσθαι, τοιαύτην μὲν οὐκ ἂν
εὐξαίμην ἔγωγε διακρῖναι δίκην, ἄμφω γὰρ φίλω,[1]
καὶ ἥ τε πατρὶς τίμιον ὅ τε βασιλεὺς αἰδέσιμος καὶ
κατὰ τὴν αὑτοῦ[2] φωνὴν ἑταῖρος καί, τὸ μέγιστον,
ἀπὸ τῶν λόγων οὓς ἀδελφοὺς ἐγώ τε κἀκεῖνος
τίκτομεν. οὐ μὴν ἀλλ' ἐπειδὴ δεῖ πάντα ὕστερα
τῆς ἀληθείας εἶναι καὶ προεῖπον ὡς οὐδὲν ὑποστει
λάμενος ἃ φρονῶ λέξω, καὶ καταστήσας ἅπαξ ἐν
τῷ συμβουλεύειν ἐμαυτὸν εἰς ἀνάγκην κατακέ
R 490 κλειμαι | τοῦ τὴν ψῆφον ἐνεγκεῖν, λεκτέον ἅ γε
φαίνεται.

17. Οὐδ' εἰ πάνυ πολλάκις, ὦ ἄνδρες Ἀντιοχεῖς,
φαίην μάτην ὑμῖν ἐγκαλεῖν τὸν βασιλέα, δυναίμην
ἂν πλὴν ὑμῶν πεῖσαί τινα. ἥ τε γὰρ περὶ θεοὺς |
εὐσέβεια τό τε πρὸς τοὺς ἀρχομένους ἥμερον ἥ τε F 1
φύσις φιλοσοφίᾳ προσήκουσα τά τε μαθήματα
συνηγωνισμένα τῇ φύσει, πάντα ταῦτα καθ' ἡμῶν
γίγνεται καὶ μαρτυρεῖ καὶ μονονουχὶ βοᾷ ὅτι μᾶλ
λον ἡ πόλις εἰς ἐκεῖνον ἥμαρτεν ἢ παρ' ἐκείνου τι
περὶ ἡμᾶς πεπλημμέληται. 18. ὁ γὰρ ἄνθρωπος
μίαν ταύτην ἡδονὴν ἥδεται τὴν ἀπὸ τοῦ μηδὲν
ἑαυτῷ συνειδέναι πονηρὸν καὶ τῶν θεῶν τῷ μὲν
σῖτον ἐσθίειν διέστηκεν, ἐν δὲ τῇ τῆς ἀρετῆς

---

[1] φίλω F., conj. Re.: φιλῶ mss.
[2] αὑτοῦ Re. (mss.): αὐτοῦ F.

case we should, if we are wise, humble ourselves and be sorry, whether we have deliberately wronged our good emperor or if some hostile spirit has given us such a reputation, for all our innocence. 16. However, since you make great play of your innocence, and he insists that he has been deeply wronged, I would not like to decide such an argument, for you are both my friends. My country demands my respect, the emperor my reverence. He, by his own admission, is my companion, and especially by the brotherhood of letters that he and I both practise.[a] Yet, since truth must prevail over all else and I have proclaimed my intention of speaking my mind without reservation, having once adopted the role of counsellor I have been faced with the necessity of delivering my verdict, and I must give my considered opinion.

17. Men of Antioch, however often I were to repeat that the emperor's charges against you are without foundation, I could never convince anyone except yourselves. His piety towards the gods, his clemency towards his subjects, his intellectual affinity with philosophy, and his studies that are allied with his intellect, all are against us. They bear witness, almost shout it aloud, that the city has offended against him rather than that he is at fault with regard to us. 18. His only pleasure is his consciousness of nothing base within him. He differs from the gods only by the fact that he eats the food of men: in

---

[a] *Cf. Or.* 15. 7, 18. 14 ff. Julian (*E.L.F.* Nos. 97-98) addresses Libanius as ἀδελφέ. This has been interpreted as the religious terminology of the brotherhood of Mithraism, but there is no evidence that Libanius had ever become an initiate, probable though it may be : more important, both contexts are literary, and indicative of the brotherhood of letters.

ἀσκήσει καὶ τῇ τῆς ψυχῆς ἐπιμελείᾳ πλησίον
αὐτῶν ἐστι, τῶν μὲν αἰσχρῶν ἐπιθυμιῶν πλέον
κρατῶν ἢ ὧν ἄρχει πόλεων, τῶν δ᾽ ἤδη τὴν αὐτὴν
βασιλείαν ἐσχηκότων τοὺς μὲν τοῦ μηδενὸς ἀξίους
ἀποφήνας, τοὺς δὲ οὐχ ὅσουπερ πρότερον, τοὺς
δὲ τῇ μὲν μιμησάμενος, ἔστι δὲ οἷς νικήσας. 19. οὕτως οὖν ἀγαθὸν ἔχοντες τὸν κατήγορον καὶ τῶν
ἐκ τῆς Εὐρώπης γενομένων τῷ Διὶ δικαιότερον
οἰόμεθα περὶ ὧν ἐγκεκλήμεθα ἐξαρνούμενοι μεθ᾽
ἡμῶν τινας τῶν ἀκρωμένων ποιήσειν; οὐκ ἔστιν.
εἰπὲ γάρ, τίνα πιστὴν ἐροῦμεν πρόφασιν; ὡς
ἀβασανίστως ὅ τι ἂν τύχῃ πράττει;[1] καὶ τίς οὕτω
τῶν ἐπ᾽ ἀγορᾶς στρεφομένων | ἔμπειρος τῶν καθ᾽ F 1
ἡμέραν πραττομένων; ἀλλ᾽ ὡς ἰσχυρότερον λογι-
R 491 σμοῦ τρέφει θυμόν; ὁ τοὺς ἀκονήσαντας | ἐπ᾽
αὐτὸν ξίφη ζῆν ἀφείς; ἀλλ᾽ ὅπως δημεύσειεν,
αἰτίας πλάττει κενάς; ὁ τὴν ἀρχαίαν τοῦ χρυσοῦ
φορὰν τοῖς δήμοις ἀνείς; ἀλλὰ θηριώδης ἄνθρωπος; ὁ βαδίζων εἰς ἱερὰ καὶ τοῖς ἀρχομένοις
ἀναμιγνὺς ἑαυτὸν καὶ δικάζων πράῳς καὶ περὶ τῶν
ἡμετέρων τέκνων ἀνερωτῶν καὶ χαίρων εἴ τι τῶν
καλῶν ἐπιτηδεύοι; 20. πολλοὶ μάρτυρες ἥξουσιν,
ὦ ἄνδρες Ἀντιοχεῖς, ἐκείνῳ βοηθοῦντες, πόλεις
μυρίαι, ἔθνη μεγάλα, γῆ καὶ θάλαττα, πάντες οἱ
νεμόμενοι τὴν μέχρι τῆς ἡμετέρας ἀπὸ τῶν τοῦ
Ῥήνου ῥευμάτων, ὑφ᾽ ὧν ἁπάντων ἀγαπώμενος
εἰς ταυτηνὶ προπεμπόμενος ἧκεν. ὅταν οὖν ἀπαρέ-
σκωμεν μόνοι καὶ μόνοις ἐγκαλῇ τοὺς ἄλλους

---

[1] Punctuation F.

[a] On this passage cf. A. D. Nock, *J.R.S.* 47 (1957), p.
122 : "Deification and Julian."

[b] Minos and Rhadamanthys : with Aeacus, the three

the practice of virtue and his concern for things
spiritual he approximates to them,[a] for he has more
control over his lower appetites than over the cities
he rules, and of previous occupants of his throne some
he has revealed as worthless, others not so worthy
as before, and others again, if he takes them as his
models in one respect, he excels in several others.
19. So then, when we have such a paragon as our
accuser, one more just than the children Europa bore
to Zeus,[b] can we expect any listener to take our part
if we deny the charges? Impossible! Tell me, what
convincing excuse can we make? That he acts without due consideration? But who of the people who
frequent the market is so expert in his daily business?
That his temper is beyond the control of reason?
What! when he allowed those who whetted their
swords against him to live?[c] That he makes up baseless charges so as to go in for confiscations? When he
has remitted to the populace its time-honoured payments of gold?[d] That is he brutal? When he walks
to the temples mingling with his subjects, shows
clemency in his judgements, inquires about our
children and expresses pleasure at any good turn he
can do them? 20. Men of Antioch, there will be
many come as witnesses to stand up for him, cities
without number, great provinces, continent and
ocean, and all that dwell between us and the river
Rhine, with whose devoted escort he has come to our
city. So, when we alone displease him, when he has

judges of the underworld. (Plato, *Apol.* 41 A, *Gorg.* 523 E).
In Homer (*Od.* 11. 568) Minos acts as the sole judge of the
shades.

[c] *Cf. Or.* 12. 85. The arguments that follow are adaptations of the *Misopogon.*

[d] The edict on *aurum coronarium* (*E.L.F.* No. 72).

ἐπαινῶν, οὐκ ἐκεῖνον εἰκὸς μεταβεβληκέναι τοὺς
τρόπους, ἀλλ' ἡμᾶς οὐκ εὐήνιον παρεσχῆσθαι τὴν
πόλιν.

21. Οὕτως ἐξετάζων, ὦ ἄνδρες πολῖται, τὰ
πεπραγμένα μᾶλλον ἡμᾶς αἰτίαις ἐνεχομένους ἢ
συκοφαντουμένους εὑρίσκω. εἰ δὲ δεῖ καὶ σαφε-
στέρων ἐγκλημάτων ἅψασθαι καὶ δακεῖν μὲν ὑμᾶς,
ὠφελῆσαι δέ, τὸ μὲν ὡς κατεκρύψατε τὰ παρὰ τῶν
R 492 ἀγρῶν καὶ | δυνάμενοι καταστῆσαι λαμπρὰν τὴν
ἀγορὰν ὅπως εἰς στενὸν ἥξει διεπράξασθε, καὶ
πόλεμον ἤρασθε πρὸς | τὴν τοῦ βασιλέως ἐπιθυμίαν, F
οὐκ ἐρῶ. ψευδοίμην γὰρ ἂν εἰδὼς ὅτι πολλοὶ τῶν
πολλὴν γῆν ἐχόντων πεινῶντας τοὺς ὑμῶν αὐτῶν
οἰκέτας ὁρῶντες ἐπαρκεῖν αὐτοῖς οὐ δύνασθε. 22.
ἀλλ' ἐκεῖνό γε ἡδέως ἂν μεμψαίμην, ὅτι μὴ τὴν
γνώμην τῆς δυνάμεως παρεσχόμεθα καλλίω. τί
δέ ἐστιν ὅ φημι; ἔστιν, ὦ ἄνδρες Ἀντιοχεῖς,
ἀδυναμίαν καὶ προθυμίαν συνελθεῖν καὶ τὸν αὐτὸν
ἄνθρωπον ἔργῳ μὲν τῷ κελεύοντι μὴ δυνηθῆναι
χαρίσασθαι, γνώμῃ δὲ καὶ τῷ σφόδρα συμβου-
ληθῆναι καὶ τῷ φαινομένης ἐλπίδος ἡσθῆναι καὶ τῷ
τῆς τοῦ πράγματος φύσεως ἐναντιουμένης ἀθυ-
μῆσαι. 23. ὧν ἡμεῖς οὐδὲν ἐδείκνυμεν, ἀλλ' ἦμεν
ἔνδηλοι[1] βαρυνόμενοι τῷ νόμῳ καὶ ποιοῦντες μὲν
ὅσα ἐνῆν, ἀηδῶς δ' ὑπουργοῦντες, καὶ τοὺς μὲν
ἐν αὐτοῖς τοῖς ἔργοις ὑποφέροντες πόνους, τὸ
πραττόμενον δὲ οὐκ ἐπαινοῦντες. ἐγὼ δ' ἠξίουν
ὑμᾶς συνερασθῆναι μὲν τῷ βασιλεῖ τῆς κατα-
στάσεως ταύτης, θαυμάσαι δὲ τὴν ὁρμήν, εἰ καὶ

---

[1] ἔνδηλοι F. (CVBM, A before correction): ἔκδηλοι Re.
(other mss.).

complaints against us alone and praise for the rest, the probability is not that he has changed his ways but that we have consigned to him a city ill controlled.

21. On this assessment of what has occurred, fellow citizens, I find that we are more open to blame than falsely slandered. If reference must be made to the most obvious grounds for accusation, and if you must be hurt while helped, I will not adduce the argument that you concealed the produce of your estates, that you had it in your power to make business boom and yet manufactured a recession,[a] and that you were active in hostility to the emperor's wishes. I would be telling a lie, for I know that many of you large land-holders saw your own servants starving to death and were unable to provide for them. 22. But this complaint I would have no compunction in making: we failed to make our willingness rise above our circumstances. Let me explain. It is possible, gentlemen, for inability and willingness to go hand in hand. One and the same person may actually be incapable of performing the service enjoined upon him, and yet do so in spirit, by his willing concurrence, by his joy at hope revealed and his dejection at the unfortunate outcome of the matter. 23. We have given no such indication. We made no secret of the fact that we resented the law, and though we complied with the letter, our service was a grudging one. In what we actually did we undertook the burdens, but with no approval for the policy. I expected you to join the emperor in your enthusiasm for this settlement, to admire his spirit, even if it were not the

---

[a] Cf. Jul. *Misop.* 368 c : πάντα γέμει, πάντα πολλοῦ. Lib. *Or.* 1. 126, 18. 195, Amm. Marc. 22. 14. 1 ff. Petit, *Libanius et la vie municipale à Antioche*, pp. 109 ff.

# LIBANIUS

τὸ ῥᾷστον[1] ἀπῆν, ὡς ψυχήν τε φιλάνθρωπον
ἐμφανίζουσαν καὶ τῇ πενίᾳ βοηθοῦσαν, δεινὸν
ἡγουμένην εἰ οἱ μὲν ὡς μάλιστα τρυφῷεν, οἱ δὲ |
τῶν ἀναγκαίων ἐνδεεῖς διατελοῖεν, καὶ τῆς ἀγορᾶς F
ἀνθούσης ὁρᾶν μόνον ἐξείη τοῖς πενεστέροις τὰς
τῶν εὐπορούντων ἀπολαύσεις. 24. ταῦτα ἔδει
R 493 φρονεῖν καὶ γενέσθαι φανεροὺς οὐ | τῷ κολάσαντι
τὰς τιμὰς μεμφομένους, ἀλλὰ τοῖς οὐκ ἀνεχομένοις
σωφρονῆσαι καπήλοις. καὶ γὰρ εἰ τὸ πρᾶγμα
μηδὲν μᾶλλον ἠκολούθει τοῖς βουλήμασιν, ἀλλ'
ὑμεῖς γε ἐν τοῖς εὐξαμένοις ἐδοκεῖτ' ἂν εἶναι μηδὲν
ἀντιπεσεῖν τῇ βασιλέως γνώμῃ. οὕτω καὶ στρατιῶται διαφεύγουσιν αἰτίαν, ὅταν τοῦ στρατηγοῦ
πρὸς τὸ δοκοῦν ἄπορον ἡγουμένου τὴν αὐτοῦ τοῦ
παρακαλοῦντος μιμησάμενοι τόλμαν οἴωνται μὲν
δεῖν χωρῆσαι διὰ παντός, ἀποκρουσθέντες δὲ τῷ
μὴ τυχεῖν τοῦ τέλους ἀλγῶσιν. 25. ἡμεῖς δὲ
τοιοῦτον λόγον γενέσθαι συνεχωρήσαμεν ὡς ἐν
μὲν ταῖς φερούσαις ἀφθονίαν ἡμέραις ἀθυμοῖμεν,[2]
τῇ σπάνει δὲ τῶν ὠνίων ἑορτάζοιμεν, ὡς ἐλεγχό-
μενοι μὲν ἐκείνῳ, νικῶντες δὲ τούτῳ. χρῆν δὲ
ἐκεῖνον γεγενῆσθαι τὸν λόγον ὡς τὴν τοῦ βασιλέως
ὑπερβάλλομεν λύπην, ὅτι μὴ καὶ ἐκ[3] τοῦ παρόντος
τῶν τιμῶν μέτρου μένει τὸ σχῆμα τῆς ἀγορᾶς. |
R 494 26. Ἐμοὶ ταῦτα σύνοισθα; | φήσειεν ἂν Εὔ- F
βουλος ἀναπηδήσας καὶ ὁ μετ' ἐκεῖνον καὶ ὁ

[1] ῥᾷστον Re. (mss.): δραστήριον F.
[2] ἀθυμοῖμεν F. (UV; IM corrected): ἀθυμοῦμεν Re. (other mss.).
[3] ἐκ Re. (mss. except VI): ἐπὶ F. (V; I before correction).

[a] Julian (*Misop.* 369 cd) accuses the wealthy decurions

226

easiest situation to deal with, as an indication of his humane character and relief to the poor, for it would be, he thought, a scandal for some to live soft while others stayed without the necessities of life, and for the market to boom while the poorer clasess could see only the luxuries of the rich. 24. That should have been our attitude. We should have shown our disapproval not of him who brought the prices down but of the merchants who would not brook constraint.[a] In fact, even if matters did not proceed in line with your wishes, at any rate it would be clear that you were of that section that desired no collision with the emperor's will. It is in this way that soldiers, too, escape blame, when their commander leads them on some forlorn hope and they follow his resolute example as he urges them on: they think they should go through thick and thin, and if they fail, they are grieved at not reaching their objective. 25. We however have acquiesced in the growth of the story of our disappointment at a time of plenty and of our delight in a dearth of supplies, regarding the first as detrimental to us, the second as advantageous. The story should have been of our annoyance surpassing that of the emperor, because the market is deteriorating even following the present limitation of prices.

26. " Are you attributing anything like that to me? " Eubulus [b] may jump up and say, and a second,

of Antioch, not the retailers, of engaging in black-market operations.

[b] *Principalis* of Antioch, attacked by the mob in the riots of A.D. 354 (Amm. Marc. 14. 7. 6, Lib. *Or.* 1. 103) and a determined opponent of Libanius (*Or.* 1. 116, 156, 163). His identification with the professional rival of Libanius has been vigorously argued: *v.* Seeck, *B.L.Z.G.* 39 ff.

τρίτος καὶ ὁ τέταρτος καὶ τῶν ἄλλων ἕκαστος.
οὐκ ἔγωγε. πάλαι γὰρ ἂν ὑμῖν ἐχθρὸς ἦν, εἴ τι
τοιοῦτον ᾔδειν. ἀλλ' οὐδ' ἂν ἐκεῖνο πεισθείην ὡς
οὐκ ἐξεφοίτησεν ἐντεῦθεν ἀφορμὴ τὸ μῖσος ἐπι-
σπωμένη. καὶ παρ' ὅτων μὲν ἀνθρώπων ἀγνοῶ,
περιτρέχουσαν δὲ τοιαύτην δόξαν ᾐσθόμην. 27.
Συκοφάντου γὰρ τὸ ἔργον. πάλιν ἡ τοῦ βασιλέως
ἀρετὴ ταύτην ἡμῖν ἀποκλείει τὴν καταφυγήν. ἄλλος μὲν γὰρ κἂν ὑπήχθη καὶ ἐξηπατήθη, τοῦτον δὲ
κἂν ταῖς δίκαις ὁρῶμεν οὐχ ἑλκόμενον ὑπὸ τῶν ψευ-
δομένων, ἀλλὰ πάντα πατοῦντα καὶ κατακλῶντα
φενακισμὸν καὶ καθάπερ φάλαγγα ῥηγνύντα τὰς
παραγωγάς, ἕως ἂν ἐπ' αὐτὸ τἀληθὲς πορευόμε-
νος ἀφίκηται.

28. Ἀλλ' εἰ δοκεῖ, τὴν ἀγορὰν ἐῶμεν καὶ πάντων
R 495 ἀέρων | τὰ ἐγκλήματα. οἱ δὲ κακῶς οὗτοι γυ-
μνούμενοι καὶ κάκιον τρέχοντες καὶ δεδωκότες
αὑτοῖς ἄδειαν τοῦ κακῶς λέγειν ὃν ἂν ἐθέλωσι, καὶ
ἃ μηδ' ἂν κατ' ἀλλήλων φθεγγόμενοι δικαίως ἀπῆλθον ἀθῷοι, ταῦτα καταχέαντες τοῦ σωφρονεστά-
του καὶ δικαιοτάτου καὶ | φρονιμωτάτου, πότερ' F
ἄμεμπτον ἡμῖν ἐποίουν τὴν πόλιν ἢ τούτων οἷς
πιέζεται νῦν ἀξίαν; 29. καὶ μὴ νομίζετε περὶ τῆς
αὑτοῦ δόξης δεδοικότα χαλεπῶς ἔχειν τοῖς εἰρη-
μένοις, μήποτε τοσοῦτον δυνηθείη ταυτὶ τὰ καθάρ-
ματα, ἀλλὰ τό τινας τῶν ἀρχομένων τοσαύτης

---

(Acacius), Förster, vol. 10, pp. 760 f., Petit, *Étudiants de
Libanius*, pp. 74, 94, Wolf, *Vom Schulwesen der Spätantike*,
pp. 93 f.
    [a] Cf. *Or.* 18. 182 ff., Amm. Marc. 22. 10.

a third, a fourth and all the rest after him. Not I. I would have been at daggers drawn with you long ago if I had known of anything like that. But I am not convinced either that from this source there did not arise some consideration that attracted this unpopularity to you. Who was responsible, I do not know, but this much I did see, that such an opinion was widely accepted. 27. " Yes. That was due to slander." Once again our emperor's goodness prevents us from having recourse to such an excuse. Any other man indeed might be deceived and led by the nose, but we see that even in the courts of law he is not taken in by lies, but that he spurns and cuts short all deceit and breaks through the array of humbug until he makes his way to the real truth.[a]

28. Then, if you please, let us put aside the question of the market and those complaints about all the vagaries of the weather. But some rascals here, whose practice is bad and performance worse, have granted themselves the licence of abusing absolutely anyone and have besmirched our wise, just and noble emperor with abuse that they would not have deserved to get away with, even if made against each other.[b] Now, have they brought no reproach upon the city or have they made her deserving of her present plight ? 29. And do not consider his displeasure at these remarks to be due to his fear for his own reputation. I trust that this riff-raff will never be able to achieve so much. What has upset him is

[b] Cf. Amm. Marc. 23. 1. 5 : after the deaths of Felix and Julianus, the mob salutes him " Felix Iulianus Augustus " : ibid. 22. 14. 3: " Cercops, victimarius." The religious struggle forms the background of many of these lampoons : cf. Misop. 357 a ff.—the Chi and the Kappa (Christ and Constantius) are proclaimed as preferable to him.

γέμειν ἀσελγείας καὶ μήτε φοβεῖσθαι τολμᾶν τε[1]
ἐν βασιλείᾳ ῥᾳδίως ὃ μηδ᾽ ἂν ἐν δημοκρατίᾳ καὶ
ταύτῃ πλείονι τοῦ συμφέροντος ἐξουσίᾳ χρωμένῃ,
τοῦτ᾽ ἔστιν ὃ τὴν ἀθυμίαν ἐμπεποίηκε.  30.
τοιούτων οὖν ᾀσμάτων διὰ τῆς πόλεως φερομένων |
R 496 τίς ἀνεβόησεν ὡς ἐπ᾽ ἀσεβείᾳ; τίς προσελθὼν ἐ-
πάταξε; τίς τὴν καρδίαν ἐπλήγη; τίς εἶπε πρὸς
τὸν πλησίον· Οὐ κωλύσομεν; οὐ συλληψόμεθα;
οὐ δήσομεν; οὐκ ἀποκτενοῦμεν; ἔπρεπε γάρ, οἶμαι, τὸν μὲν ἡσυχάζειν, ἡμᾶς δὲ εἶναι τοὺς ἀπ-
αιτοῦντας τὴν δίκην, καὶ πρὶν ἐκεῖνον ἥτις ἐστὶν
ἡ βλασφημία μαθεῖν, τοὺς ὑβριστὰς ἀπολωλέναι.

31. Ὀλίγοι, φησίν, ἦσάν τινες. οὐκοῦν καὶ διὰ
τοῦτο κεκολάσθαι χρῆν, ὅτι ἃ πλείονες ὄντες τῶν
λοιπῶν οὐδ᾽ οὕτως ἂν εἰκότως ἐτόλμων, ταῦτ᾽
ὄντες οὐδὲ εἴκοσι παροινοῦντες οὐκ ὤκνουν. |

32. Ἀλλὰ φαῦλοί τινες ἦσαν, ἄποροι καὶ κακ- F 1
οῦργοι καὶ βαλλαντιοτόμοι. δευτέραν ἀνάγκην
εἴρηκας τοῦ δεῖν αὐτοὺς διεσπάσθαι, εἰ τὰ μὲν
ἀδικήματα μεγάλα καὶ δεινὰ καὶ περιφανῆ, παρ-
R 497 αίτησις | δὲ οὐδαμόθεν.

33. Ξένοι, φησίν, ἦσαν οἱ θέοντες. οὐκοῦν οἱ
μὲν οἷς ἔλεγον ἠδίκουν, ἡμεῖς δὲ οἷς ἐπετρέπομεν.
ἴσον δὲ γίνεται τῷ δρᾶν τὸ παρὸν κωλῦσαι μὴ
βουληθῆναι, καὶ δι᾽ ὧν τις οὐκ ὀργιζόμενος τοῖς
ἠδικηκόσι φαίνεται τῆς ἀδικίας ἐπαινέτης γίγνεται. 34. Ἄνθρωπε, Φοῖνιξ εἶ καὶ πόλις ἔστι σοι;

―――――――
[1] τε UI (conj. Re. *Animadv.*) : δὲ F. (other mss.).

that some of his subjects should be so filled with insubordination and so disrespectful, and should not scruple to attempt under his imperial constitution what they would never dare do even in a democracy that enjoys a greater licence than is good for it. 30. So, when such lampoons were circulated in our city, who protested as if against impiety? Who went and administered a thrashing? Who felt any personal grief? Who said to his neighbour, "Come on! Let's stop them, arrest them, imprison them, execute them"? He, surely, should not have been called upon to act. We should have been the ones to demand their punishment, and such insolent scoundrels should have been executed before ever he learned of their enormities.

31. "But," it is objected, "they were only a handful." Then all the more reason for punishing them, for though not a score in number, they did not shrink from hooliganism such as they would never lightly venture upon even if they outnumbered the rest.

32. "But they were rascals, beggars, criminals, cut-purses." You have given another reason why this clique should have been broken up, if their misconduct was serious and substantial, clearly observed and inexcusable.

33. "Those who chased around with these stories were not citizens of ours," I am told. Then their misconduct was in what they said, ours in what we permitted. If you can prevent anything and yet refuse to do so, it is tantamount to doing it : if you show no anger at wrong-doers, you thereby approve of their wrong-doing. 34. We should have told them, "Look here, my man. You're a Phoenician, aren't you? Have you a home to go to? Then go there and

LIBANIUS

μάλιστα μὲν κἀκεῖ σωφρόνει, εἰ δὲ οὐ δύνασαι, μὴ
παύσαιο νοσῶν οἴκοι καὶ τὴν ἀσέλγειαν ὀνομά-
ζων ἑορτήν. ἡμεῖς δὲ οὐκ ἴσμεν τοιαῦτα οὔτε
ᾄδειν οὔτε ἀκούειν. ἀλλ' ἐπιθυμεῖς παρ' ἡμῖν
κορδακίζειν; ἀπόθνησκε καὶ μὴ τὰ σαυτοῦ κακὰ
τῷ κοινῷ τῆς πόλεως προστίθει.

35. Τί ἐροῦμεν; ἢ τί φήσαιμεν ἄν, διότι τούτων
οὐδὲν πεποιήκαμεν; ἐρεῖ τις, Ἐδείσαμεν, φησί,
μὴ τὰ δοκοῦντα νόμοις ἱεροῖς γίγνεσθαι κωλύοντες |
εἰς αἰτίαν τοῦ τὰς ἑορτὰς ἀναιρεῖν ἐμπέσωμεν. F 1ᵃ
R 498 ἔδει γὰρ ἡμᾶς πεισθῆναι ταῦτα | ἑορτὴν εἶναι,
κῶμον οὕτω τολμηρὸν ἐπὶ τὴν θειοτάτην χωροῦντα
κεφαλήν. 36. ἀναμεμίχθαι σκώμματά τινά τισιν
ἑορταῖς ὁμολογῶ, ἀλλὰ πρῶτον μὲν κοῦφα καὶ
φορητὰ καὶ οὐκ ἀπὸ γλώττης ἀναπεπταμένης, οὐ
γὰρ εἰς ὁμοίους, ἀπορριπτούμενα, καὶ ταύτῃ τὴν
τραχύτητα λεαίνοντα. εἰ δὲ ἐξῆν τοῖς ἐμοῖς δούλοις
τἀξ ἀνθρώπων ὀνείδη συμφορῆσαι τὴν ἑορτὴν
προστησαμένοις ἀνέδην ἐμὲ λοιδορεῖν, ἐγὼ μὲν
οὐκ ἂν ἀπεδεξάμην τοὺς ταύτῃ τῇ θεραπείᾳ
χαίροντας θεούς.

37. Ἦν μὲν οὖν φροντιζόντων πόλεως ἀνθρώπων
πάλαι ταῦτα ἐκκόψαι καὶ μηδὲ τὸν ὕπτιον Κωνστάντιον περιδεῖν ὑβριζόμενον, λογιζομένους ὡς
βασιλέως ἁπλῶς κἂν ἡ γνώμη μετέχῃ ῥᾳθυμίας,
ἥ γε τύχη τιμῆς ἀξία. εἰ δ' ἦν¹ οὐδὲν ἀπεικὸς μετὰ
R 499 τῶν ἄλλων | καὶ τοῦτο ἀμεληθῆναι, παρειληφότος

¹ δ' ἦν F. (VVat82) : δ' οὖν Re. (other mss.).

ᵃ This lampooning of Julian seems to have taken place
at the Saturnalia—hence the reference to the licence then
granted to slaves—or at the New Year festival, when a
similar practice occurred (Or. 9. 11).

232

behave yourself. If you can't, then carry on with your
lunacy at home and call your disgusting behaviour a
high day and holiday. We are here unused to making
such remarks or listening to them. Oh! so you want
to show your paces here, do you? Then you'll pay
for it with your life. Don't you get our city community mixed up in your misdeeds!"

35. What shall we say? What reason could we ever
give for not having done any of this? I shall be told,
" We were afraid that, if we sought to put a stop to
something that was accepted religious practice, we
should be blamed for abolishing the holiday." Well,
we should have assured ourselves that it was holiday
making for such unrestrained buffoonery to be aimed
at the sacred person of our emperor. 36. I agree that
some ridicule is part of some holidays, but it is light-
hearted, easily borne and not uttered from unbridled
mouths, for it is not directed against their equals,
and so it soothes its bitterness. But if my slaves were
allowed to scrape together all the insults men can
lay their tongues to and abuse me without restraint,
using the holiday as their excuse, I would never
have acknowledged the gods who enjoy such attentions.[a]

37. Hence men who had any regard for their city
should have done away with this sort of thing long
ago, and they should not have ignored the insults
offered even to the sluggard Constantius.[b] They
should consider that, however weak an emperor's
character, his position at least deserves respect. And
if this consideration might not unreasonably be ignored along with the rest, yet when there succeeded

[b] Such as happened at Edessa, also at holiday time: *Or.*
19. 48, 20. 27.

LIBANIUS

γε τὴν ἀρχὴν τοῦ πάντας ἐν ἅπασι τῆς γῆς μέρεσι
παρελθόντος οὐδὲν ἐχρῆν τῶν κόσμον ἀπαιτούντων
ὀλιγωρεῖσθαι, ἀλλὰ | μάλιστα μὲν οὔπω προσ- F 17
ιόντος τοῦ καιροῦ φόβῳ προανελεῖν τὰς ὕβρεις,
τούτου δὲ διαφυγόντος τὴν γνώμην ὑπ' αὐτῆς
κινηθῆναι τῆς ἀσελγείας. 38. ὅλως δὲ λαμπρὰν
ἔδει τῶν τρόπων γενέσθαι τὴν μετάστασιν καὶ τὴν
πόλιν ἀμείνω μεταλαβεῖν ἁρμονίαν, ὥσπερ τινὰ κι-
θάραν εἰς ἄκρου κιθαρῳδοῦ χεῖρας ἐλθοῦσαν, ταύτην δὲ τὴν ἁρμονίαν διὰ πάντων μὲν τῶν κοινῶν,
διὰ πάντων δὲ τῶν ἰδίων[1] τετάσθαι καὶ ψυχῶν
καὶ διαίτης καὶ ἀνδρῶν καὶ παίδων καὶ γυναικῶν.
39. Ἀλλ' ὅτι μὲν ἐκ τῆς ἡμετέρας μωρίας
συνέστη τε τὴν ἀρχὴν τὸ μῖσος καὶ προϊὸν ηὐξήθη,
δεδήλωται· συγχωρῶ δέ, εἰ δοκεῖ, τύχης εἶναι τὸ
ἔργον οὐ τὰ δίκαια ποιούσης. τί οὖν; ἐάσομεν,[2]
ὥσπερ κακοὶ ναῦται, κρατηθῆναι τὴν ναῦν ὑπὸ τοῦ
χειμῶνος ἤ τινα πρόνοιαν ἀντιστήσομεν τῷ κλύδωνι;
R 500 ἐμοὶ μὲν τοῦτο δοκεῖ καὶ τοῦτο βούλημα | τοῦ παρόν-
τος λόγου καμνούσῃ βοηθῆσαι τῇ πόλει, καὶ πάνθ'
ὅσα ἐπετίμησα, πρὸς μίαν ταύτην τείνει σπουδήν.
40. Τίνα δὴ τὰ φάρμακα; φανῶμεν ὡς ἀληθῶς
ἀλγοῦντες, φανῶμεν ὡς ἀληθῶς πενθοῦντες. ἀπολο-
γησώμεθα λύπῃ καὶ σωφροσύνῃ. καὶ γὰρ τοῦτο
ἕν ἐστι | τῶν ἐγκλημάτων, ὡς φρόνημα μεῖζον F 17
ἀσκοῦμεν τοῦ δέοντος καὶ φοβεῖν οὐδὲν δύναται
τὴν πόλιν. μή μοι νομιζέτω τὴν αὐτοῦ κατήφειαν

[1] ἰδίων F. (VB, I corrected): εἰδῶν other mss.
[2] ἐάσομεν F., Re. (P: inserted after ναῦται I): δράσομεν other mss.

[a] Cf. Plat. Rep. 431 e ff.
[b] Argyrius the elder, principalis of Antioch. Richtsteig
234

to the throne one who surpassed all men throughout the world, they should not belittle those qualities that required good behaviour of them. Rather, before ever the occasion offered, in fearful anticipation they should have done away with such insults: that failing, their feelings should have been altered by the very enormity of it. 38. In short, there should have been a notable change of attitude. The city should have acquired a better concord,[a] as when a lyre comes to the hand of an expert, and this concord should have extended over the whole scale of our activities both public and private, and the character and conduct of men, women and children.

39. However, it has been shown that this resentment arose originally from our stupidity and that it increased as it went on. I concede, if you like, that it is a piece of undeserved bad luck. But what then? Are we, like incompetent sailors, going to allow the ship of state to founder in the storm, or shall we devise some protection to act as a bulwark against the waves? Such is my opinion and this is the intention of my present speech, to help out city in its distress. All the reproofs I have administered have this one end in view.

40. What, then, is the cure? Let us show ourselves to be really sorry and really grieved. Let us present our plea sorrowfully and decorously. In fact it is one of the charges against us that we display more arrogance than we should and that nothing can alarm our city. And please don't let Argyrius[b]

(Förster, *Libanius*, vol. 12 (index), p. 14) and Petit, *Libanius et la vie municipale*, p. 120 *et al.*, confuse him with his grandson of the same name. Petit combines this reference with *Or.* 15. 23 to present him as *epistates* of the bakers: on which *cf. J.R.S.* 47 (1957), p. 239.

Ἀργύριος εἰς ἀπολογίαν ἀρκεῖν, ἀλλ' εἰς ἀχθηδόνα κοινὴν σχηματίσωμεν τὸ ἄστυ καὶ μιμησάσθω πένθος οἰκίας ὅλη¹ πόλις. 41. κλείσωμεν βραχὺν χρόνον τὸ θέατρον καὶ δεηθῶμεν τῶν ὀρχηστῶν τουτωνὶ καὶ μίμων μεταδοῦναι καὶ² τοῖς ἀστυγείτοσι τῶν παρ' αὐτῶν ἀγαθῶν, ἡμῖν δὲ ἐπιτρέψαι τὸ θέρος ἄνευ τέρψεως διαγαγεῖν. τὰς τῶν ἵππων ἁμίλλας εἰς ἐλάττους συστείλωμεν ἄθλους, ἐξ ἀντὶ τῶν ἑκκαίδεκα τάξαντες. τὸ πολὺ καὶ μάταιον τοῦτο φῶς καὶ τρυφὴν ἄχρηστον δεικνύον τὸ πρὸ τῶν βαλανείων κρεμάμενον εἰς πολλοστὸν τοῦ νῦν ὄντος καταστήσωμεν. δικάσωμεν ἡμῖν αὐτοῖς, ἵνα μὴ βασιλεὺς ἡμῖν. ὑπόσχωμεν ἑκόντες τιμωρίαν, ἵνα μὴ μείζω πάθωμεν ἄκοντες. οἰκείᾳ ψήφῳ τὴν ἐκείνου κωλύσωμεν. 42. κἂν οἱ τῶν θεάτρων ἐξηρτημένοι χαλεπαίνωσι, πείθωμεν αὐτοὺς ἐπιγνῶναι τὸν καιρόν, οὐ προσεχόντων δὲ μηδεὶς ἔστω λόγος. δεινὸν γάρ, εἰ τούτοις κατὰ τῆς κοινῆς σωτηρίας χαριούμεθα καὶ τὸ μὴ λυπῆσαι τοὺς ὁμολογοῦντας ἄνευ τῶν ἐπὶ σκηνῆς μὴ | δύνασθαι ζῆν ἔμπροσθεν τοῦ λῦσαι τὴν βασιλέως F 17 ὀργὴν θησόμεθα. 43. εἰ γὰρ δὴ δεδοίκαμεν στάσιν, R 501 καὶ τοῦτ' ἐγκαλεῖ | τῇ βουλῇ βασιλεύς, εἰ οὕτω κακῶς τῆς πόλεως προῦστημεν ὥστ' ἀνάγκην εἶναι τοὺς ἀμείνους τοῖς πολλοῖς ἀκολουθεῖν καὶ τοῖς ὄχλοις ἐκπορίζειν ἡδονὰς ἢ εὐθὺς ἀπολωλέναι. ἀλλὰ μὴν ἄγαν παμπόλλους εἶναι νομίζομεν τοὺς

---

¹ ὅλη ⟨ἡ⟩ F., conj. Re.
² καὶ bracketed F. (om. B).

believe his own dejection to be excuse enough. Rather let us make the town assume an air of common distress and let a whole city imitate a household in its grief. 41. Let us shut our theatre for a short time, and ask the dancers and actors here to let our neighbours too share the blessings they provide and leave us to pass the summer without amusements. Let us reduce the number of chariot races.[a] Make them six instead of sixteen. This extravagant lighting, this indication of idle luxury, that hangs over the entrances to our baths—let us make it a fraction of what it is now.[b] Let us pass sentence on ourselves, lest the emperor do it for us. Let us volunteer for punishment, lest we should willy-nilly suffer a worse, and let us prevent his verdict by our own. 42. Even if the devotees of the theatre complain, let us induce them to recognize the seriousness of the situation, and let no account be taken of those who disapprove. It would be disastrous to favour them to the detriment of the whole community, and to think more of humouring those who confessedly cannot endure an existence without their stage idols than of appeasing the emperor's wrath. 43. For if we are in fact afraid of riots, the emperor has this complaint to make against the council, that we are so inefficient in the administration of the city that the better sort have to follow the lead of the masses and must provide entertainment for the mob, or else be killed on the spot. We certainly do think that there are far too many people craving for dancing shows in time of

[a] These suggestions are deliberate adaptations of the *Misopogon* : the theatre (343 d ff.), the reduction of the horse races to six (340 a).
[b] The street lighting in Antioch was famous and unique : *cf.* Amm. Marc. 14. 1. 9, Lib. *Or.* 11. 267, 22. 6, 33. 35 f.

ἐν λιμῷ ζητοῦντας ὀρχήσεις. ἀλλ᾽ ἀνθρώπων ἐκ
τοῦ κυβεύειν εὐπορούντων κομιδῇ τινων εὐαρι-
θμήτων καὶ τούτων ξένων, ἐφ᾽ οὓς ἔχομεν τὸν τῆς
ξενηλασίας νόμον ἢν θρασύνωνται. 44. οἶμαι μὲν
οὖν εἴξειν ἅπαντας τοῖς ὑμῖν δοκοῦσιν, ἂν δ᾽ ἄρα
τις καὶ γένηται θόρυβος, σώσει τοῦτο τὴν πόλιν
τὸ φοβερόν. ὡς πολλοῦ γε ἄξιον ἀκοῦσαι βασιλέα
τῶν ἐνθένδε ἀναβαινόντων ὅτι Ἀντιοχέων οἱ μὲν
τὰ κοινὰ πράττοντες μεταρρυθμίζουσιν εἰς καρ-
τερίαν τὴν πόλιν, ὁ δῆμος δὲ ἀντιτείνει καὶ οἴεται
δεῖν ἢ τρυφᾶν ἢ στασιάζειν.

45. Ὁ δ᾽ οὐ χρηστὸν οἰωνὸν ταῦτα εἶναι νομίζων
εἰ μὲν ἀπόντος φόβου παντὸς φανεροῦ τὴν μεταβολὴν εἰσηγούμην, ἴσως ἂν ὀρθῶς εὐλαβεῖτο, θυμοῦ
δὲ ζέοντος τηλικούτου καὶ τῶν ἀπ᾽ αὐτοῦ προσδοκωμένων, ἢν αὐτοὶ τῶν ἡδονῶν τι περικόψωμεν,
τάχ᾽ ἂν ἐμπλήσαιμεν | τὸν ἐλαύνοντα δαίμονα τὰ F 1
ἡμέτερα. οὔκουν εὖ φερομένην ἐμβαλοῦμεν εἰς
κακόν τι τὴν πόλιν, ἀλλὰ σειομένην στήσομεν. 46.
σταίη δ᾽ ἄν, ὦ ἄνδρες πολῖται, βεβαίως, εἰ, ὃ τῶν
μὲν εἰρημένων ἐστὶ μεῖζον, ἐνίοις δὲ πρόσαντες,
R 502 τοῖς πλείοσι δὲ κατὰ νοῦν, νικήσειέ | τε καὶ
θαυμασθείη. εὖ γὰρ εἰδέναι χρὴ τοῦθ᾽ ὡς οὔτε
πρηνεῖς ἐπὶ γῆς ἐρριμμένοι οὔτε κλαδίοις ἐλαιῶν
αἰτοῦντες, οὐ στεφανοῦντες, οὐ βοῶντες, οὐ πρεσ-
βεύοντες, οὐ ῥήτορα δεινότατον πέμποντες σβέσετε

---

[a] A professional claque, hired to promote applause for
theatrical performers, began to turn its attention to political
and religious matters in the later 4th century, the most
notable occasion being that of the riots in A.D. 387 : cf.

famine. But they are composed of those who have made their money from gambling, and there are precious few of them, and mostly outsiders, at that.[a] We can exercise the right of expulsion against them, if they become too big for their boots. 44. So I am sure they will all retire before your resolve, but for all that, if any disturbance occurs such a threat will be the salvation of the city, for it will be worth while for the emperor to hear from those who travel up-country from here that the authorities in Antioch are trying to bring stable order to the city, though the commons opposes them and thinks it proper to live in luxury or to riot.

45. If anyone believes that my suggestion of a change of attitude, without any obvious fear to demand it, involves an evil precedent, he may perhaps be justified in his qualms. Yet when such great seething anger has been roused, with all the results that we can expect to ensue, we may perhaps, if we ourselves curtail our pleasures, satisfy the spirit that is harrying us. If the city is set on a fair course, we shall not involve it in any trouble, and if it runs adrift, we shall stabilize it. 46. And, gentlemen, stabilized it will be, if—and this is the crux of my remarks, not disagreeable to most people, though difficult for some [b]—if it wins its cause and its respect. You can be quite sure of one thing : it is not by prostrating yourselves on the ground, not by pleading with olive branches, not by presenting crowns, protestations, embassies, nor by sending an expert

Browning, *J.R.S.* 42 (1952), pp. 13 ff., " The riot of A.D. 387 in Antioch." The present demonstrations against Julian are an early example of this development.

[b] The Christians among the Antiochene decurions. The pagans are addressed in § 50 below.

# LIBANIUS

τὴν ὀργήν, ἣν μὴ παυσάμενοι τῶν ὕθλων τούτων
δῶτε τῷ Διὶ καὶ τοῖς ἄλλοις θεοῖς τὴν πόλιν, περὶ
ὧν ὑμᾶς πολὺ πρὸ τοῦ βασιλέως Ἡσίοδος διδάσκει
καὶ Ὅμηρος εὐθὺς ἐκ παίδων. 47. ὑμεῖς δὲ τῷ
πεπαιδεῦσθαι μὲν ἀξιοῦτε τιμᾶσθαι καὶ παίδευσιν
καλεῖτε τὰ ἔπη, περὶ δὲ τῶν μεγίστων ἑτέροις
χρῆσθε διδασκάλοις καὶ ὧν κεκλειμένων ἔδει
στένειν, ἀνεῳγμένα φεύγετε. εἶθ' ὅταν Πλάτωνος
καὶ Πυθαγόρου μνησθῇ τις, τὴν μητέρα καὶ τὴν
γυναῖκα καὶ τὴν ταμίαν καὶ τὸν μάγειρον καὶ τὸ
πάλαι ταῦτα πεπεῖσθαι προτείνεσθε καὶ οὐκ
αἰσχύνεσθε ταῦτα αἰσχυνόμενοι, ἀλλ' οἷς ἔδει
νομοθετεῖν, τούτων ἐφόλκια γίγνεσθε | καὶ μεγάλην F 1
ἀνάγκην ἡγεῖσθε τοῦ κακῶς διὰ τέλους φρονεῖν τὸ
πάλαι φρονεῖν κακῶς, ὥσπερ ἂν εἴ τις τὴν ὥραν ἐν
τῇ νεότητι πεπρακὼς καὶ διὰ τῶν ἄλλων ἡλικιῶν
φυλάττοι τὴν νόσον.

R 503   48. Καὶ τί δεῖ μακρολογεῖν; | νῦν γὰρ ὑμῖν
αἵρεσις ἢ μισουμένοις[1] διατελεῖν ἢ διπλῇ κερδᾶναι
τό τε τοῦ κρατοῦντος κτησαμένοις εὐμενὲς καὶ
γνοῦσι τοὺς ὄντως τὸν οὐρανὸν ἔχοντας. μόνοι
γὰρ ὑμεῖς ἐν οἷς χαριεῖσθε κερδανεῖτε καὶ σχῆμα
διδόντων ἔχοντες ἔργῳ τῶν λαμβανόντων ἔσεσθε.
49. ἀλλ' οὐδεὶς ὑμᾶς μεταστήσει λόγος, οἶδα, καὶ

---

[1] μισουμένοις F. : μισουμένους Re. (mss.).

---

[a] Libanius himself.

[b] It is commonplace that the poets, Homer and Hesiod
in particular, provide the foundations for the Hellenic
education and religion, but the special reference here is
to Julian's account of his own boyhood education under his
pedagogue Mardonius (*Misop.* 352 bc).

[c] On the tensions between the Hellenic and the Christian

240

orator[a] that you will assuage his wrath, unless you
stop your present nonsense and surrender your city
to Zeus and the other gods. Homer and Hesiod[b]
instructed you about them in earliest childhood, long
before the emperor did. 47. You expect to be
admired for your educational system, and you call
epic poetry part of it, and yet on the matters of prime
importance you employ other teachers : you turn
your backs upon instruction when the road lies open
to it, though when it was barred you should have been
loud in your laments.[c] So, whenever there is any
mention of Plato and Pythagoras, you put forward
the excuse of your mother, your wife, your house-
keeper, your cook, and your lasting trust in doctrines
like theirs, and you have no qualms about the qualms
that such doctrines inspire, but you follow the lead
of those you should command : your prolonged
perverseness you regard as the strongest reason for
its continuance, just as if, after prostituting yourself
in youth, you were to maintain the vice for all the
rest of your life.[d]

48. And what need is there for me to dwell on this ?
Now you have the choice either to continue as the
objects of his resentment or to double your profit
by gaining the good will of the emperor and by
recognizing the true gods in heaven. For you alone
will win profit by the favours you give, and though at
first sight the givers, you will in reality be gainers.
49. But no reasoned argument will cause you to

systems of education at this time, openly displayed in Julian's
ban on Christian professors (*E.L.F.* No. 61), *cf.* Festugière,
*Antioche*, pp. 91 ff., 211 ff.

[d] Adapts *Misop.* 356 b ff., 363 a ff., where the decurions
of Antioch are criticized for conniving at the proselytizing
activities of their womenfolk.

διὰ τοῦτο συνέτεμον, ἵνα μὴ τηνάλλως μηκύνοιμι.
ἀλλ᾽ ὅπως, ἡνίκα ἂν¹ ἐγγὺς ᾖ τὰ δεινὰ καὶ βασιλεὺς
μετὰ Πέρσας ὡς πολεμίαν μεταχειρίζηται τὴν πόλιν, μή μοι περιστάντες ὀδυρεῖσθε² φάσκοντες καιρὸν
ἥκειν τῶν λόγων. ὧν γὰρ αὐτοὶ καταφρονεῖτε,³ πῶς
ἂν τούτους ἀξιοίητε παρ᾽ ἐκείνῳ δύνασθαι;

50. Πρὸς δὲ τοὺς ἀδικεῖσθαι νομίζοντας, εἰ τῶν
τε ἄλλων αἰτιῶν οὐ μετέχοντες καὶ θεοῖς θύοντες
μετὰ τῶν ἀσεβούντων τε καὶ τἆλλα ὑπαιτίων⁴ ζη-
μιωθεῖεν, ἐμαυτοῦ μὲν οὐκ ἐρῶ λόγον, τὸν ἐκείνου δὲ πρὸς ἐμέ. καὶ γὰρ αὐτὸς διῄρουν ὑμᾶς
ἀπολογούμενος | πρὸς αὐτόν, τῷ δὲ ἓν ἔπος ἥρκει F 1
τοῦ τὴν δάφνην παρὰ τῶν Μουσῶν λαβόντος.
διδοὺς γὰρ εἶναί τινας οὐ πονηροὺς οὐκ εἴα θαυμάζειν εἰ μετὰ τῶν κακῶν ἀπολοῦνται.  π ο λ λ ά κ ι
γ ά ρ  φησι  κ α ὶ  σ ύ μ π α σ α  π ό λ ι ς  κ α κ ο ῦ  ἀ ν δ ρ ὸ ς
ἀ π η ύ ρ α.  51. κἀνταῦθα οὐκ ἐνῆν ἀναισχυντεῖν
R 504 οὕτω πάλαι τοῦ πράγματος | ἔχοντος. τίς γὰρ οὐκ
οἶδεν ὅπως μὲν ἀνηλώθη τῷ λοιμῷ τῶν Ἀχαι-
ῶν ὁ στρατὸς διὰ τὴν Ἀγαμέμνονος ἁμαρτίαν, οἷα
δὲ ἔπαθον ἀποπλέοντες οἴκαδε διὰ τὴν Αἴαντος
ἀδικίαν; οὐκ Ἀθηναῖοι μὲν τῆς Περικλέους εἰς
τοὺς Μεγαρέας⁵ ὕβρεως ἔτισαν κοινῇ τὴν δίκην,

---

¹ ἂν om. Re. (mss. except V, P corrected).
² ὀδυρεῖσθε Cobet: ὀδύρεσθε UIMo: ὀδύρησθε F. (other
mss.).
³ καταφρονεῖτε F. (V): καταφρονοίητε Re. (other mss.).
⁴ ὑπαιτίων F., conj. Re., Cobet: ποιούντων P: ὑπ᾽ αὐτῶν
mss. except P, I corrected: ποιούντων ὑπ᾽ αὐτῶν Re. (I).
⁵ Μεγαρέας F.: ἥρωας Re. (mss.).

ᵃ Hesiod: cf. Theog. 30.
ᵇ Hesiod, Works and Days, 240: cf. Or. 14. 31.
ᶜ Schol. PIB: ὁ Λοκρὸς Αἴας ἐν τῷ τῆς Ἀθηνᾶς ναῷ τὴν

change your attitude, I am sure : it is for this reason that I am brief, so as not to waste my breath to no purpose. But take care that, when disaster draws near and the emperor, after dealing with the Persians, treats the city as his foe, you do not come around me with your complaints and tell me that the time for my eloquence has come, for when you your-selves despise it, how can you expect it to have any influence upon him ?

50. To those of you who feel that they are harshly treated in that, though not involved in the rest of the charges and though they sacrifice to the gods, they too are punished along with the impious and those guilty of other offences, to them I will answer not with my own argument but with the one he put to me. For I too tried to draw a distinction between you in the defence I presented to him, but one line from the poet who won his crown of laurel from the Muses[a] was enough for him. He admitted that there were some who were not disaffected, but said that it was no cause for surprise that they too would suffer along with the wicked, for, said he, " often a whole city even has been punished for one wicked man."[b] 51. Here again, it was impossible to brazen it out, for this is as old as the hills. Everyone knows how the Achaean host was smitten by plague because of Agamemnon's sin, and how they suffered on their journey home because of the crime of Ajax.[c] The Athenians as a community were punished for Pericles' intransigence over Megara.[d] The Thebans

---

Κασάνδραν ἔφθειρεν, ὅθεν ᾿Αθηνᾶ ὀργισθεῖσα κοινῇ τοὺς ῞Ελληνας ἐτιμωρήσατο πνεύμασι ἀτόποις ἐκδοῦσα τούτους πλέοντας οἴκαδε.

[d] Cf. Aristoph. Peace, 606 ff., a joke that was later vested with authority ; cf. Diod. Sic. 12. 40.

Θηβαῖοι δ᾽ ἐνόσουν Οἰδίπου κτείναντος Λάιον καὶ ταῦτα ὃν ἔσφαττεν οὐκ εἰδότος; τοῦτον οὖν ὁρῶν παρὰ τοῖς κρείττοσι κεκρατηκότα τὸν νόμον φυλοκρινήσει καθήμενος ἀπὸ τῶν φαύλων ὄντων πολὺ πλειόνων τοὺς χρηστούς; βουλοίμην μὲν ἄν, πιστεύειν δὲ οὐκ ἔχω.

52. Ἕως οὖν ἔτι διαβαίνει ποταμοὺς καὶ βλέπει πρὸς τὴν τῶν Περσῶν δυναστείαν καὶ σκοπεῖ περὶ | τῆς εἰσβολῆς καὶ ποῦ καὶ πότε καὶ πῶς ἐπί- F 18 θοιτο τοῖς πολεμίοις, ποιήσωμεν ἡμᾶς αὐτοὺς καλοὺς κἀγαθοὺς καὶ καθάπερ οἱ ἡμέτεροι πρόγονοι τῆς πολλῆς τρυφῆς ἀπαλλαγέντες εἰς τὸ μέτριον μετέστησαν, οὕτω καὶ ἡμεῖς ἀλλήλους παρακαλέσαντες τὴν μὲν νῦν οὖσαν περὶ τῆς πόλεως δόξαν ἐκβάλωμεν, φανῶμεν δὲ ἄξιοι βασιλεῖ τῆς προτέρας ἐλπίδος. 53. ἐκεῖνος ᾤετο μάλιστα ταύτην ἑαυτῷ συγχορεύσειν[1] καὶ τὰς ἄλλας ἀποκρύψειν εὐνοίᾳ καὶ τῆς πατρίδος αὐτῆς[2] οἰκειοτέραν ἔσεσθαι καὶ[3] κάλλος αὐτῇ καὶ προσθήκας ἑτέρας ἑτοιμάζων ἐπορεύετο. νῦν δὲ μισεῖ καὶ μισεῖσθαι πέπεισται ὁ Ἀπόλλωνος φίλος ὑπὸ τῶν Ἀπόλλωνος τροφίμων καί φησιν ἐν Ταρσοῖς τῆς Κιλικίας χειμάσειν. |

R 505 54. ἡμεῖς δὲ εἰ τοῦτο γένοιτο, βιωσόμεθα; εἰπέ μοι, ποίαις ψυχαῖς; τί λέγοντες; πῶς ἀλλήλους ὁρῶντες; πῶς τοὺς εἰσαφικνουμένους; Ἀντι-

---

[1] συγχορεύσειν F., Re. : συγχορεύειν mss.
[2] αὐτῆς F. : αὐτὴν Re. (mss.).
[3] καὶ before κάλλος om. F., in error.

were visited with sickness because of the murder of
Laïus at the hands of Oedipus, even though he did
not know who it was he killed. So, when he sees this
law prevailing with the gods, will the emperor sit
down and pick out the good from the much greater
number of the bad? I could wish it were so, but
cannot be sure of it.

52. Then, while he is still crossing rivers, facing the
might of Persia, pondering upon his invasion, and
considering how, when and where to attack the foe,
let us make true patriots of ourselves.[a] Just as our
forefathers rid themselves of their excessive luxury
and turned to moderation, so let us by our mutual
encouragement discard the reputation that the city
now has and reveal ourselves to our emperor as
worthy of his former hopes. 53. He thought that
this, of all cities, would associate itself with him in its
joy, would eclipse all others in good will, and would
be more his own even than his home town.[b] So he
came here, ready to lavish upon it beauty and other
delights.[c] But now he loathes it, and he, Apollo's
friend, is convinced that he is loathed by us, Apollo's
nurselings,[d] and he declares that he will spend the
winter season in Tarsus in Cilicia. 54. And if this
should come to pass, shall we continue to exist? Then
with what mood, with what words, with what looks
for ourselves and for our visitors? Good Lord

---

[a] Clear indication of the date of composition, March/
April A.D. 363.

[b] Constantinople: cf. Julian ,E.L.F. No. 59 (443 b):
τὴν ἐμὴν πατρίδα Κωνσταντίνου πόλιν . . . ἐγὼ ὡς μητέρα φιλῶ.

[c] Cf. Or. 15. 52.

[d] Apollo's friend in his practice of divination: Apollo's
nurselings, under Libanius' own guidance, in their gifts of
eloquence and education.

# LIBANIUS

οχείας οὔσης, Ἥλιε, καὶ σωζομένης ἐν Ταρσοῖς
βασιλεύς; καὶ πέμψομεν πρέσβεις εἰς Κιλικίαν οἱ
δεχόμενοι τοὺς ἐκεῖθεν; καὶ Κύδνος εὐτυχέστερος
Ὀρόντου τοῦ ποταμοῦ; 55. καὶ ἡ αἰτία δι' ἣν
ταῦτα οὕτω πέπρακται, χαλεπωτέρα πτώματος.
οὐκ ἤνεγκαν ἄρχοντα ἀγαθὸν οἱ τῶν μὴ τοιούτων
γενεὰν ἐνεγκόντες ὅλην, οὐκ ἤνεγκαν ἐν βασιλεῖ
φιλοσοφίαν οἰκοῦσαν, ἀπεσείσαντο τὴν ἀρχήν.
εἶτ' οὐ πᾶς ὑμῖν ἀπὸ τῶνδε τῶν χρόνων πολέμιος
βασιλεύς; οὐ διαδέξονται μετὰ τοῦ | σκήπτρου τὸ F 1
μῖσος; οὐ φεύξονται τὴν ἀκόλαστον; οὐ συνεπι-
θήσονται τοῖς καιροῖς; οὐ τοῖς ἀεὶ τὴν πόλιν
ἔχουσι τὴν νῦν ἀγνωμοσύνην προοίσουσι;[1] καλῆς
γε προνοίας τοὺς υἱεῖς κληρονόμους καταλείψετε·
ἄνδρες, δείσατε τὸν κρημνόν. 56. τοιοῦτον ἐχθρὸν
ἐγὼ κἂν ἰδιώτην ἔδεισα. οὐκ ἔστι τοῦ Τυανέως
πόρρω κατὰ τὸν βίον, ὃς δυοῖν ῥήμασιν ἔστιξε τὴν
ἡμετέραν. εἶτ' οὐ νήψομεν; οὐχ ὅλον τὸ συμ-
R 506 βησόμενον ὀψόμεθα ταῖς ψυχαῖς; οὐκ ἐπὶ | τὰ
ἱερὰ δραμούμεθα; οὐ τοὺς μὲν πείσομεν, τοὺς
δὲ ἕλξομεν; οὐ παρὰ τοὺς βωμοὺς ταῖς ἱκετείαις
χρησόμεθα χαίρειν ἀφέντες ἱπποδρόμους; οὐκ
ἀποστελοῦμεν φήμην ἐπ' αὐτὸν Χοάσπην Ἀντι-

---

[1] προοίσουσι F., Re. (correction in B): προσοίσουσι mss.

[a] Rivers of Tarsus and Antioch respectively.
[b] Constantine and his sons : cf. the ending of Julian's
Caesars.

246

Helios, while Antioch stays safe and sound, is the emperor to fix his quarters in Tarsus ? And shall we send envoys to Cilicia, we who receive them from there ? And shall Cydnus have better luck than the river Orontes ?[a] 55. And the reason why this has occurred is worse than ruin. Those who put up with a whole brood of bad rulers[b] could not put up with a single good one. They could not put up with philosophy innate in an emperor, but they shook off his rule. Then will not every emperor from this time forth be your foe? Will they not inherit his hatred along with his throne ? Will they not flee this lawless city and set upon it in times of crisis? Will they not cast our present stupidity in the teeth of all future inhabitants ? A fine inheritance you will leave your children, to be sure! Gentlemen, pause and shudder at the abyss that yawns before you.[c] 56. Were he but a private citizen, I would fear to have such a one as my foe. In his manner of life he does not differ much from that man of Tyana who branded our city in a couple of lines.[d] Then shall we not sober ourselves and, inwardly seeing all that will come to pass, have recourse to the temples ? Shall we not persuade people to go there or drag them by main force ? Shall we not turn our backs upon the horse races and make our supplications at the altars, and, sending to the very Choaspes[e] the news that Antioch has made her

[c] A recognition of the same imperial esprit-de-corps as that appealed to in *Or.* 24.

[d] Apollonius, *cf.* Philostr. *V.A.* 1. 16 : ὁ Ἀπολλώνιος ἰδὼν τὸ ἱερὸν χαρίεν μέν, σπουδὴν δὲ ἐν αὐτῷ οὐδεμίαν . . .'Ἀπόλλον, ἔφη, μετάβαλε τοὺς ἀφώνους εἰς δένδρα, ἵνα κἂν ὡς κυπάριττοι ἠχῶσιν.

[e] Imputes to Julian the same ambition to rival the achievements of Alexander as in *Or.* 18. 260 f.

οχεῖς ἀπολελόγηνται λέγουσαν; οὐ δεξόμεθα
τὴν ἐκεῖθεν βασιλεὺς διήλλακται λέγουσαν;

57. Τούτων εἰ λέγοι τις βέλτιον, πρῶτος ὑπακού-
σομαι. εἰ δ᾽ ἐνθάδε σιγήσας οἴκοι με κακῶς ἐρεῖ,
θαυμάσεταί με τοῦ χειμῶνος ἅμα δάκρυσιν.

---

<sup>a</sup> The minatory conclusion echoes that of the *Misopogon*.

plea, receive the message back that the emperor has been reconciled with her?

57. Should any man suggest something better, I will be the first to agree. If, however, he remains silent here and reviles me in the privacy of his home, he will in winter time have cause to admire me amid his tears.[a]

# ORATION 17

# ΜΟΝΩΙΔΙΑ ΕΠΙ ΙΟΥΛΙΑΝΩΙ

R 507    1. Ὦ πόποι, ἦ μέγα πένθος οὐκ Ἀχαιίδα Fii.
γῆν μόνον, ἀλλὰ καὶ πᾶσαν ὁπόσην ὁ Ῥωμαίων
κοσμεῖ θεσμὸς κατείληφε· μᾶλλον μὲν γὰρ ἴσως
ἦν Ἕλληνες οἰκοῦσιν, ἅτε καὶ μᾶλλον αἰσθανο-
μένην τοῦ κακοῦ, | διήκει δ' οὖν καὶ διὰ πάσης γῆς, F 2ᵛ
ὡς ἔφην, ἡ πληγὴ τύπτουσά τε καὶ κατατέμνουσα
τὰς ψυχάς, ὡς οὐκέτ' ὂν βιωτὸν ἀνδρὶ βελτίστῳ τε
καὶ ὅτῳ τοῦ εὖ ζῆν ἐπιθυμία.   2. τιμαὶ μὲν
οἴχονται τῶν ἀγαθῶν, ὑψηλαὶ δὲ τῶν πονηρῶν τε
καὶ ἀκολάστων φατρίαι¹· νόμοι δὲ κωλυταὶ κακουρ-
γημάτων οἱ μὲν ἤδη λέλυνται, οἱ δὲ αὐτίκα τοῦτο
πείσονται, τοῖς δὲ μένουσι γράμμασιν εἶναι περιέσται ἔργων ἀμοίροις. πέπονθέ τε τὸ ἀνθρώπειον
γένος, οἷον αἱ πόλεις ὧν κατασείεται τείχη. καὶ
γὰρ ἐκεῖ τοῦ περιφράττοντος ἀπολωλότος τῶν μᾶλλον ἰσχυόντων γίνεται τὰ τῶν δικαίως κεκτημένων,
οἱ δὲ ἐπιπεσόντες ἁρπάζουσί τε καὶ κτείνουσι καὶ
ὑβρίζουσιν εἰς γυναῖκας ἁλούσας καὶ παῖδας. καὶ
νῦν ἀνέῳκται² κατὰ τῶν ἐπιεικῶν τοῖς ἀνόσια
δρῶσιν ὁδὸς εὐρεῖα καὶ κλισιάδες μεγάλαι, καὶ
R 508 τετείχισται οὐδὲν ἔτι.   3. τὸν μὲν οὖν | Ἕκτορα τῆς

---

¹ φατρίαι F. (mss.) : φρατρίαι Re. and editors.
² ἀνέῳκται F. (mss.) : ἠνέῳκται Re. and editors.

252

# THE LAMENT OVER JULIAN [a]

1. " ALAS, great indeed is the grief" that has beset
not just " the land of Achaïa," [b] but the whole empire
where the laws of Rome hold sway. It is perhaps the
greater in that part where the Greeks live, for they
have the greater knowledge of the disaster, but the
blow that smote and harrowed our souls with the
thought that life is a mockery for the good man who
wants to lead a good life, has, as I have said, smitten
the whole length and breadth of the world. 2. Gone
is the glory of the good: the company of the wicked
and the licentious is uplifted. Laws, the suppressors
of evil, are either laid low or soon to be so, and if they
remain, they will remain as ineffectual ciphers. The
human race has experienced the fate of cities whose
walls are laid low. Their defence is gone, and all that
the rightful owners possess passes to the stronger,
who fall upon them looting and murdering, and
ravishing their captive wives and children. Now the
broad path, the great doors lie wide open for the doers
of evil to attack the just. [c] The walls are down. 3.
Hector has, and rightly, been called the " steadfast

---

[a] *Oration* 17.

[b] Homer, *Iliad*, 1. 254. This passage is cited by Eustathius (on *Od.* 1. 344).

[c] Herod. 9. 9 : a very artful adaptation, with its undertones of civilization under attack by barbarism.

Τροίας ἤδη τις | ἐκάλεσεν ἀστραβῆ κίονα ὀρθῶς F προσειπών. πεσόντος γὰρ ἐπὶ σαθροῦ τὸ Ἴλιον εἱστήκει καὶ αὐτίκα ἔμελλε κείσεσθαι μετὰ τοῦ Ἕκτορος. νυνὶ δὲ οὐ μιᾶς περὶ τὸν Ἑλλήσποντον πόλεως οὐδέ γε ἔθνους ἑνὸς ἀνατέτραπται κίων, ἀλλ' ἡ ἀρχὴ τῶν ἀπογόνων Αἰνείου, τὸ δέ ἐστι γῆς ὅ τι κάλλιστον καὶ θαλάττης, ἐπ' οὐδενὸς ἰσχυροῦ βέβηκεν. ἀλλ' ἔστι καὶ τῶν οὐ σφόδρα βιαίων πνευμάτων κατασεῖσαι, τῶν μὲν ἔνδοθεν πονηρίᾳ λυμαινομένων, τῶν δὲ σὺν ὅπλοις ἔξωθεν ἐπιόντων τε καὶ ἐχόντων.

4. Τίνα μέντοι, τίνα θεῶν αἰτιατέον; ἢ πάντας ὁμοίως ἐκλιπόντας φρουρὰν ἣν ὤφειλον[1] τῇ γενναίᾳ κεφαλῇ ἀντὶ πολλῶν μὲν ἱερείων, πολλῶν δὲ εὐχῶν, μυρίων δὲ ἀρωμάτων, πολλοῦ δὲ αἵματος τοῦ μὲν νυκτός, τοῦ δ' ἐν ἡμέρᾳ χυθέντος; οὐ γὰρ τοὺς μὲν εὐώχει, τοὺς δὲ ὑπερέβαινεν, ὥσπερ ὁ Αἰτωλὸς ἐκεῖνος τὴν Ἄρτεμιν ἐν καρπῶν συλλογῇ, ἀλλ' ὅσους οἱ ποιηταὶ παρέδοσαν, πατέρας τε καὶ παῖδας, θεούς τε καὶ θεάς, ἄρχοντάς τε καὶ ἀρχομένους, ἅπασιν ἔσπενδέ τε | καὶ τοὺς ἁπάντων F ἐνεπίμπλη βωμοὺς ἀρνῶν καὶ βοῶν. 5. ὥστε ἔγωγε πολλάκις ἐνεθυμήθην ὅτι οὐδὲν ἂν δέοι τῷδε τῷ ἀνδρὶ τάχους τε ἵππων καὶ τοξοτῶν τέχνης καὶ ὁπλιτῶν ἀλκῆς καὶ δέκα μυριάδων, ἀλλ' ἔχων ἀμφ' αὑτὸν τοὺς θεούς, ὀλίγην στρατιὰν μέγα δυναμένην, ὀφθεὶς τοῖς ἐναντίοις πείσει γενέσθαι γυμνούς. 6. ἤλπιζον δὲ καὶ σκηπτοὺς καὶ πρηστῆρας καὶ τὰ

---

[1] ὤφειλον τηρεῖν Morel (PBM, correction in I): τηρεῖν deleted Re., F.

---

[a] Pindar, Ol. 2. 89 ff.

stay of Troy,"[a] for when he had fallen Ilium stood on rickety foundations and was soon to lie prostrate with him. But now there has fallen the stay of not just a single town by the Hellespont nor yet of a single province, but the empire of the descendants of Aeneas, the most glorious thing of land and sea, is stood on no sure foundation. Winds that blow with no great force can cause its fall, since within ill-doers ravage it by their wickedness and enemies under arms attack it from without and possess it.

4. But which of the gods—which, I ask you, can be blamed for this ? Have they all alike abandoned the guard they should have stood around his noble person in return for the many sacrifices, the many prayers, the countless offerings of incense and the blood of sacrifice that flowed both day and night? He did not feast some and ignore others, as that Aetolian of old did with Artemis in the gathering of his crop, but to all the gods whom the poets have handed down to us, fathers, sons, male and female, governors and governed, he made libation and loaded the altars of every one with sheep and oxen.[b] 5. So I often thought to myself that this man would need no speedy horses, no skilled archers, no brave infantry, no thousands of men, but with the gods about him, a small army of great might, he would induce the enemy, at the first sight of him, to lay down their arms. 6. I expected to see thunderbolts and fireballs

[b] *Cf.* Homer, *Iliad*, 9. 529 ff. Oeneus of Calydon forgot Artemis in his sacrifices, and she as punishment sent the Calydonian boar to ravage his country. From the boar hunt that followed sprang the feud that resulted in the death of Meleager.

The rôle of poets as formulators of pagan religion is here made explicit. ·

ἄλλα βέλη τὰ τῶν κρειττόνων καταβήσεσθαι ἐπὶ
Πέρσας, οἱ δὲ οὕτως ἄρα ἦσαν δίκαιοι ὥστε πολλῇ
μὲν ἑστιαθέντες κνίσσῃ, λαμπρὰ δὲ ὑποσχόμενοι
καὶ τῶν γε πρώτων οὐ φθονήσαντες τελευτῶντες
R 509 τά τε ἄλλα | συνέχεαν καὶ αὐτοῦ προσαπεστέρησαν
ἁλιέων μιμησάμενοι δέλεαρ καὶ δι' Ἀσυρίων κε-
κρατημένων ἐπὶ θάνατον ἑλκύσαντες. 7. ἀμείνων
ἄρα ἦν λογισμὸς[1] ὁ τέως καταγελώμενος ὃς πό-
λεμον ὑμῖν ἀρά|μενος πολύν τε καὶ σφοδρὸν καὶ F 2
ἄπαυστον ἔσβεσε μὲν πῦρ ἱερόν, ἐπέσχε δὲ θυσιῶν
ἡδονήν, βωμοὺς δὲ ἐφῆκε λακτίζουσιν ἀνατρέπειν,
ἱερὰ δὲ καὶ νεὼς τοὺς μὲν ἔκλεισε, τοὺς δὲ κατέ-
σκαψε, τοὺς δὲ βεβήλους ἀποφήνας πόρνοις ἐνοικεῖν
ἔδωκε, ξύμπασαν δὲ τὴν περὶ ὑμᾶς διατριβὴν καταλύσας νεκροῦ τινος θήκην[2] εἰς τὸν ὑμέτερον
R 510 ἐγκατέστησε κλῆρον. | 8. ἀλλ' ὅμως οὗτος ὁ
Σαλμωνεὺς ἢ Λυκοῦργος καὶ πρός γε ἔτι Μελι-
τίδης, οὐδὲ γὰρ νοῦ μετεῖχεν οὐδὲ πολὺ βελτίων
τῶν ἐν ταῖς γραφαῖς ἦν ἢ τῶν πηλίνων, τεσσα-
ράκοντα ἔτη κατέσχεν ἦν ἐλωβᾶτο γῆν καὶ μόλις
ποτὲ ἀπῆλθε νόσῳ. 9. ὁ δέ γε ἱεροὺς ἀνανεωσά-
μενος νόμους καὶ τὰ καλὰ ἀντὶ τῶν κακῶν εἰς

---

[1] ὁ λογισμὸς F., Cobet (B, correction in A). Om. Re.
(other mss.).
[2] τινος F., Morel (correction in C) : τινα other mss. θήκην
F., Re. (correction in A) : φήμην Morel (other mss.).

---

[a] An embittered account of Christian reaction to Julian's
religious policies, in a tone akin to that of Julian's outburst
against Christ (*Caesars*, 336 a). Pagan horror of pollution
from contact with the dead, most recently expressed by
Julian himself in his religious legislation (*E.L.F.* No. 136),
encouraged militant Christians to select pagan sanctuaries
as the burial places for their own dead (as the precinct of

and all the bolts of heaven descending on the Persians.
But the justice of the gods, it seems, was such that,
though feasted with offerings of fat, after promise of
success and initially grudging him nought, they finally
put all into confusion and robbed us of him too, bait-
ing him like fishers and luring him on to his death
at the hands of the Assyrians he had conquered.
7. A creed which we had until then laughed to scorn,[a]
which had declared such violent, unceasing war
against you, has won the day, after all. It has
quenched the sacred flame : it has stopped the
joyful sacrifices : it has set them on to spurn and
overthrow your altars : your temples and sanctuaries
it has closed, or demolished, or profaned, or given to
harlots to dwell in : it has utterly undone the reverence that was yours, and has established in your
inheritance a dead man's tomb. 8. But yet, that
Salmoneus, that Lycurgus, and Simple Simon, to
boot, for he was witless and little better than a
painted image or a figure of clay,—for forty years he
possessed this world that he defiled, and then at long
last died a natural death.[b] 9. But he who revived
sacred laws, who put virtue, not vice, in pride of

Daphne for S. Babylas), and so render them useless for the
pagan devotees.
    [b] Constantius reigned in all for 40 years (Amm. Marc. 21. 15.
3). Here, chiefly because of his persecution of paganism,
he is presented as sacrilegious, cruel and stupid, by means
of suitable mythological and literary parallels. Salmoneus,
mythical king of Elis, usurped the name and tried to imitate
the thunder and lightning of Zeus. In punishment, he was
soon slain by a thunderbolt. Lycurgus, king of Thrace,
offered violence to Dionysus and was punished with blindness and early death (Homer, *Iliad*, 6. 130 ff.). The stupidity
of Melitides, a proverbial Simple Simon, and of Constantius
is emphasized by Libanius' use of Aristoph. *Frogs*, 535 ff.

τάξιν ἀγαγών, ἐγείρας μὲν ὑμετέρους οἴκους,
στήσας δὲ βωμούς, ἱερέων δὲ γένη συγκαλέσας ἐν
σκότῳ κρυπτόμενα, λείψανα δὲ ἀγαλμάτων ἐπαν-
ορθώσας, θύσας δὲ ἀγέλας, θύσας δὲ ποίμνια, τὰ
μὲν ἔξω, τὰ δὲ ἔνδον, τὰ μὲν | ἐν νυξί, τὰ δὲ ὑφ᾿ F
ἡλίῳ, πάντα δὲ τὸν αὐτοῦ βίον ἐκ τῶν ὑμετέρων
ἀρτήσας χειρῶν, μικρὸν μὲν χρόνον ἐν[1] μικροτέρῳ
σχήματι βασιλείας, πολὺ δὲ βραχύτερον ἐν τῷ
μείζονι φανεὶς ᾤχετο γεύσας μὲν ἀγαθῶν τὴν
οἰκουμένην, κορέσαι δὲ οὐκ ἀρκέσας. 10. ἀλλὰ |
R 511 πεπόνθαμεν οἷον εἰ τῷ φοίνικι τῷ ὄρνιθι παρέστη
διὰ πάσης μὲν τῆς γῆς ἐκτεῖναι τὴν πτῆσιν, στῆναι
δὲ μηδαμοῦ μήτε ἀγρῶν μήτε ἄστεων. ἀμυδρὰ
γὰρ οὕτως ἂν ἐγένετο τοῖς ἀνθρώποις ἡ τοῦ ὄρνι-
θος ὄψις. καὶ νῦν ἦν οὗτος ἀπέδωκεν εὐδαιμονίαν
ὥσπερ ὑπόπτερος διέδραμεν οὐκ ἀνασχομένη ῥιζω-
θῆναι τῆς, οἶμαι, κακίας ἀναμαχεσαμένης τὴν
ἧτταν. 11. ὡς πολύ γε ἦν κουφότερον ἐν τοῖς
χείροσι μένειν ἀπείρους ὄντας ἁρμονίας βασιλικῆς
ἢ μεταρρυέντας ἐπὶ τὰ ἀμείνω τοῦ βίου πάλιν ἐπὶ
τὰ πρόσθεν ἀπενεχθῆναι, καθάπερ ναῦν ἀναχθεῖσαν
μὲν ἐξ ἀλιμένων χωρίων, αὖθις δὲ ἐναντίῳ πνεύματι
πεμφθεῖσαν ἐπὶ τὰς πέτρας, ὥστε καὶ περιρραγῆναι.
12. τὸ δὲ μηδὲ διὰ χρόνου γενέσθαι τὴν ἐπάνοδον
τῶν κακῶν, ἀλλ᾿ ὥσπερ παρακύψασαν τὴν ἀγαθὴν
τύχην εὐθὺς οἴχεσθαι φεύγουσαν, Ἡράκλεις, ὡς
πικρόν τε καὶ πικρῶν τινων δαιμόνων. λειμών τις
οὗτος ἀνθήσας παραχρῆμα κατερρύη. |
13. Καίτοι ἔγωγε τοὺς μὲν τικτομένους μακαρί- F

[1] ⟨τῷ⟩ μικρ. add F., conj. Re. (La.).

258

place, who raised up your dwellings, erected altars, gathered together the priesthood that was languishing in obscurity, resurrected all that were left of the statues of the gods, who sacrificed herds of cattle and flocks of sheep, out of doors or indoors, at night time or in daylight, whose whole life depended upon your support[a]—he appeared for a short time in the guise of the junior emperor and much more briefly in that of the senior, and he has gone after giving the world taste of his bounty, but not enough to satisfy.[b] 10. Our plight is such as would be if the phoenix chanced to wing its way over all the earth and settle nowhere, either in town or country: the sight of the bird would be so indistinct to humans. So now the happiness that he bestowed on us has sped by as if on wings, for when wickedness made good its defeat, it could not bear to take root. 11. How much more bearable was it to stay in our unblest state, without knowledge of this imperial harmony, than to have changed our course towards the better things of life and then be drawn back to our former plight, like a ship that puts out from a harbourless shore and is driven back upon the rocks by a contrary wind so that it is dashed to pieces. 12. That our troubles should return after such short interval, and that our good fortune should put in a fleeting appearance and then be away and gone—alas, how harsh it is, and how harsh the gods that permit it ! Here a meadow of flowers has vanished straightaway.

13. And yet I used to call babes at birth blessed in

[a] Cf. Or. 1. 119. For Julian's religious policies cf. Bidez, Vie de Julien, pp. 261 ff.

[b] Julian was Caesar from November A.D. 355 until 361 (Constantius' death), and sole Augustus thereafter.

ους ἀπεκάλουν ἐν οἵῳ δὴ χρόνῳ σπαρέντες ἦλθον
εἰς φῶς, τοὺς δ' αὖ γεγηρακότας ἠλέουν ἐν βορβόρῳ
R 512 τε βεβιωκότας πλῆθός τε | ἐτῶν ἐν ἀγνοίᾳ τῶν
καλῶν ἀνηλωκότας, πλὴν ὅσον καὶ οἵδε σκιρτή-
σαντές τε ἐν γήρᾳ καὶ χορεύσαντες ἔμελλον
πορεύεσθαι.[1] κακοδαίμονες δὲ ἄρα ὄντες ἐλάνθανον οἱ γεννώμενοι πρὸς τέλματά τε ἥξοντες καὶ
νοσήσουσαν τὴν γῆν.

14. Ὦ γλυκείας ἀκοῆς, ἣν ἀπὸ τῆς ἑσπέρας ἡ
φήμη φέρουσα τὰς πόλεις εὔφραινε, μάχας καὶ
τρόπαια καὶ Ῥῆνον πλεόμενον καὶ φόνον Κελτῶν
καὶ αἰχμαλώτους λαμβανομένους, τοὺς δὲ πρὶν
Ῥωμαίων ἁλόντας ἀποδιδομένους καὶ φόρους ἐκ
πολεμίων καὶ τὰ κείμενα ἀνιστάμενα καὶ δαίμονός
τινος ἔργα καὶ ἀρετὴν ἀπαγγέλλουσα. 15. ὦ τῶν
δευτέρων θαυμασιωτέρων, ὁδοῦ τε ἐκείνης διὰ τῶν
ἐσχάτων καὶ δρόμου λανθάνοντος καὶ ὁπλιτῶν ἐξ
φοβούντων δισμυρίους καὶ πάντων μὲν ἐπ' αὐτὸν
ὁπλιζομένων, ἀμαχεὶ δὲ τοῦ πολέμου τεθέντος. ὦ
τῶν λόγῳ δηλουμένων, ὦ τῶν | πείρᾳ δεικνυμένων. F
16. βασιλεὺς ἐξέπληξε λόγου γραφῇ περὶ Βόσπορον
ἄνδρα τὸν ὑπὸ ἀμαθίας φάσκοντα Διογένη μιμεῖ-
σθαι τὸν ἐκ Σινώπης, ὄντα δὲ πλὴν ἀναιδείας
οὐδέν. βασιλεὺς ἐπέσταλκε σὺν ἀμηχάνῳ κάλλει
καὶ περιιστάμεθα τὰς ἐπιστολάς. 17. χωρεῖ παρὰ
R 513 | τὴν μητέρα τῶν θεῶν εἰς Φρυγίαν. ἔπειτα ἐκεῖ
τι παρ' αὐτῆς ἀκούσας ἐπείγεται. εἶτα ἐκ Κιλικίας

---

[1] πορεύεσθαι Re. (mss.) : ἀπέρχεσθαι F.

[a] For Julian's successes in Gaul cf. Or. 18. 40 ff. ; Amm.
Marc. Books 16-18, 20.
[b] Julian's Danube voyage and surprise of Lucillianus at
Sirmium, here exaggerated, cf. Amm. Marc. 21. 8-9.

the time when, new-born, they came into the light of day. I used to pity those who had grown old and lived their lives in squalor and spent their tale of years in ignorance of the good, except that even they, after leaping and dancing for joy in their old age, would then go their ways. But those who were being born into the world were, after all, ill-starred, though they knew it not, for they were coming to quags and an earth plague-stricken.

14. O glad tidings that report brought from the west to bless the cities, with news of battles and triumphs, of the sailing on the Rhine, the slaughter of Celts and the capture of prisoners, of the restoration of Romans previously taken prisoner, of tribute from the foe, the uplifting of what was laid low, and the glorious deeds of some divine spirit.[a] 15. O the more wondrous news that followed—that march along the fringe of empire and onslaught unobserved, the half dozen soldiers who caused twenty thousand to panic, the arming of the world against him, and the bloodless ending to the war! Ah, for all that was shown by reason and proved in action![b] 16. The emperor composed an oration in Constantinople and routed a fellow who stupidly claimed to be a follower of Diogenes of Sinope, but yet was made up of naught but impudence.[c] The emperor sent us letters of consummate beauty and we flocked to hear them. 17. He went to Phrygia to the Mother of the Gods, and then hastened on his journey after receiving some information from her there.[d] Then from Cilicia

[c] Julian, *Or.* 7 (pp. 204 ff.), *Against the Cynic Heracleius.* Cf. *Or.* 18. 157.
[d] Cf. *Or.* 12. 87, 18. 161 ; Amm. Marc. 22. 9. 2. Julian's *Or.* 5, *On the Mother of the Gods*, had been composed in Constantinople, in the March before he left.

σχολῇ πορεύεται δοκοῦν καὶ τοῦτο τῷ Διί. ἦκεν εἰς τὴν μεγάλην τὴν Ἀντιόχου πόλιν ἤ, εἰ βούλει γε, Ἀλεξάνδρου τοῦ φίλου τε αὐτῷ καὶ οὐκ ἐῶντος καθεύδειν, ὥσπερ δή τινα στρατηγὸν στρατηγὸς Ἀθηναῖος Ἀθηναῖον. 18. οὗ δὴ μυρίαι μὲν δικαζόμεναι δίκαι, πολλῶν δὲ θέσεις νόμων, βιβλίων δὲ συγγραφαὶ βοηθούντων θεοῖς, δρόμοι δὲ εἰς τεμένη τὰ μὲν ἐν τῇ πόλει, τὰ δὲ πρὸ αὐτῆς ἐν γηλόφοις, τὰ δὲ ἐν ἄκροις ὄρεσι. καὶ οὐδὲν οὕτω χαλεπὸν οὐδὲ δύσβατον ὃ μὴ λεῖον ἐδόκει νεὼν ἔχον ἢ πρότερόν γε ἐσχηκός. | πυνθανόμενοι δὲ οἱ μέχρι τῶν F τερμάτων Αἰγύπτου τε καὶ Λιβύης ὡς ἐρρωμένως ἅπτοιτο τῶν ἱερῶν ὁ βασιλεύς, μικρὰ μὲν ἐχρῶντο ταῖς οἰκίαις, ἐν ἱεροῖς δὲ διῃτῶντο.

19. Ἔδει τότε, ὦ φίλτατε, μὴ ἀπώσασθαι τὴν Περσικὴν πρεσβείαν σπονδάς τε αἰτοῦσαν καὶ R 514 στέρξουσαν οἷς | γνοίης. ἀλλά σου τὰ παθήματα τῆς πρὸς τῷ Τίγρητι γῆς ἀνθεῖλκε τὴν γνώμην δεδῃωμένης τε καὶ ἐρημωθείσης καὶ πολλὰς ἐμβολὰς ἀνασχομένης, ὧν ἑκάστη τὸν τῇδε πλοῦτον ἐκεῖσε μετήνεγκεν. ᾤου γὰρ ὡσπερεὶ προδοσίαν εἶναι μὴ λαβεῖν δίκας ἡσυχίας ἐπιθυμοῦντα. 20. ἀλλ᾽ ἰδού, τὸ δαιμόνιον ἀντέκρουσε. μᾶλλον δὲ δίκας μὲν ἐπράξω παριούσας μεγέθει τὰ ἀδικήματα. γῆ ἦν Ἀσυρίων, τὸ κάλλιστον ὧν Μῆδοι κέκτηνται,

---

[a] For Alexander and Antiochus in relation to the foundation of Antioch cf. Or. 11. 72 ff.

[b] Plutarch (Them. 3. 3, Mor. 184 F) and Cicero (T.D. 4. 19. 44) have an uplifting but untrue anecdote that the youthful Themistocles (who had, in actual fact, been archon in 493 B.C.) was reformed from his wild ways by the consideration of the renown won by Miltiades at Marathon.

he made a leisurely way, this too being the will of Zeus, and he came to this capital city of Antiochus or, if you would have it so, of Alexander who was so dear to him [a] and allowed him no sleep, as one Athenian general affected another such.[b]  18. Here countless were the cases he judged, many the laws he enacted : there was the composition of works in support of the gods, visits to shrines inside the city, on the slopes outside it, and on the very mountain tops. Nowhere was so hard or inaccessible that did not seem smooth and easy if it had a temple or had had one in days gone by.[c] The people who dwell as far away as the borders of Egypt and Libya, upon learning how zealously the emperor clove to the temples, began to make little use of their homes and spent their time in temples.

19. You should not then, my dear friend, have rejected the Persian embassy, when it asked for peace and was submissive to your will.[d] But the sufferings of the lands near the Tigris, ravaged and derelict, the victim of many an incursion, every one of which caused the transfer of our wealth into Persian hands, diverted your attention. You thought it tantamount to treason to desire peace and to refrain from exacting punishment.  20. But there ! Heaven opposed you, or rather you tried to exact a punishment disproportionate to the crime. There was the land of Assyria, queen of the Persian domains, shaded with

For Julian and Alexander cf. Or. 18. 260 ; Amm. Marc. 16. 5. 4, 25. 4. 15 ; Socr. H.E. 3. 21.
[c] For Julian in Antioch cf. Or. 18. 164 ff., where the order of topics is reversed as compared with the present passage, i.e., justice (182 ff.), religious polemic (178 ff.), shrines (171 ff.).
[d] Cf. Or. 18. 164 f., for the rejection of Persian peace proposals.

φοίνιξι μεγάλοις δένδρων τε ἑτέρων παντοδαποῖς
εἴδεσι σκιερά, χρυσόν τε καὶ ἄργυρον αὐτοῖς ὡς ἂν
ὀχυρωτάτῃ φρουροῦσα, βασιλείων τε λαμπρῶν ἐν-
ῳκοδομημένων κάπρων τε καὶ ἐλάφων καὶ ὁπόσα
θήρα δίδωσιν ἐν χώροις τετειχισμένοις πεφυλαγ-
μένων φρουρίων τε κρειττόνων πολεμίας χειρὸς εἰς
ἀέρα μέσον ἠρμένων ἀγρῶν τε παρισουμένων ἄστεσι
τῆς τε ἄλλης εὐδαιμονίας διαφερόντως ἀνθούσης. 21.
τούτοις | δὴ προσπεσὼν οὕτως ἐπέκλυσέ τε καὶ κατ- F 2
έσυρε γελῶν τε ἅμα καὶ παρέχων τοῖς στρατιώταις κωμάζειν, ὥστε ἀποικίας εἰς αὐτὴν δέοιντ᾽ ἂν
Μῆδοι καὶ οὐδὲ ἀνδρὸς γενεᾷ τὸ πτῶμα ἀνορθῶσαι.
καὶ μὴν ὄχθης τε ἀνάβασις ἀπιστουμένη νυκτομαχία
τε ὄχλον ὅτι πλεῖστον κατενεγκοῦσα Περσῶν τρό-
μος τε ἐγκείμενος τοῖς μέλεσι καὶ τὸ πόρρωθεν ὁρᾶν
R 515 φθειρομένην τὴν γῆν σὺν ἀτολμίᾳ, ταυτὶ | μὲν τῆς
δίκης ἣν ἐπετίθει.

22. Ἀπόδος δὴ ἡμῖν, ὦ θεῶν ὕπατε, τὸν ὁμώνυ-
μον, ὃς πλεῖστα δή σε ἐκάλεσεν ἐν ἔτει ἀρχομένῳ.
τοῦ δὲ ὁμόζυγος καὶ γέροντός περ ὄντος τὸν
ἐνιαυτόν,—ὁ δὲ ἐν μέσῳ κατέδυ. καὶ ὁ μὲν ἔκειτο,
ἡμεῖς δὲ ἐν Δάφνῃ τὰς Νύμφας ἐθεραπεύομεν
ὀρχήσει τε καὶ ταῖς ἄλλαις χάρισιν εἰδότες ὧν
ἐπεπόνθειμεν οὐδέν.

23. Τίς ἄρα λόγχην ἐκείνην ἐχάλκευσε τοσοῦτον
δυνησομένην; τίς ἐπήγαγε δαίμων τῷ βασιλεῖ
θρασὺν | ἱππέα; τίς κατηύθυνεν ἐπὶ τὰ πλευρὰ τὴν F 2

---

[a] Cf. Or. 18. 217 ff., for Julian's invasion of Assyria.
[b] Cf. Or. 18. 251 ff., Amm. Marc. 24. 6. 4 ff. for the

264

tall palms and other trees of all kinds, their strongest storehouse of gold and silver, with magnificent palaces built therein, with herds of boars, deer and all the animals of the chase contained within their enclosures, with forts towering aloft into mid air beyond the strength of hostile hand, with villages comparable with cities and with unparalleled prosperity.[a] 21. Here he directed his attack, and he so harried and overwhelmed them, himself all smiles and allowing his troops to make merry amongst it, that the Persians would need to colonize it and a man's lifetime would not be enough to repair the disaster. Moreover, the incredible ascent of the bank, the night battle that slew a vast number of Persians, the trembling that seized their limbs and, in their cowardice, the vision from afar of the ravaging of their lands—all this was part of the punishment he inflicted upon them.[b]

22. Restore to us then, supreme consul of the gods, your namesake who invoked you so often at the year's beginning. His colleague, despite his advanced years,[c] you have allowed to complete his year—but he was overcome in its mid course. And while he lay slain, we at Daphne were worshipping the Nymphs with choric dance and other delights, ignorant of the disaster that had befallen us.

23. Who then was it who forged the spear that was to have such power ? What god sent a daring horseman against our emperor, or aimed the spear at his

crossing of the Tigris and the night assault; *Or.* 1. 133, Socr. *H.E.* 3. 21, the siege of Ctesiphon.

[c] Julian's colleague in the consulship of A.D. 363 was Sallustius. The incoherence in this passage is due to overpowering emotion, not to textual corruption, as Reiske and Förster imagined.

LIBANIUS

αἰχμήν; ἢ δαίμων μὲν οὐδείς, προθυμία δὲ σφοδρὰ
καταναγκάζουσα περιτρέχειν τε καὶ ἐξοτρύνειν
στρατιὰν ἀργὸν εἰωθυῖάν τε καθεύδειν καὶ τραυμάτων ἄπειρον τὴν πολλήν; ἀλλ' ὁ μὲν οὕτως
R 516 ἠμέλει τοῦ σώματος, Ἀφροδίτη | δὲ ὅπως οὐκ
ἐξήρπασεν οὐδὲ Ἀθηνᾶ θαῦμα ἂν εἴη. 24. καίτοι
παλαιάς γε βοηθείας αὐτῶν¹ ἐμιμοῦντο ἄν, ὧν ἡ
μὲν Μενέλεων ἐξέσωσεν, ἡ δὲ Πάριν, ἄνδρα
ἠδικηκότα καὶ προσηκόντως ἀγχόμενον. τίς ποτε
ἄρα τότε ἦν ἐν οὐρανῷ λόγος; τίς Ἄρεος ἀνέστη
κατήγορος, ὥσπερ πρότερον ὁ Ποσειδῶν, φερομένου μὲν ἐπὶ τῆς ἀσπίδος ἔτι ἔμπνου τοῦ βεβλη-
μένου, τῆς στρατιᾶς δὲ οἰμωγῇ διαχρωμένης, τῶν
ὅπλων δὲ αὐτοῖς τὰς χεῖρας ἐκφυγόντων,² ὥσπερ
ἐν τῷ Σικελικῷ πορθμῷ τὰς τῶν Ὀδυσσέως
ἑταίρων αἱ κῶπαι; 25. θρῆνος ἦν τότε Μουσῶν,
θρῆνος ἦν ἐν Βοιωτίᾳ καὶ Θρᾴκῃ καὶ τοῖς φίλοις
ὄρεσι θρηνουσῶν, οἶμαι, γῆν | τε καὶ θάλατταν καὶ F
ἀέρα, εἰς οἵαν ἀνομίαν ἐμπεπτώκασι, τὰ ἄλλα δέ,
ὡς ἂν ἐστερημένα τῆς τῶν βωμῶν θοίνης. 26.
ὀδυρόμεθα δὴ καὶ ἡμεῖς κατὰ συμμορίας, φιλόσοφοι
μὲν τὸν τὰ τοῦ Πλάτωνος σφίσι συνδιερευνώμενον,
ῥήτορες δὲ τὸν δεινόν τε εἰπεῖν καὶ εἰπόντος |
R 517 ἐξετάσαι, οἷς δὲ πρὸς ἀλλήλους διαφοραὶ ψήφου
δικαίας δεόμεναι τὸν ἀμείνω τοῦ Ῥαδαμάνθυος
δικαστήν. 27. ὦ γεωργοὶ κακοδαίμονες, ὡς βορά
γε ὑμεῖς ἔσεσθε τῶν εἰσπράττειν τεταγμένων. ὦ
βουλευτηρίων ἰσχὺς καταρρέουσά τε ἤδη καὶ εἰς

¹ αὐτῶν Re., Morel (mss. except C; om. M): αὐτῶν F. (C).
266

breast? Or was it no god, but his compulsive zeal to alarm and arouse an army sluggish, unused to activity and for the greater part unacquainted with wounds? Yet though he had no thought for his own safety, the wonder is that Aphrodite or Athena did not rescue him. 24. For they would have been merely imitating their ancient feats of rescue, when one of them rescued Menelaüs and the other Paris, though he was a criminal and deserved throttling.[a] But what discussion took place in heaven then? Who rose to accuse Ares, as Poseidon once did, when our wounded emperor still breathing was borne away on his shield and the whole army lamented and their weapons dropped from their hands, as the oars dropped from the hands of Odysseus' comrades in the Sicilian strait?[b] 25. Then surely there was a lament of the Muses and laments in Boeotia and Thrace and their beloved hills as they bewailed the lawlessness that had overtaken earth and sea and sky, and, besides, how they had been robbed of their altar feasts. 26. We, too, lament him according to our professions. Philosophers bewail the death of one who was their companion in their investigations of the works of Plato. Rhetors bewail one who was an expert in oratory and the criticism of oratory. Litigants requiring a just decision bewail him, a judge more upright than Rhadamanthys. 27. Ah, the poor peasantry! What a prey you will be to those appointed to collect your taxes! Alas for the power of the town councils, even now in decline and soon to become a mere shadow!

[a] Cf. Homer, *Iliad*, 4. 128 ff., 3. 370 ff.
[b] Homer, *Od*. 12. 203

---

[2] ἐκφυγόντων Re. (mss. except UI): ἐκφευγόντων F. (UI before correction).

εἴδωλον ἀφιξομένη ταχέως. ὦ πόλεων ἄρχοντες,
ὡς ἀπολεῖταί γε ὑμῖν τὸ ἔργον τοῦ ὀνόματος,
ὥσπερ ἐν ταῖς πομπαῖς καὶ ἔσται τὸ ἄρχον ὑπὸ
τῷ ἀρχομένῳ, ὦ βοαὶ πενήτων ἀδικουμένων, ὡς
μάτην γε πρὸς τὸν ἀέρα ῥιφήσεσθε. ὦ λόχοι
στρατιωτῶν, οἷς ἀπόλωλε βασιλεὺς ταὐτὰ τοῖς πολλοῖς ἐπὶ στρατείας σιτούμενος. ὦ νόμοι δικαίως
ἂν 'Απόλλωνος δόξαντες εἶναι καταπατούμενοι. ὦ
λόγοι δύναμίν τε καὶ σθένος ὁμοῦ κτησάμενοί τε
καὶ ἀποβαλόντες. ὦ χεῖρες ὑπογραφέων τῇ τῆς
γλώττης εὐμουσίᾳ κρατηθεῖσαι. ὦ πτῶμα τῆς
οἰκουμένης | κοινόν. 28. κατακλυσμός τις οὗτος F 2
ἕτερος θέρους μέσου ἢ προσβολὴ πυρός, ὁποῖον ἐν
τῇ Φαέθοντος ἡνιοχείᾳ λόγος ἀφθῆναι. μᾶλλον δὲ
πολλῷ τουτὶ τὸ πάθος ἐλεεινότερον. τὸ μέν γε ἦν
R 518 ἐρήμην εἶναι τὴν | γῆν, τὸ δὲ νῦν πάσχειν κακῶς
ὑπὸ τοῦ χείρονος τὸν ἀμείνω πόαν τε ὑπάρχειν
ὥσπερ θρέμματι τῇ κακίᾳ τὰς πόλεις ἄφθονον, ἐξ
ὧν ἂν ἔχοι τρέφεσθαι εἰς πιμελήν. 29. ὥσπερ οὖν
ἀνθρώπῳ νοσοῦντι τὴν ψυχὴν γέμοντί τε πονηρῶν
ἐπιθυμιῶν κρεῖττον ἀπελθεῖν ἢ ζῆν τυραννουμένου
τοῦ ἐν τῇ ψυχῇ βελτίονος ὑπὸ τοῦ φαυλοτέρου,
οὕτω δὴ καὶ τῇ γῇ μᾶλλον ἂν ἐλυσιτέλει κρυφθῆναι
συνεχέσιν ὄμβροις ἢ πεπολίσθαι τε καὶ τρέφειν
γένος ἀνθρώπων, ἐν ᾧ κακία μὲν τίμιον ἀρετὴ δὲ
ἄτιμον. 30. ἀναπνεύσατε, Κελτοί. χορεύσατε, Σκύθαι. παιανίσατε, Σαυρομάται. ὁ ζυγὸς ὑμῖν συν-
τέτριπται καὶ οἱ αὐχένες ἐλεύθεροι. τοῦτο ἦν ἄρα
νεὼς 'Απόλλωνος πυρὶ δαπανώμενος, ἐξέλιπεν ὁ

--------

<sup>a</sup> Cf. Herod. 1. 65.       <sup>b</sup> Cf. Ovid, Met. Bk. 2.

Alas for the governors of cities ! Vanished will be the
reality of your titles, as though in the ritual of procession, and the ruler will be under the thumb of the
ruled ! Alas for the cries of the oppressed poor ! How
fruitlessly will you rise to heaven ! Alas for the regiments of the army, who have lost an emperor who on
campaign shared the rations of the rank and file !
Alas for the laws which might justly have been held to
be those of Apollo *a* and are now trampled underfoot !
Alas for oratory, for the power and strength it won
and, no sooner won, lost ! Alas for the hands of the
secretaries, whose speed could not equal the eloquence
of his tongue ! Alas for the disaster that afflicts the
whole world ! 28. This was a second flood in mid-
summer or a visitation of fire, such as they say was
kindled when Phaëthon drove his chariot.*b* Yet
this is something far more pitiful. Then the earth
was empty : now the good are outraged by the bad,
and the cities are for wickedness as abundant fodder
for a beast, that it can fatten upon them. 29. When
a man ails in soul and is full of base desires, it is
better for him to die rather than to live with the
better part of his soul held in bondage by the worse.
So now it would be better for the whole world also
to lie hidden under perpetual storm rather than to be
girdled with cities and to produce a race of men
among whom vice is held in honour and virtue dis-
honoured. 30. Breathe freely again, you Celts.
Dance for joy, you Goths. Raise your cry of triumph,
you Sarmatians. The yoke upon you has been
broken and your necks are free.*c* This then was
what was meant when the temple of Apollo was

*c* Cf. Or. 18. 290, referring to the events of summer A.D.
364. Amm. Marc. 26. 4. 5, Zos. 4. 3. 4.

θεὸς τὴν γῆν μιαίνεσθαι μέλλουσαν, τοῦτο σει-
σμοὶ γῆν πᾶσαν δονοῦντες, μελλούσης ἄγγελοι ταραχῆς τε καὶ ἀκοσμίας.

31. Σὺ μέν, ὦ βασιλέων ἄριστε, μεγάλα ἐργαζό-
μενος | ἐνενόεις τὸν ἐπαινέτην ἐμὲ καὶ λόγους τοὺς F 2
ἐσομένους τοῖς πράγμασιν, ἐγὼ δὲ ἤσκουν τὴν
διάνοιαν ὡς μὴ λειφθείην τῶν ἔργων, ὥσπερ τις
παλαιστὴς ἐπιμελούμενος τοῦ σώματος πυνθανόμενος ἥξειν ἀντίπαλον ἰσχυρόν. ἐγὼ μὲν οὖν λέγω
τε καὶ ἐρῶ καὶ οὐκ ἀδικήσω σιγῇ τὰ ἔργα,
ἀκούσονται δὲ ἄλλοι μὲν τῶν ᾀσμάτων, αὐτὸς δὲ ὁ
τὰς νίκας ἀνῃρημένος τέθαπται καλὰς καὶ γενναίας
ἐλπίδας τῆς οἰκουμένης ἐκτεμών. 32. ἐδέξατο
πληγὴν Ἀγαμέμνων, ἀλλὰ Μυκήνης βασιλεύς, Κρε-
σφόντης, ἀλλὰ Μεσσήνης, Κόδρος, ἀλλὰ χρησμῷ
πειθόμενος, Αἴας, ἀλλὰ μικρόψυχος στρατηγός,
Ἀχιλλεύς, ἀλλ' ἥττων ἀφροδισίων καὶ θυμοῦ καὶ
R 519 ἄλλως | ταραχώδης, Κῦρος, ἀλλ' ὄντων υἱέων,
Καμβύσης, ἀλλὰ μαινόμενος. Ἀλέξανδρος ἔθνη-
σκεν, ἀλλ' οὐκ ἐχθροῦ χειρί, καὶ ἅμα ἄνθρωπος
δοὺς ἂν ἀφορμὴν κατηγόροις. ὁ δὲ ἐξ ἑσπέρας
μέχρις ἀνίσχοντος ἡλίου κρατῶν, ψυχὴν δὲ ἔχων
μεστὴν ἀρετῆς, νέος δὲ καὶ οὐκ ὢν πατὴρ ὑπ'
Ἀχαιμενίδου τινὸς κατενήνεκται. | 33. ἀκούσας F 2
ἀνέβλεπον εἰς οὐρανὸν ψεκάδας αἵματι συμμιγεῖς

---

[a] The burning of the Daphnaean temple occurred on
October 22nd A.D. 362, cf. Amm. Marc. 22. 13 (with mention
of earthquakes elsewhere), Julian, Misop. 361 b, E.L.F.
No. 105, Lib. Or. 60 (Monody on the Daphnaean Temple).

[b] i.e., Or. 18 (Funeral Oration for Julian).

[c] The revived Persian monarchy of the 3rd century A.D.
claimed descent from their predecessors of classical times :

wasted by fire, that the god abandoned the earth since it was going to be defiled. This was the meaning of the earthquakes that shook the entire world : they were harbingers of the riot and disorder to come.[a]

31. Most excellent of emperors, in all your mighty deeds, you used to spare a thought for me who praise you and for my oratory that would praise your deeds. I trained my intellect so that I should not be inadequate to deal with your achievements, like a wrestler continually in training and aware that a strong challenger was coming to meet him. Well, now I tell fo his deeds and I shall do so.[b] I shall not dishonour them by silence, but it will be others who hear my strains. He who gained the victories lies in his grave, cutting short the fine and noble hopes of the world. 32. The blow fell on Agamemnon, but he was king of Mycenae. Upon Cresphontes, but he was king of Messene. Upon Codrus, but he was acting in obedience to an oracle. Upon Ajax, but he was a weak-hearted general; and on Achilles, but he was ruled by love and anger, a turbulent character on the whole; and on Cyrus, but he had sons to succeed him, and on Cambyses, but he was mad. Alexander died, but by no enemy hand, and he was besides one who might have given grounds for criticism. Yet the emperor who ruled over all from the west to the rising sun, whose soul was filled with virtue, still a young man and with no sons to follow him, he has been done away with by some Persian.[c] 33. At the news I gazed up to heaven expecting

in this they were at one with the classicism of contemporary Greek writers, who just as willingly identify the Goths with the Scyths of Herodotus.

ἀναμένων, οἵας ἀφῆκεν ἐπὶ Σαρπηδόνι Ζεύς, οὐ
μὴν εἶδον. ἴσως μέντοι ἀφῆκεν ἐπὶ τῷ νεκρῷ, τοὺς
δὲ πολλοὺς ἔλαθεν, ἅτ᾽ ἐν μάχῃ καὶ κονιορτῷ καὶ
αἵματι τῷ ἀπὸ τῶν φόνων.

34. Ὢ νεῷ καὶ ἱερὰ καὶ ἀγάλματα βασιλείων
ἐξελαυνόμενα. ὁ μὲν ὑμᾶς ἱδρύσατο μάρτυρας
ἐγγύθεν ἐσομένους τῶν αὐτῷ πραττομένων, ὑπὸ δὲ
τῶν ἀτίμως ἐκβέβλησθε ἐπιλεγόντων ὡς καθαίροιεν
τὸν χῶρον. ὢ πολλὰ συγκινήσας ἐπὶ σαυτῷ
δάκρυα οὐκ ἐπ᾽ ἤματι κατὰ τὸ ἔπος ὀλοφυρμοῦ
τυχών, ἀλλ᾽ ἐν τῷ πένθει κατέχων ἀνθρώπους καὶ
κατασχήσων γε, ὄφρ᾽ ἂν ὕδωρ τε νάῃ καὶ
δένδρεα μακρὰ τεθήλῃ. 35. σοῦ τις ἤδη τὴν
R 520 τελευτὴν ἀγγείλας | αὐτοῦ λίθοις κατεχώσθη,
καθάπερ αὐτόχειρ γεγονὼς ἢ ὡς ἀδύνατά γε ἀγγέλ-
λων, ὥσπερ ἂν εἰ ἔφασκε τῶν θεῶν τινα τεθνάναι.
παιδὸς μὲν ἤδη τις τάφον ἀδακρυτὶ παρῆλθε, πρὸς
δὲ σὴν ὅστις τείνειε τὸν ὀφθαλμὸν εἰκόνα, πηγαὶ
δακρύων εὐθύς, τῶν μὲν παῖδα, τῶν δὲ πατέρα
καλούντων, κοινῇ δὲ ἁπάντων φύλακα. |

36. Ὢ τῆς ὀρφανίας ἢ κατείληφε τὴν γῆν, ἣν F 22
κάμνουσαν ἀνορθώσας ὥσπερ ἰατρὸς ἀγαθὸς πάλιν
ἐξέδωκας τῷ πυρετῷ καὶ τοῖς πρὶν ἀρρωστήμασιν.
ὢ δυστυχοῦς ἐμῆς πολιᾶς, ὢ διπλοῦ πένθους ἐμοῦ,
τοῦτο μὲν τὸν βασιλέα μετὰ τῶν ἄλλων θρηνοῦντος,
τοῦτο δὲ τὸν ἑταῖρόν τε καὶ φίλον. 37. σὺ μὲν
ἠπείγου πρὸς ἐμὴν βοήθειαν ποιῶν μοι κληρονόμον

---

ᵃ Cf. Homer, Iliad, 16. 459 ff. The passage is an interesting example of Libanius' scepticism in the use of classical
legend. Cf. also the story of Daphne, Or. 31. 43.

bloody drops of rain to fall, such as Zeus showered over Sarpedon, but I saw them not. Yet perhaps he did scatter them over his corpse but this was not noticed in the dust of battle and the blood of the slain.[a]

34. Alas for the shrines, the temples and the statues that are now cast out from the palaces! He set you up to be witnesses near by of his achievements, and now you are cast out in dishonour by those who proclaim that they are purging the place. Alas for the tears you cause to be shed for you! You are lamented not, as the poet says, " for the day,"[b] but you keep men stricken with grief, and shall do so, " while rivers run and trees grow tall."[c] 35. Men before now have stoned to death on the spot messengers of your passing, as though they were the actual murderers or the bearers of impossible tidings, just as if they had told of the death of some god.[d] Men before now have passed their son's grave with never a tear, but whenever they gaze upon your statue, floods of tears well up, as some address you as son, others as father, but all alike as their protector.

36. Alas for the bereavement that has afflicted the whole world. You cured it of its ills like a good physician, and then delivered it up once more to fever and its earlier ailments. Alas for my forlorn old age and my double grief! I mourn for my emperor as others do, and I mourn a companion and a friend. 37. You were eager to help me and to make my

[b] Homer, *Iliad*, 19. 229. This piece of imagery appealed to Oriental writers, *cf. Orac. Sibyll.* 4. 130.

[c] Epigram (*Anth. Pal.* 7. 153) in Plato, *Phaedr.* 264 CD. *Cf. Homeri Opera*, vol. V (ed. Allen, O.C.T.), pp. 198-199.

[d] According to Zosimus (3. 33), this actually occurred at Carrhae.

# LIBANIUS

τὸν νόθον, ἐγὼ δὲ ἀνεβαλλόμην τὴν σπουδήν, ὡς
αὐτὸς μὲν προαπαλλαξόμενος, σοῦ δὲ εἰς τόδε
ἀμυνοῦντος. Μοίραις δὲ ἄρα οὐ ταὐτὰ[1] ἐψήφιστο.
ἀλλ' ἐγὼ μὲν ἐδημιούργουν λόγον διαλλαγῶν τῶν
R 521 πρὸς τὴν | πόλιν φάρμακον, σὺ δὲ ᾤχου, σεσίγηται
δὲ τὸ φάρμακον. 38. γέγονα δὲ καὶ ὅλως ἀμβλὺς
εἰς λόγων τόκον, ὥσπερ ἔνιαι μητέρες ὑπὸ μεγάλων
κακῶν ἐπηρώθησαν τὰς γαστέρας. καὶ μὴν καὶ
ὅλως ἐξέπεσον τῶν φρενῶν καὶ οὐκ ἄνευ πόνου πάλιν
ἐπανῆκον εἰς νοῦν. ἦν δὲ ἄρα βέλτιον ἐν ἀγνοίᾳ
πάντων ὁμοίως κεῖσθαι μανίαν ἀντὶ λύπης περιφέ-
ροντα, ἐπειδή γε οὐδεὶς ἔτι δαιμόνων ποιεῖ πεν-
θοῦντα ἄνθρωπον οὐ λίθον, οὐ δένδρον, οὐκ ὄρνιν.

---

[1] ταὐτὰ F. (CAVMo) : ταῦτα Re. (PUBMLa).

---

[a] Arabius (later to be called Cimon) was born of Libanius'
union with a concubine who was probably of servile origin
about A.D. 355/6, and is noted as just beginning his ele-
mentary schooling in A.D. 361 (*Epp.* 625, 678). The boy's
future was to remain Libanius' major domestic preoccupation, since he would normally assume the legal status of
the mother and be barred from inheritance (*cf. Or.* 1. 145,

natural son my heir,[a] but I kept putting off your suggestion, for I felt that I would die before you and you would assist him on this matter. But the decision of Fate was not the same as mine. I was composing a speech of reconciliation to heal your feelings towards our city, but you have departed, and the healing words remain unspoken.[b] 38. I have become quite incapable of producing speeches, as some mothers under the influence of great disasters become barren.[c] Indeed I have been quite out of my mind and it is not without much ado that I have returned to my senses. It was, in fact, better to lie ignorant of everything alike, a prey to madness rather than grief, for no god now turns a man in his grief into stone or stock or bird.

195). In addition to Julian's proposal on his behalf, even Jovian went so far as to write a letter of promises that, naturally, remained unfulfilled (*Ep.* 1221. 6).

[b] *Oration* 15: this passage indicates that that speech never reached Julian and remained undelivered.

[c] Libanius renewed his declamations only after New Year, A.D. 364. His immediate reaction to the news of Julian's death had been to think of suicide (*Epp.* 1128, 1194, 1430; *Or.* 1. 135).

# ORATION 18

# ΕΠΙΤΑΦΙΟΣ ΕΠΙ ΙΟΥΛΙΑΝΩΙ

R 521    1. Ἔδει μέν, ὦ παρόντες, ἅπερ ἤλπιζον ἐγώ τε F ii.2
καὶ πάντες ἄνθρωποι, τὸ τέλος εἰληφέναι καὶ τὴν
μὲν Περσῶν ἀρχὴν νυνὶ καταλελύσθαι, τῆς δὲ
R 522 ἐκείνων γῆς Ῥωμαίους | ἄρχοντας ἀντὶ σατραπῶν
ἐπιμελεῖσθαι νόμοις ἡμετέροις καὶ τὰ μὲν ἱερὰ
κεκοσμῆσθαι τὰ παρ' ἡμῖν τοῖς ἐκεῖθεν λαφύροις,
τὸν δὲ ταύτην ἀνῃρημένον τὴν νίκην καθήμενον ἐπὶ
τοῦ βασιλείου θρόνου | δέχεσθαι τοὺς ἐπινικίους. F 23
ταυτὶ γὰρ ἦν, οἶμαι, καὶ δίκαια καὶ προσήκοντα
καὶ τῶν πολλῶν θυσιῶν ἃς ἐκεῖνος ἔθυσεν ἄξια.
2. ἐπεὶ δὲ μεῖζον μὲν ἴσχυσεν ὁ φθονερὸς δαίμων
τῶν εὐλόγων ἐλπίδων, κεκόμισται δὲ νεκρὸς ἀπὸ
τῶν Βαβυλῶνος ὅρων ὁ μικρὸν τοῦ τῶν ἔργων
ἀπέχων τέλους, καὶ δάκρυα μὲν ὁπόσα εἰκὸς ἀπὸ
πάντων ὀμμάτων ἐρρύη, κωλῦσαι δὲ οὐκ ἔνι τὴν
τελευτήν, ὃ λοιπὸν μέν ἐστιν, ἐκείνῳ δὲ μάλιστα
κεχαρισμένον ποιῶμεν, ἐν ἄλλοις ἀκροαταῖς περὶ
τῶν ἐκείνου τι λέγοντες, ἐπειδήπερ αὐτὸς ἐκωλύθη
τὸν ἔπαινον ὧν ἔπραξεν ἀκοῦσαι.    3. πρῶτον μὲν
γὰρ ἀδικοῖμεν ἄν, εἰ ὁ μὲν ὅπως ἐπαινεθείη πάντα
ἐτόλμησεν, ἡμεῖς δὲ αὐτὸν ἀποστερήσαιμεν τῶν

_____

ᵃ Oration 18.

278

# FUNERAL ORATION OVER JULIAN [a]

1. GENTLEMEN here present,[b] what I and all men hoped for should have come to pass: the Persian empire should now lie in ruins, and Roman governors instead of satraps should now be administering their territory under our laws : our temples here should be adorned with booty got from them, while the victor in this contest should be seated on his imperial throne, receiving the orations composed in honour of his exploits. Such, I am sure, would be right and proper, a fitting reward for all the many sacrifices he offered. 2. Yet since the spirit of envy has prevailed over our reasonable expectations, and his dead body has been brought back from the borders of Babylon, when he was so near the objective at which he aimed; since tears, as you would expect, have flowed from every eye and still could not prevent his death, let us perform the one thing left for us and most acceptable to him, and tell something of what he did, but before a different audience, for he has been prevented from hearing the praises of the deeds he wrought. 3. For first of all, it would be unjust that, though he ventured all to ensure his praises be sung, we should yet

[b] The fiction that the oration was actually addressed to an audience is, as with many others of Libanius' speeches, maintained throughout. In fact, it never received public delivery.

279

ἄθλων. ἔπειτα πάντων αἴσχιστον οἷς ζῶντα ἂν
ἐτιμῶμεν, ταῦτα τεθνεῶτι μὴ φέρειν. ἄνευ γὰρ
τοῦ τῆς ἐσχάτης κολακείας εἶναι τὸ περιόντας μὲν
θεραπεύειν ἀπελθόντων δὲ ἀμνημονεῖν, τοῖς μὲν
ζῶσιν, εἰ καὶ μὴ λόγῳ τις χαρίζοιτο, κατὰ πολλοὺς
R 523 ἂν ἑτέρους | δύναιτο τρόπους· πρὸς δὲ τοὺς οἰχο-
μένους ἐν ἡμῖν ὑπάρχει μόνον, | εὐφημίαι τε καὶ F
λόγοι τὰ πεπραγμένα μετ' ἀρετῆς εἰς ἅπαντα
παραπέμποντες τὸν χρόνον.

4. Ἀεὶ μὲν οὖν ἔγωγε τὸν ἄνδρα τοῦτον ἐγχειρῶν
ἐγκωμιάζειν ἐλάττους εὗρον τοὺς ἐμοὺς λόγους
τοῦ μεγέθους τῶν ἔργων, καὶ μὰ τοὺς θεοὺς
οὐδεπώποτε ἠχθέσθην εἰ φίλου βασιλέως ἀρετὴ
νικῴη τὴν τοῦ φιλοῦντος σοφιστοῦ δύναμιν. κοινὸν
γὰρ τοῦτό γε τῶν πόλεων κέρδος ἡγούμην τὸ τὸν
ἐπὶ σωτηρίᾳ τῶν ὅλων παρειληφότα τὴν ἀρχὴν
μηδενὶ καταλιπεῖν λόγῳ τοῖς ἔργοις ἐξισωθῆναι
τοῖς ἑαυτοῦ. ὁ δὲ οὐδὲ τὰς πρὸς Ὠκεανῷ δεδειγ-
μένας ἀνδραγαθίας οἷός τ' ὢν κοσμῆσαι κατὰ τὴν
ἀξίαν μόνας, τίς ἂν εἴην τήμερον ἀνάγκην ἔχων
ἐκεῖνά τε καὶ τὸν ἐπὶ τοὺς Πέρσας δρόμον ἑνὶ
παραδοῦναι λόγῳ; 5. οἶμαι γάρ, εἰ παρὰ τῶν
κάτω θεῶν ἀνάστασιν ἐκεῖνος εὑράμενος ἐπὶ τῷ
τουτονί μοι συμπονῆσαι τὸν λόγον λανθάνων τοὺς
ἄλλους ἅπαντας ἐκοινώνει μοι τῆς σπουδῆς, μηδ'
ἂν οὕτω τὸ μέτρον ἀκριβῶς γενέσθαι τοῖς πράγ-
μασιν, | ἀλλὰ καλλίω μὲν ἂν ἢ νῦν ῥηθῆναι, πᾶν F
δὲ ὅσον εἰκός, οὐδὲ οὕτω. τί οὖν χρή με πείσεσθαι
νομίζειν ἄνευ συμμαχίας τοιαύτης τοσοῦτον πόνον
280

rob him of his reward. Moreover, it would be utterly disgraceful not to grant him in death the honours we gave him in life. For besides the fact that it would be the grossest kind of flattery to fawn upon the living and forget the dead, one may oblige the living in many other ways, even without an oration. Yet with regard to the dead, there is but one recourse for us—the praise and narration that transmit their glorious achievements to all posterity.

4. Now, in all my attempts to speak in his praise,[a] I have ever found my words insufficient for the greatness of his deeds, and, to be sure, I did not take umbrage that my beloved emperor's genius should outstrip the powers of the teacher that loved him. I considered it advantageous to all the states of the empire alike that he who had ascended the throne for the salvation of the whole world should make it impossible for words to match his deeds. Since I cannot deal adequately merely with the high qualities he demonstrated in the West,[b] how would I go on to-day, now that I am put to it, to entrust to a single oration both that topic and his expedition against Persia? 5. Indeed, I believe that, if he secured of the gods below permission to return on condition of assisting me in this task and if, unawares to everyone else, he shared such a labour of love with me, not even so would there be a true measure of his deeds. It would be better expressed than now, but even then as an entirety it would not be treated as it should be. What then must I consider my position to be if I choose so great a task without such assistance?

[a] An echo of *Or*. 17. 31.
[b] Refers to Julian's recovery of Gaul from German ravages, A.D. 356–360. *Cf. Or*. 12; 13; *infra*, §§ 33 ff.

αἱρούμενον;[1] 6. ἀλλ' εἰ μὲν μὴ καὶ πρότερον ὑμᾶς
ᾐσθόμην οὐκ ἀγνοοῦντας μὲν ὡς ἡ νίκη τῶν
ἔργων, ὅμως δὲ ἡδομένους τοῖς λόγοις, καλῶς ἂν
R 524 εἶχέ μοι σιωπᾶν· | ἐπεὶ δὲ καὶ τότ' εὐθὺς ἐπῃνεῖτε
καὶ ἐμένετε τοὺς λόγους ἀγαπῶντες, οὐκ εἶναι
πρόφασιν ἡγούμενος τῇ σιωπῇ δικαίαν πειράσομαι
τὰ δίκαια ποιεῖν πρὸς τὸν βασιλέα καὶ φίλον.
7. Ἐγένοντο μὲν οὖν οὐκ ὀλίγοι βασιλεῖς γνώμῃ
μὲν οὐ κακοί, γένει δὲ οὐ λαμπροί, καὶ τὴν μὲν
ἀρχὴν ἐπιστάμενοι σῴζειν, αἰσχυνόμενοι δὲ εἰπεῖν
ἐξ ὧν ἐγένοντο, ὥστε καὶ τοῖς ἐγκωμιάζουσιν
αὐτοὺς ἔργον εἶναι θεραπεῦσαι τὸ τραῦμα, τούτῳ
δὲ οὐδέν ἐστιν ὃ μὴ χορηγεῖ πρὸς ἔπαινον. 8.
αὐτίκα τὸ γένος, αὐτῷ πάππος μὲν βασιλεύς, ὃς
μάλιστα δὴ χρημάτων ὑπεριδὼν μάλιστα δὴ τὰς
τῶν ἀρχομένων εὐνοίας ἐκτήσατο, πατὴρ δὲ βασιλέως μὲν υἱὸς βασιλέως δὲ ἀδελφός, δικαιότερος δὲ
τοῦ σχόντος τὴν βασιλείαν ἔχειν, ἀλλ' ὅμως
ἡσύχαζε καὶ συνεύχετο τῷ λαβόντι καὶ συζῶν |
ἀδόλως καὶ φιλῶν διετέλει. 9. γήμας δὲ ὑπάρχου F
θυγατέρα χρηστοῦ τε καὶ νοῦν ἔχοντος, ὃν ὁ
πολέμιος νενικηκὼς ᾐδέσθη καὶ τοὺς αὑτοῦ παρεκά-
λεσεν εἰς ἐκεῖνον βλέποντας ἄρχειν, ποιεῖται τουτ-
τονὶ τὸν ἄριστον καὶ τιμᾷ τὸν κηδεστὴν τῇ
προσηγορίᾳ τοῦ παιδός. 10. Κωνσταντῖνος μὲν
R 525 οὖν τετελευτήκει νόσῳ, τὸ ξίφος δὲ μικροῦ | διὰ
παντὸς ἐχώρει τοῦ γένους ὁμοίως πατέρων καὶ
παίδων. οὗτος δὲ καὶ πρεσβύτερος ἀδελφὸς ὁμο-

---

[1] αἱρούμενον Re., mss. : ἀναιρούμενον F.

[a] Constantius Chlorus.
[b] Julius Constantius, legitimate son of Constantius and
half-brother of Constantine, married as his second wife

282

6. Had I not before now observed your awareness of the fact that victory belongs to the world of action, while you yet derive pleasure from oratory, it would be best for me to stay silent. However, since on those occasions you were prompt to praise and remained in enjoyment of my orations, I feel that there is no just cause for silence, and so I will attempt to do justice to my emperor and my friend.

7. Now there have been many emperors who, though not deficient in character, were not of distinguished ancestry, and who, though knowledgeable in preserving the empire, were ashamed to mention their parentage, with the result that those who made speeches in their praise had some difficulty in salving this sore. However, in his case there is nothing that does not redound to his credit. 8. In the first place, as regards his parentage, his grandfather was an emperor who held wealth in especial contempt and won the especial affection of his subjects.[a] His father was an emperor's son and an emperor's brother and, though more fitted to rule than the actual ruler, he yet held his peace and congratulated him on his accession and continued as a loyal and affectionate member of the family.[b] 9. He married the daughter of a wise and virtuous prefect, whom the victorious enemy respected, advising his own subordinates to take him as the pattern for their administration, and he became the father of this excellent prince and honoured his father-in-law by giving his son the same name. 10. When Constantine fell ill and died, murder stalked through practically all the family, fathers and sons alike. Our prince and

Basilina, daughter of Julius Julianus, an adherent of Licinius.

πάτριος τὸν πολὺν διαφεύγουσι φόνον, τὸν μὲν
νόσου ῥυσαμένης ἢ πρὸς θάνατον ἀποχρήσειν
ἐδόκει, τὸν δὲ τῆς ἡλικίας, ἄρτι γὰρ ἀπήλλακτο
γάλακτος. 11. ἐκεῖνος μὲν οὖν πρὸς ἄλλοις μᾶλλον
ἦν ἢ λόγοις νομίζων ἧττόν γε ταύτῃ πειράσεσθαι
τοῦ φθόνου, τοῦτον δὲ ὁ λαχὼν δαίμων ἐκίνει πρὸς
ἔρωτα λόγων καὶ διέτριβε περὶ αὐτοὺς ἐν τῇ
μεγίστῃ μετὰ τὴν Ῥώμην πόλει φοιτῶν εἰς διδα-
σκαλεῖον, ὁ βασιλέως μὲν υἱιδοῦς, βασιλέως δὲ
ἀδελφιδοῦς, βασιλέως δὲ | ἀνεψιός, οὐ σοβῶν οὐδὲ F 24
λυπῶν οὐδὲ ἀξιῶν ἀποβλέπεσθαι διὰ πλῆθος
ἀκολούθων καὶ τὸν ἀπ᾿ ἐκείνων θόρυβον. ἀλλ᾿
εὐνοῦχός τε βέλτιστος σωφροσύνης φύλαξ καὶ
παιδαγωγὸς ἕτερος οὐκ ἄμοιρος παιδείας ἐσθής τε
μετρία καὶ ὀφρὺς οὐχ ὑπὲρ τὰς ἄλλας καὶ τὸ
φθάσαντα προσειπεῖν καὶ τὸ μὴ παρῶσαι τὸν
πένητα καὶ τὸ καλούμενον εἰσελθεῖν καὶ τὸ πρὶν ἢ
R 526 κληθῆναι μένειν καὶ τὸ στῆναι μὲν οὗ τοῖς | ἄλλοις
νόμος, ἀκοῦσαι δὲ ταῦτα τοῖς ἄλλοις καὶ μετὰ τῶν
ἄλλων ἀπελθεῖν καὶ μηδαμοῦ ζητῆσαι πλέον, ὥστ᾿
ἔξωθέν τις ἐπελθὼν καὶ βλέψας εἰς τὸν χορὸν οὐκ
εἰδὼς οἵτινες οὐδ᾿ ὧντινων, οὐκ ἂν εὗρεν ἐν συμβό-
λοις τισὶ τὴν ὑπεροχὴν τῆς τύχης.
12. Οὐ μὴν πάντα ἐκείνοις ἴσος ἦν, ἐπεὶ ἔν γε
τῷ συνιέναι καὶ δέξασθαι τὸ ῥηθὲν καὶ φυλάξαι

---

<sup>a</sup> The military massacres that almost wiped out the legi-
timate descendants of Constantius Chlorus occurred a few
months after Constantine's death, in autumn A.D. 337.
Julian always blamed Constantius for them, not without
reason : *cf. Ep. ad S.P.Q.Ath.* 270 cd, Zos. 2. 40. 2, Socr.
*H.E.* 3. 1, Philostorg. 2. 16. Socrates here adapts the
narrative of Libanius, with its pathetic exaggeration of
Julian's extreme youth.

his elder brother escaped this massacre, Gallus saved by an illness which was thought quite enough to be the death of him anyway, Julian by his tender years, for he was but newly weaned.[a] 11. Now while Gallus preferred to devote himself to other pursuits than eloquence, believing that he would thereby encounter less unpopularity, Julian's guardian angel urged him on to the love of learning, and therein he spent his time in the greatest city of the empire next to Rome.[b] He went to school, an emperor's grandson, an emperor's nephew and an emperor's cousin, with no swagger, causing no trouble, and claiming no attention by a host of attendants and the hubbub that they create. An excellent eunuch[c] was the guardian of his virtue and another attendant who was not without his share of learning. Julian's dress was nothing out of the ordinary: his demeanour was no more proud than that of others: he spoke to people before he was spoken to, and he did not repulse the poor: he would enter a room when invited, and until invited he would wait: he would stand where the rest usually did, listen to exactly the same as the rest, would leave with the rest, and would never claim any extra attention. So, if you had come from abroad and viewed the class without knowing who they were and who their parents, you would never have discovered from his outward appearance anything to mark the superiority of his station.

12. However, he was not on a level with them in every particular, for in his understanding and appreciation of his lessons, in his grasp and retention of

---

[b] Constantinople.
[c] Mardonius, cf. Julian, Misop. 352 a. For Julian's schooldays cf. Schemmel, Philologus, 1927, pp. 455 ff.

λαβὼν καὶ μὴ πονῶν ἀπειπεῖν πολὺ τοῖς ἄλλοις
πρὸς αὐτὸν ἐποίει τὸ μέσον. ὃ ἐγὼ καθορῶν
ἤλγουν οὐ σπείρων αὐτὸς εἰς τὴν τοιαύτην ψυχήν.
σοφιστὴς γάρ | τις πονηρὸς τοῦ κακῶς ἀγορεύειν F
τοὺς θεοὺς μισθὸν εἶχε τὸν νέον ἐν τοιαύτῃ καὶ
αὐτὸν τῇ περὶ τῶν θεῶν τρεφόμενον δόξῃ καὶ
φέροντα τὴν φαυλότητα τῶν λόγων διὰ τὸν πρὸς
τοὺς βωμοὺς τοῦ διδασκάλου πόλεμον. 13. ἤδη δὲ
πρόσηβος ἦν, καὶ τὸ τῆς φύσεως βασιλικὸν πολλοῖς
καὶ μεγάλοις τεκμηρίοις ἐμηνύετο. καὶ ταῦτα οὐκ
εἴα καθεύδειν Κωνστάντιον, δείσας δὲ μὴ πόλις
μεγάλη τε καὶ μεγάλην ψῆφον ἔχουσα καὶ πρὸς τὴν
Ῥώμην εἰκασμένη τοῖς ὅλοις ἐπισπασθῇ πρὸς τὴν
ἀρετὴν τοῦ νέου καὶ γένηταί τι τῶν ἐκείνῳ λυπηρῶν,
πέμπει μὲν αὐτὸν εἰς τὴν Νικομήδους πόλιν ὡς οὐ
φοβήσουσαν ἴσα, παιδεύεσθαι δὲ δίδωσιν ἐξουσίαν.
ὁ δὲ οὐ φοιτᾷ μὲν παρ' ἐμὲ ποιούμενον αὐτοῦ τὰς
συνουσίας ἤδη καὶ πόλιν ἀντὶ πόλεως ᾑρημένον τὴν
γαλήνην ἔχουσαν ἀντὶ τῆς κινδύνων γεμούσης, τοὺς
λόγους δὲ ὠνούμενος ὁμιλῶν οὐκ ἀνίει. 14. τὸ δὲ
R 527 αἴτιον τοῦ | τοῖς λόγοις μὲν χαίρειν, φεύγειν δὲ τὸν
ἐκείνων πατέρα, πολλοῖς καὶ μεγάλοις αὐτὸν |
ὅρκοις ὁ θαυμαστὸς ἐκεῖνος κατειλήφει σοφιστὴς ἦ F
μὴν ἐμὸν μήτε γενέσθαι μήτε κληθῆναι φοιτητὴν
μήτ' εἰς τὸν κατάλογον ἐγγραφῆναι τῶν ἐμῶν
ὁμιλητῶν. 15. ὁ δὲ τῷ μὲν ἐξορκίσαντι μεμφόμενος, τοὺς ὅρκους δὲ οὐ παραβαίνων, ἐμοῦ δὲ

---

[a] This sophist is Hecebolius, with whom Julian as emperor
dutifully remained in correspondence. Under Constantius
he had been Christian, but his record of apostasy and re-

them, and in his perseverance in his labours, he opened up a great gap between himself and the rest. I saw that and regretted that it was not I that had the cultivation of such genius. A good-for-nothing teacher had the lad as a reward for his abuse of the gods, and the boy was actually being brought up with such notions of religion and was enduring this incompetence in rhetoric because of the war waged against the altars by his teacher.[a] 13. He was now on the threshold of manhood, and the princeliness of his nature was attested by many notable signs. This allowed Constantius no rest, and so, fearful that his capital, which was so influential in the formulation of public opinion and in matters of government the peer of Rome, should be attracted to the young man's excellence, with some untoward consequences for himself, he had him packed off to Nicomedeia, since that city would cause him not nearly so much alarm, and there he provided facilities for his education. Julian did not attend my lectures, though I had established myself there and had chosen the peaceful calm of that city in preference to the teeming dangers of the capital. Still, he bought copies of my speeches and so maintained an association with me. 14. The reason for the fact that he found pleasure in my oratory and yet avoided its author was that marvellous teacher of his. He had bound him with many fearsome oaths never to be or to be called my pupil and never to be enrolled on the list of my students. 15. Though resenting his teacher's imposition of such an oath, he did not break it, but since he was

conversion in the years following A.D. 361 won him the nickname of Euripus. Socr. *loc. cit.* and 3. 23 has Libanius' narrative in mind. Both authors omit any mention of Julian's stay at Macellum.

ἐπιθυμῶν εὗρεν ὅπως μήτε ἐπιορκήσει καὶ μετα-
σχήσει τῶν λόγων, πορθμέα τινὰ τῶν καθ' ἡμέραν
λεγομένων δωρεαῖς μεγάλαις κτησάμενος. οὗ δὴ
καὶ τὰ μάλιστα τῆς φύσεως διέδειξε τὴν ἰσχύν·
αὐτῷ γὰρ ἥκιστά μοι συνὼν τῶν συνεχῶς συνόντων
ἀμείνων εἰς μίμησιν ἦν καὶ δι' ἀμυδροτέρας ὁδοῦ
τὴν εἰλικρινῆ τὴν ἐκείνων τῇ τῶν καρπῶν παρῄει
φορᾷ, ὅθεν, οἶμαι, καὶ τοῖς ὕστερον ὑπ' αὐτοῦ
πεποιημένοις λόγοις ἔνι τι πρὸς ἡμᾶς συγγενὲς καὶ
ἔδοξεν εἷς εἶναι τῶν πεπλησιακότων.

16. Ἐκείνῳ μὲν οὖν περὶ ταῦτα ἡ σπουδή, τῷ δὲ
ἀδελφῷ γίνεται μετουσία τῆς βασιλείας κατὰ τὸ
δεύτερον σχῆμα. διπλοῦ γὰρ ἐγηγερμένου τῷ
Κωνσταντίῳ πολέμου, τοῦ μὲν προτέρου Περσικοῦ,
τοῦ δ' ἐπ' ἐκείνῳ τοῦ πρὸς τὸν τύραννον, ἔδει
δήπου καὶ συνάρχοντος, καὶ πέμπεται Γάλλος ἐξ
Ἰταλίας τὴν πρὸς ἕω φρουρήσων, καὶ ὅπερ τῷ
τοῦδε πατρὶ πρότερον, τοῦτο ὑπῆρχε καὶ τῷδε,
βασιλέως ἦν ἀδελφός. 17. ἐκεῖνος | μὲν οὖν καὶ F 2
διὰ τῆς Βιθυνίας δορυφορούμενος ἐχώρει καὶ εἶδον
ἀλλήλω, τούτου δὲ τὴν γνώμην οὐκ ἠλλοίωσεν ἡ
περὶ ἐκεῖνον τύχη, οὐδὲ τὸ βασιλεύειν οἱ τὸν
ἀδελφὸν ἀφορμὴν εἰς ῥαθυμίαν ἔλαβεν, ἀλλ' ἐπηύξησε μὲν τὴν ἐπιθυμίαν ἣν εἶχε περὶ τοὺς λόγους,
ἐπηύξησε δὲ τοὺς πόνους οἷς ἐχρῆτο περὶ τὴν
τούτων θήραν νομίζων εἰ μὲν ἐν ἰδιώτου μέρει
R 528 μείνειεν ἕξειν ἀντὶ τῆς | βασιλείας τὴν σοφίαν,
κτῆμα θειότερον, εἰ δ' ἐπὶ σκῆπτρον ἄγοιτο

---

[a] Libanius takes particular pride in this : cf. Or. 1. 130,
15. 7.
[b] The revolt of Magnentius in the West broke out in A.D.

so desirous of me, he discovered a method whereby he could share in my oratory without perjuring himself. He got someone, at considerable expense, to convey to him my lectures each day. And here he proved the power of his genius in the highest degree, for with no personal association with me, he imitated my style better than any of my regular pupils. By this more obscure path he surpassed the brilliance of their approach in the fruitfulness of his labours, and this is surely the reason why, in the orations he afterwards composed, there is some affinity with my own and he was thought to have been one of my students.[a]

16. While he interested himself in this, his brother came to share the throne in a junior capacity. Constantius had two wars on his hands, first against Persia, and then against the usurper Magnentius. He certainly required a colleague, and so he sent Gallus from Italy to safeguard his Eastern empire.[b] In times past his father's position had been that of an emperor's brother: so was Julian's now. 17. Now, when Gallus passed through Bithynia with his retinue, the two brothers had an interview, but his rise to fortune did not affect Julian's outlook, nor did he make it an excuse for idleness that his brother was a ruling emperor. Instead he increased his passion for learning still further, and increased the efforts that he applied to its pursuit, for he felt that, if he remained in a private station, he would possess in place of majesty an attribute more divine—wisdom, while if he were called to the throne, he would adorn

350, with the assassination of Constans. In March A.D. 351 Gallus was promoted Caesar, married to Constantia, and sent to Antioch to govern the East: cf. Zos. 2. 45.

κοσμήσειν τῇ σοφίᾳ τὴν βασιλείαν. 18. διὰ τοῦτο
ἡλίῳ τε ἐχρῆτο πρὸς τὰς μαθήσεις καὶ νυκτὸς
ἐπελθούσης πυρὶ καὶ τὴν μὲν οὐσίαν οὐκ ἐποίει
μείζω ῥᾴδιον ὄν, τὴν δὲ γνώμην καλλίω. καί ποτε
τοῖς τοῦ Πλάτωνος γέμουσιν εἰς ταὐτὸν ἐλθὼν
ἀκούσας ὑπέρ τε θεῶν καὶ δαιμόνων καὶ τῶν ὡς
ἀληθῶς τὸ πᾶν τοῦτο καὶ πεποιηκότων καὶ σῳζόν-
των καὶ τί τε ἡ ψυχὴ καὶ πόθεν ἥκει καὶ ποῖ
πορεύεται καὶ τίσι βαπτίζεται καὶ τίσιν αἴρεται
καὶ τίσι καθέλκεται καὶ τίσι μετεωρίζεται, καὶ τί
μὲν αὐτῇ δεσμός, τί δὲ ἐλευθερία, καὶ πῶς ἂν
γένοιτο τὸ μὲν φυγεῖν, τοῦ δὲ τυχεῖν, ἁλμυρὰν
ἀκοὴν ἀπεκλύσατο ποτίμῳ λόγῳ | καὶ πάντα τὸν F 2
ἔμπροσθεν ἐκβαλὼν ὕθλον ἀντεισήγαγεν εἰς τὴν
ψυχὴν τὸ τῆς ἀληθείας κάλλος, ὥσπερ εἴς τινα
μέγαν νεὼν ἀγάλματα θεῶν πρότερον ὑβρισμένα
βορβόρῳ. 19. καὶ ἦν μὲν περὶ ταῦτα ἕτερος,
ἐσχηματίζετο δὲ τὰ πρόσθεν, οὐ γὰρ ἐξῆν φανῆναι. Αἴσωπος δὲ ἐνταῦθα μῦθον ἂν ἐποίησεν οὐκ
ὄνον λεοντῇ κρύπτων, ἀλλ' ὄνου δορᾷ τὸν λέοντα.
κἀκεῖνος ᾔδει μὲν ἃ εἰδέναι κρεῖττον, ἐδόκει δὲ τὰ
ἀσφαλέστερα. 20. τῆς φήμης δὲ πανταχοῖ φερο-
μένης πάντες οἱ περὶ τὰς Μούσας καὶ τοὺς ἄλλους
γε θεοὺς οἱ μὲν ὡδοιπόρουν, οἱ δὲ ἔπλεον σπεύ-
δοντες ἰδεῖν τε ἐκεῖνον καὶ συγγενέσθαι καὶ εἰπεῖν
αὐτοί τι καὶ ἀκοῦσαι λέγοντος. ἦν δὲ ἐλθοῦσιν
οὐ ῥᾴδιον ἀπελθεῖν· κατεῖχε γὰρ ἡ σειρὴν οὐ
λόγοις μόνον, ἀλλὰ καὶ τῷ πρὸς φίλτρον εὖ πεφυ-

---

[a] Cf. Eunap. V.S. 473 ff. Julian himself dates his conversion to A.D. 351 (E.L.F. No. 111).

[b] The citation is Plato, Phaedr. 243 D, an appropriate tag

his majesty with wisdom. 18. Thus for his studies he made use of sunlight, and when evening fell, of lamplight. His aim was not to make his possessions any greater, easy though that was to do, but to improve his intellect. Finally, he met with people who were steeped with the learning of Plato,[a] and he learned of gods and spirits and the real creators and saviours of this whole universe: he gained knowledge of the nature of the soul, its origin and its destination, the causes of its glory and elevation, and of its ruin and debasement: he discovered its bondage and its freedom, and the means to avoid the one and attain the other, and he washed a sour story clean with sweet discourse,[b] casting out all that earlier nonsense and in its place introducing into his soul the beauty of truth, no less than if he had brought into some mighty temple statues of gods that had been in times past befouled and besmirched. 19. Despite the change in his beliefs, he kept the same appearance as before, since to reveal them was out of the question. Aesop here would have composed a fable not of an ass in a lion's skin but of a lion in an ass's hide[c]: though he really knew what was right to know, he pretended a knowledge of what was safer. 20. His fame spread on all sides, and devotees of the Muses, and of the other gods too, travelled by land and sea, eager to look on him, to make his acquaintance, to address him themselves and to hear him address them. Once they came, it was not easy for them to go away again. Siren-like he detained them, not just by his eloquence, but by his natural attrac-

to round off the Platonic language in which this conversion to Neo-Platonism is described.

[c] Aesop, *Fab.* 33. Babrius, *Fab.* 139.

κέναι. τῷ δ' ἄγαν φιλεῖν εἰδέναι καὶ τοὺς ἄλλους
ἐπαίδευε καλῶς τοῦτο ποιεῖν, ὥστε συγκεραννύ-
μενοι γνησίως οὐκ ἀπόνως ἀπηλλάττοντο.

21. Ἦν οὖν ἐκείνῳ παντοδαπὴ σοφία συνει-
λεγμένη καὶ δεικνυμένη, ποιηταί, ῥήτορες, γένη
R 529 φιλοσόφων, | πολλὴ μὲν Ἑλλὰς φωνή, οὐκ ὀλίγη
δὲ ἀτέρα. τῷ δὲ | ἦν φροντὶς ἀμφοτέρων εὐχή τε F
ἀπὸ παντὸς εὖ φρονούντων στόματος γενέσθαι τῶν
πραγμάτων τὸν νεανίσκον κύριον καὶ στῆναι μὲν
τὴν φθορὰν τῆς οἰκουμένης, ἐπιστῆναι δὲ τοῖς
νοσοῦσι τὸν ἐπιστάμενον τὰ τοιαῦτα ἰᾶσθαι. 22.
οὐ μὴν φαίην ἂν ἐκεῖνον ἐπιτιμᾶν ταῖς εὐχαῖς οὐδ'
ἀλαζονεύσομαι τοῦτό γε ὑπὲρ αὐτοῦ, ἀλλὰ βούλεσθαι μὲν καὶ αὐτόν, βούλεσθαι δὲ οὐ τρυφῆς
οὐδὲ δυναστείας οὐδὲ πορφύρας ἔρωτι, τοῦ δὲ τοῖς
αὐτοῦ πόνοις ἀποδοῦναι τοῖς ἔθνεσιν ὧν ἐξεπε-
πτώκεσαν τά τε ἄλλα καὶ οὐχ ἥκιστα δὴ τὰς τῶν
θεῶν λατρείας. 23. ᾧ δὴ καὶ διαφερόντως τὴν καρδίαν ἐπλήττετο νεώς τε ὁρῶν κειμένους καὶ τελετὰς πεπαυμένας καὶ βωμοὺς ἀνατετραμμένους καὶ
θυσίας ἀνηρημένας καὶ ἱερεῖς ἐλαυνομένους καὶ τὸν
τῶν ἱερῶν πλοῦτον εἰς τοὺς ἀσελγεστάτους μεμε-
ρισμένον, ὥστ' εἴ τις αὐτῷ θεῶν ὑπισχνεῖτο τὴν
τούτων ἐπανόρθωσιν δι' ἑτέρων ἔσεσθαι, σφόδρα
ἄν μοι δοκεῖ τὴν βασιλείαν φυγεῖν· οὕτως οὐ τοῦ
R 530 κρατεῖν, τοῦ δὲ εὖ πρᾶξαι τὰς πόλεις | ὠρέγετο.

24. Ταύτης τοίνυν τῆς ἐπιθυμίας ἐν ταῖς ψυχαῖς
τῶν πεπαιδευμένων ἀκμαζούσης τοῦ τῇ τοῦδε
γνώμῃ θεραπευθῆναι τὴν γῆν ἦλθεν ἐπὶ τὸν Γάλ-
λον | συκοφαντία καὶ γράμματα ἐπιβουλὴν ἔχοντα F

---

ᵃ Julian himself admits, in allegorical narrative, that his

292

tiveness. By his gift for deep affection he instilled the capacity for it into others also, so that being so nobly compounded together they were separated not without difficulty.

21. He gathered together wisdom of every kind and displayed it—poetry, oratory, the various schools of philosophy, much use of Greek and not a little of Latin, for he interested himself in both. On the lips of every man of sense was the prayer that the lad should become the ruler of the empire, that an end be put to the ruin of civilization, and that there be put in charge of the troubled world one who knew how to cure such ills. 22. I would not go so far as to say that he disapproved of such prayers. I shall make no such boast about him. I feel that this was his desire too, but that it arose from a longing not for luxury, power or the imperial purple, but for the restoration by his own efforts of the worship of the gods in particular to the empire whence it had been expelled. 23. It was this that shook him to the core, as he saw their temples in ruins, their ritual banned, their altars overturned, their sacrifices suppressed, their priests sent packing and their property divided up between a crew of rascals. If one of the gods promised him a cure for these ills at another's doing, I am sure that he would have insisted on refusing the throne. His anxiety, therefore, was not for power but for the well-being of the cities.[a]

24. As this desire was growing in the hearts of men of learning, that the world might be cured by his will, a false accusation was brought against Gallus and a letter containing highly treasonable material was

conversion to Hellenism was accompanied by political ambitions of the kind here described (*Or*. 7. 232 a ff.).

τὴν ἐσχάτην εὕρητο, δόντων δὲ δίκην τῶν ἀδι-
κούντων, οὐ γὰρ ἔμελλεν αὐτοὺς στεφανώσειν ὁ
τὰ τοιαῦτα ἠδικημένος, ἔδοξεν ἧς εἰλήφει δίκης
ὀφείλειν δίκην ὁ λαβὼν καὶ ἀπέθνησκεν ἄφωνος
φθάσαντος τὴν ἀπολογίαν τοῦ ξίφους. 25. καὶ
αὐτίκα οὗτος ἀνέσπαστό τε καὶ ἦν μέσῳ φυλάκων
ὡπλισμένων ἄγριον μὲν βλεπόντων, τραχὺ δὲ φθεγ-
γομένων, κοῦφον δὲ ἀποφαινόντων οἷς ἐποίουν τὸ
δεσμωτήριον. καὶ προσῆν τὸ μηδὲ ἐφ' ἑνὸς
ἱδρύεσθαι χωρίου, τόπους δὲ ἐκ τόπων ἀμείβειν
ἐπὶ ταλαιπωρίᾳ. καὶ ταῦτα ἔπασχεν ἐγκαλούμενος
μὲν οὐδὲν οὔτε μεῖζον οὔτε ἔλαττον. πῶς γὰρ ὅς
γε διειστήκει μὲν τἀδελφοῦ σταθμοῖς πλείοσιν ἢ
τριακοσίοις, γράμματα δὲ ἔπεμπεν, οὐδὲ ταῦτα
πολλάκις, προσρήσεσιν ὁριζόμενα μόναις; διόπερ
οὐδ' ἦν οὐδ' ὁ συκοφαντάσων, ἀλλ' ὅμως οἷς ἔφην
ἐπιέζετο κατ' ἄλλο μὲν οὐδέν, ὅτι δ' εἷς ἀμφοτέροις
πατὴρ γένοιτο. 26. πάλιν τοίνυν ἐνταῦθα ἄν τις
αὐτοῦ θαυμάσειε τὸ μήτε τοῖς κατὰ τοῦ τεθνεῶτος
λόγοις κολακεῦσαι τὸν ἀπεκτονότα μήτε τοῖς
ὑπὲρ ἐκείνου παροξῦναι τὸν ζῶντα, ἀλλὰ τὸν μὲν
R 531 ἀφανεῖ λύπῃ τιμᾶν, | τῷ δὲ μὴ δοῦναι πρὸς φόνον
ἀφορμὴν σφόδρα γε βουλομένῳ. οὕτω | γὰρ εὖ F
καὶ καλῶς ἐκράτησε τῆς γλώττης καὶ ταῦτα τῶν
περιεστηκότων ἀνιαρῶν οὐ σφόδρα ἐπιτρεπόντων,
ὥστε ἐνέφραξε τῇ καρτερίᾳ τοῖς πονηροτάτοις τὰ
στόματα. 27. οὐ μὴν οὐδὲ ταῦτα ἤρκει πρὸς

---

ᵃ Amm. Marc. 14. 7. 9 ff., Zos. 2. 55. The fall of Gallus
occurred in A.D. 354.
294

discovered. Those responsible for it were punished, for after being the victim of such calumny he was not likely to reward them with garlands of greeting, but, by inflicting this punishment, he was held to be guilty of the crime he had punished, and he was condemned to death unheard, for his execution took place before he could make any plea.[a]  25. Julian was arrested immediately, and he was surrounded by armed guards, grim of face and harsh of tongue, whose behaviour was such that imprisonment seemed a mere trifle in comparison. Besides that, he was unable to remain in any single place: he was shifted from one locality to another to his discomfort.[b]  All this he endured without a single charge, great or small, being brought against him. How could there be, when he lived a distance of three hundred days' journey away from his brother and corresponded— and not very often, at that—by letters that were confined merely to greetings?  So, though there was none to level accusation however false against him, he was victimized as I have said for no other reason than that the pair of them had a single father.  26. Here again there is reason to admire him: he made no denunciation of his dead brother to flatter his murderer, nor did he make any pronouncement on his behalf and so inflame the living against himself. He honoured his brother with concealed grief and allowed Constantius no excuse to kill him, though he was greatly desirous of it. He kept a good tight rein on his tongue, though hardly prompted to do so by all the discomforts that beset him, so that, by his patience, he stopped the mouths of the wickedest blackguards. 27. Yet not even this served

[b] *Cf.* Socr. *H.E. loc. cit.*

σωτηρίαν οὐδὲ ἴστη τῷ μάτην θυμουμένῳ τὴν
ὀργήν, τὸν δὲ εἶδε Κάδμου θυγάτηρ Ἰνὼ χειμαζό-
μενον, ἡ Κωνσταντίου γυνή, καὶ τὸν μὲν ἠλέησε,
τὸν δὲ ἐμάλαξε καὶ πολλαῖς ταῖς ἱκεσίαις ἔλυσεν[1]
ἐρῶντα τῆς Ἑλλάδος καὶ μάλιστα δὴ τοῦ τῆς Ἑλλάδος ὀφθαλμοῦ, τῶν Ἀθηνῶν, εἰς γῆν ἐρωμένην
πέμψαι. 28. τοῦτο τοίνυν αὐτὸ πῶς οὐκ ἀτεχνῶς
ψυχῆς ἐκ θεῶν ἀφιγμένης τὸ καταστάντα εἰς
αἵρεσιν χωρίου μήτε κήπων μήτε οἰκιῶν μήτε
ὑλῶν[2] μήτε τῶν ἐπ᾽ αἰγιαλοῖς ἀγρῶν μήτε τῆς
ἀπὸ τῶν ἄλλων ὄντων οὐκ ὀλίγων ἐπιθυμῆσαι
τρυφῆς, ἃ πάντα ἦν ἐπὶ τῆς Ἰωνίας αὐτῷ, ἀλλ᾽
ἡγήσασθαι μικρὰ τὰ δοκοῦντα μεγάλα πρὸς τὴν
τῆς Ἀθηνᾶς πόλιν, τὴν μητέρα Πλάτωνος καὶ
Δημοσθένους καὶ τῆς ἄλλης τῆς πολυειδοῦς σοφίας;
29. ἧκε μὲν οὖν ἐκεῖσε θέων, ὡς προσθήσων οἷς
R 532 ἠπίστατο καὶ διδασκάλοις | ἐντευξόμενος δοῦναί
τι δυναμένοις ὧν εἶχε πλέον. | συγγινόμενος δὲ F 2
καὶ πεῖραν αὐτοῦ τε παρέχων καὶ λαμβάνων
ἐκείνων ἐξέπληττε μᾶλλον ἢ τοῦτο ἔπασχε καὶ
μόνος ἐκεῖνος νέων τῶν Ἀθήναζε ἡκόντων διδάξας
τι μᾶλλον ἢ μαθὼν ἀπῆλθε. τοιγαροῦν ἀεί τινα
σμήνη περὶ αὐτὸν ἑωρᾶτο νέων, πρεσβυτέρων,
φιλοσόφων, ῥητόρων. ἔβλεπον δὲ ἄρα εἰς αὐτὸν
καὶ οἱ δαίμονες εὖ εἰδότες ὡς οὗτος αὐτοῖς ἐπαν-
άξει τὰ πάτρια. 30. ὁ δὲ λέγων τε ἦν ὁμοίως

---

[1] ἔλυσεν MSS. : ἔπεισεν F. (conj. Re.).
[2] ὑλῶν King : αὐλῶν F., Re., MSS.

---

[a] Cf. Homer, Od. 5. 333 ff. For the intervention of
Eusebia on Julian's behalf, and for his studies in Athens,

to protect him, nor did it assuage the wrath of Constantius in his stupid ill-temper, but as he was lying tempest-tossed, an Ino Cadmus' daughter, the wife of Constantius,[a] saw him, took pity on him, and soothed her husband. With many a plea she set free this lover of Greece and especially of Athens, the most precious part of Greece, to send him to the land he loved. 28. Now this must surely be a token of a spirit sent from heaven, that in choosing a residence he showed no desire for gardens, villas, woodlands,[b] seaside estates or the luxury of the many other possessions that were all his in Ionia, but regarded all this seeming good fortune as of little account compared with Athens, the home of Plato, Demosthenes and the various other branches of learning. 29. So he went there with all speed, to add to his store of knowledge and to consort with teachers who could offer something beyond what he already had. Upon associating with them and giving proof of his qualities and gaining proof of theirs, he astonished them more than they him. He alone of the youngsters who came to Athens left after giving instruction rather than receiving it.[c] At any rate, there could always be seen about him swarms of men, young and old, of philosophers and rhetors. And the gods also fixed their eyes on him, well aware that he was the one who would restore them their age-old privileges. 30. He was equally remarkable for his eloquence and

<hr />

*cf.* Julian, *Or.* 3. 118 b ff., *Ep. ad S.P.Q.Ath.* 273 a, Amm. Marc. 15. 2, Zos. 3. 1, Socr. *loc. cit.*

[b] An implied contrast with Constantius who prided himself upon his hunting prowess (Amm. Marc. 21. 16. 7). Constantius, in his private life, was above reproach (*ibid.* 5 f.).

[c] Libanius ascribes to Julian an attitude towards Athenian teachers similar to his own ; *cf. Or.* 1. 17 ff.

θαυμαστὸς καὶ αἰδούμενος, οὐ γὰρ ἦν ὅ τι χωρὶς
ἐρυθήματος ἐφθέγγετο. τῆς μὲν οὖν πραότητος
ἅπαντες ἀπέλαυον, τοῦ πιστεύεσθαι δὲ οἱ βέλτιστοι,
κἂν τούτοις αὐτοῖς πρῶτος ἦν ὁ παρ' ἡμῶν, ὁ
μόνος ἐν ἀνθρώποις ἄμεμπτος, ὁ τὸν μῶμον ἀρετῇ
νενικηκώς.

31. Ἦν μὲν οὖν γνώμη τῷ νεανίσκῳ ταῖς Ἀθή-
ναις ἐμβιῶναί τε καὶ ἐντελευτῆσαι καὶ τοῦτο
κέκριτο πέρας εὐδαιμονίας, τῶν πραγμάτων δὲ
ἀπαιτούντων βασιλέα δεύτερον ἐφθαρμένων μὲν
τῶν περὶ τὸν Ῥῆνον πόλεων, τῶν δ' ἐκεῖσε πεμ-
πομένων στρατηγῶν μείζονα ἢ ἐξῆν ζητούντων
καλεῖται πρὸς ἀρχὴν ὁ φιλοσοφῶν Ἀθήνησιν ἐξ
αὐτοῦ τοῦ φιλοσοφεῖν παρέχων θαρρεῖν | τῷ πλεῖστα F 2
ἠδικηκότι. καὶ γὰρ εἰ φονεὺς ἐγεγόνει πατρός τε
καὶ ἀδελφῶν, τῶν μὲν πάλαι, τοῦ δὲ ἔναγχος, ἀλλ'
ἤλπιζέ γε τὰς πίστεις ἐν βεβαίῳ κείσεσθαι καὶ τὸν
ἐκείνου τρόπον κρείττω τῶν ἐγκλημάτων ἔσεσθαι.
32. ὁ μὲν οὖν καλῶν οὐ κακῶς ἤλπιζε, τὸν δὲ
R 533 οὐδὲν ἦν ὃ πιστεύειν | ἔπειθεν ὡς οὐκ εἰς ἐπιβουλὴν
ἡ τιμή τελευτήσει, ταυτὶ γὰρ ἐδίδου τὸ ῥυὲν αἷμα
μαντεύεσθαι, διαδύσεως δὲ οὐκ οὔσης καλεῖ σὺν
δάκρυσι τὴν θεὸν καὶ δεηθεὶς ἀμύνειν ἐπορεύετο.
μετασχὼν δὲ τῆς βασιλείας ἐπ' ἆθλον εὐθὺς ἀπο-
στέλλεται τῶν Ἡρακλέους χειρῶν δεόμενον. εἶχε
γὰρ ὧδε τὰ περὶ τοὺς Γαλάτας, ὧν οἱ τελευταῖοι
προσοικοῦσι τὸν ὠκεανόν.

---

[a] Identified, plausibly, by Sievers (p. 90) with Celsus,
*praeses Ciliciae* in A.D. 362 (*cf.* Seeck, *B.L.Z.G. s.v.*).
[b] Silvanus, usurper in Gaul after the suppression of the
revolt of Magnentius: *cf.* Jul. *Or.* 1. 48 c, 2. 98 d, Amm.
Marc. 15. 5.    [c] *Cf.* Julian, *Ep. ad S.P.Q.Ath.* 270 cd.
[d] *Ibid.* 274 d ff.

his shyness, for none of his utterances was made without a blush. Everyone enjoyed the kindness of his disposition, but it was only the best among them who enjoyed his confidence, and foremost among them was our fellow-citizen, the one person without reproach and by his excellence rising superior to idle gossip.[a]

31. Now, the lad's intention was to live and die in Athens, and that he thought to be the most perfect bliss. However, the situation demanded a second emperor, for the cities near the Rhine were in ruins and the commanders sent to that theatre of war aspired to something higher than their lawful station.[b] So the student of philosophy at Athens was summoned to the throne, and in consequence of his very philosophy he inspired confidence in the man who had wronged him most. Though he had been the murderer of his father and his brothers, some long before, the last but recently,[c] he still had hopes that his assurances would be loyally kept and that his disposition would be stronger than the complaints he could level against him. 32. So, in summoning him, he was not far wrong in his hopes, but Julian had no grounds for believing that this advancement would not turn out to be a snare, for the blood already shed gave him reason to come to this conclusion. However, there was no way of avoiding it, and he tearfully invoked the goddess and prayed her to help him, and so took his departure.[d] On becoming a partner on the throne, he was immediately detailed for a task that required the hands of Heracles to deal with it, for the position in Gaul, the most distant province by the ocean's edge, was as follows.

33. Μαγνεντίῳ Κωνστάντιος πολεμῶν ἀφελο-
μένῳ μὲν ἀλλοτρίαν ἀρχήν, ἄρχοντι δὲ αὐτῷ μετὰ
φυλακῆς τῶν νόμων πάντ' ᾤετο δεῖν κινεῖν ἐπὶ
τῷ τὸν ἄνδρα ἑλεῖν. καὶ ἀνοίγει δὴ τοῖς βαρβάροις
διὰ γραμμάτων τοὺς Ῥωμαίων ὅρους ἐξεῖναι φήσας
αὐτοῖς ὁπόσην δύναιντο κτᾶσθαι. 34. δοθείσης δὲ
ἐκείνοις τῆς ἀδείας καὶ τῶν συνθηκῶν λελυμένων
ταῖς ἐπιστολαῖς | εἰσχυθέντες ἐπὶ πολλῆς τοῦ κω- F 2
λύσοντος ἐρημίας, ὁ γὰρ δὴ Μαγνέντιος ἐν Ἰτα-
λίᾳ τὰς δυνάμεις εἶχε, Μυσῶν λείαν ἐργάζονται
τὰς εὐδαίμονας πόλεις, καὶ κατεσύροντο μὲν κῶμαι,
κατεσείετο δὲ τείχη, χρήματα δὲ ἤγετο καὶ γυναῖκες καὶ παῖδες, καὶ οἱ δουλεύοντες[1] ἠκολούθουν τὸν
αὐτῶν πλοῦτον οἱ δυστυχεῖς ἐπὶ τῶν ὤμων φέροντες, ὁ δὲ οὐ δυνάμενος δουλεύειν καὶ γυναῖκα καὶ
θυγατέρα ὁρᾶν ἐν ὕβρει κλάων ἀπεσφάττετο,
μετενηνεγμένων δὲ ἐκεῖσε τῶν παρ' ἡμῖν ἀγαθῶν
ἐγεώργουν οἱ κεκρατηκότες τὴν ἡμετέραν μὲν ταῖς
αὐτῶν χερσί, τὴν δὲ αὐτῶν ταῖς τῶν εἰλημμένων. |
R 534 35. αἱ δ' αὖ διαφυγοῦσαι τὴν ἅλωσιν ἰσχύϊ τειχῶν
γῆν μὲν οὐκ εἶχον πλὴν ὀλίγην κομιδῇ, λιμῷ δὲ
ἀνηλίσκοντο παντὸς ἁπτόμενοι τοῦ δυναμένου τρέφειν, ἕως εἰς τοσοῦτον σωμάτων κατέστησαν ἀριθμὸν ὥστε τὰς πόλεις αὐτὰς ἀγρούς τε εἶναι καὶ
πόλεις καὶ τὸ εἴσω τῶν περιβόλων ἀοίκητον
ἀρκοῦσαν γεωργίαν. καὶ γὰρ βοῦς ἐζεύγνυτο καὶ
ἄροτρον εἵλκετο καὶ σπέρμα κατεβάλλετο καὶ ἀνῄει

---

[1] δουλεύοντες Fabr. (most mss.): βουλεύοντες Re. (AV; CI
before correction): δουλεύσοντες F.

---

[a] A remarkable admission of Magnentius' good administration, lacking the qualification of Zos. 2. 54.

33. When Constantius was at war with Magnentius who had usurped the empire of another and was governing it himself with regard for law and order,[a] he felt that he must have recourse to every means to secure his downfall, and sending letters to the barbarians he actually opened up Roman territory to them, for he told them that he permitted them to occupy as much as they could.[b] 34. They were given a clear field and the terms of their treaties were rescinded by these despatches, and they swept in with absolutely none to stop them, for Magnentius had his forces in Italy. They ravaged the prosperous cities to their hearts' content[c]: villages were laid waste, walls were battered down: goods, women and children were carried off. The menfolk, as slaves, followed them, the poor devils carrying their own possessions on their backs. If they could not endure slavery and the sight of wives and daughters assaulted, they were murdered in the midst of their laments: the pick of what we possessed was transferred to the barbarians, and the victors farmed with their own hands the land that belonged to us and by those of their captives that which was their own. 35. Those cities that escaped the sack by the strength of their walls had no land save for a very small area: their folk were ravaged by famine and had recourse to anything that could serve for food, until the inhabitants were so reduced in number that the cities themselves formed both city and farmland and the uninhabited spaces inside the defences provided land enough for farming. Yes, oxen were yoked, furrows drawn, the seed set, and the corn grew, was

[b] Cf. Zos. 2. 53.
[c] Cf. Or. 12. 40 and note.

στάχυς, καὶ θεριστὴς καὶ ἅλως, καὶ πάντα | ταῦτα F 2·
εἴσω πυλῶν ὥστ᾽ οὐκ ἄν τις ἔφησεν ἀθλιωτέρους
εἶναι τοὺς ἁλόντας τῶν οἴκοι μενόντων.

36. Καὶ ὁ μὲν τοσούτου μισθοῦ τὴν νίκην
πριάμενος εὐθὺς μὲν ἥδετο καὶ ἐγαυρία, τοῦ πολεμίου δὲ ἡττημένου καὶ τῆς προδοσίας ἐκφανείσης
καὶ μονονουχὶ βοώσης τῆς Ῥώμης ὡς ἠκρωτηρί-
ασται, τοῖς μὲν αὐτοῦ κινδύνοις ἐξελάσαι τοὺς
κωμάζοντας οὐκ ἐτόλμα, στρατεύειν δὲ τὸν ἐκ
μουσείων ἄρτι πρὸς ὅπλα εἱλκυσμένον ἠξίου καὶ τὸ
δὴ καινότατον, τὸν αὐτὸν ὁμοῦ κρείττω τε φανῆναι
καὶ χείρω τῶν πολεμίων ηὔχετο, τῷ μὲν τῆς γῆς
ἐπιθυμεῖν ἐκεῖνο ποιῶν, φθόνῳ δὲ τοῦτο. 37. καὶ
ὅτι γε ἀπολούμενον οὐχ ἧττον ἢ κρατήσοντα ἐξ-
έπεμψεν εὐθὺς ἔδειξεν. οὔσης γὰρ αὐτῷ στρατιᾶς
ὅση πρότερον τρεῖς βασιλείας συνεῖχε, καὶ πολλῶν
R 535 μὲν ὁπλιτῶν πολλῶν δὲ | ἱππέων, ὧν, οἶμαι,
φοβερώτατον τὸ παρὰ τῆς σκευῆς ἄτρωτον, τρια-
κοσίους αὐτῷ τοὺς φαυλοτάτους τῶν ὁπλιτῶν
ἐκέλευεν ἕπεσθαι· τοὺς γὰρ ἱδρυμένους αὐτὸν ἐκεῖ
στρατιώτας εὑρήσειν. οὗτοι δὲ ἦσαν οἱ μεμα-
θηκότες ἡττᾶσθαι καὶ οἷς ἔργον ἦν πάλαι πολιορ-
κεῖσθαι. 38. τὸν δὲ οὐδὲν ἄρα | τούτων ἐτάραξεν F 2
οὐδὲ ἔδειξε περίφοβον, ἀλλὰ τότε πρῶτον ὅπλων τε
καὶ πολέμου γευόμενος καὶ μέλλων ἐπὶ τοὺς ἀεὶ
νενικηκότας ἐξάγειν στρατιώτας τρέμοντας οὕτω
μὲν ἤνεγκε τὴν σκευήν, ὥσπερ ἀντὶ βιβλίων ἐξ
ἀρχῆς ἀσπίδα μεταχειριζόμενος, οὕτω δὲ ἐχώρει

---

[a] Cf. Or. 12. 44, Amm. Marc. 16. 2. 12.
[b] Ibid. 15. 8. 1.
[c] Those of Constantine II, Constans and himself, he now
being the sole survivor of the sons of Constantine.

reaped and threshed, all inside the city gates, so that the captives could not have been said to be any worse off than they who remained at home.[a]

36. Constantius, after buying his victory at such cost, at first rejoiced and was glad, but after the final defeat of his foe, his treason stood revealed and Rome practically cried out aloud that she had been foully mutilated. He had not the courage to eject the intruders at the risk of his own skin, so he called on this student, whom he had just now fetched from college to a career of arms, to undertake the expedition.[b] But the oddest thing was his prayer that this same person should at the same time overcome and be overcome by the enemy, such emotions being due to his desire to recover his territory and to his envy. 37. He gave immediate proof that he was sending him out to death no less than to victory, for, though he had an army that in times past was big enough to keep three empires[c] in order, with masses of infantry and cavalry so invulnerably equipped as to lend them a terrible aspect, he detailed three hundred[d] of his most unreliable infantry to act as his escort: he would, he said, find his army in those already stationed there, that is, in men who had long been schooled in defeat and whose job had long been to stand siege. 38. Yet none of this worried Julian or caused him alarm. Though this was his first taste of action and campaigning, and though he was going to put into the field unsteady troops against the all-conquering foe, he wore his gear as if he had from the start been used to handling a shield instead of books, and he advanced with such confidence as if he

[a] Cf. Or. 12. 44, Julian, Eq. ad S.P.Q.Ath. 277 d, Zos. 3. 3.

θαρρῶν ὥσπερ μυρίων Αἰάντων ἡγούμενος. 39.
δύο δὲ ἄρα αὐτὸν ἐποίει τοιοῦτον· ἓν μὲν ἡ σοφία
καὶ τὸ τὰ βουλεύματα εἰδέναι χειρῶν ὄντα δυνατώ-
τερα, ἕτερον δὲ τὸ πιστεύειν αὐτῷ συστρατεύειν
τοὺς θεούς. ᾔδει δὲ καὶ τὸν Ἡρακλέα τὴν Στύγα
διαφυγόντα τῇ ῥοπῇ τῆς Ἀθηνᾶς.

40. Τῆς δὲ τῶν θεῶν πρὸς αὐτὸν εὐνοίας εὐθὺς
ἀπὸ γραμμῆς ἐναργὲς τὸ σύμβολον. κινηθεὶς γὰρ
ἐξ Ἰταλίας τοῦ χειμῶνος μεσοῦντος, ἡνίκα τὸν μὴ
στέγῃ σωζόμενον ἕτοιμον ἦν ἀπολωλέναι κρυμῷ τε
καὶ νιφάσιν, οὕτω φαιδρᾶς ἀπολαύων ἐπορεύετο τῆς
ἀκτῖνος, ὥστ᾽ ἔαρ ὀνομάζοντες τὴν ὥραν ἐχώρουν
καὶ πρὸ τῶν πολεμίων τὸ ψῦχος ἥττητο. 41. καὶ
μὴν κἀκεῖνό γε σημεῖον τῆς βελτίονος τύχης.
διεξιὼν γὰρ πολίχνιον | τὸ πρῶτον ἧς παρελάμβανε F 2
γῆς στέφανόν τινα κλάδων, πολλοὺς δὲ ἐκ καλω-
R 536 δίων τεταμένων | εἰς κίονας ἐκ τοίχων ἐξαρτῶσιν
οἱ δῆμοι μετεώρους, τούτων εἷς τῶν στεφάνων ᾧ
καλλωπίζομεν τὰς πόλεις ἐκλυθεὶς τοῦ δεσμοῦ
καταβαίνων ἦν ἐν τῇ τοῦ βασιλέως κεφαλῇ[1] καὶ
ἥρμοσε, καὶ βοὴ πανταχόθεν. ἐδηλοῦτο γάρ,
οἶμαι, τῷ στεφάνῳ τὰ μέλλοντα τρόπαια καὶ ὅτι
νικήσων ἔρχεται.

42. Εἰ μὲν οὖν ὁ πέμψας ἐπέτρεψεν εὐθὺς ἐν
ἔργοις τε εἶναι καὶ χρῆσθαι τοῖς λογισμοῖς, εὐθὺς
ἂν ἐδέχετο τἀκεῖ τὴν μεταβολήν, νῦν δ᾽ ὁ μὲν
πάντων ἦν ἄκυρος πλὴν τῆς χλαμύδος, οἱ στρατηγοὶ
δὲ κύριοι, ταῦτα γὰρ ἐδέδοκτο τῷ πεπομφότι τοὺς

---

[1] κεφαλῇ F. (most mss.: cf. Socr. H.E. 3. 1): κορυφῇ Re.
(corrections in C La).

were commander of a host of heroes. 39. There were two good reasons for such behaviour. First, there was his philosophy and his knowledge that strategy was more effective than brute strength. Secondly, he had confidence that the gods fought on his side. He knew that Heracles too had escaped the Styx because Athena tipped the scale in his favour.[a]

40. Right from the start there was a clear indication of the goodwill of the gods towards him. He left Italy in mid-winter, a season when anyone not protected under cover was liable to die from the snowstorms and frost, but his march was accompanied by such brilliant sunshine that, as they advanced, they called it the season of spring, and the cold was conquered even before his enemies were. 41. Moreover, here was another indication of his better fortune: as he was passing through the first township of the province allotted to him, one of the garlands of greenery—our parishes hang them in large numbers suspended on strings in mid-air between the pillars and the house walls and we decorate our towns with them—lost its fastenings, dropped on the emperor's head and fitted exactly. A cheer rose up on all sides[b]: for by this crown, obviously, his future triumphs were foretold, and the fact that he came to conquer.

42. Now, if the emperor that sent him had allowed him to go into action straightaway and to use his own initiative, the situation there would have been improved immediately, but in fact he had authority for nothing save to wear the uniform. Executive powers were vested in his military officers, for it had

[a] Cf. Or. 13. 28.
[b] Socr. (loc. cit.) borrows this story from Libanius.

μὲν ἐπιτάττειν τὸν δὲ ὑπηρετεῖν. ὁ δὲ Ὀδυσσέως
τε καὶ τῶν Ὀδυσσέως μεμνημένος ἠνείχετο, τοῖς
στρατηγοῖς δὲ ἄρα ἤρεσκε καθεύδειν. τοῦτο δὲ
ἐποίει τοὺς ἐναντίους μεγάλους, εἰ βασιλέως ἥκον-
τος ἔχοιεν ἃ πρότερον. 43. ἀλλ' ὅμως καὶ κεκωλυ-
μένου πράττειν, περιόντος | δὲ μόνον κατὰ θέαν τὰ F 2
ἔθνη, τουτὶ γὰρ ἐδέδοκτο[1] μόνον, τοσοῦτον ἴσχυσε
τοὔνομά τε καὶ τὸ πρόσωπον ὥστ' ἤδη τις τῶν
κατακεκλεισμένων πολύν τινα χρόνον καὶ τεταριχευ-
μένων ἐκπηδήσας εἷλε βάρβαρον πρὸς τῷ τείχει
γεωργοῦντα καὶ ἄλλος ἄλλον καὶ ἕτερος ἕτερον καὶ
τινα καὶ νυκτερινὴν ἐπιχείρησιν νεανίσκων ἀπεκρού-
σαντο πολλῶν γέροντες ὀλίγοι γήρᾳ τῶν ὅπλων
ἀφειμένοι. οἱ μὲν γὰρ κλίμακας φέροντες κατὰ
πύλας ἐρήμους προσέθεσαν, ᾧ δὴ τρόπῳ τῶν πόλεων τὰς πλείστας ᾑρήκεσαν, οἱ δὲ ὡς ᾔσθοντο,
πᾶν τὸ φανὲν ὅπλον ποιησάμενοι παρηβηκόσι πο-
R 537 σὶν ἔτρεχον | βοῶντες τὸ τοῦ βασιλέως ὄνομα. καὶ
ἐνίκων οἱ γέροντες, ὥσπερ οἱ Μυρωνίδου, τοὺς μὲν
αὐτοὶ κτείνοντες, οἱ δὲ καὶ σφᾶς αὐτοὺς ἄνωθεν ῥιπτοῦντες ἀπέθνησκον. 44. ἐγένετο δὲ καὶ
νέων ἑτέρωθεν ἐκδρομή τις ἐπὶ τοὺς βαρβάρους
οὐ πρότερον εἰωθότων. καὶ οἱ μὲν τραπέντες
ἔφευγον, οἱ δὲ ἐτρύφων ἐν ταῖς σφαγαῖς οὐχ
ὁρῶντες μὲν τὸν βασιλέα, τῷ δὲ πλησίον αὐτῶν

---

[1] ἐδέδοκτο Fabr. (mss.) : ἐδέδοτο Re., F.

[a] So Julian, *Ep. ad S.P.Q.Ath.* 277 d ff., Zos. 3. 2.
[b] At Augustodunum, *cf.* Amm. Marc. 16. 2. 1.
[c] *Cf.* Thuc. 1. 105. In 459 b.c., while the majority of
Athenian first-line troops were engaged in Egypt and Aegina,

306

been Constantius' decision that they should command
and he be subordinate to them.[a] He, mindful of
Odysseus and his companions, put up with the position, but the generals, it seemed, preferred to stay
fast asleep, and it encouraged the enemy that, after
the arrival of an emperor, they should have all they
had had before. 43. But for all that, even if action
were denied him and his tours of his provinces were
only for inspection—and that was all he was allowed
to do—the influence of his title and presence was
such that one of those who had long been cooped up
like fish in a barrel sallied out and captured a barbarian tilling the land close to the wall, and one or
two more people did the same. Finally a night attack made by a large force of young warriors was
repulsed by a few old men who had been released
from military service because of their age.[b] The
assailants, with ladders, attacked alongside an un-
guarded gate—their favourite method of capturing
a city—but the inhabitants, as soon as the alarm was
raised, used everything in sight as a weapon and
charged with aging step, shouting the emperor's name
as the battle cry. And the old fellows won, just like
those of Myronides, killing some of the assailants
themselves, while others of the attackers threw themselves to their death from the wall.[c] 44. From the
other side the young men made a sally against the
barbarians, something quite contrary to their custom
hitherto. They revelled in the killing, and the enemy
turned and fled. They did not actually see the
emperor but had been inspired by his nearness, while

the reserve forces (" the oldest and the youngest ") under
Myronides successfully defended Athens' new ally, Megara,
from Corinthian attack.

LIBANIUS

εἶναι τεθαρρηκότες. ἕτεροι μετανίστασθαι μέλ-
λοντες ἐκβαλόντες τῶν ψυχῶν τὸν φόβον ἔμενον.
45. βαρβάρων δὲ ἐκ δασείας ὕλης ἐπιθεμένων τοῖς
ἐσχάτοις | ἐν τῇ πορείᾳ τῆς στρατιᾶς πρὸς τοσοῦτον F 25
τὸ πρᾶγμα μετέστησεν ὥσθ' οἱ λυπήσειν ἐλπίσαντες
ἀπεσφάττοντο. καὶ ὁ κτείνας μάρτυρα τοῦ φόνου
τὴν τοῦ τεθνεῶτος ἐκόμιζε κεφαλήν, καὶ ἦν τις
μισθὸς ἐπὶ τῇ κεφαλῇ καὶ ἡ πολλὴ σπουδὴ κεφαλὴν
τεμεῖν. τῇ γὰρ ἐπιθυμίᾳ τοῦ κέρδους ὁ σοφώτατος
ἐκεῖνος ἐκάθηρε τὰς ψυχὰς τῆς δειλίας, καὶ τὸ
λαβεῖν ἐθέλειν τολμᾶν ἔπειθεν. οἱ δ' εἰς τὰς
νήσους ἃς ὁ Ῥῆνος ποιεῖ τῶν βαρβάρων κατα-
φυγόντες θήρα τοῖς νέουσί τε καὶ πλέουσι τῶν
ἡμετέρων ἦσαν, καὶ τοῖς ἐκείνων βοσκήμασιν αἱ
πόλεις εἰστιῶντο. 46. καὶ μὴν δυοῖν πόλεων ταῖν
μεγίσταιν τὴν μὲν εὑρὼν μυρίαις προσβολαῖς
κεκακωμένην, τὴν δ' ἔναγχος ἐφόδῳ μιᾷ κεκενω-
μένην τε καὶ κειμένην τῇ μὲν χεῖρα ὤρεξεν εἰς
ἀνάστασιν καὶ φρουρὰν ἐγκατέστησε, τὴν δ' ἀπειρη-
κυῖαν τοῖς ἅπασιν ὥστε καὶ ὅθεν οὐ νόμος ἀναγ-
κασθῆναι τραφῆναι παρεμυθήσατο ταῖς ἀμείνοσι |
R 538 τῶν ἐλπίδων. 47. ταῦτα ὁρῶν τις βασιλεὺς μοίρας
οὐ μικρᾶς βαρβαρικῆς ἧκεν ἀπολογίαν τε κομίζων
ὡς οὐ μεγάλα ἠδίκηκε, καὶ σπονδὰς αἰτῶν καὶ
συμμαχήσειν λέγων, ὡς δ' ἐδόκει | τι λέγειν, F 25
σπένδεται βραχύν τινα χρόνον ποιῶν αὐτὸν ἐπιει-
κέστερον τῷ φόβῳ τῶν δευτέρων.
48. Ταυτὶ μὲν οὖν καὶ ἔτι πλείω τούτων τὴν

ᵇ Socr. loc. cit. The Dacian campaign, illustrated on
Trajan's Column, provides a precedent for this type of total
warfare.

308

others, who were on the point of settling elsewhere,
cast away their fears and stayed. 45. And when the
barbarians launched an attack from the depths of the
forest upon the rear of the column of march, the
change in the situation was such that they who had
expected to throw him into disorder were annihilated.[a]
Their killers brought in their dead foes' heads as
proof, for there was a price set on every head, and
much eagerness for head-hunting.[b] With great cle-
verness he used their desire for gain to purge their
souls of cowardice, and acquisitiveness inspired courage. Some of the enemy sought refuge on the islands
formed by the Rhine and fell prey to those of our
people who crossed by swimming or in boats; and the
cities feasted on their cattle. 46. In fact, of the two
most important cities, he found that one had been
harried by countless inroads[c] and the other was lying
desolate and in ruins as a result of a single recent
attack. He lent a helping hand for the rebuilding of
this last, and placed a garrison in it.[d] The other,
that had become completely destitute, so that it had
been reduced to using the most outlandish things for
food, he consoled with hopes of better things. 47. On
seeing this, the chieftain of a not inconsiderable native
tribe came to him with his excuses: he pleaded that
he had done no great harm, and asked for peace and
offered to become an ally. Since there seemed to be
something in what he said, Julian made a truce with
him for a short period, rendering him better disposed
through fear of what might follow.

48. So, in his tours of inspection of the province,

[c] Brotomagus (Brumath), cf. Amm. Marc. 16. 2. 12 f.
[d] Agrippina (Cologne), ibid. 16. 3, Julian, Ep. ad
S.P.Q.Ath. 279 bc.

χώραν ἐπιὼν ἴσχυσεν οὔπω τοῦ πᾶν ὃ διανοηθείη
πράττειν εἰς ἐξουσίαν ἥκων. ὡς δὲ ἀπήλλακτο
μὲν ὁ τοὺς πολεμίους δεδιὼς στρατηγὸς εἰς δὲ
τοὺς οἰκείους ὑβρίζων, ἧκε δὲ διάδοχος ἀνὴρ τά
τε ἄλλα βέλτιστος καὶ πολέμων οὐκ ἄπειρος καὶ
τῶν κωλυμάτων τὰ πολλὰ ἐπέπαυτο, τότε δὴ τότε
τῷ βασιλεῖ καιρὸς ἐπιδείξεως ἀκριβοῦς παρῆν. 49.
σκοπείτω δέ τις· ὡς γὰρ ἐδόκει τῷ πρεσβυτέρῳ
γενέσθαι δεῖν διάβασιν ἐπὶ τοὺς βαρβάρους, τούτου δὲ ὁ νεώτερος ἦρα πάλαι καθάπερ ἵππος δρόμου καὶ πρὸς τὴν ἀνάγκην ᾗ κατείχετο ἤχθετο,
μικρὰν οὖσαν ὁ Κωνστάντιος ὁρῶν τὴν ἐκείνου δύναμιν καὶ τοῦ τολμήματος ἥττονα πέμπει τῶν αὑτοῦ
διπλασίαν, τρισμυρίους ὁπλίτας, ἐπιστήσας ἡγε-
μόνα δοκοῦντα ἐπίστασθαι δυνάμει χρῆσθαι. 50. καὶ
ἔδει δὴ στράτευμα ἐν ταῦτα ἀμφότερα γενέσθαι, καὶ
R 539 ὡς ἦν οὐ | πολὺ τὸ συνιοῦσι μέσον, δείσας ὁ πρε-
σβύτερος μὴ μετάσχῃ τῆς νίκης ἅτερος καὶ ἅμα
ἡγούμενος | ἀρκέσειν τοὺς αὑτοῦ, κελεύει τῷ μὲν F 2
μηκέτι συμμίξαι διαβῆναι δὲ μόνον. γεφυροῦντι
δὲ αὐτῷ πλοίοις τὸν ποταμὸν τεμόντες τῆς ὕλης
ἀφιᾶσιν ἄνω οἱ βάρβαροι κατὰ ῥοῦν πάχη ξύλων
ἃ προσπίπτοντα ταῖς ναυσὶ τὰς μὲν διέσπασε, τὰς
δ' ἀνέρρηξε,[1] τὰς δὲ καὶ κατέδυσε. 51. διαλελυ-

[1] δ' ἀνέρρηξε F. (mss.): δὲ διέρρηξε Re.: om. Fabr. A ends.

[a] For the deposition of Marcellus and his replacement
by Severus cf. Jul. Ep. ad S.P.Q.Ath. 278 d, Amm. Marc.
16. 11. 1.
[b] Libanius regularly uses πρεσβύτερος and νεώτερος in con-

such and more was the influence he exerted, though he had not yet reached a position where he could put all his schemes into practice. That commander who showed cowardice in face of the enemy and reserved his violence for his own people was withdrawn, and as his successor there came a first-rate man with an expert acquaintance with warfare.[a] Hence most of the obstacles were removed, and now at last the time had come for the emperor to prove himself beyond all doubt. 49. Just consider the circumstances. His senior colleague decided that a crossing of the river should be effected against the barbarians: he, the junior, had long been eager for this, like a horse for the race, fretting at the constraint that held him back. Constantius saw that Julian's forces were small, too small for the venture and sent 30,000 infantry, double the numbers that he had, putting in command a general who had a name for skilful handling of troops. 50. Both these armies should have combined into one, but when there was no great distance between them as they converged Constantius[b] became alarmed that Julian should share in the victory, and at the same time, thinking his force to be sufficient, he ordered his general not to effect a junction but to cross alone. While he was building a pontoon bridge across the river, the barbarians felled trees higher up and sent great baulks of timber floating downstream. These crashed into the boats and loosened them from their moorings, holing or sinking them.[c] 51. This first

nection with joint rulers to express not merely age but the hierarchy of imperial power, either between an Augustus and his Caesar, as here, or between two Augusti, as in *Or.* 24. 12 f.

[c] For Barbatio's failure in the campaign of A.D. 357 *cf.* Amm. Marc. 16. 11. 2 ff.

μένης δὲ τῆς πρώτης πείρας ὁ μὲν ᾤχετο φεύγων
καὶ αἱ τρεῖς μυριάδες, τοῖς βαρβάροις δὲ οὐκ
ἤρκει τὸ μὴ παθεῖν, ἀλλ' αὐτῶν ἤδη νομίσαντες
εἶναι τὸ καὶ δρᾶσαί τι διαβάντες ἐδίωκον καὶ
καταλαβόντες ἔκτεινον καὶ παιανίζοντες ἀνεχώρουν
καὶ συνῆπτον ἔργον ἔργῳ, μᾶλλον δὲ ἀπὸ λόγων
ἤρχοντο τῶν δευτέρων. 52. ὡς γὰρ ἦσαν οἴκοι
πάλιν, ὁ βασιλεὺς δὲ ἐνεπίμπλη πυρῶν καὶ φρούρια
καὶ πόλεις ἀπὸ τῶν ἐκείνοις εἰργασμένων ληΐων
ταῖς τῶν στρατιωτῶν χερσίν, ὅπως οἷόν τε ἦν, ἐπὶ
τούτῳ | χρώμενος καὶ τὰ κείμενα ἀνίστη,[1] καὶ F 2

R 540 πόρρω τοῦ Ῥήνου χειμάζοντι | βασιλεῖ τὰς τῶν
ἐχθρῶν ἐπιχειρήσεις ὀξέως μηνύσειν ἔμελλεν ἄλλων
παρ' ἄλλων δεχομένων τὸν λόγον—πρότερον δὲ τὸ
μῆκος τῆς ἐρημίας ἀφῃρεῖτο τὴν τῶν ἐπιβουλῶν
αἴσθησιν—ταῦτα δὴ πυνθανόμενοι Ῥωμαίους ἐν γῇ
Ῥωμαίων τἀκείνων ἀμῶντας ἀγανακτήσαντες ὥσπερ τῶν πατρῴων αὐτοῖς κειρομένων, πέμψαντες
κήρυκα καὶ δι' ἐκείνου δεικνύντες τὰς ἐπιστολὰς
αἳ τὴν γῆν αὐτῶν ἐποίουν, πολεμεῖν αὐτὸν ἔφασκον
τοῖς τῷ πρεσβυτέρῳ δόξασι καὶ δεῖν τοῦτο ὁμο-
λογεῖν ἢ τοῖς γεγραμμένοις ἐμμένειν ἢ μηδέτερον
βουλόμενον ἐλπίζειν μάχην. 53. ὁ δὲ τὸν μὲν ἐπὶ
κατασκοπὴν ἥκειν εἰπών, μὴ γὰρ ἂν οὕτω θρασὺν
γενέσθαι τὸν ἐκείνων ἄρχοντα, κατεῖχεν, αὐτὸς δὲ
μεμνημένος τῶν παρακελεύσεων ὧν ἤκουσεν ἐν
ταῖς συγγραφαῖς τῶν παλαιῶν ἐκείνων διεξιόντων
στρατηγῶν, καὶ καλῶς εἰδώς, ὅτι λόγος τοιοῦτος
ἔργων ἡγούμενος εὔψυχον ἐπὶ τὴν συμπλοκὴν

---

[1] ἀνίστη MSS. : ἀνέστη F.

attempt having failed, he took to his heels and ran, his 30,000 with him. The barbarians were not content to have escaped harm: they thought it was now their turn to inflict some, and so they crossed the river in pursuit, fell upon them and killed them and returned home in triumph, and began to follow up one action with another, or rather, from words they proceeded to the consequences of them. 52. For when they had returned home, the emperor began to stock his forts and towns with corn taken as booty from the lands cultivated by the enemy, employing his soldiers on this as far as possible.[a] He restored the ruined places, and when he took up winter quarters far from the Rhine the emperor was to be informed of any enemy attack by relays of messengers, the word passing from one place to the next. Previously the extent of the waste-land had deprived us of all knowledge of their plans. The barbarians, finding out that Romans in Roman territory were reaping crops that belonged to them, were as annoyed as at the ravaging of their ancestral domains.[b] They despatched an envoy to display the letter that made the land their own, and asserted that Julian was opposing his sovereign's will and that he should confess as much: he must either abide by the terms of the despatch or, if he refused, expect war. 53. Julian however alleged that he came to spy for them, for their chief would never have been so arrogant as that, and he had him arrested. Then remembering the speeches of exhortation that he had heard given by the generals of old in history books, and well aware that such an address at the start of action sends the

---

[a] *Cf.* Amm. Marc. 16. 11. 11 ff.
[b] *Ibid.* 16. 12. 3 ff.

παραπέμπει τὸν στρατιώτην, εἶπε λόγον, ὃν ἥδιστα
μὲν ἂν εἰς τὸν παρόντα λόγον ἐνέθηκα, τοῦ νόμου
δὲ τοῦ περὶ ταῦτα | οὐκ ἐῶντος τοσοῦτον εἴποιμ᾽ F 2
ἄν, ὅτι τοῖσι δ᾽ ἄφαρ πόλεμος γλυκίων γένετ᾽
ἢ πρότερον τὸ μηδὲν ποιεῖν. 54. καὶ ἐδόκει δεῖν
κέρας μὲν ἑκάτερον τοὺς ἱππέας ἔχειν, τὸ μέσον δὲ
εἶναι τῶν ὁπλιτῶν, τοὺς δὲ ἀμείνους ἑκατέρων
τούτων ἐν τῷ δεξιῷ περὶ τὸν βασιλέα. καὶ τοῦτο
ἔδει μὲν τοὺς πολεμίους λανθάνειν, λαθεῖν δὲ οὐκ
εἴασεν αὐτομόλων τινῶν κακία. γιγνομένης δὲ
R 541 τῆς ἐκείνων | διαβάσεως κωλῦσαι μὲν ἐξὸν ὁ
βασιλεὺς οὐκ ἐβουλήθη ἀλλ᾽ οὐδὲ μέρει μικρῷ
προσπεσὼν μαχέσασθαι, ἤδη δὲ ὄντων τρισμυρίων
κατέβαινε πρὶν ἐπιγενέσθαι πολλάκις τοσούτους·
ἐγνώκεσαν γάρ, ὡς ἦν ἀκούειν ὕστερον, μηδένα
τῶν μαχίμων οἴκοι μένειν. 55. ἄμφω τοίνυν ἄξια
θαυμάσαι, τὸ μήτε τοῖς πρώτοις ἀπαντῆσαι μήτε
πᾶν τὸ κεκινημένον δέξασθαι· τὸ μὲν γὰρ ἦν οὐ
μέγα, τὸ δὲ τοῦ μεγίστου κινδύνου, καὶ τὸ μὲν
μικροῦ τὴν γνώμην, τὸ δὲ ἀλογίστου. διὰ τοῦτο
πλείους μὲν ὧν ἦγε καὶ πολλῷ τινι περαιουμένους
οὐκ εἶργε, τῇ δὲ ἐφόδῳ τὸ τούτοις ἐπιρρέον ἔ-
στησε. 56. τοῖς βαρβάροις δὲ πάντα πεπυσμέ-
νοις τὸ μὲν ἀνδρειότερον τῆς στρατιᾶς πρὸς τὸ
κρεῖττον ἀντετέτακτο, τῷ δεξιῷ δὲ κέρᾳ σύμμα-
χον | ἔδωκαν λόχον ὃν ἔκρυψαν ὑπὸ ὀχετῷ μετεώρῳ F 2

---

[a] For Ammianus' version, *ibid.* 16. 12. 9 ff. The comment upon this rhetorical convention is fair illustration of
the current practice.

[b] Homer, *Iliad*, 2. 453.

[c] The most detailed account of the battle of Strasburg is

314

men cheerfully into battle, he delivered a speech which I would gladly have inserted here in my own,[a] but since that is forbidden by the tradition in such matters, I will limit my remarks to this, that "for them fighting became much more to their liking"[b] than inaction had been before. 54. It was decided that the cavalry should be posted on either flank, with the infantry in the centre and the pick of both horse and foot on the right with the emperor. This arrangement should not have come to the enemy's notice, but the treachery of some deserters prevented this. The enemy began their crossing and, although it was in his power to stop them, the emperor refused to do so, nor yet would he bring on a fight by an attack on a small section of their forces. However, when they numbered 30,000, he marched down to meet them before many times more came on the scene, for they had resolved, as was afterwards discovered, to leave none of their fighting men behind at home. 55. Both aspects of his strategy, then, were worthy of remark, first, his refusal to attack the vanguard, secondly, his refusal to engage with all the enemy in motion, for the first was of little importance, the second fraught with the greatest danger, the one indicating timidity, the other rashness in a general. Hence he did not seek to prevent the crossing of forces far greater than his own, but by his attack he put a stop to any reinforcement for them.[c] 56. Upon discovering the disposition of his forces, they opposed the bravest of their own troops to the pick of his. On the right they placed a supporting party in an ambush concealed

given by Ammianus (16. 12). Libanius' information is derived from Julian's own report (E.L.F. No. 25).

LIBANIUS

καλάμων πυκνῶν, καὶ γὰρ ἦν ὑδρηλὸν τὸ χωρίον,
τοὺς καθημένους ἀφανιζόντων. οὐ μὴν τούς γε
ὀφθαλμοὺς τῶν ἐπ' ἄκρῳ τῷ εὐωνύμῳ Ῥωμαίων
ἐλάνθανον, ἀλλ' ὡς εἶδον, ἅμα βοῇ δραμόντες τοὺς
μὲν ἀναστήσαντες ἐδίωκον, τῆς στρατιᾶς δὲ εἰς
ἥμισυ δι' ἐκείνων διετάραξαν φυγῆς φυγὴν τεκούσης
τῆς τῶν πρώτων τὴν τῶν δευτέρων. 57. γίγνεται
δέ τι παραπλήσιον ἐν τῇ μάχῃ τῷ περὶ τὴν τῶν
Κορινθίων πρὸς Κερκυραίους ναυμαχίαν. καὶ γὰρ
ἐν ταύτῃ νικᾶσθαί τε καὶ νικᾶν ἑκατέροις συνέβη.
τὸ γὰρ εὐώνυμον ἑκατέρων ἐκράτει ὥστ' ἐπιέζετο
τὸ περὶ τὸν βασιλέα Ῥωμαίων δεξιόν, λογάδες ὑπὸ
λογάδων. 58. καὶ οὐδὲ τοῖς τὰ σημεῖα φέρουσιν
R 542 οἳ φυλάττειν | δὴ μάλιστα μεμελετήκασι τάξιν ὁ
νόμος ἐσώζετο. ὡς δὲ ἐνέκλιναν, μέγα βοήσας
ὁ βασιλεὺς καὶ τοὺς τοῦ Τελαμωνίου | μιμησά- F 2
μενος λόγους, ὁ μὲν γὰρ εἶπεν οὐκ εἶναι τοῖς
Ἕλλησι διαφθαρεισῶν τῶν νεῶν ἐπάνοδον, ὁ δὲ
ἡττηθεῖσι τούτοις κεκλείσεσθαι τὰς πόλεις καὶ
τροφὴν δώσειν οὐδένα, καὶ ἐπέθηκε δὴ τελευτῶν
ὡς εἰ δέδοκται φεύγειν, αὐτὸν δεήσει κτείναντας
τότ' ἤδη δραπετεύειν, ὡς ζῶντά γε οὐκ ἐπιτρέψειν,
καὶ δείκνυσι δὴ τῶν βαρβάρων τοὺς ἐλαυνομένους
ὑπὸ τῶν τρεψαμένων. 59. ὡς δὲ τὰ μὲν ἤκουσαν,
τὰ δὲ εἶδον, καὶ τὰ μὲν ᾐσχύνθησαν, τοῖς δὲ
ἥσθησαν, ἀνέστρεφόν τε καὶ αὖθις συνέμισγον, καὶ
τὸ αἰσχρὸν ἐλέλυτο, καὶ πᾶς ἦν ἐν τῷ διώκειν·
ὥστε καὶ οἱ τῶν σκευοφόρων τῶν ἐν τῇ κορυφῇ
φύλακες ἠράσθησαν τῶν γιγνομένων μετασχεῖν.
ὡς δὲ ἠπείγοντο καὶ ὁ δρόμος δῆλος ἦν, δόξαν
316

in a water course ; a deep curtain of reeds hid the party, for the ground was marshy. For all that, it did not escape the gaze of the Romans on the extreme left : as soon as they saw them, they raised the battle cry and charged, dislodged them and followed in pursuit, and by their means set about half their army in disorder, since panic begot panic and passed from one section to another. 57. The result was not unlike that of the naval engagement between Corcyra and Corinth, for here too both sides won and lost.[a] The left wing of each side was victorious, so that the crack troops around the emperor on the Roman right were hard pressed by the crack troops of the enemy. 58. Not even the standard bearers, so strictly trained in keeping their posts, maintained their regular behaviour. They gave way, and the emperor shouted aloud copying the words of the son of Telamon.[b] He, you will remember, told the Greeks that there was no returning home for them once their ships were destroyed, and Julian told these men that if they were beaten, the cities would shut their gates against them, and no one would give them supplies : finally he added that, if they had made up their minds to flee, they would have to kill him first, for while ever he was alive, he would not let them do it, and he pointed out to them those barbarians who were fleeing before their pursuers. 59. Hearing and seeing this, they were ashamed and encouraged, and they turned and entered the fray once more. Their disgrace was erased and everyone joined in the pursuit, so that even the guards in charge of the baggage train on the crest of the hill were moved to take part in the action. They rushed forward and, their

[a] Thuc. 1. 49.        [b] Homer, *Iliad*, 15. 501 ff.

πλείονος δυνάμεως παρέσχον τοῖς βαρβάροις, καὶ
οὐκ ἦν ὁ μένειν ἔτι βουλόμενος.   60. ὥστε
ἐκεκάλυπτο μὲν τὸ πεδίον ὀκτακισχιλίοις νεκροῖς,
ἐκρύπτετο δὲ ὁ Ῥῆνος τοῖς ἀπειρίᾳ τοῦ νεῖν
ἀποπνιγεῖσι, μεσταὶ δὲ ἦσαν τῶν κειμένων αἱ
νῆσοι τοῦ ποταμοῦ τῶν νενικηκότων ἐπὶ τοὺς ἐν
ταῖς ὕλαις ἐπτηχότας ἰόντων. τοῖς δὲ πορρωτάτω
βαρβάροις νεκροὶ καὶ ὅπλα τὴν μάχην ἐμήνυον ὑπὸ
τοῦ ῥεύματος φερόμενοι.   61. τὸ | δὲ μέγιστον, F 26
σαγηνεύοντες γὰρ τοὺς ἐν ταῖς νήσοις ἐν ταύτῃ τῇ
θήρᾳ καὶ τὸν ἄρχοντα μετὰ τῶν ἀρχομένων εἷχον·
ὃν ἦγον ἐχόμενοι τῶν χειρῶν, οὐ γυμνώσαντες τῶν
ὅπλων, ἄνδρα μέγιστόν τε καὶ κάλλιστον καὶ τοὺς
ἁπάντων ὀφθαλμοὺς ἐπιστρέφοντα καὶ σώματι καὶ
R 543  σκευῇ.   62. καὶ ὁ μὲν ἥλιος τοιοῦτον ἔργον | ἐπ-
ιδὼν ἔδυ, τὸν ἄνδρα δὲ τοῦτον ὁ βασιλεὺς εἰς
εὐθύνας ὧν ἐτόλμησε καταστήσας μέχρι μὲν ἐχρῆτο
λόγοις φρόνημα ἔχουσιν ἐθαύμαζε, ταπεινὰ δὲ τὰ
τελευταῖα γενναίοις τοῖς πρώτοις ἐπιθέντα καὶ
δείσαντα περὶ τῇ ψυχῇ καὶ μνησθέντα σωτηρίας
ὥσπερ ἐμίσησεν. οὐ μὴν ἔδρασέ γε δεινὸν οὐδὲν
οὐδὲ ἔδησεν αἰδεσθεὶς τὴν ἄρτι τύχην καὶ λογιζό-
μενος ὅσον ἴσχυσεν ἡμέρα μία.
    63. Τίνα τῶν παρ᾽ Ἕλλησιν ἑορτῶν παρέβαλεν
ἄν τις τῇ τότε ἑσπέρᾳ συμπινόντων μὲν ἀλλήλοις
τῶν ἠγωνισμένων, ἀριθμούντων δὲ πρὸς ἀλλήλους
οὓς ἐν τῇ μάχῃ κατήνεγκαν, καὶ τῶν μὲν γελών-
των, τῶν δὲ ᾀδόντων, τῶν δὲ ἀπειλούντων, ὁ δὲ
εἰργόμενος σιτίων τοῖς τραύμασιν ἀρκοῦν εἶχε
παραμύθιον αὐτὰ τὰ τραύματα;   64. ἦ που κἂν

---

    ª Chnodomarius : Julian, *Ep. ad S.P.Q.Ath.* 279 c, Amm.
Marc. 16. 12. 65 ff.

advance being seen, they gave the enemy an exaggerated notion of their numbers, so that none now was ready to stand his ground. 60. In consequence, the field was littered with the bodies of 8,000 dead, and the Rhine was hidden by the corpses of those who, unable to swim, were drowned, while the islands in the river were full of the bodies of the slain, for the victors routed out those who were skulking there in the woods. To the most far distant barbarians corpses and armour carried down by the stream brought the tidings of battle. 61. Best of all, while beating the islands for fugitives, in this hunt they even caught the chief[a] along with his followers. Without stripping him of his armour, they held fast his hands and led him captive, a tall, fine figure of a man, who attracted everyone's attention by his appearance and equipment. 62. The sun sank to rest after witnessing such a feat, and the emperor made him face an inquiry into his activities. While ever he presented a bold front in his replies, he admired him, but when, after a noble beginning, he ended in tones of humility, fearing for his life and begging for mercy, he almost hated him. Still, he did him no harm : he did not even put him in chains, out of respect for his recent eminence and from consideration of the great effect a single day had produced.

63. What festival in Greece could have been compared with that evening, when the combatants were drinking together, recounting to one another how many they had killed in the battle, laughing, singing, bragging, while anyone kept away from the feast by his wounds found ample consolation in his very wounds ? 64. Why, even in their dreams they fought

τοῖς ὀνείρασιν ἐκεῖνοι τοὺς | βαρβάρους ἐνίκων καὶ F 2
τὴν ἀπὸ τῶν ἐν ἡμέρᾳ πεπονημένων ἡδονὴν καὶ
διὰ τῆς νυκτὸς ἐκαρποῦντο, χρόνιοι δή, μάλα
χρόνιοι τρόπαιον στήσαντες βαρβάρων καὶ τῷ παρ'
ἐλπίδα μειζόνως εὐφραινόμενοι. 65. καίτοι πότερον φύσει κακοὺς ὄντας Ἰουλιανὸς ἐποίησε
βελτίους ὥσπερ τις θεὸς μένος ἐμβαλών; καὶ τί
μεῖζον τοῦ μεῖζον ἀνθρώπου δύνασθαι; ἀλλὰ
χρηστὰς φύσεις ἔβλαπτεν ἡγεμόνων κακία; καὶ τί
κάλλιον τοῦ τοὺς ἀγαθοὺς εἰς ἐπίδειξιν ὧν ἴσχυον
ἀγαγεῖν; ἀλλὰ θεῶν τις ἐξ ἀφανοῦς τὰ τούτων
ἐποίει βελτίω; καὶ τίνος οὐ σεμνότερον μετὰ τοι-
R 544 ούτων ἀγωνίζεσθαι συμμάχων; | ἐπεὶ καὶ τοῖς
Ἀθηναίοις μεῖζον εἰς δόξαν, οἶμαι, τὸ μεθ' Ἡρακλέους καὶ Πανὸς πρᾶξαι τὰ λεγόμενα Μαραθῶνι
ἢ εἰ τῶν θεῶν χωρὶς ταῦτα ἐδεδύνηντο.

66. Ἄλλος μὲν οὖν ἄν τις ἐπὶ τοσαύτῃ νίκῃ τὴν
στρατιὰν διαφεὶς αὐτὸς ἂν ἥκων εἰς πόλιν ἵππων
ἁμίλλαις καὶ θεάτρων ἡδοναῖς εἱστίασεν ὀφθαλμούς,
ἀνέπαυσε τὴν γνώμην. ἀλλ' οὐκ ἐκεῖνος. ἀλλὰ
τοῖς μὲν τὰ σημεῖα φέρουσιν, ὅπως εἰδεῖεν τηρεῖν
τὴν | τάξιν, δίκην ἐπέθηκε ζῶσι τὸ μὴ καὶ ἀπο- F 2
κτεῖναι τῇ νίκῃ δούς, τὸν δὲ μέγαν ἐκεῖνον, τὸν
βασιλέα, τὸν αἰχμάλωτον πέμπει Κωνσταντίῳ τῶν
αὐτοῦ συμφορῶν μηνυτήν, οἰόμενος δεῖν αὐτὸν μὲν
πονεῖν, τῶν δὲ τοιούτων ἄθλων ἐκείνῳ παραχωρεῖν,
Ἀχιλλεὺς Ἀγαμέμνονι τῆς λείας ἀφιστάμενος. 67.
ὁ δὲ ἦγέ τε ἐπ' αὐτῷ πομπὴν καὶ ἡβρύνετο καὶ

---

[a] For the unexpectedness of the victory *cf.* Amm. Marc.
16. 12. 51.        [b] Herod. 6. 105.

and beat the enemy over again, and all night long
they enjoyed the pleasure of their labours of the day,
for at last, at long last, they had set up a trophy over
the barbarians and were the more delighted at its
very unexpectedness.[a] 65. But did Julian turn them
into heroes from being natural cowards, like some
deity infusing them with valour ? Then what can
surpass such superhuman ability ? Or had their
courage been rendered unavailing by the cowardice
of their commanders ? Then what is more glorious
than to induce good men to demonstrate their
staunchness ? Or was it some god behind the scenes
who caused their success ? Then to fight with the
gods on our side is surely the proudest boast of all.
It redounded more to the credit of Athens, for
instance, that she gained her famous victory at
Marathon with the aid of Heracles and Pan than if
she had done so without the gods to help her.[b]

66. Now, any other man after such an overwhelming
victory might have disbanded his army, retired to his
capital and feasted his eyes on horse races and
theatrical amusements, and sought mental relaxa-
tion. But not he ! To teach the standard bearers
how to remain at their posts, he punished them but
let them live : the remission of the death sentence he
attributed to his victory.[c] That great tall fellow, the
chief, his prisoner, he sent to Constantius to tell the
news of his own undoing, for he regarded it his duty
to perform the actions himself but to give the credit
for them to Constantius—an Achilles resigning his
spoils to Agamemnon.[d] 67. Constantius celebrated
a triumph over him, gave himself airs and gained fame

[c] Zos. 3. 3. 11.
[d] Julian, *loc. cit.*, Amm. Marc. 16. 12. 66.

ἦν λαμπρὸς ἀπὸ τῶν ἑτέρου κινδύνων, ἐπεὶ καὶ
τὸν τῷδε μὲν συνδιαβάντα δυνάστην παραινοῦντα δὲ
μὴ μάχεσθαι φοβήσας τοῖς γιγνομένοις εἰς τὰς
Κωνσταντίου χεῖρας φεύγοντα ἐνέβαλε, καὶ ἦν
ἀμφοῖν διὰ τοῦτον[1] βασιλέοιν δεσπότης, τοῦ μὲν
αὐτὸν δόντος, τοῦ δὲ ἁλόντος.

68. Ἀλλ' ἐπάνειμι γάρ, ὅτι μὴ ταὐτὸν τοῖς
νικῶσιν ἔπαθε πάθος οὓς ἐπὶ τέρψεις ἀφιᾶσι καὶ
ῥᾳθυμίας αἱ νῖκαι. ἀλλ' ἐπειδὴ τῇ γῇ τοὺς πε-
πτωκότας παρέδωκεν, οὐκ ἐπέτρεψε τοῖς στρατιώταις καὶ μάλα βουλομένοις καταθέσθαι τὰ ὅπλα
ἀλλ' ἡγούμενος τὸ μὲν πεπραγμένον εἶναι τῇ σφῶν
αὐτῶν βοηθούντων ἀνθρώπων, | δεῖν δὲ τοὺς ἀγα- F
R 545 θοὺς καὶ τιμωρίαν ὧν πεπόνθασι λαμβάνειν, | ἦγεν
ἐπὶ τὴν πολεμίων διδάσκων καὶ λέγων ὡς βραχὺ
τὸ λειπόμενον καὶ τρυφὴ μᾶλλον ἢ πόνος, ὡς
ἐοίκασιν οἱ βάρβαροι θηρίῳ βεβλημένῳ καὶ δευτέραν περιμένοντι πληγήν. 69. καὶ οὐκ ἐψεύσατο·
διαβάντων γὰρ οἱ μὲν ἐν ἡλικίᾳ γυναῖκας καὶ
τέκνα ταῖς ὕλαις ἐγκαταθέμενοι φεύγοντες ἐσώ-
ζοντο, ὁ δὲ πυρὶ μὲν ἀνήλισκε τὰς κώμας, ἐξῆγε δὲ
πᾶν τὸ κεκρυμμένον, καὶ τὰ δένδρα οὐκ ἐκώλυε,
καὶ παρῆν αὐτίκα πρεσβεία ταπεινοὺς φθεγγομένη
λόγους καὶ πρέποντας τοῖς παροῦσι κακοῖς. οἱ δὲ
ἦσαν αὐτοῦ στῆναι καὶ λήξαντα τοῦ φθείρειν
χρῆσθαι τοῦ λοιποῦ φίλοις. σπένδεται δή, καὶ τῶν
σπονδῶν χρόνος ὁ χειμὼν μόνος, παρ' οὗ καὶ
σπονδῶν ἄνευ τύχοι τις ἂν ἴσως ἀναπαύσεως. 70.
τοῖς μὲν οὖν ἡττημένοις τοσοῦτον ἔδωκεν, αὐτὸς

---

[1] τοῦτον F., conj. Re. (corrections in CM): τοῦτο other mss.

from another man's dangers,[a] for Julian had filled a
second chief, who had joined the other in his invasion
but had advised him not to fight, with such alarm that
he sent him fleeing into the hands of Constantius,
who now, by Julian's agency, became master of both
chieftains, one by surrender, the other by capture.

68. But to return to my theme. His reactions were
not those of a victor whom success diverts to pleasure
and idleness. After burying his dead, he did not
allow his troops to lay down their arms, though they
greatly desired it. Their performance so far, he felt,
had been simply one of defending their own country
from aggression: men of mettle should revenge
themselves for what they had suffered. So he led
them in an invasion of enemy territory, explaining to
them that there was little left to do and that it would
be more of a pleasure-jaunt than a fatigue, for the
barbarians were like a wounded beast awaiting the
*coup de grâce*. 69. And he was not wrong either:
when his army made the crossing, the barbarian
warriors hid their women and children in the forest
and sought safety in flight. He burned down their
villages and brought out all they had hidden away,
for the forest provided no hindrance. An embassy
immediately presented itself, using humble language
suited to their present plight. They proposed that
he should halt there, cease his ravages and treat
them as friends in future. He did, in fact, make
a truce with them, but only for the duration of
the winter, when even without a truce they might
perhaps have gained a respite.[b] 70. So much then
was the grace he granted his defeated foe, but he

    [a] *Cf.* Ammianus' bitter comment, 16. 12. 70.
        [b] Amm. Marc. 17. 1, Zos. 3. 4.

δὲ οὐκ ἠξίωσεν,[1] ἀλλ' ἐν χειμῶνι μέσῳ τοῦτο μὲν
Φρακτοὺς χιλίους οἷς ταὐτὸν εἰς ἡδονὴν χιών τε
καὶ ἄνθη κώμας τινὰς πορθοῦντας, ὧν ἐν μέσῳ
φρούριον ἔρημον, περιστοιχισάμενος | καὶ κατα- F 2⟨
κλείσας εἰς τοῦτο λιμῷ λαβὼν ἔπεμψε δεδεμένους
τῷ μείζονι, πρᾶγμα καινότατον, καὶ γὰρ ἐκείνοις
νόμος ἢ νικᾶν ἢ πίπτειν. ἀλλ' ὅμως ἐδέθησαν
ταὐτόν, οἶμαι, παθόντες τοῖς ἐν Σφακτηρίᾳ Λάκω-
σιν. ἐκείνους μὲν οὖν λαβὼν ὁ βασιλεὺς δῶρά τε
ὠνόμαζε καὶ τοῖς αὐτοῦ λόχοις ἀνέμιξε πύργους τινὰς σφίσιν ἐγκαταμιγνύναι πιστεύων. οὕτως ἀντὶ
πολλῶν σωμάτων ἕκαστος ἦν. 71. ἐν μὲν τοίνυν τοῦτο τοσοῦτον ἔργον χειμερινόν, ἕτερον δὲ
οὐκ ἔλαττον. ἔθνος γὰρ ὅλον ἐξαίφνης καταθέον
τὴν χώραν ἔθει μὲν αὐτὸς ὡς ἐξελῶν μετὰ τῶν
φυλάττειν τεταγμένων τὸ πιεζόμενον, οἱ δὲ αἰσθό-
μενοι τοῦ δρόμου φθάσαντες αὐτοὶ τοὺς πολεμίους
R 546 ἐξέβαλον | ἀποβαλόντας οὐκ ὀλίγους. οὕτως ὁ
βασιλεὺς παρών τε καὶ μέλλων ὁμοίως ἐνίκα. 72.
καὶ ταῦτα ἔπραττεν ἐκ μέσων ἀνιστάμενος καὶ
τότε τῶν βιβλίων, μᾶλλον δὲ χωρῶν ἐπὶ τοὺς
ἐναντίους μετὰ τούτων ἐχώρει. ἀεὶ γὰρ εἶχεν ἐν
χεροῖν ἢ βίβλους ἢ ὅπλα νομίζων μεγάλα πόλεμον
ὑπὸ σοφίας ὠφελεῖσθαι καὶ μείζω γε φέρειν ῥοπὴν
βασιλέα βουλεύεσθαι δυνάμενον ἢ μαχόμενον. 73.
αὐτίκα δύο ταυτὶ πῶς οὐ λυσιτελέστατα μὲν τοῖς
ἄλλοις γνώμης | δὲ δεξιωτέρας, τὸ τιμαῖς μὲν F 2⟨

---

[1] ἠξίωσεν Re. (mss. except VP): ἠξίωσε καθῆσθαι F. (V,
P corrected).

---

[a] Amm. Marc. 17. 2 ; cf. Thuc. 4. 38.

did not expect so much for himself : in mid-winter he had to deal with a thousand of the Franks, to whose taste snows and blossoms come alike. They were engaged in ravaging some villages in the centre of which was a deserted fort. Here he surrounded them and kept them penned up until he forced them to surrender from starvation. Then he sent them in chains to his superior—an event without precedent, for it was their way to conquer or die. For all that, they were put in chains, just like the Spartans at Sphacteria.[a] The emperor who received them described them as a gift and drafted them into his own regiments, confident that he was enrolling pillars of strength for himself, since every one was a match for many ordinary men. 71. This then was one of his major exploits in that winter, but there was another no less remarkable. When a whole enemy tribe suddenly overran part of the province, he hastened to dislodge them in concert with the forces garrisoning the threatened area, but on the news of the raid, anticipating his coming, they themselves ejected the enemy inflicting heavy losses. So the emperor, both upon his arrival and before it, was alike victorious. 72. And this feat he performed as he just then arose from the midst of his books—or rather, as he went against the foe, he went with his books for company. For he always had in his hands either books or arms, for he considered warfare to be greatly helped by philosophy, and that in an emperor ability to use his wits was more effective than belligerency.[b] 73. For instance, the two following devices were certainly beneficial to the community and indications of his superior intellect, first that he increased the eager-

[b] *Cf.* Amm. Marc. 16. 5. 3 ff.

αὐξῆσαι τὴν προθυμίαν τῶν ἀγαθῶν ἃς αὐτοῖς
προὐξένησε παρὰ τοῦ τὰ τοιαῦτα νέμοντος, ποιῆσαι
δὲ τοὺς τὰ τῶν πολεμίων λῃστεύοντας ὧν κρατή-
σαιεν δεσπότας; ἐοικὸς γὰρ δὴ τοῦτο ἐκείνῳ
σαφῶς τῷ τὸν κομίσαντα πολεμίου κεφαλὴν χρυσίον δέχεσθαι τῆς τόλμης.  74. τῆς φήμης δὲ ἐπὶ
τὴν οἰκουμένην ἄμφω φερούσης ἦρα μὲν αὐτοῦ
πᾶς στρατιώτης ὅστις ἔργων ἐραστής, ἤρων δὲ οἱ
περὶ τοὺς λόγους, καὶ τῶν Ἀθήνησι διατριβόντων
οἱ συνειδότες αὐτοῖς τι καλὸν ὡς ἐκείνων ἤεσαν,
ὥσπερ πάλαι ποτὲ εἰς Λυδίαν οἱ σοφισταὶ παρὰ τὸν
Κροῖσον. ἀλλὰ Σόλωνι μὲν Κροῖσος τοὺς θησαυροὺς τῶν χρημάτων ἐδείκνυεν ὡς ἂν οὐδὲν τοῦδε
κεκτημένος τιμιώτερον, ὁ δὲ τοῖς ἀφικνουμένοις
τοὺς τῆς ψυχῆς θησαυροὺς ἀνεπετάννυεν, ἐν οἷς[1] ἦν
τὰ παρὰ τῶν Μουσῶν, καὶ[2] ὁ βασιλεὺς ᾖδεν ἔπη
τούτοις τοὺς ἥκοντας κοσμῶν, καὶ νῦν ἔξεστιν
ἀναγνῶναι λαβόντα.

75. Τοιαῦτα τοίνυν συναναβακχεύσας τοῖς Ἑρμοῦ
τε καὶ Διὸς ὀπαδοῖς τοῦ καιροῦ τὸ σημεῖον αἴροντος
εὐθὺς στρατεύει καὶ περὶ τὸν ποταμὸν ἀστράψας
ἔθνος | ὅλον οὕτως ἐξέπληξεν ὥστ᾽ ἠξίουν μετοι- F
R 547 κεῖν καὶ μέρος εἶναι τῆς αὐτοῦ | βασιλείας, τῆς
οἰκείας τὸ ζῆν ὑπ᾽ ἐκείνῳ κρίνοντες ἥδιον, καὶ γῆν
ᾔτουν καὶ ἐλάμβανον. καὶ βαρβάροις ἐπὶ βαρβάρους ἐχρῆτο πολὺ κάλλιον ἡγουμένοις μετὰ

---

[1] ἐν οἷς F., conj. R. : ὡς mss. except V and Par. 3016 : ὃς
V ; in Par. preceded by τὸν . . . θησαυρόν.
[2] After καὶ F. inserts ἅπερ.

---

[a] e.g., Priscus: cf. Or. 12. 55, Julian, E.L.F. No. 13, Eunap. V.S. 481 ff.
[b] Cf. Or. 12. 55. f.
[c] A Platonic tag (Διὸς ὀπαδοί: Phaedr. 252 c) is here

ness of good men by the honours that he sponsored
for them from the distributor of such things, and
secondly, that in the harrying of enemy territory,
he allowed them possession of whatever they got
their hands on, for this is obviously on a par with his
proclamation that anyone who brought in the head of
an enemy should receive a gold piece for his courage.
74. His renown spread both reports over the whole
world, and he was loved by every soldier that loved
action and by men of learning. Those residents of
Athens that knew their own worth went to visit him,
as once upon a time the sages visited Croesus in
Lydia.[a] Yet Croesus displayed to Solon his treasures
of money, as though that was the most priceless
possession he had ; but Julian displayed to the
newcomers the treasures of his soul, treasures that
held the riches of the Muses, and with them the
emperor recited verses in honour of his visitors.
Even now you can obtain them and read them.[b]

75. Such then was the revelry with which he enter-
tained the servants of Hermes and Zeus,[c] but as soon
as the season called for the raising of the standard he
went on campaign.[d] He made a lightning appearance
on the Rhine, and so terrified a whole enemy tribe
that they asked permission to migrate and form part
of his empire, judging it better to dwell beneath
his sway than in their own country. They asked for
land, and they got it. And against barbarians he employed barbarians who thought it more honourable

linked with the conventional notion of Hermes as patron of
learning to indicate the pagan bias of this literary coterie in
Paris.

[d] The campaign of A.D. 358, described by Julian, *Ep. ad
S.P.Q.Ath.* 280 a ff., and Amm. Marc. 17. 8 ff., began with
operations against the Salian Franks and Chamavi.

τούτου διώκειν ἢ μετ᾽ ἐκείνων φεύγειν. 76. καὶ
ταυτὶ μὲν ἀμαχεί, γνοὺς δὲ πάλιν διαβαίνειν καὶ
σπάνει πλοίων ἵππους τε καὶ ὁπλίτας νεῖν ἀναγκάσας προῄει τὰ μὲν δῃῶν, τὰ δὲ κτώμενος,
ἐκώλυε δὲ οὐδείς. ὀψὲ δέ ποτε οἱ δυστυχεῖς
ἱκέτευον δέον πρὸ τοῦ πυρός. 77. ὁ δὲ ἥκειν τὴν
ἡμέραν νομίσας ᾗ τὰ τῶν Γαλατῶν θεραπεύσειν
ἔμελλε, τὸ μὲν πρῶτον αὐτοὺς ἀτίμως ἀπέπεμψεν,
ὡς δ᾽ αὖθις ἧκον αὐτοὺς ἄγοντες ἱκέτας τοὺς
βασιλεῖς καὶ τὸ σκῆπτρον ἔχοντες εἰς γῆν ἔκυπτον,
ἀναμνήσας τῆς πολλῆς ὕβρεως καὶ τῶν μυρίων
παθημάτων ὠνεῖσθαι τὴν εἰρήνην ἐκέλευε τῆς
ἰάσεως τῶν κακῶν πόλεις μὲν ἐγείροντας, σώματα
δὲ ἄγοντας. 78. οἱ δὲ ὡμολόγουν τε καὶ οὐκ
ἐψεύδοντο, καὶ ἐκομίζετο μὲν ξύλα τε καὶ σίδηρος
εἰς ἀνάστασιν οἰκιῶν, ἐλέλυτο δὲ πᾶς εἰς ἐπάνοδον
αἰχμάλωτος ὑπὸ τοῦ μαστιγοῦντος πρότερον θω-
πευόμενος ὅπως αὐτῷ μὴ μνησικακήσειεν, οὓς δὲ
οὐκ ἄγοιεν ὧν εἰλήφεσαν τεθνεῶτας ἐδείκνυον, τὸ
δὲ ἐν τούτοις | ἀληθὲς ὑπὸ τῶν ἀφειμένων ἐκρί- F 27
R 548 νετο. | 79. τοῖς μὲν δὴ μυρίοις[1] στρατιώταις
θάλαττα φανεῖσα τὸ πρῶτον μετὰ τὸ πλῆθος τῶν
ὁρῶν τε καὶ πόνων κραυγήν τε ἐκίνησε καὶ δάκρυα
σὺν χαρᾷ καὶ περιέβαλλον ἀλλήλους οἱ κοινωνοὶ
τῶν κινδύνων ἐκείνων, οὗτοι δὲ οὐ θάλατταν, ἀλλ᾽
ὡς εἶδον ἀλλήλους, ταὐτὸν ἔδρων, οἱ μὲν οἰκείους
ὁρῶντες ἐκφυγόντας δουλείαν, οἱ δ᾽ οἰκείους τε
καὶ τὴν οἰκείαν ἀπολαμβάνοντες. συνεδάκρυε δὲ

---

[1] μυρίοις Re., mss. : Κυρείοις F., Fabr.

---

[a] Suomarius and Hortarius : Amm. Marc. 17. 10. 3 ff.,
Zos. 3. 4.

to pursue in his company than to flee in theirs. 76. This much was achieved without a fight; but he resolved to cross the river again, and through lack of boats he set his infantry and cavalry to swim across. Then he advanced, ravaging and collecting booty, with none to say him nay. The wretched inhabitants at last offered a tardy submission, as they had to do or else be burned out. 77. But he felt that the day had come that should cure all the ills of Gaul, and so he at first sent them off contemptuously, but they came back again with their chieftains in person as suppliants, and the wielders of the sceptre abased themselves to the ground.[a] Then he reminded them of their long reign of terror and the incalculable damage they had wrought, and he told them to buy peace at the cost of healing the harm they had done, by rebuilding the towns and restoring the inhabitants. 78. They agreed to this and were true to their word. Timber and iron were brought to rebuild houses, and every captive set at liberty to return and, so that he would not bear malice, was cosseted by the man who had earlier flogged him. The captives whom they did not restore, they proved were dead, and the truth in this matter was decided by the testimony of those released. 79. In the army of the Ten Thousand, after their long toils and endless mountains, the first sight of the sea evoked shouts and tears of joy, and those who had shared those dangers embraced one another.[b] These folk now did the same at the sight not of the sea but of each other, as they saw their kinsfolk restored from slavery or as they recovered homes and kindred. Everyone else, who though not

[b] Xen. *Anab.* 4. 7. 21 ff.

καὶ ὅσον γένους μὲν αὐτοῖς οὐ μετεῖχεν, ἑώρα δὲ
τὰς περιπλοκάς, καὶ ἔρρει δάκρυα δακρύων ἀμείνω
ὧν τὰ μὲν ἦν διοικιζομένων πάλαι, τὰ δὲ συνιόντων
τότε.

80. Οὕτω Γαλάτας ὁ πόλεμος καὶ διέσπασε καὶ
συνήγαγεν, ὁ μὲν δειλίᾳ τῶν ἐφεστώτων, ὁ δὲ
ἀνδρίᾳ πολεμηθείς. καὶ βουλευτήρια δὲ ἐπίμπλατο
καὶ δῆμοι, καὶ τέχναι καὶ πόροι χρημάτων ηὔξοντο,
καὶ θυγατέρων ἐκδόσεις καὶ γάμοι νέων καὶ ἀποδη-
μίαι καὶ ἑορταὶ καὶ πανηγύρεις εἰς κόσμον τὸν ἔμ-
προσθεν ᾖεσαν. | 81. ὥστ᾽ εἴ τις οἰκιστὴν καλοίη τῶν F 2
πόλεων ἐκείνων τὸν ἄνδρα τοῦτον οὐκ ἂν ἁμαρτάνοι.
τὰς μὲν γὰρ ἤγειρεν οἰχομένας, ταῖς δὲ μικροῦ κεκε-
νωμέναις τοὺς οἰκήτορας ἀπέσωσε καὶ τὸ μηκέτι
τὸν ἴσον φοβεῖσθαι φόβον ἀπέδωκεν. οὔκουν
οὐδεὶς ἔτι βαρβάρων χειμῶνος ἐπελθόντος ἐπὶ τὰς
εἰωθυίας λῃστείας ἐξέπλευσεν, ἀλλ᾽ οἴκοι μένοντες τὰ
R 549 αὑτῶν ἤσθιον οὐκ αἰδοῖ συνθηκῶν μᾶλλον ἢ | φόβῳ
πολέμου, ἐπεὶ καὶ τοῖς οὔπω σπονδῶν τετυχηκόσι τὸ
προσδοκώμενον δέος ἡσυχάζειν παρῄνει.

82. Τίνα δὴ τὰ ἐπὶ τῆς ἡσυχίας; τὴν μεγίστην
τῶν ὑπὸ τὸν ἥλιον νῆσον ἣν ὠκεανὸς ἔχει τοῖς
λογισμοῖς ἑώρα καὶ πέμπει δὴ λογιστὰς τῆς
δαπάνης ἣ τοὔνομα μὲν ἦν στρατιωτική, τῷ δὲ
ἔργῳ πρόσοδος τῶν ἡγουμένων. καὶ τοὺς μὲν
ταῦτα ἀδικοῦντας δικαίους ἐποίησεν, ἕτερον δὲ
πολλῷ μεῖζον καὶ μάλιστα Γαλάταις σωτήριον.

---

[a] For Julian's concern with Britain in A.D. 359 cf. Julian,

connected by family ties yet saw their embraces, began to weep also, and tears flowed, tears far sweeter than those once shed at parting, for now they were tears of joy at their reunion.

80. In this way a war sundered the Gauls when it was fought under a cowardly commander and reunited them under a brave one. The council chambers and the commons of the cities were filled, and manufactures and financial revenues increased. Daughters were betrothed, young men got married, people travelled about, and holiday and festival gatherings regained their pristine splendour. 81. Thus, if this man were to be called the founder of those cities, the term would not be inappropriate, for some that had vanished he resurrected, to others that were almost depopulated he restored the inhabitants and granted them to have no such fear in future. So when winter came, no barbarian now sailed out on his usual forays. They stayed at home and ate their own stuff, not so much out of respect for agreements as of fear of war, since even those who had no treaty relations with us were warned to stay peaceful by the terror they anticipated.

82. And what of his activities in this peaceful time? He took counsel for the greatest of the islands under the sun, that lies surrounded by ocean.[a] He sent accountants there to supervise the expenditure that was nominally made upon military objectives but was in fact a source of revenue for the generals. He brought to heel those guilty of this misconduct, and he also did something else of much more importance and designed for the security of Gaul in particular.

*Ep. ad S.P.Q.Ath.* 279 d ff., Amm. Marc. 18. 2. 3 f., Zos. 3. 5.

83. τοῦ σίτου γὰρ ἀπὸ τῆς νήσου πάλαι φοιτῶντος μετὰ τὴν θάλατταν διὰ τοῦ 'Ρήνου καὶ τῶν βαρβάρων οὐκέτ᾽ ἐπειδήπερ ἴσχυσαν ἐπιτρεπόντων ὁλκάδες αἱ πάλαι μὲν ἀνειλκυσμέναι κατεσάπησαν, ὀλίγαι δὲ ἔπλεον, ὧν ἐν λιμέσι τὸν γόμον ἐξαιρουμένων ἁμάξας ἐχρῆν ἀντὶ τοῦ ποταμοῦ τῷ σίτῳ γενέσθαι, καὶ τὸ πρᾶγμα ἦν ἡ μεγίστη δαπάνη. τοῦτ᾽ | οὖν ἀνανεούμενος καὶ δεινὸν νομίζων εἰ μὴ πρὸς τἀρχαῖα καταστήσει τὴν σιτοπομπίαν, ναῦς τε ὀξέως ἔδειξε πλείους ἢ πρότερον καὶ διεσκοπεῖτο πῶς ἂν αὐτῷ δέξαιτο τὸν σῖτον ὁ ποταμός.

F

84. Ἐν τούτῳ δὲ ὄντος κλοπῆς ἐδίωκεν ἄρχοντα ἀρχόμενος, Φλωρέντιος δὲ ὡς μὲν ὕπαρχος ἐδίκαζεν, ὡς κλέπτειν δὲ εἰδὼς καὶ τότε εἰληφὼς ἐπὶ τὸν γραψάμενον τὴν ὀργὴν ἦγεν αἰδούμενος τὸν ὁμότεχνον. ὡς δὲ οὐκ ἐλάνθανεν ἀδικῶν, ἀλλ᾽ ἦσαν οἱ πρὸς ἀλλήλους φθεγγόμενοι | καὶ ὁ θροῦς αὐτῷ τὰ ὦτα ἐκέντει, τὸν βασιλέα δικαστὴν ἐκάθιζεν. ὁ δὲ τὰ πρῶτα ἔφυγεν, οὐ γὰρ αὐτῷ καὶ τοῦτο δεδόσθαι. 85. καὶ ταῦτα ἐποίει Φλωρέντιος οὐ τῷ τὰ δίκαια ἐψηφίσθαι, τῷ δὲ νομίζειν ἐκεῖνον αὐτῷ θήσεσθαι κἂν ἀδικεῖν δοκῇ. ὡς δὲ τῆς πρὸς αὐτὸν χάριτος πλέον εἶδεν ἐσχηκυῖαν τὴν ἀλήθειαν, ἤλγησέ τε τὴν ψυχὴν καὶ ἄνδρα ᾧ μάλιστα ἐχρῆτο διαβαλὼν γράμμασιν ὡς ἐπαίροντα τὸν νέον ἐξ-

R 550

---

a Julian had crossed swords with Florentius upon the question of imposing a *superindictio* on the Gallic provinces earlier in A.D. 358 (Amm. Marc. 17. 3). This incident, which occurred in winter 358/9, set the Caesar and his prefect still further at odds (*cf. Ep. ad S.P.Q.Ath.* 282 c). The ἀνδρόγυνος of *E.L.F.* No. 14 (384 d) may refer to him.

83. It had long ago been the practice to bring corn from the island, first by sea and then up the Rhine. Since the time the barbarians had gained control, they had not allowed it passage, and the ships had long been hauled ashore and left to rot. Some few continued to ply, but since they discharged their cargo in coastal ports, the corn had to be conveyed by waggons instead of river transport, and that was a very expensive undertaking. Julian therefore set about renewing the practice and was sadly disturbed should he not put the carriage of corn on its former footing. So he promptly produced more ships than before and considered means whereby the river should be opened up for the passage of his corn.

84. While he was engaged on this, one of the provincials began the prosecution of an official for peculation. Florentius, as prefect, presided over the case and, being himself well versed in the art of peculation and the recipient of a bribe in the present instance, he began to direct his anger against the prosecutor, out of respect for his partner in crime. Such misconduct did not go unobserved : people began to gossip about it and the noise of it began to disturb his ears, and so he tried to get the emperor to preside over the case. The emperor tried at first to avoid this duty, claiming that this was not one of the powers granted him. 85. This action of Florentius sprang not from being given a just verdict but from the notion that Julian would side with him, even if it appeared that he was in the wrong.[a] However, when he found that the force of truth counted for more with Julian than any partiality towards himself, he was sore at heart and, in his despatches, he traduced the emperor's intimate friend as encouraging the young

ἔβαλε τῶν βασιλείων, ὃς ἦν | ἀντὶ πατρὸς τῷ F 2
βασιλεῖ. 86. πάλιν τοίνυν τοῦτον ἐτίμησε λόγοις οἳ
τὴν ἐπὶ τῷ τότε χωρισμῷ κηρύττουσιν ἔτι λύπην,
καὶ ἅμα μὲν ἔστενεν, ἅμα δὲ τῶν ὑπολοίπων
εἴχετο. καὶ οὐκ ἐγένετο χείρων τὴν γνώμην
τοσαῦτα ἀδικούμενος. 87. οὐδ' ᾤήθη δεῖν ὧν ὑπὸ
τούτων ἔπασχε παρὰ τῆς Ῥωμαίων ἡγεμονίας
δίκην λαβεῖν, ἀλλὰ κατέβαινε μὲν ἐπ' αὐτὸν τὸν¹
ὠκεανόν, πόλιν δὲ Ἡράκλειαν, Ἡρακλέους ἔργον,
R 551 ἀνίστη. τὰ πλοῖα δὲ εἰς τὸν Ῥῆνον | εἰσῆγε τῶν
προσδοκωμένων κωλύσειν ἀποπνιγομένων μέν, εἴρ-
γειν δὲ οὐκ ἐχόντων. ὁ δὲ ἐχώρει τὴν τῶν
ἐνσπόνδων παρεξιών, ὅπως μὴ δι' αὐτῶν ἐπὶ τοὺς
πολεμίους ἰὼν ἀνάγκῃ τι βλάψειε. καὶ ἅμα τὰ
πλοῖα παρέπλει καὶ τῶν ἐναντίων ὁ στρατὸς
ἀντιπροσῄεσαν ὡς δὴ σχήσοντες ζευγνύναι πειρωμένων. 88. ἐνταῦθά μοί τις ἀθρείτω τὸν στρατη-
γικώτατον, καὶ ὡς οὐδὲν ἦν τῶν ἀμηχάνων ὃ μὴ
ῥάδιον ἐξήλεγχεν. ὡς γὰρ βαδίζων καὶ περι-
σκοπῶν τὴν ἀντιπέρας ὄχθην κατεῖδεν ἐπίκαιρον
τόπον | οἷον κατασχεθέντα παρέχειν ἀσφάλειαν τοῖς F 2
κατειληφόσι, πλοῖά τινα καὶ μοῖραν τῆς δυνάμεως
μικρὰν ἀφανῶς ἐν κοίλῳ τινὶ τῆς οἰκείας ὄχθης
χωρίῳ καταλιπὼν αὐτός τε ἐπορεύετο καὶ τοὺς
ἐχθροὺς ἠνάγκαζεν ἴσῃ πορείᾳ χωρεῖν, ἑσπέρας δὲ
στρατοπεδευσάμενος τοῖς καταλειφθεῖσιν ἐκείνοις
σημαίνει διαπλεύσασι κρατῆσαι τοῦ χωρίου. 89.

¹ τὸν inserted by Asmus.

334

man to be too big for his boots, and so expelled from
the palace one who was almost a father to the
emperor. 86. So once more he honoured him with a
speech that still expresses his grief at that separation
and in his grief he clung the closer to the friends left
to him : nor did his temperament succumb to such
injustice.[a] 87. Nor again did he think that he should
revenge himself upon the empire of Rome for the
wrongs he suffered at the hands of these people, but
he went right down to the coast and restored a city
called Heraclea, a labour of Heracles.[b] He brought
the corn convoys up the Rhine, while all who hoped
to stop him choked with rage but were unable to
prevent him. He continued his advance, skirting
the territory of the tribes at peace with him, so that
he would not have to harm them by attacking the
enemy through their land. So the fleet sailed on, and
the enemy army advanced in line with it to prevent
any attempt at bridging the river. 88. Here, if you
please, consider his consummate captaincy. There
was no impasse that he did not resolve with ease.
As he marched on and surveyed the opposite bank,
he observed a strategic point which, if taken, would
afford security to the occupying troops, and so he left
behind some boats and a small detachment of his
forces hidden in an inlet on his own side of the river,
while he himself advanced and compelled the enemy
to march parallel with him. In the evening, after
pitching camp, he signalled the party left behind to
cross and occupy the point. 89. They obeyed and

[a] Speech of consolation on the departure of Salustius,
*Or.* 8. 240 a ff. *Cf.* Julian, *Ep. ad S.P.Q.Ath.*, *loc. cit.*,
*E.L.F.* No. 14. 385 d, Zos. 3. 5.
[b] Amm. Marc. 18. 2. 4 ff. Libanius makes play with the
name.

καὶ οἱ μὲν πεισθέντες ἐκράτουν, οἱ δὲ ἀναστρέ-
ψαντες ἐζεύγνυον ὁρμώμενοί τε ἐξ οἰκείων καὶ
τελευτῶντες εἰς τὸ κατειλημμένον. ταῦτα τοῖς
βαρβάροις δόξαν πλειόνων γεφυρῶν ἐνέβαλε καὶ
τῶν περιεστηκότων αὐτοὺς κακῶν οὐκ ὀλίγα ἀγνοεῖν ἡγοῦντο. καὶ τότε δὴ τοὺς ἐπὶ τὴν εἰρήνην
καταφυγόντας ἐπήνουν καὶ ἧκον τῶν αὐτῶν ἐπὶ
τοῖς αὐτοῖς ἀξιοῦντες τυχεῖν, ὁ δὲ καὶ τὴν τούτων
αἴθων τε καὶ τέμνων, ἐπειδή ποτε ἐνεπλήσθη, διαλ-
λάττεται. καὶ πάλιν αἰχμαλώτων λύσεις καὶ τἆλλα
πάντα ἄχρι τῶν δακρύων ἐοικότα τοῖς πρώτοις.

90. Ἀντιλαβόντων δὴ τὰς τύχας ἀλλήλων Γαλατῶν τε καὶ τῶν ἐν κύκλῳ βαρβάρων καὶ τῶν μὲν
ἀνηνθηκότων, τῶν δὲ κατερρυηκότων καὶ τῶν μὲν
F 275 ἐν θαλίαις, | τῶν δὲ ἐν στεναγμοῖς | κειμένων καὶ R
τῶν μὲν ἀπολωλεκότων τὸ κράτος ὃ διὰ τέλους
ἕξειν ἐνόμιζον, τῶν δὲ ἀπειληφότων τὴν δύναμιν ἐφ'
ἧς οὐκέτ' ἤλπιζον ἔσεσθαι, καὶ πάσης φωνῆς ταὐτὸν ἀδούσης ὡς οὐχ ὅπλων ταυτὶ μᾶλλον ἢ τῆς
ἐκείνου διανοίας, ἦλθεν ἐπ' αὐτὸν φθόνος παρὰ τοῦ
στεφάνους ὀφείλοντος. καὶ τοῦ στρατοῦ τὸ μὲν
ἀκμάζον τε καὶ πρὸς τὰς χρείας ἕτοιμον ἐκάλει καὶ
μετεπέμπετο, τὸ δὲ παρηβηκός τε καὶ συνεισφέρον
ἀριθμὸν ἀντ' ἔργων εἴα μένειν. 91. πρόφασις δὲ ὁ
Περσικὸς πόλεμος καὶ τὸ μὴ δεῖσθαι τὴν Γαλατῶν
εἰρήνην στρατιωτῶν, ὥσπερ οὐ ῥᾳδίως ὅρκων
πατουμένων ὑπὸ βαρβάρων ἀπιστίας ἢ ὡς οὐ δέον

---

[a] Cf. Amm. Marc. 20. 4, Zos. 3. 8. 6.

gained control of it, and the rest retraced their steps and bridged the river, starting from their own side and finishing at the point just taken. This caused the barbarians to suppose that there were more bridges, and they began to think that they were beset by a number of troubles of which they had no idea. Then at last they concurred with those who had already had recourse to peace, and they came asking to receive the same treatment on the same terms. The emperor, burning and ravaging their lands, when satisfied at last, accepted their overtures: and once again there took place the release of prisoners, with all the incidentals and the tears as on the earlier occasion.

90. The situation in Gaul and in the surrounding barbarian tribes was now completely reversed. The Gauls had experienced a revival and were in high spirits, while the barbarians had suffered disaster and were in despair at losing the supremacy that they used to think was theirs for all time. Gaul had recovered the power she had never again expected to have, and it was on everyone's lips that this was the result not so much of military successes as of Julian's genius. As a consequence, he became the victim of the envy of the man who owed him his crowns of victory,[a] for he began to recall the pick of the army and those ready for any emergency, allowing only those past their prime, whose contribution was mere numbers instead of deeds, to stay with him. 91. The ostensible reason was the Persian war, and the fact that a now peaceful Gaul required no troops, as though it were not a simple matter for the treacherous barbarians to ride roughshod over their agreements and as if it were unnecessary

337

LIBANIUS

προσεῖναι ταῖς συνθήκαις τὸ παρὰ τῶν ὅπλων
ἐχυρόν. ἀλλ᾽, οἶμαι, στρατιᾶς μὲν μείζονος τῆς
αὐτῷ παρούσης ἐπὶ τοὺς Πέρσας οὐκ ἐδεῖτο.
μέρος τε γὰρ ἐκείνης ἐξήρκει καὶ πολλάκις τὴν
αὐτὴν ἀγείρας οὔποτ᾽ ἂν ἦλθε διὰ μάχης ἐγνωκὼς
ἀεὶ μέλλειν. 92. ἀλλ᾽ ἕτερος ἦν ὁ λογισμός. στῆ-
σαι γὰρ αὐτῷ καὶ τὰ ἔργα καὶ τὴν δόξαν ἤθελεν
αὐξομένην, μᾶλλον δὲ καὶ διαφθεῖραι τὴν ὑπάρ-
χουσαν ἐπαγαγὼν αὐτῷ τε καὶ τοῖς ὀλίγοις καὶ
σαπροῖς στρατιώταις τὴν τῶν βαρβάρων νεότητα.
93. ἐπεθύμει γὰρ τὸν ἐναντίον τῷ | τότε κομισθῆναι F 1
πανταχοῖ λόγον ὡς ὁ μὲν κατακέκλεισται καὶ
πολιορκεῖται, τοὺς πολεμίους δὲ οὐδὲν χωρεῖ, ἀλλ᾽
αἱροῦσι πόλεις καὶ κατασκάπτουσι πάλιν καὶ ἀροῦσι
καὶ σπείρουσι τὴν ἀλλοτρίαν. ᾔδει γὰρ ὡς εἰ καὶ
R 553 λίαν | στρατηγικὸς ἐκεῖνος ταὐτὸν ἂν πάθοι κυβερ-
νήτῃ μεγίστης νεὼς ἐστερημένῳ ναυτῶν. οὐδὲ
γὰρ ἡ 'κείνου τέχνη δύναιτ᾽ ἂν ἀνθ᾽ ὅλου πληρώ-
ματος γενέσθαι τῇ νηί. οὕτως ὁ βέλτιστος βασιλεὺς ἧς ἔδωκεν ἀρχῆς ἐφθόνει τῷ διασεσεικότι τὴν
βάρβαρον.
94. Πεσὼν τοίνυν εἰς ἀπορίαν ὁ γενναῖος ἐκεῖνος
καὶ τῷ τε πεισθῆναι καὶ μὴ τὸν ὄλεθρον ὁρῶν
ἀκολουθοῦντα, τό τε γὰρ γυμνωθῆναι τῆς δυνάμεως
τὴν παρὰ τῶν ἐναντίων εἶχε σφαγὴν τό τε ἔχεσθαι
τὴν παρὰ τῶν οἰκείων, μᾶλλον εἵλετο λειπόμενός[1]
τι παθεῖν ἢ δοκῶν ἀπειθεῖν κουφοτέραν κρίνων τὴν
παρὰ τῶν πολεμίων πληγὴν ἧς ἔμελλε πλήξειν ὁ
συγγενής. οὕτω δὴ πράττειν ἔδωκεν ἃ βούλοιντο
τοῖς τοῦ πρεσβυτέρου | κόλαξιν. οἱ δὲ ἀπ᾽ αὐτῶν F 2

[1] λειπόμενος Re. (mss. except for corrections in PU):
πειθόμενος F. (PU corrected).
338

for military backing to support the articles of peace. He clearly had no need of an army bigger than the one he had already to deal with Persia, for a section of that was enough for the job, and however many times he raised a force like it, he would never have gone into battle, for he was bent on procrastination. 92. No! His reasoning was something very different. He wanted to call a halt to Julian's activity and his rising fame, or rather to destroy the fame he had already won by inciting the barbarian warriors to attack him and his unreliable troops. 93. He desired a report exactly the reverse of the one then obtaining to be broadcast throughout the empire, namely that he was pent up, beleaguered, and that nothing could hold the barbarians who once again were capturing and demolishing cities, ploughing and sowing a land not their own. He knew that, even if Julian were one of the great commanders, he would be brought to the same pass as the helmsman of a great ship if he had no crew: for there too, his skill would not avail the ship without its full complement. So that fine emperor begrudged the power he had given to the one who had shaken heathendom to the core.

94. Hence our noble Julian was in a quandary. He saw disastrous consequences whether he obeyed or not, for to be stripped of his forces involved destruction at the hands of the enemy, their retenton involved it from his own side. Here he chose to have them leave him, come what might, rather than to give the appearance of disloyalty, for he judged that any blows inflicted by the enemy would be less serious than those from his own kinsman. Hence he allowed the toadies of his senior colleague a completely free hand, and they began with his personal

ἀρξάμενοι τῶν δορυφόρων καὶ οἷς μάλιστα ἐπί-
στευεν ἐκλέγοντες διὰ πάντων ᾔεσαν ἕως αὐτῷ
κατέλιπον ὁπλίτας εὔξασθαι μόνον δυναμένους.

95. Καὶ ὁ μὲν ἔστεργεν, οὐκ ἀδακρυτὶ μέν, ὅμως
δὲ ἠξίου φέρειν, κινουμένων δὲ πανταχόθεν τῶν
διεσπαρμένων λόχων οἰμωγὴ πανταχόθεν ᾔρετο
πρὸς οὐρανὸν πενήτων, εὐπόρων, οἰκετῶν, ἐλευθέρων, γεωργῶν, ἀστικῶν, ἀνδρῶν, γυναικῶν, νέων,
πρεσβυτέρων μόνον οὐκ εἰσβεβληκέναι τοὺς πολεμίους ἡγουμένων καὶ τὰ μόλις ἐκτμηθέντα κακὰ
πάλιν ἀναβλαστήσειν ἡγουμένων. μάλιστα δ' ἐξ
ὧν ἐγεγόνει τέκνα τοῖς στρατιώταις, αὗται δει-
κνῦσαι παιδία τά τε ἄλλα καὶ τὰ ἐν τῷ γάλακτι
καὶ ταῦτα ἀντὶ θαλλοῦ σείουσαι μὴ προδοῦναι σφᾶς
ἐδέοντο. 96. ταῦτα ὡς ἤκουσεν ὁ βασιλεύς,
R 554 παρῄνει τοῖς ἐξ Ἰταλίας | ἥκουσιν ἑτέραν ἄγειν
τοὺς στρατιώτας πολὺ τῆς πόλεως ἐν ᾗ καθῆστο
καὶ διέτριβεν ἀπέχοντας. ἐδεδίει γάρ, οἶμαι, μὴ
δράσειαν ὃ καλῶς ποιοῦντες ἔδρασαν. ὡς δὲ οὐ
προσεῖχον ἐκεῖνοι τοῖς λόγοις, ἀλλ' εἰσῆγον τοὺς
ἄκρους τῶν λόχων ὧν ἐξήρτηται τὸ λοιπόν, ὁ μὲν
ὄχλος αὐτῶν | ἅπας ἐδεῖτο καὶ μένειν καὶ σῴζειν F 27
ἅπαντα ὑπὲρ ὧν ἐπεπονήκεσαν, οἱ δὲ ἠλέουν τε

---

[a] *Cf.* Julian's own pungent comments, *Ep. ad S.P.Q.Ath.*
280 d ff. A detailed account of this incident and its consequences appears in Amm. Marc. 20. 4 ff. Zosimus, it
may be noted, applies this description to Julian's original
bodyguard (3. 3. 3).

[b] Libanius here combines two uses of θαλλός, (i) the olive
branch of supplication (a common usage in drama), (ii) the
proverbial waving of branches of greenstuff to entice cattle

bodyguard and his most reliable troops and worked through the whole army removing detachments, until they left him, for infantry, men just about able to muster up a prayer.[a]

95. This he put up with, not without heartburnings, it is true. Still, put up with it, he did. But when the separate drafts were everywhere sent on the move, everywhere there rose to heaven cries of lamentation from rich and poor, slave and free, peasant and townsman, women and men, young and old. They felt that their enemies had practically begun to invade again already, and that the troubles excised with such difficulty would once more rear their heads. Those women especially who had borne children to the soldiers pointed to their children, not least to the babes at the breast dandled then before them and begged their fathers not to desert them.[b]

96. Hearing of this, the emperor advised the commission from Italy to march the troops off by another route far from the city where he had fixed his headquarters and was in residence.[c] He clearly was afraid they would react in the way they did—and quite properly did. However, they ignored his warnings and persisted in concentrating there the cream of the regiments on whom all the rest depended. Then the whole populace began to beg them to stay and protect everything they had worked for, and the soldiers began to pity them for their pleas and to

home (cf. Plat. Phaedr. 230 D, imitated by Lucian, Hermot. 68, Philostr. V.S. 587, Athen. Deipn. 1. 46 (p. 25 b). The second has more immediate impact here, since many of Julian's best troops were enrolled on terms that they should not serve outside Gaul (Amm. Marc. 20. 4. 4).

[c] Decentius stupidly insists on a rendez-vous at Paris (Amm. Marc. loc. cit.).

τοὺς κελεύοντας[1] καὶ ἐδυσχέραινον τὴν ὁδόν. 97.
αἰσθόμενος δὲ ὁ βασιλεὺς εἶπεν ἐν αὐτοῖς ἀπὸ τοῦ
εἰωθότος πρὸ τῆς πόλεως βήματος ὡς οὐκ εἴη
βουλὴ περὶ ὧν ἤδη τῷ κρείττονι δέδοκται. μακρὸν
δὲ ἐκεῖνοι σιωπῇ δεξάμενοι λόγον καὶ προσειπόντες
οὐδὲν ἐσπέρας ἤδη, μᾶλλον δὲ περὶ μέσας νύκτας
ὅπλα ἐνδύντες περιστάντες τὸ βασίλειον ἐβόων
διδόντες τὴν μείζω τάξιν τε καὶ προσηγορίαν.
98. ὁ δὲ ἠγανάκτει μὲν τοῖς γιγνομένοις, δρᾶσαι δὲ
ἦν οὐδὲν ἕτερον πλὴν τοῦ μηδένα τῶν ἔνδον μοχλῶν
ἐᾶν ἅπτεσθαι. φανείσης δὲ ἡμέρας ἀνασπάσαντες
τὰς θύρας καὶ ξίφη δεικνύντες εἶλκον αὐτὸν ἐπὶ
ταὐτὸ βῆμα, καὶ μάχη μακρὰ λογισμῶν καὶ βοῆς,
τοῦ μὲν οἷς ἡγεῖτο κωλύσειν διεξιόντος, τῶν δὲ
ἀξιούντων τῇ κραυγῇ νικᾶν. 99. φεύγοντος δὲ τὴν
ταινίαν τὴν χρυσῆν καὶ καταφεύγοντος ἐπὶ τὸν
ἀρχαῖον νόμον ἀνήρ τις μέγας καὶ τἆλλα βέλτιστος
ὄπισθεν αὐτῷ παραστὰς οἷον εἶχε στρεπτὸν περὶ τῇ
'κείνου τίθησι κεφαλῇ, καὶ ἐδέδοτο τὰ μείζω. τῆς
τοίνυν ἀνάγκης ἡττηθεὶς καὶ τοσούτων ὁπλιτῶν
ὁρμὴν ζέουσαν οὐ | δυνηθεὶς προκαταπαῦσαι τοῦ F 2
R 555 φρονήματος εὐθὺς | ἀπὸ τῶν ταῦτα δεδωκότων
ἤρξατο. 100. ἀντὶ γὰρ τοῦ ζητεῖν ὅν τινα σφίσι
δώσει μισθὸν καὶ δώροις μεγάλοις κολακεύειν, ὅτι
νόμον ἡγητέον τὴν αὐτοῦ γνώμην ἐκήρυξε. δοκεῖν

---

[1] κελεύοντας Re. (mss. except for U and correction in P):
ἱκετεύοντας F. (U, P corrected).

---

[a] Libanius here omits to mention the divine guidance that
Julian (284 c) received, identified by Ammianus (20. 5. 10)
with the vision of the Genius Populi Romani.

grumble at the journey. 97. Perceiving this, the
emperor addressed them from the usual platform
outside the city : the decision of his superior, he said,
could not be reconsidered. He spoke at length and
they heard him in silence without saluting him at all,
but during the evening, or rather, about midnight,
they gathered under arms, surrounded his headquarters and begun to offer him the superior rank and
title of Augustus. 98. He was angry at this happening, but could do nothing beyond forbidding anyone
indoors to unfasten the bolts.[a] When day dawned,
they broke in the doors, and displaying their swords,
dragged him to the same platform. Then there
occurred a long exchange of argument and shouting,
he giving an explanation with arguments calculated
to put an end to this, they trying to get their way by
crying them down. 99. While he refused the golden
diadem, making ancient custom the grounds for so
doing,[b] a tall fellow, a most notable person, who was
standing behind him, placed on his head a torque such
as he himself was wearing, and therewith was
granted the supreme power. Then yielding to
necessity and unable to quench the burning passion
of so many troops, he immediately gave a demonstration of his resolve with those who had granted him
this. 100. For instead of looking round for a reward
to give them and courting them with massive
donatives, he issued a proclamation that his will was

[b] He also presents Julian's refusal of the diadem as due
to regard for constitutional propriety. Ammianus (20. 4.
17 f.) clearly indicates that it was also an appeal to military
pride : " eoque adfirmante primis auspiciis non congruere
aptari muliebri mundo." Eunap. (*F.H.G.* vol. V, *fr.* 14)
implies that the proclamation at Paris was a put-up job,
engineered by Julian.

τοίνυν αὐτῷ μηδένα τῶν ἠναντιωμένων τοῖς πεπραγμένοις μηδεμίαν ἀπαιτεῖν δίκην μηδὲ ξίφος ἐπ᾽
αὐτοὺς ἕλκειν μηδὲ βλέμματι φοβεῖν μηδὲ ῥήματι
λυπεῖν, ἀλλ᾽ οἷς ἂν ἐχρῶντο πρὸς αὐτοὺς κεκοι-
νωνηκότας, ταῦτα ποιεῖν πρὸς μεμαχημένους. 101.
καίτοι τίς οὐκ ἂν καὶ ῥᾳθυμοῦντας παρώξυνεν;
ἀλλ᾽ οὐκ ἐκεῖνος. οὐδενὶ γὰρ αἵματι τὴν βασι-
R 556 λείαν ἐβουλήθη τυραννίδος ἐγκλήματι | μολῦναι.
διὰ ταῦτα ἐπέταξε σωφρονεῖν. καὶ παρῆσαν αὖθις
οἱ τρέμοντες φαιδροὶ καὶ τεθαρρηκότες καὶ περιει-
στήκεσαν τὸν θρόνον τοῦ μὴ τεθνάναι χάριν εἰδότες.
102. ὧν οὐ προσηκούσας ἀμοιβὰς ἀπέδωκαν· ἀντὶ
γὰρ εὐεργεσίας οὐκ ἔδησαν[1] κατὰ τὴν παροιμίαν,
ἀλλ᾽ ἐβουλήθησαν ἀποκτεῖναι τῶν εὐνούχων τὸν
μάλιστα περὶ τὴν | εὐήν ἐλπίσιν ἀναπτερώσαντες. F 2
ἤδη δὲ ὄντος ἐγγὺς τοῦ φόνου στρατιώτης ἐξ
Ἀπόλλωνος ἐσείετο καὶ τὸ γενησόμενον ᾔδη καὶ
συνεκάλει τὸν ὄχλον εἰς ἐπικουρίαν, οἱ δὲ ἔθεόν τε
καὶ τὸ συντεθὲν ἀνίχνευον. καὶ τὸ μέγιστον, οὐδὲ
ὁ ταῦτα ὑπηρετῶν ἀπεσφάττετο. 103. ὁρῶν δὲ
τοὺς τἀκείνου φρονοῦντας ἐγγύθεν ἐπιβουλεύοντας
καί που καὶ τολμῶντας λέγειν ὡς ἄρα ἄμεινον εἰς
τὰ πρότερα καταβῆναι καὶ τῶν παρόντων ἀπο-
στῆναι, θεοὺς μόνους ἀξιόχρεως ἐν τοῖς τηλικούτοις

---

[1] ἔδησαν F. (VUIB corrected) : ἐδέησαν Re. (other mss.).

[a] Cf. Julian, 285 cd.
[b] A misinterpretation of the incident narrated by Ammianus (20. 4. 20 ff.). There the cause is wild rumour : no
plot exists and no investigation takes place. In Libanius'
information, there is confusion between the military *excubitor*

to be regarded as law, and it was his decree that
none should try to punish anyone who had opposed
the recent events[a]: no sword was to be drawn
against them, no intimidating looks or threatening
word directed towards them: their opponents must
be treated in exactly the same way as their supporters. 101. Any other man would have incited
them on against them, even if they were lukewarm.
But not Julian! He had no desire to defile his reign
with the shedding of blood, a charge to be levelled
against a usurper. Hence he demanded restraint.
Those who had retired in panic made their reap-
pearance, full of smiles and confidence, and they
stood around his throne, thankful to have escaped
execution. 102. But for this they made no fitting
return, for they did not, as the saying goes, oblige
him by way of recompense for his kindness, but they
plotted to murder him by inflating with great
expectations that one of his eunuchs who was most
closely in attendance at his bed. But when the time
for the deed drew near, a soldier became possessed
by Apollo and foretold the mischief afoot, and called
the people to aid. They came to the rescue and
tracked down the plot, and, to cap it all, not even
the eunuch who served as their instrument was
put to death.[b] 103. Julian saw the sympathizers
of Constantius lying in wait for him close by and
even having the impudence to suggest at times that
it would, after all, be better for him to return to the
earlier arrangement and to quit his present position,
and he felt that under such circumstances the only
reliable advice was that of the gods. So he made

(so Ammianus) and the *cubiculi praepositus* (τῶν εὐνούχων τὸν
μάλιστα περὶ τὴν εὐνήν).

ἡγησάμενος συμβούλους ἐρόμενος ἤκουσεν ὡς ἐμ-
μενετέον οἷς εἶχε. 104. λαβὼν δὴ ψῆφον τὴν ἐξ
οὐρανοῦ καὶ τὴν κοινὴν τῆς δυνάμεως ἄρχοντάς
τε ἐπὶ τὰς πόλεις ἐξέπεμπεν ἀντὶ πονηρῶν μὲν
R 557 ἀγαθούς, ἀντὶ δὲ σκαιῶν πεπαιδευμένους | καὶ
στρατόπεδον ἀπὸ τῶν ληστεύειν ἠναγκασμένων
συνήγαγεν, οἳ Μαγνεντίῳ συναράμενοι τοῦ κινδύνου
πράξαντες κακῶς τὰς ὁδοὺς κατειλήφεσαν ἀδίκοις
τρεφόμενοι πόροις. τούτους ἐφ᾽ ὅπλα καλέσας καὶ
δοὺς ἄδειαν φανῆναι τοὺς μὲν τοῦ παρανομεῖν ἀπήλλαξε, τοὺς δὲ ὁδοιπόρους τῶν φόβων. 105. ἐλθὼν δ᾽
ἐπὶ τὸν Ῥῆνον καὶ δείξας τοῖς βαρβάροις τὴν κεφα-
λὴν καὶ δευτέροις ὅρκοις | τὰς ὁμολογίας ἐνδήσας F 2
ἔτρεχεν ἐπὶ τὸν ἀκούσιον ἀγῶνα, μᾶλλον δ᾽ ἐπὶ τὴν
ἄνευ τῆς πρὸς τὸν οἰκεῖον μάχης τοῦ σκήπτρου
διαδοχήν· ᾔδει γὰρ παρὰ τῶν θεῶν ἀκούσας ὃ συμβήσεται.

106. Ἀλλὰ γὰρ ὑπερέβην τι τῶν ἀξίων εἰρῆσθαι.
τοῦτο δὴ λεκτέον. πρεσβειῶν γὰρ οὐκ ὀλίγων
ἀμφοτέρωθεν γενομένων, ὧν αἱ μὲν ἐκεῖθεν ἠξίουν
ἐπὶ τοῦ σχήματος μένοντα μηδὲν ἔργῳ πλέον ἢ
πρόσθεν ἔχειν, αἱ δ᾽ ἐνθένδε πάντως δεῖν ἀφίστασθαι τῆς τιμῆς καὶ διὰ πάντων εἶναι τὸν πρότερον,
ἐν τούτῳ δὲ ἦν αὐτὸν ἀπολωλέναι καὶ τοῦ στρατοπέδου τὸ πλέον καὶ συνήθεις καὶ φίλους, τῷ δὲ
τῆς μὲν αὑτοῦ σφαγῆς βραχὺς ἦν ὁ λόγος, δεινὸν
δὲ ἐδόκει προδότην καταστῆναι τῶν φιλτάτων.
107. ἐπειδὴ ταῦτα ἦν καὶ πάλιν ἐπὶ ταὐτὸ πάλαισμα
R 558 Κωνστάντιος ἀφῖκτο | καλῶν γράμμασι τοὺς βαρ-

---

[a] Libanius' version of the exploits of Charietto in previous
years : cf. Zos. 3. 7.

enquiry of them and received the reply that he should retain the position he held. 104. After getting a verdict from heaven and that of all the army, he sent out to the various states good governors in the place of bad, and men of culture instead of dunces. He also mustered an army from those who had been forced into banditry after sharing in the venture and failure of Magnentius, when they had beset the roads and made a living by unlawful means. These then he called to arms and, granting them to show themselves with impunity, he released them from their life of crime and wayfarers from their fears.[a] 105. Then he marched to the Rhine, showed his imperial person to the barbarians and, confirming his agreements with fresh oaths, he hastened to the struggle forced upon him, or, to be more precise, to succeed to the throne without coming to blows with his kinsman, for he had been forewarned by the gods and knew what was to come

106. However, I have omitted a matter worthy of mention and of it I must now speak. Several envoys came and went on both sides, those from Julian proposing that he should retain his present status, but with no more actual power than he had had before, those from Constantius requiring the comple abdication of his new title and the return, in every particular, to his previous station. This involved the destruction of himself, of most of his army, and of his friends and intimates, and, though Julian had but slight regard for his own life, he was most reluctant to turn traitor to all that he held dear.[b] 107. In this situation Constantius resorted to the same trick of calling in the

---

[b] For the negotiations of A.D. 360/1 cf. Amm. Marc. 20. 8 ff., Zos. 3. 9, Zonaras 13. 10. 16 ff.

βάρους ἦ πρότερον καὶ χάριν αἰτῶν καταδουλοῦ-
σθαι τὴν Ῥωμαίων, ἔπειθεν ἐπιορκεῖν ἐκ πολλῶν
ἕνα. ὁ δὲ ὁμοῦ μὲν ἐλήστευεν, ὁμοῦ δὲ ἐν τοῖς
ἀγροῖς οὓς εἰλήφει μισθὸν ἐτρύφα καὶ ὡς ἂν |
ἄκακός τις συνεδείπνει τοῖς ἐνθένδε στρατηγοῖς. 108. F 2
καὶ τὸν μὲν λῦσαι τὰς σπονδὰς ὑπομείναντα πίνοντα
εἶχε, διαβὰς δὲ εἰς τὴν ἐκείνου δίκην ἐπέθηκε
τῆς ἐπιορκίας οὐ μεμπτήν. συνδραμόντων δὲ περι-
φόβων τῶν τὰ δίκαια τετηρηκότων καὶ τοῖς ἁμαρ-
τήμασιν ἐκείνου δεινῶς αἰσχυνομένων καὶ προσ-
τιθέντων ὅρκοις ὅρκους ἀναβὰς ἐπὶ βῆμα ὑψηλὸν
ἐν μέσῃ τῇ βαρβάρῳ καὶ τοὺς ἐκείνων ἄρχοντας
ἄνωθεν ὁρῶν ἐν ὑπηκόων τάξει μετὰ τῶν πολλῶν
ἑστηκότας τὰ μὲν ἀναμνήσας, τὰ δὲ ἀπειλήσας
ἀπῆλθε. 109. καὶ ἤδη δύναμις συνείλεκτό τις ἧς
οὐ τὸ πλῆθος μᾶλλον ἄν τις ἢ τὴν προθυμίαν
ἠγάσθη. οἳ συνθήκαις τε καὶ δεξιαῖς ἀλλήλους
κατελάμβανον ἦ μὴν πᾶν μὲν ποιήσειν, πᾶν δὲ
πείσεσθαι ὑπὲρ νίκης, φοβηθῆναι δὲ ἓν μόνον, τὴν
ἐκ τοῦ μὴ φυλάξαι γενησομένην αἰσχύνην.

110. Τοῦ δὲ ὅρκου διὰ πάντων χωροῦντος Νεβρί-
διός τις ἀνήρ, μᾶλλον δὲ ἀνδρόγυνος, ὕπαρχος ὢν
παρὰ τοῦ πρεσβυτέρου τοῦτο λαβών, ἐπετίμα τοῖς
γιγνομένοις καὶ τὸν ὅρκον ἐμέμφετό τε καὶ ἔφευγε
βαρβάρους καλῶν τοὺς ὀμωμοκότας. οὕτως ἐκο-
λάκευε. πᾶσαν δὲ ὀργὴν ἐφελκυσάμενος καὶ χεῖρα
R 559 καὶ δικαίως | ἂν κατακοπεὶς ὑπὸ τοῦ πρώτου
πλήξαντος ἂν | εἰκότως ὥσπερ νεφέλῃ καλυφθεὶς F 2

---

[a] Vadomarius : cf. Amm. Marc. 21. 4, Julian, *Ep. ad
S.P.Q.Ath.* 286 ab.
[b] As in the *Iliad* hard-pressed mortals are sometimes

barbarians by letter as he had done before, and begging them as a favour to enslave Roman territory. One out of many he induced to break his word, and he began to ravage and also to make merry in the lands he had got as his reward, and he went to dine with the generals on our side as though he had done nothing wrong at all.[a] 108. This fellow, who had dared break the treaty, he arrested in his cups and, crossing over into his territory, inflicted a well-deserved punishment for his treachery. Those who had bided loyally by their agreements gathered in alarm, greatly ashamed at such misconduct, and added oath upon oath, and he mounted a tribunal in the middle of barbarian country, gazed down upon their chieftains who stood as subjects with their hordes of followers, and after issuing threats and reminders, took his leave. 109. By now he had assembled a force remarkable not so much in numbers as in morale. The men bound each other by compacts and agreements to go to every length and endure every hardship to ensure victory, and to fear only the disgrace that would be the consequence of negligence.

110. The oath was being administered to all and sundry when a man, or rather a creature half man, half woman, called Nebridius, appointed prefect by Constantius, disapproved of what was going on and refused to take the oath, describing those who did so as barbarians—such a sycophant was he ! He brought upon himself universal anger and physical threat, and though he deserved to be cut in pieces by the first man who had reason enough to strike him, he was saved enveloped in cloud, as it were.[b] Human-

whisked away by divine intervention (*e.g.*, Paris, 3. 381 ; Aeneas, 5. 345), Julian covered Nebridius with his robe.

LIBANIUS

διεσώζετο. καὶ μέμψαιτο μὲν ἄν τις τὴν ἐνταῦθα
φιλανθρωπίαν, ἡ δ' οὖν φιλανθρωπία τοῦ βασιλέως
ἡμῖν τοσαύτη.

111. Ἐκεῖθεν τοίνυν ὥσπερ χειμάρρους ἐφέρετο
παντὸς ἐμποδίσματος κρείττων ἀεὶ γιγνόμενος,
γεφύρας προκαταλαμβάνων, καθεύδουσιν ἐφιστά-
μενος, ἄλλοσε μὲν αὐτοὺς ἀναγκάζων βλέπειν,
κατόπιν δὲ αὐτοῖς προσιών, ἐλπίζειν μὲν ἕτερα
ποιῶν, πειρᾶσθαι δὲ ἄλλων, ἠπείρῳ μὲν χρώμενος
οὐχ ὁρωμένων ποταμῶν πλέων δὲ σὺν ὀλίγοις
ἡνίκα ἐξείη, τοὺς μὲν ἐν τοῖς ὅροις ἐῶν καθῆσθαι,
τὰς πόλεις δὲ αὐτὰς ἔχων ὧν προβέβληντο, πείθων,
βιαζόμενος, ἐξαπατῶν· οἷον γὰρ αὖ κἀκεῖνο· ὧν
ἐκράτησε στρατιωτῶν ὅπλοις τοὺς ἑαυτοῦ κοσμή-
σας ἔπεμπεν ἐπὶ πόλιν εὖ πεφραγμένην, οἱ δὲ
οἰκείους τε ἡγοῦντο τοὺς προσιόντας καὶ τὰς πύλας
ἀνοίξαντες ἐδέχοντο τοὺς ἐναντίους. 112. τὸ δὲ
πάντων ἥδιστον, ὅτι προσλαβὼν μὲν Ἰταλίαν τὴν
καλήν, προσλαβὼν δὲ Ἰλλυριοὺς τοὺς μαχιμωτά-
τους καὶ πόλεις πολλάς τε καὶ ἰσχυρὰς καὶ χώραν
ἀρκοῦσαν εἰς βασιλείαν μεγάλην οὐδαμοῦ μάχης
ἐδεήθη καὶ φόνων, ἀλλ' ἀπέχρησεν ἡ φρόνησις καὶ
τὸ ποθεῖσθαι τὸν ἄρχοντα. 113. μεγίστη δὲ συμ-
μαχία | τὰ τοῦ δειλοῦ καὶ προδότου γράμματα F
πρὸς τοὺς βαρβάρους ἃ πλέων τε καὶ πεζεύων
R 560 ἀνεγίνωσκε μὲν πόλεσιν, ἀνεγίνωσκε | δὲ στρατο-
πέδοις παρεξετάζων τοὺς αὐτοῦ πόνους ταῖς καλαῖς
ἐπιστολαῖς. αἱ δὲ τῷ μὲν ἐξεπολέμουν τὸν ἀκού-
οντα, τῷ δὲ προσετίθεσαν καὶ ταῦτα πολλοστὸν

---

ᵃ Ammianus speaks with some admiration of Nebridius'
loyalty here : 21. 5. 11 f.

350

ity in these circumstances might perhaps be censured, but the humanity of our emperor reached proportions like that.[a]

111. Thenceforeward he rushed on like a torrent,[b] always surmounting every obstacle, gaining control of bridges, surprising the defenders in their sleep and forcing them to fix their attention elsewhere while he came upon them from the rear: he caused them to expect one thing and experience something very different, making use of land when rivers were not to be seen but sailing down them with his small force whenever possible, leaving the frontier garrisons undisturbed but occupying the cities they were set to defend by the use of persuasion, force or stratagem. For instance, on one occasion he equipped his own troops with the armour of soldiers he had captured and sent them against a strongly fortified city, and the inhabitants opened their gates and admitted their opponents, thinking they were their own troops approaching. 112. Best of all, he gained control of the pleasant land of Italy and the warlike Illyrians—many strong cities and an area enough to form an empire in itself—and nowhere had he need to resort to fighting and bloodshed: his quick wits and the desire for him as their emperor was sufficient. 113. The despatches sent by the cowardly, treacherous Constantius to the barbarians were of the greatest assistance to him, for as he sailed or marched along, he read these out to the cities and the garrisons, contrasting his own labours with such fine missives as these. These aroused the hostility of the hearers against Constantius and gave Julian their support,

---

[b] For the advance along the Danube in summer A.D. 361 cf. Amm. Marc. 21. 8 ff., Zos. 3. 10.

ἄγοντι μέρος τῆς ἐκείνου στρατιᾶς. 114. ἀλλ'
ὅμως ἀφίσταντο μὲν Μακεδόνες εὐθέως, ἀφίστατο
δὲ ἡ Ἑλλὰς καὶ τὸν καιρὸν ἥρπαζεν ὃν ᾔτει παρὰ
τῶν θεῶν σιγῇ τε καὶ βωμῶν χωρίς, οὐ γὰρ ἦσαν.
ἀνεῴγνυτο δὴ νεώς τε ὁ τῆς Ἀθηνᾶς καὶ οἱ τῶν
ἄλλων θεῶν τοῦ βασιλέως ἀνοίγοντός τε καὶ τι-
μῶντος ἀναθήμασι καὶ αὐτοῦ τε θύοντος καὶ τοὺς
ἄλλους παρακαλοῦντος. 115. εἰδὼς δὲ ὡς καὶ θεοὶ
παρ' Ἀθηναίοις ἐκρίθησαν, εὐθύνας ἠξίωσε δοῦναι
τῶν πεπραγμένων, καὶ τοὺς Ἐρεχθείδας ὁ βασιλεὺς ἐποίει δικαστὰς πέμπων ἀπολογίαν ἐν γράμμασι. τυράννου μὲν γὰρ ἕρμαιον ἥγεῖτο τὸ μὴ
κρίνεσθαι, βασιλέως δὲ τὸ περὶ ὧν ἔδρασεν εἰς λόγον καθίστασθαι. ὁδοῦ δὲ πάρεργον, στάσιν ἐμ-
πεπτωκυῖαν ἱεροῖς γένεσι διαστᾶσαν τρόπον τινὰ
τὴν πόλιν ἐπιστολαῖς ἔπαυσεν, ὡς ἂν ἐν ὁμονοίᾳ
καὶ καθ' ἡσυχίαν τὰ πάτρια τελοῖτο τοῖς κρείττοσι.|

116. Καὶ Ἀθηναῖοι μὲν ἔθυόν τε χρόνιοι καὶ τοῖς F
θεοῖς ηὔχοντο ταῦτα ἃ καὶ μηδενὸς εὐχομένου
δώσειν ἔμελλον, ὁ δὲ ἤλαυνε τρίχα διελὼν τὴν
δύναμιν καὶ ταῦτα τῆς Θρᾴκης ὑπὸ τῶν ἐναντίων
κατειλημμένης· ἤλπιζε γὰρ τῶν μὲν εὐθὺς κρατήσειν, ἐλθὼν δὲ ἐπὶ τὸν Βόσπορον τὸ διαπλέον
σχήσειν. 117. τῷ δὲ ἄρα ἀγγέλους ἐκ Κιλικίας |
R 561 ἔφερον ἵπποι φράσοντας τὴν ἐπὶ ταῖς Κρήναις τοῦ

---

ᵃ Cf. Socr. H.E. 3. 1.

ᵇ Julian, Ep. ad S.P.Q.Ath. 268 a ff.  Cf. E.L.F. No. 20.
Corinth (Liban. Or. 14. 29 f.) and Rome (Amm. Marc. 21.
10. 7) also received similar manifestos.

ᶜ Julian halted at Naissus to consolidate and regroup,

even though his army was but a fraction of the other's.[a] 114. But despite that, Macedonia came over to his side straightaway, and so did Greece: she took the opportunity for which she had prayed to the gods in silence and without resorting to their altars, for there were none. The temple of Athena and those of the other gods were reopened by the emperor's hand and he honoured them with offerings, making sacrifice in person and bidding others to do likewise. 115. And, knowing that the Athenians had sat in judgement even over gods, he thought fit to give account of his conduct, and so the emperor set up the descendants of Erechtheus as his judges, sending them his defence in writing, for he felt that it was a godsend for a tyrant to be immune from judgement: an emperor should be called to account for his actions.[b] Incidental to his journey, by his despatches he put an end to a quarrel that had broken out between the priestly families and was tending to cause faction in the city, so that they could perform the time-honoured ritual to the higher powers in peace and concord.

116. And at long last the Athenians began to offer sacrifice and prayers to the gods for what they intended to give even without any prayer. Meantime he divided his forces into three and continued his advance, despite the fact that Thrace had been occupied by the enemy, for he hoped to get the better of them immediately and, upon reaching the Bosporus, to gain control of the crossing. 117. But just then couriers reached him from Cilicia with the news of Constantius' death at Crenae[c]: while he was

and there heard the news of Constantius' death at Mopsucrene: Amm. Marc. 21. 10 ff.

πρεσβυτέρου τελευτὴν ὃν ἀπειλοῦντα μείζω τοῦ
Ξέρξου καὶ περὶ τοῦ τί χρήσεται τῷ σώματι τοῦ
πολεμίου σκοποῦντα, τὸν γὰρ ἀντεπιόντα ἔχειν ἡ-
γεῖτο πρὶν ἑλεῖν, Ζεὺς ὁ κατὰ Σοφοκλέα μεγάλης
γλώσσης κόμπους ὑπερεχθαίρων νόσῳ πεδή-
σας ἀπήνεγκε. 118. τοῖς μὲν οὖν ἄλλοις πλάσμα
τε ὁ λόγος ἐδόκει καὶ παράκρουσις καὶ μηχάνημα
καὶ δεῖν ἀπιστεῖν, ὁ δὲ ἐκ κιβωτίου τινὸς βιβλίον
μεταπεμψάμενος ἐδείκνυ λόγια πρεσβύτερά τε πολὺ
τῆς ἀγγελίας καὶ τῇ τότε ἀγγελίᾳ βεβαιούμενα καὶ
ὡς θεοῦ | πέμποντος ἤρχοντο καθαρὰν αἵματος F
αὐτῷ τὴν νίκην ἐπηγγελμένου καὶ παραινοῦντος
ἐπείγεσθαι τοῦ μή τινα τολμῆσαι μακρὰν ἀπόντος
τὴν βασιλείαν ἁρπάσαι. 119. ἀναγινώσκων τοίνυν
καὶ τὸν πόλεμον ὁρῶν οὕτω καλὴν καὶ πολλοῦ
τινος ἀξίαν λαβόντα κρίσιν καὶ τελευτὴν ἀκούων
ἀνθρώπου συὸς ἀγρίου θυμὸν ἐπ' αὐτὸν ἔχοντος
οὐκ ἐπὶ θοίνην καὶ πότον καὶ τὰς ἀπὸ τῶν μίμων
ἡδονὰς ἐτράπετο, ἀλλ' ἐκβεβηκότων μὲν τῶν
χρησμῶν, γῆς δὲ καὶ θαλάττης ὑπ' αὐτῷ γεγενη-
μένης, ἀντιβλέποντος δὲ οὐδενός, ἑνὸς δὲ εἶναι τὰ
πάντα πάντων ὁμολογούντων, οὐδὲν δὲ ἀναγκα-
σθεὶς ὧν οὐκ ἐβούλετο δρᾶσαι, πάντων δὲ αὐτῷ
βασιλείων ἀνεῳγμένων εἰς θρῆνον κατηνέχθη καὶ
δάκρυα κατὰ τῶν λογίων ἔρρει. 120. καὶ οὐδὲν
ἦν ἰσχυρότερον τῆς φύσεως, ἀλλ' ἐρώτημα πρῶτον
ὁ νεκρὸς καὶ ποῦ τὸ σῶμα καὶ εἰ τιμᾶται τὰ
εἰκότα. οὕτως ἦν χρηστὸς περὶ τὸν τὰ τοῦ Κρέον-

---

[a] Soph. *Ant.* 127.

[b] The oracle is quoted by Amm. Marc. 21. 2. 2, Zos. 3. 9,
Zonaras 13. 11, and by Scholiast (B) on the present passage.

bandying about more threats than ever Xerxes did and was considering how to treat the person of his enemy, for he fancied he had his attacker before ever he got him caught, Zeus,—to use Sophocles' words—" in fierce anger at the boasts of his braggart tongue," [a] smote him with illness and carried him off. 118. Now everyone else believed the report to be a fiction, a deception and snare, something not to be trusted. He, however, ordered a book to be fetched from one of his chests and produced oracles received previous to this message and now confirmed by it : they had come by the will of god who had announced a bloodless victory for him and counselled him to hurry, so that no one should dare usurp the throne while he was far away. [b] 119. So, on reading this and seeing the war decided in so proper and desirable a manner, hearing too of the death of a man who had behaved towards him with the temper of a wild boar, he did not betake himself to feasting and drinking and the amusements of the stage, but now that the oracles had turned out true, when all earth and sea lay under his sway and there was none to say him nay, when there was universal agreement that the whole world should be his alone, without being forced into anything he did not wish to do, and when all the palace opened its doors to him, now he gave way to lamentation and his tears flowed about the oracles. 120. Nothing could overcome the force of his character: his first question was about the dead man, the whereabouts of his body, and whether it was received with due honour. Such was his nobility towards the man who would have played a Creon's part towards

Julian expressed much relief at this divine dispensation ; *E.L.F.* No. 28 (382 a ff ), Amm. Marc. 22. 2.

# LIBANIUS

R 562 τος ἂν ἐπ᾽ αὐτῷ μιμησάμενον. | καὶ οὐκ ἐνταῦθα
τὰ πρὸς τὸν οἰχόμενον ἔστη, ἀλλὰ κατέβη μὲν εἰς
τὸν λιμένα τῆς μεγάλης πόλεως πάντα ἀγείρας τὸν
ὅμιλον, ἔτι δὲ κομιζομένου διὰ τῆς θαλάττης
ᾤμωζεν. ἥψατο δὲ ταῖν χεροῖν τῆς σοροῦ πάντα
βασιλείας σύμβολα πλὴν τῆς χλαμύδος ἀπορρίψας |
οὐκ ἀξιῶν ἐγκαλεῖν τῷ σώματι περὶ τῶν τῇ ψυχῇ F 2
βεβουλευμένων.

121. Τετιμημένου δὲ ἐκείνου ταῖς προσηκούσαις
τιμαῖς ἀπὸ τῶν θεῶν τῶν τῆς πόλεως τῆς θεραπείας ἤρχετο σπένδων μὲν ἐν ὀφθαλμοῖς ἁπάντων,
χαίρων δὲ τοῖς ἑπομένοις, καταγελῶν δὲ τῶν οὐκ
ἀκολουθούντων καὶ πείθειν μὲν ἐπιχειρῶν, βιά-
ζεσθαι δὲ οὐκ ἀξιῶν. καίτοι φόβος ἐπεκρέματο
τοῖς διεφθαρμένοις καὶ ἦν ἐλπὶς ὡς ἐκκοπήσονται
μὲν ὀφθαλμούς, ἀποτετμήσονται δὲ κεφαλάς, ποτα-
μοὶ δὲ αἵματος ῥυήσονται τοῖς φόνοις, ἀνάγκας δὲ
καινὰς ὁ καινὸς δεσπότης εὑρήσει, μικρὸν δὲ εἶναι
δόξει πῦρ καὶ σίδηρος καὶ τὸ καταποντίζεσθαι καὶ
τὸ ζῶντα κατορύττεσθαι καὶ τὸ περικόπτεσθαι καὶ
τὸ κατατέμνεσθαι. ταυτὶ μὲν γὰρ τοῖς πρόσθεν
ἐπέπρακτο, πολὺ δὲ τούτων ἠλπίζετο χαλεπώτερα.
122. ὁ δὲ τῶν τε ἐκεῖνα δεδρακότων ὡς οὐ πρατ-
τόντων ὃ ζητοῦσι κατεγίνωσκεν αὐτός τε οὐδὲν
ὄφελος εὕρισκε τῆς ἐνταῦθα ἀνάγκης. τοὺς μὲν
γὰρ τὰ σώματα νοσοῦντας δήσαντά ἐστιν ἰάσασθαι,
δόξαν δὲ περὶ θεῶν οὐκ ἀληθῆ τέμνων καὶ καίων
οὐκ ἂν ἐκβάλοις, ἀλλὰ κἂν ἡ χεὶρ θύῃ μέμφεται ἡ
γνώμη | τὴν χεῖρα καὶ κατηγορεῖ μὲν τῆς τοῦ F

---

[a] Soph. *Ant.* 198 ff.
[b] *Cf.* Greg. Naz. *Or.* 5. 17.  This example of imperial

356

him[a] : nor did he confine his mourning for the dead to that spot, but in the capital he went down to the Great Harbour, assembled the populace, and began mourning while the body was still being conveyed by sea. He cast away all emblems of majesty but his cloak, and with his hands took hold of the coffin, disdaining to bear a grudge against the dead for the plots he had contrived in his lifetime.[b]

121. After honouring him with due ceremony, he made a beginning with the worship of the gods of the state. He offered libation to them in the full view of all and was pleased with those who followed his example and scorned those who did not. He tried to win them by persuasion and refused the use of force, but still the threat of fear hung over the corrupted, for they expected to be blinded or beheaded : rivers of blood would flow in massacres, they thought, and the new master would devise new-fangled tortures, the fire, sword, drowning, burial alive, hacking and mutilation seeming mere child's play. Such had been the behaviour of his predecessors and they expected his measures to be more severe still. 122. He however, had a low opinion of those who had indulged in such practices, for they failed in their object, he thought, and he personally found no value in compulsion of this kind. Anyone suffering from a physical disease can be cured by putting him under restraint, but a false religious creed can never be eradicated by hacking and burning : even if a man's hand performs the sacrifice, his conscience reproaches him for it and condemns him for his

esprit-de-corps, demanded of Julian's successors in *Or.* 24. 28 ff., is confirmed in Julian's own writings hereafter : *e.g.*, *Misop.* 357 bc, *E.L.F.* No. 59 (443 a ff.).

# LIBANIUS

σώματος ἀσθενείας, θαυμάζει δὲ ἃ πρόσθεν, καὶ
ἔστι σκιαγραφία τις μεταβολῆς, οὐ μετάστασις |
R 563 δόξης, καὶ συμβαίνει δὴ τοὺς μὲν τυγχάνειν
συγγνώμης ὕστερον, τοὺς δὲ ἀποθανόντας μετὰ[1]
θεῶν τιμᾶσθαι. 123. ταῦτ᾿ οὖν αἰτιώμενος καὶ ταῖς
σφαγαῖς ὁρῶν ηὐξημένα τἀκείνων ἔφευγεν[2] ἃ κατε-
μέμφετο καὶ τοὺς μὲν δυναμένους γενέσθαι βελτίους εἰσῆγεν εἰς τἀληθές, τοὺς δὲ τὰ χείρω
στέργοντας οὐχ εἷλκεν. οὐ μέντοι βοῶν ἐπαύετο·
ποῖ φέρεσθε, ὦ ἄνθρωποι; καὶ τοῦ φωτὸς
τὸν σκότον ἡγούμενοι φανότερον οὐκ αἰσχύνεσθε οὐδὲ αἰσθάνεσθε τὰ τῶν ἀσεβῶν
γιγάντων νοσοῦντες; ὧν τὰ σώματα μὲν
οὐδὲν διέφερε τῶν ἄλλων ὥστ᾿ ἀφιέναι τὰ
λεγόμενα βέλη, τὸ δ᾿ ὥσπερ ὑμεῖς ἀτιμάζειν τὰ θεῶν ἐποιήσατο τὸν μῦθον. 124.
ᾔδει γὰρ ὡς ὁ σὺν ἐπιστήμῃ τῆς θεραπείας ἁπτό-
μενος τῆς ψυχῆς πρὸ | τῶν ἄλλων φροντιεῖ καὶ τῶν F ⁝
γε τῆς ψυχῆς ἀγαθῶν τῆς εὐσεβείας πρώτου.
ταὐτὸν γάρ, ταὐτὸν δύνασθαι ταύτην γε ἐν ἀνθρω-
πίνῳ βίῳ καὶ τρόπιν ἐν νηὶ καὶ θεμέλιον ἐν οἰκίᾳ.
καὶ γὰρ εἰ πάντας μὲν ἀπέφηνεν εὐπορωτέρους
Μίδου, μείζω δὲ πόλιν ἑκάστην τῆς ποτὲ Βαβυλῶνος, πόλεως δὲ ἑκάστης τῷ περιβόλῳ περιέτηξε
R 564 χρυσόν, τῶν δ᾿ | αὖ περὶ τὸ θεῖον ἡμαρτημένων
ἐπηνώρθου μηδέν, ἴσον ἂν ἔπραττεν ἰατρῷ παρα-
λαμβάνοντι μὲν σῶμα καθ᾿ ἕκαστον τῶν μερῶν
γέμον κακῶν, πάντα δ᾿ ἰωμένῳ πλὴν ὀμμάτων.

---

[1] μετὰ Re. (mss. except VUIBa) : τὰ F. (VUIBa).
[2] ἔφευγεν Herwerden : ἔφυγεν F., Re. (mss.).

358

bodily frailty attaching itself to the same objects of devotion as before. The result is a sort of illusion of change, not a real conversion of belief, and such people are either forgiven afterwards or, if put to death, are held in honour along with the gods they worship. 123. Such then were his criticisms, and seeing that the influence of his opponents increased with persecution, he shunned methods of which his disapproved: those who could be cured he began to direct towards the truth, but he would not drag by main force those wedded to the baser way of life.[a] For all that, he never ceased exclaiming, " Where are you rushing off to, you people?[b] Are you not ashamed to think darkness more brilliant than light? Don't you see that you are sick, like the impious giants? They were no different in body from all the rest, for them to hurl their legendary bolts: it was their contempt for the gods, just like yours, that gave rise to the myth." 124. He was aware that a man who handles religion with understanding will have care for his soul more than for anything else, and for piety, first and foremost of all the blessings of the soul. It has the very same effect in human life as the keel in a ship or the foundation in a house. If he made all men richer than Midas, every city greater than Babylon ever was, if he gilded the circuit of every city wall,[c] and yet mended none of their errors of religion, he would be behaving like a doctor who received as a patient a man sick in every limb and cured all except

---

[a] For Julian's edict of toleration cf. E.L.F. No. 42 (with references).

[b] [Plato], *Clitophon*, 407 A, a passage much imitated by later writers.

[c] Cf. Plato, *Critias*, 116 B; Lib. *Or.* 1. 82 adapts, with reference to rhetoric.

125. διὰ τοῦτ' ἐπὶ πρώτην ἤει τὴν ἰάτρευσιν τῶν ψυχῶν ἡγεμὼν γιγνόμενος ἐπὶ τὴν γνῶσιν τῶν ὡς ἀληθῶς τὸν οὐρανὸν ἐχόντων καὶ νομίζων αὐτῶν συγγενῶν οἰκειοτέρους τοὺς ταῦτα παιδευομένους καὶ φίλον μὲν ἄγων τὸν Διὶ φίλον, ἐχθρὸν δὲ τὸν ἐκείνῳ, μᾶλλον δὲ φίλον μὲν τὸν ἐκείνῳ φίλον, ἐχθρὸν δὲ οὐ πάντα τὸν οὔπω Διὶ φίλον. οὓς γὰρ ᾤετο τῷ χρόνῳ μεταθήσειν οὔτ' ἀπήλαυνε κατεπᾴδων τε ἐνῆγε τὴν πρώτην τε ἀναινομένους περὶ βωμοὺς ὕστερον χορεύοντας ἔδειξε.

126. Πρῶτον μὲν οὖν, ὅπερ ἔφην, ὥσπερ φυγάδα | τὴν εὐσέβειαν κατήγαγε νεὼς τοὺς μὲν ποιῶν, F 2 τοὺς δὲ ἐπισκευάζων, εἰς δὲ τοὺς εἰσάγων ἕδη. χρήματα δὲ ἐτέλουν οἱ τοῖς τῶν ἱερῶν λίθοις σφίσιν αὐτοῖς οἰκίας ἐγείραντες. καὶ κίονας εἶδεν ἄν τις τοὺς μὲν ναυσὶ τοὺς δὲ ἐπ' ἀμαξῶν τοῖς σεσυλημένοις κομιζομένους θεοῖς, καὶ πανταχοῦ βωμοὶ καὶ πῦρ καὶ αἷμα καὶ κνίσσα καὶ καπνὸς καὶ τελεταὶ καὶ μάντεις ἐλεύθεροι φόβου καὶ ἐν ὀρῶν κορυφαῖς αὐλοὶ καὶ πρόσοδοι καὶ βοῦς ὁ αὐτὸς ἀποχρῶν θεραπείᾳ τε εἶναι θεῶν καὶ δεῖπνον ἀνθρώποις. 127. ἐπεὶ δὲ οὐ ῥᾴδιον μὲν βασιλεῖ καθ' ἑκάστην ἡμέραν ἔξω βασιλείων ἐφ' ἱερὰ βαδίζειν, λυσιτελέστατον δὲ συνεχὴς ὁμιλία θεῶν, ἐν μέσοις τοῖς βασιλείοις ἱερὸν μὲν οἰκοδομεῖται τῷ τὴν ἡμέραν ἄγοντι θεῷ καὶ μυστηρίων μετέσχε τε καὶ μετέδωκε μυηθείς τε ἐν μέρει καὶ μυήσας, χωρὶς δὲ πᾶσι θεοῖς βωμοὺς ἱδρύσατο. καὶ πρῶτον ἔργον ἐξ εὐνῆς ἀεὶ συγγενέσθαι διὰ θυσιῶν τοῖς κρείττοσι καὶ νικῆσαι ταύτῃ γε τὸν Νικίαν. 128.

---

[a] Cf. Julian, *E.L.F.* No. 83 (376 c).
[b] Cf. *Or.* 1. 119.  [c] Thuc. 7. 50.

the eyes. 125. So he proceeded first to the cure of their souls, leading men to the recognition of the real lords of heaven and regarding those so instructed as closer to him than kinsmen even. The friend of Zeus was his friend, he thought; his foe, a foe of his own, or more precisely: Zeus' friend was his friend, but not every man who was not yet a friend of Zeus was a foe of his, for he did not rebuff those he thought he could convert in time, and by the charms he exercised on them he began to lead them on and, despite their initial reluctance, he revealed them later congregating around the altars.[a]

126. First of all then, as I have said, he restored piety, as it were, from exile. Some temples he built, others he restored, while he furnished others with statues. People who had built houses for themselves from the stones of the temples began to contribute money. You might have seen pillars carried by boat or by waggon for our plundered gods. Everywhere there were altars, fire, blood offerings, fat and smoke[b]: the mystic ritual was performed, seers were freed from fear, and on the mountain tops were pipings and processions, and the same ox served as worship for the gods and a feast for men. 127. But since it was not easy for the emperor to go from the palace to the temples every day, and yet continued intercourse with the gods is a matter of the greatest moment, a temple to the god who governs the day was built in the middle of the palace, and he took part in his mysteries, initiated and in turn initiating. He also set up altars to all the gods separately, and his first task on rising from his bed was to associate with our lords by means of sacrifice, in which he was more assiduous even than Nicias.[c]

οὕτως ἐξέτεινε τῆς περὶ ταῦτα σπουδῆς τοὺς ὅρους
τὰ μὲν ἀπολωλότα πρὸς ταὐτὸν αὖθις ἄγων, καινὰ
δὲ παλαιοῖς προστιθείς. ἔπειθε δὲ ταῦτα θαρρεῖν
τὸ σωφρονεῖν. | καὶ σύνεγγυς ἔχειν ἱεροῦ τὸ δωμά- F 2
τιον ἐξῆν τῷ γε κρείττονι ἡδονῶν. οὐδὲν γὰρ ἐπράτ-
R 565 τετο τῆς νυκτὸς τῶν τοιούτων γειτόνων | ἀνάξιον.
129. ἃ μὲν οὖν ὑπέσχετο καὶ τοῖς θεοῖς καὶ τοῖς
ἀνθρώποις περὶ τῶν θεῶν πρὸ τῆς βασιλείας, οὕτω
λαμπρῶς ἐπ᾽ αὐτῆς ἀπέδωκεν, ὅς γε¹ καὶ τῶν
πόλεων αἷς μὲν ἦν ἱερὰ μένοντα, καὶ προσορῶν
ἥδετο καὶ τοῦ τὰ μέγιστα εὖ παθεῖν ἀξίας ἐνόμιζε,
τὰς δὲ ἀνεσπακυίας ἢ πάντα ἢ τὰ πλείω μιαράς τε
ὠνόμαζε καὶ τῶν ὠφελειῶν μετεδίδου μὲν ὡς
ὑπηκόοις, οὐ μὴν ἄνευ τοῦ δυσχεραίνειν. ταῦτ᾽
οὖν ποιῶν καὶ τοὺς θεοὺς ἐφιστὰς τῇ γῇ καὶ διαλ-
λάττων ἐῴκει ναυπηγῷ νηὶ μεγάλῃ τοὺς οἴακας
ἀποβαλούσῃ προστιθέντι πάλιν ἑτέρους, πλὴν ὅσον
οὗτος τοὺς αὐτοὺς ἀπεδίδου σωτῆρας.

130. Τοιαῦτα δὴ περὶ τῶν πρώτων καὶ μεγίστων
πεπολιτευμένος βλέψας εἰς τὴν βασιλικὴν θεραπείαν
καὶ κατιδὼν ὄχλον ἄχρηστον τηνάλλως τρεφόμενον,
μαγείρους μὲν χιλίους, κουρέας δὲ οὐκ ἐλάττους,
οἰνοχόους δὲ πλείους, σμήνη τραπεζοποιῶν, εὐνού-
χους ὑπὲρ τὰς μυίας παρὰ τοῖς ποιμέσιν ἐν ἦρι,
καὶ τῶν ἄλλων ἑκάστων ἐθνῶν ἀμυθήτους κηφῆνας,
μία γὰρ | δὴ τοῖς ἀργοῖς καὶ φαγεῖν ἀγαθοῖς F 2
καταφυγὴ τῶν διακόνων βασιλέως καὶ κληθῆναι
καὶ νομισθῆναι καὶ ταχὺ τὸ χρυσίον ἐποίει τὴν

¹ ὅς γε Re. (mss.) : ὥστε F.

128. So far then did he extend the limits of his zeal in this matter, since he desired first to restore the lost rituals once again to their original position, and secondly to add fresh ones to the traditional rites. His continence inspired in him this confidence, and because of his control over sensual pleasure it was possible for him to have his bedchamber next door to a temple, for nothing of his behaviour during the night was unworthy of such neighbours. 129. All the promises about the gods that he had made to both gods and men before his accession he justified most signally after it. If any city had temples still standing, he was delighted at the sight and thought them deserving of the greatest kindness, but if they had demolished all or the greater part of them, he called them polluted : he offered them a share in the benefits he dispensed, as being his subjects, but not without annoyance. In this activity, then, in setting the world under the guidance of the gods and effecting a reconciliation, he was like a shipwright who fits out a big ship with a new rudder after she has lost her old one, but the difference was that Julian restored to us our original protectors.

130. Such then were his measures on matters of first and greatest moment. He next turned his attention to the state of the imperial court, where he found a useless horde of people maintained to no purpose. There were a thousand cooks, as many barbers, and even more butlers. There were swarms of waiters, eunuchs more in number than flies around the flocks in spring, and a multitude of drones of every sort and kind. There was one refuge for such idle gluttons, to have the name and title of being one of the emperor's household, and in very quick time a

# LIBANIUS

ἐγγραφήν, τούτους τοίνυν οὓς μάτην ἔβοσκεν ἡ
βασιλικὴ δαπάνη ζημίαν οὐχ ὑπηρέτας νομίσας
ἐξέωσεν εὐθέως. 131. συνεξέωσε δὲ καὶ τοὺς πολλοὺς ὑπογραφέας οἳ τέχνην ἔχοντες τὴν τῶν
οἰκετῶν ὑφ᾽ ἑαυτοῖς ἔχειν τοὺς ὑπάρχους ἠξίουν
καὶ οὐκ ἐξῆν αὐτῶν οὐ πλησίον οἰκεῖν, οὐκ ἐντυ-
R 566 χόντα προσειπεῖν, | ἀλλ᾽ ἀπεστέρουν, ἥρπαζον,
πωλεῖν ἐπηνάγκαζον, τιμὴν οἱ μὲν οὐκ ἐτίθεσαν,
οἱ δ᾽ οὐ τὴν ἀξίαν, οἱ δὲ ἀνεβάλλοντο, οἱ δὲ τὸ μὴ
ποιῆσαι κακῶς ἀντὶ τῆς τιμῆς ὀρφανοῖς ἐλογίζοντο,
καὶ περιῇεσαν κοινοὶ τῶν καλόν τι κεκτημένων
ἐχθροί, οἷον ἵππον ἢ ἀνδράποδον ἢ δένδρον ἢ ἀγρὸν
ἢ κῆπον· αὐτῶν γὰρ μᾶλλον ἢ τῶν ἐχόντων εἶναι ταῦτα ἠξίουν. καὶ ὁ μὲν ἀφιστάμενος τοῖς
ἰσχύουσι τῶν πατρῴων βέλτιστος καὶ ἀπῄει φέρων ἀντὶ τῆς οὐσίας τὸ ῥῆμα, ὅτῳ δὲ ἐφαίνετο
δεινὸν ταῦτα παθεῖν ἀνδροφόνος, γόης, πλήρης ἀδικημάτων, πολλῶν ὀφείλων δίκας. 132. ποιοῦντες
δὲ τοὺς μὲν ἄλλους ἀπόρους | ἐξ εὐπόρων, αὐτοὺς F 29
δὲ ἐξ ἀπόρων εὐπόρους καὶ τῇ τῶν πρότερον εὐδαιμόνων πενίᾳ πλουτοῦντες καὶ τὴν ἀπληστίαν
εἰς τὰ τέρματα τῆς οἰκουμένης ἐκτείνοντες ὅ τι
βούλοιντο παρὰ τοῦ κρατοῦντος ἐπήγγελλον καὶ
οὐκ ἦν ἀρνηθῆναι, ἀλλ᾽ ἡρπάζοντο παλαιαὶ πόλεις
καὶ κάλλη νενικηκότα χρόνον διὰ θαλάττης ἤγετο
ποιήσοντα κναφέων υἱέσιν οἰκίας τῶν βασιλείων

---

[a] For this purge of the palace *cf.* Socr. *loc. cit.*, Amm.
Marc. 22. 4.

[b] *Or.* 2. 58 reveals the drastic nature of his reform.

[c] Like Dulcitius, one-time governor of Asia, *Or.* 42. 24.

piece of gold would ensure their enrolment. All these, maintained to no purpose by the imperial purse, he regarded not as servants but as nuisances, and so he expelled them forthwith.[a] 131. Besides these he expelled the many secretaries[b] who, though performing a menial function, yet required prefects to be under their thumb. No one could live near them ; none who met them could address them without them robbing, pillaging or forcing them to sell either at an unfair price or at none at all; some would put off paying, some calculated that, in the case of orphans, not to hurt them was as good as paying them their debt, and they went about, the enemies of every single man who had anything worth having, whether horse, slave, tree, farm or garden. This they felt was their property rather than that of the owner. The man who renounced his ancestral possessions in favour of these persons of influence was a gentleman, and off he would go with this title in return for his estates, while whoever objected to such treatment, he was guilty of murder and magic, crammed full of crime and liable to be punished on more than one count. 132. So they reduced the rich to poverty and raised themselves from poverty to prosperity, for they amassed money by beggaring those who previously were men of substance, and they extended their rapacity to the very ends of the earth, for in their communications from the emperor they inserted just what they liked, and it was impossible to say them nay. Ancient cities were ransacked and their beauties that had withstood the march of time were taken by sea to provide some fuller's sons[c] with

The same complaint, made from a more self-interested point of view, is met in *Or.* 62. 8 ff.

# LIBANIUS

φαιδροτέρας. 133. οὕτω δὲ ὄντων ἐκείνων οὐ
φορητῶν πολλοὶ ζηλωταὶ καθ' ἕκαστον, αἱ κύνες,
φασί, τὰς δεσποίνας μιμούμεναι. τῶν γὰρ οἰκετῶν
οὐδεὶς ἦν, ὃς οὐχ ὕβριζε δέων, σπαράττων, ἀφαι-
ρούμενος, παίων, ἐκβάλλων, ἐλαύνων, γεωργεῖν
ἀξιῶν, ἐπὶ ζεύγους φέρεσθαι, δεσπότης εἶναι καὶ
τοσοῦτός γε ὅσος ἦν ὁ δεσπότης αὐτῷ. 134. οἷς
γε οὐκ ἐξήρκει πλουτεῖν, ἀλλ' εἰ μὴ καὶ κοινωνοῖεν
ἀξιώματος ἠγανάκτουν ὡς ταύτῃ δὴ κρύψοντες τὴν
δουλείαν. καὶ ζώνην εἶχον μετὰ | τῶν κεκτη- F
R 567 μένων φρίττειν ἀναγκάζουσαν καὶ στενωπὸν | καὶ
φυλακὴν καὶ πόλιν. τούτους δὴ τοὺς Κερβέρους
καὶ πολυκεφάλους εἰς ἰδιώτας ἐξέβαλε προσειπὼν
κέρδος ἡγεῖσθαι τὸ μὴ τεθνάναι τούτους. 135.
τρίτην μοῖραν κακούργων ὑπηρετῶν κλεπτόντων
καὶ λωποδυτούντων καὶ πᾶν καὶ λεγόντων καὶ
ποιούντων ἐπὶ τῷ λαβεῖν τῶν βασιλείων ὑπερώρισε
θυρῶν οἳ τὰς αὐτῶν πατρίδας τῆς παρ' αὐτῶν
ἀπεστερηκότες χρείας βουλὰς ἀποδράντες καὶ νόμους λειτουργιῶν εἰς ἀγγελιαφόρους τελέσαντες
ἐωνοῦντο μὲν πευθῆνες καταστῆναι καὶ τὸ σχῆμα
ἦν φυλάκων, ὅπως μηδὲν ἀγνοοῖ βασιλεὺς τῶν ἐπ'
αὐτὸν συντιθεμένων, τὸ δὲ ἔργον καπήλων. 136.
ὥσπερ γὰρ ἐκεῖνοι τὰς θύρας ἔωθεν ἀνοίγοντες
σκοποῦσι περὶ τῆς ἐμπολῆς, οὕτως οὗτοι κερδῶν
ἐμέμνηντο πρὸς τοὺς τούτων προσαγωγέας οἳ

---

ᵃ For the proverb *cf.* Plat. *Rep.* 563 c.   Greek hunting
dogs appear, traditionally, as females : *cf.* Xen. *Cyneg.* 3.
ᵇ Evasion of curial duties by enrolment as *agens-in-rebus*
or *curiosus* was one of the commonest devices, as shown by
*Cod. Th.* 12. 1. *passim. Cf.* Pack, *Studies in Libanius*, pp.
18 ff.
For Julian's edict on the *cursus publicus* and the *curiosi*

houses more glorious than palaces. 133. Intolerable
as they were, each one of them had many followers—
like master, like man, as the saying goes.[a] There
was none of their servants whose behaviour was not
outrageous too : they imprisoned, harried and
robbed ; they inflicted assault, ejection and exile,
and demanded for themselves forced farm-labour,
conveyance by carriage and pair and a mastery
every bit as complete as that of their own masters.
134. Not content with amassing money, they resented it if they did not share their dignity, for in
this manner they would conceal their slavish condition. Along with their masters they wore the
belt of office that made street, fortress and city
tremble before them. These hell-hounds, these
many-headed monsters he reduced to the level of
ordinary individuals, and told them to think themselves lucky they got away with their lives. 135. A
third group of villainous underlings he ejected from
the doors of his palace, thieves and brigands who
would say and do anything for money. These were
the people who had robbed their own cities of their
services, who had fled from the town councils and the
customary civic duties, and had been enrolled among
the couriers [b] and had purchased the position of investigator. Ostensibly they were a guard, to prevent
the emperor remaining in ignorance of anything
being plotted against him, but in fact they were mere
hucksters. 136. Just as these, on opening up their
shops of a morning, look round for business, so did
this crew drop the mention of pickings to their lick-

cf. E.L.F. No. 67 (Cod. Th. 8. 5. 12). An interesting account
of the change effected by it is given by Eustathius in Julian,
Ep 72.

τοὺς χειροτέχνας σιγῶντας ὡς λοιδοροῦντας τὴν
βασιλείαν ἦγον ὑπὸ τὰς ἐκείνων μάστιγας, οὐχ ἵνα |
ξαίνοιντο, ἀλλ' ἵνα τὸ μὴ τοῦτο παθεῖν πρίαιντο. F 29
καὶ οὐδεὶς ἦν ἔξω βελῶν, οὐ πολίτης, οὐ μέτοικος,
οὐ ξένος, ἀλλ' ὁ μὲν οὐδὲν ἀδικῶν καὶ συκοφαντού-
μενος ἀπώλλυτο μὴ διδούς, ὁ δὲ καὶ σφόδρα
πονηρευόμενος προϊέμενος ἐσώζετο. 137. ὁ μέγιστος δὲ τῶν πόρων ἑλεῖν τι κακούργημα περὶ τὴν
βασιλείαν· ἀντὶ γὰρ τοῦ παραδοῦναι τῇ τῶν ἀδι-
R 568 κουμένων ὀργῇ τὸν ἁλόντα | ἀντὶ τῶν καταπε-
πιστευκότων τοῖς ἐπιβουλεύουσιν ἐπὶ τῷ λαβεῖν
ἐβοήθουν. 138. ἔτι τοίνυν τοῖς μὲν σωφρονοῦσιν
ὥρας ἐπιπέμποντες νέων καὶ καθιστάντες εἰς
ἀδοξίας φόβον, τοὺς δὲ τῶν γοήτων ἐλέγχους τοῖς
πόρρω τῆς αἰτίας προσάπτοντες δύο ταύτας ὑπερ-
βαλλούσας ἐκαρποῦντο προσόδους, μᾶλλον δὲ τρίτην
ἑτέραν ἁδροτέραν ἀμφοῖν. διδόντες γὰρ ἐξουσίαν
τοῖς τὸ νόμισμα διαφθείρειν τολμῶσιν ἀπὸ τῶν
σπηλαίων ἐν οἷς ταῦτα ἐτολμᾶτο, δόκιμον ὑπὲρ τοῦ
παρασήμου φέροντες ἐτρύφων. 139. ὅλως δὲ τῶν
ἀφορμῶν ἡ μὲν ἐν ἀφανεῖ τε καὶ συχνή, ἡ δ' ἐν
φανερῷ τε καὶ δήλη, σχῆμα δὴ νόμου[1] λαβοῦσα, καὶ
οὐ σφόδρα τῆς ἑτέρας | ἐλάττων. ὥστ' ἔθνους F 29
μεμνημένοι καὶ τὸν ἀριθμὸν τῶν χρημάτων εὐθὺς
προσετίθεσαν ὃν ὑπῆρχεν ἐκεῖθεν ἔχειν.

140. Οὗτοι τοίνυν οἱ βασιλέως ὀφθαλμοὶ καὶ
φάσκοντες ἅπαντα εἰς φῶς ἄγειν καὶ ποιεῖν τοὺς
πονηροὺς μετρίους τῷ μὴ ἐξεῖναι λανθάνειν πάσας
ἀνίεσαν εἰς πονηρίαν ὁδοὺς καὶ μόνον οὐκ ἐκήρυττον

---

[1] δὴ (δὲ Re.) νόμου F., Re. : δ' ἦν ὁμοῦ mss.

spittles, and these would bring the tradesmen under their lash on the charge of insulting the emperor, even when they had not uttered a word, not so as to give them a good drubbing, but to ensure that they bought immunity from it. No one was out of range of their assault, whether citizen, resident visitor or foreigner. The innocent victim of such an accusation was lost if he did not pay up, while the veriest blackguard was saved if he did. 137. Their chief source of income was to discover some crime committed against the emperor, for instead of handing over the guilty party to an enraged victim, they would, with an eye to profit, succour the traitors instead of their employers. 138. Moreover, they would blackmail respectable citizens by getting them into compromising situations with handsome youngsters and alarming them with fears of disgrace, or they would fasten a charge of magic on someone completely innocent. These were two superlative money-making devices, but there was one more lucrative still. By giving a free hand to counterfeiters in the dens where they dared ply their trade, they got good money in return for bad, and so made a fortune. 139. To sum up, of their sources of income one was concealed and plentiful, while the other was open and above board, being cloaked in legal form, and not so very much less than the first. So if the thought of any province recurred to them, they would immediately go on to remark upon the sum of money they could get from it.

140. These " King's Eyes,"[a] then, though pretending to bring every secret to light and to reform the wicked because of the impossibility of concealment, had opened up all the roads for wickedness and

[a] Aristoph. *Ach.* 92.

LIBANIUS

ὡς ἀκίνδυνα δράσουσιν. ὥσθ' οἱ κωλυταὶ τῶν
ἀδικημάτων αὐτοὶ τοὺς ἀδικοῦντας ἔσωζον κυσὶν
ἐοικότες συμπράττουσι τοῖς λύκοις. διὰ ταῦτα
ἴσον ἦν θησαυρῷ τε ἐντυχεῖν καὶ τούτων μετασχεῖν
τῶν μετάλλων. ὁ γὰρ ἥκων Ἶρος ἐν βραχεῖ χρόνῳ
Καλλίας. 141. ἄλλου τοίνυν ἀντλοῦντος ἐπ' ἄλλῳ
καὶ γιγνομένων τῶν μὲν πόλεων πενεστέρων, τῶν
δὲ ταῦτα καπηλευόντων εὐδαιμόνων πάλαι τε ὁ
βασιλεὺς ἡμῖν ἤχθετο καὶ παύσειν ἠπείλει δυνηθεὶς
R 569 καὶ δυνηθεὶς ἔπαυσεν ὅλην μὲν ἐκείνην | δια-
σκεδάσας τὴν φατρίαν, ἀφελόμενος δὲ καὶ προσηγορίαν καὶ τάξιν ἀφ' ἧς πάντα ἐπόρθουν τε καὶ
διώρυττον, αὐτὸς δὲ τοῖς αὐτοῦ χρώμενος μὲν εἰς
γραμμάτων πομπάς, τῆς δὲ τοῦ ταῦτα δρᾶν ἐξουσίας
οὐ μεταδιδούς. 142. τοῦτο δὲ ἦν ἀκριβῶς | ἐλευ- F 29
θέρας γενέσθαι τὰς πόλεις, ἐφεστηκότος δὲ τοῦ
ταῦτα ποιεῖν ἔχοντος οὐκ ἦν ἀναπνεῦσαι καθαρῶς.
ἀλλ' ὁ μὲν ἐβάλλετο, ὁ δὲ ἔμελλε, καὶ τῷ γε μὴ
πεισομένῳ τὸ πείσεσθαι προσδοκᾶν ἀντὶ τοῦ παθεῖν
καθίστατο. 143. τῶν τοίνυν ἀγγάρων ἡμιόνων τῇ
τε συνεχείᾳ τῶν πόνων καὶ τῷ τοὺς ἄρτι ῥηθέντας
τὰς μὲν λιμοκτονεῖν, αὐτοῖς δὲ τῷ 'κείνων λιμῷ
παρασκευάζειν Σύβαριν—ἐποίει δὲ πολὺν τὸν πόνον
καὶ τὰ νεῦρα οἷον ἐξέτεμνε τὸ τῷ βουλομένῳ
ῥάδιον εἶναι ζεύξαντα ζεῦγος ἐλαύνειν καὶ ταὐτὸν
δύνασθαι βασιλέως τε περὶ ταῦτα καὶ πευθῆνος
γράμματα. διὸ στῆναι μὲν οὐκ ἦν οὐδὲ μικρὸν
οὐδὲ ἀπολαῦσαι φάτνης, ἡ πληγὴ δὲ ἀσθενοῦσαν

---

ᵃ Cf. Ep. 143. Irus, the beggar of the Odyssey, becomes
Callias, the millionaire of Aristophanes.
ᵇ Cf. Or. 13. 42.

370

had practically proclaimed impunity for misconduct. Thus the very people there to prevent crime were the protectors of the criminal, like sheepdogs hunting with the wolf pack, and it was like coming across hidden treasure to have a share in this goldmine—rags to riches in no time![a] 141. People were bled white one after another and, as the cities were beggared, these racketeers made money. Our emperor had long been angry about it, and he swore that if he got the chance he would put a stop to it : and when he got the chance, stop it he did. He broke up that whole gang, took away their rank and title, whereby they had succeeded in spreading a trail of pillage and looting, and used his personal attendants for the conveyance of despatches, but without giving them any authority to behave like this. 142. This meant that the cities were really and truly free, for while ever they had any supervisor over them with such powers for misconduct, it was impossible for them to breathe freely. So beatings took place, or there was the prospect of them, and the possibility of such an experience was as good as the occurrence itself even for those not due to experience it. 143. Again, the mules used in the public post died of over-work or were starved to death by the above-mentioned gentry, and these by starving them got the means to live on the fat of the land.[b] The job was delayed and the beasts, as it were, hamstrung by the fact that it was easy for any Tom, Dick or Harry to hitch up a team and drive off, the investigator's credentials in this matter carrying as much weight as the emperor's. So the beasts were not allowed to stand still even for a moment; they never saw the inside of a stall; if one fell sick, the lash was never out of use

371

# LIBANIUS

οὐκ ἀνίστη πρὸς δρόμον, ἔδει δὲ εἴκοσιν ἢ καὶ
πλειόνων πρὸς ἕλξιν ὀχήματος, αἱ πολλαὶ δὲ αἱ
R 570 μὲν ἄρτι λυθεῖσαι πίπτουσαι | ἔθνησκον, αἱ δὲ ὑπὸ
τῷ ζυγῷ πρὶν ἢ λυθῆναι—κᾆτ᾽ ἐκωλύετο μὲν ἀπὸ
τοῦ τοιούτου τὰ δεόμενα τάχους, τὴν βλάβην δὲ
πάλιν εἰς χρημάτων λόγον αἱ πόλεις ἐδέχοντο.
144. τοῦ δὲ | ἀθλίως ταῦτα ἔχειν ἔλεγχος σαφέ- F 29
στερος ὁ χειμὼν τότε δὴ μάλιστα διακοπτομένης
πολλαχοῦ τῆς τῶν ὀρέων διαδοχῆς ὥστ᾽ ὀρεωκόμοι
φεύγοντες ἐν ὀρῶν ἦσαν κορυφαῖς, ἡμίονοι δὲ
χαμαί, τοῖς δ᾽ ἐπειγομένοις πλὴν βοῆς τε καὶ τοῦ
πλῆξαι τὸν μηρὸν οὐδέν. καιροὶ δὲ οὐκ ὀλίγων
πραγμάτων ἐξέφυγον τὰς ἀρχὰς ταῖς κατὰ τοῦτο
βραδυτῆσι. καὶ ἐῶ λέγειν ἵππους ὅμοια πεπονθότας καὶ ὄνους πολλῷ δεινότερα. τοῦτο δὲ ἦν
τοὺς ταῦτα λειτουργοῦντας ἀπολωλέναι. 145.
ἵστησι δὴ καὶ ταύτην Ἰουλιανὸς τὴν μέθην στήσας
ὡς ἀληθῶς τοὺς οὐκ ἀναγκαίους δρόμους καὶ τὰς
μὲν τοιαύτας χάριτας ἐπικινδύνους ἀποφήνας καὶ
δοῦναι καὶ λαβεῖν διδάξας δὲ τοὺς ἀρχομένους
ὑποζύγια τοὺς μὲν κτᾶσθαι, τοὺς δὲ μισθοῦσθαι.
καὶ πρᾶγμα ἀπιστούμενον ἑωρᾶτο, γυμνάζοντες
ἡνίοχοι μὲν ἡμιόνους, ἱπποκόμοι δὲ ἵππους. ὥσπερ
γὰρ πρότερον ἐπεπέδηντο ταῖς ταλαιπωρίαις, οὕτω δέος ἦν, μὴ καὶ τότε τῷ μήκει τῆς ἀργίας.
τουτὶ δὲ τοὺς οἴκους τῶν ὑπηκόων εὐπορωτέρους
καθίστη.

146. Ἐπεδείξατο δὲ τὴν αὐτὴν πρόνοιαν καὶ περὶ
τὰς ἐν ταῖς πόλεσι βουλὰς αἳ πάλαι μὲν πλήθεσί
τε | καὶ πλούτοις ἔθαλλον, ἔπειτα ἦσαν οὐδὲν μετερ- F 29

---

*a* Cf. Cod. Th. 11. 16. 10 (E.L.F. No. 47 a).  Even

372

for it to break into a trot; it needed twenty or more to pull a carriage, and most of them dropped down dead as soon as they were unhitched or else, before then, in the traces. As a result anything that required speed was delayed, and once again the cities had to foot the bill for the loss. 144. The winter season provided a clearer demonstration of this sorry state of affairs, for then the relays of mule teams completely broke down, with the result that the muleteers took refuge on the mountain tops, the mules sprawled on the ground, and the hurrying travellers could do nothing but shout and slap their thighs. Because of such delays the administration failed to follow up its opportunity on several critical occasions. I forebear to mention the similar treatment of horses, and a worse one still of the asses. But all this spelt ruin for those who provided such services. 145. Anyway, Julian put a stop to this sottishness. He made an end of journeys that were not absolutely necessary and declared both the grant and receipt of such favours to be equally punishable, instructing his subordinates either to buy or to hire their animals.[a] Then there was to be seen a sight beyond belief, muleteers and grooms exercising their mules and horses. Before this their ill-condition had been the cause of their delay; now the fear was that their long period of inactivity would have the same effect. But it did give more prosperity to the homes of his subjects.

146. He displayed the same consideration for the councils of the cities, too. In times past they had been flourishing in the number and wealth of their members, but at this time they had sunk to nothing,

Gregory (*Or.* 4. 75) has a good word to say for Julian on this subject.

ρυηκότων πλὴν ὀλίγων κομιδῇ τινων τῶν μὲν εἰς
R 571 τὰ στρατιωτῶν, τῶν δ' εἰς τὸ | μέγα συνέδριον.
τοὺς δ' ἦν ἕτερόν τι τὸ δεξόμενον καὶ οἱ μὲν
ἐκάθευδόν τε καὶ ἐχαρίζοντο τῷ σώματι καὶ τῶν οὐ
τὴν αὐτὴν αὐτοῖς ἐλθόντων κατεγέλων. τὸ δὲ
ὑπολελειμμένον ὀλίγον ὂν ἐβαπτίζετο, καὶ τὸ λειτουργεῖν τοῖς πλείοσιν εἰς τὸ προσαιτεῖν ἐτελεύτα.
147. καίτοι τίς οὐκ οἶδεν ὡς ἡ τῆς βουλῆς ἰσχὺς
ψυχὴ πόλεώς ἐστιν; ἀλλὰ Κωνστάντιος μὲν λόγῳ
ταῖς βουλαῖς[1] βοηθῶν ἔργοις ἦν ἐχθρὸς μετατιθεὶς
ἑτέρωσε τοὺς ἐκείνας φεύγοντας καὶ διδοὺς ἀτελείας παρανόμους. ἐῴκεσαν οὖν ῥυσοῖς γραϊδίοις
ἠσθημένοις ῥάκια καὶ ὠδύροντο μὲν οἱ σεσυλημένοι
βουλευταί, δεινὰ δὲ αὐτοὺς[2] ὡμολόγουν πεπονθέναι
τε καὶ πάσχειν οἱ δικάζοντες, βοηθεῖν δὲ ὄντες
ἕτοιμοι βοηθεῖν οὐκ εἶχον. 148. ἀλλ' ἔδει ποτὲ καὶ
ταύτας τὴν αὐτῶν ῥώμην ἀπολαβεῖν. τὸ γὰρ δὴ
πολλῶν ἐπαίνων ἄξιον ἐκεῖνο γράμμα τὸ δεῖν πάντα
ἄνδρα πρὸς βουλὴν καλεῖν καὶ μηδὲν ἔχοντα
ἰσχυρὸν | εἰς ἄφεσιν ἐγγράφειν οὕτω τὸ πρᾶγμα F
ἐπηνώρθωσεν ὥστ' ἠλέγχετο μικρὰ τῷ πλήθει τῶν
εἰσιόντων τὰ χωρία. 149. οὐ γὰρ ἦν ὑπογραφεὺς
οὐδὲ εὐνοῦχος ὁ χρημάτων ἀφήσων ἀλλ' οἱ μέν, ὡς

---

[1] βουλαῖς F., conj. Re.: ψυχαῖς mss.
[2] αὐτοὺς F., conj. Re.: αὐτοῖς mss.

---

[a] As Aristophanes did, for instance : cf. Or. 14. 10. The
term " soldier " covers both the military and the *agentes-
in-rebus.*

[b] The recruitment of a senate for Constantinople under
Themistius in A.D. 358/9 did take some influential provincials from their local *curiae* (cf. *Epp.* 40, 70, 80). Libanius,
however, dissuades some of his intimates from applying for

374

for their members, except for a very few, had scuttled off to serve either in the services[a] or in the senate.[b] For yet others there was something else to absorb them, and they lived a life of ease and bodily pleasure, mocking those who did not go their way.[c] The remnants, a mere handful, were in dire straits and for most of them civic service ended in beggary. 147. Yet everyone knows that a strong council is the life blood of a city. Constantius, while ostensibly on the side of the councils, in actual fact was their enemy, for he transferred to other spheres men who sought to avoid service there and he granted immunities illegally. Thus the councillors, despoiled, were like wrinkled old women dressed in rags, and were full of complainings, and though the governors agreed that they had been and were badly treated and were eager to help them, they were unable to do anything about it. 148. But at last the councils too were to recover their standing. That admirable rescript, that everyone should be summoned to the council and be enrolled unless he had valid reason for exemption, so improved the position that the council chambers turned out to be too small to contain the numbers of entrants.[d] 149. For there was no secretary or eunuch to get them off

the clarissimate on the grounds that the senate is a place for nonentities and that membership of it means wasted money, as well as lost influence at home (*Epp.* 34, 731). This exaggerated local patriotism prevents him from recognizing the very real gains won by such applicants.

[c] *e.g.*, law—or the Christian clergy.

[d] In Antioch Julian had increased the numbers of decurions by 200 before initiating his major curial legislation (*Misop.* 367 d ff.). In consequence of his present reform Alexandria on Issus raised the number of decurions from one to fifteen (*Ep.* 696).

εὐνούχοις προσῆκε, τὰ δούλων ὑπηρέτουν οὐδὲν
ἐπὶ τοῖς χιτῶσι φρονοῦντες, οἱ δ' ὅσα χεῖρα καὶ
μέλαν ἀπαιτεῖ καὶ κάλαμον ἐπλήρουν, τἄλλα δὲ
ἠπίσταντο σωφρονεῖν μαθόντες ὑπὸ τοῦ διδασκάλου
R 572 | πενίαν δικαίαν ἀγαπᾶν. τοιγαροῦν καὶ νῦν πολ-
λοὺς ἂν εὕροις ἀπ' ἐκείνης τῆς συνουσίας φιλοσόφων
βελτίους. οἶμαι δὲ καὶ τοὺς ἄλλους ἅπαντας τοὺς
ἐν ταῖς τάξεσιν ἥκιστα δὴ τότε κέρδη θαυμάσαντας
μάλιστα δόξης ἐπιθυμῆσαι. 150. μέμνησθε δὲ ὡς
ὧν πρότερον προϊόντων πρηνεῖς κατεπίπτομεν
ὥσπερ ἐν ἀστραπαῖς, τούτοις ἐκ τῶν ἵππων ἀπο-
βαίνουσιν ἐπ' ἀγορᾶς ἐμβάλλοντες δεξιὰν διαλεγό-
μεθα καὶ τὸ μὴ μείζω τῶν ἄλλων φρονεῖν τοῦ
φοβεῖν ἡγοῦνται κάλλιον. |

151. Ἀλλὰ μὴν νόμους βασιλεῦσι θεῖναι μὲν F
ῥάδιον, ἔξεστι γάρ, συμφέροντας δὲ οὐ ῥάδιον,
φρονήσεως γὰρ ἤδη τοῦτό γε. ὁ δὲ τοιούτους μὲν
ἔθηκεν οἷς εὗρεν ὥστε μεγάλα τοὺς πρὸ τούτων
γενομένους ἀνθρώπους ἐζημιῶσθαι, τοὺς δὲ τούτοις
μὲν ἐοικότας τῶν πάλαι κρατούντων, λελυμένους
δὲ αὐθαδείᾳ δυνάστου πάλιν κυρίους ἀπέφηνε τὸ
τοῖς εὖ ἔχουσι συμφέρεσθαι τοῦ μάτην τῶν κειμένων ἐπιλαμβάνεσθαι κάλλιον εἰς φιλοτιμίαν
ἡγούμενος.

152. Φέρε δὴ καὶ περὶ τῶν δίκην δεδωκότων
σκεψώμεθα. οὐκοῦν τριῶν ὄντων οἳ σφαγαῖς ἐτε-

---

ᵃ e.g., Cod. Th. 5. 20. 1 (E.L.F. No. 139 : De longa con-

for a price : the eunuchs, as eunuchs should, performed menial duties and put on no haughty airs
because of their liveries, and the secretaries fulfilled
all tasks that required hand, pen and ink, but in all
else had learned how to behave themselves, being
schooled by their master not to demur at honest
poverty. Why, even now you can find many of them
better than philosophers as a result of their association with him, and my own belief is that all others
besides in the various grades of service had at that
time the least regard for gain and the greatest desire
for glory. 150. Bear in mind, too, that whereas we
used to fall on our faces, as though struck by lightning, at their approach, now, as they descend from
their carriages in the city square, we shake hands
with them and hold conversations with them, and
they regard it as a better thing not to put on more
airs and graces than other folk than to instil fear into
them.

151. What is more, it is easy enough for emperors
to make ordinances, for that is their prerogative, but
not for them to make beneficial ones, for that requires
intelligence. But he did make such ordinances, and
by them he ensured that people living before his time
had missed a great deal. He also renewed the validity of laws like them, enacted by emperors in days
gone by but now discarded by a tyrant's whim, for in
his opinion it was a nobler object of ambition to
support institutions of merit than to direct frivolous
attacks against already established practices.[a]

152. Now let us consider the case of the men who
were punished. Of the three people executed, one

*suetudine*) ; *ibid.* 13. 3. 4 (*E.L.F.* No. 75 : *De archiatris*),
*cf.* Julian, *Ep.* 25 b.

λεύτησαν ὁ μὲν συκοφαντῶν ἐπεληλύθει τὴν οἰκουμένην καὶ ταῖς ἠπείροις ἀμφοτέραις μυρίους
R 573 θανάτους ὤφειλεν ὥστ᾽ | ἤλγουν οἱ τὸν ἄνθρωπον
εἰδότες, ὅτι μὴ οἷόν τε ἦν καὶ τεθνεῶτα κτεῖναι καὶ
τρὶς τοῦτο ποιῆσαι καὶ πολλάκις. ὁ δ᾽ ἄνευ τοῦ
τὸν Κωνστάντιον δεδουλῶσθαι δοῦλος αὐτὸς ὢν
καί, τὸ τοῦδε δεινότερον, εὐνοῦχος, αἰτιώτατος
ἐγεγόνει τῷ Γάλλῳ τῆς ὠμοτάτης τελευτῆς. ὅ γε
μὴν τρίτος ὀργῇ μὲν τῆς στρατιᾶς | ἀνηρπάσθη F
δώρων βασιλικῶν αὐτούς, ὡς ἔλεγον, ἀπεστερηκώς,
ἔτυχε δὲ καὶ μεταστὰς παραμυθίας τινὸς τῇ θυγατρὶ
τοῦ βασιλέως μοῖραν οὐ μικρὰν τῶν πατρῴων
ἀφέντος. 153. οἵ γε μὴν εἰς αὐτὸν ὑβρικότες, ἦσαν
γάρ, ἦσαν οἳ παρεκάλουν τινὰς ἐπὶ τὸ σκῆπτρον
οὐδενὸς κατ᾽ οὐδὲν φειδόμενοι ῥήματος, τὴν μὲν
ἀξίαν δίκην οὐκ ἔδοσαν, οὔκουν ἀπέθανον, νήσοις
δὲ ἐνδιατρίβοντες τῆς γλώττης ἐπαιδεύοντο κρατεῖν. οὕτως ἐκεῖνος ἑτέροις μὲν ἠδικημένοις ἠ-
πίστατο τιμωρεῖν καλῶς, ἐν δὲ τοῖς εἰς αὐτὸν
μεγαλόψυχος ἦν.

154. Εἰσῆλθε καὶ εἰς τὸ συνέδριον καὶ τὴν μεγάλην βουλὴν περὶ αὐτὸν ἐκάθισε πολὺν δὴ χρόνον
ταύτης τῆς τιμῆς ἐστερημένην. εἰς μὲν γὰρ τὸ
βασίλειον εἰσεκαλεῖτο πρότερον ἐστήξουσά τε καὶ
μικρὰ ἀκουσομένη, βασιλεὺς δὲ οὐκ ᾔει παρ᾽ αὐτὴν
συγκαθεδούμενος· τῷ γὰρ μὴ δύνασθαι λέγειν

---

[a] This first victim of the trials at Chalcedon was Paulus
" *Catena* " ; *cf.* Amm. Marc. 22. 3.

[b] Eusebius, chamberlain of Constantius : *cf.* Amm. Marc.
22. 3. 10, Socr. *loc. cit.*

[c] Ursulus. Ammianus (20. 11. 5, 22. 3. 3) thoroughly—

had travelled through the whole world spreading his
false charges broadcast.[a] Both in Europe and in Asia
he deserved to die thousands of times, so that those
who knew the fellow were aggrieved that they could
not put him to death over and over again. The second, despite the fact that he had Constantius under
his thumb, was a slave and, worse still, a eunuch. He
had had been primarily responsible for the cruel death
of Gallus.[b] The third of them, however, had fallen
victim to the anger of the soldiery, having allegedly
deprived them of donatives from the emperor, but
even after his death he had some consolation, for the
emperor renounced a large portion of her father's
property in favour of his daughter.[c] 153. However,
persons guilty of offences towards him—and there
actually were people who invited pretenders to bid
for the throne and abused him in every possible way
—these were not punished as they deserved to be.[d]
They were certainly not executed but relegated to
islands, where they learned how to keep a still tongue
in their heads. Thus he knew how to avenge others
for the wrongs they had suffered, but with regard to
those offered to himself he exercised a noble
generosity.

154. He made his entry into the senate house, too,
and seated around him the Grand Senate that had
long been deprived of this honour. Until now it had
been summoned to the palace to stand and listen to a
few remarks, and the emperor did not come to attend
its sessions, for because of his incapacity for public
speaking, he shunned a place that required an

and properly—disapproved of this condemnation, an attitude
obviously shared by Libanius here.
[d] *Cf.* Amm. Marc. *loc. cit.* (Palladius, Taurus, Florentius).

# LIBANIUS

ἔφευγε χωρίον δεόμενον ῥήτορος, ὁ δέ, ὥσπερ
Ὅμηρος ἔφη τὸν δεινὸν λέγειν, ἀσφαλέως ἀγο-
ρεύων ἐδίωκε τοὺς τοιούτους συλλόγους διδοὺς
μὲν τῷ βουλομένῳ παρρησιάσασθαι πρὸς αὐτόν,
διεξιὼν δὲ καὶ αὐτὸς νῦν μὲν παῦρά τε | καὶ F 3
λιγέως, νῦν δὲ νιφάδεσσιν ἐοικότα χειμε-
ρίῃσι τοὺς Ὁμηρικοὺς ἐκείνους δημηγόρους νῦν
μὲν μιμούμενος, νῦν δ' ἐν ᾧπερ ἑκάτερος εὐδοκίμει
παριών. 155. λέγοντος δὲ αὐτοῦ καὶ τὰ μὲν ἐπ-
R 574 αινοῦντος, τὰ δὲ ἐπιτιμῶντος, | τὰ δὲ νουθετοῦντος
ἀγγέλλει τις προσιέναι τὸν διδάσκαλον, ἄνδρα
Ἴωνα, φιλόσοφον ἐξ Ἰωνίας κεκλημένον, ὁ δὲ ἐκ
μέσων ἀναπηδήσας τῶν γερόντων ἔθει πρὸς τὰς
θύρας τὸ τοῦ Χαιρεφῶντος πρὸς Σωκράτην πεπον-
θώς, ἀλλ' ἐκεῖνος μὲν Χαιρεφῶν τε ὢν καὶ ἐν τῇ
Ταυρέου παλαίστρα, ὁδὶ δὲ πάντων τε κρατῶν κἂν
τῷ μεγίστῳ συνεδρίῳ δεικνὺς ἅπασι καὶ κηρύττων
τοῖς ἔργοις ὅτι σοφία βασιλείας τιμιώτερον καὶ
ὡς ὅ τι ἐν αὐτῷ καλὸν ἐνείη, τοῦτο δῶρον φιλοσοφίας. 156. περιβαλὼν οὖν καὶ ἀσπασάμενος ᾗ
νόμος τοῖς ἰδιώταις ἀλλήλους ἢ βασιλεῦσί γε ἀλλή-
λους εἰσῆγεν οὐ μετέχοντα τῆς βουλῆς, | κοσμεῖν F 3
ἡγούμενος οὐ τὸν ἄνδρα τῷ τόπῳ, τῷ δὲ ἀνδρὶ τὸν
τόπον, καὶ διαλεχθεὶς ἐν ἅπασιν οἷος ἐξ οἵου δι'
ἐκεῖνον γένοιτο, τῆς δεξιᾶς ἐχόμενος ἀπηλλάττετο.

---

ᵃ Cf. Homer, Od. 8. 171, Iliad, 3. 214, 222. This uncon-
ventional behaviour of Julian's, so much at variance with
Constantius' stern composure, earned him many detractors:
cf. Amm. Marc. 25. 4. 17, Lib. Or. 1. 129, Socr. loc. cit.
ᵇ An adaptation of Plato, Charm. 153 A, where Chaerephon welcomes his teacher Socrates who has unexpectedly
returned from the wars. Julian's mentor in philosophy,

orator's presence. Julian however, as Homer says of the able speaker, " with unerring discourse " attended such debates, allowing any who so desired to speak his mind freely before him and delivering speeches himself, sometimes " with words brief and clear," sometimes " with words like snowflakes in winter," now imitating those speakers in Homer, now excelling each of them in his own particular technique.[a] 155. Once, as he was in the middle of an oration with expressions of praise, censure and advice, he was told that his teacher, the Ionian philosopher whom he had summoned from Ionia, was coming. Then " he leapt up from the midst " of the elders and dashed to the door, affected just as Chaerephon was by Socrates, but while he was just a Chaerephon in Taureas' wrestling school, Julian was emperor of the world and in the supreme senate, proving to all and proclaiming by his actions that wisdom was more precious than royalty and that whatever nobility there was in him was the gift of philosophy.[b] 156. So he embraced him and welcomed him in the way that ordinary citizens do, or in which emperors greet one another. Then he introduced him, though he was no senator, for he thought he was not so much honouring the man by the place as the place by the man. He delivered an address, explaining to all the fundamental change that Maximus had effected in him,[c] and then he left, still holding his

Maximus of Ephesus, had been summoned to court (Eunap. V.S. 476 ff.). His arrival is described by Eunapius and by Amm. Marc. 22. 7. 3. Libanius, not to be outdone, narrates a similar exhibition of enthusiasm evinced towards himself by Julian on the occasion of the delivery of Or. 12 (Or. 1. 129).

[c] For Julian's conversion by Maximus cf. Eunap. loc. cit.

τί διὰ τούτων ποιῶν; οὐκ ἀμοιβάς, ὡς ἄν τις
ὑπολάβοι, μόνον ἐκτίνων τῆς παιδείας, ἀλλὰ καὶ
τὴν πανταχοῦ νεότητα, προσθείην δ' ἂν καὶ γῆρας,
πρὸς παιδείαν παρακαλῶν, ἐπεὶ καὶ γέροντες ἤδη
πρὸς μαθήσεις ἐκινήθησαν. πᾶν γὰρ ὑπὸ τῶν ἀρχόντων ἀτιμαζόμενον μὲν ὑφ' ἁπάντων ἀμελεῖ-
ται, τιμώμενον δὲ ἀσκεῖται.

157. Ὁ δὲ νομίζων ἀδελφὰ λόγους τε καὶ θεῶν
ἱερὰ καὶ τὸ μὲν ὅλως ἀνηρημένον ὁρῶν, τοῦ δὲ τὸ
πλέον, ὅπως τελέως καὶ τὸ τούτων ἔχοι καὶ πάλιν
ἐρασθεῖεν ἄνθρωποι λόγων ἔπραττε, τοῦτο μὲν ταῖς
τῶν ἐπισταμένων τιμαῖς, τοῦτο δὲ τῷ λόγους αὐτὸς
ποιεῖν. δύο γοῦν εὐθὺς τότε ἔδειξεν, ἔργον μιᾶς
R 575 ἡμέρας, μᾶλλον δὲ νυκτὸς ἑκάτερον, | ὧν ὁ μὲν
ἐπάταξεν ἄνθρωπον νόθον Ἀντισθένους μιμητὴν
ἀλογίστῳ θράσει τὸ πρᾶγμα ὁριζόμενον, ὁ δὲ πολλά
τε καὶ καλὰ λέγει περὶ τῆς μητρὸς τῶν θεῶν.
158. τῆς αὐτῆς δὲ διανοίας καὶ τὸ τὰς πόλεις ὑπὸ
τοῖς λέγειν ἐπισταμένοις ποιεῖν καὶ παῦσαι τοὺς
βαρβάρους τῶν | ἐθνῶν κυβερνήτας, οἳ γράφοντες F
μὲν σὺν τάχει νοῦν δὲ οὐκ ἔχοντες ἀνέτρεπον τὰ
σκάφη. ὁ δὲ τοὺς πεπληρωμένους ποιητῶν τε καὶ
λογοποιῶν καὶ παρ' ὧν ἦν εἰδέναι τίς ἄρχοντος
ἀρετή, τούτους παρεωσμένους ὁρῶν ἔδωκε τοῖς
ἔθνεσι. 159. τοιγαροῦν ἕκαστος αὐτὸν ἐπὶ Συρίας
ἐλαύνοντα λόγῳ περὶ τοὺς ὅρους ἐδέχετο, δώρῳ
πολὺ βελτίονι συῶν τε καὶ ὀρνίθων καὶ ἐλάφων

---

[a] Antisthenes, follower of Socrates and founder of the
Cynic school, whose teachings were diametrically opposed
to those of Plato. This feud was maintained by neo-Cynics
and neo-Platonists under the empire.

[b] Julian, Or. 7 (Against the Cynic Heracleios : 204 a ff.) ;
Or. 5 (To the Mother of the Gods : 158 a ff.). Cf. Or. 17. 16.

hand. What was his idea in all this, you may ask. He was not merely paying a debt of gratitude for his education, as you might suppose, but inviting the youth throughout the world, yes, and, I would add, the old men too, to the pursuit of learning, for even old men were now stimulated towards study, since, if a thing is despised by our rulers, it suffers universal neglect, if honoured, it becomes the fashion.

157. Also, considering learning and religion to be akin, and seeing the one nearly ruined, the other totally so, he directed his actions to the complete restoration of learning to its position and its renewal in men's regard, first by honouring its exponents, and again, by personally composing discourses. At any rate, he then delivered two straightaway, each the labour of a single day, or rather, of a single night. One of these belaboured a bogus follower of Antisthenes [a] whose definition of his creed was irrational and impudent, and the other is a fine sustained oration on the Mother of the Gods.[b] 158. It was with the same intention that he put the cities under the government of persons of ability in rhetoric and put a stop to the employment as provincial governors of those savages who, for all their skill in shorthand, had not a scrap of sense and upset the boat. Seeing that men full of poetry, prose and subjects from which the art of government could be learned had been slighted, he once more put them in charge of provinces.[c] 159. So, as he journeyed towards Syria, each successive governor welcomed him at the borders of his province with an address, a gift more acceptable than the boars, birds and bucks

---

[c] *e.g.*, Salustius (*Ep.* 1224), Nymphidianus (Eunap. *V.S.* 497).

# LIBANIUS

ἃ σιγῇ τοῖς βασιλεῦσιν ἤγετο, τότε δὲ ἀντὶ τούτων
οἱ λόγοι. καὶ διεδέχοντο τὴν παραπομπὴν ἄρχοντες
ῥήτορες. ὧν ὁ τῆς Κιλικίας, ἐμὸς μὲν ὁμιλητής,
ἐκείνῳ δὲ φίλτατος, τεθυκότι τε καὶ παρεστηκότι
τῷ βωμῷ τὸν ἔπαινον διῆλθε. καὶ ἱδρὼς ἀφ᾽
ἑκατέρου πολὺς ἔρρει, τοῦ μὲν ὁ τοῦ λέγοντος, τοῦ
δὲ ὁ τοῦ τὸν λέγοντα φιλοῦντος.

160. Ἀπὸ τούτων πολὺς αὖθις ὁ λειμὼν τῆς σοφίας. καὶ αἱ τῶν τιμῶν ἐλπίδες ἐπὶ τὴν τῶν λόγων
μεθειστήκεσαν κτῆσιν, καὶ τοῖς σοφισταῖς τὰ
πράγματα βελτίω τῶν μὲν ἀπ᾽ αὐτῶν τοῦ μανθάνειν
ἀρχομένων, τῶν δὲ ὀψὲ παρ᾽ αὐτοὺς μεταχωρούν-
των πώγωνας | ἐκεῖσε φερόντων καὶ τὸ τῶν δακ-
τύλων ἔργον. | οὕτως αὖθις παρεσκεύασε τὰ τῶν
Μουσῶν χλοῆσαι καὶ τὰ ὡς ἀληθῶς ἄριστα κάλλιστα νομισθῆναι καὶ μὴ τὰ τοῖς δούλοις προσήκοντα
τῶν τοῖς ἐλευθέροις πρεπόντων δύνασθαι πλεῖον.

161. Καίτοι τί μεῖζον εἴποι τις ἂν τοῦ θεούς τε
καὶ θεῶν δῶρον τὸ μέγιστον, τοὺς λόγους, ἐκ τῆς
ἐσχάτης ἀτιμίας εἰς τὸ τιμᾶσθαι προαγαγεῖν παρέ-
χοντα μὲν αὐτὸν διὰ πάσης τῆς πορείας σοφισταῖς,
ἐκτρεπόμενον δὲ τῆς εὐθείας ὁδοῦ κατὰ θέαν ἱερῶν,
ἐνεγκόντα δὲ ῥᾳδίως καὶ μῆκος ὁδοῦ καὶ χαλεπό-
τητα καὶ θάλπος. 162. οὗ δὴ καὶ μέγαν τῆς
εὐσεβείας τὸν μισθὸν ἠνέγκατο γνοὺς παρὰ τῶν
αὐτόθι δαιμόνων ὅτι τε ἐπιβουλεύοιτο καὶ ἥτις ἡ
σωτηρία. διὰ τοῦτο τῆς πορείας τὸν ῥυθμὸν

---

ᵃ Celsus : cf. Ep. 736, Or. 62. 61 f., Amm. Marc. 22. 9. 13.
384

that used to be offered to the emperors without a
word said. Now there were speeches instead of this
stuff, and the successive governors who received his
royal progress were orators. Such was the governor
of Cilicia, my old pupil and his dear friend, who
delivered a speech in his honour after the performance
of the sacrifice as he stood before the altar. Sweat
rolled off them both, from the one the sweat of
delivery, from the other that of affection for the
speaker.[a]

160. In consequence of this, the field of philosophy
was once again highly cultivated. The expectation
of honours, too, transferred students to the acquisition of learning, and there was an improvement in
the teachers' position, as their pupils either began
their education with them, or else late in the day
betook themselves to their classes, wearing beards
and bearing the work of their hands.[b] In this
way also he ensured that the Muses would flourish,
that true ideals should be held in the highest esteem,
and that pursuits appropriate to slaves should not
carry more weight than those suited to free men.

161. Yet what more important could be mentioned
than his restoration of religion and oratory, religion's
greatest gift, from a position of utter disgrace to one
of honour? Throughout his whole journey he was
easy of access to teachers, and he turned aside from
the high road to inspect temples, bearing with ease
the length, toil and heat of the road. 162. And there,
indeed, he got great reward for his piety from the
local deities, who informed him of plots against him
and of the manner of his salvation. Thus he altered

[b] *i.e.*, they had already earned their living as shorthand-
writers.

μεθαρμόσας θᾶττον ἢ πρόσθεν ἐχώρει καὶ διέφευγε
τὴν ἐνέδραν.

163. Καὶ ἐπιβὰς Συρίας χρέα τε λύσας ταῖς
πόλεσι καὶ φανεὶς ἐν τεμένεσι καὶ λαλῶν βουλευ-
ταῖς πρὸς ἕδεσιν ὥρμησε μὲν εὐθὺς ἐπὶ τὴν Περσῶν
τιμωρίαν καὶ οὐκ ἠξίου μέλλειν οὐδ' ἐν τῇ καθέδρᾳ
R 577 | τὴν ὥραν ἀναλοῦν, ὁπλιτῶν δὲ καὶ ἵππων ἀπειρη-
κότων καὶ μικρὰν αἰτούντων ἀναβολὴν ἄκων μέν,
ὡς ἂν ἐν | τῇ ψυχῇ τοῦ θυμοῦ ζέοντος, εἶξε δὲ F
ὅμως ταῖς ἀνάγκαις τοσοῦτον ἐπιφθεγξάμενος ὡς
ἔσται τις ὁ σκῶμμα ἐπ' αὐτὸν ἀφήσων ὡς ὄντως
εἴη τοῦ προτέρου συγγενής.

164. Σκοπῶμεν δὴ κἀν τῇ καθέδρᾳ τὸν βασιλέα
καὶ εἰ καιρὸς ἅπας εἶχε πράξεις ἐγκωμίων ἀξίας.
ἧκεν αὐτῷ γράμματα Περσικὰ δέξασθαι δεόμενα
πρεσβείαν καὶ λόγῳ τὰ διάφορα τεμεῖν. οἱ μὲν
οὖν ἄλλοι πάντες ἐπηδῶμεν, ἐκροτοῦμεν, ἐβοῶμεν
δέχεσθαι, ὁ δὲ ῥῖψαι κελεύσας ἀτίμως τὴν ἐπι-
στολὴν πάντων ἔφη δεινότατον εἶναι κεῖσθαι μὲν
τὰς πόλεις, αὐτοὺς δὲ διαλέγεσθαι καὶ ἀντεπέ-
στειλέ γε μηδὲν δεῖν πρέσβεων αὐτοῦ τάχιστα
ἐκεῖνον ὀψομένου. οὐκοῦν τοῦτο ἦν νίκη πρὸ
συμβολῆς καὶ πρὸ μάχης τρόπαιον ὁ συμβαῖνον

---

a For the visit to Pessinus and the shrine of the Magna
Mater cf. Amm. Marc. 22. 9. 5. The cult of Cybele (the
Idaean Mother) was transferred to Rome from Pessinus in
204 B.C., and the Megalensian games instituted in her
honour ; cf. Livy 29. 10 ff. Note that Libanius leaves aside
any provocative mention of the decree of June, A.D.
362, whereby on the eve of his departure from Constantinople Julian had banned Christians from the practice of
teaching.

the order of his march and, proceeding faster than
before, he escaped the ambush.[a]

163. And as soon as he set foot in Syria,[b] he cancelled
the debts of the cities: he made his appearance in
temple precincts and conversed with town councillors
close to the statues. He was eager to begin reprisals
against Persia and had no liking for delay or yet for
wasting the campaign season by staying where he
was, but he allowed his infantry and cavalry a break,
for they were exhausted and asked for a short rest.
He did so unwillingly, it is true, for his anger was
seething within him: nevertheless, he gave way to
necessity, merely exclaiming that the joke would be
made about him, that he was certainly of the same
breed as his predecessor.

164. Now let us consider our emperor during his
stay here and see whether each event was accompanied by activities worthy of praise. A despatch
reached him from Persia, asking him to receive an
embassy and to settle any point at issue by discussion.[c] All the rest of us jumped up, clapped hands
and shouted to him to accept the offer, but he ordered
the despatch to be rejected out of hand, for it was
intolerable that they should talk of peace while his
cities were in ruins.[d] He returned the reply that
envoys were not needed: the Persian would see him
soon enough. Now this was to win the victory before
entering the engagement and to erect a trophy
before the start of battle—the sort of thing we know

[b] Julian entered Antioch on July 18th (cf. Amm. Marc.
22. 9. 10 ; Bidez, Vie, p. 400). His first meeting with
Libanius is described in Ep. 736 and Or. 1. 121.

[c] Cf. Or. 12. 76, 17. 19. For Julian in Antioch cf. Lib.
Or. 1. 119 ff., Julian, Misopogon, Amm. Marc. 22. 9 ff.

[d] Cf. Amm. Marc. 22. 12.

ἴσμεν ἐν τοῖς γυμνικοῖς ἀγῶσιν, ὅταν τῷ πολὺ
διαφέροντι φανῆναι μόνον ἀρκῇ. 165. καὶ τὸ μὲν
ἤδη τοῦ βασιλέως παρόντος ἐκεῖνον τοῦτο παθεῖν
οὐ σφόδρα ἄν τις θαυμάσειε, καίτοι καὶ τοῦτο
θαυμαστὸν τρέμειν τὸν εἰωθότα φοβεῖν, τὸ δὲ
Κωνσταντίου μὲν γεγυμνωκότος τήνδε τὴν χώραν
ὅπλων, Ἰουλιανοῦ δὲ τἀκείνου μὲν λαβόντος, ἔτι
δὲ τῶν τῇδε | ἀπόντος ἤδη μηδένα Πέρσην μηδε- F
R 578 μιᾷ πόλει | προσβαλεῖν ἀλλ' ἀπὸ ψιλῆς τῆς
προσηγορίας ἠρεμεῖν πῶς οὐ πάντα ἀποκρύπτει
θαύματα;

166. Καὶ ταυτὶ μὲν ἔγνω περὶ τῆς πρεσβείας
ὅπλων, οὐ λόγων δεῖσθαι τὰ πεπραγμένα, τῶν δ'
αὖ στρατιωτῶν, οὓς μὲν ἐκέκτητο πρότερον, πάντα
ἔχειν ἡγεῖτο καλῶς, καὶ γὰρ τὰ σώματα ἔρρωντο
καὶ ταῖς μάχαις ἔχαιρον καὶ τὰ ὅπλα αὐτοῖς τέχνης
οὐ φαύλης καὶ θεοὺς καλοῦντες ἐμάχοντο, οὓς δ'
αὖ προσειλήφει, καλοὺς μὲν ἑώρα καὶ μεγάλους καὶ
ὅπλα ἐπίχρυσα φέροντας, τῷ δὲ πεφευγέναι τοὺς
πολεμίους πολλάκις πάσχοντας πρὸς τὴν θέαν τῶν
Περσῶν, ὅπερ ἐν ὄρεσιν Ὅμηρος ἄνθρωπον ἔφη
πρὸς δράκοντα, ἤ, εἰ βούλει γε, ὅπερ ἔλαφοι πρὸς
κύνας. 167. νομίσας οὖν αὐτοῖς βλάπτεσθαι τὰς
ψυχὰς οὐχ ἡγεμόνων φαυλότητι μόνον, ἀλλὰ καὶ
τῷ θεῶν ἄνευ πολεμεῖν μῆνας ἐννέα ταύτην αὐτοῖς
ἐκάθητο προξενῶν τὴν ῥοπήν, νομίζων καὶ πλῆθος
σωμάτων καὶ σιδήρου κράτος καὶ ἀσπίδων ἰσχὺν
καὶ πάνθ' ἁπλῶς φλυαρίαν εἶναι θεῶν οὐ συμπολε-

---

[a] Homer, *Iliad*, 3. 33 ff.
[b] *Cf. E.L.F.* No. 50.

occurs in athletic contests when all that is needed is for the favourite to walk into the ring. 165. It may be no great cause for surprise to find the Persian so affected during our emperor's presence here, though it is surprising enough that the man who usually caused others to tremble should himself be the one to tremble. What surely eclipses all other marvels is that, after the stripping of military protection from the area by Constantius, upon Julian's accession to the throne and before his arrival here, not a single Persian had attacked any one of our cities, but remained inactive as a result of the mere mention of his name.

166. Such then was his decision about the embassy, that the events of the past required weapons, not words. Of his troops, those that he had with him originally he thought to be in good shape, for they were sound physically, their fighting spirit was high, their equipment of no bad manufacture, and they entered the fight with the names of the gods on their lips : his recent acquisitions, however, despite their handsome appearance, tall stature and gilded armour were, as he saw, owing to the long acquaintance with defeat at the hands of the Persians, affected by the sight of them as the man in Homer was at the sight of a snake in the mountains,[a] or, if you like it better, as stags at the sight of the hounds. 167. So, feeling that their morale was lowered not just by bad leadership but also because they went into battle without the gods supporting them, he stayed where he was for nine months procuring for them the turning of the scales, for he considered superiority in numbers, force of steel, strength of shield, and every single thing to be quite pointless if the gods were not on his side.[b]

μούντων. 168. ὅπως οὖν συμπολεμοῖεν, ἐποίει
πείθων τὴν ἀψομένην δόρατος δεξιὰν ἅπτεσθαι καὶ
σπονδῆς καὶ λιβανωτοῦ ὥστ' ἔχειν βελῶν φερο-
μένων εὔχεσθαι | τοῖς ταῦτα δυναμένοις κωλύειν. F 3
οὐκ ἀρκούντων δὲ τῶν λόγων χρυσὸς καὶ ἄργυρος
συνέπραττεν εἰς πειθώ, καὶ διὰ κέρδους μικροῦ
μεῖζον εἶχε κέρδος ὁ στρατιώτης, διὰ χρυσίου
φιλίαν θεῶν πολέμου κυρίων. 169. οὐ γὰρ ᾤετο
δεῖν ὁ βασιλεὺς Σκύθας καλεῖν εἰς ἐπικουρίαν οὐδὲ
ὄχλον ἀθροίζειν βλάψοντα τῷ πλήθει καὶ πολλὰς
ἐμποιήσοντα τὰς ἀπορίας, ἀλλὰ τὴν πολὺ βαρυ-
τέραν χεῖρα τὴν τῶν κρειττόνων. τούτους γὰρ
ἐδίδου τοῖς θύουσι συμμάχους, τὸν Ἄρη, τὴν Ἔριν,
τὴν Ἐννώ, τὸν Δεῖμον, τὸν Φόβον, ὧν τὰ νεύ-
R 579 ματα ποιεῖ τροπάς· ὥστ' εἴ τις αὐτὸν | φαίη
βάλλειν Πέρσας καὶ τιτρώσκειν ἐπ' Ὀρόντῃ διατρίβοντα, μετ' ἀληθείας ἂν λέγοι.

170. Περὶ ταύτην τὴν σπουδὴν οὐκ ἀρνοῦμαι
πλοῦτον ἀνηλῶσθαι μέγαν, καλλίων δὲ ἄρα ἥδε ἡ
δαπάνη τῆς περὶ τὰ θέατρα καὶ τοὺς ἡνιόχους καὶ
ὅσοι τεταριχευμένοις ἀπαντῶσι θηρίοις. ὧν οὐδὲν
ἐπεσπάσατο | τὸν ἄνδρα τοῦτον ὅς γε καὶ καθι- F 3
ζούσης αὐτὸν ἀνάγκης ἐν ἱπποδρόμῳ πρὸς ἄλλοις
εἶχε τὰ ὄμματα τιμῶν ὁμοῦ τήν τε ἡμέραν καὶ
τὰ αὑτοῦ, τὴν μὲν τῷ παρεῖναι, τὰ δὲ τῷ μένειν
ἐπ' αὐτῶν. 171. οὐδεμία γὰρ ἔρις οὐδὲ ἅμιλλα
οὐδὲ κραυγὴ τὴν γνώμην μετέστησεν ἀπὸ τῶν φρον-

---

<sup>a</sup> Greg. Naz. Or. 4. 82 f.
<sup>b</sup> As Constantius had done in A.D. 360 (Amm. Marc. 20.
8. 1). In fact, Julian did have a Gothic contingent (ibid.
23. 2. 7).
<sup>c</sup> Homer, Iliad, 4. 439.
<sup>d</sup> As Julian himself asserts, Misop. 344 a.

168. His actions were designed to secure their active support: he induced the hand that grasped the spear to grasp offerings of incense and libation, so that they would be able to pray, when the weapons were flying, to those who had it in their power to forestall them. If persuasion proved insufficient, gold and silver co-operated to ensure adherence, and through this petty profit the soldiery secured a greater gain : by accepting a piece of gold, they won the friendship of the gods, the lords of war.[a] 169. For our emperor did not think it proper to call upon the Goths for assistance[b] nor gather a force that would do harm by its very numbers and raise many problems : the assistance on which he ought to rely was the much weightier power of the gods. For these were the allies he offered to such as performed the sacrifice— the gods of War, Strife, Fury, Terror and Fear, at whose nod foes are routed.[c] So, if you were to assert that he smote and wounded the Persians while he was still staying by the Orontes, you would not be far wrong.

170. I do not deny that considerable sums were spent on this objective, but, after all, such expenditure is more creditable than any made upon the theatre,[d] the races or the fights with beasts that have been kept cooped up in a cage. Nothing of that sort attracted Julian. Why, when he did have to sit in the hippodrome,[e] he kept his eyes fixed on something else and did honour to the day by his presence and to his thoughts by his concentration upon them. 171. For no struggle, no contest, no cheers could divert

[e] *Ibid.* 340 a, *Letter to a Priest*, 304 b ff. Libanius throughout this passage takes the *Misopogon* as his main source.

LIBANIUS

τισμάτων, ἐπεὶ καὶ ἑστιῶν ὄχλον σύμμικτον κατὰ
τὸν νόμον πίνειν ἄλλοις ἐπιτρέπων αὐτὸς λόγους
ἀνεμίγνυ τῷ πότῳ τοσοῦτον τῆς θοίνης μετέχων
ὅσον μὴ δοκεῖν ἀπεσχῆσθαι. τίς γὰρ οὕτω πώποτε
γαστρὸς ἐκράτησε τῶν ἐν οἰκήματι μικρῷ φιλοσοφούντων; τίς οὕτως ἄλλοτε ἄλλων ἀπέστη σιτίων
ἄλλοτε ἄλλον θεραπεύων θεόν, τὸν Πᾶνα, τὸν Ἑρμῆν, τὴν Ἑκάτην, τὴν Ἶσιν, τῶν λοιπῶν ἕκαστον;
τίς οὕτω πολλὰς ἀσιτίας μεθ᾽ ἡδονῆς ἤνεγκε θεοῖς
συνών; 172. ὁ γὰρ δὴ τῶν ποιητῶν λόγος ἔργον ἦν,
καί τις αὐτοῦ τῆς κόμης ἥψατο τῶν ἐξ οὐρανοῦ
καταβάντων καὶ εἰπών τι καὶ ἀκούσας ᾤχετο. καὶ
τὰς μὲν ἄλλας συνουσίας μακρὸν ἂν εἴη λέγειν, ἀλλ᾽
εἰς τὸ Κάσσιον ὄρος παρὰ τὸν | Κάσσιον ἀναβὰς F
Δία μεσημβρίας σταθερᾶς εἶδέ τε τὸν θεὸν καὶ
ἰδὼν ἀνέστη καὶ συμβουλὴν ἐδέξατο δι᾽ ἧς πάλιν
R 580 διαφεύγει | λόχον. 173. εἰ μὲν οὖν οἷόν τ᾽ ἦν ἄνθρω-
πον οὐρανοῦ κοινωνῆσαι θεοῖς, μετ᾽ ἐκείνων ἂν
ἦν αὐτῷ[1] τῆς αὐτῶν μεταδιδόντων χώρας, τοῦ σώματος δὲ ταῦτα οὐκ ἐῶντος αὐτοὶ παρ᾽ ἐκεῖνον
ᾔεσαν διδάσκαλοι τοῦ τί δεῖ ποιεῖν καὶ τί μὴ ποιεῖν γιγνόμενοι. τῷ μὲν γὰρ Ἀγαμέμνονι Νέστωρ
σύμβουλος ἦν ὁ Πύλιος, πάνυ μὲν γέρων, ἄνθρωπος δέ γε· τούτῳ δὲ ἀνθρώπων οὐδενὸς πρὸς ταῦτα
ἔδει, πάντων γὰρ ἦν ἀνθρώπων ἐν βουλαῖς ὀξύτα-
τος, παρὰ δὲ τῶν ἅπαντα εἰδότων ἦσαν αἱ παρ-
αινέσεις.

---

[1] αὐτῷ F. (αὐτω PU) : αὐτῶν Re. (other mss.).

[a] *Misop.* 346 a.
[b] Christian hermits and Cynic philosophers.

392

his mind from its speculations. For instance, even when entertaining a motley assemblage according to custom, though he allowed the rest to drink as usual, he interspersed his drinking with rhetorical discussion, partaking of the banquet only so far as not to seem to avoid it.[a] Now who of those practitioners of philosophy in a little hut has ever had such control over his appetites?[b] Who in worshipping the different gods at different times, Pan, Hermes, Hecate, Isis and the rest, has ever been so abstinent with the various foods?[c] Who ever kept so many fasts with such pleasure in his association with the gods? 172. The legend told by the poets was turned into fact. One of the immortals descended from heaven, took him by the hair, spoke to him and listened to his reply, and departed. Other such colloquies it would be tedious to narrate, but on ascending Mount Cassius to worship Zeus Cassius, at high noon he beheld the god and, on beholding him, rose up and received some advice, whereby he avoided a second trap.[d] 173. If it were possible for a human to share heaven with the gods, he would have done so with them, and they would have made room for him: but since this could not be done by reason of his body, they came in person to him to instruct him what to do and what not to do. For Agamemnon Nestor of Pylos was an adviser, a very old man, it is true, but human, none the less. Julian needed no humans for this purpose, for he was the most alert of men in counsel, and his advice came from the omniscient ones.

[c] *Misop.* 346 b: *cf.* Lib. *Or.* 1. 121, 15. 79. For Julian's orgy of sacrifices in Antioch *cf.* Amm. Marc. 22. 12. 6 f., 25. 4. 17.  [d] *Ibid.* 22. 14. 4.

174. Τοιούτοις μὲν σωτῆρσιν ἐφυλάττετο καὶ
τὰ πολλὰ συνῆν, νήφων δὲ συνεχῶς καὶ τὴν γαστέρα
οὐ βαρύνων τοῖς περιττοῖς τούτοις φορτίοις, ὥσπερ
πτηνὸς διὰ τῶν πραγμάτων ἤρχετο, πρεσβείαις
ἀποκρινόμενος συχναῖς ἐπὶ μιᾶς ἡμέρας, πόλεσιν
ἐπιστέλλων, στρατοπέδων ἄρχουσι, πόλεων ἄρχουσι, φίλοις ἀποδημοῦσι, φίλοις ἐπιδημοῦσιν,
ἀκούων ἐπιστολῶν, | δοκιμάζων αἰτήσεις, βραδείας F
ἀποφαίνων χεῖρας ὑπογραφέων τῷ τάχει τῆς
γλώττης. μόνος δὲ ἐκεῖνος τριῶν ἔργων εἰργάσατο
σύνοδον, ἀκοῆς, λόγου, γραφῆς· τῷ μὲν γὰρ ἀνα-
γινώσκοντι τὰ ὦτα παρεῖχε, τῷ γράφοντι δὲ τὴν
φωνήν, τοῖς δὲ αὐτοῦ ζητοῦσι γράμματα τὴν δεξιάν,
καὶ τὸ μηδὲν ἁμαρτεῖν πανταχοῦ προσῆν. 175. τὸ
μὲν οὖν ἀναπαύεσθαι τῶν διακόνων ἦν, αὐτοῦ δὲ
ἐπ᾽ ἔργον ἀπ᾽ ἔργου μεταπηδᾶν. ὁπότε γὰρ
λήξειε τοῦ διοικεῖν, ἀριστήσας ὅσον παρεῖχε ζῆν,
οὐκ ἐλείπετο τῶν τεττίγων, ἀλλ᾽ ἀφιεὶς αὐτὸν ἐπὶ
τοὺς σωροὺς τῶν βιβλίων ᾖδεν ἕως αὐτὸν πάλιν
ἐκάλει δείλης ἡ πρόνοια τῶν ὅλων, καὶ τὸ δεῖπνον
R 581 μᾶλλον τῆς προτέρας τραπέζης κεκολασμένον | καὶ
ὕπνος ὃς ἂν ἐκ τοσούτου γένοιτο μέτρου σιτίων,
καὶ πάλιν ὑπογραφεῖς ἕτεροι τὴν ἡμέραν ἐπ᾽ εὐνῆς
ἀνηλωκότες. 176. τοῖς μὲν γὰρ διακόνοις διαδοχῆς
ἔδει καὶ παρ᾽ ἀλλήλων εἶχον τὰς ἀναπαύσεις· ὁ δὲ
εἴδη μὲν πόνων ἤμειβε, πάντα δὲ ἐπόνει μόνος τὰς
Πρωτέως μεταβολὰς ἐν τοῖς πραττομένοις παριών,
ὁ αὐτὸς ἱερεύς, λογογράφος, μάντις, δικαστής, στρατιώτης, διὰ πάντων σωτήρ. 177. ἔσειε μὲν ὁ

---

[a] The sweet song of the cicada was proverbial: cf. Hom.
Il. 3. 151, Hes. Op. 580, Plat. Phaedr. 262 D. Julian's oratory is compared with this.

174. By such saviours was he guarded and with them he especially associated: in continued sobriety and without burdening his belly with the excessive amounts of food that are now the fashion, he went through all his business with the speed of flight. In a single day he would reply to many embassies, send despatches to many cities and governors, both civil and military, and to his friends, whether travelling abroad or visiting his court. He would listen to despatches, examine pleas, and by the speed of his words reveals the hands of his shorthand writers as laggardly. He alone performed three functions combined, hearing, speaking and writing : he would lend an ear to readers, his voice to writers, and his hand to any that required his personal signature— and, what is more, with never a mistake ! 175. Rest was for his subordinates : for himself, there was a leap from one task to another. When he relaxed from affairs of state, after breakfasting on just enough to keep body and soul together, not to be outdone by the cicadas,[a] he would make for his piles of books and read aloud until, in the evening, his care for the empire recalled him to his task. Then would follow a meal even more frugal than the first, and a sleep such as you might expect to result from such an abstemious diet. Then there would appear more secretaries who had spent the day in bed.[b] 176. His servants, in fact, needed to work in shifts, and they would rest in relays. He however, exchanged one form of work for another and alone performed them all. He outdid Proteus in the changes of role that he assumed, for he was priest, writer, seer, judge, soldier and universal saviour, all in one. 177. When

[b] *Cf.* Amm. Marc. 25. 4. 5 f.

Ποσειδῶν τὴν μεγάλην ἐν Θρᾴκη πόλιν, ἀγγελίαι δὲ
ἐφοίτων ὡς εἰ μή τις διαλλάξει | τὸν θεὸν περιέσται F
τῆς πόλεως τὸ κακόν· ὁ δὲ ὡς ἤκουσε στὰς ἐν
μέσῳ τῷ κήπῳ καὶ τῷ σώματι δεχόμενος τὸν
ὄμβρον τῶν ἄλλων ὑπὸ ταῖς ὀροφαῖς ὄντων τε καὶ
ὁρώντων καὶ ἐκπληττομένων διακαρτερήσας ὁ δαι-
μόνιος εἰς δείλην ὀψίαν τὸν μὲν θεὸν ἐπράϋνε, τὸν
δὲ κίνδυνον ἔλυσε, καὶ μετ' ἐκείνην ἰόντες ἐμήννον
λογιζόμενοι[1] τὴν ἡμέραν ᾗ ἔληξε τὸ κινοῦν, καὶ
οὐδὲ αὐτοῦ τῷ σώματι λυπηρὸν οὐδὲν ὁ ὄμβρος
ἐνέβαλε. 178. τοῦ χειμῶνος δὲ τὰς νύκτας ἐκτεί-
νοντος ἄνευ πολλῶν καὶ καλῶν ἑτέρων λόγων
ἐπιθέμενος ταῖς | βίβλοις αἳ τὸν ἐκ Παλαιστίνης F
ἄνθρωπον θεόν τε καὶ θεοῦ παῖδα ποιοῦσι, μάχῃ τε
μακρᾷ καὶ ἐλέγχων ἰσχύι γέλωτα ἀποφήνας καὶ
φλήναφον τὰ τιμώμενα σοφώτερος ἐν τοῖς αὐτοῖς
δέδεικται[2] τοῦ Τυρίου γέροντος. ἵλεως δὲ οὗτος ὁ
R 582 Τύριος | εἴη καὶ δέχοιτό γε εὐμενῶς τὸ ῥηθέν, ὡς
ἂν υἱέος ἡττώμενος.

179. Ταυτὶ τοῦ μήκους τῶν νυκτῶν ἀπολέλαυκεν
ἡμῖν ὁ βασιλεύς· ἑτέροις δὲ ἐν ταῖς τηλικαύταις
τῶν Ἀφροδίτης ἐμέλησεν. ὁ δὲ τοσοῦτον ἀπέσχε
τοῦ ζητεῖν εἴ τῳ θυγάτηρ ἢ γυνὴ καλή, ὥστ' εἰ μὴ
θεσμῷ γάμων | ἐζεύχθη παρὰ τῆς Ἥρας, ἐτελεύτα F

---

[1] λογιζόμενοι Re. (mss.) : λογιζομένῳ F.
[2] δέδεικται Socr. H.E. 3. 23, p. 196 D : δέδεικτο Re., F.
(mss. except V) : ἐδέδεικτο V.

---

[a] Cf. Or. 15. 71, where the incident is presented with
reference to Antioch, not to Constantinople. This is the
earthquake of 2 Dec. A.D. 362 (Amm. Marc. 22. 13. 5).
[b] Quoted by Socr. H.E. 3. 23.

Poseidon[a] caused earthquakes in the capital in Thrace, messengers came repeatedly with the news that if the god were not appeased, the ruin of the city would be complete. On hearing this, he took his stand in the garden, his person drenched with pouring rain, while all the rest looked on in awe from under cover, and our blessed prince steadfastly endured until, late in the evening, he soothed the god and put an end to the danger. Afterwards they came and informed him, calculating the day when the tremors ceased. Nor did the rain-storm cause him any personal harm. 178. As winter lengthened the nights,[b] besides many other fine compositions, he attacked the books in which that fellow from Palestine is claimed to be a god and son of god.[c] In a long polemic and by dint of forceful argument, he proved such claims to be stupid, idle chatter. On the same subject he showed himself wiser than the old sage from Tyre: and right pleased and happy may this Tyrian be to accept this statement, beaten as it were by his son.[d]

179. Such were our emperor's enjoyments during the long winter nights, when other people are usually more interested in matters of sex. But so far was he from enquiring whether any man had a good-looking daughter or wife that, had not Hera once bound him in the rites of marriage, he would have

[c] The *Contra Galilaeos* (*cf.* Julian, ed. Wright (Loeb), vol. 3, pp. 313 ff.). Julian also composed the *Caesars* and the *Hymn to Helios the King* in the December. Libanius, again avoiding provocation, omits all reference to the burning of the temple of Apollo at Daphne in October, which had infuriated Julian.

[d] Porphyry of Tyre, *Adversus Christianos* (ed. von Harnack, *Abh. Berl. Akad.* 1916).

ἂν λόγῳ μόνον τὰς ἀνθρώπων ἐπιστάμενος μίξεις.
νῦν δὲ τὴν μὲν γυναῖκα ἐπένθησεν, ἑτέρας δὲ οὔτε
πρότερον οὔθ᾽ ὕστερον ἥψατο φύσει τε δυνάμενος
σωφρονεῖν καὶ τῆς ἐν ταῖς μαντείαις διατριβῆς
συμπαρακαλούσης.   180. ἐν αἷς διῆγε μάντεών τε
τοῖς ἀρίστοις χρώμενος αὐτός τε ὢν οὐδενὸς ἐν τῇ
τέχνῃ δεύτερος ὥστε μηδ᾽ ἐξεῖναι τοῖς μάντεσι
παρακρούεσθαι συνεξεταζόντων τὰ δεικύμενα τῶν
ὀφθαλμῶν ἐκείνου.  καί που καὶ τῶν ἐν τούτῳ
ἐπισταμένων ἀπῆλθε κρατῶν, οὕτως εὐρεῖά τε καὶ
πάμφορος ἡ ψυχὴ τῷ βασιλεῖ, καὶ τὰ μὲν εὕρισκε
τῇ φρονήσει, περὶ δὲ τῶν ἀνεκοινοῦτο τοῖς κρείττοσιν.  ἐντεῦθεν οἷς τε οὐκ ἐδόκει δώσειν ἀρχὰς
ἔδωκεν οἷς τε ἐνομίζετο δώσειν οὐκ ἔδωκε, ψήφῳ
θεῶν καὶ διδοὺς καὶ μὴ διδούς.

181. Ἀλλὰ μὴν ὡς γνήσιος ἦν κηδεμὼν τῆς
ἀρχῆς καὶ ὡς τἀκείνης ἦγε πρὸ τῶν ἑαυτοῦ πολ-
λαχόθεν μὲν δεδήλωται, σαφέστερον δ᾽ ἂν ὡδὶ
γένοιτο. παρακαλούμενος γὰρ ἐπὶ γάμον παρὰ τῶν
ἐπιτηδείων ὅπως παῖδας φυτεύσειε κληρονόμους
τῆς ἀρχῆς, τοῦτ᾽ αὐτὸ δεδιὼς ἔφη μέλλειν, μὴ
κακοὶ φύντες νόμῳ | παραλαβόντες διαφθείρωσι τὰ F
πράγματα τὸ τοῦ Φαέθοντος παθόντες.  οὕτω τὴν
ἀπαιδίαν τὴν αὐτοῦ τῆς εἰς τὰς πόλεις λύμης
κουφότερον ἔκρινεν.

182. Οὐ τοίνυν οὐδὲ τὸν περὶ τὰς δίκας πόνον ὡς

---

[a] Hera is the presiding deity of wedlock.  For Julian's conduct after Helena's death cf. Amm. Marc. 25. 4. 2.

[b] Especially so in his criteria for his pagan priesthood, cf. Letter to a Priest, 305 a ff.

[c] Phaëthon, son of Helios, the sun-god, demands of his father the right to drive his chariot for a day.  The horses run away with him and, when earth and heaven are near

ended his days knowing nothing of sexual intercourse of humans save by report. As it was, he went into mourning for his wife and never touched another woman before or afterwards,[a] for he had a natural bent towards continence and his preoccupation with soothsaying tended in the same direction. 180. On this he spent his time, employing the most capable soothsayers, and himself being second to none in the art, so that the seers could never mislead him since his gaze too scrutinized the omens. Indeed, at times he surpassed specialists in the subject, so wide and all-embracing was our emperor's intellect, and his discoveries were made either as a result of his own insight or of his association with the gods. So it was that he bestowed office upon persons to whom it was thought he would not give it, and withheld it from those to whom it was thought that he would, the giving and the withholding both being dictated by the decision of the gods.[b]

181. Moreover, though there is ample evidence to show how genuine a guardian of his empire he was and how much more importance he placed on its welfare than on his own, this may make it clearer still. His intimates tried to persuade him to remarry so that he would have sons to succeed to the throne, but he replied that that was the very thing that deterred him, lest his children, if degenerate, should be legal heirs to the throne and bring ruin on themselves, suffering Phaëthon's fate.[c] So, childlessness for himself he judged to be of less importance than any harm done to the empire.

182. Nor again did he seek to avoid the task of

destruction from the sun's fire, Zeus strikes him down by lightning; cf. Ovid, Met. 1. 748–2. 343.

# LIBANIUS

R 583 ἂν εἰς | τοσαῦτα μέρη τὴν ψυχὴν διανέμων ἔφευγεν,
ἀλλὰ καὶ τοῖς δικάσαι δεινοτάτοις καὶ πάντων
ἀδωροτάτοις ὑπάρχοις ἔχων ἀφεῖναι τὸν περὶ ταῦτα μόχθον ὅμως ἕνα καὶ αὐτὸν τῶν δικαζόντων
ἀπέφηνε καὶ πρὸς τὸν ἆθλον ἀπέδυ, πλὴν εἴ τις
ἐπιλαμβάνοιτο τοῦ ῥήματος φάσκων οὐκ ἆθλον,
ἀλλὰ καὶ ῥᾳστώνην αὐτῷ καὶ παιδιὰν γενέσθαι
τὰς δίκας.    183. οὕτως ἀπεκρούετο μὲν εὐχερῶς
τῶν συνηγόρων τὰς ἀπάτας, τὸ δὲ ἐν ἑκάστῳ
δίκαιον ἀμυθήτῳ τάχει τῆς γνώμης ᾔρει λόγοις
λόγους κρίνων ἀληθέσι ψευδεῖς καὶ νόμοις νικῶν
σοφίσματα. καὶ οὐ τοῖς μὲν πλουτοῦσιν ἠναντιοῦτο
καὶ δίκαια λέγουσι, μετὰ δὲ τῶν πενομένων καὶ
ἀναισχυντούντων ἦν, ὡς ἄν τις τοῖς μὲν φθονῶν τῆς
τύχης, πρὸς δὲ τοὺς ἐλέῳ καιρὸν οὐκ ἔχοντι χρώμενος, ἀλλ' ἀφιστὰς τὴν γνώμην τῶν ἀγωνιζο-
μένων τῇ φύσει τῶν πραγμάτων προσῆγε τὴν
κρίσιν, ὥστ' ἀπῆλθέ ποτε καὶ πλούσιος νενικηκὼς
καὶ πένης ἡττημένος.    184. καὶ εἶχε μέν, εἴπερ
ἐβούλετο, παραβαίνειν τοὺς νόμους καὶ οὐκ ἔμελλεν
εἰς | δικαστήριον εἰσαχθεὶς δώσειν δίκην, οὕτω δὲ F 3
ἀκριβέστερον τῶν πικροτάτων[1] δικαστῶν ᾤετο δεῖν
τοῖς κειμένοις ἐπὶ τῶν κρίσεων ἐμμένειν ὥστε τινὸς
τῶν διὰ τὴν ἄλλην ἀδικίαν ὑπ' αὐτοῦ μισουμένων
γράμμασι πεπλασμένοις βιαζομένου τὸ δίκαιον
ᾔσθετο μέν, τοῦ δὲ ἀδικουμένου γράφεσθαι τὸ
γράμμα οὐκ ἔχοντος ἔκρινε τὸν ἀδικοῦντα νικᾶν
ἐπειπὼν ὡς οὐκ ἀγνοήσειε μὲν τὴν κακοτεχνίαν,
ἡσυχάζοντος δὲ τοῦ βεβλαμμένου, τῷ νόμῳ δου-

---

[1] πικροτάτων Norman (cf. Amm. Marc. 22. 9. 9 : " iudici-
bus Cassiis tristior ") : σμ- or μικροτάτων (mss.), F., Re.

400

dispensing justice,[a] since he was able to divide his personality into so many compartments as it were. He could delegate such tasks to expert judges and incorruptible prefects, but he still made his appearance as one of the judges and stripped for the contest, unless perhaps you wish to criticize the term and say that the courts were for him not a contest but a diversion and amusement. 183. Thus he would rebut with ease the tricks of the advocates and seize upon the point at issue with incredible quickness of intellect, comparing false arguments with true and confuting their subterfuges with legal precedent. It was not his way to attack the wealthy when they were in the right, or to side with the poor if they were barefaced liars, out of envy of the rich for their good fortune or an ill-timed sympathy for the poor. He made no distinction of person between the litigants but applied his judgement to the facts of the case, so that at times a rich man came off best and a poor man lost. 184. He could, if he so desired, have broken the laws without any likelihood of his being brought into court to be punished for it. Yet he thought that he should abide by the established legal procedure more consistently than the most unbending of officials. Hence when a person whom he detested for his misconduct perverted the course of justice by forged documents, he saw where justice lay but, since the victim was unable to bring any complaint against the document, he gave the verdict to the guilty party, but he ended by stating that he was not unaware of the fraud but the inaction of the injured party caused him, in obedience to the law, to give a

---

[a] For which he is praised by Ammianus (22. 9. 9) and, naturally, derided by Gregory (*Or.* 5. 20 f.).

λεύων διδοίη τὴν ψῆφον τῷ κεκακουργηκότι. ὥστε
μετὰ μείζονος ἀπῄει λύπης ὁ νενικηκὼς τοῦ
νενικημένου, ὁ μὲν εἰς γῆν,[1] ὁ δὲ εἰς δόξαν ζημιω-
R 584 θείς. οὕτως εὗρε μήτε τὸν νόμον | κινῆσαι καὶ
τὸν ἀδικοῦντα κολάσαι. 185. ἀνεῳγμένου δὲ τοῦ
βασιλέως δικαστηρίου καὶ πᾶσιν οὔσης ἐξουσίας
ἐκεῖσε καταφυγεῖν πάντες ὅσοι δι' ἰσχύος ἀδίκου
τὰ τῶν ἀσθενεστέρων εἶχον, οἱ μὲν ἀναιδῶς ἁρπά-
σαντες, οἱ δὲ ἐν πράσεως σχήματι, οἱ μὲν ἐγκαλοῦ-
σιν, οἱ δὲ καὶ σιωπῶσιν ἀποδώσοντες προσῄεσαν
φθάνοντες τὰς κρίσεις τῷ φόβῳ, καὶ δικαστὴς ἦν
αὐτὸς αὑτῷ τῶν ἠδικηκότων ἕκαστος. 186. ὥσθ'
ὅπερ ἐφ' Ἡρακλέους γενέσθαι φασὶ τοὺς ὅπου δὴ
γῆς ἢ θαλάττης πάσχοντας | κακῶς ἐκεῖνον καὶ F
ἀπόντα καλεῖν καὶ τοὔνομα πρὸς ἐπικουρίαν ἀρκεῖν,
τοῦτο καὶ τὴν τοῦδε προσηγορίαν δεδυνημένην
ἴσμεν. καὶ πόλεις καὶ κῶμαι καὶ ἀγοραὶ καὶ
οἰκίαι καὶ ἤπειροι καὶ νῆσοι καὶ νέοι καὶ γέροντες
καὶ ἄνδρες καὶ γυναῖκες τῷ τὸν δεῖνα βασιλεύειν
λέγειν τοὺς λυποῦντας ἀπεωθοῦντο, καὶ χεῖρα πρὸς
πληγὴν ἕτοιμον τὸ ῥῆμα τοῦτο συνέστειλε πολλάκις. 187. ἐδέξατο δὴ τὸ δικαστήριον ἐκεῖνο
καὶ πόλεις ὑπὲρ πρωτείων ἀμφισβητούσας αἳ τῶν
ἐν Συρίᾳ μετὰ τὴν ἡμετέραν μέγισται, κάλλος δὲ
θατέρᾳ πλέον ἅτε καὶ τὴν θάλατταν καρπουμένη.
λόγων δὲ μακρῶν εἰρημένων καὶ τῶν μὲν ἄλλα τε
διεξελθόντων ἃ τῆς ὥρας ἦν καὶ πολίτου τινὸς
σοφίαν, τῶν δὲ ἐν μεσογείᾳ ξένου τε καὶ πολίτου,
τοῦ μὲν ταύτην προκρίναντος ἐμφιλοσοφεῖν, τοῦ

---

[1] γῆν F. (mss.) : κτῆσιν Re. (gloss in I).

verdict in favour of the criminal. Thus the winner
left more deeply hurt than the loser who had suffered
the loss of his land alone, while he had lost his reputation. In this way he contrived the punishment of
the wrongdoer without infringement of the law.
185. When the emperor's court was opened and all
were at liberty to have recourse to it, all those
people who had got possession of the property of
some weaker party by illegal means, either by barefaced robbery or by a trumped-up sale, came to make
restitution, in some cases to complainants, in some,
even to those who made no outcry. These anticipated the verdict in their fear, and each of the wrong-
doers passed judgement on himself. 186. So, as they
say happened in the case of Heracles, people in distress everywhere on land and sea invoked his name,
even in his absence, and it served as protection
enough. Here too we know that his name had the
same effect. Cities, villages, markets, households,
continents and islands, the young and the old, men
and women began to repel their persecutors by the
mere mention of him upon the throne, and his name
often stayed a hand that was raised to strike. 187.
That court also undertook to decide the issue between two cities in a dispute about precedence.
These were the greatest in Syria next to our own, and
one had the advantage of beauty since it enjoyed the
proximity of the sea. Long speeches were delivered,
where the representatives of the one adduced their
various claims to beauty and also the wisdom of a
citizen of theirs,[a] while those of the inland town
dwelt upon the wisdom of the alien who resided
there, having chosen the place as the site for his

---

[a] Laodicea : *cf.* Suidas, *s.v.* Ἀπολινάριος Λαοδικεύς.

δὲ ἐκεῖνόν τε καὶ τοὺς ἀκολουθοῦντας ἐκείνῳ
πανταχόθεν ἀσμένως δεξαμένου, τὴν μὲν τῶν
λίθων αὐγὴν χαίρειν ἀμφοτέροις | ἀφείς, τοὺς | F
R 585 ἄνδρας δὲ ἀλλήλοις παραθεὶς προτέραν ἐποίησε τῇ
τιμῇ τὴν τούτοις κρατοῦσαν. 188. ταυτὶ δὲ ψηφι-
σάμενος ἆρ' οὐ πρὸς ἀρετὴν παρεκάλει τὰς πόλεις
ἀμελήσας τοῦ τῶν ἀψύχων κάλλους, ὡς οὐ δυναμένου φέρειν παρὰ κριτῇ σπουδαίῳ πλεονεξίαν;

189. Ἄρτι μὲν οὖν τῆς ἐν τοῖς ἱεροῖς ἐμεμνήμην
κοινότητος, νῦν δὲ ἔχω τι μεῖζον εἰπεῖν ὅτι καὶ
δικάζων πλείστῳ τούτῳ πρός τε τοὺς ῥήτορας καὶ
πρὸς ἐκείνους ὧν οἱ ῥήτορες προέκαμνον ἐχρῆτο,
διδοὺς ἐξουσίαν καὶ βοῆς ἀμετρίᾳ καὶ χειρὸς ἀνα-
σείσει καὶ πᾶσι σχήμασι καὶ τοῖς εἰς ἀλλήλους
σκώμμασι καὶ οἷς ὅλως ἑκάτεροι κρατήσειν ἐπί-
στευον. καὶ πολὺ πρὸς ἕκαστον, ὦ ἑταῖρε. 190.
τουτὶ μὲν καὶ πρὸς ἅπαντας, οὐ μόνον πρὸς
ῥήτορας νῦν δὴ πρῶτον ἀρχομένοις ὑπὸ τοῦ
κρατοῦντος δοθὲν ῥῆμα ἴυγγος δυνατώτερον εἰς
εὔνοιαν. οὐ γὰρ τοὺς φόβους καὶ τὰς σιγὰς καὶ τὸ
εἴσω τὴν χεῖρα ἔχειν καὶ τὸ κύπτειν εἰς γῆν καὶ τὸ
βλέπειν εἰς τὸ ὑπόδημα μᾶλλον ἢ τὸ πρόσωπον καὶ
τὸ δούλους ἀντ' ἐλευθέρων ὁρᾶσθαι κἂν τοῖς λεγο-
μένοις κἂν τοῖς πραττομένοις, οὐ ταῦτα ἡγεῖτο |
τὴν βασιλείαν αὔξειν, ἀλλὰ τὸ μηδένα τῶν ἐκείνῳ F 3
R 586 συγγινομένων μὴ¹ αὐτὸν ἔχειν μᾶλλον | ἢ 'κεῖνα

¹ μὴ inserted F., ἢ Fabr. (following ἢ omitted).

ᵃ Apamea: ibid. s.v. Σώπατρος Ἀπαμεύς. Iamblichus
and Sopater are the philosophers here mentioned, whose
404

philosophical studies,[a] and also of one of their citizens
who had given an enthusiastic welcome to him and
his followers from every quarter. Julian put aside
any question of the gleaming marble buildings they
might both possess and compared the men, and he
gave the precedence in honour to the city that was
superior in this respect. 188. In such a verdict, did he
not encourage the cities to the pursuit of virtue,
ignoring the beauties of inanimate creation, since
that can have no influence upon a balanced judgement?

189. Just recently I mentioned his affability in the
temples. Now I can say something more on the
subject. He applied this quality in the highest
degree towards the advocates and the clients for
whom they toiled when he sat in judgement. He
gave them full freedom to raise their voices, to shake
their fists and to make all sorts of gestures and comments to each other—in short, to use all the tricks of
the trade that each party relies on to win a case.[b] He
frequently addressed them as " My friend." 190.
And this expression applied to everyone, not just to
advocates, was now for the first time used by an
emperor towards his subjects, and it was more pro-
ductive of good will than any talisman. He did not
think that it heightened his majesty for them to be
frightened and silent, to fold their hands, to prostrate
themselves to the ground and to study his shoe-toe
in preference to his face, and in all their words and
actions to be seen as slaves rather than free men.
What mattered to him was that everyone about him
should be able to admire him for himself instead of

fame wins Julian's verdict for Apamea; *cf.* Eunap. *V.S.*
462 ff.       [b] *Cf.* Amm. Marc. 22. 10.

# LIBANIUS

θαυμάσαι. 191. ἐπεὶ καὶ τὴν ἁλουργῆ χλαμύδα
φέρων ἦν οὐκ ἦν βασιλεύοντα μὴ φορεῖν ὡς οὐδὲν
τῶν ἄλλων διαφέρουσαν ἔφερεν. οὔκουν αὐτὸν
περιεσκόπει φορῶν οὐδὲ ἐβασάνιζε βαφὴν οὐδὲ
βελτίω λαβὼν ἡγεῖτο γεγονέναι βελτίων οὐδὲ τὴν
ἀρίστην ἄριστος, οὐδὲ τῇ τῆς χρόας ὑπερβολῇ τῆς
ἀρχῆς τὴν εὐδαιμονίαν ἐμέτρει, ἀλλ' ἐκεῖνο μὲν
ἠφίει βαφεῦσι καὶ ὑφάνταις ὅ τι βούλοιντο δρᾶν,
αὐτὸς δὲ ἐν τῇ τῆς φρονήσεως φορᾷ καὶ τῇ τῶν
πόλεων ἐκεῖθεν ὠφελείᾳ ὑψηλήν τε ᾤετο τὴν
βασιλείαν ποιεῖν καὶ διὰ τούτων εἶναι λαμπρότερος.
192. ἔμεινε δὲ καὶ ὁ χρυσὸς περὶ τῇ κεφαλῇ θεῶν
οὕτω γνόντων· δι' ὅ,[1] θεῶν, οἶμαι, καὶ τοῦτο
εἰδέναι. ὡς ἐκεῖνός γε οὐκ ὀλιγάκις ὥρμησεν
ἄχρυσον ποιῆσαι τὴν κεφαλήν, ἀλλ' ἦν ἀμείνων ὁ
κωλύων.

193. Ὁ χρυσὸς δὲ οὗτος ἀνέμνησέ με χρυσῶν
στεφάνων οὓς αἱ μὲν πόλεις ἔπεμπον διὰ πρέσβεων
ἀλλήλας ὑπερβάλλουσαι τῷ σταθμῷ, χιλίων οὗτος
στατήρων, δισχιλίων δὲ ἐκεῖνος, τούτων ὁ παρ'
ἑτέρων ἕλκων πλέον. ὁ δὲ ἐπιτιμήσας τῷ μεγέθει
σαφῶς εἰδὼς ὡς οὐκ ἄνευ πόνου τὰ τοιαῦτα συλ-
λέγοιτο, νομοθετεῖ | τὸν στέφανον ἀπὸ στατήρων F 3
ἑβδομήκοντα φοιτᾶν τὴν μὲν τιμὴν ἴσην νομίζων
R 587 ἑκάτερον δύνασθαι, φιλοχρημάτου δὲ | εἶναι κέρδη
ζητεῖν ἐν τιμῶν σχήματι. 194. καὶ τούτους οἱ
κομίζοντες τοὺς νόμους καὶ πολλὰ ἕτερα γράμματα, τὰ μὲν οὐ χείρω τὰ δὲ καὶ βελτίω, τοσοῦτον

---

[1] δι' ὅ, F.: διὸ Fabr. (mss.): διὰ Re.

[a] Cf. Amm. Marc. 22. 9. 11.
[b] The extant legislation on *aurum coronarium* is dated
April 29, A.D. 362 (*Cod. Th.* 12. 13. 1; *E.L.F.* No. 72).
406

all that. 191. Even when he wore the purple cloak that had to be worn by an emperor, he did so as if it were nothing out of the ordinary.[a] In wearing it, he did not look himself up and down and examine its hue, nor did he think of himself, if he got a richer dye, as any the better man, nor if he got the richest, as being without peer. No, he did not measure the happiness of his reign by the depth of his purple. He let the dyers and weavers do as they thought fit with that : he believed the sublimity of his reign was due to the exercise of his intellect and the aid he granted the cities therefrom, and that that was what gave him more prestige. 192. The golden crown remained encircling his head, for the gods decided it so. As for the reason, it was, I think, for the gods to know that too ; at any rate, he personally was quite often minded to leave his head uncrowned, but always there was some higher power to prevent it.

193. This gold is a reminder to me of those crowns of gold that the cities used to send by their envoys, striving to outdo one another in the weight of them. One would weigh a thousand staters, another two thousand, one from another town more still. He disapproved of such excessive amounts, for he knew quite well that these contributions were made not without difficulty, and so he ordained that crowns of seventy staters only should be sent, for he valued the compliment just as highly whatever the amount, and regarded it as mere avarice to seek profit under the pretext of honour.[b] 194. And as for the couriers who delivered his decrees and the many other communications that were as good as, if not better than that, so

That Julian later ordained an upper limit of 70 *solidi* is noted only here.

ἀπεῖχον τοῦ μισθὸν ἐπὶ τοιούτοις αἰτεῖν ὥσθ'
ἑκόντων διδόντων οὐ προσίεντο· τοσοῦτος ἐπῆν
κίνδυνος τοῖς οὐ καλοῖς λήμμασι, καὶ ἦν δῆλον ὡς
εἰληφότι λαθεῖν τε οὐκ ἔσται καὶ δοῦναι δίκην
ἀνάγκη. οὕτως ἀγαθοῦ βασιλέως οὐ κατῃσχύνετο
δόξα τῇ τῶν ὑπηρετούντων κακίᾳ.

195. Καὶ ὁ μὲν ἐν τούτοις ἦν, βοὴ δὲ ἐξαίφνης
ἐν ἱπποδρόμῳ δήμου πεινῶντος, ὡς τῆς μὲν γῆς
ὑπὸ τῶν ἀέρων ἠδικημένης, τῆς πόλεως δὲ ὑπὸ
τῶν εὐπόρων οὐ φερόντων εἰς μέσον χρονίου συλλογῆς θησαυροὺς ἀλλὰ τοῦ σίτου τὰς τιμὰς συνι-
στάντων. συγκαλέσας δὴ γεωργοὺς καὶ χειροτέχνας καὶ καπήλους καὶ πάντων ἁπλῶς τιμητὰς
ὠνίων ἀναγκάσας νόμῳ σωφρονεῖν καὶ πρῶτος
αὐτὸς ἀκολουθήσας τῷ · νόμῳ τοὺς αὐτοῦ πυροὺς
εἰς ἀγορὰν ἐνεγκών, ἐπειδὴ τῷ νόμῳ | μαχομένην F 3
ᾔσθετο τὴν βουλὴν καὶ τοῖς μὲν αὐτοῦ χρωμένην
τὰ δὲ αὐτῆς κατακρύπτουσαν, οἴεταί τις ἀκοῦσαι
τῶν οὐκ ἐπισταμένων τὰ τότε δόρυ καὶ ξίφος καὶ
πῦρ καὶ θάλατταν, ταῦτα γὰρ ὀφείλειν δοκοῦσιν οἱ
τῶν ὑπηκόων πολεμοῦντες βασιλεῖ, καὶ γὰρ οὗτος |
R 588 ἄνευ ὅπλων πόλεμος ἐξεπίτηδες ἀπειθεῖν καὶ παρὸν
συνᾴδειν διαφωνεῖν καὶ ἃ κυροῦν ἐκεῖνος ἐσπούδακε,
πάσῃ τῇ τέχνῃ ποιεῖν ἄκυρα. 196. τὸ μὲν οὖν τῆς
ἀρχῆς δίκαιον καὶ ταῦτα εἰσηγεῖτο καὶ τούτων χαλεπώτερα, καὶ πάντως ἂν ἄλλος σκηπτοῦ δίκην ἐπὶ

---

[a] For famine in Antioch cf. *Misop.* 350 a, 368 c ff., Lib.
*Or.* 15 and 16, *Or.* 1. 126, Amm. Marc. 22. 14. 1, Socr.
*H.E.* 3. 17. Discussion by Downey, *An Economic Crisis at
Antioch* (Studies in hon. of A. C. Johnson, Princeton, 1951),
De Jonge, " Scarcity of Corn and Corn-prices in Amm."
408

far from demanding payment for their services, they refused to accept it when it was freely offered. Ignoble gain was attended by such risks, and clearly it was impossible for the recipient to escape detection and punishment was inevitable. Thus the fame of a good emperor was not besmirched by the shortcomings of his subordinates.

195. While he was thus engaged, all of a sudden there arose in the hippodrome the outcry of a starving populace; they complained that the soil had suffered from a bad season and the city from the wealthy, who failed to produce their long-hoarded stocks for public consumption but forced up the price of corn.[a] He called together the farmers, manufacturers and shopkeepers, in fact all who had anything to do with fixing market prices, and forced them by edict to charge a reasonable price, and he himself was the first to bring his own wheat to market in obedience to the edict. When he saw the city council actively opposing it and using his contributions while hoarding their own, you might, if you were unacquainted with the events of the time, expect to hear of executions by spear and sword, by burnings and drownings—for these are the punishments that subjects who rebel against the emperor are held to deserve: for, indeed, deliberate disobedience and non-co-operation when co-operation is possible, and the sparing of no effort to nullify such measures as he was set on ratifying— this was indeed unarmed rebellion. 196. Such punishments, and those still more severe, were consonant with the claims of his imperial state, and anyone else would certainly have come down like a

Marc.," *Mnemosyne*, 1948, pp. 238 ff., Petit, *Vie municipale*, pp. 109 ff,

τοὺς ὑβρικότας ἠνέχθη, ὁ δὲ πανταχοῦ τε τὸν θυμὸν ἀνέχων καὶ τότε δὴ διαφερόντως νενικηκὼς
τὰς μὲν προσηκούσας τιμωρίας ἀφῆκε δεσμωτηρίου δὲ ὀνόματι μᾶλλον ἢ δεσμῷ τὴν δίκην ἐπράξατο.
οὔκουν εἴσω θυρῶν ἐγένετο τῶν πολιτευομένων οὐδείς. ἀλλ᾿ οὐδὲ νὺξ ἐπεγένετο τῷ βραχεῖ τούτῳ
καὶ κούφῳ, ἀλλ᾿ ὀλίγον τὸ μέσον ἑκατέρων τῶν
διακόνων, ὧν¹ οἱ μὲν ἦγον ἐκεῖσε, οἱ δὲ ἀπήλλατ-
τον. καὶ οἱ μὲν ἐδείπνουν τε καὶ ἐκάθευδον, ὁ
δὲ οὐδέτερον. οἱ μὲν γὰρ οἷς οὐκ ἐπεπόνθεσαν
ἔχαιρον, ὁ δὲ οἷς ἐπεπόνθεσαν ἤλγει καὶ τοῦτο ἔφη
μέγιστον ἠδικῆσθαι παρὰ τῆς πόλεως τὸ τοιαύτην
δίκην ἀναγκασθῆναι λαβεῖν. 197. οὕτω τοῦτο |
καίτοι σμικρότατον ὂν μέγιστόν τε ἡγεῖτο καὶ τοὺς F 3?
αὑτοῦ τρόπους ἐκβαίνειν καὶ οὐκ ἀνέμεινε τῶν
φίλων τινὰ μέμψασθαι τὸ πεπραγμένον, ἀλλ᾿ αὐτὸς
ᾐτιᾶτο τὸ ἔργον οὐχ ὡς εἰς ἀναμαρτήτους, οἶμαι,
γεγενημένον, ἀλλ᾿ ὡς αὑτῷ προσῆκον μηδ᾿ ἐπ᾿
ἀδικήμασιν εἴς γε βουλὴν τῶν τοιούτων τι ποιεῖν.

198. Μικρὸν γοῦν ὕστερον ἑτέρων τῇ πόλει
R 589 μειζόνων τετολμημένων, καὶ γὰρ εἰ περὶ | πατρίδος
οἱ λόγοι, τῆς γε ἀληθείας οὐδὲν πρεσβύτερον, τὰς
τῶν δυναστευόντων τιμωρίας ὑπερβὰς ἐπὶ τὴν τοῦ
ῥήτορος ἧκε καὶ παρὸν στρεβλῶσαι καὶ ἀποκτεῖναι
λόγῳ τὴν πόλιν ἀμύνεται, ταὐτόν, οἶμαι, καὶ
πρόσθεν πεποιηκὼς πρὸς ἄνδρα Ῥωμαῖον θρασυνό-

¹ ὧν inserted F. (conj. Re.).

---

ᵃ For a comparison of this account of Julian's relations
with Antioch and those of *Or.* 1. 126, 15. 20, 16. 21, *cf.*
Petit, *Historia*, 5 (1956), pp. 481 ff. Julian's rancour is
significantly toned down here.

thunderbolt on such insubordination, but he generally
kept his temper in check and on that occasion exercised a singular self-control, for he refrained from
imposing the punishments that they deserved and
penalized them with an imprisonment more nominal
than real, since none of our city fathers found himself
inside the jail gates. Not even a night closed on this
brief, light imprisonment, for practically no time
elapsed between one set of officers taking them to
jail and another bringing them out of it. They went
to have dinner and to bed, but he did neither. They
were glad at what they had not suffered, he was
grieved at what they had, and he asserted that this
was the crowning insult he had suffered from our city,
to be forced to inflict such a punishment. 197. So
this event, despite its pettiness, he regarded as of the
greatest moment and quite foreign to his behaviour:
nor did he wait for any of his friends to censure what
he had done, but he had no good word for it himself,
not because it was directed against innocent people,
obviously, but because it did not become him to
inflict any such punishment on a city council, whatever their misdeeds.[a]

198. At any rate, when a little later the city behaved with even greater insubordination—yes, even
though I speak of my own birthplace, truth must
prevail—then he scorned the punishment that
despots inflict and proceeded to apply that of an
orator, for, though he had it in his power to use
torture or execution, he chose to avenge himself on
our city by an oration,[b] as he had done previously,
to be sure, with a Roman citizen who had behaved

[b] The *Misopogon*, written in February, A.D. 363 : *cf.*
Zos. 3. 11.

411

# LIBANIUS

μενόν τι τοιοῦτον ἐφ' ᾧ δικαίως ἄν, εἰ καὶ μηδὲν
ἕτερον, ἐξέπεσε τῶν ὄντων. ὁ δὲ τῆς μὲν οὐσίας
οὐκ ἀπεστέρησε, βέλει δὲ αὐτὸν ἔβαλεν ἐπιστολῆς.
199. ἀλλ' ὅμως τὸν οὕτω βραδὺν εἰς φόνον πάλιν
ἐβούλευσαν ὁπλῖται δέκα κτεῖναι καὶ μελέτης τῶν
τακτικῶν ἀνέμενον ἡμέραν. μέθη δὲ εὖ ποιοῦσα
προλαβοῦσα τὸν καιρὸν πάντα ἐξήλεγξε καὶ τὸ τέως
λανθάνον ᾔδετο.

200. Θαυμάζει τις οὖν ἴσως εἰ πρᾷος καὶ ἥμερος
καὶ δίκας τὰς μὲν οὐ λαμβάνων τὰς δ' ἐλάττους
τῶν | τεταγμένων, εἶχεν ἀεί τινας ἐν τοῖς ἀρχο- F 3
μένοις δυσμενεῖς. ἐγὼ δὲ τούτου τὴν αἰτίαν ἐν
τῇ μνήμῃ τῆς ὀδυνηρᾶς ἐμοὶ τελευτῆς φράσω. νῦν
δ' ἄξιον εἰπεῖν περὶ τῶν συνήθων τῶν ἐκείνου
τοσοῦτον ὅτι τῶν ἐκείνῳ γενομένων συνήθων οἱ
μὲν ἦσάν τε ἀγαθοὶ καὶ ἐδόκουν, οἱ δὲ ἐδόκουν μέν,
ἦσαν δὲ οὐ τοιοῦτοι. καὶ τοὺς μὲν τῶν πάντων
οὐδὲν μετέβαλε, τοὺς δὲ ὁ χρόνος διήλεγξεν. 201.
ὡς γὰρ ἐλάβετο τῆς βασιλείας καθαρῶς καὶ κύριος
κατέστη τῶν τε θησαυρῶν καὶ τῶν ἄλλων ὅσα
τὸν πλοῦτον ποιεῖ τὸν βασιλέως, οἱ μὲν προῖκά
R 590 τε αὐτῷ συνῆσαν | καὶ οὐκ ἐποίουν τὰ αὐτῶν
μείζω ταῖς παρ' ἐκεῖνον εἰσόδοις, ἀλλ' ἱκανὸν
ἡγοῦντο κέρδος φιλεῖν τε καὶ φιλεῖσθαι καὶ τὸν
αὐτῶν ἐρώμενον ὁρᾶν ἄρχοντά τε τὴν τηλικαύτην
ἀρχὴν καὶ σὺν ἐπιστήμῃ καὶ πολλάκις γε αὐτοῦ
κελεύοντος λαμβάνειν, καὶ νὴ Δία γε καὶ δεομένου,
γῆν, ἵππους, οἰκίαν, ἀργύριον, χρυσίον, εὐπορεῖν

---

[a] E.L.F. No. 82 (443 c ff.), the letter against Nilus,
written before the end of A.D. 362 : cf. Lib. Ep. 758.
[b] Cf. Greg. Naz. Or. 4. 84. The incident appears to be

with an impudence rather similar.[a] He would have been justified in confiscating his property, at the very least, but he did not deprive him of his possessions; the weapon he used was a letter directed against him. 199. Still, though he was so reluctant to shed blood, ten soldiers formed another conspiracy to kill him. They waited for the day of the manœuvres, but fortunately drink forestalled their attempt and revealed the whole affair, and the plan hitherto secret was proclaimed aloud.[b]

200. Now, one may perhaps be surprised that, for all his kindliness and mildness and though the punishments he inflicted were either none at all or less than normal, he yet encountered from time to time some disloyalty among his subjects. The reason for this I shall tell in my account of his end, so lamentable to me. At present this much needs to be said of his intimate friends, that of those intimates some were good both in appearance and reality, and nothing at all could change them, while others had the appearance without the reality, and time revealed them for what they were. 201. For after he had beyond dispute gained control of the empire and had become master of the treasures and all else that constitutes the emperor's wealth, some associated with him without thought of gain. They did not try to increase their possessions through their audiences with him, but thought it gain enough to love and be loved and to see the man who loved them ruler over such a mighty empire, and a wise ruler too. Though he bade them often enough, and in fact begged them, to accept land, horses, house, silver, gold, they

connected with the executions of Juventinus and Maximinus (*cf.* Peeters, *Analecta Bollandiana*, 42. 77 ff.).

LIBANIUS

λέγοντες διέφευγον τὰς δόσεις. 202. οἱ βέλτιστοι
μὲν οὕτως. οἱ δὲ χρημάτων πάλαι μὲν ἐπιθυ-
μοῦντες, προσποιούμενοι δὲ καταφρονεῖν, καιρὸν
δὲ ἀναμένοντες ἐχρῶντο φανέντι καὶ ᾔτουν καὶ
λαμβάνοντες ᾔτουν πάλιν καὶ λαβόντες οὐκ ἔληγον,
οὐδ᾽ ἦν ὅ τι αὐτοῖς ἴστη τὴν ἀπληστίαν. ὁ δὲ
μεγαλοψυχίᾳ μὲν προΐετο, χρηστοὺς δὲ οὐκέτ᾽ ἐνό-
μιζεν. ἀλλ᾽ ἠπατημένος μὲν ἤλγει, τὸν χρόνον δὲ |
αἰσχυνόμενος ἠνείχετο καὶ τὸ δοκεῖν εἶναι βέβαιος F 3
εἰς φιλίαν τοῦ τοιούτων ὄντων ἀπηλλάχθαι κρεῖττον
ἡγεῖτο. 203. ὥστ᾽ ἠγνόει μὲν οὐδενὸς τῶν πλησια-
ζόντων τὴν φύσιν, χαίρων δ᾽ αὐτῶν τοῖς σπου-
δαίοις καὶ συμφορὰν τοὺς ἑτέρους κρίνων τῶν μὲν
εἴχετο, τοὺς δὲ οὐκ ἀπήλαυνεν, ἀλλὰ καὶ σοφιστὴν
κρείττω τῆς προσηγορίας παρεχόμενον τὸν τρόπον
ἐθαύμαζε καὶ φιλόσοφον χείρω τοῦ σχήματος
ἐλεγχόμενον ἐκάκιζε, τὸ δὲ μὴ δοκεῖν ἐν τῇ βασιλείᾳ παλαιὰς ἀτιμάζειν συνηθείας πάντα ἔπειθε
φέρειν.

204. Ἀλλὰ γὰρ ἐπιθυμεῖν μοι δοκεῖτε τῆς τῶν
τελευταίων καὶ μεγίστων ἀκοῆς, ἃ Πέρσας καὶ
τὴν ἐκείνων γῆν ἐπιστρατεύσας διέθηκε. καὶ
θαυμαστὸν οὐδὲν εἰ πάλαι πρὸς ταύτην τὴν μερίδα
κεχήνατε τὸ μὲν κεφάλαιον εἰδότες ὡς νικῶν
ἔπιπτε, τῶν δὲ ἐν μέρει τὰ μὲν οὐδὲ ἀκούσαντες, τὰ
δ᾽ οὐχ ὡς ἔχει. 205. ποιεῖ δὲ ὑμᾶς ὡρμῆσθαι πρὸς

_a_ Such, Libanius claims, was his own attitude : _Or._ 1.
125, 51. 30, _Ep._ 1158.
_b_ As asserted by Greg. Naz. _Or._ 5. 19, and hinted by Lib.
414

replied that they were quite satisfied and declined his offers.[a]  202. That was the way with the best of them.  However, others had long been greedy for money, though they pretended to despise it, and they awaited their opportunity, and made full use of it when it came, to ask and to receive, and then to ask for more, and there was no end to their receiving, for nothing could satisfy their greediness.[b]  In his generosity he lavished all this upon them, but he no longer looked upon them as men of worth.  He was vexed at being deceived, but he put up with them out of regard for their long association and considered his reputation as a loyal friend more important than ridding himself of such as these.  203. Thus, being unaware of the character of none of his acquaintances, he rejoiced in them if they were good, and if they were not, he was sorry, but though he held tight to the good, he did not send the bad packing.  He would admire a sophist whose character rose superior to that title, and he would scorn a philosopher who, upon test, turned out to be below that standard, and he was induced to put up with anything by his desire not to be thought, as emperor, to be turning his back on old acquaintance.

204. But I think that you are eager for the recital of his last and greatest exploits, his treatment of Persia and the Persians in his invasion.  Nor is it any wonder that you have long been waiting open-mouthed for this portion, for you know the simple fact that he fell in the hour of victory, but as for the details, what you have heard is either nothing at all or else false.  205. Your eagerness to hear the narrative

*Or.* 1. 123 ff., probably with Maximus in mind : *cf.* Eunap.
*V.S.* 477 f.

R 591 τὴν ἀκρόασιν λογισμὸς | τῆς Περσῶν ἰσχύος καὶ
ὅσην οὖσαν ἐνίκων τὴν Κωνσταντίου δύναμιν καὶ
ἐφ᾿ ὅσον φρόνημα καὶ θάρσος οὑτοσὶ χωρῶν οὐκ
ἔδεισε. Κωνστάντιος γὰρ χωρὶς τῶν τε ἄλλων
νήσων καὶ τῶν ἐν ὠκεανῷ κειμένων τὴν ἐξ αὐτῶν
τῶν ἠόνων ὠκεανοῦ[1] γῆν μέχρι τῶν | Εὐφράτου F
ῥευμάτων ἐκέκτητο τά τε ἄλλα φέρουσαν πάντα
πολλὰ καὶ σωμάτων μεγέθη καὶ ψυχῶν ἀνδρίαν ἀφ᾿
ὧν ἂν γένοιτο στρατόπεδον ἀρραγές. 206. ἀλλ᾿
ὅμως οὗτος ὁ μέγας ταῖς παρασκευαῖς, ὁ τὰς
μυρίας πόλεις καὶ λαμπρὰς ἔχων, ὁ τοὺς πολλοὺς
δεχόμενος φόρους, ὁ τὸν πολὺν χρυσὸν ἐκ τῶν
μετάλλων ἐξαγαγών, ὁ καλύψας ἱππέων σιδήρῳ
σώματα Περσῶν ἀκριβέστερον, ὁ καὶ τοὺς ἵππους
ὅπλοις ῥυόμενος τραυμάτων, οὗτος πόλεμον παρὰ
τοῦ πατρὸς ἐκδεξάμενος θάρσους δεόμενον βασιλέως καὶ ψυχῆς ἐπισταμένης δυνάμει χρῆσθαι
καλῶς, ὥσπερ συμπολεμήσειν τοῖς ἐναντίοις ὀμω-
μοκώς, ὅπως μὲν λήψεται τἀκείνων ἢ μή τι τῶν
αὐτοῦ γένοιτο ὑπ᾿ ἐκείνοις οὐκ ἐσκέψατο, στράτευμα δὲ ἄγων καθ᾿ ἕκαστον ἔτος ἀρχομένου
θέρους ἅμα ἦρι τειχομαχούντων διαβὰς Εὐφράτην
καὶ περὶ αὑτῷ τοσαύτην στρατιὰν καθίσας καὶ
διανοούμενος εἰ φανεῖεν οἱ πολέμιοι φεύγειν, τῶν
πολιορκουμένων μόνον οὐκ ἀκούων τὰς οἰμωγάς,
στρατηγικώτερον ἡγεῖτο τὸ μὴ μάχεσθαι μηδὲ τοῖς
οἰκείοις ἀπολλυμένοις ἀμύνειν. 207. τίς οὖν ὁ τῆς
καθέδρας καρπός; ὁ μὲν κατέσειε τείχη καὶ κατ-

---

[1] ὠκεανοῦ F. (mss.) : om. Re.

[a] For Constantius' Persian campaign cf. Or. 59. 61 ff.,
Julian, Or. 1. 18 b.

is aroused by your reflections upon the might of Persia, and the great army of Constantius that they overcame, and their overweening pride against which Julian advanced undeterred. Besides the islands, including those situated in the Atlantic, Constantius held all the territory from the very shores of Ocean to the River Euphrates, which can muster many a tall man and many a brave heart, and plenty besides, and from them an invincible army would have been composed. 206. However, that emperor, so mighty in his preparations with his countless famous cities, his vast income from taxes, and all the gold from his mines, who covered his cavalry with mail more carefully than the Persians and used armour to protect even his horses from being wounded, he inherited from his father[a] a war that required an emperor of daring and an intelligence capable of using his forces to advantage. However, it was just as though he had sworn to act in league with his opponents; he took no thought for capturing anything of theirs or for seeing that they won nothing of his; every year, at the beginning of the summer, they meantime laying siege to his fortresses in early spring, he would lead his army across the Euphrates and halt the best force he had mustered, intent on beating a retreat if the enemy put in an appearance, and though he could almost hear the laments of the beleaguered citizens,[b] he thought it better tactics not to fight or aid any of his own subjects who were in the process of being destroyed. 207. What, then, was the consequence of his dilatoriness? While the enemy was battering down his fortifications, de-

[b] As at Amida (Amm. Marc. 19. 1-8), or Singara (*ibid.* 20. 6-7).

# LIBANIUS

ἔσκαπτε πόλεις καὶ χρήματα καὶ | σώματα ἄγων
ἀνέστρεφεν, ὁ δὲ τοὺς ὀψομένους τὴν ἐρημίαν
ἔπεμπε καὶ τοῦ μὴ πλέον τι πεπονθέναι χάριν ᾔδει
τῇ Τύχῃ καὶ διὰ τῶν πόλεων ἐπανῄει μεθ᾽ ἡμέραν
R 592 τὰς ἐπὶ νίκῃ νενομισμένας φωνὰς | παρὰ τῶν
δήμων δεχόμενος. καὶ τοῦτο ἦν ἔργον ἔτους
ἑκάστου· διέβαινεν ὁ Πέρσης, ὁ δὲ ἔμελλε. προσέ-
βαλλε περιβόλοις, ὁ δὲ ἐκινεῖτο. ἐγγὺς ἦν ἑλεῖν,
ὁ δὲ ταῦτα ἐπυνθάνετο. ᾔρει, τῷ δὲ ἤρκει μὴ
μεμαχῆσθαι. ὁ μὲν αἰχμαλώτων ἡβρύνετο πλή-
θεσιν, ὁ δὲ ἵππων ἁμίλλαις. τὸν μὲν ἐστεφάνουν
αἱ πόλεις, ὁ δὲ τοὺς ἡνιόχους. ἆρ᾽ οὐκ εἰκότως μοι
προσείρηται Περσῶν οὗτος σύμμαχος; τὸ γὰρ
παρὸν κωλύειν ἐπιτρέπειν ἐγγὺς ἂν εἴη τοῦ ταῖς
χερσὶ συντελεῖν. 208. καὶ μή με οἰέσθω τις
ἀγνοεῖν μήτε τὴν νυκτομαχίαν ἐν ᾗ δράσαντές τι
καὶ παθόντες διεκρίθησαν, μήτε τὴν ἐν ἠπείρῳ
ναυμαχίαν ἐν ᾗ μόλις τὴν πολλὰ παθοῦσαν πόλιν
ἔσωσαν. αὐτὸ γὰρ δὴ τοῦτο καὶ τὸ σχέτλιόν
ἐστιν ὅτι ψυχὰς παραλαβὼν εἰδυίας πολεμίους
φοβεῖν φοβεῖσθαι συνείθισε καὶ πονηρᾷ μελέτῃ
γενναίας φύσεις ἐξέλυσεν. 209. ὅση δὲ ἡ τῆς
μελέτης ἰσχὺς ἐν ἅπασι πράγμασι δηλοῦσι | μὲν
οἱ σοφοί, δηλοῖ δὲ καὶ ὁ μῦθος. αὕτη καὶ τὸν
βελτίω καὶ τὸν χείρω πρὸς τοὐναντίον ἂν μετα-
στήσαι τῷ μὲν χείρων τῆς φύσεως, τῷ δὲ δοθεῖ-
R 593 σα βελτίων. αὕτη καὶ γυναῖκας | ἐφ᾽ ἵππους ἀνεβί-
βασε καὶ κρείττους ἀνδρῶν ἐν ὅπλοις ἐποίησε,

---

[a] At Singara, A.D. 348, described at length and claimed
as a victory for Constantius in *Or.* 59. 99 ff. : *cf.* Jul. *Or.* 1.
23 b, Amm. Marc. 18. 5. 7.

[b] At the third siege of Nisibis, A.D. 350 : *cf.* Jul. *Or.* 1.
27 b ff., Zonaras 13. 7. 3.

molishing cities and making off with captives and booty, he would send his forces to inspect the desolation and thank his lucky stars that no worse harm had been done. Then he made his way back through the cities and every day receive a welcome from the populace in terms usual after a victory. Year after year this is what went on: the Persians would cross the river, and he would be thinking about it: they would be attacking the forts, and he would start to move: they would be just about to take them, and he would get the news: they would take them, and he was content not to have fought an engagement. They revelled in their hordes of captives, he in the horse-races: the cities presented their crowns to the Persian, he to his race-drivers. Am I not justified in saying that he was in league with Persia? To permit such goings-on when he could stop them is tantamount to helping with his own hands. 208. And let nobody think me unaware of that night battle where the combatants disengaged after casualties had been inflicted and suffered by both sides,[a] or of that sea-battle on land, whereby they saved, with difficulty, that long-suffering city.[b] The sum of his disgrace is this—that he inherited an army of high morale, schooled to inspire fear into the foe, and accustomed it to feel fear, and by bad training ruined this fine morale. 209. Both philosophy and legend bear witness to the efficacy of training in every activity. It can cause a good man and a bad to turn into the opposite, according as to whether it comes as inferior or superior to his natural character. It has mounted even women [c] on horseback and has given them the better of men in war. If

[c] The Amazons.

κἂν τὸν ἀρετῆς φύσει μετειληφότα ζῆν ἐν κώμοις
καὶ μέθαις ἀναγκάσῃς, ἡ μὲν αὐτὸν ἀπολείπει,
μαθὼν δὲ ταῦτα ἀντὶ τῶν ἐκείνης καλῶν ζῇ τούτοις
ἡδόμενος, ἐχθρὰ δὲ αὐτῷ τὰ πρότερα, καὶ ἡ
συνήθεια τὴν φύσιν ἐξέκρουσε. 210. τοιοῦτόν τί
φημι καὶ τοὺς ἐκείνου στρατιώτας ὑπ' ἐκείνου
πεπονθέναι τὰ μὲν ὅπλα λαμβάνοντας, συμπίπτειν δὲ
κωλυομένους καὶ διδασκομένους ὑπὸ σκηναῖς καθεύδειν συγγενῶν ἁλισκομένων καὶ μὴ φοβεῖσθαι
τὴν αἰσχύνην καὶ δεδοικέναι τὴν τελευτήν. ἃ τὸ
μὲν πρῶτον ἐδυσχέραινον, ὡς εἰκὸς εὐψύχους,
ἔπειθ' ἧττον, εἶτα προσίεντο, εἶτα ἐπήνουν. 211.
διὰ ταῦτα πόρρωθεν κονιορτὸς ἀρθεὶς οἷος ἂν ἐξ
ἵππων γένοιτο οὐκ ἀνίστη πρὸς συμβολήν, ἀλλ'
ἔτρεπεν εἰς φυγήν. ἴλης μὲν γὰρ ἐπιφανείσης
ἱππέων οὐδὲ ταύτης μεγάλης χανεῖν αὐτοῖς εὔχοντο
τὴν γῆν πᾶν παθεῖν αἱρούμενοι μᾶλλον ἢ Πέρσην
ἐγγύθεν προσιδεῖν, ἐξῃρημένης δέ σφισι τῆς ἀνδρίας
συναφῄρητο καὶ ἡ παρρησία, καὶ | οὕτως ἀνω- F
μολόγητο τὸ δέος ὥσθ' ὁπότε παρ' οἷς καταλύοιεν,
ὑπὸ τούτων ἠξίουν θεραπεύεσθαι, τοὔνομα τὸ
Περσῶν ἔπαυεν ἐνοχλοῦντας. καὶ πᾶς ἂν εἶπεν
ἐπισκώπτων ὅτι Πέρσης ἐκεῖνος ἔρχεται, οἱ δ'
ἄρ' ἠρυθρίων τε καὶ ἀπεπήδων. ἐπὶ μὲν οὖν τοὺς
ὁμοφύλους ἀγόμενοι καὶ πλήττειν ᾔδεσαν καὶ
πληγῆναι, Περσικὸς δὲ αὐτοῖς οὕτω πολὺς ἐνίδρυτο

---

ᵃ The parallel is unfortunate. Constantius lived a very
sober life : cf. Amm. Marc. 21. 16. 5.
420

you force a naturally good man to live among drunken revelry, his goodness deserts him and he learns these vices instead of the glories of virtue, and he lives with pleasure in them and loathes his previous life, and so habit becomes the ruin of his character.[a] 210. Something of the sort, I assert, befell Constantius' soldiery at his hands, since they took up their arms but were prevented from making an attack, and learned how to doze in their tents while their kinsmen were led away captive, and how to feel no shame and to be afraid of death. They resented all this for a start, naturally enough, being men of courage, but then their resentment faded and turned into acceptance and, finally, outright approval. 211. So, if a dust cloud rose in the distance such as horses would make, it did not spur them on to the fight, but turned them in flight. If a troop of cavalry made its appearance, and no large one either, they would pray for the earth to open and swallow them up, for any fate was preferable to seeing the Persians close to them.[b] As their courage dwindled, so did their self-confidence, and so openly confessed was their fear that, if ever they demanded attention from the people on whom they were billeted, the word " Persian " was enough to stop them making nuisances of themselves, and if any practical joker told them, " The Persians are coming," up would come their colour and away they would dash. So, in fighting against their own people they had learned to give and take hard knocks,[c] but so deeply ingrained was the dread of the Persians that had grown during many

---

[b] e.g., ibid. 19. 8.

[c] Constantius had a genius for handling civil wars : ibid. 21. 16. 15.

# LIBANIUS

φόβος ἐν πολλοῖς ἔτεσι συλλεγείς, ὥστ᾿ ἔφη τις ἂν
R 594 αὐτοὺς καὶ τοὺς ἐν ταῖς γραφαῖς | πεφρικέναι.

212. Τούτους δὴ τοὺς οὕτω διεφθαρμένους οὗτος
ὁ θαυμάσιος ἐπὶ Πέρσας ἦγεν, οἱ δὲ ἠκολούθουν
κατὰ μικρὸν ἀναμιμνησκόμενοι τῆς ἀνδρίας ἣν
εἶχον, καὶ πιστεύοντες διὰ πυρὸς ἐλθεῖν ἂν ἀπαθεῖς
ταῖς ἐκείνου βουλαῖς. 213. τίνες οὖν αὗται; μεγάλην οὖσαν εἰδὼς ἐν ἀπορρήτοις ῥοπήν, ὃ γὰρ
οὐδὲν ἂν ὀνῆσαι προρρηθὲν μέγα ἂν ὠφελῆσαι
κρυφθέν, οὐκ εἰσόδου χρόνον, οὐκ εἰσβολῆς ὁδόν,
οὐ μηχανημάτων τρόπον, οὐδὲν ὧν ἔστρεφεν ἐπὶ
τῆς ψυχῆς ἐξήνεγκεν εἰδὼς ὅτι πᾶν ἐκλαληθὲν
εὐθύς ἐστιν ἐν ὠσὶ κατασκόπων. 214. ἀλλὰ πλοίων
ἐμπλῆσαι τὸν Εὐφράτην καὶ τροφῆς τὰ πλοῖα πρὸς
τὸν ὕπαρχον εἴρητο, πρὶν δὲ τὸν χειμῶνα | ἐξήκειν F
ὑπερβὰς τὰς ἁπάντων ἐλπίδας καὶ κατὰ τάχος
διαβὰς τὸν ποταμὸν οὐκ ἐπὶ τὴν πλησίον μεγάλην
τε καὶ πολυάνθρωπον πόλιν[1] ἦλθεν ὡς ἴδοι τε καὶ
ὀφθείη καὶ τὰ εἰωθότα τοῖς βασιλεῦσι τιμηθείη,
ἀλλ᾿ ὀξύτητος δεῖσθαι τὸν καιρὸν εἰδὼς ἧκε μὲν
εἰς πόλιν ἔχουσαν μέγα Διὸς ἱερὸν ἀρχαῖον, θαυμάσας δὲ καὶ εὐξάμενος δοῦναί οἱ κακῶσαι τὰ
Περσῶν ἀποσχίσας τῆς δυνάμεως μυριάδας ὁπλιτῶν δύο τούτους μὲν ἐπὶ τὸν Τίγρητα πέμπει
φυλάξοντάς τε τὴν γῆν εἴ τι ταύτῃ προσίοι δεινὸν
καὶ παρεσομένους αὐτῷ κατὰ καιρὸν καλοῦντι.

---

[1] After πόλιν, Re. and editors insert Σαμόσατα καλουμένην
(following gloss τὰ σαμόσατα in B): om. F. (mss.).

---

[a] For the narratives of Julian's Persian campaign cf.
Amm. Marc. 23. 2 ff., Zos. 3. 12 ff., Lib. Or. 1. 132 f. Julian's

years, that you might say that they could not look at
pictures of them without a shudder.

212. This then was the army, so corrupted, that
our glorious emperor led against the Persians. They
followed, gradually recovering the courage they once
possessed and the confidence to walk through fire
unscathed in consequence of his strategy. 213. This
was as follows[a]: he knew the great advantages of
secrecy; the broadcasting of information is valueless,
whereas its concealment can be of great assistance ;
and so he did not reveal the time of his invasion, its
proposed route, or his tactics. In fact, he disclosed
nothing of what he had in mind, for he was well
aware that news once blurted out is picked up by
spies.[b] 214. His instructions to the prefect had been
to concentrate boats on the Euphrates and to load
them with stores,[c] and before the end of winter he
surprised everyone by crossing the river at speed.
He did not march by way of the great populous city [d]
near by, to see and be seen and to collect the formal
greetings usually paid to an emperor. He knew that
now was the time for speed, and he made his way to a
city [e] that has a grand old temple of Zeus, where he
reverently prayed that it be granted him to be the
ruin of Persia. Here he detached from his forces
twenty thousand infantry, and sent them to the
Tigris to cover the area, should danger threaten in
that direction, and to support him if he summoned

last letter to Libanius (*E.L.F.* No. 98) covers the route to
Hierapolis.
   [b] Amm. Marc. 23. 2. 2.          [c] Zos. *loc. cit.*
   [d] Edessa : *cf.* Sozom. 6. 1. The editors, reading Samosata
without mss. authority, ignore this information and that of
Ammianus, above.
   [e] Carrhae : *cf.* Amm. Marc. 23. 3. 1, Sozom. *loc. cit.*

215. χρῆν δὲ ἄρα καὶ τὸν Ἀρμένιον παραπλήσιόν τι ποιεῖν, διὰ γὰρ τῆς ἐκείνου γῆς τῆς ἀρίστης ἐλθόντα μετὰ πυρὸς ὥσπερ εἰκὸς τὸν ἐχθρὸν συμμῖξαι τῷ βασιλεῖ, καὶ γενομένους ἀθρόους ἢ ἐκβαλεῖν τῶν ὅρων τοὺς ἐναντίους φεύγοντας ἢ καταπατῆσαι μένοντας. τούτων δὲ παρηγγελμένων αὐτὸς ἐχόμενος Εὐφράτου πιεῖν τε παρέχοντος καὶ παραπέμποντος τὴν ἐν τοῖς πλοίοις R 595 τροφὴν | ἐχώρει. 216. πλῆθος δὲ καμήλων θεώμενος, κάμηλον ἐξηρτημένην καμήλου φορτίοις βαρυνομένας, τὰ δὲ ἦν οἶνός τε ἥδιστος ἄλλος ἐξ ἄλλης γῆς καὶ ὅσα | εἰς ἡδίω πόσιν οἴνου τοῖς ἀν- F 3 θρώποις μεμηχάνηται, τί φέροιντο ἐρόμενος ἐπειδὴ ἐπύθετο, μένειν κελεύει τὰς πηγὰς τῶν ἡδονῶν. πρέπειν γὰρ στρατιώταις ἀγαθοῖς πίνειν οἶνον ὃν αὐτοῖς κτᾶται τὸ δόρυ, τῶν στρατιωτῶν δὲ εἷς καὶ αὐτὸς εἶναι καὶ προσήκειν αὐτῷ τοῖς πολλοῖς ἰσοδίαιτον εἶναι.

217. Οὕτω δὴ τὰ τρυφὴν ἔχοντα πάντα ἀποκόψας, ὧν μάλιστα καὶ μόνων ἐδεῖτο τὰ παρόντα, ταῦτα ἔχων ἐπορεύετο τῆς γῆς αὐτῷ τὰ ὑποζύγια βοσκούσης πόα χρηστῇ, τὸ γὰρ ἔαρ ὑπὲρ ἐκείνης ἤδη τῆς χώρας εἱστήκει. 218. καὶ προϊόντες φρούριον εἶδον ἐν χερρονήσῳ τοῦ ποταμοῦ κείμενον, πρῶτον καὶ φανὲν καὶ ληφθὲν οὐχ ὅπλοις ἀλλὰ φόβῳ. ὡς γὰρ εἶδον τοὺς ἀπαντικρὺ λόφους ὑπὸ τῆς στρατιᾶς κεκαλυμμένους οὐκ ἐνεγκόντες τὰς μαρμαρυγὰς τῶν ὅπλων ἀνέῳξάν τε τὰς πύλας καὶ δόντες

---

<sup>a</sup> This corps was to operate under his kinsman, Procopius, and Sebastianus, acting in concert with Arsaces of Armenia

them as occasion demanded.[a]  215. Arrangements were also made for the Armenians to perform a similar duty. If the enemy advanced through their most fertile districts burning and looting as was likely, they were to link up with the emperor, and together they were either to expel the enemy from their land in flight, or, if he stayed, crush him. After issuing such instructions he continued his advance, his own forces hugging the Euphrates, which provided drinking water and convoy for the stores in the boats. 216. On seeing a big camel train, with one animal tied behind another and all loaded with freight, this being composed of the finest wines from all over the world and all the devices people have discovered for the increased pleasure of wine drinking, he asked what they were carrying, and on being told what it was, he gave orders for these wells of pleasure to stay behind. Good soldiers, he said, should drink the wine they won at sword-point[b]; he was one of the soldiers, and it was proper that his rations should be the same as the rest.

217. So he pruned everything that involved easy living, and marched on with only the stuff that the present situation demanded, the land providing rich pasture for his baggage train since spring was now well advanced in that region. 218. As they moved on, they saw a fortress lying on a neck of land formed by the river, and this was no sooner seen than taken, not by assault but by panic, for the inhabitants saw the slopes opposite covered by the army, were frightened by the glint of arms, opened their gates

to provide support from the north. In this it was a signal failure : *infr.*, § 260. Amm. Marc. *loc. cit.*
  [b] *Cf.* Amm. Marc. 24. 1. 14 f.

αὐτοὺς ἦλθον τὴν ἡμετέραν οἰκήσοντες. τὸ δὲ τῶν
ἐπιτηδείων πλῆθος πολλῶν ἡμερῶν ἦν ἑκάστῳ
τροφὴ ὥστε δι᾽ ἐρήμου τῆς ἐχομένης ἰόντες
ὅσωνπερ ἐν ἄστεσιν ἀπολαύειν εἶχον.

219. Φρούριον ἕτερον ἦν ἐν νήσῳ περιεξεσμένῃ |
καὶ τεῖχος περὶ πᾶσαν ἐληλαμένον μηδὲν ἔξω F
καταλελοιπὸς αὐτοῦ[1] μηδ᾽ ὅσον δοῦναι χώραν |
R 596 ποδί. μακαρίσας δὴ τοὺς οἰκοῦντας τῆς τοῦ τόπου
φύσεως καὶ γνοὺς ὡς εἰ τοῖς ἀνηνύτοις ἐπιχειροίη
χαρίζοιτ᾽ ἂν τοῖς πολεμίοις καὶ ὅτι τῆς ἴσης ἀνοίας
παριέναι τε ἃ λαβεῖν ἔνι καὶ προσπαλαίειν τούτοις
ἃ λαβεῖν οὐχ οἷόν τε, ταχέως ἐπ᾽ αὐτοὺς ἥξειν
εἰπὼν καὶ δέος σφίσιν οὐ μικρὸν ἐγκατοικίσας καὶ
ταράξας τὴν γνώμην τοῖς ῥήμασι πάλιν δι᾽ ἐρήμου
πορευθεὶς ἅπτεται τῆς Ἀσυρίων γῆς, ἣ ποιεῖ τοὺς
οἰκήτορας εὐδαίμονας τοῦτο μὲν πλήθει καὶ κάλλει
καρπῶν ἀπ᾽ ὀλίγου σπέρματος, τοῦτο δὲ ἀμπέλων
τε καὶ φοινίκων τόκῳ καὶ τοῖς ἄλλοις ἀγαθοῖς ἃ
δῶρα γῆς ἀγαθῆς. 220. ταῦτα βλέποντες καὶ
τούτων μετέχοντες οἱ στρατιῶται πολλῶν ὄντων ἐν
ἑκάστῃ κώμῃ, πολλαὶ δὲ αἱ κῶμαι καὶ μεγάλαι καὶ
πόλεσιν οὐ σφόδρα μεγάλαις αἱ πολλαὶ παρισού-
μεναι διὰ πάσης τῆς Ἀσυρίων ἐκτισμέναι,[2] τούτοις
οὖν ἐντυχὼν ὁ στρατὸς οὐκ ἐμέμψατο τῇ περὶ τὴν
πορείαν ταλαιπωρίᾳ. τὸ γὰρ ἆθλον ἄξιον ἦν τῶν
πεπονημένων διὰ τῆς ἐρήμου τὴν ἥμερον ἔχειν.
221. ἐνταῦθα φοίνικας ἐξέτεμνον, ἀμπέλους ἀνέ-

---

[1] αὐτοῦ Re. (mss. except P) : αὐτοῦ F. (P) : αὐτῆς Fabr.
[2] ἐκτισμέναι F. (mss.) : ᾠκισμέναι Re. (gloss in B).

426

and surrendered, and went to live in our country.[a]
The stocks of provisions gave many days' rations for
all, so that, although they passed through the desert
further on, they had as much to eat as they had in
cities.

219. There was another fortress on an island[b] that
rose sheer out of the river. The whole island was
encircled by fortifications so that not enough room
was left outside there to give even a foothold. He
thought the inhabitants lucky in the natural strength
of the place, and recognizing that if he attempted the
impossible, he would be doing the enemy a favour,
and that assaulting impregnable positions was no less
madness than neglecting those that could be taken,
he told them that he would soon be back to deal with
them, inspiring great fear in them and sapping their
resolution by his words. He resumed his march
through the desert and arrived in Assyria, a land
that bestows prosperity on its inhabitants by the
quantity and quality of what it produces from a
small amount of seed, and by the production of vines
and palms and all other good things of a fertile
country. 220. The soldiery looked at it and made
free of the plentiful supplies in every village. These
villages are many in number and large in size, mostly
comparable with fair-sized towns, and they are
situated throughout the length and breadth of
Assyria, and on coming upon them, the army had no
grumbles about the rigours of the march, for the
reward of occupying the cultivated land was worth all
their struggles through the desert. 221. Here they
cut down the palm trees, tore up the vines, ransacked

---

[a] Cf. Amm. Marc. 24. 1. 6 (Anatha).
[b] Ibid. 24. 2. 1 (Thilutha).

σπων, | ἐκένουν¹ ταμιεῖα, κατέσκαπτον μετ' ὀργῆς, F 3
ἤσθιον, ἔπινον, οὐ μὴν μέχρι μέθης, οὐ γὰρ εἴα τοῦ
διὰ μέθην ἀρτίως ἀποσφαγέντος ὁ φόβος, ἀλλὰ
τὴν μὲν δύναμιν συνεῖχον, ὅπως δὲ καὶ νήψουσιν
ἐσκόπουν. οἱ δὲ δυστυχεῖς Ἀσύριοι πόρρωθεν ἀπὸ
τῶν ὁρῶν ἑώρων τὰ σφῶν αὐτῶν κακά, φεύγοντες
μέντοι καὶ τὸ πεδίον ἐκλιπόντες πολέμιόν σφισι
R 597 σύμμαχον ἀντιστήσαντες | τὸν ποταμὸν οὕτως
ἀπῆλθον. 222. πῶς οὖν τοῖς μὲν ἐπεκούρει, τοῖς δ'
ἐμάχετο; πολὺς ὢν ὁ ποταμὸς Εὐφράτης καὶ πολλῶν ποταμῶν ἀντίρροπος μικρὸς μὲν οὐδέποτε,
μέγιστος δὲ αὐτὸς αὑτοῦ γίνεται τῶν ἠρινῶν
ὄμβρων λυόντων εἰς ὕδωρ τὴν ἐν Ἀρμενίᾳ χιόνα
τοῦ χειμῶνος οἰκοδομηθεῖσαν, οἱ δὲ περὶ αὐτὸν
γεωργοὶ διώρυγας ἔνθεν καὶ ἔνθεν κατατέμνοντες,
ὁπόσα Αἰγύπτιοι τῷ Νείλῳ, χρῶνται καὶ οὗτοι
τῷ ποταμῷ, καὶ ἔστιν ἀμφοῖν ὁ γεωργὸς κύριος
εἰσδραμεῖν τε τὸ ὕδωρ καὶ μή. 223. τοῦ στρατοῦ
τοίνυν ἐπιόντος ἀνέντες πάσας εἰσόδους τῷ ῥεύματι
τάς τε διώρυχας ἔπλησαν καὶ δι' ἐκείνων τὴν ἄλλην
γῆν. οὗτος μόχθων ἐκείνοις ὁ χαλεπώτατος παντὸς
μὲν τοῦ λιμνάζοντος λυποῦντος, τοῦ δὲ ἐν ταῖς
διώρυξι τοῖς μὲν εἰς στέρνον ἀναβαίνοντος, τοῖς δ'
εἰς πρόσωπον, | ἔστι δὲ οὓς καὶ ὑπεραίροντος. F 3
ἀγὼν οὖν ἔσχατος αὑτόν τε σῶσαι καὶ ὅπλα καὶ
τροφὴν καὶ ὑποζύγια. 224. καὶ τοῖς μὲν ἐπισταμένοις νεῖν βοηθὸς ἦν ἡ τέχνη, τοῖς δ' ἀπειροτέροις
μείζων ὁ πόνος. ὥσθ' οἱ μὲν ἐγεφύρουν, οἱ δ' ἀντὶ
τοῦ μέλλειν ἐτόλμων. καὶ τοῖς μὲν δι' ὄχθης
ὑψηλῆς τε καὶ στενῆς ἐλαύνουσι τὸ μὴ βραχῆναι
ὑπῆρχε, σφαλερὸν δὲ ἡ στενότης, οἱ δ' ἐκεῖνο

¹ ἐκένουν Herwerden : ἐκίνουν F., Re. (mss.).

and demolished the barns furiously: they ate and they drank, but not so much as to get drunk, for the fear caused by the recent execution of a man for drunkenness acted as a deterrent: they retained their faculties and saw that they stayed sober. The unhappy Assyrians from far off in the hills gazed upon the disaster that had befallen them, but for all their flight and evacuation of the level country that was now their foe, as a counter-balance before their departure they had made the river their ally. 222. As for the manner in which it assisted the one side and opposed the other, the Euphrates is a mighty river, the equal of many others put together, its flow, never small, coursing in spate when the spring rains melt the masses of snow built up during winter in Armenia. Then the neighbouring farmers cut canals in all directions and utilize the river, just as the Egyptians do the Nile. In both cases the farmer controls whether or not to allow the water to flow in. 223. So, as the army advanced, they opened all the sluices and flooded the canals, and by means of them, the rest of the country. This was the most difficult task for our troops, for all this area became a lake and hampered their progress, the water in the canals coming breast-high or chin-high in places and, at times, even beyond their depth. So there was a grim struggle to save oneself, one's weapons, rations and baggage animals. 224. Those who knew how to swim got some help from their skill and pressed on hardily instead of delaying, whereas those who did not found their labours increased by the need for bridging operations. Some advanced along a high narrow causeway and escaped getting wet, but the very narrowness was a hazard that others

φεύγοντες ἐν τοῖς ὕδασιν ᾠχοῦντο,[1] καὶ δεσπότῃ τε
δοῦλος χεῖρα ὤρεγε καὶ δοῦλον ὁ δεσπότης ἀνέσπα.
225. καὶ διὰ τοσούτων γε περαιούμενοι τῶν δεινῶν
οὐκ ᾤμωξαν, οὐκ ἐδάκρυσαν, οὐκ ἐμέμψαντο τὴν
στρατείαν, οὐ ῥῆμα ἀπέρριψαν πικρόν, οὐ πρὸς
αὑτοὺς ἐνενόησαν, ἀλλ᾽ ὥσπερ διὰ τῶν Ἀλκίνου
κήπων ἰόντες οὕτως ἥδοντο τοῖς παροῦσιν ἐλπίδος
R 598 τε, οἶμαι, | βελτίονος ὑπούσης καὶ ἅμα τοῦ βα-
σιλέως ταὐτὰ τοῖς πολλοῖς ἑκόντος ταλαιπωροῦν-
τος. 226. οὐ γὰρ ταῖς τῶν στρατιωτῶν ἐπιτείνας
κεφαλαῖς σανίδας, ὅπερ[2] ἂν ἄλλος ἴσως[3] ἐποίησεν,
ἐβάδιζεν ἀπόνως ἐν πονοῦσι μόνος, ἀλλὰ πρῶτος τῷ
σώματι πηλὸν καὶ ἰλὺν καὶ | ὕδωρ τέμνων οὕτω F
παρεκάλει τοὺς ἄλλους ἔργοις οὐ λόγοις, διά-
βροχον στρατιώταις καὶ σκευοφόροις τὴν χλαμύδα
δεικνύων.

227. Καὶ οἱ μὲν τὴν λίμνην εἰργασμένοι τὴν
πολλὴν Ἀσύριοι τὸ σόφισμα ἤλπιζον ἢ ἀποστρέ-
ψειν τὴν στρατιὰν ἢ ἀποπνίξειν, οἱ δέ, ὥσπερ
ὑπόπτεροι πάντες ἢ τοῦ Ποσειδῶνος αὐτοῖς δι-
ϊστάντος τὸ ὕδωρ, οὕτω διαφυγόντες οὐκ ὀλίγοι
προσέβαλλον οὐκέτι φρουρίοις, ἀλλ᾽ ἦν πόλις
Ἀσυρίων μεγάλη τοῦ μὲν τότε βασιλεύοντος ἐπώ-
νυμος, τεῖχος δὲ εἴσω τοῦ τείχους ἔχουσα δεύτερον
ὥστ᾽ εἶναι πόλιν ἐν πόλει βραχυτέραν ἐν μείζονι
κατὰ τοὺς κάδους τοὺς ἐν ἀλλήλοις κειμένους.
228. γιγνομένης δὲ τῆς ἐφόδου συνῆγε τοὺς οἰκήτορας ὁ φόβος εἰς τὸ βραχύτερον τεῖχος, ὡς

---

[1] ᾠχοῦντο F. (VU): ἐχοῦντο Fabr. (other mss.): εἰλοῦντο
Re.
[2] ὅπερ F. (mss.): ὥσπερ Re.
[3] ἴσως inserted F. (mss.): om. Re.

avoided by riding through the water, and then
slaves stretched out a hand to help their masters
and masters pulled their slaves to their feet. 225.
As they passed through such perils, they made no
moan, shed no tear, had no grumbles for the campaign, gave vent to no harsh word nor kept it
privately to themselves, but they enjoyed their
situation as though they were taking a stroll through
the gardens of Alcinoüs,[a] for they were full of high
hopes and their emperor of his own free will shared
the same toils as the common soldier. 226. For he did
not, as another man might perhaps have done, have
planks laid down on top of his men's heads to that he
could walk along, the only one without discomfort
while they all laboured on. With his own person he
was the first to force his way through mud and slush
and water, and so he encouraged the rest by deeds
not words, as he showed his dripping cloak to soldiers
and sutlers alike.

227. The Assyrians who had caused this huge
morass expected their device either to divert the
army or to drown it, but they, as though all taking
wing or as if Poseidon parted the waters for them,
made their escape from it and began a mass assault
not upon fortresses now, but upon a great Assyrian
city.[b] This was named after the reigning king, and
it contained a second line of defences inside its walls,
so that there was a smaller city inside the larger, just
as jars are stacked one inside another. 228. The
assault began, and the inhabitants in their fear retired inside the smaller fortification, thinking it the

---

[a] Cf. Or. 13. 18, and note.
[b] Pirisabora, which includes the name Sapor: Amm.
Marc. 24. 2. 9. (Bersabora, Zos. 3. 17.)

ἰσχυρότερον. οἱ δὲ τὸ μὲν ἔχοντες, τῷ δὲ προσιόντες βάλλονται μὲν ὑπὸ τῶν ἄνωθεν τοξοτῶν καὶ
ἀπέθανόν τινες, χώματα δὲ αἴροντες ὑπὲρ τὸ τεῖχος παρεστήσαντο τοὺς συνειλημένους[1] ὁμολογίᾳ. ἡ
δὲ ἦν μηδὲ ἐν σπονδαῖς ποτε ἐκείνους ἀποδοῦναι
Πέρσαις. ᾔδεσαν γὰρ τὰς παρ' ἐκείνοις δοράς. ὃ
καὶ σημεῖον τοῦ μὴ βλακεύοντας, παντὶ δὲ σθένει
μαχομένους εἰλῆφθαι. |

229. Οὕτω πάντα ἦν τοῦ βασιλέως ἥττω καὶ F 3
οὐδὲν τὸν ἄνδρα ἔφερεν. ἀλλ' ἦν χαλεπὸς μὲν
πολεμίοις, χαλεπὸς δὲ τῶν οἰκείων τοῖς οὐκ εἰδόσιν
ἢ κρατεῖν ἢ πίπτειν. τῶν τοίνυν προβεβλημένων
τῆς προνομῆς τῶν ἱππέων κακῶς ἠγωνισμένων
ὥστε αὐτοῖς καὶ τὸν ἵππαρχον ἀποθανεῖν, τοὺς
R 599 ἀξιοῦντας τιμᾶσθαι πρὸ | τῶν πολλῶν τοῖς ἀπο-
κτενοῦσι παρέδωκεν οὐκ ἀπὸ τῆς σκηνῆς ἐκπέμπων τὴν τιμωρίαν, ἀλλ' εἰς μέσους ἀναστρέφοντας
εἰσελθών, καταβιβάζων ὡπλισμένους πολλοὺς αὐτὸς
ἔχων δορυφόρους οὐδὲ τρεῖς. οὕτως ἦν πεπαι-
δευκὼς ἄρχεσθαι τοὺς στρατιώτας καὶ πᾶν τὸ
δοκοῦν τῷ κρατοῦντι δέχεσθαι. 230. τοῖς οὖν
ἱππεῦσιν ἀπαντήσας σὺν βοῇ τὸν ἀπολωλότα
ζητοῦσι καὶ δίκην τὴν ἀξίαν ἐπιθεὶς τοῖς οὐκ
ἐπαμύνασι καὶ δείξας τοῖς ἄλλοις ἅπασιν οἷα
μένει τοὺς ἀπορραθυμοῦντας, εἰσῆλθεν εἰς τὴν
σκηνὴν θαυμαστότερος γεγονώς. 231. βουλόμενος
δὲ ὡς πλείστην τῆς πολεμίας κακουργεῖσθαι πυκνὰς
ἐποιεῖτο τὰς ἀναπαύλας ὅπως τὸ μὲν ἄλλο στρατό-

---

[1] συνειλημένους F., conj. Re. : συνειλεγμένους Fabr. (mss.).

[a] Cf. Amm. Marc. 24. 3. 1-2, Zos. 3. 19.

stronger. Our men, having gained the outer ring, advanced against the other and became the target for the archers on top, and some of them were killed ; but by raising mounds to overtop the wall they forced the beleaguered garrison to surrender on terms. These were that not even in the general treaty of peace should they ever be restored to the Persians, for they were well acquainted with the Persian habit of flaying alive such people as themselves. This proves that they surrendered not out of faint-heartedness but after an obstinate resistance.

229. In this way the emperor rose superior to every check and nothing could withstand him. But he was a hard man to his enemies and to those of his own troops who did not know how to conquer or die. For instance, a detachment of cavalry sent ahead to cover a foraging party fought an unsuccessful engagement and lost their commander killed.[a] Those who expected to be honoured above the rest he handed over to execution, but he did not send an impersonal order from his headquarters : instead he made his way into the middle of them on their return, and though they were many and armed and he had barely three of his escort with him, he had them de-graded on the spot. He had so trained his men to obey and to accept their commander's every decision. 230. So by meeting the squadron which with great outcry was looking for its dead commander, and by inflicting suitable punishment on those who had not rallied to his support and making it plain to all the rest what was in store for any dereliction of duty, he returned to his tent with his prestige higher than ever. 231. In his desire to inflict the greatest possible damage on enemy territory, he made frequent halts so that, with

πεδον ἐν χαρακώματι μένοι, τοῖς δὲ κούφοις τε καὶ
εὐρωστοτέροις εἴη διερευνᾶσθαι τὴν γῆν ἄλλοις
ἄλλοσε σκεδαννυμένοις. οἱ καταγείους τε οἰκήσεις
ἀνεῦρον καὶ ἧκον ἄγοντες Ἀσυρίων τέκνα μετὰ
μητέρων ὥστε τὸν τῶν αἰχμαλώτων ἀριθμὸν πλείω
τοῦ τῶν κτησαμένων εἶναι. σπάνις δὲ τροφῆς
οὐδὲ οὕτως. |

232. Ἐντεῦθεν τοίνυν ἐχώρουν ἐπὶ τὸν αὐτὸν F 3
ἆθλον, τὰς διώρυχας, μᾶλλον δὲ ἐπ᾿ αὐτὸ τοῦ
ἄθλου τὸ χαλεπώτατον· πλείους γὰρ αἱ τομαὶ τῆς
γῆς, κἂν τῷ βάθει πάλιν τὸ πλέον. οὗ δὴ καὶ
σαφέστατα σωτὴρ ἐγένετο τῆς στρατιᾶς πάσης.
233. ἐπαινουμένης γὰρ ὑφ᾿ ἑτέρων ἑτέρας ὁδοῦ
μακροτέρας μέν, τῶν δὲ ὑδάτων ἔξω, τοῦτ᾿ αὐτὸ
τῆς ὁδοῦ μάλιστα φήσας δεδοικέναι τὸ διψῆν τε
ὁμοῦ καὶ παντὸς εἴδους ὑδάτων ἐστερῆσθαι καὶ
R 600 προσθεὶς ὡς ἐν τούτῳ μὲν | εἴη πόνος, ἐν ἐκείνῳ δὲ
ὄλεθρος, καὶ πολὺ βέλτιον παρ᾿ ὑδάτων ἐνοχλου-
μένους βαδίζειν ἢ ζητοῦντας ὕδωρ οὐκ ἔχειν, καὶ
μνησθεὶς δή τινος παλαιοῦ Ῥωμαίων στρατηγοῦ
διὰ τοιαύτης ἀβουλίας αὐτόν τε καὶ οὓς ἦγεν
ἀπολέσαντος καὶ δείξας εὐθὺς ἐκ βιβλίου τὴν
πανωλεθρίαν, τοιαῦτα λέγων τοὺς μὲν οὐ τὰ συμ-
φέροντα εἰπόντας αἰσχυνθῆναι κατηνάγκασε, τοὺς
δὲ ἔπεισεν ὀκνῆσαι μηδέν. 234. καὶ αὐτίκα
πλείους μὲν ἐπὶ γῆς οἱ φοίνικες, συχναὶ δὲ ἀπὸ
τούτων αἱ γέφυραι, ῥᾳστώνη δὲ ὑπερβῆναι τοῖς
πλείοσιν. εἶχε δὲ πολλὴν φιλοτιμίαν καὶ τὸ φθάσαι

---

[a] Julian here uses Plutarch's account of the disaster at
Carrhae for his homily ; cf. Plut. Crassus, 20 ff.

the main forces confined to the perimeter of the camp, the light forces and more mobile troops could scatter in all directions and scour the countryside. They discovered underground dwellings and returned with the women and children of the Assyrians, so that the captives exceeded their captors in number. Yet not even so was there a scarcity of rations.

232. From there they proceeded to the same task, the irrigation canals, or rather to the worst part of the whole task, for there were more cuttings than there was land, and in depth too they were more than the normal. Here indeed he proved himself the saviour of the whole army without a shadow of doubt. 233. For some people recommended a different route which, though longer, lay outside the water-logged area. His reply to this was that the only thing he was afraid of on the march was to suffer from thirst and to have no water at all. He added that, while their present route was laborious, the alternative would be disastrous, and they would do far better to advance despite the impediment of the water than to look for water and have none. He reminded them of a Roman general of bygone days who, through such imprudence, had brought ruin on himself and all his men, and there and then he produced a book[a] and read them the account of his annihilation. By such arguments he made the authors of such unhappy counsel ashamed of themselves and induced the rest to fear nothing. 234. Presently, palm trees became more plentiful in the district, and from them many bridges were constructed, so that the passage became easier for the majority of the troops. This involved much rivalry, and the men, in their desire to get across before the

τὸν διὰ τῆς γεφύρας ἐρχόμενον ἐμβάντα αὐτὸν εἰς
τὸ ὕδωρ. καὶ τὸ μὲν ἰσχυρὸν τῶν πολεμίων οὕτως
ἐξελήλεγκτο καὶ τὸ ὕδωρ ἐνενίκητο πάνυ δὴ νι-
κήσειν ἐλπισθέν. |

235. Ἔμελλε δὲ ἄρα καὶ ἕτερον ἰσχυρὸν οὐκ εἰς F 3
μακρὰν ἀσθενὲς ἐπιδειχθήσεσθαι. ἦν γάρ τι φρούριον καρτερὸν καὶ τοῦτο ἐν νήσῳ ὄχθου τε καὶ
τείχους μέτρῳ πρὸς ἀέρα ἀνεστηκός, τοσοῦτον ἦν
ἑκατέρου τὸ ὕψος. τὸ μὲν οὖν κάτω πλὴν κομιδῇ
τινος μικροῦ περιέζωστο δονάκων πυκνότητι κρυπ-
τούσῃ τοὺς ὑδρευομένους οἳ διὰ καταβάσεως ἀδή-
λου τοῖς ἔξω κατὰ πολλὴν ἐξουσίαν ὑπὸ ταῖς τῶν
δονάκων κόμαις ἐχρῶντο τῷ ποταμῷ, τὸ τεῖχος δὲ
κρεῖττον ἦν μηχανημάτων, τοῦτο μὲν ἐπὶ νήσου
πεποιημένον ἦν εἴσω πᾶσαν εἶχεν αὐτοῦ, τοῦτο δὲ
ἐφ᾽ οὕτως ὑψηλῆς, καὶ προσῆν τὸ πλίνθον ὀπτὴν
πρὸς ἑαυτὴν ἀσφάλτῳ δεδέσθαι. 236. ἡ μὲν οὖν
ἰσχὺς τοῦ φρουρίου συνεβούλευε μὴ πειρᾶσθαι, τὸ
δὲ ἐκδραμόντας τινὰς τοῖς πρώτοις τῆς στρατιᾶς
προσπεσεῖν καὶ μικρὸν ἀποσχεῖν τοῦ καὶ τὸν
βασιλέα τρῶσαι θυμῷ πρὸς πολιορκίαν τοὺς πεπονθότας ἦγε. καὶ οἱ μὲν προσεκάθηντο, Πέρσαι δὲ
601 ἄνωθεν ἐγέλων, ἐτώθαζον, ὕβριζον, | ἐτόξευον,
ἐτύγχανον· ἴσον αὐτοὺς ἡγοῦντο ποιεῖν ὥσπερ ἂν εἰ
καὶ τὸν οὐρανὸν ἐπεχείρουν ἑλεῖν. 237. ὁ δὲ
πρῶτον μὲν καὶ αὐτὸς πέτραις καὶ βέλεσι τῶν ἐπὶ
τοῦ | τείχους ἥψατο, καί τις φέρων τὸ βέλος ἐν τῷ F 3
σώματι κατέπιπτεν, ἔπειτα γεφύρᾳ τὴν νῆσον πρὸς

---

[a] Amm. Marc. 24. 3. 10 ff., Zos. 3. 19.
[b] Maiozamalcha: cf. Amm. Marc. 24. 4, Zos. 3. 20 ff.

436

troops marching over the bridge, would enter the
water and wade. This bulwark on which the enemy
had relied thus proved ineffective and the water was
overcome, though they had quite expected it to
prevail.[a]

235. Another of the enemy's bulwarks also was to
show its weakness, and after no long interval. There
was a strong fortress,[b] this too situated on an island,
and because of the combination of bank and wall,
both of them being so high, it soared up to the sky.
At its foot, except for a very small area, there was an
encircling growth of dense reeds that concealed the
water-carriers who, by means of a pathway down,
invisible to anyone outside, made full use of the river
under the cover of the reed-bed. The wall was too
high to be attacked by engines, first because it was
built on an island and encircled it completely, and
again, because the island was so sheer; finally, the
baked bricks of which it was composed were bound
together by bitumen. 236. The strength of the place
counselled him not to attempt it, but a party sallied
out, attacked the vanguard of the army and very
nearly wounded the emperor himself, and this made
the victims hot to besiege it. So they invested it,
and the Persians from above sent down a rain of
jeering, insult and abuse, and aimed their arrows at
them and found their targets ; such tactics, they
thought, were as stupid as trying to storm the heights
of heaven. 237. First then he personally directed the
fire of stones and missiles against the defenders of the
wall, and one or two tumbled down with the bolt still
in them. Then he linked the island to the mainland

This incident is discussed by Norman, Chalmers and
Cameron in articles in *Class. Qu.* 1957, 1960 and 1963.

LIBANIUS

τὴν ἤπειρον συνῆψεν, οἱ δὲ ἐργαζόμενοι φυλακὴν
εἶχον τὰ σκύτινα τῶν πλοίων· τούτων γὰρ τὰ ἄνω
κάτω ποιήσαντες καὶ δύντες ὑπ' αὐτοῖς καὶ τοὔδαφος τῶν πλοίων ἀντ' ὀροφῆς πεποιημένοι οἱ
μὲν εἴσω τῶν τοίχων τὸ αὐτῶν[1] ἕδρων, Πέρσαις δὲ
ἦν καὶ πᾶν βέλος ἐπὶ ταῦτα μάταιον ἅ γε οὐκ ἦν
ἀκίσιν [βαλεῖν],[2] οὐ συντρίψαι λίθοις, οὐ καῦσαι
φλογί. 238. οὐ μὴν παρὰ τοῦτο ἐθορυβοῦντο, ἀλλ'
εἰδότες μὲν ὀρύττοντας τοὺς πολεμίους, εἰδότες δὲ
πᾶν τεχνωμένους, νύκτα καὶ ἡμέραν ἐκώμαζον, ὡς
ἂν ἀπέραντα πονούντων. οἱ δὲ ἐνέκειντό τε καὶ
οὐκ ἔκαμνον καὶ πρὸς τὰ ἄνω χωροῦντες ὡδο-
ποίουν. τοῦ δὲ ὀρυττομένου τὸ εὖρος ἦν ἀνθρώπου, καὶ ὁ πρῶτος ἀναρριχώμενος ἐν μέσαις νυξὶν
εἰς μέσα πύργου τινὸς διαδὺς ἔλαθε, τῷ | δὲ εἵ- F 34
πετο δεύτερος, καὶ τρίτος ἐκείνῳ, καὶ πᾶς ἐβούλετο τῶν ἀναβαινόντων εἶναι. 239. γραῦν δ' αὐτοῦ
μόνην σὺν παιδίῳ κατακειμένην, ἐπειδὴ ᾔσθετο,
σιγᾶν ἀναγκάσαντες τὰς θύρας τῶν πύργων καταλαβόντες σύνθημα τοῖς κάτω πρὸς βοὴν δείξαντες
ῥαγείσης πολλῆς ἐκείνης καὶ τῶν φυλάκων σὺν
ἐκπλήξει τῶν εὐνῶν ἐκπηδώντων οὐδὲν ἔδει ἢ τοὺς
ἐπιστάντας σφίσι φονεύειν ἅπαντας, οἱ γὰρ δὴ
R 602 πλείους αὐτοὺς ἀπώλλυσαν ταῖς ἀπὸ τοῦ | τείχους
ῥίψεσι, θήρα τε ἦν πολλὴ τῶν πειρωμένων λαθεῖν
καὶ οὐδεὶς ἔχειν αἰχμάλωτον ἐβούλετο μᾶλλον ἢ
διαφθείρειν ὥστ' ἀφίεσαν ἄνωθεν, αἱ δὲ αἰχμαὶ
κάτωθεν ἀπήντων τοῖς ζῶσι, τοῖς ἡμιθνῆσι, τοῖς

[1] αὐτῶν F., conj. Re. (correction in M) : αὐτὸ Fabr. (mss.).
[2] βαλεῖν (Mo and insertions in CM) bracketed F. ; who
suggests ἦν ⟨διαπεῖραι⟩ ἀκίσιν.
438

by bridging, the engineers using the hides of the boats as protection. They would turn them upside down, get underneath them, and make a roof of the boat bottoms, and they continued doing their job inside the walls, and against these tactics neither fire nor any kind of missile was of any use to the Persians, for they could not pierce them with barbs, crush them with stones or burn them with flame. 238. For all that, they were not perturbed. They know that their enemy was mining and employing every device, but they spent night and day revelling, convinced that their labours would be interminable. However our men pressed on without tiring and progressed on their way upwards. The tunnel was wide enough to take one man at a time, and at dead of night the first man scrambled up and came out unnoticed in the interior of one of the towers,[a] to be followed by another and yet another, and all the sappers were eager to be members of the party completing the climb. 239. An old woman was sleeping there alone with a child. When she noticed them, they forced her to keep silent, and occupying the gates of the towers, they gave the signal to the men below to sound the attack, and as it blared forth, the guards jumped out of bed in alarm. All they had to do then was to kill any they came across, the greater part committing suicide by hurling themselves down from the walls. There was much hunting out of those who tried to hide, and nobody wanted to take prisoners, preferring to give no quarter, and they flung them down on to the spears below that welcomed them living, unconscious or dead, for the descent itself was

---

[a] *Cf.* Ammianus and Zosimus, *loc. cit.*, Suidas, *s.v.* ἀνασχοῦσα, and articles cited above.

τεθνεῶσιν. ἤρκει γὰρ ἡ φορὰ πρὸς θάνατον. 240.
τοιαῦτα ἐχόρευσαν μὲν ἐν νυκτὶ τοῖς πολεμικοῖς
δαίμοσιν, ἔδειξαν δὲ ἀνίσχοντι τῷ θεῷ. καὶ τοῦτο
μόνον ἠπείθησαν τῷ βασιλεῖ. ὁ μὲν γὰρ ἐκέλευε
ζωγρεῖν καὶ τὸν εἰλημμένον ἐλεεῖν, οἱ δὲ μεμνημένοι τῶν βελῶν καὶ τοὺς βεβλημένους εἰδότες καὶ
τῆς ὀργῆς τὴν δεξιὰν κινούσης παρεμυθοῦντο τὴν |
ἐπὶ τοῖς πόνοις λύπην τῷ φόνῳ καὶ ἐδέοντο F 34
βασιλέως συγγνώμην ἔχειν εἰ δρῶσι πεπονθότες.
241. ἀπολωλόσι δὴ τοῖς ἀνθρώποις ἐπαπώλλυτο τὸ
φρούριον μάλιστα δὴ τῶν ἐκεῖ φρουρίων ἐκτριβέν.
ὅσῳ γὰρ κατασκευῇ τῶν ἄλλων διέφερε, τοσούτῳ
τὴν παντελῶς ἀφανίζουσαν ἐπεσπάσατο ψῆφον.
διχόθεν γὰρ ἡ βλάβη Πέρσαις ἀντικαθιστᾷ τε καὶ
R 603 μὴ τὸ φρούριον. 242. οὕτω δὴ | λαμπρὸν καὶ
μεῖζον ἀνθρωπείας φύσεως τὸ πεπραγμένον, ὥσθ'
οἱ μὲν ᾑρηκότες οὐδὲν ἔτι αὐτοὺς ἐνόμιζον οἴσειν,
τῶν δὲ ἐναντίων συγκατενήνεκτο τὸ φρόνημα τῷ
τείχει καὶ ᾤοντο δὴ σφίσι πάντα εἶναι σαθρά. καὶ
βασιλεὺς ἀεὶ μὲν ἐργαζόμενος μεγάλα, μικρὰ δὲ
πάντα ἡγούμενος οὐκ ἔσχε τοῦτο μὴ νομίσαι πάμ-
μεγα. ἐφθέγξατο γοῦν ὅπερ οὐ πρόσθεν ὡς εἴη
τῷ Σύρῳ δεδωκὼς ἀφορμὴν εἰς λόγον, ἐμὲ δὴ
λέγων. ἀλλ' ἡ μὲν ἀφορμὴ θαυμαστή, πάντων
ἐμοὶ φίλτατε, σὲ δὲ οὐκ ἔχοντι τίς ἡδονὴ τοῦ βίου;
243. Ἀλλ' ἐκεῖσε ἐπανέρχομαι, ὅτι τὸ φρούριον
παθὸν ἃ διεξῆλθον, τῇ φήμῃ τοῦ πεπραγμένου
πολλὴν ἐπὶ πλεῖστον τῆς ὁδοῦ τῶν ἐναντιωσομένων
ἐρημίαν ἐποίησεν. ὥστε καὶ τὰς κώμας ἐπῇεσαν

---

<sup>a</sup> Cf. § 1, above.

enough to kill them. 240. Such was the carnival
they held during the night to the gods of war and
revealed to the Sun God at his rising. In this alone
they disobeyed their emperor, for he had given
orders to take prisoners alive and show them mercy.
The troops, however, remembering the missiles and
knowing their losses, and impelled to the action by
their fury, found in the massacre some consolation
for the rigours they had endured, and they begged
the emperor's pardon for getting their own back.
241. As well as the massacre of the garrison, the
fortress itself was destroyed, razed more completely
than any of the forts in the district. It had surpassed
all others in its defences, and so now it brought upon
itself the order for its utter destruction, and the
Persians, whether they replaced the fortress or not,
suffered a set-back in either case. 242. So glorious
was the event, so far beyond ordinary human endeavour, that the victors began to think that nothing
could stop them, and the enemy's morale was brought
as low as their walls and they felt utterly insecure.
The emperor himself, though ever engaged on mighty
tasks and regarding them all as mere trifles, could
not but consider this a magnificent feat of arms. At
any rate, he passed a remark he had never made
before, that he had given the Syrian (me, that is,)
matter to talk about.[a] My dearest friend, the
matter was indeed wonderful, but what pleasure in
life is there left for me, if I have not you ?

243. But to resume: the razing of the fortress in
the manner I have described, by the rumour of the
event, rendered would-be opponents conspicuous by
their absence over the greater part of the route. Thus
the camp-followers would even enter villages and lay

οἱ σκευοφόροι λαμβάνοντες ἃ μὴ λαβόντες οἱ κατοι-
κοῦντες ᾤχοντο. μᾶλλον δὲ τὰ μὲν ἐλάμβανον, ἃ
δὲ φέρειν οὐκ ἦν τὰ μὲν ἐδίδοσαν τῷ ποταμῷ τὰ δὲ
τῷ πυρί, ὥσπερ ἀμέλει καὶ | βασίλεια τοῦ Πέρσου F 3
κείμενα μὲν ἐπὶ τῷ ποταμῷ, κάλλος δὲ ἅπαν
ἔχοντα Περσικὸν ὅσον τε ἐν οἰκοδομήσεσι καὶ ὅσον
ἐν κήποις τε καὶ φυτῶν ὥραις καὶ ὀσμαῖς ἀνθέων,
συῶν δὲ ἀγέλην ἀγρίων ἔτρεφεν ἀπαντικρὺ χωρίον
ἐν οἷς αὐτὸν ἐγύμναζεν ὁ Πέρσης, τότε δὲ Ῥωμαίους εὐώχουν ἅπαντας. ταῦτα ἐνεπρήσθη τὰ
βασίλεια τῶν ἐν Σούσοις οὐδέν, ὥς φασιν, ἀτιμό-
τερα καὶ δεύτερα ἐπὶ τούτοις καὶ τρίτα ἐπὶ κάλλει |
R 604 μὲν ἐκείνων λειπόμενα, κάλλους δὲ οὐκ ἄμοιρα.

244. Τοιαῦτα δρῶντες ἐπὶ τὰς πάλαι ποθουμένας
ἀφικνοῦνται πόλεις αἳ τὴν Βαβυλωνίαν γῆν ἀντὶ
Βαβυλῶνος κοσμοῦσι. ῥεῖ δὲ αὐταῖν μέσος Τίγρης
ὁ ποταμὸς καὶ παραμείψας οὐ μικρὸν δέχεται τὸν
Εὐφράτην. ἐνταῦθα οὐκ ἦν εὑρεῖν ὃ ποιητέον·
εἴτε γὰρ παρίοιεν οἱ στρατιῶται τοῖς πλοίοις, οὐκ
ἦν προσελθεῖν ταῖς πόλεσιν, εἴτ' ἐπ' ἐκείνας ἴοιεν,
ἀπώλλυντ' ἂν αὐτοῖς αἱ νῆες, εἴτ' ἀναπλέοιεν διὰ
τοῦ Τίγρητος, μόχθος τε μέγας καὶ μέσαι[1] ταῖν
πόλεων ἐγίγνοντ' ἄν. 245. τίς οὖν ἔλυσε τὴν
ἀπορίαν; οὐ Κάλχας οὐδὲ | Τειρεσίας οὐδ' ἄλλος F 3
οὐδεὶς τῶν μάντεων. λαβὼν γὰρ αἰχμαλώτους
τῶν αὐτοῦ που πλησίον οἰκούντων ἐζήτει διώρυχα
ναυσίπορον καὶ ταύτην ἐκ βίβλων, ἔργον μὲν παλαιοῦ βασιλέως, ἄγουσαν δὲ τὸν Εὐφράτην ἐπὶ

---

[1] μέσαι F., Re. (M, I corrected): μέσαιν Fabr. (other mss.).

---

[a] Amm. Marc. 24. 5. 1.
[b] Coche (the successor to Seleuceia-on-Tigris) on the

hands on whatever the inhabitants had left in their
flight, or, to be more precise, some of their stuff they
took, and what they could not carry they hurled
either into the river or into the fire. For instance,
a palace of the Persian king, lying on the river bank,
with all the Persian elegance in building, in gardens,
fine plantations and scented flowers, with a herd of
wild pigs in a park opposite for the Persian to keep
in practice with his hunting, all this provided a feast
for the whole Roman army, and then the palace was
burnt down.[a] It was, so it is said, not at all inferior
to that at Susa. After that they burnt another, and
then a third which, though inferior to the other two
in beauty, was not without its share of it.

244. Engaged on such activities, they reached the
cities that had long been their objective. These have
taken the place of Babylon as the adornments of the
land of Babylonia, and midway between them flows
the river Tigris, which unites with the Euphrates a
little further downstream.[b] Here it was impossible
to find out what was to be done. If the soldiers continued past them in their vessels, they could not
attack the cities; if they attacked the cities, they
would have to give up their boats; if they sailed
up the Tigris, the task would be enormous and the
boats would be caught midway between the two
cities. 245. It was no Calchas, no Teiresias or any
other seer who then resolved the difficulty. Having
taken some captives from the inhabitants of the
surrounding area, Julian began to enquire about a
navigable channel, his information here also derived
from his books. This, the work of a king of days gone

western bank, Ctesiphon, the Persian capital, on the east of
the river : *cf.* Amm. Marc. 24. 5. 3, 6 ; Sozom. 6. 1.

τὸν Τίγρητα ταῖν δυοῖν ἀνωτέρω πόλεων. 246.
τῶν δὲ αἰχμαλώτων τοῦ μὲν τῆς νεότητος οὐδὲν
ἐπισταμένης, τοῦ δ' ἐν γήρᾳ πάντα ὑπ' ἀνάγκης
εἰπόντος, καὶ γὰρ ἑώρα τὸν βασιλέα περὶ τῶν
τόπων οὕτως ἀκριβῶς τοῖς λόγοις χρώμενον ὥσπερ
τινὰ τῶν ἐπιχωρίων, οὕτως ἐν τοῖς γράμμασιν
ἀπὼν ἑωράκει πάλαι τὴν χώραν, φράζει τοίνυν ὁ
πρεσβύτης οὗ τέ ἐστι καὶ ὡς κέκλειται καὶ ὡς
ἀναχωσθεῖσα τὸ πρὸς τῷ στόματι σπείροιτο. 247.
νεύσαντος δὲ τοῦ κρατοῦντος ἅπαν τὸ κώλυμα
R 605 ἐξῄρητο | καὶ τοῖν ῥείθροιν τὸ μὲν ξηρὸν ἑωρᾶτο,
τὸ δὲ ἦγεν ἐπὶ τὸν Τίγρητα πλοῖα παραπλέοντα τῷ
στρατῷ, καὶ τοῖς ἐν ταῖς πόλεσι μείζων ἐπελθὼν ὁ
Τίγρης ἅτε προσλαβὼν τὸν Εὐφράτην | φόβον F 344
ἐπήνεγκε μέγαν ὡς οὐ φεισόμενος τῶν τειχῶν.
248. ἐκφαίνεται δὴ Περσῶν τὸ δοκιμώτατον καὶ
κατεῖχον τὴν ὄχθην ἀσπίσι τε λαμπούσαις καὶ
ἵπποις χρεμετίζουσι καὶ τόξοις ἠσκημένοις καὶ
μεγέθεσιν ἐλεφάντων οἷς ἴσον ἔργον δι' ἀσταχύων
ἐλθεῖν καὶ φάλαγγος. οὗτοι μὲν οὖν ἦσαν ἀντι-
μέτωποι, ποταμὸς δὲ ἔνθεν καὶ ἔνθεν, ὁ μὲν ἐγγὺς
ὁ[1] βεβιασμένος, ὁ δέ τις ἀπωτέρω, καὶ στρατιὰ
Περσῶν ἑτέρα, τὰ δὲ κατόπιν ὠμῶς πεπορθημένα
καὶ οὐ διδόντα τὴν αὐτὴν πάλιν ἐλθεῖν. 249.
ἐδεῖτο δὴ τόλμης ὑπερφυοῦς ὁ καιρὸς τοῖς οὐ μέλ-
λουσιν ἀπολεῖσθαι λιμῷ, καὶ πάντες τεταραγμένοι
πρὸς ἕνα ἔβλεπον. ὁ δὲ πρῶτον μὲν ἃ τῶν εὐθυ-

---

[1] δὲ after ὁ (mss.) bracketed F., Re.

---

[a] The Naharmalcha (King's Canal): Amm. Marc. 24.
6. 1; Zos. 3. 24. Herod. 1. 193 is the source of Julian's

444

by, led from the Euphrates to the Tigris upstream of the cities.[a] 246. Of the captives, one was a mere boy and knew nothing of it, but the other, an old man, was forced to tell all about it, for he saw the emperor as accurately informed about the geography of the region as if he had been born there, such long acquaintance with the terrain had his books given him even when he was far away. The old fellow, then, told where it was situated and revealed that the channel had been closed and that the blockage at its mouth was under cultivation. 247. At the emperor's command the whole obstruction was removed, and of the channels the old one was seen to dry up, while this other conveyed the boats parallel with the army to the Tigris. The Tigris, descending with greater volume upon the inhabitants of the cities since it had also been swollen by the water of the Euphrates, caused great panic among them, for it seemed that it would not spare their walls. 248. The cream of the Persian army now made its appearance and occupied the bank, shields glittering, horses neighing, with bows trained and huge elephants that could burst through a phalanx as easily as through a field of corn. These then faced them: on either side was a river, the one near by being the one diverted from its course, with another at some little distance guarded by another Persian army. To the rear lay the area of savage devastation that offered no hope of return by the same route. 249. The time had come when, if they were not to die of starvation, some superhuman courage was required, and the whole army in perturbation looked to a single man. His first actions were

information rather than Polybius (5. 51), an author with whom Libanius, at least, was unacquainted.

445

μουμένων ἐστίν, ἐποίησεν ἱππόδρομόν τε λεάνας
καὶ ἱππέας ἐπ᾽ ἀγῶνα καλέσας καὶ ἆθλα κέλησι
θείς, θεαταὶ δὲ τῶν δρωμένων οὕτω πρὸς τοῖς
οἰκείοις ἦσαν οἱ πολέμιοι, οἱ μὲν κάτω περικαθή-
μενοι τὰς ἁμίλλας, οἱ δὲ ἀπὸ τῶν ἐπάλξεων, τὸν
μὲν μακαρίζοντες ὡς ἂν ἐν ταῖς εὐφροσύναις τῶν
νενικηκότων ὄντα, σφᾶς δὲ αὐτοὺς ὡς ἂν οὐκ
ἔχοντας ταῦτα κωλύειν θρηνοῦντες.  250. ἐν ᾧ δὲ
τοῖς δρόμοις τῶν ἵππων ὁ στρατὸς ἐψυχαγωγεῖτο,
κεναὶ τῶν φορτίων ἐκ παραγγέλσεως ἦσαν αἱ νῆες,
τῷ λόγῳ μὲν ὅπως ὀφθείη | τὸ σιτηρέσιον εἴ πη F 3
παραναλωται, τὸ δὲ ἔργον ἦν, οὐ προειδότας
R 606 ἐξαίφνης ἐμβιβάσαι | τοὺς στρατιώτας ἐβούλετο.
δεδειπνηκότας τοίνυν ἀγείρας τοὺς ἐν τέλει καὶ
δείξας ὡς μία λέλειπται μόνη πρὸς σωτηρίαν ὁδὸς
Τίγρητα διαβάντας γῆς ἀκεραίου πάλιν ἀπολαύειν
ἔχειν, τοὺς μὲν ἄλλους εἶχε σιγῶντας, ὑφ᾽ ᾧ δὲ ἦν
τῆς δυνάμεως τὸ πλέον ἀντέλεγε τῷ τε ὕψει τοῦ
κρημνοῦ καὶ τῷ πλήθει τῶν πολεμίων φοβῶν.
251. ὁ δὲ τὴν μὲν τοῦ τόπου φύσιν καὶ διαμελλόν-
των τὴν αὐτὴν εἰπὼν ἔσεσθαι, τοὺς πολεμίους δὲ
πλείονας, ἕτερον ἄνδρα ἐκέλευε καὶ προεῖπεν ὡς
κρατήσει μὲν οὗτος, οὐκ ἄνευ δὲ τραύματος.  τοῦτο
δὲ αὐτὸν τῇ χειρὶ δέξεσθαι καὶ οὗ τῆς χειρὸς
προσέθηκε καὶ τούτῳ πάλιν τὸ μικροῦ δεήσειν
φαρμάκου.  252. καὶ αἱ μὲν νῆες εἶχον ἤδη τοὺς
μαχομένους,[1] ὁ δ᾽ εἱστήκει βλέπων εἰς οὐρανόν, ὡς
δὲ ἔλαβεν ἐκεῖθεν τὸ σύνθημα, δίδωσιν αὐτὸ τοῖς

---

[1] μαχομένους Re. (mss.) : μαχουμένους F., Cobet.

---

[a] Cf. Or. 1. 133, 24. 37 ; Ruf. Fest. Brev. 28 ; Sozom. loc.
cit.

446

indicative of confidence: he levelled out a race-track and summoned cavalrymen to a contest, offering prizes for the horses.[a] Not only his own troops but also the enemy were spectators of what went on, some encamped on the plain around the course, and others watching from their battlements, counting him lucky for engaging in the festivities of the victorious and full of self-pity at not being able to put a stop to it. 250. While the army was enjoying some recreation at the horse races, the ships were ordered to be emptied of their cargoes, ostensibly so that there might be a check on any deficiency of rations. In actual fact, however, he wanted to embark his troops suddenly and without giving them advance notice.[b] After they had had a meal, then, he called his commanders to a council of war and explained that there was only one recourse left to them, to cross the Tigris and once more live off a land that had not suffered devastation. This silenced the rest, but the commander of the main body opposed the plan with alarming reports both of the height of cliff and the numbers of the enemy. 251. He replied that the geographical situation would remain unaltered, however long they dallied, but the enemy's numbers would increase. So, bidding another officer take command, he foretold that he would succeed, but at the cost of a wound that he would receive in the hand, and he added whereabouts on the hand this would be, and also that it would not require much curing.[c] 252. The storming party was already aboard when he stood gazing up to heaven. Receiving the signal from there, he passed it on to his colonels, and

[b] *Cf.* Amm. Marc. 24. 6. 4 ff., Zos. 3. 25.
[c] Victor: *cf.* Amm. Marc. 24. 6. 13.

ταξιάρχοις, οἱ δὲ τοῖς ἄλλοις ὡς οἷόν τε μάλιστα δι'
ἡσυχίας. οἱ δὲ ἔπλεόν τε καὶ | ἐξέβαινον αἴσθησίν F 3
τε ἤδη τοῖς ἐγγὺς παρέχοντες καὶ βαλλόμενοι, ἀλλ'
ὅμως ὃν οὐκ ἂν ἐν εἰρήνῃ τε καὶ μηδενὸς εἴργοντος
μεθ' ἡμέραν εὔζωνοι κρημνὸν ἐθάρρησαν, διὰ νυκτὸς
ὁπλῖται τοὺς πολεμίους ὑπὲρ κεφαλῆς ἔχοντες
ἀναβεβήκεσαν· ὅπως μέν, οὐδ' ἂν νῦν ἔχοιμεν
ἐρωτηθέντες εἰπεῖν. οὕτως οὐκ ἀνθρώπων μᾶλλον
ἦν τὸ ἔργον ἢ θεοῦ τινος ταῖς αὐτοῦ χερσὶ μετεωρί-
ζοντος ἕκαστον. 253. τῇ δ' οὖν ἀναβάσει τὸν
φόνον συνάψαντες τοὺς μὲν ἀνισταμένους κατήνεγκαν, τοῖς δὲ κακὸν ἐπιστάντες ὄναρ ἔτι καθεύ-
δοντας ἔκτεινον. οἱ δὲ ἀφυπνισθέντες τοσοῦτον
εἶχον τῶν κοιμωμένων πλέον ὅσον ᾔδεσαν ἃ πά-
σχουσιν, ἐπεὶ ἀμύνεσθαί γε τοὺς ἐπικειμένους οὐδὲ
τούτοις ἦν. 254. οἷα δὲ ἐν νυκτὶ καὶ σκότῳ, πολλὰ
R 607 μὲν ἐφέρετο | κατὰ τῶν σωμάτων ξίφη, πολλὰ δὲ
κατὰ τῶν δένδρων, ἐδήλου δὲ ταῦτα ὁ κτύπος, οἰμωγὴ δὲ ἠκούετο τετρωμένων, τιτρωσκομένων, μελλόντων, ἀπολλυμένων, ἱκετευόντων. οἱ δὲ προῄε-
σαν σφάττοντες, καὶ τῆς γῆς τοσοῦτον ἐκέκρυπτο τοῖς
τῶν πεπτωκότων σώμασιν ὅσον ἂν καλύψαιεν ἑξα-
κισχίλιοι νεκροί. 255. εἰ δὲ μὴ σκύλων ἐπιθυμίᾳ περὶ
τοὺς τεθνεῶτας διέτριψαν ἀλλ' ἐπὶ τὰς | πύλας F 3
ἀΐξαντες ἢ ἀνέσπων ἢ κατέσχισαν, εἶχον ἂν Κτη-
σιφῶντα τὴν πολυύμνητον. νῦν δὲ χρυσὸν μὲν καὶ
ἄργυρον καὶ ἵππους τοὺς τῶν οἰχομένων ἐκτῶντο,
ἅμα δὲ ἡμέρᾳ πρὸς ἱππέας ἠναγκάζοντο μάχεσθαι οἳ

---

<sup>a</sup> Festus (*Brev.* 28) confirms Libanius' statement. Am-
mianus (*loc. cit.*) gives a more favourable version of the
failure to advance on Ctesiphon.

they to their men with the utmost possible secrecy.
They set sail and disembarked, but by now had been
observed by the enemy near by and had become a
target for their weapons; but for all that it was night-
time with the enemy in occupation of the crest, in full
armour they scaled the cliff before which men might
have quailed, even if they attempted it in peace time,
without opposition, in daylight, and unhindered by
their equipment. As to how they managed it, it is
impossible still to answer that question. The job was
done not so much by human endeavour as by some
god who lifted up each man with his own hands.
253. The ascent was followed by a massacre, where
they exterminated all who got up to oppose them
and, coming upon others like a nightmare, slew any
still asleep. Those awakened had just this much advantage over their sleeping comrades, that they
realized what was happening to them, for not even
they could repulse their assailants. 254. And, as
happens in pitch darkness, sword blows in plenty fell
on the bodies of men and upon trees, and then the
thud betrayed what had happened. There was
heard the groaning of men who were or had been
injured or who were soon to be so, of men dying, of
men begging for quarter. Our troops continued their
murderous advance, and the earth was covered with
the bodies of the slain to the number of six thousand.
255. And had they not dallied around the dead in
their eagerness for spoil, but if instead they had made
a dash for the gates and pulled them up or torn
them down, they would have gained possession of
far-famed Ctesiphon.[a] As it turned out, they got
their hands on the gold, silver and horses of the slain,
but at day-break they were forced to engage with the

τὰ μὲν πρῶτα ἐλύπουν, ἔπειτα δὲ ὑφ' ἑνὸς ἐξ
αἱμασιᾶς ἀναδραμόντος στρατιώτου κυκηθέντες
ἔφυγον. διαβαίνει δὲ τὸ λοιπὸν στρατόπεδον, καὶ
τούτων πανταχοῖ τοὺς ὀφθαλμοὺς φερόντων μετὰ
θαύματος οἱ κτείνοντες περιέπλυνον αὐτοὺς τῷ ποταμῷ, καὶ ὁ Περσῶν Τίγρης τῷ Περσῶν αἵματι
χρωσθεὶς ἔρρει.

256. Λογιζέσθω δή τις τὰς ἐκείνων εἰς τὴν
ἡμετέραν εἰσβολὰς καὶ τὸ καθ' ἕκαστον ἔργον καὶ
παραβαλλέτω ταύτην τὴν μίαν ταῖς συχναῖς ἐκεί-
ναις καὶ τάχα εὑρήσει λαμπρὰ μὲν κἀκεῖνα, πολὺ
δὲ μείζω ταῦτα καὶ τὰ μὲν οὐδενὸς ἀπαντῶντος
πεπραγμένα, τὰ δὲ ὄντων τῶν μαχομένων τετολ-
μημένα, ὥστ' εἴ τις | ἤρετο Πέρσας εἰ ἐβούλοντ' F 34
ἂν μήτε ἃ δεδράκασι δεδρακέναι μήτε ἃ πεπόνθασι
πεπονθέναι, πάντας ἂν εἰπεῖν ἀπὸ τοῦ βασιλέως
R 608 ἀρξαμένους ὡς ἐπὶ πολλῷ | τὰ τότε ἐνίκων. 257.
γνοίη δ' ἄν τις κἀκεῖθεν· Κωνστάντιος γὰρ ἐν
οὐδεμιᾷ τῶν εἰσβολῶν εἰς αἴτησιν σπονδῶν ἠναγ-
κάσθη πεσεῖν, ὁ δὲ ὧν ἔφην πεπραγμένων ἔπεμψε
τὸν δεησόμενον ἐνταυθοῖ στῆναι τὸν πόλεμον καὶ
τὸν νενικηκότα τοῦ πλείονος ἀποσχόμενον φίλην
ἔχειν καὶ σύμμαχον τὴν αὐτῶν ἀρχήν. 258. καὶ ὁ
μὲν ἐπὶ τούτοις ἥκων τῶν εὖ γεγονότων εἰσελθὼν
ὡς τὸν ἀδελφὸν τοῦ πέμψαντος μεθ' ἡμῶν ἐπ'
ἐκεῖνον ἰόντα γονάτων ἁπτόμενος ἐδεῖτο κοινῶσαι
βασιλεῖ τὸν λόγον. ὁ δὲ κατὰ σπουδήν τε καὶ

a Hormisdas, brother of Sapor, who had sought refuge
with Constantius. Libanius repeatedly insists on Sapor's
overtures for peace at this time (cf. Or. 1. 133, 30. 41),
although no confirmation may be obtained from either
450

cavalry, which caused them trouble at first, but finally retired in disorder before a single soldier who set upon them from behind a stone wall. The remainder of the army then made the crossing, gazing in wonderment at all about them, while the killers washed themselves in the river, and the Persian Tigris flowed on dyed red with Persian blood.

256. Now consider the Persian invasions of Roman territory and their successes on each occasion, and compare this one invasion of ours with their numerous incursions. You will perhaps find that though their successes have been spectacular, this is much more so. Theirs were won without opposition; this venture was undertaken in face of fighting troops, so that if you asked the Persians whether they would want their victories undone provided that their disasters were cancelled, they would all have answered, from their king downwards, that their past victories had been paid for very dearly. 257. You may gather this from the following consideration also. In none of their invasions was Constantius ever reduced to such straits as to ask for a truce. The Persian king, however, after the events I have narrated sent an envoy to request an end to the war then and there, and to beg the victor to refrain from further hostilities and to have the Persian empire as a friendly allied state. 258. The envoy sent on this errand was one of the nobility, and he approached the brother of the king who had sent him, he being a member of our army of invasion against him,[a] and embracing his knees, besought him to arrange an interview with the emperor.

Ammianus or Zosimus. This insistence must be due to his use of another source of information: it can hardly be merely rhetorical falsification to heighten the pathos of Julian's end.

μεθ' ἡδονῆς ὡς δὴ χρηστόν τι μηνύσων ἦλθε
μειδιῶν καὶ διηγεῖτο καὶ δῶρα προσεδόκα τῶν
λόγων. ὁ δὲ αὐτόν τε σιγᾶν ἐκέλευε καὶ τὸν
ἥκοντα ἀποπέμψαι σιγῶντα καὶ συγγένειαν τὴν
πρὸς αὐτὸν ἐκείνου πλάσαι τῆς συνουσίας πρόφασιν.
οὔτε γὰρ καταθέσθαι τὸν πόλεμον ἠξίου τό τε τῆς
εἰρήνης ὄνομα δεινὸν ἐνόμιζεν ἀμβλῦναι στρατιώτην. ὁ γάρ, οἶμαι, πεισθεὶς ὡς ἔξεστι μὴ μάχε-
σθαι, κακῶς ἂν¹ ἀναγκαζόμενος μάχοιτο. 259. διὰ |
τοῦτο εἴσω τῶν ὀδόντων προσέταξε μένειν τὸ F 3
γλυκὺ τῶν σπονδῶν ὄνομα.  καίτοι τίς οὐκ ἄν,
ἐνδεικνύμενος τοῖς ἑαυτοῦ πόσον τι δεδύνηται |
R 609 στρατηγῶν, ἤγειρε σύλλογον ἐπ' ἀκροάσει τῶν
ῥημάτων; ἀλλ' οὗτός γε ἐπὶ συνθήκας καλούμενος
τῷ τείχει προσελθὼν ἐπὶ μάχην τοὺς τειχήρεις
ἐκάλει γυναικῶν μὲν εἶναι λέγων ὃ πράττουσιν,
ἀνδρῶν δὲ ὃ φεύγουσι.  260. τῶν δὲ εἰπόντων δεῖν
τὸν βασιλέα ζητεῖν κἀκείνῳ δεικνύειν αὐτὸν ἐπε-
θύμησε μὲν Ἄρβηλα καὶ ἰδεῖν καὶ διελθεῖν ἢ ἄνευ
μάχης ἢ καὶ μαχεσάμενος ὥστε μετὰ τῆς Ἀλεξάνδρου νίκης τῆς αὐτόθι καὶ ταύτην ὑμνεῖσθαι,
καὶ γνώμην δὲ εἶχεν ἐπιβῆναι πάσης ὅση Πέρσαις
ὁρίζει τὸ κράτος, μᾶλλον δὲ καὶ τῆς ὁμόρου, καίτοι
μηδετέρας αὐτῷ μοίρας ἐλθούσης μήτε τῆς οἰκείας
μήτε τῆς συμμάχου, τῆς μὲν ἀδικίᾳ τοῦ τὸ ἔθνος
ἔχοντος, ἡ δέ, ὥς φασι, κατ' ἀρχὰς εὐθὺς τοξευ-

---

¹ ἂν inserted F.

---

ᵃ In any case, in his march north up the Tigris, he would
pass close to Arbela. Socrates (3. 21) uses this passage of
Libanius, and adds the notion of a divinely-inspired infatua-

452

He then came in haste and with joy, as the bearer of good news, and all smiles, he said his say, confidently expecting to be rewarded for his message, but the emperor bade him be silent and send the envoy away in silence, and pretend that his relationship with the Persian king had been the reason for the interview. He rejected any cessation of hostilities, and he felt the word " peace " to be the surest means of blunting an army's fighting spirit, for if men are convinced that fighting is not inevitable, they fight less effectively when forced to do so. 259. Hence he bade these pleasant words " treaty of peace " stay unspoken on his lips. Yet who would not, to prove to his men the success of his generalship, have called an assembly of the troops to listen to the terms ? He, however, though invited to conclude an agreement, advanced against the walls and challenged the besieged to battle, telling them that their actions were those of women, and they were avoiding behaving like men. 260. Upon their reply that he should seek their king and show himself to him too, he conceived the idea of seeing and passing through Arbela, either with or without a battle, so that his victory would be celebrated along with that won by Alexander there,[a] and he also formed the plan of setting foot on all the territories of which the Persian empire is composed and upon the adjacent countries too. But neither our own nor the allied reinforcements had linked up with him. The allied sovereign had played him false, and our own forces, so it is said, right at the outset had suffered some casualties from archers as they were

tion. This seems to be an inference from the change of route sketched by Zos. 3. 26 and Ammianus (24. 7. 3: " mediterraneas vias arripere proposuit ").

θέντων τινῶν ἐν τῷ Τίγρητι λουομένων, μεῖζον
αὐτοῖς ἡγήσατο τὸ μάχεσθαι πρὸς αὐτούς. καὶ
ἅμα ἡ τῶν ἡγεμόνων πρὸς ἀλλήλους φιλονεικία
ῥαθυμεῖν τοῖς | ἀρχομένοις ἐπέτρεπεν. ὁπότε γὰρ F 3
ἅτερος κινοίη, μένειν ἅτερος παραινῶν χαριζόμενος
R 610 ἔπειθεν. 261. οὐ μὴν χείρω | γε ταῦτα ἐποίει τὸν
βασιλέα. ἀλλ' οὐκ ἐπήνει μὲν ἀπόντας, πράττειν
δὲ ὅσαπερ ἄν, εἰ παρῆσαν, ἠξίου καὶ πρὸς τὴν
Ὑρκανίαν ἔτεινε τὸν λογισμὸν καὶ τοὺς Ἰνδῶν
ποταμούς. ἤδη δὲ τῆς στρατιᾶς ἐπὶ ταῦτα ὡρμη-
μένης καὶ τῶν μὲν πορευομένων, τῶν δὲ συσκευαζο-
μένων, θεῶν τις τοῦ μὲν ἀφίστησι, νόστου δὲ κατὰ
τὸ ἔπος παρῄνει μεμνῆσθαι. 262. τὰ πλοῖα δὲ
πρὸς τὴν προτέραν βουλὴν ἀφεῖτο πυρί, κάλλιον
γὰρ ἦν ἢ τοῖς πολεμίοις. ταὐτὸν δ' ἂν εἰκότως
ἐδρᾶτο καὶ τοῦ προτέρου μὲν οὐ βουλευθέντος,[1] τοῦ
δὲ ἐπανιέναι νικῶντος. ὀξὺς γὰρ καὶ πολὺς ὁ
Τίγρης ἐμπίπτων ταῖς πρώραις πολλῶν ἠνάγκαζε
δεῖσθαι χειρῶν τὰ πλοῖα καὶ ἔδει τοὺς ἀνέλκοντας
ὑπὲρ ἥμισυ τῆς στρατιᾶς γενέσθαι. τοῦτο δὲ ἦν
κρατεῖσθαι μὲν τοὺς μαχομένους, ἔχεσθαι δὲ ἀμαχεὶ
μετ' ἐκείνους τὰ ἄλλα. 263. πρὸς δὲ τούτοις καὶ
τὴν εἰς τὸ μαλακίζεσθαι παράκλησιν ἀνῃρήκει τὸ
πῦρ. ὁ γὰρ μηδὲν ποιεῖν ἐθέλων ἀρρωστεῖν
σκηπτόμενος ἔκειτο καθεύδων ἐν | πλοίῳ, πλοίων F
δὲ οὐκ ὄντων ἅπας ἦν ἐν ὅπλοις. ὡς τοίνυν οὐδὲ
σφόδρα βουλομένοις ἦν ἔχειν ναῦς τοσαύτας, ἔδειξε

---

[1] βουλευθέντος F. (Par. 3016, corrections in IM): βουλη-
θέντος Re. (other mss.).

454

bathing in the Tigris, and thought it better to fight
these native opponents. Moreover, the rivalry
between the commanders produced slackness in the
men, for whenever one of them gave the order to
march, the other would recommend a halt, and by
this appeal to popularity, he would get his way.[a]
261. Yet this did not discourage the emperor at all.
Though deploring their absence, he insisted on
behaving as he would have done had they joined him,
and he began to extend his view even to Hyrcania
and the rivers of India. But with the expedition now
directed to these objectives and with the army either
already in motion or preparing for it, one of the gods
deterred him from it and bade him, in Homer's
words, to bethink him of a return home.[b] 262. In
accordance with the earlier plan, the boats had been
consigned to the flames—better that than to the
enemy. He would probably have done the same, had
this previous plan never been devised, as now when
plans to return won the day, for the Tigris, meeting
their bows with fierce strong current, made the
vessels need many to man-handle them, and more
than half the army would have been required to tow
them, and that would have meant the defeat of
the fighting men, and after them the capture of the
rest of the army without a struggle. 263. Moreover,
the burning of the boats had disposed of any inclina-
tion towards slackness, for all the idlers would lie
sleeping in the boats on the excuse of sickness,
whereas, if there were no boats at all, every man
would be under arms. That they could not keep so
many vessels, however much they wanted to do so,
was shown by the fact that they were incapable of

[a] Amm. Marc. 24. 7. 7.  [b] Homer, *Iliad*, 10. 509.

τὸ μηδὲ τὰς ὑπολειφθείσας, αἱ δὲ ἦσαν πεντε-
καίδεκα γεφυρῶν εἴνεκα πεφυλαγμέναι, μηδὲ ταύτας ἀρκέσαι σῶσαι. βιαιότερος γὰρ ὢν καὶ
ναυτῶν τέχνης καὶ τῆς ἄλλης πολυχειρίας ὁ πόρος
R 611 αὐτάς τε | καὶ τοὺς ἐμπλέοντας εἰς τὰς τῶν πολε-
μίων χεῖρας ἐξέβαλεν ὥστ᾿ εἰ δεῖ κατηγορεῖν
ἐκείνου τοῦ πυρὸς τοὺς ἐζημιωμένους, ὁ Πέρσης
ἂν εἰκότως ὁ μεμφόμενος εἴη. καὶ πολλάκις γε,
ὥς φασιν, ἐμέμψατο.

264. Οὕτω μὲν τοῦ Τίγρητος πίνοντες ἐχώρουν
κατ᾿ ἀριστερὰν χεῖρα τὸν ποταμὸν ἔχοντες καὶ διὰ
χώρας ᾔεσαν τῆς προτέρας ἀμείνονος ὥστε οἷς
εἶχον αἰχμαλώτοις θαρροῦντως προσετίθεσαν. ἐπεὶ
δὲ τῆς μὲν πεφυτευμένης ἐπὶ τέλει, τῆς δὲ ψιλῆς τε
καὶ οὐδὲν[1] φαυλοτέρας ἦσαν ἐν μέσῳ, κηρύττει
σιτία φέρεσθαι τὸν στρατὸν ἡμερῶν εἴκοσι, τοσαύτη
γὰρ ὁδὸς ἐπὶ τὴν ἀρίστην τε πόλιν καὶ ἅμα τῆς
ἡμετέρας ὅμορον. τότε δὴ πρῶτον ὁρᾶται Περσικὴ
παράταξις, πλῆθος οὐκ ἄτακτον, καὶ χρυσὸς πολὺς
ἐν τοῖς ὅπλοις. πεσόντος δὲ ἡμετέρου τινὸς
προμάχου καὶ συμπεσόντων ἁπάντων οὔθ᾿ ἱππεὺς
οὔθ᾿ ὁπλίτης ἤνεγκε τὰς παρ᾿ | ἡμῶν ἀσπίδας, ἀλλ᾿ F 3
εὐθὺς ἐγκλίναντες[2] ἔφευγον ἐν εὖ[3] τοῦτο ἠσκηκότες
τοῦ πολέμου τὸ μέρος. 265. καὶ τοῦ λοιποῦ
παράταξις μὲν οὐδεμία, κλοπαὶ δὲ καὶ ἀγεννεῖς
ὀλίγων ἱππέων ἔφοδοι τοῖς ὑστάτοις ἐκ τάφρων

---

[1] πολὺ conj. Re. : οὐδεμιᾶς οὐ suggested F. : καίπερ οὐδὲν ?
[2] ἐγκλίναντες Herwerden (V) : ἐκκλίναντες F., Re. (other
MSS.).
[3] ἐν εὖ F. (VU) : ἐν om. La : εὖ om. Re. (CBMoMP).

---

[a] Their capture is reported by Zosimus (3. 28. 2), but not
in the manner here narrated by Libanius.

keeping safe even the remainder,[a] which, fifteen in number, had been held back for bridging operations: the current was too strong both for skilled boatmen and for manhandling, and it swept them and those that sailed in them into the clutches of the enemy. Thus if there was anybody to feel aggrieved and criticize that burning of the boats, it was the Persians who had the more reason for complaint. And as a matter of fact, complain they did, and often, so it is said.

264. So they marched on with the Tigris to drink, keeping the river on their left. Their route lay through a country more hospitable than before, so that they confidently added to the number of the prisoners they held. When they had passed beyond the cultivated area and were in the middle of a bare district that still was not too bad, he issued orders for the army to take twenty days' rations with them, that being the distance to the fine city that marks the boundary of the Roman empire.[b] Then for the first time the Persians were seen in battle array, a well-disciplined force with the glitter of gold in their armament.[c] One of our forward troops fell, whereupon our men charged *en masse*, and neither horse nor foot withstood our infantry's shields, but they all gave ground and fled, having become well versed in this particular aspect of warfare. 265. Thereafter no pitched battles took place, only ambuscades and paltry attacks on our rear by small parties of horse

[b] Since Julian's aim was to retire on Corduene, this would appear to be Bezabde. Libanius, however, shows little appreciation of the gravity of Julian's position.

[c] Dated to June 16th by Ammianus (24. 8. 2). Libanius omits any mention of the Persian "scorched earth policy," which effectively undermined Roman morale.

ἐπιπηδώντων οὐδὲ τότε κτεινόντων μᾶλλον ἢ
θνησκόντων. τοῦ γὰρ ἱππέως ὑπιὼν ὁ ὁπλίτης τὸ
R 612 δόρυ | ξίφει τὸν ἵππον ἀναρρηγνὺς ἀμφοτέρους
εἶχεν ἐπὶ γῆς καὶ ἕτοιμόν γε εἰς πληγὴν τὸν ἐν τῷ
χιτῶνι τῷ σιδηρῷ. 266. οἱ μὲν οὖν προσιόντες
τοιαῦτα ἔπασχον, οἱ δὲ πόρρωθεν ἰσχύοντες, οἱ
τοξόται, τὸ βέλος ἀφιέντες ἐπὶ γυμνὰ τοῦ στρατιώτου τὰ δεξιὰ πρὸς αὐτούς τε βλέπειν ἠνάγκαζον
καὶ σχολῇ προϊέναι. προῇεσαν μέντοι καὶ τὸ
νέφος οὐκ ἐκώλυε τῶν βελῶν εἰς ἅπαν. ἐλαύνων
γὰρ πανταχῇ τὸν ἵππον ὁ βασιλεὺς ἐπεκούρει τῷ
πιεζομένῳ λόχους τε ἀπὸ τῶν ἐν ἀδείᾳ τοῖς δεομένοις ἄγων καὶ τοὺς ἀρίστους τῶν στρατηγῶν ἐπ'
οὐρὰν πέμπων.

267. Μέχρι μὲν οὖν τούτων ἐκεῖνός τε νικῶν |
ἐχώρει καὶ ἐμοὶ λέγειν ἡδύ, τὸ δὲ ἐντεῦθεν, ὦ F
θεοὶ καὶ δαίμονες καὶ μεταβολαὶ τύχης, ἐφ' οἷον
ἄγομαι λόγον. βούλεσθε σιγήσω τὰ λοιπὰ καὶ
στήσω τὸν λόγον ἐν τοῖς εὐφημοτέροις; πολλὰ
ὑμῖν, ὦ παρόντες, ἀντὶ τῆς οἰμωγῆς ἀγαθὰ γένοιτο.
τί οὖν δὴ δοκεῖ; κλαίωμεν ἢ λέγωμεν;[1] ἐοίκατε
τῷ μὲν ἔργῳ πλήττεσθαι, τὸν δὲ λόγον ἀπαιτεῖν.
ῥητέον δὴ καὶ δόξαν οὐκ ἀληθῆ περὶ τῆς τελευτῆς
παυστέον.

268. Ἀπειρηκότος γὰρ ἤδη τοῦ Πέρσου καὶ
σαφῶς καταπεπολεμημένου καὶ δεδιότος μὴ τὰ

[1] κλαίωμεν F., Cobet (BVIM): κλαίομεν CMoLaU:
κλείομεν Re., Fabr. λέγωμεν F., Cobet (BVIMUP): λέγομεν
Re., Fabr. (CMoLa).

[a] This address to an imaginary audience serves, as at

descending on them from the cover of ditches. Even then they did not kill more than they lost in killed, since our infantry, dodging under the lances of the cavalry, hamstrung the horses, fetched them and their riders to the ground, and had the mail-clad warriors at their mercy. 266. So fared all who came to close quarters, but the archers, effective at long range, aimed at the unprotected right flanks of our troops and forced them to face them and proceed more slowly. Their progress however was maintained, and the cloud of arrows did not bring them to a complete halt. The emperor, riding up and down the line, came to the help of those in distress by bringing up reinforcements from sections where all was quiet to the places where they were needed and by sending the best of his commanders to guard the rear.

267. So far his progress was a triumphant one and a pleasant tale for me to tell, but hereafter—alas, you gods and spirits and fickleness of fortune !—what a story I am forced to relate ! Would you prefer me to draw a veil over the sequel and to stop my tale on this note of success ? Blessings light upon you, gentlemen, for your cries of grief ! What then is your wish ? That I give way to lamentation or say on ? It appears that, sorrow-stricken at the event as you are, you yet demand an account of it, and so I must speak on, and put a stop to a false report current about his death.[a]

268. The Persians were now in despair : they had been brought to their knees, and feared that our army, already in possession of the best of their terri-

the start of the oration, to increase the suspense and to heighten the pathos.

κράτιστα τῆς αὐτοῦ γῆς κατασχόντες ἐπιχειμάσωσι
καὶ πρέσβεις ἑλομένου καὶ δῶρα ἀριθμοῦντος, ἐν
οἷς ἦν καὶ στέφανος, καὶ μέλλοντος δὴ ταῦτα τῆς
ἐπιούσης σὺν ἱκετηρίᾳ πέμπειν καὶ ποιεῖν ἐκεῖνον
R 613 τῶν συνθηκῶν ὁριστὴν διασπᾶται | μέν τι τῆς
τάξεως τῶν μὲν τοὺς προσβάλλοντας ἀμυνομένων,
τῶν δὲ οὐκ αἰσθανομένων προϊόντων,[1] αἰγίδος δὲ
ἐξαίφνης λαμπρᾶς κόνιν τε ἐπεγειρούσης καὶ νέφη
συναγούσης καὶ τοῖς βουλομένοις τι κακουργεῖν συν-
αιρομένης ὁ μὲν βασιλεὺς ὡς συνδήσων τὸ διαρραγὲν
ἔσπευδεν | σὺν ἑνὶ θεράποντι, δόρυ δὲ ἱππέως ἐπ᾽ F 3
αὐτὸν ἐνεχθὲν ἄοπλον, τῷ γάρ, οἶμαι, σφόδρα κρατεῖν οὐδὲ ἐφράξατο, διὰ τοῦ βραχίονος δραμὸν εἰς
τὴν πλευρὰν εἰσέδυ. 269. καὶ πεσὼν ἐπὶ γῆς ὁ γενναῖος τὸ αἷμα ὁρῶν καταρρέον κρύπτειν ἐθέλων τὸ
συμβὰν ἐπὶ τὸν ἵππον αὖθις ἀναβάς, ἐπειδὴ τὸ αἷμα
τὴν πληγὴν ἤλεγχεν, ἐβόα καθ᾽ οὓς ἀεὶ γίγνοιτο μὴ
δεδιέναι τὸ τραῦμα, μηδὲ γὰρ θάνατον ἔχειν.
ἔλεγε μὲν ταῦτα, τοῦ δεινοῦ δὲ ἡττᾶτο. καὶ
κομίζεται πρὸς τὴν σκηνὴν καὶ τὴν μαλακὴν
εὐνήν, τὴν λεοντῆν καὶ τὸν φορυτόν, ταυτὶ γὰρ ἡ
᾽κείνου στρωμνή. 270. τῶν ἰατρῶν δὲ μὴ εἶναι
σωτηρίαν λεγόντων δεξαμένη τοῦ θανάτου τὸν
λόγον ἡ στρατιά, πάντες μὲν ὠλοφύροντο, πάντες
δὲ ἐκόπτοντο, παρὰ πάντων δὲ ἡ γῆ δάκρυσιν

---

[1] τῶν δὲ οὐκ αἰσθανομένων om. F.

---

[a] In view of Ammianus' account of the straits to which
the Romans were reduced, Libanius' suggestion of wintering in Persian territory is the perversion of a panegyrist.

tory, would make their winter quarters there. They
had chosen their envoys and were counting out the
gifts to send, including even a crown, and they
intended to despatch the embassy next day to plead
for peace, leaving Julian to define the terms.[a] Then
part of the column was detached from the rest;
some of the troops were engaged in defending themselves against their assailants and the rest, without
noticing, continued on their way, while a violent
storm suddenly arose, gathering clouds of dust
and whirling them along, an encouragement to any
who wished to do us hurt.[b] The emperor was riding
in haste with only one attendant as escort to repair
the gap in the ranks, when a cavalryman's spear
pierced him. He was without armour: confident
in his success, apparently, he had taken no precautions, and the spear passed through his arm
and penetrated his side. 269. Our noble emperor fell
to the ground and, seeing the blood gushing out, he
wanted to conceal what had occurred. He remounted straightaway, but when the bloodstains
showed that he was wounded, he called out to everyone he met not to be afraid about his wound, for it
was not fatal. That was what he said, but he was
already beginning to succumb. He was carried to his
tent, to his soft bed and the lion skin and straw of
which it was made.[c] 270. The doctors said that there
was no hope, and the army, hearing the news that he
was dying, all began to wail and beat their breasts
and drench the ground with tears. Their weapons

He does, however, insist upon the imminence of peace talks,
and in *Or.* 1. 133 represents them as actually taking place.
  [b] A detail confirmed by Festus (*Brev.* 28).
  [c] *Cf.* Amm. Marc. 25. 3—with slight variations in detail.
The account of *Or.* 24. 6 ff. develops the present passage.

LIBANIUS

ἐβρέχετο, τὰ ὅπλα δὲ τὰς χεῖρας ἐκφυγόντα ἔρ-
ριπτο, ᾤοντο δὲ μηδ' ἄγγελον ἐκεῖθεν ἀναστρέψειν
οἴκαδε. 271. ὁ δὲ δὴ Πέρσης δῶρα μὲν ἃ τούτῳ
πέμπειν ἔδει θεοῖς σωτῆρσιν ἀνέθηκεν, αὐτὸς δὲ
τὴν εἰωθυῖαν παρέθετο τράπεζαν πρότερον τοὔδαφος ἀντ' ἐκείνης ποιούμενος ἐκόσμησέ τε τὴν κό-
μην κατὰ τὸν νόμον κατερραθυμη|μένην πάντα τὸν F 3
τῶν κινδύνων χρόνον, ἃ δὲ χάσματι γῆς ἀφανισθέν-
των πασσυδὶ τῶν ἐναντίων ἔπραττεν ἄν, τούτοις
ἑνὸς ἐκείνου τελευτῶντος ἐχρῆτο. ἀμφότεροι τοίνυν ἔθεντο ψῆφον εἰς τὴν ἐκείνου γνώμην τὰ
R 614 πράγματα ἀνακεῖσθαι | Ῥωμαίοις, οἱ μὲν οἷς
ἐπένθουν, οἱ δὲ οἷς ὠρχοῦντο, καὶ οἱ μὲν οἷς ἡγοῦντο
ἀπολωλέναι, οἱ δ' οἷς ἤδη κεκρατηκέναι.
272. Ἴδοι δ' ἄν τις αὐτοῦ τὴν ἀρετὴν κἀκ τῶν
τελευταίων ῥημάτων. ἁπάντων γὰρ τῶν περιεστηκότων εἰς θρῆνον πεπτωκότων καὶ οὐδὲ τῶν
φιλοσοφούντων δυναμένων καρτερεῖν ἐπετίμα τοῖς
τε ἄλλοις καὶ οὐχ ἥκιστα δὴ τούτοις εἰ τῶν βεβιω-
μένων αὐτὸν εἰς Μακάρων νήσους ἀγόντων οἴδε ὡς
ἀξίως Ταρτάρου βεβιωκότα δακρύοιεν. ἐῴκει δὴ
ἡ σκηνὴ μὲν τῷ δεξαμένῳ δεσμωτηρίῳ τὸν Σωκράτην, οἱ παρόντες δὲ τοῖς ἐκείνῳ παροῦσιν, ἡ πληγὴ
δὲ τῷ φαρμάκῳ, τὰ ῥήματα δὲ τοῖς ῥήμασι, τῷ δὲ
μὴ δακρύσαι τὸν Σωκράτην μόνον τὸ μηδὲ τοῦτον.
273. δεομένων δὲ τῶν φίλων ἀποφῆναι τῆς ἀρχῆς
κληρονόμον οὐδένα αὐτῷ παραπλήσιον ἐγγὺς ὁρῶν
ἀφῆκε τῇ στρατιᾷ τὴν ψῆφον. | οἷς δὴ καὶ ἐπιστέλ- F 3

15 ff.
ᵇ For the comparison with the death of Socrates cf. Plato,
462

fell from their hands and were cast aside, and they thought that no messenger even would ever get back home from there with the news. 271. But the Persians offered the gifts destined for Julian to the gods of their salvation ; they began to dine at their usual table, when up to now they had used the ground instead; they dressed their hair in its accustomed style, having neglected to do so during the whole time of crisis, and their behaviour at the death of that single man was just as though their enemies had utterly disappeared, swallowed up by the earth. Both sides then were convinced that the Roman success depended on his genius, the Romans by their lamentations, believing they were lost, the Persians by their rapturous rejoicing, believing that they were already victorious.

272. You can gather his courage even from his last words. When all about him gave themselves up to lamentation and not even the philosophers could restrain themselves, he reproved them all, but especially the philosophers. The exploits of his lifetime would take him to the Islands of the Blest, he said, yet they bewailed him as though he had lived a life worthy of Tartarus.[a] His tent was like the prison that had held Socrates, the company like the company there, his wound the poison, and his words those of Socrates. Socrates was the only one not to be in tears : so was he.[b] 273. His friends begged him to appoint a successor to the throne, but he saw nobody anything like himself and remitted the decision to the army, bidding them do their

*Phaedo*, 117 c ff. The Libanian *Apologia Socratis* (*Decl.* 1) may also be regarded as a disguised justification of Julian and his career.

λει πάντα τρόπον σώζειν αὐτούς, καὶ γὰρ αὐτὸν
ἐκείνους σώζοντα πάντα ἀνατλῆναι πόνον.

274. Τίς οὖν ὁ κτείνας ποθεῖ τις ἀκοῦσαι. τοὔνομα μὲν οὐκ οἶδα, τοῦ δὲ μὴ πολέμιον εἶναι τὸν
κτείναντα σημεῖον ἐναργὲς τὸ μηδένα πολέμιον ἐπὶ
τῇ πληγῇ τετιμῆσθαι. καίτοι διὰ κηρύκων ὁ
Πέρσης ἐπὶ γέρας ἐκάλει τὸν ἀπεκτονότα καὶ
μεγάλων ὑπῆρχε τῷ φανέντι τυχεῖν. ἀλλ' ὅμως
οὐδεὶς οὐδ' ἔρωτι τῶν γερῶν ἠλαζονεύσατο. 275.
καὶ πολλή γε τοῖς πολεμίοις ἡ χάρις, ὅτι ὧν οὐκ
ἔδρασαν οὐ προσέθεντο τὴν δόξαν ἀλλ' ἔδοσαν ἡμῖν
παρ' ἡμῖν αὐτοῖς τὸν σφαγέα ζητεῖν. οἷς γὰρ οὐκ
ἐλυσιτέλει ζῶν, οὗτοι δὲ ἦσαν οἱ ζῶντες οὐ κατὰ
τοὺς νόμους, πάλαι τε ἐπεβούλευον καὶ τότε
δυνηθέντες εἰργάσαντο τῆς τε ἄλλης ἀδικίας αὐτοὺς
ἀναγκαζούσης οὐκ ἐχούσης ἐπὶ τῆς ἐκείνου βασι-
R 615 λείας ἐξουσίαν καὶ μάλιστά | γε τοῦ τιμᾶσθαι τοὺς
θεούς, οὗ τὸ ἐναντίον ἐζήτουν. |

276. Ἃ δ' ὑπὲρ τοῦ Περικλέους ὁ Θουκυδίδης F 3⁵
φησὶν ὅτι τῇ τελευτῇ λαμπρότερον ἔδειξεν ὅσον
ἦν αὐτὸς τοῖς πράγμασι, ταῦτ' ἂν ἔχοι τις εἰπεῖν
καὶ περὶ τοῦδε. τῶν γὰρ ἄλλων ἁπάντων τῶν αὐτῶν ὦνπερ καὶ πρότερον ὄντων, τῶν ἀνδρῶν, τῶν
ὅπλων, τῶν ἵππων, τῶν ταξιαρχῶν, τῶν συνταγμά-
των, τῶν αἰχμαλώτων, τῶν χρημάτων, τῆς τροφῆς,
ἐν μιᾷ τῇ περὶ τὸν βασιλεύοντα μεταβολῇ τὰ πάν-

---

ᵃ Amm. Marc. 25. 3. 20.

ᵇ A question resumed at length in *Or.* 24. 6 ff. This
passage is cited by Sozom. 6. 1.

ᶜ The Christians—as alleged by Libanius (*loc. cit.*) and

utmost to save themselves, for he had spared himself no toil in saving them.[a]

274. Who was it that killed him, you would like to know. I do not know his name, but that his murderer did not belong to the enemy is clearly proved by the fact that none of the enemy received any reward for killing him.[b] But the Persian king issued a proclamation and invited his killer to claim a reward, and if he had come forward he could have obtained a great prize, yet nobody boasted of doing it, not even in his desire for reward. 275. Indeed, we should be very grateful to the enemy for not claiming credit for what they had not done, and for allowing us to seek his murderer from among ourselves. For those fellows, who found his existence detrimental to themselves and whose whole manner of life was contrary to the law, these had long conspired against him, and then at last seized their chance and acted. The motives that drove them to it were their natural wickedness, that had no scope under his government, and more especially, the honours paid to the gods, where their ambitions were poles apart from his.[c]

276. What Thucydides says about Pericles, that by his death he gave clearer proof of his importance to the state, can be said of him too.[d] Everything might be as before, men, equipment, horses, commanders, regiments, prisoners, money, rations, but all was brought to ruin by the single accident of the change

regarded as probable by Sozomen (6. 2). Ammianus (25. 6. 6) notes that, in the fighting after Julian fell, a report of Roman responsibility was already circulating.

[d] Thuc. 2. 65. The comparison is between the disasters suffered by Athens in the Peloponnesian War and by the Romans in the Parthian campaign consequent upon the deaths of the two leaders.

τα συνετρίβη. 277. πρῶτον μὲν γὰρ οὐκ ἤνεγκαν
οὓς πρότερον ἤλαυνον, ἔπειτα[1] δελεασθέντες εἰρήνης ὀνόματι, τὸ γὰρ αὐτὸ προσήνεγκαν οἱ πολέμιοι
μηχάνημα, πάντες ἐβόων δέχεσθαι καὶ στέργειν,
καὶ πρῶτος ὁ βασιλεύων εἵλκετο. λαβὼν δὲ αὐτοὺς πρὸς τὴν ἡσυχίαν ὡρμηκότας ὁ Μῆδος διῆγε,
διέτριβεν ἐρωτῶν, ἀποκρινόμενος, τοῦτο δεχόμενος, ἕτερον ἀναβαλλόμενος, ἐν πλήθει πρεσβειῶν
ἀναλίσκων αὐτοῖς τὴν τροφήν. 278. ὡς δὲ σίτου
τε καὶ τῶν ἄλλων ἁπάντων ἐσπάνιζον καὶ ᾔτουν
καὶ πάντα δεινὴ δὴ συγχωρεῖν ἀνάγκη περιειστή-
κει, τότε | δὴ τὸν κουφότατον ᾔτει μισθόν, πόλεις F 3
καὶ χώρας καὶ ἔθνη, τὰ τείχη τῆς Ῥωμαίων ἀ-
σφαλείας. ὁ δὲ ἐπένευέ τε καὶ παντὸς ἀφίστατο
καὶ δεινὸν οὐδὲν ἐδόκει. 279. ὡς[2] ἔγωγε πολλάκις
ἐθαύμασα τοῦ Μήδου ὡς παρὸν πλείω λαβεῖν οὐκ
R 616 ἠθέλησε. τίς γὰρ | ἂν ἀντεῖπεν ἐπὶ τὸν Εὐφράτην
προάγοντι[3] τὴν ἐπιθυμίαν, τίς δ' ἂν ἐπὶ τὸν
Ὀρόντην, τίς δ' ἂν ἐπὶ τὸν Κύδνον, τίς δ' ἂν ἐπὶ
τὸν Σαγγάριον, τίς δ' ἂν ἐπὶ τὸν Βόσπορον αὐτόν;
ἦν γὰρ ὁ διδάξων τὸν Ῥωμαῖον πλησίον ὡς
ἀρκέσει καὶ τὸ λοιπὸν εἰς ἀρχὴν καὶ τρυφὴν καὶ
μέθην καὶ λαγνείαν. ὥστ' εἴ τις χαίρει τούτων οὐ
πεπραγμένων, Πέρσαις ἴστω τὴν χάριν οἳ πολλοστὸν μέρος ὧν ἐξῆν ἔχειν ἐπήγγειλαν. 280. ὡς
οὗτοί γε τὰ ὅπλα ῥίψαντες ἐκεῖνοι ἔχειν, ὥσπερ ἐκ

---

[1] δὲ after ἔπειτα inserted F.
[2] ὡς Re. (mss.) : ὥστ' F.
[3] προάγοντι F., conj. Cobet. (I corrected) : προσάγοντι Re. (other mss.).

---

[a] The new ruler was Jovian. On this judgement cf. Amm.
Marc. 25. 5. 8.        [b] Amm. Marc. 25. 7. 5 ff.

of ruler.[a]  277. In the first place, they did not stand up
to those whom they previously used to put to flight :
secondly, ensnared by this word " peace," for the
enemy applied the same technique again, they all
demanded its acceptance without demur, and the
new emperor was the first to be taken in by it. The
Persian found them hankering after peace and
dillied and dallied with question and answer, accepting this point, deferring that, and exhausting their
supplies with a string of parleys.[b]  278. Reduced to
dire straits for food and everything else besides,
they began to plead and were forced to the grim
realization that beggars cannot be choosers, and then
he finally presented his minimum terms, the cities,
territories and provinces that formed the defensive
bulwarks of the Roman empire.  Our new emperor
agreed and evacuated them all, and made no bones
about it.[c]  279. How often have I wondered why the
Persian refused to take more when he had the
chance !  Who would have said him nay, if his ambitions had extended to the Euphrates, the Orontes,
the Cydnus, the Sangarius, or to the Bosporus itself ?
The Roman had enough people about him to inform
him that even what was left was sufficient to provide
him with an empire, luxury, drunkenness and glut-
tony.[d]  So, if you are grateful that such things did
not happen, you can save your gratitude for the
Persians, for demanding only a fraction of what they
could have had.  280. And so our men came home
leaving their weapons for the enemy to keep, naked

[c] For the details of this peace *cf.* Amm. Marc. 25. 7. 9 ff.,
Zos. 3. 31.
[d] Characteristics confirmed by Amm. Marc. 25. 10. 15.
Libanius contemptuously refuses to mention the name of
Jovian in his orations.

ναυαγίας, γυμνοί, προσαιτοῦντες οἱ πλείους, ἐπανῆεσαν, ὁ δὲ ἀσπίδος ἥμισυ φέρων ἢ δόρατος
τρίτον ἢ τῶν κνημίδων τὴν ἑτέραν ἐπ᾽ ὤμων Καλ-
λίμαχος ἦν οὗτος, | ἀπολογία δὲ μία πᾶσι τοῖς F 35
ἀσχημονοῦσιν ἡ τελευτὴ τοῦ ταῦτα ἂν τρέψαντος[1]
εἰς τοὺς ἐναντίους.

R 617    281. Διὰ τί οὖν, | ὦ θεοὶ καὶ δαίμονες, μὴ ταῦτα
ἐκυρώσατε; διὰ τί μὴ τὸ μὲν ὑμᾶς ἐπιστάμενον
γένος εὔδαιμον, τὸν δὲ τούτοις εὐδαιμονίας αἴτιον
κατεστήσατε; τί μεμψάμενοι τῆς γνώμης, τί δὲ
οὐκ ἐπαινοῦντες τῶν πεπραγμένων; οὐ βωμοὺς
ἀνέστησεν; οὐ νεὼς ἐποίησεν; οὐκ ἐθεράπευσε
μεγαλοπρεπῶς θεούς, ἥρωας, αἰθέρα, οὐρανόν, γῆν,
θάλατταν, πηγάς, ποταμούς; οὐκ ἐπολέμησε τοῖς
ὑμῖν πεπολεμηκόσιν; οὐ σωφρονέστερος μὲν Ἱπ-
πολύτου, δίκαιος δὲ κατὰ τὸν Ῥαδάμανθυν, συνετώ-
τερος δὲ Θεμιστοκλέους, ἀνδρειότερος δὲ Βρασίδου;
οὐ τὴν οἰκουμένην ὥσπερ λειποψυχοῦσαν ἔρρωσεν;
οὐ μισοπόνηρος, οὐ πρᾷος δικαίοις, οὐκ ἀκολάστοις
ἐχθρός, οὐκ ἐπιεικέσι φίλος;    282. ὦ στρατιᾶς
μεγάλης, ὦ πολλῶν κατασκαφῶν, ὦ πολλῶν τροπαίων, ὦ τέλους τῆς διανοίας ἀναξίου. ἡμεῖς μὲν
ᾠόμεθα τὴν Περσῶν ἅπασαν μέρος τῆς Ῥωμαίων
ἔσεσθαι καὶ νόμοις τοῖς ἡμετέροις οἰκήσεσθαι καὶ
ἀρχὰς τὰς ἐνθένδε δέξεσθαι καὶ φόρους οἴσειν καὶ
γλῶτταν ἀμείψειν καὶ στολὴν μετακοσμήσειν καὶ
κερεῖν κόμας καὶ σοφιστὰς ἐν Σούσοις Περσῶν

---

[1] ἂν τρέψαντος F., Cobet : τρέψαντος V : ἀνατρέψαντος
other mss. : ἂν ἀνατρέψαντος Re.

---

[a] Besides the obvious pun on the meaning of the name,
there is also a reference to Marathon, where Callimachus was
polemarch ; cf. Herod. 6. 109 ff.

and for the most part beggars, as though from ship-wreck. Anyone who brought with him half a shield, the stump of a spear, or one of his greaves slung over his shoulder, was a real hero,[a] and the sole excuse for all these ragamuffins was the death of the one man who would have inflicted this upon the enemy.

281. Why then, you gods and immortal powers, did you not bring it to pass? Why did you not make man-kind happy in its knowledge of you, and him the au-thor of their happiness? What fault had you to find in his character? Which of his actions did not meet with your approval? He erected altars, built temples, worshipped in magnificence gods and heroes, air and heaven, land and sea, fountains and rivers. He took up the fight against those who had fought against you. He was more continent than Hippolytus, as just as Rhadamanthys, more intelligent than Themis-tocles, braver than Brasidas.[b] He restored to health a world that lay sick unto death. He was a hater of wrong, kindly to the just, foe to the wicked, friend to all good men. 282. Alas for that mighty army, the wide destruction it wrought, the many trophies it erected, and the end so unworthy of the conception. We expected the whole empire of Persia to form part of that of Rome, to be subject to our laws, receive its governors from us and pay us its tribute[c]: they would, we thought, change their language and dress, and cut short their hair, and sophists in Susa would

---

[b] For these virtues, all cited from literary sources, cf. Euripides, *Hippolytus*; Plato, *Apol.* 41 A (Rhadamanthys: cf. *Or.* 16. 19); Thuc. 1. 138 (Themistocles); Thuc. 4. 81 (Brasidas).

[c] An example of the regular rhetorical device of resuming in peroration the theme presented in the introduction to the speech. (*Cf. Or.* 11 (*init.* and *fin.*), *Or.* 1. 1 and 155).

# LIBANIUS

παῖδας ἐκκροτήσειν | ῥήτορας, ἱερὰ δὲ τὰ παρ' F 36
ἡμῖν τοῖς ἐκεῖθεν κοσμηθέντα λαφύροις διδάξειν
τοὺς ἐπιγιγνομένους τὸ τῆς νίκης μέγεθος, τὸν δὲ
ταῦτα εἰργασμένον ἀγωνοθετήσειν τοῖς ἐγκωμιά-
ζουσι τὰ πεπραγμένα τοὺς μὲν θαυμάζοντα, τοὺς
δὲ οὐκ ἐκβάλλοντα, καὶ τοῖς μὲν ἡδόμενον, τοῖς δὲ
οὐκ ἀχθόμενον, λόγους δὲ εἴπερ ποτὲ ἔσεσθαι
ἡδίους καὶ τοῖς ἱεροῖς ὑποχωρήσειν τοὺς τάφους
πάντων ἑκόντων ἐπὶ τοὺς βωμοὺς τρεχόντων καὶ
τῶν πρότερον ἀνατρεπόντων αὐτῶν ἱδρυομένων
καὶ τῶν τὸ αἷμα φευγόντων αὐτῶν θυόντων, τοὺς
δὲ ἰδίους ἑκάστων οἴκους εἰς εὐπορίαν ἐπιδώσειν
ἄλλαις τε ἀφορμαῖς καὶ σμικρότητι τῶν εἰσφορῶν,
R 618 καὶ γὰρ αὖ καὶ τοῦτο λέγεται | τοῖς θεοῖς ἐν μέσοις
εὔξασθαι τοῖς κινδύνοις, οὕτω λυθῆναι τὸν πόλεμον
ὥστ' αὐτῷ γενέσθαι τὴν εἰσφορὰν εἰς τἀρχαῖα
πάλιν ἀπενεγκεῖν.

283. Ταῦτα καὶ ἔτι πλείω προσδοκώμενα χορὸς
φθονερῶν ἀφείλετο δαιμόνων καὶ τὸν ἀθλητὴν
ἐγγὺς | ὄντα τοῦ στεφάνου κεκρυμμένον ἡμῖν ἐν F 36
σορῷ κεκόμικεν. εἰκότως ἄρα διὰ πάσης γῆς καὶ
θαλάττης ὁ θρῆνος ἦλθεν, εἰκότως οἱ μὲν ὡς
ἥδιστα μετ' ἐκεῖνον ἐτελεύτησαν, οἱ δ' ἀλγοῦσι τῷ
μὴ τεθνάναι νύκτα μὲν συνεχῆ τὰ πρὸ ἐκείνου
νύκτα δὲ τὰ μετ' ἐκεῖνον νομίζοντες, τὸν δὲ τῆς
ἐκείνου βασιλείας χρόνον ἀκτῖνα ὡς ἀληθῶς κα-
θαράν. 284. ὦ πόλεων, ἃς ἐποίησας ἄν, ὦ τῶν

---

[a] Libanius agrees wholeheartedly with Julian's argument
of the kinship between rhetoric and religion (v. above, § 157).
470

turn Persian children into orators : our temples here,
adorned with Persian spoils, would tell future generations of the completeness of the victory, while he who
had accomplished all this, would set up prizes for
those who celebrated his exploits in panegyric, with
admiration for some and without disdain for others,
with pleasure or without annoyance at their efforts,
and there would be more delight in oratory than ever
before[a] : dead men's tombs[b] would give place to
temples, and every man of his own free will would
make his way to the altars : their one-time desecra-
tors would themselves restore them, and the very
people who had shunned the offering of blood would
offer up sacrifice : the home of every man would, we
hoped, become more prosperous by countless other
accessions but especially by the lightness of taxation,[c]
for it is said that in the midst of his dangers he prayed
heaven for the war to end in such a way that he would
be able to reduce taxation to the level of old times.

283. These hopes, and more besides, were snatched
from us by a host of envious spirits which have
brought back to us our champion hidden in his
coffin, after the prize was all but in his grasp. Not
without reason, then, has the cry of lamentation
re-echoed all over land and sea, and after his death
men have been either glad to die or sorry to be alive.
For them the time before him is one of unbroken
night, the time that followed him the onset of
darkness once again, and the brief period of his
reign a ray of purest sunshine. 284. Alas, for the
cities you would have built, for their decay that you

---

[b] The Scholiast here recognized the anti-Christian polemic
(τάφους, ἀσύνετε, ἀλλ᾽ ἀνάστασιν βρύοντας).

[c] Amm. Marc. 25. 4. 15.

σαθρῶν, ἃς ἐπηνώρθωσας ἄν, ὦ λόγων, οὓς ἦρας
ἂν εἰς ἀξίωμα, ὦ τῆς ἄλλης ἀρετῆς, ὅσον ἴσχυσεν
ἄν, ὦ δίκης, ἣ κατέβη μὲν ἐξ οὐρανοῦ πάλιν εἰς γῆν,
ᾤχετο δὲ πάλιν ἐνθένδε εἰς οὐρανόν, ὦ μεταβολῆς
ἀγχιστρόφου, ὦ κοινῆς εὐδαιμονίας ἀρξαμένης τε
ὁμοῦ καὶ πεπαυμένης. παραπλήσιον γὰρ δή τι πεπόνθαμεν οἷον εἴ τις ἀνδρὸς διψῶντος καὶ προσάγον-
τος τοῖς χείλεσι φιάλην ψυχροῦ τε καὶ διαφανοῦς
ὕδατος γευσαμένου τὸ πρῶτον ἁρπάσας οἴχοιτο.
285. ἡμᾶς δέ, εἴπερ ἐχρῆν εὐθέως στέρεσθαι, κρεῖττον ἦν μηδὲ μετασχεῖν τὴν ἀρχὴν ἢ πρὸ τοῦ κόρου
R 619 στερηθῆναι.   νῦν δ' οὐχ ἵνα ἀπολαύσαιμεν | ἀλλ'
ἵνα οἵων οὐκέτ' ἀπολαύομεν εἰδότες στένοιμεν,
γεύσας ἀφείλετο, ὥσπερ ἂν εἰ τοῖς ἀνθρώποις
δείξας τὸν ἥλιον ὁ Ζεὺς ἐπεῖχε παρ' ἑαυτῷ μηκέτι
ποιῶν ἡμέραν. |

286. Καίτοι καὶ τοῦ ἡλίου ταῦτα μὲν ἔτι δρῶντος, F 36
τὴν αὐτὴν δὲ ἰόντος, οὐχ ὁμοία τοῖς βελτίστοις ἡ
χάρις. ἡ γὰρ ἐπὶ τῷδε λύπη βαπτίζουσα μὲν τὴν
ψυχήν, συνθολοῦσα δὲ τὴν γνώμην ἀχλύν τινα καὶ
τοῖς ὄμμασιν ἐπιφέρει, καὶ μικρόν τι διαφέρομεν
τῶν ζώντων ἐν σκότῳ. οἷα γὰρ αὖθις ἐπεισῆλθε
τῇ τοῦ βασιλέως σφαγῇ. σεμνοὶ μὲν οἱ κατὰ τῶν
θεῶν δημηγοροῦντες, ἱερεῖς δὲ ἐν εὐθύναις παρανό-
μοις. οἷς δὲ ἐθεραπεύθη τὸ δαιμόνιον ἱεροῖς καὶ ὁ
τὸ πῦρ ἔλαβε, τούτων ἡ τιμὴ τίθεται, μᾶλλον δὲ
ὁ μὲν εὐπορῶν οἴκοθεν ἔθηκεν, ὁ δ' οὐκ εὐπορῶν

---

[a] Julian himself claimed, citing Aratus (*Phaen.* 101 ff.),
that Justice had returned again to earth during his reign :
Amm. Marc. 25. 4. 19.

[b] A pathetic resumption of the phrase (from Thuc. 2. 53)
used to describe Julian's accession to supreme power in *Or.*
13. 20.

would have repaired, for oratory that you would
have raised to honour, and for all other merit and the
power it would have possessed ! Alas, for justice that
came down again to earth from heaven, [a] only to leave
us and return there once more. Alas, for the sudden
change of fortune, [b] for universal happiness ended as
soon as begun ! Our case is like that of a man
athirst who, lifting up to his lips a cup of cool clear
water, has just one sip before it is snatched from him
and gone. 285. If we were bound to suffer the loss so
soon, it would have been better never to have had a
taste at all rather than to lose it before we had our
fill. As it is, he gave us this taste and withdrew it,
not for us to enjoy but to realize sorrowfully all that
we enjoy no more, just as though Zeus reveals the
sun to mankind and then detains it with him, and lets
it never be daylight again.

286. In fact, the sun may still run his same course
and perform his same functions, but there is not the
same pleasure for good men any more. Our grief for
him has seared our souls, clouded our minds and
veiled our eyes in mist, so that we are little different
from men that live in darkness. What further
tribulations have followed upon the murder of our
emperor ! Rabble rousers who prate against the
gods give themselves airs, while our priests are subjected to illegal inquisitions, [c] and the offerings with
which the gods were worshipped and which the fire
has taken have a fine imposed upon them, or rather,
the wealthy pays the fine out of his own family
fortune, but the poor man is arrested and put to

[c] A reference to the violent anti-pagan reaction initiated
under Valens (for examples *cf.* Seeck, *B.L.Z.G. s.v.* " Seleucus, Lemmatius ").

δεθεὶς τέθνηκε. 287. νεῶν δὲ οἱ μὲν κατεσκάφησαν,

R 620 οἱ δ᾽ ἡμιτέλεστοι γέλως ἑστᾶσι | τοῖς μιαροῖς,
φιλοσόφων δὲ ἀνδρῶν αἰκίζεται σώματα, καὶ τὸ
εἰληφέναι τι βασιλέως διδόντος ὄφλημα γέγονε καὶ
πρόσεστιν αἰτία κλοπῆς καὶ δεῖ γεγυμνωμένον
μέσου θέρους ἐν μεσημβρίᾳ ταῖς ἀκτῖσι πιεζό-|
μενον, πρὸς οἷς εἴληφεν, ἃ μήτε φαίνεται λαβὼν  F 3(
μήτε δύναται δοῦναι διδόναι καταναγκάζεσθαι, οὐχ
ἵνα δῷ, πῶς γάρ, ἃ μὴ δυνατόν; ἀλλ᾽ ἵνα τῷ μὴ δύνασθαι στρεβλούμενος καὶ φλεγόμενος κατατείνηται.
288. ῥητορικῆς δὲ διδάσκαλοι συζῶντες πρότερον
τοῖς ἀρχὰς ἔχουσιν ἀπελαύνονται τῶν θυρῶν ὥσπερ
ἀνδροφόνοι, πλήθη δὲ νέων τὰ περὶ αὐτοὺς πρότερον
ταῦτα ὁρῶντες φυγόντες ὡς ἀσθενεῖς τοὺς λόγους
ἄλλην ἰσχὺν ζητοῦσι. βουλευταὶ δὲ τὴν δικαιοτάτην
θεραπείαν ὑπὲρ τῶν πατρίδων ἀποδράντες τὴν
ἄδικον ἐλευθερίαν ἐδίωξαν, ὁ δὲ ἐπισχήσων τὸν
πλημμελοῦντα οὐκ ἔστι. 289. πάντα δὲ μεστὰ
πρατήρων,[1] ἤπειροι, νῆσοι, κῶμαι, πόλεις, ἀγοραί,
λιμένες, στενωποί· πωλεῖται δὲ οἰκία καὶ ἀνδράποδα
καὶ τροφεὺς καὶ τροφὸς καὶ παιδαγωγὸς καὶ προγόνων τάφοι, πανταχοῦ δὲ πενία καὶ πτωχεία καὶ
δάκρυα, καὶ τοῖς γεωργοῖς ἄμεινον εἶναι δοκεῖ προσαιτεῖν ἢ γεωργεῖν, ὁ δὲ τήμερον δοῦναι δυνάμενος
αὔριον χρῄζει τοῦ δώσοντος. 290. Σκύθαι | δὲ  F 3(
καὶ Σαυρομάται καὶ Κελτοὶ καὶ πᾶν ὅσον βάρβα-
R 621 ρον ἠγάπα ζῆν ἐν σπονδαῖς, αὖθις | τὰ ξίφη θή-

---

[1] πρατήρων F. (P corrected) : πρακτήρων Fabr. (MoLaU) :
πρακτόρων Re. (VB, corrections in CMI).

death. 287. The temples are either demolished, or, half-finished, they stand as a laughing stock for that accursed crew. Philosophers are visited with physical violence,[a] and the acceptance of any gift from our emperor is made out to be a debt to the treasury, and a charge of embezzlement is tacked on to it. Stripped naked in the noon of mid-summer and suffering under the glare of the sun, he must be forced to repay not just what he did get, but what he obviously never got and cannot repay. Repayment is not the intention— it would be impossible, anyway : it is to have him tortured by burning and the rack because of the impossibility. 288. The teachers of rhetoric, previously the intimates of the governors, are turned away from their doors like murderers.[b] The flocks of students who used to attend them see this happen, and shun oratory as a broken reed, and look for other kinds of support. The city councillors evade doing their bounden duty on behalf of their community and chase after illegal immunity, and there is no one to check the defaulter. 289. Everywhere is full of carpet-baggers—lands, islands, villages, cities, markets, harbours and back-streets. Houses and slaves are put up for sale, foster parents, nurses, attendants, even the tombs of their ancestors. Everywhere there is poverty, beggary and tears ; farmers think it better to be beggars than farmers, and the man to give alms today is tomorrow himself in need of alms. 290. Goths, Sarmatians and Celts, and every barbarian tribe that thought itself lucky to live in peace,

[a] Maximus of Ephesus suffered persecution from A.D. 365 onwards : cf. Eunap. V.S. 478 ff. Priscus was also examined, but escaped more lightly.

[b] Libanius draws his inspiration from his experiences under Festus, consularis of Syria in A.D. 365 : cf. Or. 1. 156.

LIBANIUS

ξαντες ἐπιστρατεύουσι, διαπλέουσιν, ἀπειλοῦσι,
δρῶσι, διώκοντες αἱροῦσι, διωκόμενοι κρατοῦσιν,
ὥσπερ οἰκέται πονηροὶ δεσπότου τετελευτηκότος
ὀρφανοῖς ἐπανιστάμενοι.

291. Ἐπὶ τούτοις τίς οὐκ ἂν νοῦν ἔχων ἐκτείνας
ἑαυτὸν ἐπὶ γῆς καὶ καταχεάμενος τέφραν καὶ
τίλλων νέος μὲν ἴουλον, γέρων δὲ πολιάς, αὐτόν τε
καὶ τὴν οἰκουμένην, εἰ δεῖ δὴ τοῦτ᾽ ἔτι προσειπεῖν
αὐτήν, πενθήσειεν; 292. ἡ μέν γε Γῆ καλῶς τε
ᾔσθετο τοῦ πάθους καὶ προσηκούσῃ κουρᾷ τὸν
ἄνδρα ἐτίμησεν ἀποσεισαμένη, καθάπερ ἵππος
ἀναβάτην, πόλεις τόσας καὶ τόσας, ἐν Παλαιστίνῃ
πολλάς, τὰς Λιβύων ἁπάσας. κεῖνται μὲν αἱ μέγισται Σικελίας, κεῖνται δὲ Ἑλλήνων πλὴν μιᾶς αἱ
πᾶσαι, κεῖται δὲ ἡ καλὴ Νίκαια, σείεται δὲ ἡ κάλλει μεγίστη καὶ θαρρεῖν περὶ τοῦ μέλλοντος οὐκ
ἔχει. 293. ταῦτα αὐτῷ παρὰ τῆς Γῆς ἤ, εἰ βούλει
γε, τοῦ Ποσειδῶνος, παρὰ δὲ αὖ τῶν Ὡρῶν λιμοὶ
καὶ | λοιμοὶ φθείροντες ὁμοίως ἀνθρώπους τε καὶ F 36
βοσκήματα, ὡς οὐκ ὄν[1] θέμις ἐκείνου μεθεστηκότος
εὐθενεῖν τὰ περὶ γῆν.

294. Τί οὖν θαυμαστὸν εἴ τις τούτων ὄντων
τοιούτων, ὥσπερ ἐγώ, ζημίαν ἡγεῖται τὸ μήπω
τεθνάναι; καίτοι ἔγωγε τοὺς θεοὺς ἠξίουν οὐ
ταύτῃ γεραίρειν τὸν θαυμαστὸν ἐκεῖνον, ἀλλὰ

[1] ὄν F. (mss.): ἂν Re.

---

[a] Cf. Or. 17. 30, Amm. Marc. 26. 4. 5, Zos. 4. 3.
[b] The earthquakes of A.D. 365 were noteworthy: cf.
Amm. Marc. 26. 10. 15 and Jerome/Eusebius II, p. 197:
"terrae motu per totum orbem facto mare litus egreditur, et
Siciliae multarumque insularum urbes innumerabiles populos
oppressere." In Antioch (ἡ κάλλει μεγίστη) portents of doom

476

have whetted their swords once again : they are
descending upon us, crossing the rivers, threatening,
acting ; if they pursue us, they take us captive, if
pursued, they beat us, like wicked slaves who, on
their master's death, rise up against his orphaned
children.[a]

291. At all this every thinking man would prostrate
himself upon the ground and cover himself with
ashes. If a youth, he would tear his newly sprouted
beard, if an old man, his grey hairs, and he would
bewail the fate of himself and of the civilized world, if
we can still call it that. 292. Earth, at least, was duly
aware of her loss and has honoured our hero with
fitting mourning. Like a horse tossing its rider,
she has destroyed ever so many cities—in Palestine,
many, in Libya, all. The greatest cities of Sicily lie
in ruins, as does every city in Greece except one :
Nicaea the lovely is laid low, and our loveliest of
cities is shaken and can have no confidence for the
future.[b] 293. Such is the honour paid him by Earth
or, if you would have it so, by Poseidon : but from the
Seasons have come famine and plague, afflicting man
and beast alike, as though it is not right that creatures
upon earth should flourish once he has departed.

294. What wonder is it then, under these circumstances, that such as I think it so much loss not to be
dead already. And yet I prayed the gods to grant
that wondrous man no such honour as this, but

abounded, and from his letters of this year it appears that
some notables, in fear of earthquake and attendant visita-
tions, did actually retire from the city. In his neurotic state,
Libanius was particularly open to such alarms.

These references date the composition of the speech to
the last part of A.D. 365 or very soon after, not to A.D. 368,
as stated by Sievers (*op. cit.* p. 253) and P. Petit.

παίδων γενέσει καὶ γήρᾳ βαθεῖ καὶ μήκει βασιλείας.
295. ἀλλὰ Λυδῶν μὲν βασιλεῖς, ὦ Ζεῦ, σπέρμα |
R 622 Γύγου τὴν χεῖρα οὐ καθαροῦ, ὁ μὲν εἰς ἔτη προῆλθεν ἐννέα καὶ τριάκοντα, ὁ δὲ εἰς ἑπτὰ καὶ πεντήκοντα καὶ αὐτὸς δὲ ἐκεῖνος ὁ δυσσεβὴς δορυφόρος
εἰς δυοῖν δέοντα τετταράκοντα, τούτῳ δὲ τρίτου
προσάψασθαι μόνον ἐπὶ τοῦ μείζονος θρόνου δέδω-
κας, ὃν ἔδει πλείονος, εἰ δὲ μή, μήτοι γε ἐλάττονος
ἢ Κῦρον τὸν μέγαν ἀξιῶσαι χρόνου τὰ πατέρων
καὶ αὐτὸν πρὸς τοὺς ἀρχομένους τετηρηκότα.
296. Ἀλλὰ γὰρ ἐννοήσας τὴν ἐπιτίμησιν ᾗ τῶν
ἐν τῇ σκηνῇ δακρυόντων καθήψατο, καὶ νῦν αὐτὸν
ἡγοῦμαι τὴν ἐν τῷ θρήνῳ μερίδα τοῦ λόγου
μέμψασθαι, καί μοι δοκεῖ κἂν δεῦρο εἰσελθών,
εἴπερ ἐνῆν, | τοιούτοις ἂν πρὸς ἡμᾶς χρήσασθαι λό- F 36
γοις, ὅτι τὴν ἐμὴν ὑμεῖς ὀδυρόμενοι πληγὴν
καὶ τὸν ἐν τῇ νεότητι θάνατον, εἰ μὲν τὸ
συνεῖναι θεοῖς χεῖρον ἡγεῖσθε τοῦ τοῖς
ἀνθρώποις, οὐκ εὖ φρονεῖτε. εἰ δ' οὐκ οἴ-
εσθέ μοι ταύτης μεταδεδόσθαι τῆς χώρας,
πᾶν τοὐμὸν ἀγνοεῖτε καὶ πρᾶγμα πεπόν-
θατε ἀτοπώτατον τοῦτον ἥκιστα εἰδότες
ὃν σφόδρα εἰδέναι πέπεισθε. 297. ἔτι τοίνυν
μηδὲ τὸ ἐν πολέμῳ καὶ διὰ σιδήρου δεινὸν
ὑμῖν δοκείτω. οὕτως ἀπῆλθε Λεωνίδας,
οὕτως Ἐπαμινώνδας, οὕτω Σαρπηδών, οὔ-

---

rather the birth of children, ripe old age and length of reign. 295. Lord Zeus! of the kings of Lydia, the descendants of Gyges impure of hand, one had a reign of thirty-nine years, another of fifty-seven, and that traitorous guard himself one of thirty-eight years. Yet you granted Julian to attain only his third year as supreme ruler, when you should have thought him worthy of a longer, or at least no less a span than Cyrus the Great, for he too maintained the attitude of a father towards his subjects.[a]

296. However, when I reflect upon the reproof he administered to the mourners in his tent, I feel that now too he disapproves of this part of my oration that consists of lamentation.[b] I believe that, if it were possible to be, he would come among us and address us in words like these [c]: " You bewail the fatal stroke that carried me off in my youth, but if you think association with the gods to be inferior to that with men, you do not think aright. And if you suppose that room has not been made for me there, you know me not at all, and you are in parlous plight, since you know least about the one you felt sure you knew best. 297. Moreover, let it not trouble you, either, that I died in war and by the steel. So did Leonidas and Epaminondas, so Sarpedon and Memnon, sons of

Gyges, Cyrus), but with an inaccurate recollection of the length of Ardys' reign—49 years.

[b] Cf. Or. 1. 135, where similar reflections deter him from his first idea of suicide.

[c] Rhetorical reminiscences of Julian's death-bed address (cf. Amm. Marc. 25. 3. 15 ff.), but with an implied progression from the heroes of history to mythical heroes of divine origin, and thence to a combination of the two in Alexander. He, after being hailed as son of Zeus by the priest of Zeus Ammon in Egypt, allowed increased currency to the story. Cf. Quint. Curt. 4. 7. 8.

τω Μέμνων, οἱ τῶν θεῶν. εἰ δ' ὁ χρόνος τῇ
βραχύτητι λυπεῖ, φερέτω παραμυθίαν ὑμῖν
Ἀλέξανδρος ὁ Διός.

298. Ταυτὶ μὲν ἐκεῖνος ἄν, ἐγὼ δὲ τούτοις ἔχοιμ'
ἄν τινα προσθεῖναι, ἐν μὲν πρῶτον καὶ μέγιστον
R 623 ὅτι τὰ | μὲν τῶν Μοιρῶν ἀνίκητα, Μοῖρα δὲ ἴσως
ἐπέχει τὴν Ῥωμαίων, ὁποία ποτὲ τὴν Αἴγυπτον.
καὶ ἐπειδὴ | κακῶς μὲν ἔδει ταύτῃ γενέσθαι, ζῶν δὲ F 36
ἐκεῖνος ἐκώλυεν εὐδαιμονίαν εἰσάγων, ὑπεχώρησε
τῇ φορᾷ τῶν χειρόνων ὅπως μὴ εὖ πράττοιεν οὓς
ἐχρῆν κακῶς. 299. δεύτερον ἕτερον λογιζώμεθα
πρὸς ἡμᾶς αὐτούς, ὡς εἰ καὶ νέος ἀπῆλθεν, ἀλλὰ
πᾶν γήρας βασιλέων νικήσας ταῖς πράξεσι. τίνος
γὰρ οὕτω πολλὰ καὶ μεγάλα μνημονεύει τις τρι-
πλάσιον βεβιωκότος χρόνον; δεῖ τοίνυν ἀντ' ἐκείνου τὴν ἐκείνου δόξαν ἔχοντας φέρειν καὶ μὴ διὰ
τὴν τελευτὴν μᾶλλον ἀλγεῖν ἢ διὰ τὰ πρὸ ταύτης¹
εὐφραίνεσθαι. 300. οὗτός ἐστιν ὁ τῆς Ῥωμαίων
γῆς ἔξω τε ὢν ὁμοῦ καὶ κρατῶν καὶ τὸ μὲν σῶμα
ἔχων ἐν τῇ πολεμίᾳ, τὴν δ' οἰκείαν ὑπὸ τῇ βασιλείᾳ καὶ ταὐτὸν δυνηθεὶς πρός γε τὸ πάντα
ἡσυχάζειν ἀπών τε ὁμοίως καὶ παρών. οὔτε γὰρ
βάρβαρος ὅπλων ἥψατο παρὰ τὰς συνθήκας οὔτ'
ἔνδοθεν ἀνεφύη θόρυβος οὐδὲ εἷς, οἷα πολλὰ καὶ
βασιλέων ἐφεστηκότων ἐτολμήθη πολλάκις. καίτοι τοῦτο εἴτε φίλτρον εἴτε φόβος ἐποίει, μᾶλλον
δὲ εἰ φόβος μὲν | ἐπεῖχε τοὺς βαρβάρους, φίλτρον F 36
δὲ τοὺς ὑπηκόους, πῶς οὐκ ἄξιον ἑκάτερον θαυμάσαι, καὶ τὸ τοῖς ἐναντίοις δέος ἐμβαλεῖν καὶ τὸ
τοῖς οἰκείοις εὔνοιαν ἐνθεῖναι ἤ, εἰ βούλει γε,

---

¹ μᾶλλον after ταύτης (mss.) bracketed F.

the gods. If the shortness of the time allotted me causes you grief, then let Alexander, son of Zeus, afford you consolation."

298. So might he say, but I would have something to add, first and foremost, that the decrees of fate are unalterable, and perhaps the same kind of fate as once threatened Egypt now afflicts the Roman empire. It was destined that things should go awry here, but he in his lifetime blocked the ways of destiny and brought us happiness. So he retired to make way for the onset of a degenerate age, so that those doomed to misery should not be happy. 299. Again, let us consider in our inmost hearts this second point, that even if he died a young man, he yet surpassed the longest lived of emperors in his achievements. Who can call to mind so many mighty deeds wrought by any who lived three times as long as he ? Instead of his presence, then, we must keep his fame and endure the loss, not sorry at his death so much as happy at what happened before it. 300. He it is who passed beyond the boundaries of the Roman empire and still ruled over it : physically he might be in enemy territory, but he retained his own empire under his sway, and whether present or absent, he had the same ability to enforce universal peace. No barbarian in breach of his agreements took to arms, nor did a single mutiny arise at home, the kind of misconduct that has often been ventured upon even during an emperor's supremacy. Whether this was due to affection or to fear, or, to be more precise, whether fear kept the barbarians under control and affection his subjects, he deserves the fullest admiration both for striking fear into his foes and for instilling loyalty into his subjects, or if you prefer it so, for

481

LIBANIUS

ἀμφοτέροις ἀμφότερα; 301. οὐκοῦν καὶ τοῦτο τῆς
λύπης ἡμῖν ἀφαιρείτω καὶ πρὸς τούτῳ γ' ἐκεῖνο τὸ
μηδένα τῶν ἀρχομένων ἔχειν ποτὲ πρὸς αὐτὸν
εἰπεῖν ὡς ἄρα οὐχ ὑπὸ κρείττονος ἄρχοιτο. τίς |
R 624 γὰρ ἐκείνου δικαιότερος βασιλεύειν, εἰ τὸν καὶ τῷ
φρονεῖν καὶ τῷ δύνασθαι λέγειν καὶ ταῖς ἄλλαις
ἀρεταῖς διαφέροντα τῶν ἄλλων τοῖς ἧττον ἀγαθοῖς
ἐπιστατεῖν ἄξιον; 302. αὐτὸν μὲν οὐκ ἂν ἴδοιμεν,
τοὺς δὲ ἐκείνου λόγους ἔστιν ἰδεῖν τοὺς πολλοὺς
καὶ πάντας σὺν τέχνῃ. καίτοι τῶν ἐν τῷ γράφειν
καταγεγηρακότων οἱ πολλοὶ πλείους ἔφυγον λόγων ὁδοὺς ἢ ὅσας ἐλθεῖν ἐθάρρησαν ὥστε μὴ εἶναι
πλείω φιλοτιμίαν αὐτοῖς ἐκ τῶν πεποιημένων ἢ
ψόγον ἐκ τῶν μὴ γεγραμμένων, ὁ δὲ πολεμῶν
τε ὁμοῦ καὶ πλάττων λόγους πάσας μορφὰς καταλέλοιπεν ἁπάσαις μὲν ἅπαντας νικῶν, τὰ δ' αὐτοῦ
τῇ τῶν ἐπιστολῶν. 303. ταῦτα ἐγὼ λαμβάνων
παραμυθίαν πορίζομαι, διὰ τούτων ὑμεῖς τῶν ἐκ-
γόνων τὴν λύπην οἴσετε. παῖδας | τούτους ἐκεῖνος F 3
ἀθανάτους καταλέλοιπεν οὓς οὐκ ἂν ὁ χρόνος δύναιτο μετὰ τῶν ἐν ταῖς σανίσιν ἐξαλεῖψαι χρωμά-
των.

304. Ἐπεὶ δὲ εἰκόνων ἐμνήσθην, πολλαὶ πόλεις
ἐκεῖνον τοῖς τῶν θεῶν παραστήσαντες ἕδεσιν ὡς
τοὺς θεοὺς τιμῶσι, καί τις ἤδη καὶ παρ' ἐκείνου δι'
εὐχῆς ᾔτησέ τι τῶν ἀγαθῶν καὶ οὐκ ἠτύχησεν.
οὕτως ἀτεχνῶς παρ' ἐκείνους τε ἀναβέβηκε καὶ τῆς
R 625 τῶν κρειττόνων δυνάμεως παρ' αὐτῶν | ἐκείνων

---

a A point resumed in Or. 24. 37.
b For the portraits of the emperors painted on boards
482

inspiring each emotion in both alike.[a] 301. So let that consideration remove some of our grief, and also this, that none of his subjects can ever say to himself that his sovereign was not a better man that he. Who had a better right to be emperor than Julian, if the man who excels all others in intellect, in rhetorical ability and other virtues deserves to be in charge of those less well endowed ? 302. We may not see him in the flesh, but we can see his compositions, so many in number and all of supreme art. Yet of the writers who have grown old in the service of literature, the majority have been afraid of more approaches to learning than the number they have actually ventured upon, so that they can be no less blamed for what they have refused to write than praised for their compositions. He, however, composing speeches at the same time as waging war, has left behind him works of every kind, and in every one has surpassed those of everyone else, in his correspondence surpassing even himself. 303. When I take these works, I get some consolation. By means of them, his offspring, you will endure your grief, for he has left them as his offspring for all eternity, and time cannot remove them as it does the colours on his official portraits.[b]

304. And since I have made this mention of portraits, many cities have set up his in the temples of the gods and honour him as they do the gods, and before now people have offered up prayers to him also, asking some blessing, and they have not been disappointed.[c] So obviously has he ascended to heaven and has partaken of the power of the divine

(σανίδες) cf. Or. 22. 7, (on which cf. Browning, " The Riots in Antioch in A.D. 387," J.R.S., 1952, p. 15 (note)).

[c] On this extraordinary passage cf. Nock, " Deification and Julian," J.R.S., 1957, pp. 115 ff.

μετείληφε. βέλτιστοι δὲ ἄρα ἦσαν οἱ καὶ τὸν πρῶτον ἄγγελον τῆς τελευτῆς μικροῦ καταλεύσαντες ὡς θεοῦ καταψευδόμενον. 305. παραμυθοῦνται δέ με καὶ Πέρσαι γραφαῖς αὐτοῦ δηλοῦντες τὴν προσβολήν. λέγονται γὰρ αὐτὸν εἰκάσαντες κεραυνοῦ πυρὶ γράψαντες κεραυνὸν προσπαραγράψαι τοὔνομα δεικνύντες ὡς μείζω φύσεως ἀνθρωπίνης ἀφῆκεν εἰς αὐτοὺς κακά. 306. τοῦτον ἐδέξατο μὲν τὸ πρὸ Ταρσῶν τῆς Κιλικίας χωρίον, εἶχε δ' ἂν δικαιότερον τὸ τῆς Ἀκαδημίας πλησίον τοῦ | Πλάτωνος ὥστ' αὐτῷ παρὰ τῶν ἀεὶ νέων τε καὶ F 37 διδασκάλων ἃ καὶ τῷ Πλάτωνι τελεῖσθαι. τούτῳ[1] ποιεῖν σκόλια, τούτῳ παιᾶνας, τούτῳ πᾶν εἶδος ἐγκωμίων, τοῦτον σύμμαχον ἐπὶ βαρβάρους ἀρχομένους πολέμων καλεῖν, ὃς ἔχων τὸ μέλλον ἅπαν ἐκ μαντικῆς ἑλεῖν τὸ μὲν εἰ κακώσει Πέρσας ᾠήθη δεῖν προμαθεῖν, τὸ δ' εἰ σῶς ἐπάνεισιν οὐκ ἠξίωσεν, ἔργῳ δείξας ὅτι δόξης ἦν οὐ ζωῆς ἐπιθυμητής. 307. βασιλεύεσθαι μὲν οὖν ὑπὸ τοιαύτης ἀρετῆς πάντων εὐδαιμονέστατον, ἐστερημένους δὲ φάρμακον δεῖ ποιεῖσθαι τῆς λύπης τὸ 'κείνου κλέος ὃν καὶ μετὰ θεῶν ὀμνύναι τοῦ σήματος ἁπτομένους μᾶλλον εὔλογον ἤ τισι τῶν βαρβάρων τοὺς παρ' αὐτοῖς δικαιοτάτους.

308. Ὦ δαιμόνων μὲν τρόφιμε, δαιμόνων δὲ μαθητά, δαιμόνων δὲ πάρεδρε, ὦ μικρὸν μὲν τῆς γῆς μέρος κατέχων διὰ τοῦ τάφου, πᾶσαν δὲ τῷ R 626 θαύματι τὴν οἰκουμένην, | ὦ νενικηκὼς μάχαις μὲν τοὺς ἀλλοφύλους, ἀμαχεὶ δὲ τοὺς ὁμοφύλους, ὦ

---

[1] After τούτῳ, δεῖ inserted F. : ἔδει conj. Re.

[a] A topic resumed in *Or.* 24. 18 f.
[b] *Cf.* Amm. Marc. 25. 9 : Zos. 3. 34 cites his epitaph.

484

by the will of the gods themselves. They were right, then, those people who nearly stoned to death the first messenger to bring the news of his end for telling lies about a god. 305. Even the Persians provide me with some consolation when they show his invasion in pictures. They have, it is said, compared him with the fire of the thunderbolt, and they paint a thunderbolt with his name at the side, showing that the calamities he inflicted on them were beyond any human power.[a] 306. A grave just outside Tarsus in Cilicia received his body.[b] It ought more properly to have been in the Academy next to Plato's tomb, so that he too might receive the honours paid to Plato by each successive generation of students and teachers. Compose songs of jollity, songs of triumph, all kinds of praise in his honour. Summon him to help us against the barbarians who are taking to warfare once again, for when he had it in his power to learn all the future from divination, he thought the subject of his enquiry should be whether he would do harm to Persia, not whether he would return home safe, thereby showing his eagerness for glory, not for life. 307. It was the sum of happiness to be ruled by such excellence; bereft of it as we are, we must seek balm for our grief in his glory, and we may lay our hand upon his tomb and take our oath by him along with the gods with better reason than do the barbarians when they swear by the most righteous men among them.

308. Nurseling of gods, disciple of gods, companion of gods, who in your tomb possess your little patch of earth, and yet possess the whole world by its wonder, who conquered foreigners in fight, your own folk without fight, more sadly missed than sons by their

# LIBANIUS

πατράσι μὲν παίδων, παισὶ δὲ πατέρων, ἀδελφοῖς
δὲ ἀδελφῶν | ποθεινότερε, ὦ μεγάλα μὲν δράσας, F 37
μείζω δὲ μέλλων, ὦ θεῶν μὲν ἐπίκουρε, θεῶν δὲ
ὁμιλητά, ὦ πάσας μὲν ἡδονὰς καταπατήσας πλὴν
ὅσαι λόγων, ταυτί σοι παρὰ τῶν ἡμετέρων λόγων
τῶν μικρῶν οὓς αὐτὸς ἦγες μεγάλους.

fathers, than fathers by their sons, than brothers by
brothers, you who have done great things, and shall
do greater, defender of the gods, pupil of the gods,
who spurned all pleasures save only those of eloquence, this is the offering I make to you from my
paltry eloquence that you yourself did once deem
great.

# ORATION 24

# ΠΕΡΙ ΤΗΣ ΤΙΜΩΡΙΑΣ ΙΟΥΛΙΑΝΟΥ

R ii. 27 1. Οὐκ ἀρκεῖ τοῦτο τοῖς πράγμασιν, ὦ βασιλεῦ, F ii
λύπη καὶ ὀδυρμὸς καὶ ἀγρυπνία μάτην ἀναλισκο-
R ii. 28 μένη. εἰ γάρ | τι τούτων οἷόν τ᾽ ἦν ἐπανορθῶσαί τι
τῶν συμβεβηκότων, πάλαι ἂν ἅπαντα εἶχε καλῶς
ἕνεκά γε καὶ τῆς σῆς καὶ τῆς τῶν ἄλλων ἡμῶν
ἀθυμίας. δεῖ τοίνυν τούτων ἀπαλλαγέντα[1] βου-
λεύσασθαί τι μέγα καὶ καλὸν καὶ ὅθεν ἂν δράσαιμεν
τοὺς πολεμίους ἃ νῦν ἡμᾶς ἐκεῖνοι. οὕτω γὰρ
ἀντὶ τοῦ στένειν ἐν ταῖς ἀπὸ τοῦ πράττειν ἡδοναῖς
εἴημεν ἄν. 2. ἔδει μὲν οὖν | τὰ μαντεῖα ποιεῖν ἔτι F 5
R ii. 29 νῦν ἃ πρότερον, | καὶ τοῖς δεομένοις ἀκοῦσαι τί
ποιοῦντες ἄμεινον ἂν πράξαιεν λέγειν τε καὶ
μηνύειν, οὐδὲν γὰρ ἂν ἔδει σοι νυνὶ βουλῆς οὐδὲ
συμβούλων ἀνθρώπων παρ᾽ αὐτῶν τῶν θεῶν τῆς
περὶ τῶν συμφερόντων γνώμης ἀφικνουμένης· ἐπεὶ
δὲ τὰ μὲν σεσίγηκε καὶ πεποίηκεν ἀτυχεστέραν
τὴν γῆν, εἰς δὲ ἀνθρωπίνους ἧκε λογισμοὺς ἡ τῶν

---

[1] ἀπαλλαγέντα Re. (mss. except BaI): ἀπαλλαγέντας F.
(BaI).

---

[a] *Oration* 23 Re.: 24 F. Two mss. (UI) add πρὸς Οὐάλεντα
to the title, but the oration is composed after his death at the
battle of Adrianople in A.D. 378 (*cf.* § 4). The recipient of the

# UPON AVENGING JULIAN [a]

1. It is of no use to us in our present plight, Sire, to grieve and groan and pass sleepless nights to no purpose. If we could correct any of our misfortunes in this way, everything would have been put right long ago, at least as far as your disappointments and those of the rest of us are concerned. You must have done with such behaviour and adopt some notable and honourable course of action whereby we may do to our enemies all that they now do to us. In this way, instead of lamentation, we would enjoy the pleasures of action. 2. The oracles should now once more perform their previous function and give advice and information to those who ask what they should do to improve their position. There would be no need of human counsel or counsellor now, since the decision about our welfare would come from the gods themselves. However, the oracles are silent and have made the world an unhappier place for it,[b] and in our

oration is Theodosius, newly created emperor of the East (January A.D. 379).

[b] Divination, long a target for imperial legislation, was repressed with particular ferocity by the Christian emperors, and especially after its revival under Julian. The judicial reign of terror that followed the conspiracy of Theodorus in A.D. 371 occasions Libanius' present remarks : cf. Or. 1. 171 ff., Amm. Marc. 29. 1-2, John Chrysostom, P.G. 60. 273 ff.

# LIBANIUS

συμφερόντων εὕρεσις, ἀνάσχου μου περὶ τῆς παρούσης κακοπραγίας λέγοντος, ὦ βασιλεῦ, καὶ δο-
κοῦντι μέν τι λέγειν πρόσεχε, ληροῦντα δὲ τῆς
μὲν προαιρέσεως ἀποδέχου, τρέπου δὲ ἐπ᾽ ἄλλο τι
τῶν συνοίσειν μελλόντων.

3. Εἰσὶ μὲν οὖν οἱ κατηγοροῦσι τῶν στρατηγῶν,
ἕτεροι δὲ τῶν στρατιωτῶν, οἱ μὲν ἐκείνων ὡς οὐ
πεπαιδευκότων τοὺς ὑπ᾽ αὐτοῖς, οἱ δὲ τούτων ὡς
φύσει δειλῶν, ἐγὼ δὲ αἰσχύνομαι μὲν τὰς πολλὰς
αὐτῶν μάχας, αἰσχύνομαι δὲ τὸν θάνατον ὃν
τηροῦντες τὴν τάξιν ἐδέξαντο, αἰσχύνομαι δὲ τὴν
αἵματι χρωσθεῖσαν Θρᾴκην καὶ Μακεδονίας οὐ
μικρὸν καὶ τῆς Ἰλλυριῶν τὴν πολλήν. 4. ἀλλὰ
τοῦτο μὲν ἀνεῖλον ὄμβροι καὶ χρόνος, σώζονται δὲ |
R ii. 30 οἱ τῶν ὀστῶν κολωνοί. ἐν δὲ τοῖς ὀστοῖς τούτοις
ἐνεῖναί φασι καὶ τὰ ταξιαρχῶν καὶ λοχαγῶν καὶ
τῶν ἐν τοῖς ἄλλοις σχήμασιν. ἐν | μέσοις δὲ F 51
αὐτοῖς ὁ βασιλεὺς μαχόμενος ἔπεσε παρόντων μὲν
ἵππων τῶν βασιλείων οἷς ὅσον μέτεστι τάχους οὐκ
ἀγνοοῦμεν, παρεχόντων δὲ αὐτῷ τῶν ἱπποκόμων
καὶ δεομένων ἀναβάντα φυλάξαι τοῖς πράγμασιν
ἑαυτόν, ὁ δ᾽ εἰπὼν ὡς οὐκ ἄξιον ζῆν ἐπὶ τοσούτοις
κειμένοις, ἀντὶ τάφου τὸ πλῆθος τῶν ἐπ᾽ αὐτῷ
κατενεχθέντων ἔσχε.

R ii. 31    5. Μὴ | οὖν μοι λεγέτω τις δειλίαν ἢ μαλακίαν

---

[a] Cf. Sebastianus' arguments before Adrianople for the
formation of a corps d'élite. Zos. 4. 23.

[b] The Gothic invasions of the Balkan provinces, culminating in the disaster at Adrianople, A.D. 378.

[c] A deliberately selective account of Valens' death,
approximating to the story (Amm. Marc. 31. 13. 12) that he

quest for well-being we have had recourse to human calculations : so bear with me, Sire, when I speak of our present ill-success, and attend to me if you think that I am talking sense ; if nonsense, then receive my good intentions favourably, but turn to some other counsel that is likely to be advantageous.

3. Some people accuse our generals, others their men, asserting that the generals have not properly trained the men under their command, or that the men are naturally cowards.[a] I however cannot bring myself to say this, in view of the many battles they have fought and the way they have died in their ranks, and have stained with their blood Thrace, much of Macedonia and the greater part of Illyria.[b] 4. Rain and time have erased those stains, but the piles of bones remain, and among them, so it is said, you can see those of generals and colonels and those of lesser rank, and in the midst of them the emperor fell fighting. The emperor's horses were there, and we know how swift they can be, and the grooms offered them to him, begging him to mount and save himself for the empire, but he replied that it was wrong to live on after so many had fallen, and so he got, instead of a tomb, the massed heaps of the slain above him.[c]

5. So let there be no talk of cowardice, weakness or

fell in battle and his body was never found. Ammianus' alternative account, however, agrees largely with Zosimus (4. 24) and the Church historians (Socr. 4. 38, Sozom. 6. 40, Theodoret 4. 31) who dwell upon divine vengeance, that Valens, wounded, sought refuge in a near-by farm and died when it was fired by a Gothic raiding party. A hint of this story may be found in πυρὶ καὶ σιδήρῳ (§ 5, below). Eunapius (V.S. p. 480) also regards the manner of his death as an example of divine vengeance—but for the execution of the pagan philosopher, Maximus.

LIBANIUS

ἢ ἀμελετησίαν μηδὲ τὸ κρείττους γεγενῆσθαι τοὺς
βαρβάρους εἰς ταῦτα ἀναφερέτω, ἀλλ' αἱ μὲν
φύσεις τῶν στρατιωτῶν καὶ τῶν τούτοις ἐπιστα-
τούντων ταῖς τῶν ἔμπροσθεν παραπλήσιαι, κατὰ δὲ
τὴν τέχνην καὶ τὴν ἐπιμέλειαν οἶδ' ἐκείνων οὐχ
ὕστεροι, δόξης δὲ τοσοῦτος αὐτοῖς ἔρως ὥστε
ὁμοῦ καύματι καὶ δίψει καὶ πυρὶ καὶ σιδήρῳ
μαχόμενοι τὴν τελευτὴν ἡδίω τῆς φυγῆς ἐνόμισαν.
τῷ ποτ' οὖν ἡμῶν πεπλεονεκτήκασι; δοκεῖ μοι
θεῶν τις ἡμῖν ὀργιζόμενος ἐκείνοις συμπολεμεῖν.
τὴν δὲ ὀργὴν ὅ μοι μάλιστα δοκεῖ πεποιηκέναι
φράσω.

6. Ἐδέξατο μὲν ὑπὸ τῇ πλευρᾷ τὴν πληγὴν |
Ἰουλιανὸς ἐκεῖνος πειρώμενος τῆς ἑαυτοῦ φάλαγγος F 5
συνάψαι τὸ διασπασθὲν καὶ τὸν ἵππον ἅμα βοῇ καὶ
ἀπειλαῖς ἐπὶ τοῦτο ἐλαύνων, ὁ δὲ προσπεσὼν ἦν
R ii. 32 καὶ τρώσας | Ταϊηνός[1] τις ἐντολὴν πληρῶν τῷ
σφῶν αὐτῶν ἄρχοντι. τῷ δὲ ἄρα τοῦτο μισθὸν
οἴσειν ἔμελλε παρ' ἐκείνων οἷς ἦν ἐν σπουδῇ τὸν
ἄνδρα ἀποθανεῖν. χρησάμενος οὖν καιρῷ τῇ τότε
συμβάσῃ ταραχῇ καὶ τοῖς ἀνέμοις καὶ τῇ πολλῇ
κόνει πλήξας ἀπῆλθεν. 7. ὁ δὲ εὐθὺς μὲν κατέ-
R ii. 33 πεσεν, | ἔπειτ' αὖθις ἐπὶ τὸν ἵππον ἀναβὰς ἐπε-
μελεῖτο τῶν συμφερόντων τῇ φάλαγγι καὶ τὸ αἷμα

1 Ταϊηνός τις Re., F. [mss., except PB (ταϊκνός τις), Ba
(ταϊανός τις), I (ταηνότις, before corrections), La (ταϊην ὅστις)].
χριστιανός τις conj. Olearius, Cobet.

a This account of Julian's death repeats that in Or. 18.
268 ff. The details agree largely with those of Ammianus
(25. 3) and differ significantly from the story of Or. 1. 133.
Julian's death quickly became a subject of apocryphal
stories, of which Gregory Nazianzen (Invective, 2. 13) pro-

494

lack of training, if you please. Let the barbarian victory not be imputed to this. The morale of the soldiers and their officers was like that of their forebears, and they were no whit inferior to them in skill and training. Their love of glory was such that they fought heat and thirst, fire and sword, and preferred death to flight. How then have the enemy gained the upper hand of us ? I am convinced that some god is angered with us and fights on their side, and of what I believe to be the cause of this anger I will go on to speak.

6. Our renowned Julian received that blow in the side as he strove to unite part of his line that had broken,[a] spurring his horse towards them, cheering and threatening. The assailant who inflicted the wound was a Taiene,[b] acting in obedience to their leader's command. This action, indeed, would probably secure for the chief a reward from the people who were keen to have him killed. So he made the most of the opportunity offered by the prevailing confusion and the winds and swirling dust to strike him and retire. 7. He fell immediately but then remounted and supervised the dispositions for the safety of the line, and though he saw his blood

vides the earliest examples. Gregory gleefully canvasses the possibility of Christian responsibility, which Libanius here alleges and Sozomen (6. 2) regards as probable. Hence the pagan assertion that it was murder. *Cf.* Büttner-Wobst, *Philologus*, 51 (1892), pp. 561 ff. : " Der Tod des Kaisers Julianus."

[b] The Taienes were a tribe of Saracens (Sozom. 6. 1. also has a story of Saracen responsibility). These, acting independently of Romans and Persians alike, were often the cause of border incidents. Libanius here hints that the Saracens were hired by Christian dignitaries on the Roman side.

# LIBANIUS

ρέον ὁρῶν οὐ προκατέλυσε τὰς φροντίδας, ἕως
ἐλειποψύχησεν. οὕτω δὲ ἐπὶ τὴν σκηνὴν κο-
μισθεὶς καὶ μόνος ἐν δακρύουσιν ἅπασι τοῖς
περιεστηκόσι τοῦτο οὐ παθὼν οὐκ ἐμέμψατο τὴν
στρατείαν, ἀλλὰ ταύτης τε ἑαυτὸν ἐπαινέσας καὶ
λυπεῖσθαι φήσας οὐκ εἰ δέοι θνήσκειν ἀλλ᾿ ἐπὶ τῇ
τοῦ στρατεύματος ὀρφανίᾳ, τοὺς θεοὺς ὁρῶν ἤδη
παρ᾿ οὓς ἔμελλεν ἥξειν, ἀφῆκε τὴν ψυχήν.   8.
ἐγένετο βασιλεὺς ἕτερος. | τοῦτον εὐθὺς ἐχρῆν F 5
ἀμῦναι τῷ τετελευτηκότι καὶ προοίμιον τῆς βασιλείας τὴν τιμωρίαν ποιήσασθαι. τούτῳ δὲ τοῦτο
περιττόν τε καὶ μάταιον ἔδοξε. καὶ ὁ μὲν νεκρὸς
ἐκομίζετο, οἱ δὲ κακὸν τοσοῦτο κατεσκευακότες
R ii. 34 ἐγέλων. | ἐπιμιξιῶν δὲ πολλῶν ὑπὲρ εἰρήνης πρὸς
τοὺς Πέρσας γιγνομένων ἦν ἀκούειν ὡς οὐδεὶς
ἐκείνων ἐπὶ τῷ φόνῳ τετίμηται καὶ ταῦτα τιμῆς
ἐλπιζομένης.

9. Πρὸς ἐκεῖνον τοίνυν ἡγοῦμαι χαλεπῆναι τοὺς
R ii. 35 θεοὺς καὶ διὰ τοῦτο καταναγκασθῆναι | τοιαύτην
εἰρήνην ποιήσασθαι, δι᾿ ἧς μείζονα ὧν εὔξαντο ἂν
ὑπῆρξε τοῖς πολεμίοις, ᾿Αρμενία πᾶσα, πόλις ἡ
ἐπὶ τοῖς ὁρίοις, πλεονέκτημα μέγα, φρούρια πολλὰ
καὶ καρτερά.   10. ἀλλὰ τούτῳ μὲν ἴσως οὐκ ἐξῆν
τὰ τοιαῦτα ζητεῖν, οἶμαι δὲ εἶναι δῆλον ὃ λέγω,
R ii. 36 τελευτῆς | δὲ αὐτῷ ταχείας συμβάσης καὶ τοῖν

---

ᵃ Cf. Amm. Marc. 25. 3.
ᵇ Jovian—left contemptuously unnamed by Libanius in
the Orations.
ᶜ The argument is resumed from *Or.* 18. 274 f.
ᵈ The disgrace of this treaty is emphasized by contemporary historians (Amm. Marc. 25. 9, Eutrop. 10. 17, Ruf.
Fest. *Brev.* 29) and even by Church historians (Socr. 3. 22).
Christian propaganda (Greg. Naz. *Inv.* 2. 15, Aug. *Civ.*

496

gushing out, he did not stop busying himself with such considerations until he lost consciousness. So he was carried to his tent and, when all around him stood weeping, he was the only one to shed no tear. He uttered no word of regret for his campaign but commended himself for it, and remarked that he was sorry, not at the necessity of dying, but at leaving his army leaderless. Then, with his gaze already on the gods to whom he was soon to be translated, he gave up his life.[a] 8. Another man took his place as emperor.[b] He should have supported his dead predecessor without delay, and should have marked the commencement of his reign by punishing his death, but he decided that this was superfluous and pointless. So the dead body was brought home, to the jeers of those who had contrived such a crime. In the many peace parleys held with the Persians not a whisper was heard that any of them had been rewarded for the murder, even though a reward was to be expected.[c]

9. I feel that the gods were angered against that emperor and so he was compelled to make peace on terms such that the enemy gained more than they could ever have dreamed of,[d] the whole of Armenia, the acquisition of the important frontier city of Nisibis, and many strong fortresses.[e] 10. However, he may not have been able to institute such an enquiry for reasons that I think are obvious, the speedy death

Dei, 4. 29) tried to throw the blame on Julian, but the fact was that this was one of the rare occasions when the Romans were compelled to cede territory by treaty, and the disgrace was thus more apparent.

[e] Nisibis and fifteen fortresses, with large tracts of territory in Mesopotamia, were ceded under this treaty (Amm. Marc. 25. 7. 9, Zos. 3. 31).

# LIBANIUS

ἀδελφοῖν ἐπὶ τὰ σκῆπτρα παρελθόντοιν ἡ αὐτὴ
περὶ τὴν τιμωρίαν ἀργία. καίτοι τοῦ μνήματος οὐ
R ii. 37 μικρά τις ἡ πρόνοια καὶ | ταῦτα δαπάνης γινο-
μένης, ἀλλ᾿ ὅμως προΐεντο καὶ τοὺς σκεψομένους
ἔπεμπον καὶ ἠρώτων ἐπανήκοντας καὶ ὅλως ἐβούλοντο δοκεῖν ἐσπουδακέναι περὶ τὴν ἐνταῦθα λαμ-
πρότητα. 11. τουτὶ μὲν οὖν καλῶς, ἐκεῖνο | δὲ οὐ F 5
καλῶς. οὐ γὰρ οἷς ἐποίουν ἐχαρίζοντο μᾶλλον ἢ
οἷς οὐκ ἐποίουν ἐλύπουν, καὶ βελτίους γ᾿ ἂν ἦσαν
ποιοῦντες μὲν ὧν ὠλιγώρουν ὀλιγωροῦντες δὲ ὧν
ἐπεμελοῦντο, ἢ ὡς νῦν ἐποίησαν. οὐδεὶς γὰρ ἂν
οὕτως ἡσθείη τῶν ἀδίκως ἀποθανόντων κάλλει
μνήματος ὡς τῇ τοῦ κτείναντος δίκῃ. ὄντος τοίνυν
πολλοῦ τοῦ λόγου τοῦδε ὡς ἐξ ἡμῶν ὁ ἀπεκτονὼς
εἴη καὶ ὡς δεινὸν εἰ μή τις ἐπέξεισιν, οὐδὲν μᾶλλον
οὓς ἐχρῆν ἐκινοῦντο οὐδὲ συνῆγον τοὺς τῶν βουλευ-
R ii. 38 μάτων κοινωνοὺς ἐπὶ ζητήσει τοῦ | αἵματος καὶ
ταῦτα τῶν συμφορῶν εἰς ἔννοιαν τοῦ πράγματος
ἀγουσῶν. 12. διέβησαν τὸν Ἴστρον Σαυρομάται
τὴν ἄρρηκτον στρατιὰν τοῦ πρεσβυτέρου μὴ δείσαντες, κατέσυραν ἀνθοῦν τοῖς ἅπασιν ἔθνος τὸ
Ἰλλυριῶν, μετήνεγκαν εἰς τὴν αὐτῶν μεγάλην
εὐδαιμονίαν, ἔργον χρόνου μακροῦ. καὶ τὴν μὲν

---

   [a] Jovian died after only an eight-month reign, before
reaching Constantinople (Amm. 25. 10. 12).
   [b] Valentinian and Valens: cf. Or. 19. 15.

that befell him [a] : but when the two brothers came to
the throne,[b] there was the same slackness in avenging
him. They showed great concern about his tomb,
and for the expense it involved also, but still they were
ready to meet it, and sent supervisors whom they
questioned on their return. In short, their desire was
to appear enthusiastic for a magnificent memorial
for him.[c] 11. So far, so good ; not so the sequel, for
they did not so much please by their action as displease by their inaction. It would have been better
for them to have done what they shirked and to
have shirked making such arrangements in preference to behaving as they actually did. Nobody is
pleased with a handsome monument to innocent victims of murder as much as with the punishment of
the murderer. Well, it was the current story that the
murderer was from our side, and that it was a
scandal that he was not brought to book, but they
were not moved by it as they should have been, and
they did not summon the members of their council
to make enquiries into the murder, even though the
disasters they suffered constantly reminded them of
the matter. 12. The Sarmatians crossed the
Danube with no fear of the invincible army of the
senior of the two,[d] and they ravaged the wholly
prosperous province of Illyria, and transferred to
their own country all that prosperity, the fruits of
many a long year. One may well wonder at the

[c] Julian's body was brought home immediately and
buried in Tarsus (Or. 18. 306, Amm. 25. 9, Zos. 3. 34), in a
royal cemetery (Philostorg. H.E. 8. 2). A much later story
speaks of his burial among the royal tombs at Constantinople
(Cedren, p. 304).

[d] Sarmatians and Quadi invade Valentinian's Illyrian
provinces, A.D. 374 (Amm. Marc. 29. 6. 6).

τοῦ ταύτης τῆς χώρας ἄρχοντος θαυμάσαι τις ἂν[1]
λύπην δι' ἣν δακρύων οὐχ ὑπάτου[2] στολῆς |
R ii. 39 ἡγήσατο εἶναι τὸν ἐνιαυτὸν αὐτῷ, τὴν τόλμαν δὲ
τῶν ἀσθενεστέρων πόθεν χρὴ νομίσαι γεγενῆσθαι;
13. ἐγὼ μὲν γὰρ ἐντεῦθεν ἡγοῦμαι, ἐπεὶ καὶ τὴν
ἐπανάστασιν τοῦ τυράννου τὴν εἰς ἅπασαν φθορὰν
R ii. 40 ἀγαγοῦσαν τὰς | πόλεις, δι' ἣν ὁ νεώτερος πολλὰ    F 52
μὲν ἔδρασε | πολλὰ δὲ ἔπαθεν, ἐντεῦθεν ἡγοῦμαι
γεγενῆσθαι, καὶ πολύ γε πλέον τὴν δευτέραν. ὁ
μέν γε, εἰ μηδὲν ἕτερον, οἰκεῖός τε ὢν ἐτύγχανεν
R ii. 41 Ἰουλιανῷ καὶ δεδιὼς καὶ κρυπτόμενος | καὶ ἀεὶ
ληφθήσεσθαι προσδοκῶν καὶ φεύγων ἐλπιζόμενον
θάνατον οὕτως ἀνέρριψε τὸν κύβον, τὸ δὲ ἄνδρας
εὖ πεπονθότας, τιμῶν τετυχηκότας, ἐν φίλοις
ἀριθμηθέντας ὁμοῦ τε κοινωνεῖν τραπέζης καὶ
R ii. 42 τοιαῦτα ἐπιβουλεύειν, | πῶς οὐχ ὅθεν ἔφην ὥρ-
μηται; 14. ὁ πολὺς δὲ φόνος ὅ τε τῇδε ὅ τε ἐν
Ῥώμῃ δαιμόνων ὀργὴν μηνύει, δι' ἣν οἱ μὲν
ἀπέθνησκον, οἱ δὲ ἔμελλον. ὁ Φόβος γῆν τε ἔσειε |
R ii. 43 καὶ θάλατταν. καὶ οὐκ ἐπιλαμβάνομαι μὲν τοῖν
βασιλέοιν ὡς οὐ δίκαια ἔδρων τοῖς ἐξελεγχομένοις
τὴν ἐκ τῶν νόμων ἐπιτιθέντες δίκην, αὐτὸ δὲ τὸ
τῆς ἐσχάτης δίκης ἀξίους πεφηνέναι μυρίους, ὧν

---

[1] ἂν inserted F. (V) : om. Re. (other mss.).
[2] ὑπάρχου conj. Olearius.

---

[a] Probus (Amm. Marc. loc. cit.). Ammianus describes
him as praefectus praetorio in A.D. 374, his consulship
occurring in A.D. 371. The confusion of title is probably the
deliberate act of Libanius, to dramatize the seriousness of
the disaster, rather than due to manuscript corruption.

grief of the local governor [a] that caused him to be of
the opinion that his was a year of mourning, not of
consular rank : but what must we consider the origin of such venturesome activities by our inferiors ?
13. In my opinion, it is to be found here. Also, the
revolt of the pretender, that brought the cities to
utter disaster and caused the junior of the two emperors to inflict and to experience great suffering, may
be ascribed to the same cause [b]—and much more
so in the case of the revolt that followed. [c] Procopius
at least, whatever else he might be, was a relative of
Julian. In fear and hiding and in daily expectation
of arrest, fleeing from the death he anticipated, he
made his final throw ; but for men, on whom he had
lavished kindness, to whom he had granted honours
and whom he accounted his friends, for them to share
his table and yet engage in such a plot against him,
this must surely arise from the cause I have assigned.
14. The bloodshed both here [d] and in Rome denotes
the wrath of heaven, [e] and in consequence of this some
met their doom and others expected it. Panic
reigned over land and sea. I am not criticizing the
emperors : they were within their rights to impose
on proven criminals the penalty prescribed by law,
but the very fact that countless people proved deserving of the extreme penalty, and that the majority of

[b] Procopius revolted against Valens in Asia Minor late in
A.D. 365 (Amm. Marc. 26. 5 ff., Zos. 4. 5 ff.).
[c] Identified by Reiske with Eugenius' revolt of A.D. 395,
by Förster (vol. 2, p. 508) with that of Procopius—both
wrongly. *Or.* 1. 171, a parallel passage written at almost
the same time as this, shows that the reference is to the
conspiracy of Theodorus in A.D. 371, which Valens punished
with great severity.                     [d] In Antioch.
[e] The reign of terror conducted by Maximinus against
the Roman senate (Amm. Marc. 28. 1).

οἱ πλείους οἰκιῶν ὀνομαστῶν, βεβαιοῖ μου τὸν
λόγον τὸν ὑπὸ δαιμονίου τινὸς ἐλαύνεσθαι λέγοντα
τὴν γῆν. |

15. Τὰ δὲ τελευταῖα ταῦτα πῶς οὐ σαφῶς F 521
κακοδαιμονώντων; ἀπόλωλεν ἡμῖν ἔθνη πέντε καὶ
R ii. 44 εἴκοσι τῶν μὲν ἔξω τειχῶν ἡρπασμένων, τῶν | δὲ
εἴσω πάντα φαγόντων, οἷς οὐδὲ ταφῆναι τῷ λιμῷ
τεθνεῶσιν ὑπῆρξεν, ἀλλ' ἀνάγοντες αὐτοὺς οἱ προσ-
ήκοντες ἐπὶ τὸ τεῖχος ἀφίεσαν γυμνοὺς φέρεσθαι
τοὺς ταλαιπώρους κάτω. 16. τοιαῦτα ἐκώμασαν
οἱ Σκύθαι φρίττοντες ἀεὶ πρὸς τὴν ἀκοὴν τῆς
Ῥωμαίων περὶ τὸν πόλεμον τέχνης, ἀλλὰ νῦν ὅσα
ἐμαχέσαντο, τοσαῦτα νενικήκασι καλῶς μὲν ἡμῶν
καὶ ὡς προσῆκεν ἄνδρας ἀγαθοὺς ἀποθνησκόντων,
ἀναλουμένων δ' οὖν. καὶ νῦν ἐπὶ τοὺς γεωργοὺς
ἥκομεν τῶν ἐν τοῖς ὅπλοις βεβιωκότων οἰχομένων.
αἱ προσδοκίαι δὲ δειναὶ καὶ χρηστὸν οὐδὲν ἐν
ἐλπίσι, πλὴν εἰ πεισθείης μοι, βασιλεῦ, καὶ λύσαις
ὅ φημι τὴν αἰτίαν ἔχειν τῶν κακῶν.

17. Φήσουσι τοίνυν με πλάττειν οὐκ ὄντα φόνον[1]
τινές· τῶν γὰρ ἐναντίων ἕνα εἶναι τὸν ἀπεκτονότα. |
R ii. 45 ἐγὼ δὲ ὅτι μὲν οὐκ ἂν εἰς μέσην τὴν στρατιὰν
ἐτόλμησεν ἀνὴρ Πέρσης ἐλθεῖν μὴ θανατῶν καὶ
ὡς εἰ | πλείους ἦσαν πλείους ἂν καὶ διέφθειραν, F 522
νῦν δὲ ἀποθνήσκει μόνος οὐδενὸς τῶν ἐγγυτάτω καὶ

---

[1] φόνον F., Olearius, Cobet : φόβον Re. (mss.).

---

[a] The overrunning by the Goths of the Balkan provinces
after Adrianople. Libanius' language is a reminiscence of
his descriptions of the ravaging of Gaul before its deliverance
by Julian. Cf. also Zos. 4. 25. 2.

[b] This passage indicates that the date of composition of

them belonged to families of renown, confirms my assertion that the world is harassed by some super-natural power.

15. These last disasters are obviously those of an ill-starred people. We have lost twenty-five pro-vinces,[a] and the natives who lived outside walled towns have been taken off as prisoners, while those inside eat up everything they have and then, when they die of starvation, they are not even buried, but their relatives drag them up to the top of the wall and throw the poor wretches down from there, naked. 16. Such is the carnival that the Goths have held. Up to now they used to shiver every time they heard mention of the Romans' skill in warfare, but now they are victorious, and we die, nobly and as befits brave men, but perishing all the same. And now that those who have spent their lives in arms have gone, we resort to our peasantry. We can expect the worst and have no gleam of hope unless you take my advice, Sire, and do away with what I affirm to be the cause of our troubles.[b]

17. Some persons, I suppose, will say that I am inventing a murder that never happened, for, accord-ing to them, his murderer was one of the enemy. Now I will not argue the point that a Persian would never have dared to come into the midst of our army unless bent on suicide, or that if their numbers had been greater, the number of these killed would have been greater too. The fact remains that he was the only one to be killed, and no one near him and none

this oration is before November A.D. 379, when the victory of the imperial forces over Goths, Alans and Huns was announced. So Förster (vol. 2, p. 509) and Olearius (in Fabricius, *Bibl. Gr.* vii. 145). For peasantry *cf.* Themist. *Or.* 14, p. 181 B.

# LIBANIUS

ὑφ' ὧν ἐφρουρεῖτο παθόντος οὐδέν, ἀλλ' οὐδὲ μελλήσαντος, ὁ γὰρ ἆθλος οὗτος ἦν καὶ ἐφ' ὃν ἀπέ-
R ii. 46 σταλτο, τουτὶ μὲν ἐάσω. 18. ἀλλὰ | γεγένηνται δήπου πρεσβεῖαι πολλαὶ μετ' ἐκεῖνον τὸν χρόνον ὡς τὸν Πέρσην, πάλιν γὰρ ἐρῶ ταὐτό, καὶ εἰώθασί γε Πέρσαι φιλοτιμεῖσθαι τῇ μνήμῃ τῶν κατωρθωμένων καὶ διηγοῦνται δὴ πολλάκις ἃ Ῥωμαίους ἔπληξαν καὶ εἰ τῶν τινα βασιλευόντων κατήνεγκαν· ἀλλ' ὅμως οὔτ' αὐτὸς ὁ βασιλεὺς ἐκείνων οὔτ' ἄλλος οὐδεὶς τῶν ἐν ταῖς τάξεσιν ἀλλ' οὐδὲ ἰδιώτης τοῦτό γε εἰπὼν φαίνεται τὸ τὸν θάνατον ἐκεῖνον ἄνδρα Πέρσην εἰργάσθαι. 19. ἀλλ' οὐδὲ ἐν εἰκόνι τοῦτο δείκνυσθαί φασι μάλιστ' ἂν γραφέν, εἰ ἐπέπρακτο, τοσοῦτόν γε ὂν εἰς δόξαν. ἀλλ' ἐν εἴδει μὲν λέοντος πεποίηται πῦρ ἀποπνέοντος. ἃ δὲ ἔπαθον γράψαντες ἃ μὴ συνῄδεσαν αὑτοῖς δεδρακόσιν οὐ προσέθηκαν οὐδὲ ἐκαλλωπίσαντο τοῖς οὐ γεγενημένοις. 20. τὸ δὲ μέγιστον ἁπάντων, Βίκτωρα καὶ Σαλούστιον καὶ τοὺς ἄλλους τοὺς
R ii. 47 ὑπὲρ | τῆς εἰρήνης πρεσβεύοντας ἤρετο Σαπώρης εἰ μὴ αἰσχύνοιντο Ῥωμαῖοι | μηδεμίαν ὥραν τῆς F 523 ὑπὲρ Ἰουλιανοῦ δίκης πεποιημένοι μόνου πεσόντος, ὃ μάλιστα δὴ βοᾷ τί ποτέ ἐστι τὸ πρᾶγμα. ἐγὼ δέ, ἔφη, τεθνεῶτός μοί τινος τῶν ἡγεμόνων τοὺς οὐ πεσόντας περὶ αὐτὸν ἔδειρα καὶ τοὺς τοῦ τετελευτηκότος οἰκείους ταῖς ἐκείνων παρεμυθησάμην κεφαλαῖς πέμψας αὐτὰς εἰς χεῖρας αὐτοῖς. ταῦτα οὐκ ἂν εἶπεν

---

ᵃ Cf. § 8 above. The validity of this *argumentum ex*
504

of his bodyguard suffered a scratch, nor indeed was likely to, since Julian was the prize and Julian the target against whom he was despatched. 18. I repeat what I have stated previously[a]: since that time there have many embassies to the Persian king, and it is the usual thing for Persians to plume themselves on the recollection of their successes, and they often tell the tale of the disasters they have caused the Romans and of any emperor they have slain. Yet neither the Persian king himself, nor any of his generals nor any private individual even is known to have claimed for any Persian the responsibility for his death. 19. It is said that there is no representation of this even in the picture,[b] where it certainly would have appeared if this was how it happened, since it would have been so much to their credit, but he appears there as a lion breathing out fire. They have depicted all that they suffered, but they have not added anything they knew they had not done, nor did they take credit for what had not occurred. 20. The most telling point is that Victor, Salustius and the rest of the envoys sent to arrange a peace settlement were asked by Sapor if the Romans were not ashamed to have shown no concern for avenging Julian after he had been the only one to fall. That is the clearest possible indication of the real nature of the business. " Why !" he exclaimed, "when one of my commanders was killed, I flayed alive the men who failed to die at his side, and I sent their heads to console his kinsmen." Sapor would never have used

*silentio* is open to question, Philostorgius, for instance, asserting that Julian's killer was himself cut down by a member of the emperor's bodyguard.

[b] *Cf. Or.* 18. 305, where the Persians are said to have depicted Julian as a thunderbolt.

LIBANIUS

ὁ Σαπώρης οὐδὲ ἐπετίμησεν εἰ τὸ ἔργον ἑνὸς ἦν
τῶν πολεμίων. πῶς γὰρ ἂν ὃν οὐκ εἶχον ὑφ᾽
αὑτοῖς ἐτιμωροῦντο;

21. Εἰ τοίνυν ὑπὸ μὲν αἰχμῆς ἀπέθανε, χειρὶ δὲ
Πέρσου τοῦτο οὐ πέπρακται, τί λοιπὸν ἢ ἐν τοῖς
R ii. 48 ἡμετέροις εἶναι τὸν φόνον[1] ἢ χαριζομένοις | τινὶ τὸ
μηκέτ᾽ ἐκεῖνον εἶναι ἢ καὶ σφίσιν αὐτοῖς, ὅπως ἐν
ἀτιμίᾳ τὰ τῶν θεῶν εἴη ὧν τιμωμένων ἀπεπνίγοντο.

22. Ἀλλ᾽ οὐδεὶς ἐφειστήκει κατήγορος
οὐδ᾽ οἱ καταμαρτυροῦντες. ἀλλ᾽ ὑμᾶς γ᾽
ἐχρῆν καὶ οὕτως ἀνιχνεῦσαι τὸ πρᾶγμα πολλάς τε
ἡμέρας ἐπ᾽ αὐτῷ καθημένους καὶ οὐκ ἀνιέντας καὶ
τοὺς ἔχοντας μὲν ἐλέγχειν ὀκνοῦντας δὲ ἐπεγεί-
ροντας, θαρρύνοντας, προτρέποντας, ἆθλα τιθέντας,
ἐπὶ δωρεὰς καλοῦντας | καὶ νὴ Δία γε καὶ ταῖς δι᾽ F 524
ἀπειλῶν ἀνάγκαις μὴ ἐᾶν σιωπᾶν. 23. εἰ ταῦτα
παρ᾽ ὑμῶν ἐγίγνετο, πολλοὺς ἂν εἴχετε[2] τοὺς
βοῶντας, τοὺς λέγοντας, τοὺς διδάσκοντας τίς ὁ
ἀρχιτέκτων τοῦ φόνου, τίς ὁ πρῶτος ἀκούσας
R ii. 49 τοῦτο, τίσιν ὁ κτείνας ἀνεπείσθη λόγοις, | ἐπὶ
πόσῳ μισθῷ, τίνες οἱ συνειδότες, ποῖ τρώσας
ἀπεχώρησε, τίνες αὐτῷ συνέπιον καὶ συνεπαιώ-
νισαν. 24. ὑμῶν μὲν γὰρ ἡσυχαζόντων καὶ τοῖς
δυναμένοις διώκειν ἀσφαλὲς ἐφαίνετο τὸ μηδὲν
λέγειν, κεκινημένων δὲ τῶν βασιλέων καὶ τῶν

---

[1] φόνον mss. except U : φονέα F. (U).
[2] εἴχετε F., Cobet : εἴδετε Re. (mss.).

---

[a] For members of at least two missions to the Persians,
apparently combined by Libanius, cf. Amm. Marc. 25. 7. 7
and 12. He appears to have obtained this information at
first-hand, either from Salustius, whom he met on his return
and with whom he corresponded after Julian's death, or
from Victor, who visited him during the reign of Valens

506

such words of reproof if the deed had been done by one of the enemy, for how could they punish anyone they could not lay their hands on ?[a]

21. If then he died by a spear thrust, and this was not inflicted by a Persian, it follows that the murderer was one of our people, who did themselves or somebody else[b] a good turn by assassinating him so that the religion of the gods should fall into dishonour, for they almost burst with rage at the honour in which it was held.

22. But there has been none to come forward as accuser or informant, it may be retorted. But for all that, you[c] ought to investigate the matter and sit in judgement upon it for many a day without relaxing. To those who were reluctant to produce proof though able to do so, you should have applied suasion, encouragement and incentive. You ought to offer rewards, promise gifts and, by Heaven ! use threats so as not to let them stay silent. 23. If you did this, you would have plenty to proclaim the news and to inform you who it was who engineered the assassination, who first got wind of it, by what arguments the murderer was induced to act, the amount of the bribe, the accessories to the crime, where he betook himself after inflicting the wound, and the identity of those boon companions who shared in his triumph. 24. If you made no move, obviously the safest course for anyone who could set up a hue and cry was to keep his mouth shut. Had the emperors stirred

---

(*Or.* 2. 9). Sapor's habit of flaying his subjects alive as punishment for cowardice or surrender is noted in *Or.* 18. 228.

[b] Jovian.

[c] The joint emperors after Valens' death, Gratian and Theodosius.

# LIBANIUS

ἀρχόντων δηλούντων ὡς οὐ στήσονται ζητοῦντες
μέχρις ἂν εἰς φῶς ἔλθῃ τὰ κεκρυμμένα, ταχέως εἰς
φῶς ἔμελλεν ἥξειν, ἐπεὶ καὶ νῦν ἦσαν οἱ ἐν γωνίαις
λέγοντες ὅπως ἅπαν τὸ δρᾶμα συνετέθη· οἱ πολλῆς
ἐνόμιζον εἶναι μανίας οἷς μάλιστα προσῆκεν ἀγανακτεῖν ἥκιστα τοῦτο ποιούντων ἑτέρους σφᾶς αὐτοὺς εἰς πράγματα ἐμβάλλειν οὐκ εἰδότας μὲν εἴ
τινι χαριοῦνται, δεδιότας δὲ μὴ καὶ ζημία προσ-
γένηται.  25. ἤδη τις | ὁδοιπορῶν αὐτὸς μὲν ἔ- F 525
κειτο κατακοπείς, ὁ δ᾽ ἀποσφάξας ἀπελθὼν οἷς
ἀφείλετο ἐτρύφα καὶ ὁ τοῖς νόμοις αὐτὸν παρα-
δώσων οὐκ ἦν. ὁ δικάζων δὲ οὐκ, ἐπεὶ μηδεὶς
ἐδίωκεν, ἀνεξέταστον ἀφεὶς τὸ τετολμημένον ἐκάθ-
ευδεν, ἀλλὰ πάντα κινῶν καὶ παριεὶς οὐδὲν τὸ
R ii. 50 τοῦ Λυγκέως ἔδοξε | τῷ νῷ πεποιηκέναι, καὶ ὁ
αὐτόχειρ ᾕρητο πάνυ δὴ πιστεύων ἀνωτέρω πάσης
ἰδέας ἐλέγχων ἠδικηκέναι.  26. πολλὰ τοιαῦτα ἐν
ταῖς ἐρημίαις πραχθέντα οὐκ ἔλαθε, πολλὰ τοιαῦτα
ἐν ἄστεσι. καὶ οὐκ ἀπόχρη τοῖς τῶν φυλῶν
ἐπιμεληταῖς τῇ γῇ παραδοῦναι τὸν ἀπεσφαγμένον,
ἀλλ᾽ ἦκον παρὰ τὸν ἄρχοντα, ἐμήνυσαν, ἔφρασαν,
ὁ δ᾽ αὐτοῦ νομίζει τὸ μὴ τὸν δεδρακότα ἀγνοηθῆναι.

---

[a] A sneer at the gossip about the divine revelation of
Julian's death current among the Christians (cf. Sozom.
H.E. 6. 2).  By insinuation, this is held to be tantamount to
plotting against him.

[b] Lynceus, proverbially sharp-eyed: cf. Pindar, Nem. 10.
60 ff., Theocr. 27. 137 ff.

[c] Libanius takes his illustration from the procedure then
in operation at Antioch, where these minor officials exercise
some rudimentary powers of police. The eighteen local
tribes of which the city was composed (Or. 11. 231, 19. 62)

508

themselves, if the governors made it plain that they
would not cease their enquiries until the secret came
to light, it very quickly would have come to light, for,
as it was, there were mutterings in dark corners to
tell how the whole business was contrived.[a] Such
people considered it the height of folly, when
persons who were in duty bound to show their displeasure failed to do so, for others to ask for trouble
in their uncertainty whether their action would meet
with any approval and in their fear that some harm
even might be the consequence. 25. Before now,
wayfarers have been murdered, the killers have gone
off and enjoyed themselves on the proceeds, and there
was nobody to hand them over to the law, but the
judge did not give up the case as hopeless and doze
off because no prosecutor appeared. No ! he moved
heaven and earth, let nothing go by default and
resolutely applied the sharp eye of intuition.[b] As a
result, murderers have been arrested when they were
sure that the crime was beyond proof of any kind.
26. The truth has been discovered about many such
crimes committed both in cities and far from human
habitation. The watch committee do not think it
enough merely to consign the victim to his grave,
but they approach the governor, make their deposition and describe the incident, and he thinks it his
duty to have the miscreant brought to book.[c]

still retained some corporate existence in his day (*cf. Or.*
11. 245, 5. 43 f.). These *epimeletae*, probably of curial
standing, are responsible to the governor for the maintenance
of public order and services (*e.g., Or.* 23. 11, they are called
upon, under threat of physical punishment, to produce the
culprits after the riots of A.D. 387. *Or.* 33. 35 f., on the
governor's instructions, they enforce the order increasing the
public lighting of Antioch).

27. Εἶθ' ὑπὲρ μὲν τῶν τυχόντων σπουδασόμεθα,
τῷ δ' ἀρίστῳ τῶν ἀνδρῶν οὐ τιμωρήσομεν; καὶ
τοῖς μὲν ἔθνους ἄρχουσιν ἔστιν εἰς τὸ τὰ τοιαῦτα
ἐκκαλύπτειν δύναμις, ἡ δ' ὑμῶν τῶν βασιλέων
ἀσθενεστέρα τῆς θήρας; οὐκ ἔστι.   δεῖξον ὡς
ἥδιστ' ἂν τοὺς ἀνθρώπους ἕλοις, καὶ οἱ παρα-
δώσοντές σοι τὰ θηρία | φανοῦνται, ἣν αὐτοῖς F 52
ἀφέλῃς μόνον τὸν φόβον ὡς οὐδὲν δεινὸν αὐτοῖς ὁ
ἐκείνων πλοῦτος ὃν ἀπὸ τῶν ἀρχῶν ἔχουσι.  τοῦτο
R ii. 51 γάρ, τοῦτο οὐκ ἔχον ἐστὶν ὑπερβολήν, | φόνου
τοιούτου δίκην ὀφείλοντες, ὥσπερ τὸν Πέρσην
ἀπεκτονότες, ἀρχὰς ἐκαρπώσαντο.

28. Μάλιστα μὲν οὖν, εἰ καὶ μὴ τοσαύτην ὅσην
ἐδείκνυον ἄρτι βλάβην εἶχεν ἡ περὶ τὴν δίκην
νωθεία, καὶ οὕτω χρῆν ἐπιστραφῆναί τε καὶ
φυλακήν τινα ταυτηνὶ τοῖς ἐπὶ τὰ σκῆπτρα καλου-
μένοις παρασχεῖν.   ἐν μὲν γὰρ τῷ πράξασθαι
τιμωρίαν παύσετε τοὺς τὰ τοιαῦτα ἀδικοῦντας,
ποιήσαντες δὲ ἄδειαν ἐφ' ὑμᾶς αὐτούς, ἀλλ' οὐκ
ἐρῶ γε τὸ βλάσφημον.   ὥστε τήμερον τῷ μὲν
δοκεῖν Ἰουλιανῷ βοηθήσων ἀφῖγμαι, τῇ δὲ ἀλη-
θείᾳ τοῖς ζῶσιν ὑμῖν.   τῷ μὲν γὰρ οὐκ ἔστιν
ἀποδοῦναι τὴν ψυχὴν διὰ τῆς δίκης, ὑμῖν δὲ
διατηρῆσαι.   ποιήσατε τοίνυν τοὺς στρατιώτας
τῶν ἀρχόντων προκινδυνεύειν ἤ, εἰ μὴ τοῦτο
βούλοιντο, μήτοι γε ἀντὶ τῶν πολεμίων αὐτοῖς
καθίστασθαι.

29. Ἐγὼ μὲν εἰ καὶ στρατηγὸς ἐπεπόνθει τι |
τοιοῦτον ἢ καί τις τῶν στρατείᾳ ἐφεστηκότων, F 5
R ii. 52 ἠξίουν | ἄν σε χωρεῖν ἐπὶ τοὺς ἐκείνων σφαγέας
δείσαντα τὴν τοῦ πράγματος μελέτην μὴ καὶ πρὸς
τὸ μέγιστον ἀπὸ τῶν ἐλαττόνων βαδίσῃ· νῦν δ'

27. So, if we are to be so zealous for any Tom, Dick or Harry, shall we not avenge this prince without peer? If provincial governors have the power to bring such matters to light, shall your imperial power be ineffective in the quest? No indeed! Just show that you will be glad to have the fellows arrested, and people will appear to hand the beasts over to you, once you rid them of the fear that they may suffer some harm in consequence of the wealth the murderers have amassed from their positions of office. The fact is, without a word of exaggeration, that though they ought to be punished for a murder like this, they have reaped the fruits of office, as if it were the Persian king they had murdered.

28. Thus, even if your neglect of punishment has not produced the disastrous results I have just related, you ought certainly to give some attention and provide some such protection for those who are summoned to the throne. By the imposition of punishment you will put a stop to such criminals, but if you let them go scot free, you will stir up for yourselves—just what, I will forbear to mention: it does not bear thinking upon! So I have come today, on the face of it, to speak on behalf of Julian, but in fact, on behalf of yourselves, the living emperors. By punishing his death, you cannot give him back his life, but you can at least protect your own. So ensure that your soldiers risk their lives for their leaders, or, if they refuse to do so, that at least they do not behave like enemies towards them.

29. If a general or military officer had met some such fate, I would expect you to attack their murderers, in case the continuance of the practice should result in a progression from lesser victims to the

ἐπὶ τὸ κεφάλαιον τῶν πραγμάτων ὁ ἱππεὺς ἐκεῖνος
καὶ ὁ σίδηρος ἧκεν ἐν ἀκμῇ τῆς μάχης ὑπ᾽
ἐργαστηρίου πονηροῦ πεμφθεὶς ἀπὸ σκηνῆς μιαρᾶς
καὶ βουλευμάτων ὀλεθρίων. γένοιντ᾽ ἂν καὶ ἄλλοι
τινὲς ἴσως πονηροί, βασιλεῦ, μίαν σκηνὴν ὑπιόντες
ἐχθροὶ τοῖς ἄρχουσι. τούτους ἡ μὲν φύσις οὐκ ἂν
ποτε ποιήσειε βελτίους, κατάσχοι δ᾽ ἂν ἴσως ὁ
φόβος.

30. Ἀλλ᾽ ἐκεῖσε ἐπάνειμι, ὅτι ἦν μὲν ἄν, εἰ καὶ
μηδεὶς ἐπῆν περὶ τῶν ὅλων κίνδυνος, καὶ δίκαιον
καὶ λυσιτελὲς ὑμῖν παῦσαι τὸ θράσος διὰ τῆς ἐπὶ
τοῖς πεπραγμένοις ὀργῆς, νῦν δ᾽ οὐδὲ βουλομένῳ
σοι μὴ ταῦτα ποιεῖν ἔνι. οἱ γὰρ βαρεῖς οὗτοι καὶ
τοῖς τὴν Ῥώμην οἰκοῦσιν αὐτὴν ἐπιστήσαντες φό-
R ii. 53 βους | καὶ ταῦτα οὕτω πολλῶν ἡμερῶν ὁδὸν ἀπ-
έχοντες σύμβουλοι καθίστανταί σοι τῆς περὶ τὴν
τιμωρίαν ἐπιμελείας, ἧς γενομένης οὐκέθ᾽ ὑβρι-
οῦσιν οἱ Σκύθαι.

31. Τοσούτου γὰρ ἄξιος τοῖς θεοῖς ὁ τεθνεώς; ἐρεῖ τις. πάνυ γε. καὶ παλαιός γε οὗτος
αὐτῶν νόμος ὑπὲρ τῶν πεπονθότων ἀγανακτεῖν. ἡ
δίκη | δὲ ὧν τινες ἀδικοῦσι πολλάκις τείνεται καὶ F 5?
ἐφ᾽ ἅπασαν πόλιν. ἐνόσησαν μὲν Ἀθηναῖοι διὰ τὸν
Ἀνδρόγεω θάνατον καὶ τῷ πατρὶ τοῦ τετελευτηκότος τὸν δασμὸν τοὺς δὶς ἑπτὰ ἤνεγκαν ὀλίγων

---

ᵃ After their great victory over the Romans at Adrianople
the Goths raided as far as the environs of Constantinople.

greatest. As things are, it was against the head of
state that that horseman and his steel delivered the
stroke in the heat of battle, sent upon that errand by
a wicked cabal from some foul tent of dire conspiracy.
Sire, there may perhaps be yet other rascals lurking
in a solitary tent, enemies of their own leaders.
Nature could never improve them, but fear perhaps
may restrain them.

30. But to revert to my point: even if no danger
to the empire were involved, it would still be right
and proper for you to put an end to their enormities
by means of your anger at what they have done. In
fact, however unwilling you may be, you cannot help
doing so. These aggressors who inspire panic in the
inhabitants of Rome itself, though they be many
days' distance removed from it, counsel you to take
thought for avenging him; and when that is done,
there will be no more trouble from the Goths.[a]

31. Did the deceased really deserve to be so highly
esteemed by the gods, it may be asked. He did
indeed. It is an old habit of theirs to show their
displeasure over persons foully wronged. The vengeance for the misdeeds of individuals often ex-
tends over the whole community.[b] The Athenians
were smitten with plague because of the death of
Androgeos and they presented the father of the
victim with the tribute of twice seven of their children, even though the perpetrators of the deed were

With sophistic exaggeration, Libanius concentrates upon the
apprehension inspired by this event in Rome itself.

[b] An adaptation of *Or.* 16. 50 f., with its references to the
divine retribution following the offences of Oedipus, Agamemnon and the lesser Ajax. In the earlier passage they
had served to underline offences against Julian in his lifetime: here, after his death.

# LIBANIUS

ὄντων οἷς ἐτολμήθη τοὖργον, ἐνόσησε δὲ ἡ Θηβαίων
πόλις διὰ τὸν Λαΐου φόνον, οὗτος δὲ ἦν ὁ θάνατος
ἔργον τῆς Οἰδίπου χειρὸς μόνης. λιμὸς ἐν Δελφοῖς
R ii. 54 ἦν Αἰσώπου παρ᾽ αὐτοῖς | ἐπὶ σκώμματι πληγέντος.
καίτοι πόσους εἰκὸς ἀπεκτονέναι τὸν ἄνθρωπον;
ἀλλ᾽ ὅμως ἡ πόλις ἐλιμώττε, καὶ μία λύσις, εἰ
δοῖεν δίκην. 32. τί λέγεις; οὐκ ἐποίησε χαλεποὺς
Ῥωμαίοις τοὺς θεοὺς οὕτω μὲν πεσὼν Ἰουλιανὸς
οὕτω δὲ ἀμεληθείς, οὕτω μὲν χαλεπήναντος τοῖς
Ἀχαιοῖς τοῦ Ἀπόλλωνος διὰ τὸ μὴ ἀποδοῦναι τῷ
Χρύσῃ τὴν θυγατέρα τὸν δεῖνα, οὕτω δὲ βοῶν τινων
εἵνεκα τοῦ Ἡλίου, ὥστε τοιαῦτα ἀπειλῆσαι τοῖς
ἄλλοις θεοῖς εἰ μὴ λάβοι δίκην; καίτοι πεινώντων
τὸ ἔργον ἦν, ἀλλ᾽ ὅμως ἡ ναῦς αὐτοῖς κεραυνῷ
διεσκέδαστο καὶ ὁ τὰ βέλτιστα παραινῶν μετὰ τῶν
οὐ πεισθέντων ἐξέπιπτε. 33. τί τοὺς σὺν Ἀγαμέμνονι ἑλόντας τὴν Τροίαν ἀπώλεσεν; ὁ χειμών.
R ii. 55 τὴν | θάλατταν δὲ τίς ἐξέμηνεν; ἡ Ἀθηνᾶ. διὰ F 52
τί; ὅτι τῶν περὶ Κασάνδραν Αἴαντι πεπραγμένων
οὐκ ἔλαβε τὸ στρατόπεδον δίκην, ὥσπερ οὐδὲ νῦν
ἡμεῖς τοῦ φόνου. εἶτ᾽ οἴεταί τις τὴν Πριάμου
κόρην τιμιωτέραν τῇ Ἀθηνᾷ γενέσθαι πρότερον ἢ
νῦν ἅπασι τοῖς θεοῖς τοῦτον; τῆς δὲ ἐν Λεύκτροις
ἥττης τῆς ἀνελπίστου, μεθ᾽ ἣν ἔμεινε κειμένη τῶν
Λακεδαιμονίων ἡ πόλις, τίς οὐκ οἶδε τὴν ἀρχὴν
καὶ τὴν ὑπόθεσιν;

---

[a] Cf. Plut. *Thes.* 15, Paus. 1. 27. 10. Androgeos, son of
Minos, was killed by the Athenians while visiting a festival.
In punishment Minos exacted the annual tribute of seven
boys and seven girls destined for the Minotaur. From this
follows the story of Theseus and Ariadne.

[b] Cf. Aristoph. *Wasps*, 1446 and scholiast.

[c] Odysseus : cf. Homer, *Od.* 12. 270 ff.

514

a mere handful.[a] Thebes, too, was visited with plague because of the murder of Laïus, yet this death was caused by the hand of Oedipus alone. There was famine in Delphi when Aesop was murdered there because of one of his jests. How many do you think were the murderers? But for all that, it was the whole city that suffered from famine, and their one remedy was to pay the penalty.[b] 32. Well then? Has not the manner of Julian's death and this neglect of it aroused the anger of the gods against the Romans, if Apollo's wrath was kindled against the Achaeans because Chryses did not have his daughter restored to him by one of them, or if Helios was so wroth, because of a few oxen, that he threatened the rest of the gods as he did, unless the offenders were punished? The act was that of men starving, but, for all that, their ship was shattered by the thunderbolt, and the man who had given the best counsel was hurled overboard along with them that had refused to listen to him.[c] 33. The storm caused the deaths of those who had shared in the sack of Troy with Agamemnon, but it was Athena who roused the sea to madness. And her reason? That the army had not punished the outrage that Ajax had committed upon Cassandra, just as now we have failed to exact punishment for this murder. Yet can it be thought that Priam's daughter was then more precious to Athena than Julian now to all the gods? And for that unlooked-for defeat at Leuctra after which the state of Sparta remained prostrate, everyone knows the source and the reason.[d]

[d] Cf. Plut. *Pelop.* 20, Diod. Sic. 15. 54. A legendary curse laid upon the Spartans was held to have had a potent influence in ensuring their defeat at Leuctra.

34. Μέλει, μέλει καὶ τεθνεώτων ἀνθρώπων τοῖς θεοῖς, ὦ βασιλεῦ, ὧν καὶ τοῖς ζῶσιν ἔτι ἀνθρώποις μέλειν βούλοιντ' ἄν. εἰ δὲ μὴ τοῦτο τοιοῦτον ἦν, οὔτ' ἂν εἰς Μακάρων νήσους ἤγαγον οὓς ἐθαύμασαν οὔτ' ἂν ὀστᾶ λογίοις ἐτίμησαν, ὥσπερ τά τε Ὀρέστου τά τε Θησέως. 35. καὶ νῦν οἶμαι τοὺς θεοὺς πολλάκις ἐν ταῖς αὐτῶν ἀγοραῖς πεποιῆσθαι |

R ii. 56 λόγον ἅ τε ἔπαθεν οὗτος ὧν τε ἠτύχησε τεθνεώς, μεμφομένους τε καὶ παρακαλοῦντας ἀλλήλους ἐπὶ τὴν δίκην. εἰ γὰρ θρήνου μὲν ἄξιος Ἕκτωρ τῷ Διὶ διὰ τὸ πλῆθος τῶν θυσιῶν, ἐγκαλεῖται δὲ ὁ Ζεὺς ὑπὸ τῆς Ἀθηνᾶς ἐν τοῖς Ὀδυσσέως πλάνοις ὡς ἀμελῶν ἀνθρώπου τεθυκότος, τίνα εἰκὸς εἰρῆσθαι περὶ τούτου τοῦ τὰς | ἁπάντων τῶν Ἑλλήνων F 5 ἐν τοῖς δέκα[1] ἔτεσι παρελθόντος θυσίας; 36. οὗτος γάρ ἐστιν ὁ μερίσας αὑτοῦ τὸν βίον εἴς τε τὰς ὑπὲρ τῶν ὅλων βουλὰς εἴς τε τὰς περὶ τοὺς βωμοὺς διατριβάς, οὗτος ὁ τελεταῖς μυρίαις ὁμιλήσας δαίμοσιν, οὗτος ὁ ὑπὲρ τῶν ὑβρισμένων ἱερῶν

R ii. 57 στενάξας | μὲν ἕως τοῦτ' ἐξῆν μόνον, ὅπλων δὲ ἁψάμενος ἐπειδὴ καιρὸς παρῆν, οὗτος ὁ τὰ κατεσκαμμένα μὲν ἀποδοὺς τοῖς χωρίοις, τὰς τιμὰς δὲ καὶ τούτοις καὶ τοῖς ἄλλοις ἅπασιν, οὗτος ὁ τὸ θύειν καὶ σπένδειν ὥσπερ ἐκ φυγῆς καταγαγών, οὗτος ὁ τὰς πεπαυμένας ἑορτὰς ἀνανεωσάμενος,

R ii. 58 οὗτος ὁ τοὺς ἐπὶ τῇ θεραπείᾳ τῶν | κρειττόνων κινδύνους ἀνελών, οὗτος ὁ μηδαμοῦ τὴν διάνοιαν

---

[1] δέκα Re. (mss.): δύο F., Cobet.

---

[a] Orestes, cf. Herod. 1. 67.    Theseus, Plut. *Thes.* 36, *Cimon*, 8.    [b] Homer, *Iliad*, 24. 66 ff., *Od.* 1. 59 ff.
[c] Julian himself (*E.L.F.* No. 111, 434 d) dates his conversion to A.D. 351. Libanius here adopts the round figure

34. Yes, Sire. The gods are concerned about men even when they are dead, and they would wish men still alive to show concern for them too. Were it not so, they would never have translated those they admired to the Islands of the Blest, nor would they have honoured their bones with oracles, as they did with those of Orestes and Theseus.[a] 35. And now, I believe, the gods in their assemblies have taken note of Julian's fate and his neglect after death, and they are indignant and call upon each other to avenge him. If Hector deserved to be lamented by Zeus because of his many sacrifices, if Zeus is accused by Athena during the wanderings of Odysseus for neglecting a man who had sacrificed to him,[b] what were the remarks they made about Julian, do you think, since he in ten years offered more sacrifices than all the rest of the Greeks put together?[c] 36. He it was who divided up his life into preoccupation for the state and devotion to the altars, associating with gods in countless initiations, mourning for our desecrated temples, while ever mourning was all that he could do, but then, when the opportunity came, taking up arms for them. He restored the ruined temples to their places, and he restored their ritual to them and all others: he brought back, as it were from exile, sacrifice and libation, and renewed the festivals that had fallen into abeyance. He did away with the danger that was attached to the worship of the higher powers, never allowed his

of ten years to describe the period from then until his death as a parallel to the ten years' war at Troy, implied in the references to Hector and Odysseus. Julian's career is thus presented as one of prolonged religious struggle. The conjecture δύο, referring specifically to his reign as Augustus, loses the point of this literary allusion.

ἀποστήσας τῆς περὶ[1] θεῶν ἐννοίας,[2] οὗτος ὁ πολλῶν ἐξελάσας ἀχλὺν καὶ πάντων δ' ἄν, εἰ μὴ
προαπῆλθε.

37. Τούτου Διὶ μὲν μέλει, βασιλεῖ βασιλέως, ὡς
ὁμοτέχνου, Ἀθηνᾷ δὲ τῇ τοῦ Διὸς θυγατρὶ διὰ τὴν
φρόνησιν, Ἑρμῇ δὲ διὰ τοὺς ἐν πᾶσιν εἴδεσι
λόγους, | Μούσαις δὲ διὰ τὰ ἔπη, τῇ δὲ Ἀρτέμιδι  F 531
διὰ τὴν σωφροσύνην, Ἄρει δὲ διὰ τὴν ἐν πολέμοις
ἀρετήν· ὃς ἅπαν οὕτω γένος ἐταπείνωσε βαρβάρων ὑπ' ἄλλῳ τε ἄρχων καὶ τὸ πᾶν κτησάμενος,
R ii. 59 ὥστε τὴν Περσῶν μὲν ἐπιστρατεύσας | ἀνάστατον
ἐποίει, τὰ δ' ἐφεστηκότος καὶ παρόντος ἠρεμοῦντα
γένη ταὐτὸν ἐποίει καὶ ἀφεστηκότος. καὶ ὁ μὲν
ἐγγὺς Βαβυλῶνος κέλησιν ἠγωνοθέτει, βασιλεὺς δὲ
Ῥωμαῖος ἐν γῇ Ῥωμαίων οὐκ ἦν, πάντα δὲ
ἡσύχαζεν ἀντὶ τῆς παρουσίας ἀρκοῦντος τοῦ δέους,
ὃ καὶ διὰ τὸ τοὺς Πέρσας ἐλαύνειν ἐνεποίει.

38. Πᾶς οὖν ὁ μετ' ἐκεῖνον βασιλεὺς ἴστω χάριν
ὀφείλων ἐκείνῳ. τουτὶ γὰρ δὴ καὶ αἱ γυναῖκες
εἴποιεν ἄν, ὅτι τοῦ μὴ πάντα ταῦτα εἶναι Περσῶν
ἐκεῖνος αἴτιος. καὶ οὔτε τειχίζομεν οὔτε σῖτον
εἰσκομιζόμεθα οὔτε ποῖ πλεύσαντας σωθῆναι σκο-
R ii. 60 πούμεν | οὔτε φόβῳ συνοικοῦμεν οὔτε μή τι συμβῇ
τοιοῦτον οἷον καὶ ἐπὶ τῶν προγόνων δεδοίκαμεν,
οἷς ἐν τῷ θεάτρῳ συγκαθημένοις ἐφειστήκεσαν οἱ

---

¹ περὶ Re., Olearius (mss.) : παρὰ F.
² ἐννοίας Re., Olearius (API) : εὐνοίας F. (other mss.).

ᵃ Cf. Libanius' language in Or. 1. 118 f.
ᵇ Cf. Or. 17. 22.
ᶜ Julian as poet, cf. Or. 12. 55, ibid. 92, 18. 74.  Amm.
Marc. 16. 5. 7.  E.L.F. pp. 218 ff.
ᵈ i.e., as Caesar under Constantius until A.D. 361, and as
Augustus thereafter.

518

intellect to be diverted from his consideration of the gods, dispersed the mist that enveloped so many, and would have done the same for us all, had he not been untimely taken from us.[a]

37. Zeus is concerned for him, an emperor for an emperor, as one of his own craft[b]: Athena, Zeus' daughter, also, because of his gifts of intellect: Hermes, because of his oratory of every kind; the Muses, because of his poetry[c]: Artemis, because of his continence, and Ares, because of his valour in war. He brought the whole brood of barbarians to such straits, both as a ruler under another and as ruler supreme,[d] that in his campaign he made a wilderness of Persian territory, and provinces, at peace while he was present and in control of them, behaved in exactly the same way when he had left. He instituted horse races before the walls of Babylon,[e] and there was no Roman emperor in the Roman empire, but everything was just as peaceful as if he were there in person, for the fear he inspired by his harrying of the Persians was enough.

38. So let every one of his successors acknowledge the debt he owes him. Our womenfolk too would agree that it was due to him that all this region does not belong to Persia. We build no walls, we import no stocks of corn, we do not look round for a place of refuge to which we can sail: we do not live with fear to keep us company, nor are we afraid that any such disaster will befall us as occurred in the days of our ancestors, when they were attacked as they sat in the theatre by archers who had occupied the moun-

---

[e] Cf. Or. 1. 133, 18. 249; Ruf. Fest. Brev. 28; Sozom. H.E. 6. 1. This incident actually occurred before Ctesiphon. Libanius' classical allusiveness causes the change.

# LIBANIUS

τοξόται τὸ ὄρος κατειληφότες. | ἀλλ' οὐδὲ τοῖς ἐπὶ F 532
τῶν ὅρων στρατιώταις ἱδρυμένοις θαρροῦμεν, ὧν
ὅσον ἄριστον ἐπὶ τὸν Σκυθῶν μετενήνεκται πόλεμον.

39. Ταῦθ' ἡμῖν δῶρα Ἰουλιανοῦ, ταῦτα ἐκείνων
τῶν πόνων, ταῦτα ἐκείνης τῆς στρατείας, ὃς
ἀνθρώπους ὀρχουμένους ἐπὶ τῆς ἡμετέρας ἐδίδαξεν
ὑπὲρ τῆς αὐτῶν τρέμειν. ἀντὶ τούτων οὖν καὶ
πολλῶν ἄλλων ἃ τίς ἂν δύναιτο διελθεῖν; οὐ
βοηθήσεις, οὐ ζητήσεις, οὐ κολάσεις τοὺς ἀποκτεί-
R ii. 61 ναντας ἄνθρωπον ὃς τῆς ὑστεραίας | ἐδέξατ' ἂν
πρεσβείαν δῶρα παρὰ Περσῶν ἄγουσαν, ὡς αὐτῶν
ἦν ἀκούειν ἐκείνων;

40. Λάβε πεῖραν, ὦ βασιλεῦ, τῆς γνώμης, ἅψαι
τῆς βοηθείας, καὶ κεκτήσῃ τὴν τύχην. τοῦτό σοι
δείξει γεωργουμένην τὴν Θρᾴκην, τοῦτο Θερμο-
πύλας ἀνοιγομένας, τοῦτο τοὺς ἀλωμένους ἐπανά-
ξει, τοῦτο μεταποιήσει τὰ νῦν, τὰς φυγὰς καὶ τὰς
διώξεις. ὄψει τοὺς αὐτοὺς στρατιώτας ἐρευνω-
μένους τὴν ὕλην καὶ τὰ ἄντρα καὶ τοὺς μὲν σφάτ-
R ii. 62 τοντας, τοὺς δὲ ζῶντας | ἕλκοντας δοῦναι τοῖς F 53
βουλομένοις ὠνεῖσθαι. τούτων συνεφάψεται Ἰουλιανὸς πάντα καθιστὰς ῥᾴδια τοὺς μὲν ὀφθαλμοὺς
τῶν στρατιωτῶν διαφεύγων τοῖς δὲ ἔργοις γνωρι-
ζόμενος.

41. Καλὸν δέ σοι κατ' ἄμφω σπουδάσαι περὶ τὴν
τιμωρίαν· ἢ γὰρ ἐπ' ἐλέγχῳ λήψῃ τὴν δίκην, οὗ
τί γένοιτ' ἂν δικαιότερον; ἢ δυνηθέντων, ὃ μὴ γέ-

[a] For this incident, which occurred at some date unknown,
c. A.D. 250, cf. Amm. Marc. 23. 5. 3; Lib. Or. 60. 2-3, and

520

tain top.[a] And our confidence does not lie in our
frontier defence force, for the best of them have
been drafted to the war against the Goths.

39. These are the gifts that Julian has bestowed
upon us, the fruits of those labours and of that campaign of his. He schooled those fellows who were
tripping it over our land to fear for their own. In
return for all this, and much besides that beggars
description, will you not lend your aid, begin an investigation, and punish the murderers of the man who,
next day, would have received an embassy with gifts
from Persia, as we have been told by the Persians
themselves ?[b]

40. Put my recommendation to the test, Sire. Begin to proffer such aid and you will have good fortune. It will show you Thrace under cultivation and
Thermopylae unbarred[c]; it will restore the wander-
ing exiles and alter what we now suffer in the way
of defeat and rout. You will see these same soldiers
scouring forest and caves, killing or taking captives
alive to offer to those ready to buy. Julian will support all this and will render its accomplishment easy,
unseen by the eyes of the soldiers but recognizable
by his deeds.

41. In either case, it behoves you to be zealous in
avenging him. You will either exact punishment
after proof, and nothing could be fairer than that, or
if, as I pray may not happen, the miscreants should

the discussion in Downey, *History of Antioch in Syria*, pp.
252 ff.

[b] Cf. *Or.* 1. 133, 18. 268 ff. Socr. *H.E.* 3. 21.

[c] In the chaos following Adrianople the Goths had
ravaged all Macedonia and Thessaly, *i.e.*, as far as Thermopylae, where a semi-permanent guard was instituted: *cf.*
Zos. 4. 31; Themist. *Or.* 34. 24 (p. 466 D).

νοιτο, τῶν δεδρακότων διαδῦναι κατὰ τὴν προ-
αίρεσιν εὐδοκιμήσεις καὶ παρὰ τοῖς ἀνθρώποις καὶ
παρ' ἐκείνῳ καὶ παρὰ τοῖς θεοῖς, ὥσθ' ἅπερ ἦν
ἄν[1] σοι τετιμωρημένῳ, ταῦτα ἔσται ἐθελήσαντι.

<hr />

[1] ἄν inserted F. (V), conj. Re., Monnier.

be able to make their escape, you will gain fame in the eyes of men, of him, and of the gods because of your resolve, so that the blessings you would have obtained had you avenged him, will accrue to you because of your will to do so.

# INDEX OF PROPER NAMES: A

(Includes those contemporaries of Libanius to whom specific reference, whether by name or allusion, is made in the text. Numerals indicate the identifications proposed by Seeck, *B.L.Z.G.*)

525

# INDEX

# INDEX OF PROPER NAMES: B

(Names derived from religion, mythology, classical history
and literature)

# INDEX

# INDEX

*Printed in Great Britain by* R. & R. CLARK, LIMITED, *Edinburgh*

# THE LOEB CLASSICAL LIBRARY

## VOLUMES ALREADY PUBLISHED

### LATIN AUTHORS

AMMIANUS MARCELLINUS. J. C. Rolfe. 3 Vols.

APULEIUS : THE GOLDEN ASS (METAMORPHOSES). W. Adlington (1566). Revised by S. Gaselee.

ST. AUGUSTINE : CITY OF GOD. 7 Vols. Vol. I. G. E. McCracken. Vol. II. W. M. Green. Vol. III. D. Wiesen. Vol. IV. P. Levine. Vol. V. E. M. Sanford and W. M. Green. Vol. VI. W. C. Greene.

ST. AUGUSTINE, CONFESSIONS OF. W. Watts (1631). 2 Vols.

ST. AUGUSTINE : SELECT LETTERS. J. H. Baxter.

AUSONIUS. H. G. Evelyn White. 2 Vols.

BEDE. J. E. King. 2 Vols.

BOETHIUS : TRACTS AND DE CONSOLATIONE PHILOSOPHIAE. Rev. H. F. Stewart and E. K. Rand.

CAESAR : ALEXANDRIAN, AFRICAN AND SPANISH WARS. A. G. Way.

CAESAR : CIVIL WARS. A. G. Peskett.

CAESAR : GALLIC WAR. H. J. Edwards.

CATO AND VARRO : DE RE RUSTICA. H. B. Ash and W. D. Hooper.

CATULLUS. F. W. Cornish : TIBULLUS. J. B. Postgate ; and PERVIGILIUM VENERIS. J. W. Mackail.

CELSUS : DE MEDICINA. W. G. Spencer. 3 Vols.

CICERO : BRUTUS AND ORATOR. G. L. Hendrickson and H. M. Hubbell.

CICERO : DE FINIBUS. H. Rackham.

CICERO : DE INVENTIONE, etc. H. M. Hubbell.

CICERO : DE NATURA DEORUM AND ACADEMICA. H. Rackham.

CICERO : DE OFFICIIS. Walter Miller.

CICERO : DE ORATORE, etc. 2 Vols. Vol. I : DE ORATORE, Books I and II. E. W. Sutton and H. Rackham. Vol. II : DE ORATORE, Book III ; DE FATO ; PARADOXA STOICORUM ; DE PARTITIONE ORATORIA. H. Rackham.

CICERO : DE REPUBLICA, DE LEGIBUS, SOMNIUM SCIPIONIS. Clinton W. Keyes.

# THE LOEB CLASSICAL LIBRARY

CICERO : DE SENECTUTE, DE AMICITIA, DE DIVINATIONE. W. A. Falconer.

CICERO : IN CATILINAM, PRO MURENA, PRO SULLA, PRO FLACCO. Louis E. Lord.

CICERO : LETTERS TO ATTICUS. E. O. Winstedt. 3 Vols.

CICERO : LETTERS TO HIS FRIENDS. W. Glynn Williams. 3 Vols.

CICERO : PHILIPPICS. W. C. A. Ker.

CICERO : PRO ARCHIA, POST REDITUM, DE DOMO, DE HARUSPICUM RESPONSIS, PRO PLANCIO. N. H. Watts.

CICERO : PRO CAECINA, PRO LEGE MANILIA, PRO CLUENTIO, PRO RABIRIO. H. Grose Hodge.

CICERO : PRO CAELIO, DE PROVINCIIS CONSULARIBUS, PRO BALBO. R. Gardner.

CICERO : PRO MILONE, IN PISONEM, PRO SCAURO, PRO FONTEIO, PRO RABIRIO POSTUMO, PRO MARCELLO, PRO LIGARIO, PRO REGE DEIOTARO. N. H. Watts.

CICERO : PRO QUINCTIO, PRO ROSCIO AMERINO, PRO ROSCIO COMOEDO, CONTRA RULLUM. J. H. Freese.

CICERO : PRO SESTIO, IN VATINIUM. R. Gardner.

[CICERO] : RHETORICA AD HERENNIUM. H. Caplan.

CICERO : TUSCULAN DISPUTATIONS. J. E. King.

CICERO : VERRINE ORATIONS. L. H. G. Greenwood. 2 Vols.

CLAUDIAN. M. Platnauer. 2 Vols.

COLUMELLA : DE RE RUSTICA, DE ARBORIBUS. H. B. Ash, E. S. Forster, E. Heffner. 3 Vols.

CURTIUS, Q.: HISTORY OF ALEXANDER. J. C. Rolfe. 2 Vols.

FLORUS. E. S. Forster ; and CORNELIUS NEPOS. J. C. Rolfe.

FRONTINUS : STRATAGEMS AND AQUEDUCTS. C. E. Bennett and M. B. McElwain.

FRONTO : CORRESPONDENCE. C. R. Haines. 2 Vols.

GELLIUS. J. C. Rolfe. 3 Vols.

HORACE : ODES AND EPODES. C. E. Bennett.

HORACE : SATIRES, EPISTLES, ARS POETICA. H. R. Fairclough.

JEROME : SELECT LETTERS. F. A. Wright.

JUVENAL AND PERSIUS. G. G. Ramsay.

LIVY. B. O. Foster, F. G. Moore, Evan T. Sage, A. C. Schlesinger and R. M. Geer (General Index). 14 Vols.

LUCAN. J. D. Duff.

LUCRETIUS. W. H. D. Rouse.

MARTIAL. W. C. A. Ker. 2 Vols.

MINOR LATIN POETS : from PUBLILIUS SYRUS to RUTILIUS NAMATIANUS, including GRATTIUS, CALPURNIUS SICULUS, NEMESIANUS, AVIANUS, with " Aetna," " Phoenix " and other poems. J. Wight Duff and Arnold M. Duff.

2

# THE LOEB CLASSICAL LIBRARY

OVID : THE ART OF LOVE AND OTHER POEMS. J. H. Mozley.

OVID : FASTI. Sir James G. Frazer.

OVID : HEROIDES AND AMORES. Grant Showerman.

OVID : METAMORPHOSES. F. J. Miller. 2 Vols.

OVID : TRISTIA AND EX PONTO. A. L. Wheeler.

PETRONIUS. M. Heseltine ; SENECA : APOCOLOCYNTOSIS. W. H. D. Rouse.

PHAEDRUS AND BABRIUS (Greek). B. E. Perry.

PLAUTUS. Paul Nixon. 5 Vols.

PLINY : LETTERS, PANEGYRICUS. B. Radice. 2 Vols.

PLINY : NATURAL HISTORY. 10 Vols. Vols. I-V and IX. H. Rackham. Vols. VI-VIII. W. H. S. Jones. Vol. X. D. E. Eichholz.

PROPERTIUS. H. E. Butler.

PRUDENTIUS. H. J. Thomson. 2 Vols.

QUINTILIAN. H. E. Butler. 4 Vols.

REMAINS OF OLD LATIN. E. H. Warmington. 4 Vols. Vol. I (Ennius and Caecilius). Vol. II (Livius, Naevius, Pacuvius, Accius). Vol. III (Lucilius, Laws of the XII Tables). Vol. IV (Archaic Inscriptions).

SALLUST. J. C. Rolfe.

SCRIPTORES HISTORIAE AUGUSTAE. D. Magie. 3 Vols.

SENECA : APOCOLOCYNTOSIS. *Cf.* PETRONIUS.

SENECA : EPISTULAE MORALES. R. M. Gummere. 3 Vols.

SENECA : MORAL ESSAYS. J. W. Basore. 3 Vols.

SENECA : TRAGEDIES. F. J. Miller. 2 Vols.

SIDONIUS : POEMS AND LETTERS. W. B. Anderson. 2 Vols.

SILIUS ITALICUS. J. D. Duff. 2 Vols.

STATIUS. J. H. Mozley. 2 Vols.

SUETONIUS. J. C. Rolfe. 2 Vols.

TACITUS : AGRICOLA AND GERMANIA. Maurice Hutton ; DIALOGUS. Sir Wm. Peterson.

TACITUS : HISTORIES AND ANNALS. C. H. Moore and J. Jackson. 4 Vols.

TERENCE. John Sargeaunt. 2 Vols.

TERTULLIAN : APOLOGIA AND DE SPECTACULIS. T. R. Glover ; MINUCIUS FELIX. G. H. Rendall.

VALERIUS FLACCUS. J. H. Mozley.

VARRO : DE LINGUA LATINA. R. G. Kent. 2 Vols.

VELLEIUS PATERCULUS AND RES GESTAE DIVI AUGUSTI. F. W. Shipley.

VIRGIL. H. R. Fairclough. 2 Vols.

VITRUVIUS : DE ARCHITECTURA. F. Granger. 2 Vols.

# THE LOEB CLASSICAL LIBRARY

ACHILLES TATIUS. S. Gaselee.

AELIAN : ON THE NATURE OF ANIMALS. A. F. Scholfield. 3 Vols.

AENEAS TACTICUS, ASCLEPIODOTUS AND ONASANDER. The Illinois Greek Club.

AESCHINES. C. D. Adams.

AESCHYLUS. H. Weir Smyth. 2 Vols.

ALCIPHRON, AELIAN AND PHILOSTRATUS : LETTERS. A. R. Benner and F. H. Fobes.

APOLLODORUS. Sir James G. Frazer. 2 Vols.

APOLLONIUS RHODIUS. R. C. Seaton.

THE APOSTOLIC FATHERS. Kirsopp Lake. 2 Vols.

APPIAN'S ROMAN HISTORY. Horace White. 4 Vols.

ARATUS. *Cf.* CALLIMACHUS.

ARISTOPHANES. Benjamin Bickley Rogers. 3 Vols. Verse trans.

ARISTOTLE : ART OF RHETORIC. J. H. Freese.

ARISTOTLE : ATHENIAN CONSTITUTION, EUDEMIAN ETHICS, VIRTUES AND VICES. H. Rackham.

ARISTOTLE : THE CATEGORIES. ON INTERPRETATION. H. P. Cooke ; PRIOR ANALYTICS. H. Tredennick.

ARISTOTLE : GENERATION OF ANIMALS. A. L. Peck.

ARISTOTLE : HISTORIA ANIMALIUM. A. L. Peck. 3 Vols. Vols. I and II.

ARISTOTLE : METAPHYSICS. H. Tredennick. 2 Vols.

ARISTOTLE : METEOROLOGICA. H. D. P. Lee.

ARISTOTLE : MINOR WORKS. W. S. Hett. " On Colours," " On Things Heard," " Physiognomics," " On Plants," " On Marvellous Things Heard," " Mechanical Problems," " On Indivisible Lines," " Situations and Names of Winds," " On Melissus, Xenophanes, and Gorgias."

ARISTOTLE : NICOMACHEAN ETHICS. H. Rackham.

ARISTOTLE : OECONOMICA AND MAGNA MORALIA. G. C. Armstrong. (With METAPHYSICS, Vol. II.)

ARISTOTLE : ON THE HEAVENS. W. K. C. Guthrie.

ARISTOTLE : ON THE SOUL, PARVA NATURALIA. On BREATH. W. S. Hett.

ARISTOTLE : PARTS OF ANIMALS. A. L. Peck ; MOTION AND PROGRESSION OF ANIMALS. E. S. Forster.

ARISTOTLE : PHYSICS. Rev. P. Wicksteed and F. M. Cornford. 2 Vols.

# THE LOEB CLASSICAL LIBRARY

ARISTOTLE : POETICS ; LONGINUS ON THE SUBLIME. W. Hamilton Fyfe ; DEMETRIUS ON STYLE. W. Rhys Roberts.

ARISTOTLE : POLITICS. H. Rackham.

ARISTOTLE : POSTERIOR ANALYTICS. H. Tredennick ; TOPICS. E. S. Forster.

ARISTOTLE : PROBLEMS. W. S. Hett. 2 Vols.

ARISTOTLE : RHETORICA AD ALEXANDRUM. H. Rackham. (With PROBLEMS, Vol. II.)

ARISTOTLE : SOPHISTICAL REFUTATIONS. COMING-TO-BE AND PASSING-AWAY. E. S. Forster ; ON THE COSMOS. D. J. Furley.

ARRIAN : HISTORY OF ALEXANDER AND INDICA. Rev. E. Iliffe Robson. 2 Vols.

ATHENAEUS : DEIPNOSOPHISTAE. C. B. Gulick. 7 Vols.

BABRIUS AND PHAEDRUS (Latin). B. E. Perry.

ST. BASIL : LETTERS. R. J. Deferrari. 4 Vols.

CALLIMACHUS : FRAGMENTS. C. A. Trypanis.

CALLIMACHUS : HYMNS AND EPIGRAMS, AND LYCOPHRON. A. W. Mair ; ARATUS. G. R. Mair.

CLEMENT OF ALEXANDRIA. Rev. G. W. Butterworth.

COLLUTHUS. *Cf.* OPPIAN.

DAPHNIS AND CHLOE. *Cf.* LONGUS.

DEMOSTHENES I : OLYNTHIACS, PHILIPPICS AND MINOR ORATIONS : I-XVII AND XX. J. H. Vince.

DEMOSTHENES II : DE CORONA AND DE FALSA LEGATIONE, C. A. Vince and J. H. Vince.

DEMOSTHENES III : MEIDIAS, ANDROTION, ARISTOCRATES, TIMOCRATES, ARISTOGEITON. J. H. Vince.

DEMOSTHENES IV-VI : PRIVATE ORATIONS AND IN NEAERAM. A. T. Murray.

DEMOSTHENES VII : FUNERAL SPEECH, EROTIC ESSAY, EXORDIA AND LETTERS. N. W. and N. J. DeWitt.

DIO CASSIUS : ROMAN HISTORY. E. Cary. 9 Vols.

DIO CHRYSOSTOM. 5 Vols. Vols. I and II. J. W. Cohoon. Vol. III. J. W. Cohoon and H. Lamar Crosby. Vols. IV and V. H. Lamar Crosby.

DIODORUS SICULUS. 12 Vols. Vols. I-VI. C. H. Oldfather. Vol. VII. C. L. Sherman. Vol. VIII. C. B. Welles. Vols. IX and X. Russel M. Geer. Vols. XI and XII. F. R. Walton. General Index. Russel M. Geer.

DIOGENES LAERTIUS. R. D. Hicks. 2 Vols.

DIONYSIUS OF HALICARNASSUS : ROMAN ANTIQUITIES. Spelman's translation revised by E. Cary. 7 Vols.

EPICTETUS. W. A. Oldfather. 2 Vols.

# THE LOEB CLASSICAL LIBRARY

EURIPIDES. A. S. Way. 4 Vols. Verse trans.

EUSEBIUS: ECCLESIASTICAL HISTORY. Kirsopp Lake and J. E. L. Oulton. 2 Vols.

GALEN: ON THE NATURAL FACULTIES. A. J. Brock.

THE GREEK ANTHOLOGY. W. R. Paton. 5 Vols.

THE GREEK BUCOLIC POETS (THEOCRITUS, BION, MOSCHUS). J. M. Edmonds.

GREEK ELEGY AND IAMBUS WITH THE ANACREONTEA. J. M Edmonds. 2 Vols.

GREEK MATHEMATICAL WORKS. Ivor Thomas. 2 Vols.

HERODES. Cf. THEOPHRASTUS: CHARACTERS.

HERODIAN: C. R. Whittaker. 2 Vols. Vol. I.

HERODOTUS. A. D. Godley. 4 Vols.

HESIOD AND THE HOMERIC HYMNS. H. G. Evelyn White.

HIPPOCRATES AND THE FRAGMENTS OF HERACLEITUS. W. H. S. Jones and E. T. Withington. 4 Vols.

HOMER: ILIAD. A. T. Murray. 2 Vols.

HOMER: ODYSSEY. A. T. Murray. 2 Vols.

ISAEUS. E. S. Forster.

ISOCRATES. George Norlin and LaRue Van Hook. 3 Vols.

[ST. JOHN DAMASCENE]: BARLAAM AND IOASAPH. Rev. G. R. Woodward, Harold Mattingly and D. M. Lang.

JOSEPHUS. 9 Vols. Vols. I-IV. H. St. J. Thackeray. Vol. V. H. St. J. Thackeray and Ralph Marcus. Vols. VI and VII. Ralph Marcus. Vol. VIII. Ralph Marcus and Allen Wikgren. Vol. IX. L. H. Feldman.

JULIAN. Wilmer Cave Wright. 3 Vols.

LIBANIUS: SELECTED WORKS. A. F. Norman. 3 Vols. Vol. I.

LONGUS: DAPHNIS AND CHLOE. Thornley's translation revised by J. M. Edmonds; and PARTHENIUS. S. Gaselee.

LUCIAN. 8 Vols. Vols. I-V. A. M. Harmon. Vol. VI. K. Kilburn. Vols. VII and VIII. M. D. Macleod.

LYCOPHRON. Cf. CALLIMACHUS.

LYRA GRAECA. J. M. Edmonds. 3 Vols.

LYSIAS. W. R. M. Lamb.

MANETHO. W. G. Waddell; PTOLEMY: TETRABIBLOS. F. E. Robbins.

MARCUS AURELIUS. C. R. Haines.

MENANDER. F. G. Allinson.

MINOR ATTIC ORATORS. 2 Vols. K. J. Maidment and J. O. Burtt.

NONNOS: DIONYSIACA. W. H. D. Rouse. 3 Vols.

OPPIAN, COLLUTHUS, TRYPHIODORUS. A. W. Mair.

PAPYRI. NON-LITERARY SELECTIONS. A. S. Hunt and C. C.

# THE LOEB CLASSICAL LIBRARY

Edgar. 2 Vols. LITERARY SELECTIONS (Poetry). D. L. Page.

PARTHENIUS. *Cf.* LONGUS.

PAUSANIAS : DESCRIPTION OF GREECE. W. H. S. Jones. 5 Vols. and Companion Vol. arranged by R. E. Wycherley.

PHILO. 10 Vols. Vols. I-V. F. H. Colson and Rev. G. H. Whitaker. Vols. VI-X. F. H. Colson. General Index. Rev. J. W. Earp.
Two Supplementary Vols. Translation only from an Armenian Text. Ralph Marcus.

PHILOSTRATUS : THE LIFE OF APOLLONIUS OF TYANA. F. C. Conybeare. 2 Vols.

PHILOSTRATUS : IMAGINES ; CALLISTRATUS : DESCRIPTIONS. A. Fairbanks.

PHILOSTRATUS AND EUNAPIUS : LIVES OF THE SOPHISTS. Wilmer Cave Wright.

PINDAR. Sir J. E. Sandys.

PLATO : CHARMIDES, ALCIBIADES, HIPPARCHUS, THE LOVERS, THEAGES, MINOS AND EPINOMIS. W. R. M. Lamb.

PLATO : CRATYLUS, PARMENIDES, GREATER HIPPIAS, LESSER HIPPIAS. H. N. Fowler.

PLATO : EUTHYPHRO, APOLOGY, CRITO, PHAEDO, PHAEDRUS. H. N. Fowler.

PLATO : LACHES, PROTAGORAS, MENO, EUTHYDEMUS. W. R. M. Lamb.

PLATO : LAWS. Rev. R. G. Bury. 2 Vols.

PLATO : LYSIS, SYMPOSIUM, GORGIAS. W. R. M. Lamb

PLATO : REPUBLIC. Paul Shorey. 2 Vols.

PLATO : STATESMAN, PHILEBUS. H. N. Fowler ; ION. W. R. M. Lamb.

PLATO : THEAETETUS AND SOPHIST. H. N. Fowler.

PLATO : TIMAEUS, CRITIAS, CLITOPHO, MENEXENUS, EPISTULAE. Rev. R. G. Bury.

PLOTINUS. A. H. Armstrong. 6 Vols. Vols. I-III.

PLUTARCH : MORALIA. 16 Vols. Vols. I-V. F. C. Babbitt. Vol. VI. W. C. Helmbold. Vol. VII. P. H. De Lacy and B. Einarson. Vol. VIII. P. A. Clement, H. B. Hoffleit. Vol. IX. E. L. Minar, Jr., F. H. Sandbach, W. C. Helmbold. Vol. X. H. N. Fowler. Vol. XI. L. Pearson, F. H. Sandbach. Vol. XII. H. Cherniss, W. C. Helmbold. Vol. XIV. P. H. De Lacy and B. Einarson. Vol. XV. F. H. Sandbach.

PLUTARCH : THE PARALLEL LIVES. B. Perrin. 11 Vols.

POLYBIUS. W. R. Paton. 6 Vols.

7

# THE LOEB CLASSICAL LIBRARY

Procopius: History of the Wars. H. B. Dewing. 7 Vols.
Ptolemy: Tetrabiblos. *Cf.* Manetho.
Quintus Smyraenus. A. S. Way. Verse trans.
Sextus Empiricus. Rev. R. G. Bury. 4 Vols.
Sophocles. F. Storr. 2 Vols. Verse trans.
Strabo: Geography. Horace L. Jones. 8 Vols.
Theophrastus: Characters. J. M. Edmonds; Herodes, etc. A. D. Knox.
Theophrastus: Enquiry into Plants. Sir Arthur Hort. 2 Vols.
Thucydides. C. F. Smith. 4 Vols.
Tryphiodorus. *Cf.* Oppian.
Xenophon: Anabasis. C. L. Brownson.
Xenophon: Cyropaedia. Walter Miller. 2 Vols.
Xenophon: Hellenica. C. L. Brownson.
Xenophon: Memorabilia and Oeconomicus. E. C. Marchant. Symposium and Apology. O. J. Todd.
Xenophon: Scripta Minora. E. C. Marchant and G. W. Bowersock.

# VOLUMES IN PREPARATION

### GREEK AUTHORS

Aristides: Orations. C. A. Behr.
Musaeus: Hero and Leander. T. Gelzer and C. H. Whitman.
Theophrastus: De Causis Plantarum. G. K. K. Link and B. Einarson.

### LATIN AUTHORS

Asconius: Commentaries on Cicero's Orations. G. W. Bowersock.
Benedict: The Rule. P. Meyvaert.
Justin–Trogus. R. Moss.
Manilius. G. P. Goold.

*DESCRIPTIVE PROSPECTUS ON APPLICATION*

CAMBRIDGE, MASS.                    LONDON
HARVARD UNIV. PRESS      WILLIAM HEINEMANN LTD